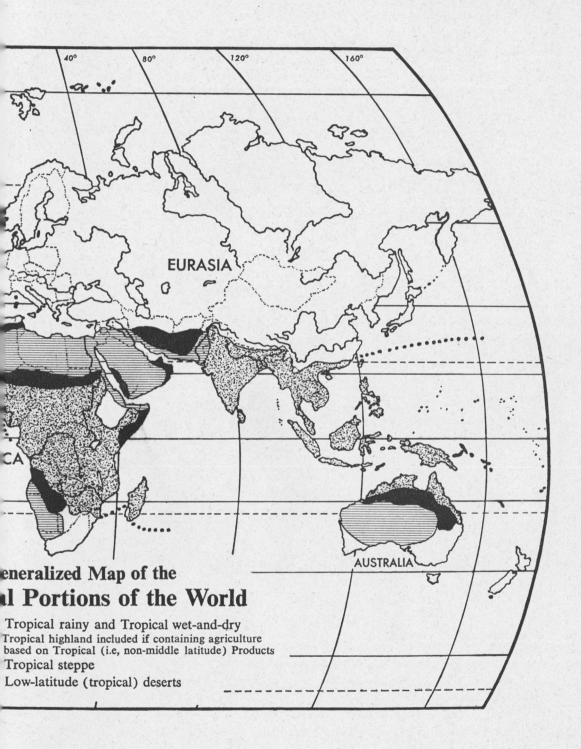

40° 80° 120° 160°

EURASIA

AUSTRALIA

CA

...eneralized Map of the
...l Portions of the World

Tropical rainy and Tropical wet-and-dry

Tropical highland included if containing agriculture
based on Tropical (i.e, non-middle latitude) Products

Tropical steppe

Low-latitude (tropical) deserts

Economic Geography

► LOYAL DURAND, JR.   *University of Tennessee*

Economic Geography

THOMAS Y. CROWELL COMPANY   *New York, Established 1834*

Preface

This book deals with the economic geography of the world. The subject is tied both to economics and to geography, for the complex of man's economic activities takes place on the earth's surface, and the production of raw materials, agricultural and manufactured products, and countless other goods is regionally distributed on the earth's surface.

The world's population is not equally spread, but rather is highly regionalized. The markets of the world and its regions differ in size, in per capita buying power, and in demand, so that raw materials, animal feeds, food for human beings, and manufactured goods are often transported widely, for use in regions distant from those of their production. The commercial world has become one of regional specialization; thus there are manufacturing regions, ones specializing in forest products, and agricultural-specialty regions, such as wheat belts or dairy areas. The interchange of goods between countries or regions in a single nation is normal and expected. Man's advancing technology and his increasing use of sources of energy and machines are resulting in marked advances in the economic world and in shifts in the spatial arrangement of his activities on the globe. Thus economic geography is a dynamic subject and one basic to the understanding of the economic activities distributed upon the lands and seas of the world.

This book is organized by products or groups of products (such as the vegetable oils or the fiber crops) whose final uses are similar or interchangeable. A single product is carried through from its raw material source to its final manufacture and use. Thus sugar cane, the sugar beet, and the sugar refinery are dealt with in a single chapter; iron and steel manufacture, the aluminum industry, and others based upon metals as original raw materials are with the chapter on metals; and wheat-growing and flour-milling are together.

This book also contains a group of chapters concerned directly with the manufacturing of the world—the general features of manufacturing, its necessary components, and its world locations and the reasons therefor. The United States, the Soviet Union, the manufacturing countries of western Europe, and Japan are given particular attention, and outlying manufactural centers are dealt with as well. Manufacturing, so important in the developed modern world, thus is treated both topically—through a particular raw material of importance—and spatially—through its regional distribution on the earth.

The concluding chapter, "A World of Change and Increasing Interdependence," summarizes the broad geographical patterns of economic activity in the present world, patterns which are the bench mark from which future changes may depart—the patterns of agriculture, fishing and ocean resources, forest lands, energy and mineral resources, manufacturing, commerce and transportation, service and recreational industries. The broad outlines of these patterns will probably continue to hold true, but some aspects are bound to change as the highly developed nations and regions continue to develop, and the so-called underdeveloped and undeveloped portions of the world are brought increasingly into the commercial scene.

Economic geography is dynamic and is ever-changing in detail. The basic principles of the subject remain constant, but the world competitive situation, the relative advantage gained by new producers or regions, the relative costs of labor and transport, man-made factors such as quotas or tariffs, shifts in technology, the growth or decline of markets through population increases or shifts, and many, many other factors result in changes in the location of the production, transfer, and exchange of goods. Change is, and always has been, expected in the economic activities of man, and changes have been exceedingly rapid in recent years.

A useful supplement to this book is a 1961 revision of John E. Kieffer's popular workbook, *Studies in World Economic Geography.* Published by Thomas Y. Crowell Company, it has been specially keyed to this text.

April, 1961   LOYAL DURAND, JR.

Contents

Maps

Economic Geography

I Economic Geography in the World

Economic geography deals with the complex web of man's economic activities as distributed upon the earth. It deals with the production, transportation, and exchange of goods in the world. The production may be from farms and plantations, from mines and quarries, from the woodlands and forests, from the sea, or— in the modern commercial world—production may be the partially manufactured or completely manufactured goods of the present. The farms, mines, forests, and seas yield raw materials for manufacture—examples being rubber, cotton, tobacco from agriculture; the metals and fuels from mines; the wood for lumber, newsprint, or rayon yarn; and fish for fertilizers. Farms and the sea yield also the raw materials for foods, most of which now reach the markets after having been processed or manufactured. Thus the production of goods involves both primary materials obtained directly from the soil, forests, and mines of the earth or from the seas, and secondary materials manufactured from the raw materials. Our machines, for example, are fabricated from metals, powered by mineral fuels (coal, oil, natural gas) or by electricity generated either from the mineral fuels or by the use of the energy of falling water; and they in turn produce a legion of present-day goods fabricated from the raw materials furnished by the earth. Man is still earth-bound; even the nuclear fuels are metals from the earth, and the multitude of chemical and "synthetic" products of the present are all fashioned from some raw materials originally, even though changed in form or structure.

In ancient times the production, transport, and exchange of goods at the market place was simple; often all three activities were consummated within a very limited area. Today the ramifications are complex and even world-wide in scope. And man's economic activities include occupations and extend to areas not known to the ancient world. Increasing urbanization in the highly developed areas of the world has resulted not only in the rise of a branch of the field—urban geography—but has enlarged and concentrated the markets and has resulted in the advent of many occupations in the professional and educational industries, the service industries, and in transportation personnel within the cities themselves. The commercialization of agriculture in the highly developed world, the specialization in crops and animals within regions most favorable by climate, soil, or market, has resulted in additional patterns of production, transport, and consumption at markets. And the advent of technical changes, such as the refrigerated railroad car, truck, or ship, the processes of freezing perishable foods, and many others, has resulted in the highly developed countries "reaching" to distant locations for materials. Tropical plantations produce bananas for world markets; fresh pineapples and other tropical fruits are commonplace. Industry today depends upon ores, fibers, vegetable oils, and other materials from areas which not long ago were outside the realm of commercial activity.

The "underdeveloped" and "undeveloped" portions of the world (terms relative to the highly developed regions or countries) have been brought into the world commercial pattern to some degree, certain ones more than others. True, some subsistence economies—hunting and fishing, gathering, subsistence agriculture—remain in some regions; but even the countries in which these are found have connections with the outside world, and all have some commercial activities within their boundaries.

Economic geography, as dealt with in this book, will include the products and regions which contribute to the economic activities of the world of the present. It will not deal with the subsistence regions; the people of these regions support themselves and provide their own needs of food, clothing, and shelter, but contribute little or nothing to the commercial world. This does not mean that they will not do so in the future. It does not mean that products do not leave these regions in return for manufactured goods from time to time—the gathering of wild rubber from the forests of the Amazon was resumed when the Japanese captured the Asian rubber plantations during World War II and a demand for rubber arose in the West—but it does mean that these areas, at present, contribute little. Even so, there is hardly a part of the world untouched by outside contacts or goods; the most inaccessible portions of parts of tropical Africa have paths worn originally by the feet of the natives, and now ridden upon by bicycles of European make. All portions of the world are accessible by airplane, provided there is a spot to land; and prospectors, seekers of petroleum and of other materials, travel the world over in their searches.

A World of Regional Specialization

Modern man in the commercial world lives in a world of specialization. Some regions or countries engage mainly in manufacturing. Some are noted for agricultural specialties. Certain nations have a large percentage of their citizens engaged in commerce. In some commercial fishermen constitute more than two million of their citizens; these, with their families, constitute a sizable population.

The countries very large in area, such as the United States, the Soviet Union, Canada, China, and Brazil, contain contrasting regions or sections, each of which is more specialized in some activities than in others. Manufacturing is a leading source of employment in southern New England; the mining industry employs many in the Appalachian coal fields, as in West Virginia, eastern Kentucky, and—by percentage—in large areas of the Rocky Mountain states; working in the forests and in the industries associated with forest raw materials is a leading activity in large portions of the Pacific Northwest and British Columbia, and specialized regions of commercial agriculture have evolved in relationship to climatic environments and transportation to markets. Thus there are wheat belts, dairy regions, animal-specialty areas, cotton-growing regions, areas specializing in citrus fruits, and a host of others around the world. Cities have specializations which stand out among their varied activities; there are manufacturing cities, ones very important in commerce (banking, wholesaling, and distribution centers), educational centers, governmental cities. In fact the highly developed portions of the world are characterized by regional specializations; the "underdeveloped" areas are ones in which some of these are emerging; the "undeveloped" areas have only a few specialized regions, or may have almost none, and a large part of their population remains at a subsistence level even in the modern world.

The development of regional specializations is owing to many factors. Climatic conditions vary. The sources of energy and of minerals are not evenly distributed. Educational and technical training varies around the world. Historical developments have played a part. The invention and perfection of machines was not evenly spread world-wide; some areas have been fortunate in providing a milieu in which inventiveness thrived and in having inventors among their citizens. Capital accumulation differed in the past, and those nations or regions in which it was accumulated were able to reinvest it in home industries, agriculture, or in distant sources of raw materials to support home industry. These, and many more are but a few factors—factors so interwoven and complex that no one may be said to be dominant in all regions, though certain ones are (or were) outstanding in some.

The nearly three billion inhabitants of the earth are not equally distributed over its surface. This very fact makes for regionalization of the markets for goods. The standards of living and the per-capita buying power of even the peoples of the densely inhabited areas differs. Half of the world's people dwell in Southeast Asia; India, China, and Java furnish a large total market but one of low buying power per person or per family; Japan, now heavily industrialized, furnishes a larger per-capita market for both home products and imported goods and raw materials. The industrialized countries of western Europe, Canada, and the United States supply very different market conditions. Each has a large and important home market as well as world-wide connections. Australia, New Zealand, Argentina, Uruguay, and the Union of South Africa, each with relatively small populations with respect to resources, and each with highly developed commercial agriculture as well as other modern economic activities, offer different market conditions with high per-capita purchasing power. The Soviet Union, very important in modern industry and agriculture, has chosen a different course; most of its materials and trade is within its own boundaries, and to date its manufactural emphasis has been upon producer goods (machines and so on) rather than consumer goods for its inhabitants.

There is regionalization in the distribution of energy—the power for modern machines. Coal, oil, and natural gas are distributed with respect to geological conditions, not to population centers. Water-power resources are related to conditions of climate and terrain. Some regions and countries are fortunate in their possession of energy resources; others lack them; still others—China is an example—are just now developing theirs. Thus time is a factor; England had a head start in the harnessing of sources of power for machines during the Industrial Revolution. China, with more extensive coal fields, is engaging in the process more than two hundred years later. Only if and when nuclear power becomes a peacetime or civilian reality can energy resources, at least theoretically, be provided around the world in proportion to the needs of the inhabitants.

The raw materials in use in today's manufacturing are not all produced in any one place, but are dispersed regionally. These raw materials may be products only of tropical agriculture; they may be farm crops only of certain climatic settings in the middle latitudes; they may be materials from the earth itself such as the mineral products; or they may be from the forested regions of the world, the seas, or even the air. The raw materials from plantations and farms cannot be grown in all climates. Even in a single broad climatic region the terrain is not everywhere suitable for specialization in a given crop; soil quality differs, giving some districts an advantage in costs and quantity of production not possessed by others. The mineral raw materials, of which the metals are of particular importance in our machine age, are distributed in relationship to geological conditions—not to the distribution of the population of the world or to the regions of major manufacturing where the machines are made. And the machines themselves, though used principally in the manufacturing regions and countries—to produce more goods—are not all marketed in the regions in which they are manufactured.

The early start of certain peoples or countries in such activities as commerce, commercial agriculture, and manufacturing has led, too, to great regional differentiation in the world. The Industrial Revolution, starting in England in the middle of the eighteenth century, spread to the western part of the continent of Europe in time, and to New England in the United States. These manufacturing areas used local power—either the water power or coal of England or the water power of New England—local labor, and, at first, home raw materials, such as wool. But as factories grew, markets expanded and trade increased, and distant raw materials, such as cotton from the American South, was transported to the factories for processing and manufacture. As time went on there arose, thus, specialized manufacturing regions in the world. The early start, the shipping and commerce, and the "know-how" of the people engaged in manufacturing were all factors leading to regional specialization in this activity. Thus, today, just as other activities are regionalized in different portions of the world, so also is intensive manufacturing. The inhabitants of the manufacturing districts or regions receive their food supplies from elsewhere—today even from halfway around the world for certain foods, as those shipped from Australia or New Zealand to Great Britain.

Enough has been said or illustrated to indicate the regional diversity in the activities of the present economic world. The specialized regions—whether associated with manufacture, agriculture, forestry, fishing, or other activities which support their inhabitants—exist. The reasons for their rise to eminence are varied and complex. The subsistence agriculture (even the subsistence "economy") of the past in Europe and in North America, wherein each farmer produced only enough to feed his family and perhaps had only a very small surplus to barter or sell in exchange for a few necessities he could not produce, has passed from the scene in the highly developed regions of the world. Commercial agriculture and specialization in a few farm crops most suited to the environment or the market has become the rule. Subsistence agriculture remains in parts of the so-called "undeveloped" world, but even these underdeveloped or undeveloped lands have been drawn into the commercial world and furnish—from certain districts within their boundaries—raw materials in the form of minerals, forest products, or agricultural materials grown on relatively few specialized farms or plantations. And every continent, save Antarctica, contains highly developed regions of world economic importance somewhere within the continental limits, whether the continent as a whole is rather well developed, such as North America, Europe, or Australia, or whether the continent contains much underdeveloped or undeveloped lands or areas, such as South America, Africa, or Asia.

Transportation

Transportation binds the world together. Transportation is extremely important to the understanding of the economic geography of the world. The most used transport routes, whether landways such as railroads or highways, waterways such as navigable rivers and canals, seaways, or airways are within the highly developed areas of the world, or connect them. The raw materials, feeds and foods, manufactured goods, and other articles of commerce are moved on these transport routes by the various kinds of carriers. In fact the transportation systems and the development went hand in hand; as railroads were built a hundred or more years ago to regions then distant from the seacoast and shipping, these regions were made accessible to the commercial world of the time. A market was made available for their products; in turn the railroad carried the manufactured or other products of the seacoast districts to the newly opened inland areas—expanding the market region of the seacoast area. Further specialization developed. The commercial grain farming of the American Great Plains, the cattle specialization of the West, and similar developments resulted from the advent of railroad transport to market. The pattern continues today; the maps depicting densest railroad and highway nets show, in effect, the highly developed regions of the world. The densest network of airways is within these regions. The seaways and the overseas airways connect them, and the ships and planes carry more traffic from one highly developed region to another than they do from any highly developed region to an underdeveloped or undeveloped one. One of the fastest methods to aid an undeveloped or underdeveloped area expand and "develop" is to provide adequate transportation within the area.

Transportation is so important to man in the commercial world that he takes it for granted—unless he is inconvenienced by its interruption. And yet, just the food he eats daily, the material of which his machines are fabricated, the energy to power those machines, the paper he writes on, his clothing, and nearly every other item he uses daily in the commercial world has been grown, mined, manufactured, or produced in a wide variety of places or regions, and is being used in a place other than the source region of most of the materials. And a part of the costs of the goods or foods in daily use in the commercial world is the transport (or transfer) cost.

Mechanization

The highly developed countries and regions of the world are mechanized. Machines are the servants of man and make each worker highly productive. The outstanding productivity of the present in these regions has been made possible by the use of machines and by man's constant improvement of old ones, invention of new ones, and by advancing technology. The machines of the present are far more efficient, in most cases, than the machines of even twenty-five years ago. Agriculture is highly mechanized in the world's major regions of commercial agriculture—almost completely so in some, like Australia, the United States, and Canada. Manufacturing and mining are almost completely dependent today upon the machine. Commercial fishing is becoming a mechanized activity. The effect of the machine is too far-reaching to be summarized; the mining of metals, such as iron ore and copper, has increased to tremendous proportions; coal fields and oil fields have been developed; the world is searched for new oil fields; the standards of living have risen; leisure time has been expanded—to mention but a few; and the social effects have been almost incalculable.

The Subject

The chief raw materials and products of the present will be discussed in the ensuing chapters.

The products of agriculture include far more than foods for human beings and feeds for animals. Many are industrial crops, and these become important raw materials in manufacturing industries; cotton and tobacco are examples. Some food or feed crops are used also in industry; corn in the United States and potatoes in Europe are used as food, feed, and in manufacturing of importance. Clothing fibers, originally of plant and animal origin, today are also synthetic products. And agriculture contributes a host of by-product materials basic to certain industries. The farmer rears cattle for milk or meat, sheep for wool or meat; but the hides and skins of these animals become basic raw materials for the tanning and leather-goods industries. The major agricultural products of the world, grouped by type—such as grain crops, the fibers, the vegetable oils, the beverage crops, and others—will be discussed and the world pattern of their distribution, and the reasons therefor, interpreted and explained.

The extractive industries of fishing and forestry, each providing an array of materials, will also be dealt with.

Discussion of the sources of energy and of the mineral industries precedes the sections on manufacturing. Energy is, of course, basic to all modern activities; American farms are so completely mechanized that they are just as dependent upon the distant oil refinery or the power plant as are some other commercial enterprises. But energy is applied in large and concentrated quantities to power the machines of industry, and it is applied in quantity within limited areas. Thus the major users of the energy resources are the regions of intensive manufacturing.

The mineral industries provide the array of metals, the mineral fuels (which are raw materials of industry as well as sources of energy), many chemical materials, fertilizer minerals, and earth materials such as sand, clay, and building stone that are used in manufacturing and in the construction industry. Iron ore, the non-ferrous metals (such as copper and zinc), and the ferroalloy metals are particularly important in the mechanized and highly developed portions of the world. It has been said that roughly half of all the mined tonnage of a given metal —such as copper—has been mined from the dawn of history to about 1900, the other half since that date. And the last sixty to seventy years have witnessed all of the mining of "new" metals (for which uses have been found) such as aluminum. Even "newer" ones, such as uranium and thorium, have even shorter commercial histories.

Manufacturing of importance centers in four major regions of the world. There are smaller, outlying centers. Manufacturing uses basic raw materials and uses partially fabricated materials. In fact, nearly two-thirds of the "raw materials" of manufacturing are products already partially processed; the steel from a steel mill is the material purchased and used by the manufacturer of machines, the refined copper from the concentrator or smelter is an important material in the electrical industry, the products of many factories are assembled into automobiles, airplanes, or ships. The fact that partially manufactured or processed materials are major ones in industry tends to hold manufacturing of many goods to existing manufactural regions, no matter for what reason or reasons they may have developed originally.

In conclusion, the commercial, transportational, and service activities of man —activities supporting millions of persons in the world—afford a summation of the complexities of the economic world of the present.

▶ QUESTIONS

1. What are some of the factors which promote regional specialization in today's world?
2. What is the function of transportation in the commercial and industrial world?
3. List several points of difference between the so-called "highly developed" countries or regions of the world and the "underdeveloped" or "undeveloped" lands.

II Sugar and Sugar Refining

The tropical world lies, roughly, between about 30° north latitude and 30° south latitude. These approximate boundaries are zones, not lines. And the border zones themselves are irregular; in some regions the poleward limit of the tropics is considerably short of 30°, and lies toward the equator from these stated latitudes; elsewhere fingers of a tropical environment extend beyond 30° north or south. But for the purpose of understanding commercial production of many of the world's products that originate in a tropical setting, these latitudes serve as rough outer boundaries, for man grows most tropical products in the zonal regions.

The middle latitudes are those of the 30's, 40's, and 50's, north and south. These latitudes are the location of the United States, of Europe, of much of Asia, and of southern Canada. Parts of Australia, all of New Zealand, the southern narrow portion of South America, and the extreme northern shores of Africa as well as the southern tip, also lie in the middle latitudes.

The transitional regions between the tropics and the middle latitudes, on the world scale, straddle the 30th parallel. Within these transitional areas certain of the "short-season" tropical products may originate, ones which reach maturity in less than a year and so will not be affected by the occasional frosts of the zone.

Truly tropical products are those requiring continuous warmth, ones which will not withstand cool weather or frosts. The middle latitudes of the world

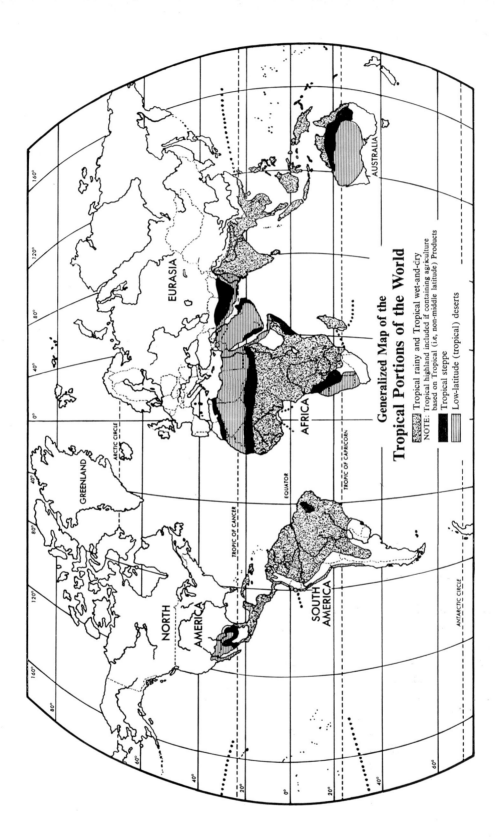

Generalized Map of the
Tropical Portions of the World

Tropical rainy and Tropical wet-and-dry

NOTE: Tropical highland included if containing agriculture based on Tropical (i.e, non-middle latitude) Products

Tropical steppe

Low-latitude (tropical) deserts

cannot produce these products, among which are natural rubber, cacao (cocoa), bananas, pineapples, coffee, and a host of others. Some tropical products are foods; some are raw materials of manufacturing. And yet many, many tropical products are in demand in the nations of the middle latitudes. This results, in the modern, commercial world, in trade between the tropics and the middle latitudes, a trade whose general direction is north-south. And because most middle-latitude consumers of these products live in the Northern Hemisphere of the world, the specific direction of most of this trade is from the tropics northward to market.

The United States is an importer of tropical foods and raw materials. Only one state, Hawaii, is entirely in the tropics. Only Hawaii, the very south of Florida, and small areas in the Southwest can grow tropical products—the southern third of Florida being in a wet-tropical setting, the southwestern areas in the arid tropics and so able to supply tropical products only from districts in which there is water for irrigation. Thus the United States, Canada, and all of Europe—to mention but a few commercially significant market regions—are almost completely or completely dependent upon trade with the tropical world for certain things that the inhabitants now look upon as necessities.

Some few tropical products compete with middle-latitude products; the same end product is obtained from two very different plants. Sugar is an example. And it is with sugar that we introduce this phase of world commercial production, for sugar is considered a necessity by practically all peoples and is a chief ingredient of the food preserving and manufacturing industry.

► SUGAR

Sixty per cent of the world's supply of commercial sugar is obtained from sugar cane, a perennial plant of the tropics. Forty per cent of the commercial sugar is from the sugar beet and originates in the middle latitudes of the world. Thus two distinctly different world regions compete in the sugar trade, competing particularly for the markets of the nations of North America and Europe, but also for the Japanese market. In addition the people of the tropics furnish themselves with cane sugar, brown sugar, or partially refined sweetenings from their home-grown sugar cane. Some middle-latitude countries supply themselves with home-grown beet sugar. The United States draws upon both sources through an elaborate quota system, and grows and refines some of each kind of sugar.

Cane and Beet Sugar

The sugar resulting from the crushing of sugar cane, and the refining of the extracted cane juice, is called cane sugar. That from the processing of sugar beets is beet sugar. Formerly there was usually a slight color differential as well as price differential between cane and beet sugar; today the refining processes have been so developed that few persons can distinguish between the two.

Historically, sugar cane and cane sugar were known long before the advent of a commercial beet-sugar industry. One of the products of tropical India and the tropical Indies was sugar; Europeans traded for this, and prized it highly, for it was a supplement to their usual sweetening material of the Middle Ages—honey. Shortly after the discovery of the New World, sugar plantations were established in the European possessions in the West Indies. Sugar and its by-products of rum and molasses were shipped to European markets. The rapid expansion of sugar-cane acreage in the West Indies and in coastal Brazil was a chief cause of the rapid introduction of African slaves there, as labor in the industry.

The sugar beet, on the other hand, did not enter world markets until after the period of the Napoleonic Wars. France was blockaded by the British Navy, and sugar from her colonies in the West Indies was unobtainable. Napoleon offered a reward for a home source of sugar. A result was the rapid introduction of the beet as a home supply; previous to this period the sugar content of the beet had been known as a result of experimentation by Prussian chemists.

Economically, sugar cane and sugar beets are produced on farms of radically different types and organization. The growing of sugar cane is chiefly a plantation industry—actually a large part of the sugar entering world trade has originated on a tropical plantation. In contrast, sugar beets originate principally upon family-operated farms of the middle latitudes. The plantation in the tropics draws upon outside capital and management, and uses either local labor or labor "imported" from elsewhere in the tropics for plantation work. Farmers growing sugar beets supply their own capital, management, land, and labor; during times of peak labor demands, such as the thinning of young plants, temporary migrant workers may be hired.

The growing of sugar cane on family farms (owned or rented) in the tropics is not unknown. This is the situation in India. But India, and most other "farming" (rather than plantation) areas in the tropics consume their sugar locally. Their sugar does not enter world trade in any significant quantity. Thus it is mainly the tropical plantation and the middle-latitude family farm which supply the raw material for the sugar refineries of the great sugar-consuming nations, and it is the raw or refined sugar from these two source regions which moves in world trade.

► SUGAR CANE

Sugar cane is a tropical perennial plant. It attains a height of from eight to twelve or fifteen feet, and has a tough canelike stalk which may reach an inch or so in diameter. The leaves of the sugar cane plant are broad. Topping the plant, during the blooming season, is a lavender tassellike bloom; but, at the poleward margins of its growth, sugar cane rarely blooms. From a distance a field of sugar cane, during the medium stages of growth, looks not unlike a mature corn field.

Sugar cane requires continuously high temperatures and a great deal of water during the period of its growth. Temperatures continuously in excess of 70° to 75°F are preferable; temperatures in the lower 60's are harmful if they occur for any length of time. Frost is fatal. Only on the poleward margins of its growth is sugar cane subjected to climatic conditions which are not the optimum.

The moisture requirements of growing cane are met by the heavy rainfall of the tropical rainy climate, and by the natural rainfall plus heavy supplementary irrigation in the tropical wet-and-dry climate. In fact nearly all modern plantations use supplementary irrigation to a degree. Those located in leeward, less rainy locations in the wet-and-dry tropics depend heavily upon irrigation and are able to increase and control their yields of cane through controlled water supplies. Total water use, for irrigation and for a sugar mill on a plantation, may reach astronomical proportions: one 8,800-acre plantation in Hawaii alone uses almost as much water per day as does the city of San Francisco, and three times more than the city of Honolulu. Thirty gallons of water have been used in the production of one pound of sugar.

Sugar cane is propagated from cuttings, not from seeds. Pieces of cane, each a foot to eighteen inches in length, are placed in shallow trenches and covered with soil. The cane grows from the cuttings, which send out extensive root systems from which the plants grow. In "primitive" sugar-cane areas the field is plowed by several yoke of oxen or other work animals, and the planting is done by hand, as is the ensuing harvest; workers cut the mature cane by using a machete, or some other type of knife. In highly organized and mechanized sugar-cane regions, such as the Hawaiian Islands, machines have been developed for use in nearly all operations on the plantations, from the plowing of the fields and the planting of the cuttings to the final harvest.

Sugar cane reaches maturity in from a year to eighteen or more months, in some regions twenty-four, depending upon the climatic conditions of the region and the species grown. Normally, in most plantation regions of the tropics, the elapsed time between planting and harvest is from fifteen to sixteen months. As the plant reaches maturity the stalk itself accumulates more and more sugar. Harvest is ideally at the time of maximum sugar content. As it is the stalk, rather than the leaves, which is valuable for sugar, a practice on some plantations is the burning of the field of cane just prior to harvest. The leaves and other excess vegetation are burned off; only the stalk itself, charred and brown but not consumed by the flames, is then cut and transported to the sugar mill.

One planting of sugar cane will yield more than one crop, or harvest, for the plant is a perennial. A second, third, or succeeding crop is known as a ratoon crop. Some plantations, operating in regions of optimum climatic conditions, may harvest seven or eight ratoon crops. Others may harvest only three to five. In any case, after a few ratoon crops the yields of sugar begin to decline; on most commercial operations only some two to five ratoon crops are harvested before the field is replanted. Management must decide, with respect to costs, yields, wages of labor, transportation charges, and prices of sugar on the world market whether to invest in replanting or continue with a ratoon crop from a specific field.

The harvesting of sugar cane varies from a highly seasonal activity in some regions to a year-round activity in other areas. In locations in the wet-and-dry tropics planting occurs toward the end of the dry season. The cane grows during the ensuing wet season, continues through the dry season following, then the second wet season, and then is harvested eighteen months after planting—at the beginning of the second dry season. This is the situation in much of Cuba. In some rainy tropical locations, planting and harvesting occur every month of the year. In some wet-and-dry locations, where heavy continuous irrigation is practiced on the plantations, planting and harvesting may take place side by side, in different fields, any month of the year. Obviously, a continued work program, if possible under the environmental conditions, permits a uniform use of plantation labor throughout the year. Peaks of work and valleys of idleness for plantation hands are avoided.

Harvest is actually somewhat seasonal, varying among producing regions. Cuban sugar harvests usually start during January, in the dry season. Elsewhere different months witness increased activity in the fields. Hawaiian harvests are well spread from February through November, permitting not only an even usage of labor, but long-time operation of sugar mills and their expensive machinery and a relatively even flow of raw sugar by ship from the islands to the mainland United States. Plantations and farms at or near the poleward limits of cane, in contrast, must cut their cane during the short period before the advent of cool or cold weather. In fact, the Louisiana sugar-cane growers, because of annual frosts, must replant annually and harvest nine to ten months later; under these conditions immature cane must often be cut, resulting in decreased yields per acre; no ratoon crop is possible.

Sugar Mills

A large and expensive sugar mill (called this in English-speaking areas, a centrale in Cuba, and other names elsewhere) is a feature of a tropical sugar plantation. Modern sugar mills are intricate factories which convert cane stalks into raw sugar. The investment in a sugar mill runs into hundreds of thousands of dollars. The end product of the mill (raw sugar) becomes the raw material of the sugar refinery, this last being located near the consuming centers rather than in the producing regions.

The cane is brought to the mill by ox team, tractor-drawn wagons, plantation railroad, or cane-hauling trucks, the mode of transport varying regionally in the tropics. Ox teams are still important on some West Indian plantations; the completely mechanized Hawaiian plantations use cane-haulers. Cane-haulers are mounted on six-foot-high rubber tires and are capable of transporting 3,600 tons or more of cane from field to mill during a normal working day.

Fɪɢ. 2-1. Sugar mill in Louisiana, a few miles from the Gulf Coast. Notice the piles of harvested sugar cane. (Standard Oil Company, N.J.)

From the truck, or other conveyance, or from a storage yard, the harvested cane is fed into a sugar mill on conveyor belts. A constant stream of cane enters the mill. During lunch hours the cane from storage yards is used so that the mill can continue in operation; to avoid deterioration cane must be milled within 24 hours of harvest in order to yield its highest sugar content. During its trip into the mill the cane is washed, rocks and mud are eliminated by flotation, trash extractors remove loose vegetation and excess material, and the cane is cut into small lengths.

Crushers—sets of rollers under very high pressure—extract about 70 per cent of the juice as the chopped cane is conveyed into the mill proper. More crushers squeeze out additional juice. Finally more water is added to the almost dry cane, which soaks it up like a sponge; at the final crushing, the added water and remaining sugar juice is pressed from the cane. So thorough is the process that the crushed and completely dry cane stalk, now called bagasse, is conveyed directly to the boilers of the mill, where it is burned immediately to generate steam to run the machinery of the mill, for much power is required; or in some mills the bagasse becomes a raw material for the manufacture of wallboard. Clarifiers, heaters, evaporators, vacuum pans, centrifugals, and other apparatus continue the process of producing raw sugar and separating the by-products.

Investment in a sugar mill—the capital in the mill—is in itself a factor in the continuance of the tropical plantation as a producing unit. Through planned management the plantation furnishes its own material and yields a "finished product" in the form of raw sugar. Large, modern sugar mills which have tried to depend upon small farmers in the tropics for supplies of cane have found planning to be inefficient, supplies erratic in delivery, and expenses of operating the mill to mount in response to intermittent operation or inability to plan for operation during a continuous period of several months. In addition the plantation operation, with perhaps miles of irrigation ditches, fertilization costs, and weed and insect-control programs, is run as an integrated unit; on modern mechanized plantations even the mud washed from the cane as it enters the mill is settled in ponds and returned eventually to the fields.

Competitively, thus, the tropical plantation continues to play a significant role in the growing of sugar cane, its milling, and the production of raw sugar. Its part, collectively, in world sugar-cane production is also considerable. Nonplantation areas supply some sugar to world markets. On the whole, however, the small-farmer portions of the tropics grow local sugar-cane supplies, crush it in small (and sometimes primitive and inefficient) mills, and obtain low yields of sugar per acre or per work input. And yet some such areas—India for example—are among the leaders in total acreage and production in the world; many persons produce the sugar for many in the market. In plantation agriculture few persons, relatively, produce the sugar for the many of the middle-latitude world.

Sugar Refineries

Sugar refineries are located principally at the markets of the consuming country. Moreover, they are mainly in seacoast cities, and directly at the water's edge. Shiploads of raw sugar from the producing areas of the tropics are docked at the refinery. Raw sugar is unloaded directly from the ship to the refinery. European sugar refineries are located in the principal port cities of the maritime nations. Those in Great Britain are especially important because Britain does not have a large sugar-beet industry at home, and depends upon imported raw sugar derived from cane. Sugar refineries in the United States are in port cities such as New Orleans, Savannah, Baltimore, Philadelphia, New York (Brooklyn), and Boston. On the West Coast the large sugar-refining center is at Crockett, California, on a navigable river or strait entering San Francisco Bay. Sugar refineries serving the Canadian market are in Halifax, St. John, and Montreal—Atlantic ports—and in Vancouver, British Columbia, on the Pacific.

Raw sugar from the tropics is the raw material of the sugar refinery. Refined sugar, the white granulated sugar of the grocery, is the manufactured or end product. Investment in a sugar refinery is large. Not only must the raw sugar be treated and recrystallized after the refining process is completed, but the end product must be bagged or boxed and then distributed from the refinery to wholesale and retail merchants. The refinery itself is a large plant, with investment in machinery and equipment (such as pipes and boilers) and in waterside land, docking facilities, and freight-forwarding facilities.

Some sugar is refined in the tropics, as for example in Cuba, and some refined sugar as well as raw sugar is exported. Certain tropical nations wish to develop their own refining industry, but this is opposed by business and labor in the middle-latitude nations on the ground that workers there would be forced into competition with less expensive labor in the tropics. Refineries in the sugar-growing nations have also been retarded in development as a result of tariff policies in the consuming nations; duties upon raw sugar are less than on the final refined product. Thus the imports are generally of the raw sugar. In effect this policy also results in employment of refinery workers in the consuming nation and near the eventual markets rather than in the sugar-producing country.

Many refineries, located in sugar-producing areas, are likewise in the consuming nation. This is the case in the part of Louisiana which grows sugar cane and completes the refining process. And, of course the beet-sugar refineries are in the middle-latitude nations, which both produce and refine sugar beets.

► SUGAR-CANE REGIONS

Sugar cane is believed to have been indigenous to the Indian Peninsula and the Ganges Valley of northern India. From India sugar cane was transported to southern China and the East Indies in very early times, as early as the third century after Christ, according to some authorities.

Arab traders with India introduced sugar cane to Arabian oases in early times. The westward spread of the Arab world between the years 600 and 800 resulted in the introduction of sugar cane to the Nile Valley, northern Africa, and to southern Spain following the Arab conquest of these regions. None of these areas furnished optimum climatic conditions for cane; Europeans continued to trade for limited supplies of sugar from India and the Indies.

The introduction of sugar cane to most of the humid tropical world occurred following the period of its discovery by Europeans. Cane was introduced to tropical Africa, near the mouth of the Congo, in 1472; to the West Indies in 1506; to Brazil and Mexico about 1530, and to other areas in the 1600's. Its introduction to the Louisiana portion of the United States Gulf Coast was relatively late— about 1750.

The West Indies became the great source of sugar for Europe during the 1500's and 1600's. The islands were prized highly by their owners, Spain, France, and England, for their contributions of sugar to the home markets; in fact, the French prized their West Indian islands more than they did Canada. The American colonies received their sugar from the West Indies also, and carried on a brisk trade in the sugar-cane by-products of molasses and rum.

Sugar for the United States, after it became an independent nation, continued to be furnished by the West Indies. But during the period of about a hundred years ago, the tropical plantation based upon sugar cane developed in many overseas locations. The Hawaiian sugar industry started during the 1850's. The source region of sugar began to widen in response to improved and faster ships and the increased demand for sugar in the rising industrial centers of Europe and America.

The Importance of Islands and Shore Locations

Tremendous areas of flat to gently rolling land in the tropics are suitable for the growing of sugar cane. Only the tropical deserts (unless there is water for irrigation, as locally in Peru or Egypt), hilly and mountainous regions, and high-altitude plateaus are excluded from production. But obviously, only a small part of the available acreage of potential sugar land in the tropics is devoted to sugar. The determinative factors of sugar location are other than climate, although, of course, all sugar cane must be grown in areas which are climatically suitable. Climate provides the over-all framework, but actual location of the industry is owing to a combination of many factors. Among these—not all operative in any single region—are political ownership (colony), access to market, availability of local or imported labor, transportation facilities and costs, investments from abroad or by nationals of the producing country, and the size of the market itself. Within recent years, the sugar quota systems, adopted by some consuming nations, have also been factors in either the expansion or contraction of the cane acreage and production of the producing countries.

Islands have been of utmost importance as focal points for the location of sugar plantations in the tropics. Merely a naming of "sugar islands" illustrates this principle—the West Indies, the East Indies, Taiwan, the Philippines, Mauritius, Reunion, the Fijis, the Hawaiian Islands. No plantation on an island is far from the sea. Ports are nearby. Islands are on shipping lanes, or, if they are not and their sugar production is large, ships will come to the islands, for there is business and there is cargo to be handled. Cheap water transportation from island to market is an asset in competition with other areas; inland plantations, in continents, are unable to compete in world markets owing to the costs of land transport.

Shoreline locations are a second favored location for sugar plantations, particularly shorelines near present ports. Originally some tropical sugar areas, like that of northeastern Brazil, were along the seacoast because of settlement accessibility. Ports developed in response to the export of sugar to Portugal. Today, in locating a new sugar plantation, transport is taken into account—transport by rail or road to a not-too-distant port, and transport as represented by the port itself and its facilities. Chief sugar-cane areas in continents, unless serving a local market, are thus at or very near the continental margins.

Plantation Labor

One problem, that of plantation labor in the tropics, has had to be solved by nearly all of the present sugar-cane producers. The problem of "lack of labor" existed, in large part, not because the plantation areas were uninhabited, but because of either the inability or the unwillingness of the original native inhabitants to engage in the day-to-day confining work in the fields of sugar cane.

The original Indian inhabitants of the West Indies proved unsuitable to the work; moreover, many had been killed during the period of Spanish conquest. The developing plantations of the past turned to African slaves for a supply of workers; this was the case, too, in Brazil. Some English colonies, such as Trinidad off the north coast of South America, imported indentured labor from India as field workers.

Sugar planters on the Pacific Islands and in southeastern Africa tapped the Orient for labor, and found an almost inexhaustible supply. The plantations of the British-owned Fiji Islands were manned by Indians from India, as were South African plantations. The native Polynesians of the Hawaiian Islands were unwilling to perform daily tasks on a continuing basis. Hawaiian planters brought, in succession (although there was overlap), Chinese, Portuguese, Japanese, Korean, Spanish, Puerto Rican, and Filipino workers. In total 360,000 Oriental workers were imported, half of them from Japan; 31,500 were brought from Portugal, the Madeira Islands off Africa, Spain, and Puerto Rico. The present composition of the population of many tropical sugar regions thus reflects the past labor shortages in commercial sugar areas.

► WORLD'S LEADING SUGAR-CANE REGIONS

Nearly every portion of the tropical world grows some sugar cane. More than thirty-four countries, on the average, have an annual production of 100,000 tons or more. But eight regions, and about a dozen nations, contribute the bulk of the sugar to world markets. It is these regions and nations which are important, commercially, in the sugar trade. The small farms of India, however, grow about a sixth of the world's sugar cane; however, yields per acre are low so that the country does not produce this percentage of the world's tonnage of sugar. And India's sugar is used at home. It does not figure in world trade to any extent. The small, primitive sugar mill, powered by cattle walking in a circle, is an almost ever-present feature of every Indian village. Surplus sugar, marketed in the cities, is mainly from the Ganges Valley of the north. Cuba follows India in production and heads the list of nations or regions engaged in commercial production.

(1) The West Indies are the world's leading sugar-cane area by far. Among the many islands, Cuba alone produces more sugar cane than even the second world region in production, and alone accounts for one-eighth of the world ton-

nage. In the commercial sugar trade and in the export of sugar, no other area even approaches the West Indies in significance. In this respect, too, Cuba dominates the archipelago. Sugar is the barometer of the Cuban economy; it accounts for one-fourth of the national income and about four-fifths of the total exports of the nation. Three-fourths of Cuba's railroad traffic is associated with sugar. Through the United States sugar quota system (until the revision of 1960) Cuba supplied a third of the annual total of all sugar to this market. Puerto Rico, Haiti, the Dominican Republic, Jamaica, Martinique, and Trinidad are also producers. British islands, such as Jamaica and Trinidad, have market contacts in Britain and Canada; French islands export raw sugar to France. Cuba exports to both the North American and European markets.

(2) Southeast Asia is a significant producer of sugar. India, Pakistan, and southern China serve the large home markets. The islands of the East Indies, especially Java, and the Philippine Islands and Taiwan export raw sugar. Japan taps these producers, as do European nations, and Japan also has small quantities of home-grown cane on its farthest southern island of Okinawa in the Ryukyus.

(3) The Hawaiian Islands in mid-Pacific are among the world's leading producers of raw sugar. The Hawaiian setting has been extremely favorable, as the islands have been (and are) in the economic framework of the United States, first as a territory, now as a state. Hawaiian sugar has thus had duty-free access to the American market, and the more than a million tons of annual production are all marketed in this country. The Fiji Islands in the southwest Pacific are likewise sugar islands, oriented toward the British and Australian-New Zealand markets.

(4) Islands of the Indian Ocean, particularly Mauritius and Reunion, are likewise "sugar islands." For a time Mauritius occupied a place in British imports comparable to Cuba in American sugar, but this position has been lost recently.

Collectively, (5) mainland Latin America, from Mexico to northern Argentina, can and does grow large acreages of sugar cane. Brazil leads among these nations. The northern part of the eastern coast of Brazil has long engaged in the sugar industry. During colonial days it was the source region of sugar for Portugal. The slave trade from Africa to Brazil, and the long-time continuance of slavery (1889) was largely associated with the sugar region. But Colombia, British Guiana, Peru, Mexico, and Ecuador, among others, possess significant acreages of sugar cane. Peruvian sugar plantations, unlike others, are located in irrigated valleys in the Peruvian desert. The cane is watered by exotic streams whose sources are in the high Andes, and which descend to the desert valleys of Peru.

(6) Africa and (7) Australia grow sugar cane. In the Union of South Africa the state of Natal, on the Indian Ocean, is the sugar producer. Natal leads all African areas in production, but some cane is grown in all political units of the continent. Labor from India was imported to work the cane fields of Natal; this was the start of the present large Indian population of both Natal and other parts of eastern Africa. Egypt, which irrigates its cane fields from the Nile, follows Natal in importance but consumes its own supply and is not a factor in sugar exports.

Australian sugar is grown along the tropical coast of Queensland, in the northeast of the continent. Unlike other tropical regions, Australian cane is grown on farms rather than plantations, and by white farmers and laborers. Government policy prohibits the importation of workers from elsewhere in the tropics. Through a high tariff, Australia now supplies itself with its needs of cane sugar.

(8) The Gulf Coast of the United States lies at the poleward limit of sugar cane. In this area, subject to annual killing frosts, sugar cane must be replanted each spring; it is harvested after a ten- to eleven-month period of growth. Were it not for tariffs and quotas, the competition of the region with the nearby West Indies would be more severe than it is. There are two areas of production. By far the larger is in Louisiana and includes part of the delta of the Mississippi and the bayou country to its west and northwest. There are both plantations and farms engaged in the activity; many of the sugar farmers (in contrast to the plantations) of the area are the Acadian French, who were moved to Louisiana from eastern Canada in the 1750's, and constitute the inhabitants of this rural French-speaking

FIG. 2-2. Air view of a sugar plantation in Louisiana, one located on the natural levees of the Mississippi River. The mill and the homes of the workers occupy a higher portion of the levee, toward the river. The cane fields stretch beyond, toward the wooded and poorly drained portion of the inner levee. (Standard Oil Company, N.J.)

part of the state. The second Gulf sugar-producing area lies in southern Florida, near Lake Okeechobee. True plantations are the operating units here. Unlike Louisiana, frosts may occur only one year in two—or three—and some cane fields survive the "winter" and resume growth as a perennial.

Regional Sugar Cane Production

Two principal commercial producers of raw sugar will be described as samples of the modern industry. Each illustrates the pattern of sugar production in the tropics. Each is outstanding in the production and export of raw sugar. These producers, Hawaii and Cuba, are alike in some ways, unlike in others. The two are the present large commercial producers in the world. They are unlike some of the primitive producing areas, of course—oxen-powered areas and plantations, or the small-grower region of India, whose sugar is ground in primitive village mills, these often animal-powered. But it is these modern areas and producers which figure in the world trade picture and in the commercial production, export, and transportation of raw sugar to distant markets.

▶ HAWAIIAN SUGAR PRODUCTION

The Hawaiian sugar plantations and sugar industry are the most mechanized and modern in the world. Every field operation, from plowing and planting to final harvest, is mechanized. Gigantic cane-haulers transport the cane to the mills, where it is unloaded mechanically and transferred by machinery from storage yard or cane-hauler to the endless belts which move the cane into the sugar mills. Some plantations, employing 800 or more persons, have nearly as many employees in office and mill positions as in the fields. Only the care and maintenance of irrigation systems and the control of irrigation pumps and valves remain hand jobs. On those plantations which use portable pipes for irrigation, instead of open ditches for the water, even the pipe is moved from field to field by mechanical transport. No longer is the importation of plantation labor from the Orient a necessity; in fact, aliens who have retired with assurance of benefit funds and wish to return home are encouraged to leave if they so wish.

The geographic setting of Hawaii in the American economic scene has been largely, even if indirectly, responsible for the mechanization of Hawaiian sugar plantations. This is owing to two factors—Hawaii's planters must compete with "cheap-labor" tropical areas, all of which are outside of the American economic realm; and Hawaii's raw sugar, all of which is marketed on the United States mainland, in the western two-thirds of the nation, faces severe competition in its marketing area with beet sugar, nearly all of which is produced and refined in the western United States.

Hawaiian sugar plantations must pay American minimum wages to sugar field

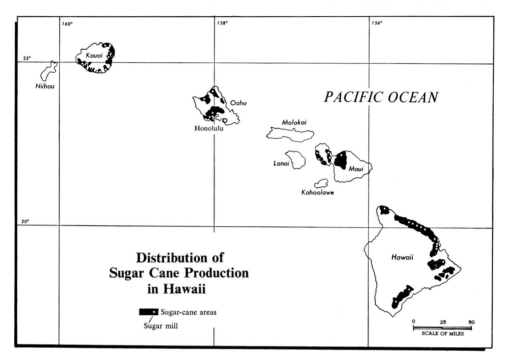

Distribution of Sugar Cane Production in Hawaii

■ Sugar-cane areas
Sugar mill

PACIFIC OCEAN

workers. Competitively, with other tropical areas not included in the United States framework, this places Hawaiian sugar workers as "the highest paid in the world." Moreover, the plantation workers of Hawaii are unionized, and persons of different skills receive wages which are higher than the legal minimum. As a "high-labor cost area" (relative to other tropical producers of sugar) Hawaii has become an area wherein management has sought to replace labor with machinery wherever possible. In addition, normal American inventiveness and tinkering have prevailed; many of the present labor-saving machines have been perfected in Hawaii. Local companies are now marketing them elsewhere in the tropics.

Secondly, Hawaiian sugar (all refined at Crockett, California) faces severe market competition. It is refined and marketed in the heart of the sugar-beet area of the nation, which stretches from the West Coast to east of Denver, Colorado. Freight charges preclude the marketing of Hawaiian sugar east of about St. Louis. Beyond this point the cane-sugar refineries of the Gulf Coast and the East Coast possess a freight-rate advantage. Competition in and for the market also has been a potent factor in causing Hawaiian plantations to be extremely efficient and in cutting production costs through mechanization in order to survive. Even so, some Hawaiian plantations have ceased operations during post-war years—mainly plantations whose fields were too rolling or hilly for efficient mechanization.

The efforts to reduce costs in Hawaii to meet tropical and market competition are apparent in other ways. Raw sugar, for example, is not bagged, as in Cuba. It is transported from sugar mill to dock in bulk, either in trucks or on conveyor belts.

It is stored in bulk on the docks, loaded in bulk, and conveyed in bulk in the holds of the sugar ships directly to the refinery. The Sugar Planters Association conducts a large-scale research program and grows experimental plots. The results of this research are shown in the development of species of cane particularly suited to the Hawaiian environment, where cane takes nearly two years to ripen, and in greatly increased yields of sugar per acre. Hawaiian plantations, even in rainy areas, depend also upon heavy irrigation; 85 per cent of the crop is irrigated. Heavy fertilization of cane fields is practiced also.

Twenty-eight sugar plantations and 27 sugar mills constitute the entire producing units in the Hawaiian Islands. The plantations, American-owned (many of them with a dominant number of stockholders resident in the islands) and operated, are located on only four of the individual islands—Kauai, Oahu, Maui,

Fig. 2-3. The highest irrigation ditch separates the two chief crops of Hawaii, which do not compete for land on the small islands. Sugar cane, to the left, is irrigated; pineapples, to the right, are unirrigated and can therefore be grown on rougher land. This ditch, on Oahu, is about 600 feet above sea level at this point. The agricultural land from this elevation to the sea is dominantly in sugar cane; pineapples are grown to altitudes of 1,200 to 1,400 feet or more—in many places on rolling to very sloping land. This is a field of young pineapple plants. (Dole Photo, Courtesy Hawaii Visitor Bureau)

and Hawaii. All plantations are at low elevations, usually less than 600 feet above sea level. Some 255,000 acres of land are devoted to sugar cane; 50,000 persons are directly or indirectly dependent upon the industry. More than a million tons of raw sugar are produced annually. Bulk sugar handling terminals are located at the exporting port of each island—at Nawiliwili, Honolulu, Kahului, and Hilo. With a ten- to twelve-month continuous harvest, the sugar fleet is on a constant and continuous move. Operations on plantation and sea thus have a relatively smooth and efficient yearly flow, without pronounced peaks of work or periods of idleness.

There is one sugar refinery in the Hawaiian Islands, at Aiea on Oahu, refining only for the local market. Thus, despite economic framework in the American scene, the Hawaiian sugar industry is oriented to an "overseas" middle-latitude market, and to a market at least 2,400 miles away, far more distant than Cuba's market. Yet the Hawaiian sugar shipments are "internal trade" of the United States, while Cuba's shorter shipments are foreign trade.

► CUBAN SUGAR PRODUCTION

The island of Cuba, the size of Pennsylvania, possesses an extremely favorable natural environment for sugar cane. In fact, some consider the environmental conditions to be the optimum in the world for the crop. Sugar cane reaches maturity in Cuba in fourteen to fifteen months, a shorter period than in most competing areas. Cuba is 700 miles long and averages less than 50 miles in width; plantations and sugar-cane farms are not far from the sea. And nearly all of the area is a level to undulating plain, well-watered during the rainy season, with adequate ground water for the dry season, and with rich and deep red clay soils of high productivity, the Matanzas clay being especially fertile. Large fields of cane are possible. Furthermore the island is well supplied with good natural harbors, no one of which is far removed from the sugar plantations.

Economically, Cuba is fortunate in being located at the "front door" of the large American market. Short transport by sea reaches American ports; European ports can be reached by low-cost (as compared to land transport) sea journeys. Labor is relatively efficient and inexpensive. Home labor may be supplemented, when needed, from the other islands of the West Indies, nearly all of which are much more crowded than Cuba.

Politically, Cuba has had favorable treatment in the market of the United States. After gaining its freedom from Spain in 1898, Cuba was granted a favorable tariff position. With the advent of the sugar import quota system, Cuba was assigned a prime place in the market. After 1934 the United States stimulated the sugar industry of the island by paying Cuba more than two cents a pound above the world price for sugar. This continued despite the upsetting of Cuban governments and revolutions: each Cuban government recognized the dependence of

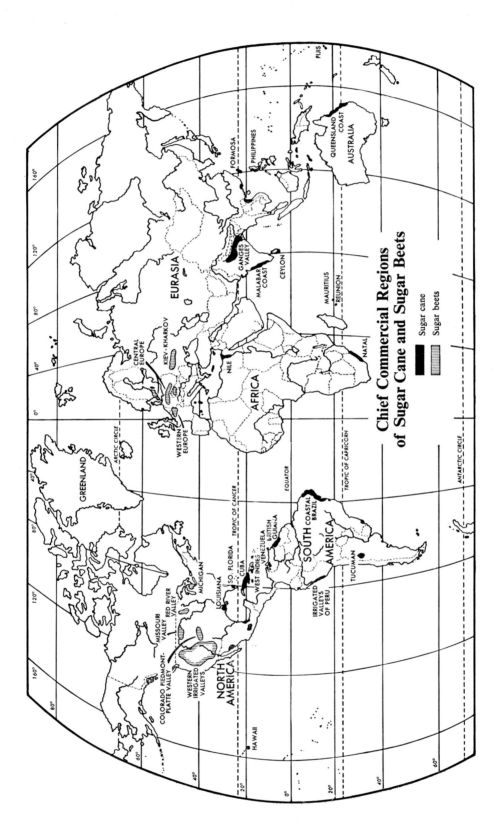

Chief Commercial Regions of Sugar Cane and Sugar Beets

the country upon sugar exports and did not disturb the economic and monetary base of the nation; however, the advent of the Castro government in 1959 resulted in a "land reform" act and government seizure of what was called "excess" plantation land. The plantations, many of them American-owned, were able to retain only a stated maximum acreage, and some were confiscated entirely. Certain plantations were changed in their form of operation to a "sugar co-operative" and others were broken up and the land distributed among the peasants. Presumably the same acreage of sugar cane is to be grown, but a higher percentage of the crop will be raised outside of the boundaries of large landholdings. Under the Castro regime, Cuba sought other markets than those of the United States. Two examples of the changed attitude were negotiated in the early months of 1960. Barter arrangements were made with the Soviet Union and with Communist China. A million tons of Cuban sugar (equivalent to the annual production from the American state of Hawaii) is to be shipped to Russia each year in exchange for Russian petroleum and machinery; half a million tons of sugar is to be shipped to Communist China annually in exchange for Chinese merchandise and household goods. In each case Cuba is to receive one-fifth of the payment in American dollars, the rest in petroleum, machinery, and merchandise; original agreements were for five years. And, to refine the petroleum, the Castro government seized the American-owned and -operated oil refineries of the island.

The attitude of the Cuban government has changed the form of sugar production but not the regions of production, to be described in this section.

The reaction to these events in the United States resulted in the Congress directing, in mid-1960, that the sugar quota allotted to Cuba be reduced somewhat in amount. Early in 1961 diplomatic relations between the United States and Cuba were terminated, and all sugar exports from Cuba to the United States were stopped. The elimination of Cuban imports was made up by increasing the quota from Mexico, Central American and West Indian areas, by a large increase in the quota of the Philippines, and by raising the quotas of the domestic producers of sugar—mainland cane and mainland beet sugar growers.

The conditions just described illustrate the "political" or man-made influence upon economic geography and the markets of a given time or year. With completely free trade Cuba could—at least theoretically—supply the sugar needs of the United States. With high duties and a high tariff wall for protection the domestic sugar-beet industry could expand to serve the market; this is the case in several European countries, which, because of past experience with wars and shipping shortages, prefer to have a home supply at all times. With a quota or allotment system in use since the 1930's, the United States spread its source regions, Cuba being the dominant one, even under the 1960 revision. But with any system Cuba remains the largest commercial producer of sugar in the world. Despite its man-made changes, the environment remains the same; the soils, level surfaces of large extent, and optimum conditions for the growing of sugar cane are not changed. If Cuba has to change its marketing pattern, or reduce its sugar-cane acreage either

temporarily or permanently, it will not be owing to any change in the environmental conditions or to any change in its geographical location at the "door" of
the largest sugar market in the world. It will be a result of political and man-made
factors in the scene.

Capital from the United States was invested heavily in the Cuban sugar industry prior to 1959. One-quarter of the plantations, including the largest ones in
Cuba, were American-owned; one candy manufacturer operated the largest of
all. Propinquity to the market attracted capital from the market. Moreover, Cuban
capital has been accumulated and invested—the existence, in large part, of the
steady United States market making this possible. Nearly all of the modern plantations and sugar mills in Cuba date from the present century, after Cuban freedom and United States protection, despite the over-all antiquity of sugar production in the island. Negatively, of course, American capital interested in sugar had
little alternative choice. Puerto Rico is mountainous, only some 3,400 square miles
in area, and its flat lands are on discontinuous and fragmented deltas and river
flood plains. The American Virgin Islands contain only 133 square miles of rough
terrain. Other islands are small, mountainous; their investment is tied to Europe
through ownership of the islands, or—as in the case of the republics of Haiti and
the Dominican Republic which share the island of Hispaniola—constant revolution, change of government, and general unrest have not been attractive to outside
investors.

Sugar production stretches from just west of the city of Havana eastward almost to the eastern mountainous tip of Cuba. The older producing regions are
near Havana and in the western half of the island, except for hilly Pinar del Rio
in the far west; the newer areas are eastward. No plantation is far from a shipping
center, a result of the narrowness of the island. The deep clay soils are all in the
areas suitable for sugar cane, areas on the plain at low elevations. One-third of
Cuban sugar is grown on the Matanzas clay; two-thirds of all cane is grown at
elevations of less than 300 feet above sea level and accessible to the ports; nearly
all sugar cane is grown at elevations lower than 900 feet.

Some 160 sugar mills, or centrales, grind the cane of Cuban plantations and
small farmers and bag the raw sugar for export. Of these, in the late 1950's,
114 were Cuban-owned and 40 were American-owned. Beginning in March
1960 some of the American-owned centrales were taken over by the Cuban government, and the American personnel evicted. In the "newer" sugar region of eastern
Cuba, the average centrale is far larger than in the older sugar lands of western
Cuba; three mills in the far east are among the largest in the nation.

Cuba is well supplied with pouch-shaped, indented natural harbors. With
one or two exceptions these all have deep water. Ports for the export of the bagged
raw sugar have been built at these harbors. Both north shore and south shore ports
engage in sugar export. In total, there are 23 exporting ports handling Cuban
raw sugar, but five of these handle 40 per cent of the trade. Nuevitas, on the north
shore, leads with 15 per cent of Cuba's exports, but is followed closely by Havana

Fig. 2-4. Cane carriers lined up awaiting delivery of harvested cane to a cooperative sugar mill in a district where cane is grown on farms rather than plantations. (Standard Oil Company, N.J.)

(north shore) and Júcaro (south shore). Of the two remaining "chief" ports, Cardenas and Cienfuegos, one is on each coast. The wide distribution of ports, and their presence on two sides of the long and narrow island, reflects the widespread distribution of Cuba's sugar plantations, and small farmers (*colonos*) who also contribute to the production of sugar cane.

Some sugar is refined in Cuba. Refineries are concentrated in and near Havana, in response to the Cuban home market. Cubans would like to add to their refinery capacity and export the finished product. To date the differential tariffs and quotas in the consuming nations, differentials between duties on raw sugar and refined sugar, have retarded the expansion of local refining.

► BEET SUGAR

The growing and processing of sugar beets is confined to the middle-latitude countries of the Northern Hemisphere. It is in these countries that the 40 per cent of world sugar contributed by the beet is grown and refined. The trade in beet sugar is a domestic trade in most of the producing nations, and it does not often cross international boundaries. However, in part of western Europe it becomes foreign trade from nation to nation, owing to the small areas of the differing political units. In contrast to the middle latitudes of the Northern Hemisphere, the nations of these latitudes in the Southern Hemisphere produce little beet sugar; except for New Zealand and Chile each country can, and does, grow sugar cane somewhere within the home area. However, sugar-beet acreage is not appreciable, even in these two countries. Thus, the sugar beets of the world are produced, almost entirely, in the United States and Canada, in western and central Europe, and in the Soviet Union. In Asia only the Manchurian Plain has a very limited acreage.

Historical Development

A Prussian scientist, Andreas S. Marggraf, called attention to the sugar content of the beet in a paper published in 1747. The King of Prussia helped sponsor the development of the industry, as Prussia was without tropical colonies and had to import its entire supply of sugar. A sugar-beet factory, or refinery, was built in Silesia in 1802. It remained, however, for the French under Napoleon to place the activity on a commercial basis, owing to the difficulties encountered by the nation in obtaining cane sugar during the blockades and unrest of the Napoleonic wars. By the close of the Napoleonic period nearly 100,000 acres of sugar beets were under cultivation in France.

Agricultural scientists and chemists have had a major part, through the years, in the development of a sugar beet which contains a high percentage of sugar. Originally the beet yielded about 5 per cent of sugar, or it took some twenty pounds of beets to yield a pound of sugar. Today the sugar content of the beet has been so improved that the yield is nearly 20 per cent; five to six pounds of beets produce a pound of sugar. Furthermore, the beet tonnage per acre has been increased greatly.

The Crop and Its Requirements

The sugar beet is a large, white beet. A long taproot descends six to eight feet into the soil, to moisture-bearing levels. Soils for beet production must be loose and friable to permit the manyfold expansion of the small young beet into the very large beet of the harvest; heavy clays do not permit the proper growth of the plant.

The sugar beet is a cool-summer crop. Preferably the summer months should not average above 70°F. Bright, clear autumn days, days of warm midday temperatures but cool, crisp nights, aid in the concentration of sugar content. Thus the harvest of sugar beets is late in the growing season, as compared to other farm crops. October usually witnesses the peak harvests, but digging of beets is often continued, or completed, in November, after the advent of frosts in most of the producing areas. The cool marine climates of western Europe and the Pacific Northwest, and the cool-summer continental climates of the northern border states of the United States and of the south-central part of the Soviet Union in Europe offer optimum conditions. Their cool summers and sunny autumns are ideal for promoting sugar content. But in addition, the cool and high irrigated valleys of the western United States offer optimum temperate conditions, and in these valleys the paucity of rainfall can be compensated for by irrigation. Thus the crop becomes a significant one in many irrigated districts. In addition (discussed later) economic conditions of irrigated areas in the West are very significant in the concentration of beets in many irrigated areas.

Beet-Sugar Refineries

The beet-sugar refining industry is located in the various producing regions. Beets are too bulky to be shipped any great distance to refining centers; the relative cost of land transport is too high, considering the weight of the raw material. Furthermore, most producing areas are in inland locations (United States or the Soviet Union) or, if not far removed from the sea (Northern France), are close to the eventual market of the refined sugar in the industrial centers of the country. Thus, in contrast to cane-sugar refineries, those working with beets are in the beet-growing areas rather than in the market areas. The refined beet sugar is then shipped to the consuming centers. A second contrast to the cane-sugar industry is that the beet industry has no intermediate stage, such as raw sugar or brown sugar; refined beet sugar is the direct product of the processing of sugar beets.

The Growing of Sugar Beets

Sugar beets are planted from seeds. As the seed is exceptionally small the young beet plants come up thickly. This necessitates the thinning of young plants. It is this stage in the industry that requires the greatest labor input, although recently machine planting of more widely spaced seeds and machine thinning of young plants have had some success. Thinning has ordinarily been done by hand; gangs of workers walk down the rows of beets, stooping over to pull up the un-needed young plants. This permits the remaining beets to grow to large size and to have uncrowded room in which to develop.

Thinning of beets in Europe is commonly accomplished by local agricultural labor. Women and children work in the fields at this process. Thinning of beets in United States producing regions is commonly dependent upon migratory sea-sonal labor, particularly from Mexico. In some northeastern growing areas local workers and high-school students are recruited for this purpose. Because, however, much of the nonmachine thinning is accomplished by migratory workers, the workers are also housed temporarily in the region and used later in the season for hoeing, weeding, and other operations in the fields—operations which could be performed by machine were it not for the need of the recruitment of the migratory workers for the thinning.

The abundant leaves of the sugar-beet plant shade the ground by midsummer. Agencies then direct the migratory labor to other areas, for hand operations such as picking fruit. The sugar-beet grower, from midsummer on, handles his crop by machine, digs it by machines which lift the beets from the ground, and transports the harvested beets to the sugar refinery.

Beet-sugar refineries operate seasonally. Operations begin as the crop is delivered. During the winter operations continue; beets are piled high in the storage yards or are delivered by rail or truck from outlying storage yards at railroad sidings or trucking terminals. From the refinery the boxed or bagged granulated sugar is shipped to markets.

The beet-sugar industry has some important by-products. One is the beet tops. This leafy vegetation is removed from the beet at the time of harvest. It is stored in pit-silos or in gigantic piles, or, in some cases, is chopped and blown into upright silos. The fodder provided by the tops is fed to animals during the winter season. In Europe the animals are on the farms; beet silage is a supplementary feed. In most beet regions of the United States the farmers purchase feeder cattle or sheep from elsewhere after the beet harvest. These are fed in part upon the beet silage, which, with other feeds, fattens the stock for market. In western beet areas the usual feeder stock is sheep, which have been grazed on mountain pastures during the summer and are driven to the irrigated valleys for winter feeding and fattening for market.

Beet pulp is a by-product of a sugar refinery. This is the remaining portion of the beet after the sugar has been extracted. Sugar-beet pulp may be fed to animals directly. Commonly now in the United States it is mixed with molasses and the resulting mixture is dried and bagged. The sugar-beet pulp-molasses mixture has proved to be excellent concentrated feed for cattle. The refineries ship it all over the nation, to the Hawaiian Islands for their cattle industry, and export it as well. An interesting sidelight on this product is that the beet refineries purchase the molasses from cane-sugar refineries; thus the two industries, competitors for markets and for quotas, are complementary in this by-product activity.

Leading Producing Areas

Two outstanding beet-producing regions are the western irrigated valleys of the United States and the plains region of western Europe and of part of the Soviet Union.

▶ WESTERN VALLEYS OF THE UNITED STATES

The sugar beet fills the need of the western irrigated valleys for an intensive crop, one which produces a large yield per acre and whose total value is high per acre. In irrigated agriculture there are costs which are not present in humid farming areas. Ditches, dams, and other irrigation and water-control works must be paid for. They must be kept in repair. Water must be paid for. Charges, obvious and hidden, are numerous. Farm operators cannot, usually, meet the high charges of irrigation agriculture without growing a valuable and intensive crop. A field of low-value hay, or a field of oats, fails to pay for itself—to produce a product whose value is greater than the charges for the water and the works to grow it, and whose value, in addition, will yield enough to pay for the cost of labor, and for the taxes on the land. Every irrigated region, unless subsidized in some way, must grow a high-value, intensive crop.

Fruits are a usual irrigated product of many western valleys—peaches in Colorado, apples and soft fruits in Washington, citrus in parts of Arizona and California. But most high-altitude irrigated valleys have too short a growing season for fruits or nights which are too cool as the dry air which has heated rapidly by day cools rapidly by night. Cool nights handicap a high-yielding crop such as corn. Other intensive crops are eliminated for one environmental reason or another. Thus, through environmental handicaps, particularly climatic ones, many irrigated regions find sugar beets to be their highest value crop. Furthermore, and equally important, the cool nights and sunny and cool days of high-altitude valleys are *ideal* for the sugar beet. The very conditions which handicap many fruits, cotton, or corn offer optimum conditions for the sugar beet.

Warmer southern and low-altitude irrigated valleys, such as the Salt River Valley of southern Arizona and the Imperial Valley of southeastern California, can grow two crops—their growing season is one of twelve months. These valleys can grow an intensive hot-season crop (cotton) and an intensive cool season or "winter" crop, such as out-of-season vegetables or sugar beets.

Thus, in ten to a dozen western states of the United States, sugar beets occupy a significant place in the economy of irrigated districts. In high-altitude valleys they are a summer crop, harvested in the fall. In low-altitude and warm valleys the sugar beet is a winter crop following another intensive product.

The growing of sugar beets, and the refining of beet sugar, is concentrated in the western United States, both for economic and geographic reasons. The cities of Denver and Salt Lake City are important regional centers in the industry. Western senators at times combine as a "sugar-beet bloc." And western sugar-beet interests compete vigorously with Hawaiian sugar-cane interests for the western market. And, of course, the western sugar industry is a competitor for "upping" its United States quota and thus reducing tropical quotas—say, from Latin America. It is here that the stiff competition between more than 100,000 American farmers—who are voters—and a few Latin American plantations reaches the halls of Congress; and here, within the economic framework of the United States, where middle-latitude family farms of the irrigated West compete with the two dozen tropical plantations of the state of Hawaii.

► EUROPE

Sugar-beet concentrations in European nations reflect political and geographic situations, in contrast to the economic and geographic factors in the United States.

In each area the environment of the sugar-beet-growing regions is at the optimum, and yields are high. Thus, European nations choose to emphasize and even subsidize a sugar-beet industry in order to have a home supply of sugar. They are desirous of being free from complete dependence upon tropical sources of sugar. The degree of their success is shown by the general abundance of sugar in most European countries during World War II and the lack of sugar and consequent necessity of sugar rationing in the United States during the same period. As soon as shipping was affected by submarine warfare, or commandeered for troop movements, the United States felt the shortage; European production and consumption continued.

Sugar-beet acreage in western Europe is highly concentrated and is grown in small and specialized producing districts. All of these are within the large area which offers optimum climatic conditions for the crop. Only in Germany is there a beet acreage in all parts of the country; even so, there is a concentration in part of the North German Plain, on loessial soils.

French and Belgian acreage is mainly near the joint frontier; French growers depend, in part, upon cheaper Belgian labor for thinning, weeding, and other hand operations. Central Europe has an ample supply of inexpensive labor. German farmers use their family labor, or draw upon refugees from the East. Soviet production, concentrated principally in the Ukraine near Kiev and Kharkov, draws upon the home labor resident on the collective farms.

The countries of central Europe usually produce a surplus of beet sugar. Considering the political situation this is exported to the East, to the Soviet Union. France, Belgium, and Denmark usually have a small surplus. This is directed to Germany and Britain, densely inhabited areas whose home supply of beet sugar must be supplemented by imported beet and cane sugar. Germany, in particular, imports quantities of beet sugar, despite her large home production, while Britain's imports lean toward cane sugar from her tropical lands.

► QUESTIONS

1. Why is one of the fundamental divisions in the world that between tropical areas and the middle latitudes?
2. Why is the tropical plantation so important in the production of certain agricultural products—both foods and raw materials of manufacture?
3. How does a plantation differ from a farm in its organization?
4. What environmental conditions restrict the major world production of sugar cane to the tropics?
5. Why are the specific sites of sugar (and other) plantations commonly on islands, peninsulas, isthmuses, or along shores?
6. Although sugar cane is grown in the tropics, sugar refineries are commonly in the middle latitudes. Explain why.

7. How is the Hawaiian sugar industry especially favored by its location within the United States? How is it affected competitively in the world sugar scene by this location?

8. Why do certain European countries promote a home sugar-beet industry?

9. Why is the sugar-beet crop so important to farmers of the American West?

10. In your opinion, would it be possible for the United States to produce its sugar requirements within the fifty states and possessions? Indicate the reasons for your answer. In your opinion, would this be wise or unwise? Support your answer.

11. Look up the latest figures of the sugar quota of the United States. Make a map to show the source regions or countries.

III Bananas, Pineapples, and Dates

The tropical world is a large and diverse one, peopled by groups of vastly different backgrounds, cultures, and stages of civilization and economic development.

The tropical world, on a broad scale, has only slight temperature changes, and temperatures are continuously high, usually in the 70's and 80's by day. Nights are warm to hot. But there are major rainfall differences in the tropics, and it is these rather than the temperature which distinguish the different climates. In general there are three tropical climates—(1) the rainy tropics, with adequate to excessive rainfall during all months; (2) the wet-and-dry tropics (called the savanna climate in many areas, the monsoon climate in southeast Asia), broad areas characterized by alternating rainy and dry (or less rainy) seasons during the course of a year; and (3) the dry tropics, or arid tropics, whose area comprises the great tropical deserts of the world, such as the Sahara.

The systems of livelihood in the tropics are diverse from place to place, and within the same climatic type. Some tribal groups engage in gathering, fishing, and hunting; these peoples do not plant seeds, they do not harvest. There are primitive agricultural systems, many involving "shifting cultivation," or the shifting of a crop to newly cleared fields as the soil of old fields wears out. There are subsistence agricultural economies. There are highly organized and productive economies such as in most of India and tropical southern China. There are plantation economies, wherein the plantation is organized for the complete purpose of the production of one crop, or product, for distant overseas markets in the countries of the middle latitudes. In the arid tropics there are nomadic peoples and advanced, complex irrigation economies almost side by side—the one in the barren desert, the other along exotic streams such as the Nile. There are livestock ranchers in parts of the tropical world, and there are people who have no animals and no experience with them.

We shall have to confine our interest to the major commercial products of the tropical world—products which are exported from it or which maintain significant industries within the tropics themselves. These products may furnish food, raw materials for industry, and major items of trade between nations. We will not discuss all of the noncommercial economies. These support thousands of persons within the tropics, but the products of these subsistence economies do not leave the area, do not enter world trade, and, while very important locally, are of little commercial consequence at present to other parts of the world. Let us take the banana as an example. Bananas are a most significant and widely used food throughout the wet tropics; they help contribute to the sustenance of thousands of people. But, the commercially significant "banana regions" are those which grow bananas for distant markets, those which, as a result, have shipping lines calling at their ports, and have commercial ties with other areas. The farmers and the plantations of these regions purchase outside necessities; they live in "the modern business world" and are an integral part of it.

Present subsistence areas may be "brought" into the commercial world as a result of many factors. The demand for bananas in middle-latitude New Zealand is being supplied now by the Samoan Islands. Until a few years ago the banana was one of the subsistence items of Samoa; it is now sold for cash, and the Samoans use the income to purchase items they previously went without. Present interest of the United States, the United Nations, and other organizations in the so-called "undeveloped" or "underdeveloped" countries is resulting, among many changes, in the creation of demand for "outside products."

From these many products of the tropics some fruits and vegetables have emerged as leaders in commercial trade; there is a demand for them elsewhere. From time to time others gain wide acceptance. No doubt still "new" tropical fruits and vegetables may enter world markets as freezing and preserving methods are perfected and transportation is pushed to remote areas.

We will discuss the chief tropical fruits and vegetables of world trade. The regions wherein these are produced commercially will be treated. Other products —for example, the taro of the Pacific Islands, important food of the Micronesians and, as poi, of the native Polynesians of Hawaii—will not be dealt with; like other tropical products which have not attained wide acceptance, taro does not enter the commercial world in quantity, despite its extreme importance as a basic food of certain peoples.

The tropical fruits and vegetables are produced as close to middle-latitude markets as possible because transportation is an important item. But they must be grown in an environment which is at least permissive, and ideally should be very favorable. The West Indies and Central America are close to the markets of the United States by sea, for no place in these islands or on the isthmus is far from ports. One might think that parts of southern Mexico were closer; they may be by air, but many tropical-products areas of Mexico are inland. The expense of a combined land journey to a port and sea shipment is greater—mainly because of the land shipment. Shore and island locations thus possess a cost advantage over inland locations.

Theoretically, with large tropical regions south of North America, of Europe, and of eastern Asia, the inhabitants of these continents should get their tropical foods and raw materials from "due south"; but this is not necessarily so in practice. Tropical areas possess very different stages of commercial development. And their political situation and foreign investments vary. Thus, as we will see, the tropical producers are not "parceled out" among the middle-latitude markets. But the United States is fortunate in that many—but by no means all—of its requirements from the tropical world are met by the regions of Latin America to our south and southeast. In this respect, the areas "closest" from the point of view of cost, do contribute heavily to the market, and practice is close to theory.

Tropical fruits number hundreds. The banana and the pineapple are the best known and most widely distributed. Bananas and pineapples are shipped in large quantities from specialized regions of production to world markets. The foreign trade in these fruits is from both tropical farms and plantation agriculture.

► BANANAS

The banana and its relative, the plantain, grow throughout the wet tropics or the wet-and-dry tropics. It is a principal source of food for the people of wide areas. There are many varieties of the fruit, and these range from types used entirely for cooking to many which are eaten directly. Skin colorations of bananas are variable, also; reds and yellows are common. Only a few species of bananas withstand shipment to distant markets, and it is these with which the middle-latitude consumer is familiar.

The range of the banana in the New World is from lowland regions of Mexico to northern Argentina and southern Brazil. In Africa the banana grows from the grasslands of the Sudan (south of the Sahara Desert) to Rhodesia. It grows also on the islands off of northwestern Africa, along protected shores in Algeria, and, if irrigated, all along the Nile Valley. The Asian-Australian range of the banana is throughout India and Pakistan, and from southern China southward throughout the islands of the East Indies, and to the northern and northeastern shores of Australia. In many primitive areas, such as portions of the Amazon Basin, the

Congo Basin and elsewhere in Africa, and on some of the islands of the East Indies, the banana is a principal source of native food. This is true also even in certain more highly developed areas, such as eastern Brazil; and nearly the entire production of India is consumed at home.

The banana tree is a soft-stalk tree. It grows from a planted rhizome. The stalk bears one bunch of bananas in twelve to sixteen months. After the bunch has been harvested, the stalk itself is cut down and another from the same root takes its place. By planting in blocks or sections, plantations or growers can count on almost continuous harvests.

The banana leaf is large and watery and shreds or tears easily, or dips under its own weight as it increases in size. The soft stalk is not resistant to sudden forces. Thus the entire tree is very subject to being blown down by high winds; when the bunch of bananas is near maturity it is lost. Gales and hurricanes—and even strong winds—will flatten a field of banana trees. Thus a plantation located in a hurricane or typhoon region faces the hazard of the total destruction of the planting. It is this combination of circumstances that is faced by the West Indian planters. Annually hurricanes cross some part of the West Indies, and their devastating effects are wreaked, in part, upon banana plantings, causing the loss of an entire planting at one time.

Bananas yield well in a wide variety of lowland soils. The alluvial soils of the river flood plains, natural levees, and deltas are especially productive, but bananas are grown on residual and volcanic soils as well as in alluvial plains. Perhaps more important than soil type is the need of continuously high temperatures, preferably in the 70's and 80's Fahrenheit. Man has found that he can provide water to plantings in dry areas, but he still is bound to certain temperature regions for optimum conditions of production. Temperatures in the lower 60's or higher 50's are "fatal" to bananas. Toward the margin of the tropics the plant may grow ornamentally but will rarely yield fruit. In marginal regions, when cool weather—or even light frost—appears, the tree collapses onto the ground.

Optimum commercial conditions, despite the widespread distribution of the banana, appear to be in the rainy tropical lowlands, especially upon alluvial soils. The rainy tropical areas of the equatorial calms are also almost windless. Bananas will yield well, too, in the wet-and-dry tropics, provided that they are irrigated during the dry season, or watered, as in native gardens. The control of plant diseases is easier in the periodically dry tropics, and it is to these climates that commercial plantings have been shifted in recent years, especially since the advent of two diseases. One is the dreaded leaf blight, sigatoka. Whole plantations in eastern Central America have been abandoned by the fruit companies following the advent of this disease, and former banana lands planted to other tropical crops. A second serious banana disease is the Panama disease, caused by a soil fungus. Even large organizations, such as certain American fruit companies, have abandoned or given up approximately 10 per cent of the banana plantings on some of their plantations in eastern Central America because of this infection.

Commercial Cultivation of Bananas

Wide areas of the tropical world possess geographical conditions which are suitable for the commercial cultivation of bananas. Actual producing areas, however, are few. They exist in areas favored by: (1) easy access to the markets of the middle latitudes, via (2) established shipping lanes and connections, with (3) adequate labor supplies, in (4) areas suitable for outside investment. The investment factor may be that of citizens of a distant nation (as a United States company investing in a Costa Rican plantation) or of home subsidy and loans by a tropical country (Ecuador, through government loans, enabling small farmers to establish banana plantings).

The transportation factor is one of the most important, if not the most. Many

FIG. 3-1. A banana plantation on the lowlands of Guatemala, with the mountains in the background. The company headquarters are in the middle distance, facing the road. The plantation villages, with homes for the workers, occupy the other open or unplanted areas; note the playing fields for worker recreation. The white "arches," rising high above the banana trees, are from the nozzles of the overhead spray irrigation. The extensiveness of a tropical plantation is evident. A good road leads to the shipping port. (United Fruit Company)

geographically favored areas lack the needed transportation facilities. Producing regions must have access to the markets of the United States, Canada, and Europe —the nontropical consuming areas. A bunch of bananas is picked green. It must be transported to a port and loaded on shipboard within twenty-four hours, and preferably within twelve or less. Thus good local transportation, by road or railroad, as well as good overseas transportation is a requisite of the industry.

The plantation portion of the industry is efficiently organized. A ship belonging to one of the fruit companies sails, say, to a port in Panama or Colombia. The bananas of the plantation are harvested just prior to the ship's arrival and are delivered to the docks at the time of arrival. Within a few hours the ship has been loaded (much of the loading now being mechanical rather than by porters each carrying one bunch), and the bananas have been refrigerated and ventilated. The vessel departs for its destination, and its time in port has all been used for the loading process.

Banana receipts at an exporting port must be large enough to justify the shipping cost. This means that plantations, or banana farms, must be concentrated in a given area to supply the quantity of fruit needed to fill a ship every few days. Ideally, and usually, the producing district is very near the port, and this means, in fact, along coastlines, on islands, and (if somewhat inland) on hard-surfaced roads, railroads, or navigable rivers. But some of the newly established plantations in the wet-and-dry tropics on the western, or Pacific, side of Central America are now nearly 300 miles by road or rail from Caribbean ports across the isthmus. Extremely careful organization is necessary in picking, shipping, and loading to ensure minimum timing between the cutting of the bananas and the loading and sailing of the ship. Some new ports have been developed on the Pacific side, too, in response to the West Coast market of the United States.

There is an almost unlimited amount of land suitable for banana production in the wet tropics. Few regions, however, meet adequately the combined requirements for home commercial production and easy accessibility to the ultimate consuming market in the middle latitudes. Throughout the one-hundred-year history of the trade, four or five areas have met the overall requirements. (1) The nations of Central America have shipped bananas to the United States; (2) and (3) the West Indies and the Canary Islands have supplied western Europe, and (4) small Pacific Islands have supplied Australia and New Zealand, and (5) Formosa has shipped to Japan.

Producing Regions

The lowlands of the Central American isthmus, the islands of the West Indies, and the northwestern coasts of South America (both on the Caribbean and the Pacific) constitute the largest commercial banana-producing portion of the tropics. *Regionally,* Central America leads, although the production from country to country is highly variable; *politically,* Ecuador, on the Pacific coast of South Amer-

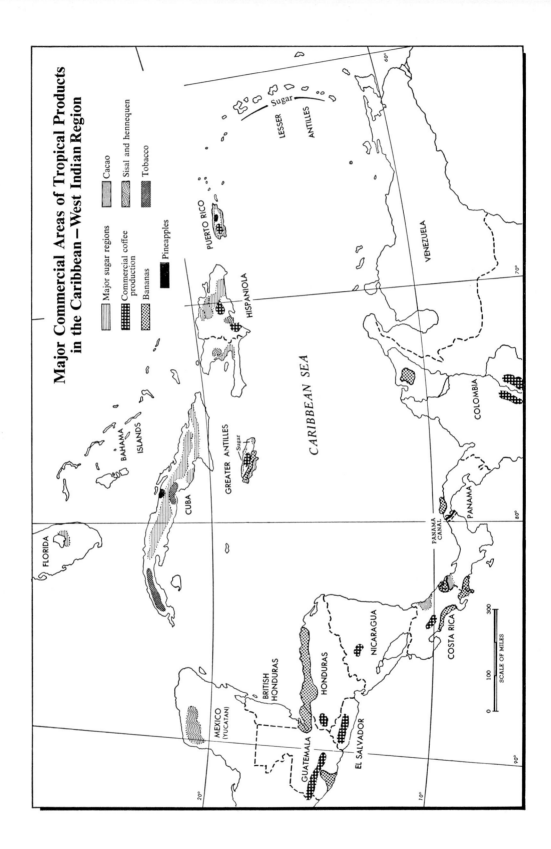

Major Commercial Areas of Tropical Products in the Caribbean—West Indian Region

Major sugar regions

Commercial coffee production

Bananas

Cacao

Sisal and henequen

Tobacco

Pineapples

FLORIDA

BAHAMA ISLANDS

CUBA

Sugar

GREATER ANTILLES

HISPANIOLA

PUERTO RICO

LESSER ANTILLES

Sugar

CARIBBEAN SEA

VENEZUELA

COLOMBIA

PANAMA

PANAMA CANAL

COSTA RICA

NICARAGUA

HONDURAS

EL SALVADOR

GUATEMALA

BRITISH HONDURAS

MEXICO (YUCATAN)

0   100   300

SCALE OF MILES

20°

10°

60°

70°

80°

90°

ica, is now the world's leading banana-exporting nation. These Latin-American areas supply 75 per cent of the world's bananas; at one time the lands touching the Caribbean alone had nearly all of this trade; their share is now a little over 50 per cent, and Ecuador has attained nearly a quarter of the banana trade. Bananas are mainly plantation-produced in Costa Rica, Panama, Honduras, and Colombia. Elsewhere, except in Ecuador and Jamaica, they originate on both plantations and farms. Ecuadoran bananas are nearly all grown by individual farmers on plots or farms of from 50 to 200 acres in size. Jamaica has more than 10,000 banana growers, each operating a miniscule plot of land.

The Canary Islands, in the Atlantic off the west coast of Africa, and the shore-land regions of Africa near the ports on the Gulf of Guinea ship bananas to European markets. These shippers account for much of the one-quarter of the banana trade not held by Central America–the West Indies–Ecuador. But Brazilian shippers join in with the Canaries and Africa in supplying Europe, although Brazilian shipments are relatively small.

The islands of Oceania grow bananas for their own use, and, on the Fijis and western Samoa, for export. Fijian bananas reach Australian markets, supplementing home-grown bananas from Carnarvon and the Queensland coast. Samoan bananas, all shipped from Apia, are marketed in middle-latitude New Zealand; bananas alone account for two-thirds of the Samoa–New Zealand trade. Islands near Japan, plus Formosa, supply that market.

Banana Consumption

Bananas were unknown, essentially, in the middle-latitude markets until the perfection of refrigeration in the 1870's and 1880's. The trade, as we know it today, dates only from the early 1900's. Following the development of the trade, the United States offered the major market. The European market was less significant until recently.

Market orientation has changed sharply since World War II. The European market has expanded with postwar recovery and with increased prosperity. Just between the middle 1930's and the middle 1950's, Europe's banana imports rose nearly 50 per cent. In contrast, the United States consumption of bananas has remained about the same since World War II, despite the increase in population. Imports of bananas are only slightly more than in prewar days; per capita consumption each year in the United States dropped from 22 pounds in the 1930's to 17 in the middle 1950's. The total market is still the world's largest, but consumption has not kept pace with increasing population.

Two Leading Producers

Costa Rica in Central America and Ecuador in Pacific South America are two leaders in present banana acreage and production. The organization of the industry in the two is different; and Costa Rica is an "old" banana area, Ecuador a "new" one. Each will be described briefly as a sample. West Indian nations and colonies, in their banana industry, have characteristics like each of these two. But, unlike Costa Rica and Ecuador, West Indian growers face the environmental hazard of hurricanes.

► COSTA RICA

The original banana plantations of Central America were on the rainy tropical plain of the east coast. The United Fruit Company, an American organization, operated many of the plantations, a fleet of ships, and unloading and distributional facilities in New Orleans and other receiving ports. Needed labor on the plantations was brought from the densely inhabited smaller islands of the West Indies. But sigatoka and the Panama disease have almost eliminated commercial banana culture on east-coast plantations; only a few small-farm producers remain. Former plantations have been abandoned or have been replanted in abaca (manila hemp), rubber, palm oils, and cacao, or with forests of teak and mahogany. Even prior to partial or complete abandonment, banana plantings in eastern Costa Rica had to be "shifted" within the plantation boundary. One planting served for six to eight years, then was replaced by a new planting in another location. But this practice permitted the plantations, all railroad-oriented to the port of Puerto Limon, to continue shipments.

With the advent and the expansion of the devastating diseases, the United Fruit Company, by the late 1930's, decided to relocate its banana plantations on the Pacific plain of Costa Rica, in the wet-and-dry tropics across the mountain range from the eastern shore. New plantings were made on the western plain. Existing small-farmer banana groves were purchased for additions to the plantations. The output of other farms was purchased for shipment. And many thousands of acres of bananas were planted by the company on its relocated holdings.

Irrigation is necessary during the dry season of three to four months; this is in contrast to the situation on the rainy eastern plain. The plantation company became a pioneer in the development of overhead spray irrigation for the banana groves. Water is forced under pressure from nozzles which revolve on a thirty-minute schedule and is sprayed over more than a 200-foot radius. Spray irrigation, now used in many world regions and on many crops, had one of its testing grounds in the Costa Rican banana lands.

The relocation of plantations had profound effects on western Costa Rica. The United Fruit Company built over 100 miles of plantation railway lines, constructed a new port at Golfito on the Pacific, built a town to house 7,000 people, added hospital and recreational facilities, and improved communications. Nearby areas profited by the new market, and vegetable production increased. Small farms were cleared on adjacent nonplantation land. In total, the whole economy of the west coast moved at an increased pace, and incomes rose in the area; this is a sample of the developments in many tropical locations with the advent of commercial agriculture and the replacement of a subsistence economy by it.

The experience of the eastern coastlands has resulted in diversification of tropical crops there. As banana plantings cease to be productive, the remaining plantations replant in new areas (not previously in bananas) and replace the former bananas with other tropical crops. Thus Costa Rica continues with a plantation economy, but it is becoming more diversified. And, of the Caribbean area lands, Costa Rica is one of five wherein commercial banana production is mainly from the large and corporate tropical plantation.

► ECUADOR

Ecuador's gain in the banana industry to its present importance has been the result of the problems in Central America and the West Indies. Plant diseases in Central America, hurricanes in the West Indies, floods, and labor troubles plagued both areas. Ecuador has arisen, since 1947, to challenge the former leaders, to surpass Costa Rica, the former chief exporter, and to profit by the postwar increase in the demand for bananas, particularly in the European market. And Ecuador has arisen to its significance in the banana trade through the development of small banana farms, independently owned and operated.

The Panama Canal was opened in August 1914. The canal completely changed Ecuador's situation with respect to the rest of the world. Direct water shipments of bulky products such as bananas from Ecuador's ports on the Gulf of Guayaquil, and through the canal to eastern North America and to Europe became possible. There was a small banana industry before the canal, but it became commercial following its opening. However, the speciality of the country was cacao, and coastal Ecuador, the narrow hot and tropical lowland between the Andes and the Pacific, had long been an important cacao area. But the witches' broom disease affected cacao trees, and the industry declined rapidly during the 1920's. Some of the abandoned cacao land was put into bananas. These, grown in small quantity along the levees, were shipped down-river to Guayaquil and exported, either through Panama or northwest on the Pacific Ocean to the markets of California. But the banana trade did not make up for the loss of the cacao industry.

Ecuador's boom in bananas, which made it skyrocket to the position of the leading exporting nation, started about 1947. Many factors, all favorable, combined to set the stage. Former cacao land was available for settlement by small farmers. The government had removed an export tax on bananas. The nation embarked upon a road-building program, financed by the United States and by the International Bank, to which the United States is a major contributor. The roads opened up new land and made it accessible. As much of this was Ecuadoran government land, the government offered it for sale to settlers; to obtain title to 120 acres a settler had to have thirty acres under cultivation in five years. Bananas could be planted immediately between the stumps of forest trees or cacao trees, and the requirement met. Railroads to the Pacific were improved, ports improved or built, and a few navigable rivers were reached from the interior by the new roads. The results were magic; small farmers obtained land, and the new highways, the railway lines, and the navigable rivers became lined with banana plantings.

Ecuador's entry into an important banana trade coincided with the postwar rise of the European market. During recent years a quarter of Ecuador's bananas have been shipped to Europe; the rest, except for a small annual shipment to Chile, reach United States markets. Some proceed directly on the Pacific to West Coast ports. Others, and the European shipments, utilize the Panama Canal. And, after the ship is on the Atlantic side, it may proceed to New Orleans, the principal port for the receipt of bananas in the nation, no matter what their source region. Or, on the Gulf, bananas from Ecuador and Central America may be unloaded at Galveston or Tampa. On the east coast, Charleston, Baltimore, and New York are significant in banana imports. From these port cities trainloads and truckloads of bananas—refrigerated in warm weather and heated and ventilated in cold weather —are dispatched to the consuming markets. European receipts are at the chief ports of the individual countries, with London, Amsterdam, and Hamburg of special importance.

Ecuador has certain problems in its banana trade. There are no regular company-owned fruit ships, as serve the Caribbean and west coast of Central America. And the harbors are shallow, so that ships cannot dock next to the shore. Bunches of bananas have to be loaded on lighters, towed to ships anchored offshore, and then reloaded for export. Full cargoes have to be obtained from many small, individual growers, and at greater effort and expense than a cargo is obtained from the efficiently managed Central American plantations.

► PINEAPPLES

The pineapple, a tropical and warm subtropical fruit, has found wide acceptance in the markets of the middle latitudes. Especially, this has been the case since about 1900 when James B. Dole experimented with species of pineapples in the Hawaiian Islands and selected the Smooth Cayenne as the one most suitable for large-scale plantation production. Dole's experimental plots, near the center of the island of Oahu, became the fountainhead of the Hawaiian pineapple industry, with its canning and shipment center at Honolulu. Later, in 1913, an employee of the Hawaiian industry invented the Ginaca machine. This peels, cores, and slices pineapples in one process and can handle dozens of pineapples each minute—a ton of pineapples every five minutes. Mass-production techniques made possible the large-scale pineapple industry, and the product reaches the market in canned form—mainly as slices, chunks, or juice. Recently, to broaden the market, pineapple juice has been mixed with other juices for canning as well.

Fresh pineapple, common in the tropical growing regions, is not common outside the tropics. On the whole the fresh fruit does not keep too well, although some species are more suitable for shipment than others. The fresh fruit is grown as near its ultimate market as possible. For example, that in the markets of the eastern United States is mainly from southern Florida, Cuba, or Puerto Rico. It is not obtainable at all seasons.

Environmental Requirements

The pineapple, ideally a product of the tropical wet-and-dry climate, is able to endure the dry season. It will grow in the rainy tropics in areas of good sub-surface drainage but will not withstand the combination of heavy rainfall and poor drainage. Pineapples are planted from crowns or slips, and the fruit matures in sixteen to twenty months. Temperatures must be high, preferably above 70°F at all times; low temperatures, or cool nights, are unfavorable. For this reason the poleward limit of the pineapple is well within the tropical border.

The fact that the pineapple plant is able to endure the dry season is related to its character. Narrow, shiny, waxy leaves reduce the transpiration of water. Insolation is reflected by the leaves. And the entire plant itself (like a camel in the animal world) is able to store water in a reservoir at the base of the stem. Actually, of course, the length of the dry season in this climatic type varies. Also, the so-called "dry season" is rarely completely rainless. Nevertheless, the high temperatures promote rapid evaporation, and so the available moisture is less than might be surmised from rainfall totals alone. The ability of the pineapple to adjust to the dry season is significant, and a factor of importance in the location of commercial agriculture, especially of plantation agriculture, specializing in the pineapple.

Research by the Hawaiian Pineapple Institute has shown that the pineapple will grow and yield in areas formerly considered too dry—areas such as the margins of the tropical steppes. To date there has been no advance of production into these areas, in part because of their inaccessible locations, in part because of the competitive marketing situations among the fruits. Thus many juices not canned formerly have entered the market and spread the consumer demand. Pineapple juices and others have held their own absolutely but declined relatively with new juices; the increasing yields per acre have almost permitted present producing areas to increase their output and maintain their share of the market.

Regions of Production

The ability of the pineapple to yield well in the wet-and-dry climate is important in several regions of its commercial production—especially in commercial agriculture on tropical islands. Islands usually do not contain large areas of arable land; this is true, especially, on many islands which engage in plantation agriculture, such as the islands of the West Indies (except Cuba) and in the islands of Hawaii. Furthermore, such islands are usually hilly or mountainous, and contain contrasting climates within short distances. Under these situations, pineapples do not compete for land with the rainy tropical products. Instead pineapples are complementary to these products, not competitive. For example, (1) bananas, cacao, sugar cane, or similar crops are in a rainy tropical setting, and pineapples in a neighboring wet-and-dry setting; this is the case in areas of the West Indies. Or (2) the rainy land products are grown on wet, windward sides of the islands, the pineapples on dry, leeward sides; this is the situation on some of the islands of Hawaii. Or (3), if the wet-and-dry area is irrigated, sugar cane and similar crops occupy flatter, lower irrigable lands, and pineapples are grown on hillier, unirrigated land; this is the situation in Oahu and Kauai, islands of Hawaii. The two major plantation crops of the Hawaiian Islands, sugar cane and pineapples, do not compete at all for land but are completely complimentary, enabling a full use of all types of arable land.

Four major commercial pineapple regions are the Hawaiian Islands, the Philippine Islands, the West Indies Islands, and the island of Formosa. In addition, as natural rubber production has declined, relatively, in Malaya, pineapples have been substituted on the plantations.

Commercial production of pineapples is scattered elsewhere in the tropics. The African plateaus of East Africa, Natal in South Africa, Mexico and other Latin American regions, Queensland in Australia, and southern China all have an output. Fresh fruit is grown near the market, in the West Indies, mainly, for the American market. But the large-scale growing of pineapples, and large-scale canning of the product, is principally an activity of Hawaiian and Philippine plantations. Hawaii has contributed as high as 80 per cent of the pineapple pack in certain years. Although sugar cane outranks pineapples in Hawaii in value and acreage, sugar cane is important elsewhere, too. Thus the uniqueness of Hawaiian agriculture in the world picture is related to its outstanding position in pineapples.

▶ HAWAII

Pineapple plantations are located on five of the eight principal islands of Hawaii. They are features of Kauai, Oahu, Molokai, Lanai, and Maui. In addition, small independent farmers on Kauai and Maui grow pineapples as part of a system of diversified agriculture of several crops and depend heavily upon the sale of pineapples for their farm income. One island, Lanai, is owned in its entirety by a pineapple company; its company town, Lanai City, is peopled entirely by persons engaged in the pineapple industry; and the pineapple fields of the island occupy the rolling to rough surface of the crater of an extinct volcano. The entire

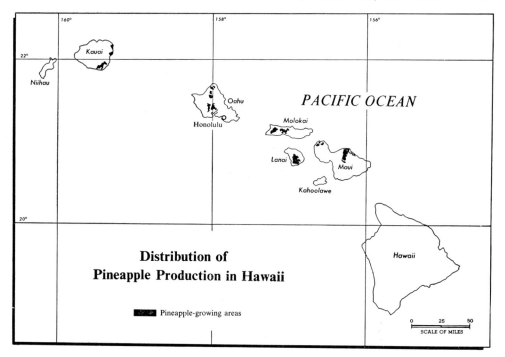

160° 158° 156°

22°

Kauai

Niihau

Oahu

PACIFIC OCEAN

Honolulu

Molokai

Lanai

Maui

Kahoolawe

20°

**Distribution of
Pineapple Production in Hawaii**

Hawaii

Pineapple-growing areas

0   25   50
SCALE OF MILES

economy of Lanai depends upon the one plantation crop; some beef cattle are grazed on land temporarily "at rest" between pineapple plantings, but only these few cattle interrupt, for a time, the "pineapple landscape" of the arable land of the island.

The pineapple industry of Hawaii supports nine canneries, three each on Oahu, Kauai, and Maui. The largest, by far, are the three on Oahu, all located in the city of Honolulu, occupying sites within two blocks of the docks of Honolulu harbor. To these canneries the pineapples from central Oahu are trucked, and the pineapples of Molokai and Lanai are barged. During the canning season a constant procession of tugs, each pulling a string of barges loaded with pineapples, cross the waters between the shipping docks of Molokai and Lanai and the receiving docks of Honolulu. The smaller canneries on Kauai and Maui are supported by the flow of trucked-in pineapples from island plantations and farmer-delivered fruit by the independent operators.

The magnitude of the pineapple industry in Hawaii is shown by figures alone. From only 100 cases of canned pineapples in 1900, and 7,700 cases in 1920, the output mushroomed to 20 million cases in 1940, and 32 million in 1957. Of the present canned output, some 18 million cases are of fruit in the form of sliced pineapples or of chunks, and 14 million cases are of pineapple juice. The industry reflects inventiveness and know-how, millions of dollars spent in research and experimentation, the constant adoption and readoption of the most modern methods, and, above all, the economic advantage possessed by the Hawaiian Islands of being within the American economic framework, with duty-free access to American markets ever since the inception of the industry. And, in the mainland markets, the advertising by the pineapple packers of Hawaii has resulted in the acceptance of pineapple products, the widespread use of the juice, and the expansion of sales. As of the last few years, too, the Hawaiian packers have entered the "combined juice" market, and maintain a plant at San José, California, where pineapple-orange, pineapple-grapefruit, and other blended juices are packed.

The Plantations

Hawaiian pineapple plantations occupy leeward sites in the islands or are located on rolling, higher lands above sugar plantations—lands too rough or rolling for the irrigation of sugar cane. It is the occupance of rolling sites, plus the contour-planting of pineapples, which makes the pineapple landscape so unique. The "waving" and "undulating" pineapple fields, with their curved rows of plants, form a pleasant and striking pattern on the landscape, whether viewed from a rise or hill, from a low spot looking upward to the fields on distant slopes, or from the air. Pineapple fields end abruptly, too, either against the base of mountainous terrain or against an irrigation ditch, where they occupy the higher, unirrigated side and sugar cane is grown on the lower, irrigated side of the master ditch. Thus, too, pineapples occupy inland locations, and, unlike sugar cane, are not grown right to the seacoast.

Pineapples are planted by using either the crowns or suckers from the stems. The fields are prepared carefully, contours are measured, fertilizers added to the red soils of volcanic origin, and road strips are surveyed prior to planting. The roads are to function during spraying and harvest, and the striplike curving fields between the roads are all of equal width—half the width of the boom on the pineapple harvester (see later section).

The places where the row is to be located are covered with long strips of paper. The planting of the suckers and crowns is accomplished by punching a hole in the paper and inserting the plant material into the soil beneath. The paper serves two purposes: it prohibits the growth of weeds by mantling the bare ground, and it provides fertilizer as it deteriorates in time into a mulch. Cultivators then retard and eliminate weeds until the pineapple plant is large enough to shade the ground between rows.

At intervals during the eighteen- to twenty-month period of growth of the pineapples, sprayers are driven down the network of fieldside roads. The arms of the sprayers reach halfway across each field. Thus, by doubling back on the adjacent road, the sprayer completes the spraying of insecticides on a particular field, and another arm sprays half of the adjacent field. For this reason the individually planted plots of pineapples are long and narrow, a factor in the distant or air-view beauty of the landscape.

The pineapple harvester has been perfected in Hawaii for Hawaiian conditions. It is a large and high machine, from one side of which a long boom extends. The harvester is driven slowly along the field road; the boom extends halfway across the adjacent field. Endless belts run on the boom. Twelve to fifteen field workers follow the boom as it moves slowly over the rows, just above the vegetation of the plants. The workers pick the pineapples, cut off the top leaves, and throw the pineapple itself on the endless belt, which transports the fruit to bins in the machine. As fast as the bins are filled, they are unloaded mechanically into lugs on trucks driven alongside. The trucks then depart for the canneries; fruit picked in the morning may be canned by afternoon. In any case, fruit picked one day will be canned or juiced by the following day. For this reason, the bargeloads of the day's harvest on Molokai and Lanai depart from these islands in the evening and are landed at Honolulu early the following morning for immediate canning.

The pineapple workers who pick the fruit perform the only hand operation

FIG. 3-2. Machine-spraying of pineapples in Hawaii. Temporary roads are left between the strips of pineapple plantings. The pipes for spraying and the booms on the harvesting machines extend halfway across each planting-strip, and the strips are planted on the contour to prevent soil erosion. This plantation lies on a sloping surface, a terrace above the sea, a surface too rough for satisfactory irrigation of sugar cane. (Dole Photo, Courtesy Hawaii Visitor Bureau)

FIG. 3-3. Two hand operations remain in the highly mechanized Hawaiian pineapple industry. One is shown. The workers, wearing heavy gloves and leather or heavy rubber trousers (because of the sharp-edged pineapple leaves), pick the pineapple, cut off the cluster of leaves, and throw the fruit on the boom, which transports it to the truck. The other hand operation is the packing of rounded pineapple slices in the cans at the cannery. (Dole Photo, Courtesy Hawaii Visitor Bureau)

remaining in the field industry. They wear heavy leather trousers and gloves so as not to be cut and scratched by the sharp-edged rubbery leaves of the plants.

The extreme mechanization of the Hawaiian pineapple industry reflects the setting of Hawaii in the economic framework of the United States. As such, the islands are subject to American minimum-wage laws. Like the sugar workers, the plantation workers are the highest paid in the world because of this, and Hawaiian competition is not with the American mainland but with *competing tropical areas* where wages are low. In order to compete at all with the low-cost tropical areas, Hawaiian pineapple plantations have been forced to economize on labor costs by mechanization. Iron works in the islands manufacture the machine parts and booms, a response to the home market. And, had the industry been in its present mechanized form fifty years ago, there would have been no need to import the thousands of workers from the Orient to man the pineapple (and sugar) plantations. Thus the time factor is significant in explaining the need for plantation labor, and the resulting composition of Hawaii's population.

Pineapple Canneries

The pineapple harvest in Hawaii proceeds all year, but well over half—in fact nearly two-thirds—is concentrated in the three "summer" months. This fortunate circumstance permits the canneries to maintain a year-round permanent force of workers and to supplement them during the busiest season with school personnel and students on vacation, and with housewives. Summer employment in the canneries finances many an education. During the height of the canning season field harvesting of pineapples continues all night, the machines being equipped with floodlights, and cannery operations are on a twenty-four-hour, three-shift basis.

Pineapples are washed as they enter the cannery and directed to endless belts which distribute them. From time to time they are conveyed across openings which sort them as to size. From bins, into which the various sizes drop, they fall by gravity to chutes which lead to the Ginaca machines. In an instant they are peeled, cored, and sliced. The peels and cores are conducted one way for juicing, the slices go to the packing tables. The actual filling of the cans with slices of pineapple is a second hand operation in the entire industry, and is performed by workers seated at long tables and wearing antiseptic uniforms and rubber gloves. Cans of chunks and juice are filled automatically by machine.

There are by-products of the pineapple industry. One of the most important is pineapple bran, manufactured from the shells and butt ends of the fruit. The bran is an important feed for dairy cattle in Hawaii. Like the meat-packing industry, the pineapple people claim that no part of the fruit goes to waste. And a subsidiary industry to the presence of the canneries is the manufacture of cans by companies which import sheet steel and make the cans in factories located adjacent to the pineapple canneries.

The overseas shipments of cases of pineapple products, and of bulk raw sugar, are Hawaii's basic exports. Shipments reach not only the mainland United States, but European and Canadian markets as well.

▶ THE PHILIPPINE ISLANDS

The commercial pineapple industry and the canning of pineapples in the Philippine Islands reflects the American economic framework. But it does so in a very different manner from the Hawaiian industry.

The Philippine industry has been made possible by the "high wages" and other costs in Hawaii. As discussed heretofore, Hawaii is subject to American minimum-wage laws, social laws, and other modern labor legislation as enacted in the United States, and yet is the only tropical state in the nation; and so its agricultural competition is with other tropical areas rather than with the mainland United States, which it supplements. Thus the "economic" in economic geography permits a place such as the Philippines to compete with Hawaii, even though it is much more distant from American markets. And it is possible for Philippine plantations to produce and can pineapples cheaply without resorting to labor-saving devices and machines. In addition, taxes are lower, suitable pineapple land is more abundant owing to the large size of the Philippine Islands, and the land is not—as in Hawaii—in competition with urban uses or for military installations. American-operated pineapple companies now have plantations in the Philippines and are developing others. They are able to place canned slices, chunks, and juice in the home market in competition with Hawaii.

The leading commercial plantation area of the Philippines is in the northern part of the southern-most island, Mindanao; home production, however, is spread widely in the Philippine archipelago. Some 25,000 acres of government land comprise the largest plantation. Although only ten airline miles from the sea north of Mindanao, the plantation lies on a plateau which has an average elevation of 3,000 feet above the sea, and the pineapple fields are at altitudes of 1,500 to 2,500 feet, occupying intermontane and plateau-surface sites. As in Hawaii, the pineapple lands are somewhat fragmented by deep canyons and gullies incised into the rolling upland surfaces. Soils of the pineapple area are of volcanic origin, comparable to those of the Hawaiian Islands. The cannery serving the plantation is in a port city, Bugo, fifteen road miles down the escarpment from the plantation settlement.

Philippine plantation labor is not expensive. Thus, although American operated, through a Philippine subsidiary, there is little incentive to mechanization. Planting, fertilization of the growing pineapple plants, and harvest are all hand operations. Cultivation is principally by animal power, both the carabao and the "Brahma bullock," a hybrid offspring of an Indian Brahma bull and a native Philippine cow, being used. During harvest the worker carries the pineapples to the edge of the field, where he tops and trims them and leaves them in piles. Other workers then hand-load the fruit into trucks for transport to the cannery.

The Philippine plantation areas, although in a wet-and-dry climatic setting, lie in regions of large total rainfall, and the "dry" season still receives from two to four inches of monthly precipitation. The good underdrainage of the plateau, however, takes care of the heavy moisture. The high afternoon heat, and the possibility—indeed probability—of late afternoon convectional showers, regulates the working day in the fields, which usually is from 5 a.m. to 2 p.m. By regulating and timing planting, an eleven-month evenly distributed harvest season is obtained, and the canneries close for but one month, mainly for overhaul and repair. Thus, competitively, the Philippine crop is more evenly spread, both in harvest and canning, than the Hawaiian, and this permits a more uniform yearly use of the labor supply. And, within the last fifteen years, enough large-scale plantations have developed to give the plateau lands of Mindanao a "pineapple landscape" and to cause concern to competing tropical areas such as Hawaii.

The favorable factors in the Philippines, such even as the downgrade haul to the canneries, are offset in part by other factors. One is the distance from the American market. Another is the necessity of importing, also by long sea journeys, the tin plate for cans or the cans themselves. A third, directly related to the more humid climate, is increased expense for pest and disease control. Nevertheless, outside capital has been attracted to the pineapple industry, and potential pineapple lands remain, even in the Mindanao area, where the main commercial production of the present is concentrated.

► OTHER TROPICAL FRUITS

Tropical fruits, other than bananas and pineapples, are produced and marketed commercially in minor quantities. Among these, some of which are raised in the tropics alone and some of which have a range well into the subtropics, are the guava, avocado, papaya, mango, passion fruit, and pomegranate. Some of these are tree fruits; others are vine fruits. And the date is a product of the oases and irrigated valleys of hot and arid tropical lands. All of these fruits are marketed fresh locally throughout the regions of their growth. Except for dates, the markets of such countries as Mexico, Brazil, India, and of such a state as Hawaii are filled with these fresh fruits in season, for all have "seasons" despite the continuous warmth of the tropics. Certain of the above listed fruits can be produced in Florida and in the warmer parts of California and marketed fresh for a short season. In general, however, these fruits reach middle-latitude markets only in the form of preserves, jellies, or in cans; and dates are dried. Those fruits which can be juiced, particularly the guava and the passion fruit, are now being marketed from Hawaii in that form.

The production of papayas is an orchard industry in Hawaii. The papaya tree, which is not tall, has a long thin trunk, from the top of which the branches spread only a short distance. As the ground is not shaded completely, vegetables can usually be grown beneath the trees and two "crops" obtained from the same acreage. The market of Hawaii is large enough to support full-time commercial papaya growers.

► DATES

The date is the fruit of the date palm. This tree grows in watered areas of the exceedingly hot deserts of the low latitudes, the tropical deserts of the world. It is characteristic today in the desert oases of the Old World, along the exotic streams such as the Indus, the Nile, and the lower parts of the Tigris and Euphrates, and has been introduced to the irrigated lands in the low-latitude deserts of the New World, such as the Salt River Valley of Arizona and the Coachella Valley of California.

The date palm is said to grow "with its feet in pools of water and its head in the fires of heaven." Daytime temperatures during the high-sun (summer) period in the tropical deserts usually exceed 100°F, and rise occasionally to 120° and even 130°. The tree withstands this intense, dry heat provided it is adequately watered. During low-sun (winter) period nights, desert temperatures may drop to 50°F or into the 40's for a few hours before sunrise. To these temperatures, which would destroy bananas, pineapples, or the tender tropical fruits, the date palm is resistant, provided they do not last too long. The rapid warming of the dry air after sunrise offsets the cooling. In a few oases of the northern Sahara a minimum temperature slightly below freezing is recorded for an hour or so on certain winter nights, without serious effect upon the tree.

Despite the large diurnal range of temperature in the deserts, the date palm does not grow in nondesert environments. It is tolerant of slightly alkaline water, the usual water of many desert oases, and so will grow and yield its fruit in situations not possible for other trees or crops.

The date palm was indigenous to the oases of the Arabian Peninsula and now is cultivated in oases throughout the desert regions which extend from the Indus River in Pakistan, westward through southern Iran, Arabia, and the Sahara Desert of northern Africa. In fact, some authorities claim the Indus region as the home area of the date palm. All agree, however, that the tree was distributed westward from Arabia into the Nile Valley and the Sahara during very early times, probably well prior to the Christian era. However, date production along the Nile does not enter world trade. The large population of Egypt consumes the home production.

The date provides food for the oasis dwellers of the Old World. Dates are prepared and served in dozens of different ways. The fruit can be kept for a long time. The fronds of the palms serve as roofing or thatching materials. The trunk provides fiber for ropes and wood for fuel and for simple construction. A date sugar is obtained from the fruit. All told, date palms are the most useful item in these oases, and a man's wealth is determined by his ownership of trees.

Commercial Production

One compact region and one broad region supply the dates sold commercially from the Old World. The compact region lies along the Shatt-el-Arab, the combined stream formed by the junction of the Tigris and the Euphrates. One bank is in Iran, one in Iraq. The broad region is the Saharan oases, but particularly those of Algeria to the south of the Atlas Mountains. Iraq, Iran, and Algeria are the chief exporters of dates.

New World dates are supplied by the growers of the tropical deserts of the extreme southeast of California and of southern Arizona. The production is now equal to demands of the United States market. The industry of the American Southwest is a highly organized, modern commercial enterprise; the Old World industry is more primitive and is based on the selling of only the surplus crop, not needed at home. Most small oases do not engage in it—in fact, they may be perennially short of a home supply in relationship to their population.

▶ THE SHATT-EL-ARAB

The Shatt-el-Arab flows from Basra to the Persian Gulf. In Iraq and Iran along its course are uniquely irrigated date gardens, extending for 110 miles along the waterfront. The high tides of the Persian Gulf back up or dam the river water. Gates in the banks are opened, and water flows into the gardens, each being surrounded by a low embankment. Thus the trees stand in pools of water and the sun furnishes the "fires of heaven." At low tide the dikes are opened again, and the unused water drains back into the river, now at a lower level.

Arabs climb the 100- to 150-foot high palms to harvest the large clusters or bunches of dates. These are lowered to the ground, where the dates are sorted and packed for export. Boxing material must be imported. The gardens, which have yielded from two-thirds to three-fourths of the world's commercial crop, contain an estimated 30 to 35 million date palms, owned by individuals in small plots of separate ownership.

Commercial production extends eastward of the mouth of the Shatt-el-Arab into oases on the plain at the head of the gulf in southwestern Iran.

▶ ARIZONA-CALIFORNIA

American date production from the irrigated Salt River Valley of Arizona and the irrigated Imperial and Coachella Valleys of southeastern California now meets American market demands. Dates are pasteurized for the market.

Picking methods, in contrast to the Old World, are modern. Tractor-drawn high platforms are pulled through the groves. The height of the platform can be raised or lowered by machinery. Ladders or walkways lead to the platform, and from it steel extensions, guarded by side railings, can be swung horizontally into the trees. Thus several pickers can work at once and reach the clusters of dates from the platform itself, or from the side extensions.

The feathery top of the date palm, whether in the New World or the Old, does not shade the ground completely: "filtered" sepulchrelike light seeps through. Thus vegetable crops, and even small fruit trees like the grapefruit, can be grown beneath date palms. As the growing season in the tropical desert climate is twelve months in length, or nearly so on the poleward margin, this permits continuous use of the land for two products, each at a different level. Particularly in the small oases of the Old World, in Arabia and in the Sahara Desert, is this a factor of great consequence. Oasis populations per unit of cultivated land can be high. This advantage of a tropical oasis is not possessed by the dry lands of the middle latitudes, where only one crop a year can be harvested before the advent of winter.

▶ QUESTIONS

1. What are the three broad climatic types in the tropics of the world?
2. Why can Central America, the West Indies, and northern South America supply tropical products in quantity to the United States at relatively less cost than the tropics of Mexico or the Amazon River basin of Brazil can supply them?
3. In what two types of tropical climates are the banana plantations of Central America located? How do production methods differ in the two?
4. What part does modern and rapid transportation play in the banana industry —from plantation to consumer?
5. What several factors—both natural and man made—have been operative in the recent rise of Ecuador to its present importance in the growing and export of bananas?
6. Why does Hawaii have a virtual monopoly of much of the commercial production of pineapples in the world?
7. In Hawaii sugar cane and pineapples supplement one another—they do not compete for the agricultural land. Explain.
8. Hawaii has been a pioneer in the mechanization both of sugar cane plantations and of pineapple plantations. What factors have been operative in this and have led the industries to experiment with and develop special machines?
9. Compare the date-growing methods and harvest of the Arizona-California producing region with that of the Shatt-el-Arab.

IV Citrus Fruit Production and Processing:

Other Subtropical Fruits

The subtropical fruits, as the term is here used, include those whose commercial production is mainly in the "warm temperate"—really subtropical—lands and those which, while not produced in this marginal zone, are grown commercially at the very outer edge of the tropics. These last are not tolerant of any frost, but yield best toward the frost line. Commercially, also, these are marketed principally in the middle latitudes and their location is thus closer to market than if they were grown in the body of tropical climates.

Some of the subtropical fruits—the orange is an example—are grown within parts of the tropics for local sale; in fact, the wild orange tree is common in both tropical southern China and those parts of China in the subtropics. Wild and cultivated orange trees are common in tropical Paraguay, and swine are orange-fed at times. But the quality oranges, grown commercially, and those destined for major markets are all produced in subtropical-tropical marginal zones. Although the tree will not withstand severe freezes, the threat of frost seems to be beneficial to it, and the groves can be protected against light frosts which may occur periodically.

Many of the subtropical fruits are from the Mediterranean subtropical lands. These areas, of which southern California and the Mediterranean Basin lands

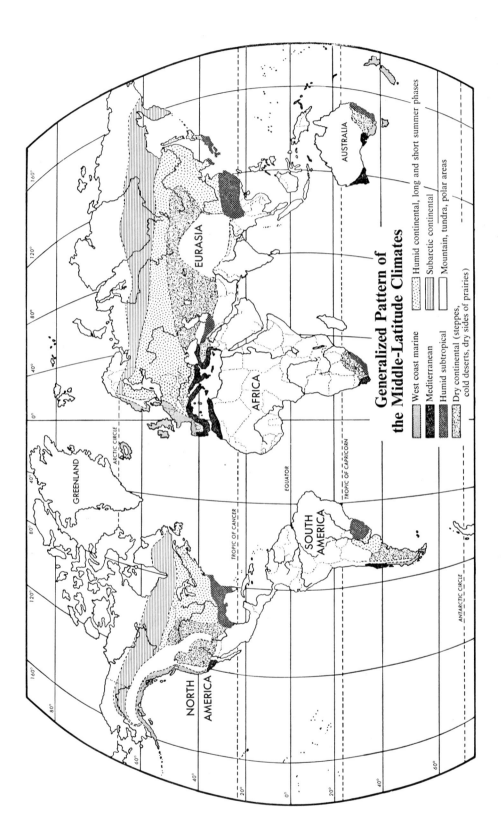

Generalized Pattern of the Middle-Latitude Climates

West coast marine

Mediterranean

Humid subtropical

Dry continental (steppes,
cold deserts, dry sides of prairies)

Humid continental, long and short summer phases

Subarctic continental

Mountain, tundra, polar areas

of Europe, Asia, and Africa are examples, possess a rainy but mild winter and a warm to hot, and essentially rainless, summer. Certain of the fruits and nut trees resist the period of summer drought; for example the fig tree and chestnut and walnut trees yield well despite the dry summer. Other subtropical fruits, such as citrus, are irrigated during the rainless season; this permits the Mediterranean subtropical lands to enter into competition with humid subtropical areas or tropical fringe areas in the supplying of world markets.

The world areas in which subtropical fruits can be grown are large in area. Economic factors, such as the cost and the supply of labor, access to markets, transportation routes and costs of transports, tariff considerations, and others are often the specific determining factors in the location of producing regions—but all must be, of course, within the framework of favorable, or at least a permissive, geographical environment.

▶ THE CITRUS FRUITS

The many species of citrus fruits belong to the same family of low evergreen broadleaf trees and evergreen broadleaf shrubs. The fruits of these species are characterized by their content of citric acid in the skin (or outer cover—endocarp), by the content of vitamin C, and by both a content of citric acid and of sugar in the pulpy and segmented interior, and by the juices contained in the fruit. The skin of the various citrus fruits may be of several different colors, such as orange, yellow, yellow-brown, or green.

Among the citrus fruits are the orange, lemon, grapefruit, lime, pomelo, kumquat, mandarin, citron, and tangerine. There are others, too, and different species of a given one—such as naval oranges, Valencia oranges, Satsuma oranges, and blood oranges. Commercially, the orange and the lemon are of chief importance in the various producing regions. The pomelo or grapefruit is of major commercial importance in the producing and consuming regions of the United States but does not attain major importance elsewhere, except locally. The lime is prominent in the true tropics; lime trees are the least resistant to frost of all types of citrus, and limes or concentrated lime juice are shipped to middle-latitude markets from distant producing regions. In contrast, oranges, lemons, and grapefruit are grown, commercially, as close to market as possible, and reach middle-latitude markets from subtropical producing regions. Of the chief commercially marketed citrus fruits, oranges and grapefruit withstand some cool periods and even very light frosts; they can be grown farthest poleward in the tropical-subtropical margins. Lemons withstand but little frost; commercial regions are slightly warmer in the "winter" than orange areas. The lime, however, is truly a product only beyond (equatorward) of the frost line, for the lime tree will not withstand even the slightest frost.

Environmental Requirements

The citrus fruits are indigenous to southeast Asia, in the monsoon lands of southern China, Indochina, the Malay Peninsula, and the western islands of the East Indies. Wild orange trees still are to be found in the open monsoon forests of the region. The various citrus trees, considering the environment of their original habitat, are large users of water. Also, as trees of the tropics and warm edge of the humid subtropics, all stages of development of the fruit—from bud and flower to partially mature and fully mature fruit—are to be found on the tree at any given time.

Citrus trees were transported to other warm to hot environments during early times, beginning with the period of trade between Europe and the Indies. Thus citrus was transplanted to desert oases; they withstand the dry heat of the desert but must be irrigated continuously. The chief region, however, to which oranges, lemons, and other citrus trees were introduced was the Mediterranean subtropics. In this environment the trees must be irrigated constantly during the dry summer—and, as noted, citrus is a large user of water. In fact, some Mediterranean areas are unable to engage in commercial production of oranges because of water shortages. During the warm and rainy winter season of this realm the citrus trees are not irrigated. But, as occasional although infrequent frosts are to be expected the growers of a Mediterranean climatic region must provide some sort of frost protection. This is an expense over and above the costs of water. In contrast, growers at the warm edge of the humid subtropics depend upon the natural rainfall of the realm and have little or no need to provide protection from frost —the exception to this statement is Florida; this warm producing area lies open to importations of cold continental air from inner North America two or three times during each winter. Thus Florida growers, like those of Mediterranean California, must invest in equipment to ward off frost in their groves.

The three regions just mentioned contain the commercial citrus production of the world. In addition, nearly all of the tropics now have local production to serve their own needs; orange, lemon, tangerine, lime, and other citrus trees are common in tropical gardens or the patios and plazas of tropical homes and towns. Several species of citrus fruit, notably the lime, grow only in the true tropics, as they will not withstand the slightest frost.

Oranges constitute the major citrus fruit of agriculture and commerce, and of total production in both tonnage and value. Lemons are of considerable importance, but far behind oranges; moreover, lemon-producing regions are more concentrated regionally than is orange production. The grapefruit, an improvement of the pomelo, is of particular importance among the citrus fruits in the United States alone. The other citrus fruits are grown in smaller quantities for the market, which does not absorb the entire possible production. The citron is often candied, and is marketed in this form. The citron, also, is in demand in Orthodox Jewish homes and communities for certain religious festivals, particularly the Feast of Booths, during which its use is a necessity. Israel now supplies most of the citron for this purpose, the fruit coming from ungrafted trees—that from grafted trees is not acceptable religiously. Morocco, Tunisia, the island of Corsica, and southern Italy also supply citron (called *etrog* in the Jewish ceremony) for this specialized market.

Rise of the Citrus Trade

Citrus fruits have long been known and consumed locally in the regions of their origin, in the desert oases to which they were transported, and in Mediterranean lands—as well as in the tropical highlands of Latin America, to which the fruit was brought by the Spanish. The spectacular rise of world trade in citrus fruits awaited the period of the 1870's, when ventilation and refrigeration of railroad cars and ships was developed and perfected. Oranges and lemons, formerly a seasonal luxury, found ready acceptance in the middle-latitude markets of northern and western Europe and of the United States and Canada. New groves were

FIG. 4-1. Orange grove in the Valencia region of eastern Spain, near the Mediterranean Sea. Valencia oranges command top prices in the markets of the British Isles and other countries of northern Europe. This is the "home region" of the Valencia orange, one of two major types grown in southern California. (Spanish National Tourist Office)

established and former groves enlarged in producing regions in response to high prices for the fruit and the expanding markets. The important citrus trade between Mediterranean Europe and the British Isles increased at this time. The 1870's and 1880's, decades following the completion of the original transcontinental railroad to California, and during which the railroads to Los Angeles were completed, witnessed the rise of a commercial citrus industry in the Los Angeles Basin. Florida plantings were expanded—even overexpanded to areas too far north for safety —setting the stage for the disastrous freezing-out of orange groves in north Florida during the 1890's.

The canning of citrus juices became important during the early portion of the twentieth century, but particularly so after the discovery of the vitamin C content of the juice. The attribute of citrus fruit to ward off scurvy, a dread disease of sailors on long voyages, had long been known; the British navy furnished limes to its sailors, and found them healthy as a result; but the actual reason for this awaited the work of the 1930's on vitamin research. As a result of the research discovery, orange, grapefruit, lemon and other juices were canned. This increased the market considerably—originally only surplus fruit, not marketed as fresh fruit, was juiced.

The advent of quick-freezing, basically in the 1940's, enlarged the citrus market tremendously. Today much of the citrus production of certain regions is marketed as canned or frozen juice; no longer is the "juicing" of citrus a by-product activity. Can factories, frozen food plants, and other industries have arisen in citrus-producing areas such as Florida and southern California. The United States today is not only the chief producing country of citrus fruits, but offers the chief market for the canned and frozen juices; so rapidly has the market accepted the product that other kinds of fruits have "declined" relatively with respect to the increase in population, and to market.

▶ ORANGES

The orange tree, a native of the tropical Orient from southern China southward throughout the Malay Peninsula—and possibly, also, of the western islands of Indonesia—was transported to Arabia and the Mediterranean lands during the early days of trade with the Far East. By the early 900's the oases of eastern Arabia were growing oranges. By the year 1000 orange culture had been established in the Mediterranean subtropical lands at the eastern end of the Mediterranean Sea. Some records even indicate an early production by the time of the second century—on a small scale. The year 1150 is said to be the date at which orange trees were first planted and cultivated in southern Spain. Citrus was introduced to other Mediterranean subtropical regions at varying dates. The settlers at the Cape of Good Hope in Africa received orange trees in 1654. The introductions to Australia occurred in 1788.

FIG. 4-2. Citrus groves, vineyards, and vegetables near the Cape of Good Hope in the Union of South Africa. This region of Mediterranean climate in the Southern Hemisphere places its citrus and other agricultural products on the markets of western Europe during the off-season of agriculture in Europe. The area is irrigated, water being derived from mountain streams. (South African Tourist Corporation)

Columbus is credited with the introduction of citrus to the New World in 1493. By 1518 oranges had been introduced to both Mexico and Brazil, and the Spanish explorers of the middle 1500's had brought the tree to Florida, where it was established by 1565 in the Spanish settlements.

From Mexico the orange tree was carried northwestward, planted in the gardens of the chain of twenty-one Spanish missions, and so reached the Mediterranean lands of southern California during the early 1700's. Actual commercial production of oranges in California, however, did not begin until settlement of the region by American settlers—this phase of California orange production dates only from about 1870; the "local first" large planting, producing fruit for the region, was made in 1805 at San Gabriel Mission.

The orange tree, like other citrus fruits, was transported from a humid and wet subtropical and tropical environment in southeast Asia to the dry-summer Mediterranean lands. Here it was necessary to irrigate orange groves during the three to five months of the rainless summer. From the Mediterranean environment of Spain the introductions to the West Indies were "back" to a humid setting, comparable to the environment of the region in which citrus was indigenous. But, eventually the transport of citrus trees from Mexico to southern California was a reintroduction to the Mediterranean subtropics. Today both types of regions—the warm edge of the humid subtropics and the Mediterranean subtropics—engage in the commercial production of oranges and other citrus fruits. Florida is an example of the warm and humid setting, southern California of the Mediterranean. The differing producing regions have to engage in different practices so far as cultivation is concerned. Mediterranean-type areas have heavy costs of irrigation; in contrast, humid regions have no water costs, as moisture is supplied by the natural rainfall—although, during recent years, Florida growers have begun the use of spray irrigation during dry spells, or during periods when the rainfall is not plentiful. The oranges of Mediterranean lands are bright in color, there is less juice in the fruit, but the juice is more concentrated in vitamin content; oranges from humid lands are more yellow in color (packers often add artificial color to the skin, and label the fruit "color added"), they contain more juice, but it is less concentrated. There are seasonal differences in harvest, also, and other regional differences in the crop.

Producing Regions

The orange crop or "pick" of the United States is the largest among the nations of the world, and a third of the total tonnage. Brazil usually follows in total production, then Spain, India, Italy, and Japan. The yield of oranges in China is not specifically known, but undoubtedly is great. Spain, Israel, and some other Mediterranean lands are most significant in the export trade to northern Europe.

There is production of oranges in the New World from the southern borders of the United States southward through some part of every nation of Latin America. Orange groves are to be found in all the countries fronting on the Mediterranean Sea in Europe, Asia, and Africa, and in West Africa, on the plateaus of East Africa, and near the Cape of Good Hope in the Mediterranean lands of the Union of South Africa.

Oranges are grown under continual irrigation in the oases of the hot desert climates. Egypt, especially, has an important production; the Egyptian crop is consumed at home and does not enter world trade. The Arizona orange crop is from a desert climatic environment also.

In the Orient, India, the Indochina region, the Philippines, and southern China supply themselves. Kyushu, the warm southern island of Japan, and the island of Okinawa in the Ryukyus supply Japanese markets and provide a small surplus for export. The Satsuma orange, a species which is more resistant to frost than others, is important at the northern limit of production in Japan. Satsumas are grown, also, along the Gulf Coast of the United States, as in Alabama; this is poleward of the limit of "normal" orange production.

Australia, from growing regions in its Mediterranean climatic areas near Perth and Adelaide, supplies oranges to its own markets, exports to New Zealand, and has a small additional surplus for shipment to Europe, especially to Britain. Oranges are grown, also, in the warmer northern sections of the east coast of Australia.

World Trade in Oranges

The United States is both the world's leading producer of oranges and a leading exporter, usually second among the nations. Collectively, however, a group of nations surrounding the Mediterranean Sea export more in quantity, shipping their oranges to the industrial countries of western Europe; thus Morocco, Algeria, Tunisia, Israel, Italy, and Spain combined lead in regional exports. Spain has long been a supplier of its well-known Valencia oranges to English and German markets. Its long establishment in this, the long-time market contacts, and propinquity to western European consuming regions are factors in Spain's retention of the position of leading exporter. The orange groves of Spain are in the warm and sunny southeast, and in the Valencia lowland of the eastern coast, both locations being near seaports. Italian oranges (and other citrus) are grown chiefly on the island of Sicily. Ports are near the producing regions, and it is almost as cheap to export by sea as to move the oranges to Italian markets—especially since the per capita income of the Italian people is not high.

The spectacular rise, recently, of Israel in orange production and export is a postwar phenomenon. Colonies of refugees from Jewish centers in Europe were established along the plain at the eastern end of the Mediterranean. Citrus production furnishes the economic base for many of the settlements. Israeli oranges now compete with those from the United States, the Union of South Africa, Spain, and Sicily in European markets. North African and Brazilian oranges enter the continental markets also, especially in France and Belgium.

The advent of concentrated orange juice—either in canned or frozen form—has revolutionized the commerce in this citrus fruit, especially so in the United States (domestic commerce) and Canada (foreign commerce). It has made less impact, to date, upon the fresh fruit trade to Europe but each year witnesses increases of the concentrates in these markets.

▶ ORANGES IN THE UNITED STATES

Orange production in the United States accounts for over a third of the world commercial crop (excluding China), and in tonnage and value exceeds all of the other citrus fruits. Five separate regions engage in the growing of oranges. Each

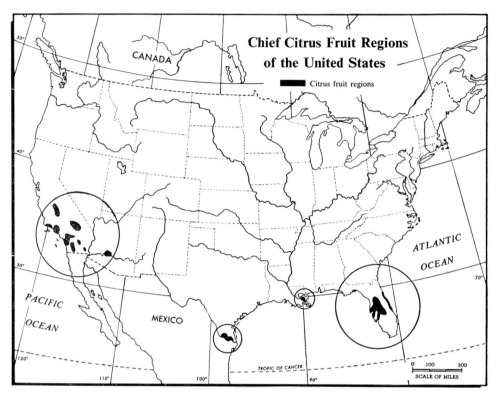

Chief Citrus Fruit Regions of the United States

region lies along the warm subtropical border of the nation. The five are located, from east to west, in Florida, Louisiana, Texas, Arizona, and California. The first two named are in the humid subtropics; the Texas area is at the dry-land border, and orange groves are irrigated from the Rio Grande; Arizona orange groves, like those of Egypt, lie in the tropical desert climate and are dependent wholly upon irrigation; the producing regions of California are in the Mediterranean subtropics of southern California and in warm, but dry, situations on the slopes of the great Central Valley of the state. Thus, in three of the five producing areas, irrigation is an absolute necessity—seasonally or annually.

Shifts in Orange-producing Regions

There have been major changes in the relative importance of the orange-producing regions of the United States during recent years. These changes and shifts have been particularly rapid in the period since the close of World War II. Southern California, the leader in the orange industry prior to World War II, has lost its position to Florida. Within California itself the south, or Los Angeles Basin, has declined in relative and absolute importance, and new producing regions elsewhere in the state have been established. These changes continue at present.

Florida orange production first surpassed that of California in 1945–1946 and has continued to expand, whereas there has been an absolute as well as a relative decline in California. The percentage of orange production in California dropped from 75 of the national production in 1920 to less than 40 by 1950. By 1955 the California percentage was down to slightly less than 30. In contrast, during the same years, the Florida percentage of the crop rose from 25 in 1920, to 55 in 1950, and reached 69 in 1955. In some years since the Florida share of orange production in the United States has exceeded 70 per cent. The three other producing regions contribute only 1 or 2 per cent apiece, and the Arizona and Texas areas are more significant in the total percentage of the citrus crop in grapefruit than in oranges.

► CALIFORNIA

The postwar decline of the citrus industry in southern California has been the result of the rapid increase of population in the Los Angeles area, which has been one of the key focal points for the large in-migration of people. The in-movement has resulted in expanding housing developments and suburbanization. New highways (freeways) built from the city through citrus areas resulted in new houses and factory developments. Many of these were scattered, originally, and orange groves remained between and among them. But, then, two events occurred to force elimination of orange acreage. One was increasing taxes, coincident upon the need for new schools, sewers, and other city services; growers could not pay the taxes and make a profit, and so sold to subdividers. A second event, with scattered groves, was the objection of the persons in the housing developments to the sprays—many of which are poisonous—smudges, and other necessary ingredients used in the control of frost and pests; thus, as a result, and with rising land costs and taxes, more growers sold to suburban subdividers.

California's acreage of oranges has thus declined both relatively and absolutely. Orange County, California—the leading county—lost 80,000 acres of orange groves (from 315,000 acres to 235,000) following the period when superhighways (freeways) were built, permitting urban expansion into the area. Declines in Los Angeles County were higher in proportion to area. One survey showed that in six months alone about 1,500 acres of orange groves were removed to make room for housing developments.

There were four separate and compact orange areas in the Los Angeles Basin. Two of these, the San Gabriel Valley and the San Fernando Valley, are now largely out of production and in urban land use. A third, the San Bernardino Valley, is losing its groves to rapid urban and industrial expansion. Most of the present production lies southeast of the city in the Los Angeles Plain—toward and in Orange County—but even this region, as mentioned above, is experiencing rapid urbanization.

The California orange crop of the Los Angeles basins and plains is divided among the Valencia, a summer-maturing orange grown in the cooler areas near the coast, and the navel or winter-maturing orange, of greatest importance inland, where temperatures are higher. Heavy irrigation and, during cool spells in the winter, orchard heating are necessary. Because of temperature inversions on cool or cold nights, the still, cold air settles to ground level. Frost protection is provided by smudge pots, set between the trees, and orchard heaters. Also, wind machines—really giant fans set on top of a tower in the orchard—are operated at these times to stir the air and keep it in motion so that frost pockets do not develop. Even the use of low-flying helicopters, whose blades stir and displace several million cubic feet of air in a few minutes, has proved effective in the frost protection of small and medium-sized acreages.

California oranges are marketed through a cooperative organization, one of the largest cooperatives in the nation. Special rates have been obtained in order to permit California citrus to compete in the markets of the eastern United States. In some areas these are spoken of as "postage-stamp rates" because eastward of certain stated points the rate is a uniform one for carload lots. The navel orange is harvested during the winter months; the "summer" orange is generally the Valencia. But, as in all citrus areas, winter harvest is predominant, a factor in the growth period of citrus which permits the fresh fruit to be placed on the market in quantity during the time that other fresh fruits are not in production. More than two-thirds of the California production is marketed as fruit; this is in contrast to Florida, where processors concentrate and juice the majority of the crop.

The southern part of the Central Valley of California, near Tulare, has had a small orange industry for some time—the second area of the state. Today this region is one wherein new groves are being planted, mainly by orchardists who have sold out in southern California and moved here; many, however, who have sold out have ceased agricultural activities and retired.

The Tulare area experiences more extremes of temperature than the Los Angeles Plain. Particularly, the hotter and drier summers cause earlier ripening of the fruit, with resulting shifts in time of access to market. Also, new plantings, which are chiefly of the navel (winter) orange, take at least eight years of growth to come to full production.

▶ ARIZONA, TEXAS, LOUISIANA

The irrigated Salt River Valley of Arizona is the locale of the orange and grapefruit industry of the state, and there is production, too, in the irrigated valleys westward of this region, such as the Coachella Valley of the desert area of southeastern California. The acreage near rapidly expanding Phoenix and its suburbs has, like southern California, felt the effects of urbanization and outlying subdivisions.

The Texas citrus groves are in the lower Rio Grande Valley, on the United States side of the river for reasons of access to market. Grapefruit are more important than oranges. Within the same region there is important production, also, of out-of-season vegetables. The Mexican side of the river is devoted mainly to cotton, marketed in Mexico, and the growing of citrus is purely for the local market. The international boundary is the determinative factor in the differing land utilization in this irrigated region. Tariffs and other regulations make it difficult for citrus or vegetable growers in Mexico to reach the American market.

Louisiana has a small orange acreage, but the groves yield a sweet and highly valued orange. Consumption of the crop is nearly all local or regional, the total yield being too small to reach national markets. New Orleans is the destination of much of the pick. The orange groves occupy long and narrow sites on the natural levees of the Mississippi, downstream from New Orleans.

► THE FLORIDA CITRUS INDUSTRY

Florida is the largest producer of citrus fruit in the world. More than a fourth of the world's total commercial production of citrus fruits now originates in Florida, and the state contributes annually from two-thirds to more than 70 per cent of the American output.

The most continuous and concentrated acreage of citrus trees in the world are in the lake-dotted "ridge" section (a common local name) of the north central portion of the interior of the Florida Peninsula. Here, in an area of gently rolling countryside, some 100 miles in length from north to south, and 40 miles in width, are more than 33 million citrus trees, two-thirds of the total plantings of such trees in the state. Here, interspersed among the numerous lakes, are the groves, large and small, which are the basis of an essentially "one-crop" activity within the region. Orange trees outnumber grapefruit trees about five to one, and the marketing of oranges is more important, in quantity, than grapefruit; but, nevertheless, Florida groves now produce three-fourths of the total world output of grapefruit. Three contiguous counties on the ridge alone contain half of the state's total area planted to citrus.

Two outlying citrus areas complete the picture of the commercial industry in Florida, although individual orange or grapefruit trees, whose fruit is used at home, are to be found in nearly every garden in the peninsular portion of the state. One region, the larger in area, lies in the western coastal section around Tampa Bay, and southward to the vicinity of Fort Myers. In some districts the groves of this region are almost connected with the ridge region; but this region lies in a somewhat warmer area in the winter season, is less hilly so far as surface configuration is concerned, and the growers have local problems, particularly insect control owing to warmer winters, which differ from those of the ridge. The other important commercial citrus region is a long narrow strip of territory along the central portion of the eastern or Atlantic coast; the name "Indian River" is associated with this region, as many of the groves are in the immediate vicinity of this long, narrow lagoon, particularly in the Brevard County section.

Within the Florida citrus area, and especially in the interior ridge section, many small towns are organized, functionally, around the citrus industry. Their surrounding service areas are associated with this agricultural enterprise, which, in effect, is one-crop agriculture. Residents work in the citrus groves, in canneries, in freezing plants; merchants depend upon the growers for a large part of their sales; wholesale establishments or cooperatives furnish sprays, fertilizers, and other necessities to the growers; bank deposits and the general state of business activity reflects the ups-and-downs of the citrus market. Only the larger towns, which may combine other activities—such as a resort industry on nearby lakes— are not almost completely dependent, directly or indirectly, upon the citrus enterprise.

The Florida citrus regions lie at the warm edge of the humid subtropics, and in the transitional area to the true tropics. Four summer months average over 80°F; during five months the average daily maxima are above 90°. But it is the winter that is the critical season. Although the "normal" winter day has a maximum temperature just over 70°, occasional frosts are expectable; the Florida peninsula lies wide open to the importation of cold air during the advent of cold waves from the broad continent to its north. But the quality oranges and grapefruit are best produced where this hazard exists, rather than in the truly tropical settings. Yet the occurrence of very severe frosts and heavy freezes is not desirable; the commercial districts of the present lie south of the region of heavy and frequent freezings. The original location of citrus production in Florida was in the St. John's River valley not far from Jacksonville. This area is "cool" in the winter—the coolest month averages a little over 50°—and the area is susceptible to several cold waves; the great Florida freeze of 1894–1895 virtually wiped out the groves of the St. John's area; the trees were killed, and commercial production eliminated. In part through the experience of trial and error, the new plantings farther south in the ridge and lake country proved to be beyond the limit of winter killing, and became the nucleus of the present intensive citrus region. Today the services of the Weather Bureau and of special frost-warning stations maintained by it warn the grower of the advent of inclement weather with the appearance of cold waves. Detailed research work today has also demonstrated the spottiness of frost at this "southern limit" of the frost line; and a combination of certain selections of a safe site for an orchard and vegetation conditions within the grove itself makes frost a not-too-severe hazard.

The important factors within the ridge citrus region are microclimatic—small local climates within the general climatic setting. These are related to the presence of more than 4,000 named lakes and ponds, the gently sloping hillsides, and air drainage. The lakes, which, of course, remain as open bodies of water all winter, moderate the temperatures along their shores, especially so on leeward shores. Citrus groves planted between large lakes are almost immune to frost; citrus groves on southeast or south shores are quite protected by the warmer air off the lake, for the cold waves advance into Florida from the northwest or north (although this is not the usual day-by-day wind direction during normal weather periods). The rolling terrain permits good subsurface drainage, which promotes stronger, healthier trees. These are then less susceptible to frost damage. The rolling surface, plus air drainage, protects the uplands and slopes from severe frost damage. As cold air is heavier than warm, it sinks into the lowlands on clear, cool nights when the temperature is near the freezing point. The low spots have frosts, the ridges and slopes do not in this critical setting. To the casual visitor

Fig. 4-3. Orange groves in the lake-dotted rolling lands of the "ridge" in central Florida. Note the continuous plantings on the rolling slopes beyond the lake. Both the slopes and the open water help provide frost protection through air drainage and through the moderation of the temperature of cool or cold air by the warmer lake waters. (Greater Orlando Chamber of Commerce)

or the outsider the ridge seems only undulating. It varies from 100 feet above sea level to just about 300; the local relief is enough, considering its overall climatic setting, to offer frost protection through air drainage. In more northerly latitudes this would not be the case; in hilly regions the ridge would barely be discernible.

The natural frost protection afforded by certain sites on the ridge is added to, when necessary, by man. During cold waves the growers supply heat from orchard heaters burning coal, coke, oil, or wood. Open fires are used by some. A few burn old rubber tires to provide smudges. Grove heating in Florida, however, is practiced generally only at the northern edge of the citrus belt. It is unusual in the southerly portions of the main producing district, or in the Tampa Bay and Indian River producing areas.

The expectancy of low temperatures varies with the year, and within the area varies within short distances. Some soil types seem to have colder air above them, for a short distance, than others. Research has established exact points for the beginning of freezing of citrus bloom, fruit, and foliage (as citrus is from the tropical margins of the world, flowers and ripe fruit may be on the same tree at the same time—usual to plants indigenous to the tropics). Orange flowers are damaged at 30°F, green oranges and grapefruit at 29°, ripe oranges and ripe grapefruit at 28°, young growth at 28°, and green foliage at 23°. The tree itself is killed if exposed to temperatures much lower than 26° for any length of time—two to three days. These research results show that some frost, or temperatures below 32°, is not detrimental—in fact, may have benefits in insect control. But prolonged cold spells or several successive cold nights are harmful. The citrus belt lies south of the "always-kill" region, north of the "truly-warm" belt. However, the severe freezes of 1957–1958 did considerable damage. Twenty per cent of the state's normal production of fruit was killed. Tree and grove losses were high on the northern fringe of the belt. In the lakeside locations, however, they averaged less than 2 per cent. According to the Federal-State Frost Warning Service at Lakeland the average number of frosty nights in the citrus belt (20-year average) is 48; the range is from a low of 23 in one season, to 66 during the coolest year. The cool-to-cold night is nonperiodic and may occur from November through February.

The citrus areas of the west coast and the east coast do not experience the number of cool nights, nor the frost, of the interior. Frost expectancy is less than half, in some areas less than a third that of the ridge. But, in contrast, the "warmer" winter permits insect infestations to be serious. Florida red scale, one of the serious citrus pests, is usually winter-killed on the ridge but is a major problem of growers in the southern half of the east coast region and the coastal sections south of Tampa Bay.

The soils of the Florida citrus regions are gray or yellow sands or red sandy loams. All of the soils have developed, within the climatic setting, under a vegetation cover of pines and blackjack and scrub oaks. On the whole the soils themselves are not fertile—in this respect the California and other citrus regions exceed the Florida area. But the soils are well drained, a great advantage; only locally are there poorly drained hardpan soils, and their presence is often marked by sharp citrus boundaries. Man has been able to overcome the naturally low fertility of the Florida soils, however, by the generous and continuous use of commercial fertilizer. In fact, in the region, the expenses for fertilizer are among the heaviest costs of the proprietors of orange groves, and, on the average, the cost of fertilizer is about one-fourth of the total cost of the production of citrus in the region.

The majority of Florida citrus groves are small in area; more than half are less than twenty acres in size. But the landscape is one of nearly continuous groves because of the numerous operators, each with his own planting. Several company-owned or cooperative groves exceed seven square miles in planted area. Many operators of the groves live in nearby towns; thus the casual traveler receives the impression that individual groves are larger than they are—houses and other buildings do not occur on each individual citrus farm.

The Florida citrus year shows a marked rhythm of activities and operations. Cover crops of grasses and citron vines (sometimes even weeds) are grown under the trees during the rainy summer season. The cover crops prevent soil erosion from the heavy convectional thunderstorm downpours and protect the soil from the heat of the summer sun. When plowed under in the fall they provide some organic matter for the sandy soils. For the rest of the year the surface beneath the groves is clean-cultivated. The clean tillage permits free air drainage and also, since there is no vegetation between individual trees, permits the moisture to be absorbed by the trees alone. The pruning of citrus trees is accomplished during the summer, when labor is not needed for harvest. Fertilization is a three-times-a-year activity, and the fertilizers are distributed by mechanical spreaders. Spraying, for control of insects and for tree diseases, is usually done four times a year.

The picking of orange and grapefruit is mainly a winter activity; there are early, midseason, and late varieties of each, so that the harvest season may last from November into late May. January normally witnesses its peak. Some fruit may be harvested in all months—a relationship to the tropical origin of the tree. A plentiful labor supply is needed during the winter harvest, as all fruit must be picked by hand; costs of labor are normally about half of the costs of production. The usual practice in the citrus belt is for the packing houses to supply the picking crews, and for the grower of citrus to sell his crop "on tree." The pickers are paid by piece work—the quantity picked.

Packing houses now process two-thirds or more of the Florida citrus production. These firms may be canning plants, condensing plants, frozen juice processors, or companies handling and selling all types of citrus products. The oranges and grapefruit marketed in fresh form are shipped from the state by rail and truck; shipments are under the regulations of two organizations, one a growers one, the other a state agency, and the State and Federal Departments of Agriculture enforce the regulations.

Florida citrus fruit that is marketed fresh reaches the markets of the eastern half of the United States. The freight-rate situation virtually gives Florida the southern market without serious competition. In the Northeast, Florida and California citrus compete. In the Middle West, especially in certain cities, the citrus from the two areas receives strong competition from the growing area in Texas—the last-named state enjoying a high-quality name in given markets. With the decline of the California production, Florida fresh fruit now reaches a wider market area than was formerly the case.

► OTHER CITRUS FRUITS

Grapefruit, lemons, limes, and other citrus fruits are produced regionally. Although there is overlap, as the plantings of oranges and grapefruit in Florida, the specialized commercial regions tend to emphasize a particular product.

The demand of the consumer differs between grapefruit and lemons. In general a large and juicy grapefruit is the type the market desires. Preference is for a compact lemon—with its concentrated juice, of course—but not a "soft" and exceedingly juicy product. The grapefruit is grown mainly in humid lands, for they produce the desired juicy fruit; if grown under irrigation a large quantity of water must be supplied. In contrast, the lemon is grown, principally, in the Mediterranean subtropics. The differing environmental settings are illustrated by the location of the commercial regions in the United States; Florida and Texas produce, on the average, more than 85 per cent of the grapefruit—in some years, 90 per cent—and the citrus regions of Arizona and California only some 10 per cent, this last all from irrigated valleys (oases) in the desert climate. In contrast, California growers of the Mediterranean subtropics produce almost all of the American-grown lemons. Thus, even in California, the grapefruit and the lemons originate in different regions, environmentally.

The United States is by far the leader in both the production and consumption of grapefruit. The new plantings of grapefruit in Israel, part of the "citrus-support" for the Jewish agricultural colonies, have brought that nation into second position, and into command of the export trade to Europe, but the total production is only a very small fraction of that of the United States—even less, usually, than the production in the minor American producing areas. Beyond these two producers, grapefruit are significant only in the islands of the West Indies, particularly in Puerto Rico, Jamaica, and Trinidad. The North American importance of grapefruit is illustrated, further, by the fact that Canada is a leader in the import of grapefruit and concentrates; in fact, despite the difference in total population, Canada and Great Britain—the two leading importers—consume approximately equal quantities of grapefruit.

Florida grapefruit, as noted previously, is grown on the ridge and in other of the state's orange-growing areas. Texas grapefruit, more important in the Rio Grande Valley than oranges, are irrigated in part. The introduction of the pink-fleshed grapefruit from Texas provided an impetus for expansion of the groves,

Fig. 4-4. Irrigated grapefruit groves in the lower Rio Grande Valley at the southern tip of Texas. The irrigation ditch receives its water from the river. The vegetable farms in the distance produce "off-season" or winter vegetables for marketing in the cities of the northern United States. The season of chief agricultural activity is the winter— for both citrus fruits and vegetables. (Standard Oil Company, N.J.)

as the "pinks" found ready market acceptance; newer plantings in Florida now contain some of the pink-fleshed varieties. The desert-valley settings of the Arizona and California producing regions are similar. In Arizona the Salt River Valley citrus area is the producing region; in California the irrigated desert valleys of the southeast—near Imperial Valley—and particularly the Coachella Valley, comprise the producing area. Large quantities of water must be provided many times a year to both the Arizona and California groves.

The lemon, like the orange, was transferred during early days from its indigenous habitat in southeast Asia to the Mediterranean Basin. Improvement and perfection of the lemon tree has taken place under the conditions of the Mediterranean environment. World commercial production of lemons is almost entirely in the Mediterranean realm. The largest producers are four separate areas of this climatic setting—southern California, Sicily, Spain, and Greece. California supplies the American market, the others the European. Were it not for a tariff Sicilian lemons would (and do, occasionally) appear in eastern United States markets. Latin American producing regions yield some lemons for their local markets.

The small plains along the northern and eastern shores of the mountainous island of Sicily constitute the lemon (as well as other citrus regions) of Italy. Sicily is fortunate in its protection from frost during the winter and from hot winds in the summer. Cold waves, which reach peninsular Italy, are moderated by the warm waters of the Tyrrhenian Sea north of Sicily. Hot sirocco winds, blowing from the Sahara in the summer, are moderated by the Sicilian mountains which provide protection to the north-coast lemon groves of the island. The groves of the east coast receive some protection, and in Calabria on the nearby mainland of Italy, small pocket plains, tucked along the shore between mountain spurs, are moderated enough to have a citrus industry. In Sicily the production of lemons is about half that of oranges; relatively the island is Europe's most important producer of lemons. In the Valencia lowland of Spain, in contrast, orange production far exceeds that of lemons. In European markets Spain has the name for quality oranges, Sicily for lemons.

The lemon groves of California are in discontinuous and fragmented coastal lowlands to the north and northwest of the Los Angeles region. The Ventura lowland is especially important. Lemons thrive under the moderately "cool" summer temperatures of the coastal strips, and under the higher humidities present along the littoral. Cool sea breezes delay maturity somewhat, throwing the picking season into the months of early summer (rather than late winter, as in interior groves, located in warmer settings). Thus the lemon harvest in the coastal valleys is just prior to the market demand for lemons, for the greatest consumption in the United States is during the summer; the advent of heat waves in the eastern half of the country promotes the sale of lemons for use in cooling drinks. Some of the packing houses near the sea are able to store lemons under "natural refrigeration" from the sea breeze and market the fruit later in the season. As with other citrus fruits, lemons are also marketed in concentrated form as canned or frozen juice.

California growers produce practically the entire American production of lemons. The virtual market monopoly and high prices received for lemons made "lemon land" relatively more valuable than that for oranges, particularly in the seaward cooler sides of the coastal lowlands. In the Ventura lowland orange acreage was lost during the 1930's and 1940's, and many orange groves were pulled up and replaced by plantings of lemons. Drainage projects in the flattish near-shore areas permitted the expansion of lemon acreage onto the newly drained lands, and resulted in increased production when the trees came into bearing. By the early 1950's the Ventura lowland alone was producing more than one-third of the lemons grown in the United States.

Urbanization has reached the California lemon regions. Growers must compete for land with subdivision developers and factories. The lemon acreage of the Los Angeles region is undergoing the changes described for oranges. And even the outlying coastal valleys have felt the impact. Oxnard, the central city of the Ventura lowland, has expanded. A recent estimate made for one of the valleys contends that ten years will see the elimination of agriculture from the area. The overall situation facing the lemon industry is, in most respects, more serious than that faced by other citrus fruits—largely because, to date, the prime lemon-growing regions have been so concentrated; and environmentally there are fewer potential producing regions than for other citrus.

The lime tree will not tolerate frost; limes are truly a citrus fruit of the tropics. Within the United States only a few areas on the Florida Peninsula south of the latitude of Miami and a few islands of the Florida Keys engage in production. One town south of Miami is the leading lime-shipping center of the nation. Otherwise, limes for the United States market are imported from the West Indies. The tropical state of Hawaii has a small but strictly local production of limes and other citrus fruits, but not enough for the home market.

▶ OTHER SUBTROPICAL FRUITS

There are many tender fruits that are raised in the subtropical realms—both the humid subtropics and the Mediterranean subtropics. Some favored spots within these realms can also grow some of the tropical fruits, usually on south-facing slopes in the Northern Hemisphere, or in small areas favored by an especially long and warm growing season. Some of the subtropical fruits—the fig, for example—can be grown and matured farther poleward than others. Among these subtropical fruits are such as the persimmon, pomegranate, alligator pear or avocado, loquat, guava, and the fig. A few locations can grow mangoes and papayas, but these are mainly from the true tropics.

Commercial persimmons are the Japanese variety. They are grown in and exported from Japan and Korea. Introduction of this variety to southern California and the Mediterranean shores of France and Italy has resulted in an industry in these locations. Boxed persimmons reach American markets in the fall. A wild persimmon is indigenous to the entire southeastern United States, but it is astringent because of a high content of tannin; after the first hard frost of late fall or early winter it is edible. This persimmon does not reach commercial markets as it is very small in size.

Pomegranates, guavas, loquats, and avocados are grown in both California and Florida, and in a few locations of the Mediterranean Basin. Fresh fruit for salads, preserves, jellies and other preservatives are made from some of these. The avocado, indigenous to the tropics of the West Indies, lowland Mexico, and lowland Central America is of extreme importance to tropical peoples; it is a source of protein for people who otherwise consume little meat or fish. The Hawaiian Islands have an important commercial production of avocados and papayas, and export some to the mainland United States. In general, however, because of the perishability and softness of all the tender subtropical and tropical fruits they are shipped only seasonally, or to specialty and fancy markets. Within the tropics, of course, such is not the case; the mango, for example, is a common fruit for all classes of people in India.

The fig tree is able to withstand the dry Mediterranean summer, and to grow on rocky hillsides and other land surfaces in Mediterranean Europe that are not suitable for crop cultivation. In the Central Valley of California, with extensive land areas, there is less severe competition for the land, and fig orchards are planted on the better soils of the level plains. In Mediterranean Europe and Asia such land, except in parts of Turkey, which has less population pressure, is not used for figs.

Fig leaves are few compared to the size of the tree; this characteristic is one which aids the tree in surviving during the summer drought. The fig is presumably indigenous to the Near East; it has long been grown on stony soils there, as well as in irrigated oases, such as Mesopotamia. But its spread throughout the Mediterranean Basin was early enough in time to enable writers of the early day to mention its presence throughout the region. The fruit of the fig tree may be yellow, green, white, black, or purple in color.

Figs must be subjected by man to a process called caprication, wherein clusters of the wild inedible caprifig are hung in the trees. A fig wasp is in the caprifig, and as the wasps fly from these clusters to the tame figs they pollinate the flowers; these are either male or female, and pollination requires an outside agency, such as the wasp. Before the fig trees introduced to California bore fruit, the fig wasp had to be transferred and acclimatized there. Today fig orchards in that state are pollinated in this and other ways, sometimes even by hand.

Italy is the leading fig-producing country. The southern portion of the Italian Peninsula has by far the largest concentration of fig orchards in the world. These are located south of the latitude of Rome on the Ionian Sea side of the peninsula and south of the latitude of Pescara on the Adriatic Sea side, as well as throughout the "toe" and the "heel" of the southern shores. Turkey and Greece are outstanding, also, in production of figs; and all European, Asian, and African shorelands around the Mediterranean Sea have a considerable crop. Izmir, in Turkey, formerly called Smyrna, has a reputation for high-quality Smyrna figs. The figs of the Mediterranean Basin lands are generally dried in the brilliant sunshine and marketed commercially as dried figs, principally in Europe. The fig production of Italy alone is about half of the total.

California serves the North American market for figs. Its fig crop, from several specialized fig-orchard areas, particularly in the hot Central Valley of the state, is only about a tenth that of Italy. The market demand in the United States is principally for canned figs, and the bulk of the production reaches the consumer in this form. Thus the market competition is mainly with other canned fruits (such as peaches or pears), rather than with dried fruits. In California the fig orchards are planted on level to sloping ground with deep soils; unlike the Mediterranean Basin, there has been no land pressure, competitively, in the fig-growing districts, to "force" planting on steep or stony submarginal lands.

Fig culture has been introduced to some of the hot, irrigated desert valleys of southeastern California and Arizona, and has proved successful.

Figs grow well in the warmer parts of the American humid subtropics. They are grown northward into Georgia, but their distribution is sporadic and is determined principally by the interest of individual farmers or orchardists in their cultivation. There are commercial fig orchards in several portions of the American South, notably in parts of Georgia and of Texas.

Mediterranean-type climatic regions in South Africa, Australia, and central Chile engage also in fig production. The fruit is particularly common in Chile.

▶ NUT CROPS

Chestnuts are a most important food item in the Mediterranean subtropics of Europe. Not only are they eaten daily during the autumn (following harvest) and winter by peasant peoples, but in some lands a chestnut flour is produced. Chestnut trees grow well on rocky hillsides and yield a return from this uncultivable land. In the lowlands field crops are planted among widely spaced chestnut trees, and two harvests are obtained from different levels.

Walnuts and almonds are grown in the Mediterranean subtropics of California and the Mediterranean Basin. Both of these nut trees survive the dry summer, but they are irrigated if water is plentiful. Filberts and other varieties of nuts are also raised in these regions and, on the West Coast, northward into Oregon.

The pecan tree grows wild in the lower Mississippi Valley of the United States, and westward to central Texas. Planted pecan groves are now common in many parts of the American humid subtropics, particularly in the southern or warmer third. Florida, Georgia, Alabama, Mississippi, Louisiana, and Texas all have important commercial production of this nut.

▶ QUESTIONS

1. Why is the lime grown commercially in different areas than the orange?
2. Explain why the European trade in citrus fruits and citrus juices is mainly foreign trade, whereas the much larger trade in the United States is domestic commerce.
3. What developments enlarged the market for citrus fruits and juices?
4. What have been the regional shifts in orange-growing in the United States during the period since World War II? Explain the reasons for these.
5. What is the effect of the United States–Mexico boundary on the land use and the markets of the irrigated region near the mouth of the Rio Grande?
6. Explain why the Florida citrus belt is more susceptible to cold waves during the winter than are the citrus regions of Arizona and southern California.
7. Why is fresh citrus fruit usually least costly during the winter (when other fresh fruits are expensive) and highest in price during the summer?
8. Name some of the fruit and nut crops which originate in either California or Florida and are marketed throughout the United States and Canada.

V Middle-Latitude Vegetables and Fruits

The vegetable and fruit crops are utilized almost entirely for food; but the potato is, in addition, an important feed for animals and an industrial raw material from which starch, alcohol, and other products are manufactured.

A vegetable is any of the many herbs that are cultivated for table use. The portion eaten may be the whole or a part; the turnip is a root, lettuce or cabbage are leaves, peas and beans are the fruit, and broccoli is a flower. Although the sweet potato is an enlarged portion of the root of the plant, the completely unrelated white potato is an underground tuber which receives its ingredients for growth from both the aboveground vine and underground roots. The number of kinds of vegetables now on the markets has increased, in part because plant breeders have developed new types, in part because some plants not formerly considered of value are now consumed.

The fruits are tree-fruits, bush fruits, and certain berries. The tree fruits include the citrus fruits (see Chapter IV) and the deciduous fruits; these last are divided into prunus fruits and pome fruits. The prunus fruits are drupaceous—they have a thin skin and a fleshy interior that encloses a single stone, or seed; the apricot, cherry, peach, plum, and prune are examples. The pome fruits include the apple and pear. Bush fruits are of several types; in growth they may be from small bushes (raspberries, gooseberries) or from vines (grapes); several new types, such as the boysenberry, have been developed by plant breeders. The strawberry, not a true "fruit," is an example of a berry which grows on a low herb rather than a bush.

▶ RISE OF THE TRADE IN VEGETABLES AND FRUITS

The vegetable and fruit industry, as we now know it, dates back less than a hundred years. The large-scale industry of the present has been made possible by a sequence of developments, and by the advent of rapid transportation. First, during the 1870's, the refrigerator car was perfected and perishables could be shipped to markets. Secondly, the manufacture of artificial ice was developed in the early 1890's; this resulted in out-of-season fresh vegetables from Florida being placed on northern markets. Thirdly, about 1900 the canning of vegetables became well established; although the art of canning was perfected about 1810 in France, and there was some canning beginning with the period of the Civil War, it was not until toward the end of the nineteenth century that fruit and vegetable canning became a significant industry. Fourthly, during the late 1930's the advent of the quick-freezing of vegetables occurred. Following World War II freezing establishments multiplied in numbers and began extending their operations to include prepared and cooked products and the freezing of extracted and concentrated fruit juices. And, in this century, mechanical refrigeration on railroad cars, trucks, and in groceries and homes permits widespread sale and storage of vegetables and fruits, as well as other products.

The growing of vegetables and fruits existed before the sequence of developments outlined above occurred. But markets were purely local. Perishables had to be consumed within a few days. Only a few of the root crops and cabbages could be stored in "root cellars" for the winter season. Thus the turnip, rutabaga, onion, and potato were the important "winter" table vegetables. Carrots and a few others were buried in sand for storage, and apples were packed in barrels and stored in cellars. This is still the case in large parts of the world. Only in the electrified areas where present refrigeration is possible are out-of-season fresh vegetables and fruits common.

The United States is the chief commercial producing area of vegetables, and its inhabitants are among the largest consumers on a per capita basis. Europe follows. Japan's commercial industry is expanding. No doubt China and India have a larger total production and consumption than in the United States, but in these countries the industry is still tied largely to the immediate market, around which vegetable farms cluster. The use of vegetables in quantity in China reflects the dense habitation and lack of land which can be used for pasture, or for feed crops for animals; the land is used directly to feed humans. In India the large use reflects the Hindu religion and its attitude toward animals; Hindus are vegetarians by choice—Chinese by necessity in many districts.

FIG. 5-1. Vegetables and rice constitute two of the chief agricultural products of Japan. Emphasis upon these food crops is a necessity because of the dense population and limited area of land suitable for cultivation. Every square yard of land is put to use, and cultivation is stretched onto hillsides by terracing. Notice the terraced fields devoted to vegetables, the vegetable fields on the plain below the slopes, the rice paddies along the river bottoms (the flooded fields in the strip in the middle distance), and the city on the plain beyond the rice fields. The high snow-capped mountain is Fujiyama. (Japan Tourist Association)

The trade in vegetables and fruits is less developed in Europe than in the United States but is expanding in response to present increases in incomes and changing food habits. Britain and Germany have been the principal markets for foreign-grown vegetables and fruits. France and other European nations generally supply themselves. The all-year growing of vegetables under glass, in hothouses, is an important industry in the Netherlands and Belgium. The warm Mediterranean lands, able to produce vegetables for the winter and spring markets of the north, are the exporters during these seasons. Thus vegetables from Spain and Italy reach English and German markets. And the Atlantic islands are also source regions; one of the prominent exports from the Canary Islands are winter-grown tomatoes for the English trade.

► THE VEGETABLE INDUSTRY OF THE UNITED STATES

The growing of vegetables, their transport to market, and the marketing itself is a highly organized activity in the United States. The availability of fresh, canned, and frozen vegetables at all seasons of the year, plus several other factors, has resulted in a large collective and individual consumption—one rising by the year.

The rising per capita consumption of vegetables in the United States has been a phenomenon of the last twenty to thirty years. Food habits have changed appreciably. There are many reasons. The discovery of vitamins in the 1910's, 1920's and 1930's, and the vitamin content of vegetables has been a factor. The American desire to be thin—or at least not unduly fat or heavy—has resulted in many persons replacing some of the "fat" foods with vegetables and salads. Vegetables have been made available in all forms at all seasons. Balanced diets have been stressed. The industry has advertised extensively and promoted their product. Fresh vegetables are marketed in attractive form, even packaged in transparent materials. New

FIG. 5-2. Market gardens are small in area, and are cultivated intensively. (Standard Oil Company, N.J.)

packaging materials of all kinds have been utilized when they have become available. The ease of cooking already prepared frozen vegetables is a factor. And, no doubt, the rising costs of certain other foods relative to the costs of vegetables is of importance. It is difficult to assess and weigh all factors, but the vitamin situation and the "American look" are given special credit by many authorities.

Vegetables are grown on three types of farms—market gardens, truck farms, and as a cash crop on general farms or dairy farms.

Market gardens are in the immediate vicinity of their market, at the fringes of cities. A market gardener does not specialize but grows nearly all of the types of vegetables for the adjacent urban market; he plants a succession of quick-maturing and longer-season vegetables so that his harvest (and income) will extend from late spring until frost. Market gardens are small in area, usually only a few acres, and are ordinarily a family enterprise.

Truck farms are located at a distance from the eventual markets, and the farmer specializes in one or two vegetables. He becomes expert in the raising of these, but is subject to vagaries of weather, costs, and availability of hired labor, transportation charges, and fluctuations of prices in the distant market. Truck

FIG. 5-3. Bunched carrots from truck farms, ready to be loaded into railroad refrigerator cars for shipment to distant urban markets. (Standard Oil Company, N.J.)

Fig. 5-4. Mexican labor picking string beans on a truck farm in the Rio Grande Valley of southern Texas. This truck-farm district, like those of parts of California and of Florida, is oriented to distant urban markets and grows vegetables only during the winter, when northern market gardens and truck farms are out of production. (Standard Oil Company, N.J.)

farms in southern Florida, southern Texas, and the warm valleys of Arizona and California produce the out-of-season vegetables and place them on the city markets of the rest of the United States during the winter. Truck farms in the Chesapeake Bay region, in New Jersey, on Long Island, in western New York State, Ohio, and elsewhere in the North produce the supply crop of vegetables and market some of them even in the cities of Florida during late summer. A truck farm is usually large in area; some of those in south Florida plant as many as 1,200 acres (nearly two square miles) of the special crop, such as pole beans; some in California grow 2,000 or more acres of a single crop, such as carrots. Truck farms are dependent upon large numbers of temporary workers, usually itinerants who move with the seasons and crop to be picked. Some of the farms have direct telephone connections with the produce buyers of the cities, and the owner or manager directs his field foreman and workers by walkie-talkie from his office.

General or dairy farms, on which a vegetable is grown as a cash crop, usually produce one which can be handled by machinery. Thousands of dairy farmers in Wisconsin grow peas. When ripe, the peavines are cut by machine, are handled like hay, and delivered to a peaviner located at a crossroads. Here the peas are separated from the pods by machine and then delivered to the cannery or freezing plant. The vines and pods are stacked for silage and fed to sheep in the winter. Other vegetables handled by machine, such as carrots and beets, are lifted mechanically from the ground in the fall. Farmers of southern Minnesota grow much sweet corn; hand labor, usually provided by the farm family, is necessary only for the picking of the ears. But some few areas specialize in a crop that is more demanding of labor; tomatoes are important on general and Corn Belt farms in large parts of Indiana, for example, and during harvest the handling of the crop necessitates recruitment of both local and itinerant workers. As might be expected from the organizational pattern, the production of vegetables on general farms (as opposed to market gardens or truck farms) is largely for the manufactural market —canneries and freezers—rather than for the fresh vegetable trade.

Vegetable growing and the existence of an out-of-season market in the United States permits "commuting" vegetable growers. Some operators in New Jersey close their activities with frost and move to Florida. Here they produce for the winter trade, which lasts until more northern areas, such as South Carolina and Georgia, come into production. As these growers are closer to market, and are able to reach it in less time and at lower costs, they capture it. As Florida goes out of production, the "commuting" grower moves back to the North and prepares for the crop year there. When he and others in New Jersey have crops for sale they, being closer to the eastern urban markets, capture them from South Carolina and Georgia. "Commuting" growers from Ohio produce a large share of the Florida radishes.

Specialized vegetable-growing regions have arisen in the United States. And a few special-crop vegetable areas have developed. The specialized regions are closely related to soils, climatic factors, and markets. The specialized crop areas are in environments which are unusually suitable for the vegetable being grown.

California, as a state, leads the nation in the production of vegetables; Florida is second. Regionally, rather than by states, the Middle Atlantic region is the outstanding one.

The largest and most important of the vegetable-farming regions is on the sandy and sandy loam soils of the Coastal Plain, in a latitude where the growing season is long because of the moderating influence of nearby bodies of water, and is close to the urban markets of the almost continuous city (Megalopolis) which extends from Washington to New York—through Baltimore, Wilmington, Philadelphia, and Trenton—a megalopolis 250 miles long, containing some 25 million inhabitants. The region, named the Middle Atlantic truck-farming region, includes southern New Jersey and the Delmarva Peninsula—the area in Delaware, Maryland, and Virginia which lies between Chesapeake Bay and the Atlantic Ocean. This bay, and Delaware Bay farther north, margin the truck-farming region on the west; the Atlantic is to the east. The growing season of 180 to 200 days is nearly as long as that of the Coastal Plain in North Carolina. This long season, with an early spring and late autumn, provides the region with a distinct competitive advantage—early vegetables mature two or three weeks after those of North Carolina—and the adjacency to markets provides the region with an economic advantage. Growers in North Carolina have only a very short time with the market to "themselves." The advantageous overall competitive position of the Delmarva area is shown by the situation in the spring of the year; winter vegetables originate in Florida, early spring ones in southern Georgia and South Carolina, then the major production jumps more than 450 miles northward to the Chesapeake Bay countryside.

Soils for vegetable growing are important, but less so than formerly. Warm, loose, friable soils are a necessity, but are usual in much of the Coastal Plain. It is the heavy fertilization, practiced at present, that makes soils less critical. It is economically feasible to spend heavily for fertilizers and utilize them abundantly

Fig. 5-5. Large-scale truck farming in southern New Jersey near urban markets. The ground is being prepared for extensive plantings of vegetables. The warm and friable sandy loam soils are excellent for vegetable crops, but must be fertilized heavily. (Standard Oil Company, N.J.)

on a vegetable crop—for the crop is high in value per unit of weight or of area.

Muck soils of swampy districts are now used for the growing of vegetables. The discovery that these organic (rather than mineral) soils were suitable, following their drainage by ditch or underground tiles, has resulted in the rise of new vegetable areas, particularly in southern Florida. Heavy addition of certain fertilizers is necessary, but the costs are more than repaid. The drained lands of the Everglades, especially those near Lake Okeechobee, whose warm waters furnish frost protection to nearby areas, are the locale (with California) of the largest vegetable farms in the nation. The region is almost frostless, has rapid transport to eastern markets, and has become the East Coast center of winter-season production. Farms are mechanized so far as possible, are very large in size, and draw upon labor from the southeastern United States. The centers of Florida vegetable production have shifted southward with this development. The efficiently managed, highly mechanized large truck farms have obtained a growing share of the market. They are able to sell in quantity; smaller truck farms farther north, in older vegetable areas, have felt their competition. Moreover, if a crop is lost by frost, the large grower is in better position to absorb the loss; the small farmer is apt to lose his entire investment.

California vegetables, grown in differing environments in a large and diverse state, are being harvested somewhere all year. The warm southern valleys, such as the Imperial Valley, are significant during the winter; other areas are the centers of summer production. Market-gardening and truck-farming districts in the Central Valley produce most of the year, and supply the urban centers of the San Francisco Bay area and the Los Angeles region. Some districts produce for canneries and freezing establishments. Trainloads of out-of-season vegetables are shipped to middle western and eastern markets. At a point en route—usually a junction in the plains area—the cars may be reassembled into separate trains destined for the location where the market conditions are best for the particular vegetable at the particular time; for example, if the St. Louis market is weak at the moment, carlots will be diverted to Dallas, or to Minneapolis, or cities wherein, at the time, the demand is strong and the vegetable in short supply. The marketing arrangements are highly organized. Thus it is mainly only for the out-of-season winter and spring market that California and Florida produce come into competition in the fresh vegetable market.

The transportation factor is very important in the vegetable trade. There is competition among carriers. In general, from the regions of principal commercial production, the major movement to market is by truck in the 200-mile zone, but there is some long-distance shipment by motor carrier. The truck and the railroad compete in the 200-to-800-mile zone. The longer shipments, as from California to eastern markets, are mainly by rail. Special rates on a given commodity have an effect. And towns not on rail lines must be served by truck only. Intermediate marketing and sorting centers have developed. Two of the largest such in the East Coast trade are Columbia, South Carolina, and Atlanta. One kind of vegetable from a growing-area in Florida may be shipped as a full truck load to Columbia;

here, at the market (a specially built facility) there is interchange and transfer, and truckloads containing an assortment of vegetables are forwarded northward. Columbia has an advantageous location for this activity; it is halfway between south Florida and New York. The market at Atlanta serves a somewhat similar function for Florida produce being directed to middle western cities; as Atlanta lies at the southern end of the southern Appalachians, the trucks routed northward—to Chicago and other cities—do not have to cross the mountains.

The irrigating of vegetables is very important. It is and always has been necessary in the dry climatic settings, such as in many of the producing districts in California. But irrigation by overhead spray methods is increasingly significant even in the humid climates of the eastern Coastal Plain. The investment in portable pipes, overhead spray equipment, and pumps is repaid by the yield; vegetables can be saved during a dry spell, "forced" somewhat even following moderate rains, and water added when needed during periods of rapid evaporation. Again, as in the "frost situation" it is chiefly the large grower who can afford the investment. He may thus harvest his crop, in certain years, a few days earlier, and in so doing, presumably obtain a price advantage over the small producer; this is true especially in the out-of-season market.

Scientific forecasts and the applying of climatological data to the vegetable industry is a practice on some recently established giant vegetable farms. One integrated operation in southern New Jersey serving all types of the market from fresh table vegetables to packaging and freezing its output on the home farm has been noted for its use of scientists in its planning, in forecasting its needs for the adding of water, and in preparations for a specific forecasted harvest date.

The overall trend in the American industry has been toward the large-scale operation financed by individuals or corporations. Increasingly the share of the market commanded by the giant farm has tended to increase with respect to the share held by the thousands of small market gardens and truck farms.

▶ MIDDLE-LATITUDE FRUITS

California is outstanding in the vegetable and fruit industry. A most important part of the state's agriculture is associated with horticulture. And when horticultural activities such as the growing of flowers and ornamental plants are added to the more usual vegetable industry and orcharding, the importance of the state's farms in this division of agriculture is apparent.

California's position as the leading agricultural state in *value of products* is owing to the significance of horticulture. Fruits, vegetables, and flowers are high in value; an acre of carrots or of bearing peach trees is more valuable than an acre of hay or of oats; the annual returns from an acre of carrots are larger than from hay; of course, the seed, labor, and other costs are higher, but the net income left after these charges have been met still exceeds that from the field crops such as hay or oats. California does not lead the nation's agriculture when it is measured by a method other than value of production. Twenty states have more *land* in farms than California has; fourteen states have more *harvested cropland*. Many exceed in the field and feed crops.

But it is in the cultivation of high-value products that California exceeds. The vegetables and fruits discussed in this chapter are examples. Others are the citrus industry, the viticulture—for table grapes, wine grapes, and raisins—and the many specialized horticultural activities which range from an important flower industry to the growing of such products as artichokes and olives.

The high-value products are in response to several factors. The Mediterranean subtropical climate permits a wide choice of products; summer-grown ones are irrigated, winter-grown ones yield in the mild temperatures and winter rainfall. The sunny, dry summer permits outdoor drying of fruits. A high value per acre product is a necessity in much of the state's farming districts to pay the costs of irrigation water. Diverse microclimates permit production for out-of-season markets in some parts of the state, warm temperate crops elsewhere, cool-season ones at higher altitudes. There are large local markets in the urban centers on the Pacific Coast of the state. And the produce which is to be marketed eastward in the central and eastern United States, or northward in the Pacific Northwest, must be valuable enough to pay its costs of transport, the labor expenses, taxes and other items, and still leave a profit for the grower.

California's relative position in the United States, though first in vegetable production, is far greater in the fruit-growing industry. Nearly 40 per cent of all farms in the country that are classified by the Census as fruit farms are in California. The state has three times more such farms than the second state in number. In value, the fruit grown in the state is more than 40 per cent of the national total. And, for most of the individual fruits, California is the leading producer; there are a few exceptions—apple production is one, and oranges another (see Chapter IV).

The several kinds of fruit of the middle latitudes are divisible, so far as producing districts or regions are concerned, into those of the warmer temperate areas and those of the cooler-summer regions. The peach is the most widely distributed of the warm-temperate fruits, the apple is the chief of the cooler regions. In the United States the peach is the major deciduous fruit tree of the South and of California; the apple predominates in the northeastern quarter of the country and in the state of Washington. The peach is important in warm southern Europe, the apple in northern Europe. Altitudinally, the apple is grown in cool highlands, the peach in lower lands; the Piedmont of the Carolinas is peach country, and apples are a product of the mountainous Appalachian uplands. The leading peach-producing states are California, South Carolina, and Georgia; the leaders in apple growing are Washington and New York.

There is overlap of apples and peaches in the latitudes of the Ohio and Potomac Valleys. Some lowland districts north of this are significant in peaches. Highland and upland areas south of these latitudes, particularly the Shenandoah Valley of Virginia, are leading centers of the apple industry. And, farther north, peaches

FIG. 5-6. The apple country in Tasmania, the island state south of Australia. Orchards are planted on slopes to ensure frost protection through air drainage. Tasmanian apples are shipped halfway around the world to British markets. (Australian News and Information Bureau)

are grown in orchards planted in sheltered districts, especially on the lee side of the Great Lakes. The peaches of Michigan originate in such a setting, parallel to the eastern shore of Lake Michigan.

All of the deciduous fruits enter foreign trade in moderate quantities. But the apple is the major fruit which is shipped long distances to world markets. It is less perishable than the "soft fruits," as most of the other deciduous fruits are termed in the trade. It is packed more easily, is less apt to bruise or deteriorate in transit, and can be stored at a market center relatively longer.

Canada, the island state of Tasmania in Australia, the Alpine area of northern Italy, the Netherlands, Argentina, the United States, New Zealand, and Denmark are the countries that are the chief exporters of apples. The United Kingdom and Germany are the chief importers; markets in one or two port cities are the primary destination; in these centers the fruit is wholesaled and distributed throughout the nations. France is the most important apple-growing country of Europe, and

Fig. 5-7. The Great Lakes fruit belts are on the eastern or leeward sides of the lakes. The cool spring season delays blooming of the trees until after the danger of a late frost has passed. This is an apple orchard on the Niagara Peninsula. (Standard Oil Company, N.J.)

its annual tonnage usually exceeds that of the entire United States. The apple orchards are concentrated in the cool northwest, near the English Channel in Brittany and Normandy; the chief use of these apples is in the manufacture of cider, the principal beverage of the entire northwest of France—the only portion of the nation wherein the use of cider exceeds the use of wine.

The fruit canning, juicing, and freezing industry is located with respect to its raw material—the fresh fruit. Nearly half of the peach crop is grown in California orchards. Peaches are utilized in the fresh-fruit trade, for drying, and for processing or canning. California is the principal center of peach drying and canning in the nation. Distance from markets of the East, as well as quantity of the California peach crop, are factors: Georgia and South Carolina peaches, marketed as fresh fruit, dominate the eastern urban markets during early summer, and Michigan and southeastern Pennsylvania peaches have the advantage of propinquity in the late summer. Washington, some distance removed from the markets of California and the eastern United States, is the center of the processing of apples that do not enter the fresh-fruit or export trade. Apple juices and apple sauces are the processed products. The apples grown in New York state and Virginia are sold mainly as fresh fruit, but there is processing of any surplus.

Apple exports from North America are from both West Coast and East Coast ports. A large quantity from Washington and British Columbia are shipped from Seattle and Vancouver to Britain, via the Panama Canal. Halifax is a major export point on the East Coast; the apples shipped from there originate in eastern Canada. The Annapolis-Cornwallis Valley of Nova Scotia is a leading apple-growing area, oriented toward the British market.

The specific site or location of orchards is determined by the conditions of the

Fig. 5-8. The apple orchards of the state of Washington—the leading state in production—are in the irrigated Yakima, Wenatchee, and Okanogan valleys east of the Cascade Mountains. The brilliant sunshine in these dry valleys helps induce a brightly-colored fruit. Note the irrigation canal, the dense concentration of orchards on the gently sloping land—the slopes having excellent air drainage—and, beyond, the open-field farming in the flatter valley lands, which are more subject to killing frosts. The individual apple grower maintains about twenty to forty acres of apples, hence the blocked appearance of the landscape. Other hardy fruits are grown in the Yakima Valley, but the Wenatchee and Okanogan valleys specialize in apples. (James S. Rayner)

local environment. The general location of orcharding districts or regions is related to the suitability of weather and climate, and, with respect to the commercial production of the present, also to markets; these markets may be ones wherein fresh table fruit is sold in quantity or ones furnished by a cannery or freezing establishment. Districts which have proved to be of unusual suitability for orchards —an example is the Yakima Valley of Washington—have attracted fruit-processing establishments; in turn, the additional local market furnished by these plants and their ability to process surplus production, have resulted in further expansion of orchards and a continued concentration of the fruit growing, packing, canning, and freezing industries. Thus well-defined fruit districts or fruit belts have developed. No longer is the "kitchen-garden" orchard, one which dots thousands of farmsteads over the nation, the chief source of fruit.

Fig. 5-9. "Apple row" in Yakima, Washington, during apple-picking season. The packing plants, storage warehouses, and apple-processing plants face both railroad and truck facilities. (James S. Rayner)

The specific site of a commercial orchard, whether planted to apples, peaches, pears, cherries, or other fruits is generally on sloping ground. Two forms of drainage—water and air—are significant in this. Fruit trees need adequate underdrainage; they will not tolerate standing waters, high water tables, or poorly drained heavy clay soils. And air drainage is equally, if not more, important, especially in the spring and fall of the year. Cold air is heavier than warm and on clear cool nights of spring will slide down the slopes, to collect in the swales and valley bottoms. When the temperature is near the freezing point, the lowlands will have frost, but the slopes are protected as a result of the air drainage and temperature inversion. Early budding trees on slopes are protected thus; the fruit has a chance to set. Water bodies provide protection, also—not in air drainage, but in delaying budding in the spring until the danger of a killing frost has passed; the waters, still cold from winter, delay the advent of spring on their lee shores; this is the protection afforded the fruit belts east of Lakes Michigan and Erie, and on the Niagara Peninsula between Lakes Erie and Ontario, and the Door Peninsula of Wisconsin.

The Central Valley of California, the lower slopes of the Sierra Nevadas above it, and some of the coastal valleys in the area of San Francisco Bay dominate in the western fruit industry. The Willamette, Hood River, and other valleys in Oregon, and certain valleys in the Rockies of Colorado, have significant acreages and production. But, overall, Washington follows California in the western industry. The apples of Washington are highly concentrated in irrigated valleys on the eastern slopes of the Cascades—the Tieton division of the Yakima Valley, the Wenatchee Valley, and the Okanagan. Orchards lie northward too, in British Columbia. At lower elevations in the Yakima Valley peaches and other soft fruits are important; the state thus produces some of the warmer-season fruits at low altitudes, as California also produces apples at higher elevations in its latitudes.

▶ POTATOES

The white potato is a plant native to the high, cool plateaus of the Andes in South America. In its present production it is grown mainly in Europe; that continent plus western Siberia in the Soviet Union produces nearly three-quarters of the world's potato crop. In the United States a quarter of the total potato acreage and 30 per cent of the total production is from Aroostook County, Maine, and the Snake River Plains of the state of Idaho.

The Spanish explorers of what is now highland Colombia, Ecuador, Peru, and Bolivia found the white potato being grown by the Incas and other Indians; at the time it was a product completely unknown in Europe or anywhere else in the world. In time, the potato was introduced to Spain, and eventually it was distributed northward into France and the British Isles. But, except in Ireland, the cultivation of the potato in Europe did not become important until the middle of the eighteenth century. A colony of Scotch-Irish settlers in New Hampshire introduced the potato in 1719 to what is now the United States—hence the misnomer of "Irish potato" originated.

Relatively cool conditions during the growing season are most favorable for the potato. In its indigenous region, in which plants still grow wild, all months average in the 50's and 60's Fahrenheit, for the "home area" is at very high altitudes and in mountain climates, although in latitudes near the equator. In the marine lands of western Europe and the cool continental lands of northern Europe the potato thrives; the warmest month of these realms is only in the 60's. Such is the case, also, in the northern border states of the United States, the chief American producers. Potatoes thrive also in the cool, high-altitude valleys of the Rockies, and at cooler higher altitudes in lower latitudes, such as on the Cumberland Plateau in Tennessee. And, in "out-of-season" potato-growing districts, as in Florida, the crop is grown during the coolest period of the year—mainly, of course, to reach the off-season markets—but production is possible only during the late fall, winter, and spring seasons in the state. In California, an important producer, the supply crop is grown in cooler districts, the out-of-season crop in the winter.

The relative humidity of the air is a minor factor in potato growing, except at high temperatures. Thus the Corn Belt and the American South, with their combination of high temperatures and high humidity during the summer, are unimportant in potato growing. But the plant does well in cool but dry lands, as in many of the western irrigated valleys.

Soils must be loose and friable to permit the very large expansion of the developing tuber. Sandy loams are ideal; some of the true sands are suitable providing organic material is added to the soil. Negatively, heavy clays are unsuitable for potatoes; their compactness retards the development of the tuber, and the "crop" may be only the size of marbles or small balls.

► THE EUROPEAN POTATO BELT

The extensive agricultural region which extends from near the Rhine in Germany eastward across the plains of Poland and north central Russia is the Rye-Potato Belt of Europe. Within this belt, all of which lies in the medium-summer phase of the humid continental climate the intensity of potato production reaches its peak. But, even in the parts of Europe margining this belt, and not included within it agriculturally, the growing of potatoes is outstanding. Thus the potato is significant in the United Kingdom, Ireland, France, Czechoslovakia, Denmark, and other countries. The crop of France alone exceeds the annual production of the entire United States.

The extreme importance of the potato in western and northern Europe is owing to several factors, some positive and some negative. The sandy soils of the glaciated Baltic Plain are ideally suited to rye and potato production. The soils of central Russia likewise are suited to the crops, whereas to the south the

Fig. 5-10. Digging potatoes in the Soviet portion of the European Potato Belt. The field is on a collective farm near Ivanovo, at 57° north latitude. The coniferous forest of this farm-and-forest region can be seen in the background. Machines such as this can be used on several root crops, such as sugar beets and mangels as well as potatoes. (Sovfoto)

prairie and steppe lands comprise the wheat belts; the two regions are complimentary in this respect. The potato in Europe is a basic multiple-purpose crop utilized for food, feed for animals, and for industrial purposes. The high yields per acre in a region of generally small farms, needing an intensive product, fit into the economy of the continent, for labor is abundant relative to land. Potatoes can be stored in root cellars and used as needed, without the expense of special refrigeration. And, negatively, nearly all of the important potato-producing regions and districts lie in a climatic setting with a summer season too cool for corn. In Europe, thus, the potato replaces the corn of the United States in many aspects of the rural and industrial economy—swine are potato-fed in Europe; industrial alcohols, starches, and flours are manufactured from potatoes; beverages are distilled from potatoes; and the crop is a basic food of millions of people. In the continent as a whole, about 40 per cent of the total annual production is consumed as direct human food; 60 per cent is used for feeding animals and for manufacture. In contrast, the uses in the United States are quite different, proportionately, and the crop is consumed as a food in far larger proportions; even so, the American per capita consumption is well below the per capita consumption of Europeans.

► POTATOES IN THE REST OF THE WORLD

The United States potato production follows that of Europe but totals less than that of individual countries such as the Soviet Union, Poland, Germany, and France. Production elsewhere in the world is small, although Canada's is important relative to the number of its inhabitants. Elsewhere only Japan and South Korea produce moderate quantities, and nearly every country which is located outside of tropical lowlands contains a small acreage. And, in environments admirably suited to potatoes, such as New Zealand and the extreme southeast of Australia, the acreage and production is related to the demands of the home market.

The American supply crop of potatoes is grown principally in Maine (chiefly Aroostook County), New York, Michigan, Wisconsin, Minnesota, North Dakota, and Idaho. Specialized farms in these states also grow certified seed potatoes,

FIG. 5-11. The Aroostook district of northern Maine specializes in the growing of late potatoes—the supply crop for eastern markets. This is one of the most intensive potato-growing areas of the nation. (Standard Oil Company, N.J.)

cuttings from which are planted in the South for the out-of-season or early potato crop. This crop, winter-grown in Florida and California, shifts northward with the advent of the spring season and is in every way comparable to the northward shifts of vegetable production. And, similarly, it "ends" in the Middle Atlantic truck-farming region, whose truck farms and market gardens are important producers of the early and midsummer crop. Similarly, early-, middle-, and late-summer districts characterize the industry in California, and there are additional supply districts in the West in Colorado and Washington.

Maine dominates the supply crop of Eastern markets. Michigan, Wisconsin, Minnesota, and North Dakota potatoes reach the markets of the Middle West and the South to the west of the Appalachians. Idaho potatoes are marketed nationally. This is the result of the specialization in the growing of a baking potato. The Idaho potato is graded rigorously, advertised nationally, and only top-quality potatoes are shipped—in part because only the best potatoes can bear the costs of shipment to distant markets, and in part to protect the reputation earned through specialization and advertising. As is the case, also, in the western fruit-growing regions, the portion of the crop which does not leave the state is processed locally.

▶ QUESTIONS

1. What series of developments and inventions permitted the rise of the vegetable trade?
2. What changes in food habits and consumption have resulted in the expansion of the trade in vegetables to its present importance?
3. Differentiate between a market garden and a truck farm.
4. What different economic problems are faced by market gardeners and truck farmers?
5. Describe, briefly, the source regions of vegetables found on the markets of Chicago and New York during the course of a year, from January through December.
6. Will the same variety of source regions provide vegetables for the San Francisco or Los Angeles markets during a year? Why or why not?
7. Explain why California ranks as the leading agricultural state—although some other states contain more land in farms or more harvested cropland.
8. What environmental factors have been important in the localization of fruit-growing regions?
9. Compare, in other parts of the world as well as in the United States and Canada, the relative locations of apple and peach production.
10. Why does the potato occupy a more important position in the agriculture, in the farming economy, and as a raw material for manufacture in northern Europe than it does in the United States?

VI Vegetable Oils and the Manufacturing

Industries Based upon Them

The various oils of vegetable origin have become of great importance in the world. A broad grouping of the vegetable oils is one dividing them into two types —those which are edible and can be used in the food industry as well as in other types of manufacturing, and those which are inedible and are used only by industries other than the food group. But the oils of each type are all processed before use, and so are raw materials for manufacture. A second classification of the vegetable oils is based upon the condition of their production. In this there are three groups: those oils of tree origin, those yielded by certain field crops, and the by-product oils. Olive oil is an example of a tree oil; the fruit of the olive tree is pressed to extract the olive oil. Linseed oil, obtained from flaxseed, is an example of an oil from a field crop, in this case the flax plant, a small grain. Cottonseed oil is a by-product vegetable oil. Cotton is grown for its lint. Cottonseeds, formerly a waste material to be discarded, are now a valuable by-product for the oil contained in them.

In point of time certain of the vegetable oils have been in use for centuries, others are relatively recent in use. The oils from the olive and from sesame seed are mentioned in early writings of the Mediterranean Basin; soybean oils have been used for thousands of years by natives of northern China and Manchuria, but their entry into world trade is a feature of only a hundred or so years. Tung oils and peanut oils are relatively "new" in their commercial production.

The chief edible oils, in estimated order of world importance, are those from the soybean, the coconut, cottonseed, peanut, the olive, and sesame. Regionally the situation is quite different. Olive oil is outstanding in the Mediterranean lands of Europe and northern Africa, soybean oil in the Orient. Within the United States the coconut, cottonseed, and peanut oils are of chief significance, both for the manufacture of vegetable shortenings and for the making of oleomargarines, as well as for other uses. The shortenings and margarines made from these oils compete with the animal fats such as lard and butter.

The chief "industrial" oils in quantity of production are rapeseed oil, linseed oil, and the palm oils. Oil from rapeseed is the major vegetable oil of large parts of China and of nearly all of India. It is used as an illuminant. Linseed oil, for use in paints and other products, is extracted from flaxseed grown in the world regions of commercial grain agriculture. The oil from the tropical palm-oil tree is used chiefly in the manufacture of soap—though nearly all of the vegetable oils are used to some extent in this industry, and names such as palm, coconut, olive, and others are combined in the trade names of some soaps. The industry also uses animal oils, such as whale oils.

Parts of the world produce vegetable oils which are used locally, and whose tonnage does not rank with the above listed. But these are of great local consequence. Sunflowers are one of the major crops of southern European Russia. The oil from the sunflower seed is used not only as an edible oil, but is also the source of some of the high-grade machine oils in use in the Soviet Union. And Russians eat the sunflower seed itself as a "nut." The babassu kernel yields an oil in Brazil, the kukui nut in Hawaii. This last was the illuminant of the early Hawaiians and received the name candlenut from the explorers and missionaries.

Vegetable oils of small total tonnage but wide use are several of the medicinal oils. Castor oil from the castor bean is illustrative.

► CLIMATIC SETTING

The tropics and the warmer portion of the subtropics constitute the source regions of nearly all of the raw materials from which the vegetable oils are obtained. Only the soybean, flaxseed, and sunflower seed are entirely from the cooler middle latitudes. And the animal fats and oils are principally products of the middle latitudes. Thus, following the development of manufacturing in Europe and the United States and Canada, the local animal products were the major sources of edible oils. When the tropical vegetable oils were introduced to the manufacturing regions in quantity—about the beginning of the present century—they came into competition with the animal products. Despite the distance of shipment by sea, the vegetable oils were produced more cheaply by tropical labor. Thus there ensued a period of severe competition in the markets, a competition between vegetable shortenings and lard, between margarines and butter. Today

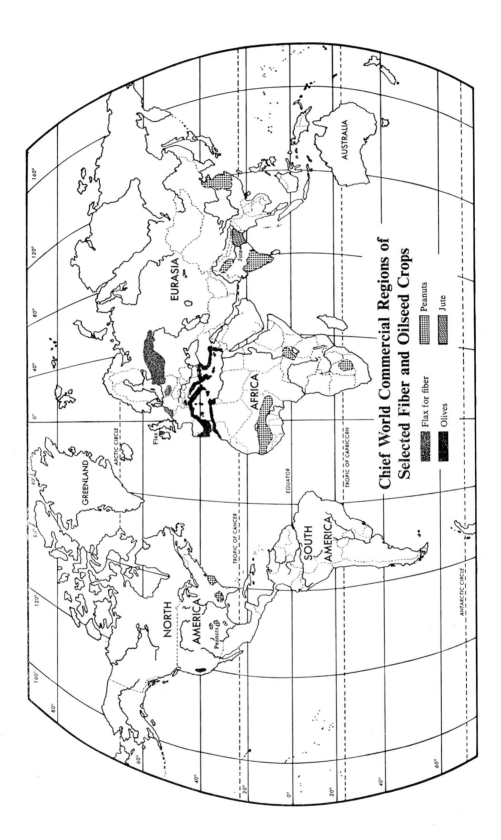

**Chief World Commercial Regions of
Selected Fiber and Oilseed Crops**

Flax for fiber

Olives

Peanuts

Jute

the increase in population has cared for the situation; Europe's inhabitants, especially, are dependent upon all of the home supply plus large imports of vegetable oils. In the United States the several food laws require a listing of the ingredients on the label, or, in some cases, a different name if the manufactured product is roughly similar. Thus we have ice cream, if butterfat is a raw material, and the ice custards and other mellorines if vegetable fats have been used in the manufacture; some manufacturers have copyrighted a name for their product (such as a shortening) and sell it under their trade name.

Two of the vegetable oils originate in the wet tropics. These are the coconut oils and the palm oils. The meat of the coconut is dried into copra, and the copra is exported. The oils are obtained from the processing of copra in the markets of the middle latitudes. In contrast, the palm nuts are sometimes pressed in the growing regions, and palm oil is exported in drums.

Cotton and peanuts are important crops in two climatic realms—the wet-and-dry tropics, and the warm humid subtropics, such as in the American South; these realms are competitive, agriculturally, in these products. The nations of Europe draw heavily upon tropical sources; in fact, much of the commercial interest of Britain and France in the interior region of West Africa is associated with cotton and peanuts. Marseilles, the large center of soap manufacture in France, is the chief port for connections with the African source regions of the oils. The United States, in contrast, has its own sources of cotton and peanuts in the South and of cottonseed in California (see Chapter VIII). Cottonseed and peanuts enter trade in their original forms; the oil is extracted in the manufacturing regions.

The Mediterranean subtropics are the only producer of olives—the olive is a representative tree of these lands, and particularly so in the Old World, to which it was indigenous. Olive oil is the major edible and industrial vegetable oil of southern Europe. It is indispensable to the inhabitants of such nations as Greece, Italy, and Spain. The use of olive oil is nearly entirely at home; exports of olive oil are mainly directed to the markets furnished by Italian settlers (even into several generations) in the United States, Argentina, and other countries of the New World. In the olive-growing region of the United States, in California, the fruit is marketed in pickled form, as ripe olives or green olives; there is little demand in the United States for olive oils, and the home industry is not large.

► COCONUT OIL AND PALM OILS

The coconut palm, distributed along shorelines of the wet tropical world, yields the coconut. Another palm tree, indigenous to the Congo Basin and West Africa (from Sierra Leone and Liberia eastward to Nigeria and the Cameroons) yields the palm nut, from whose kernel the palm oils are expressed. The coconut palm is mainly a tree of the littoral, or shore zone. The African oil palm is important in the forests of interior regions. The largest supply of copra, from which the coconut oils are expressed, is from the Philippine Islands, the islands of the East Indies now mainly in Indonesia, Ceylon, and the small islands of the southwest Pacific—the islands of Oceania. In contrast the principal sources of palm oils are all in Africa, except for a production in Indonesia, and are dominantly from Nigeria and the Congo, but also from other neighboring countries such as Ghana and Liberia. Thus the sources of coconut oils are principally in tropical Asia, of palm oils, tropical Africa.

The coconut palm is an all-purpose tree to many of the inhabitants of tropical Asia and is fundamental to the existence of many of the natives of the Pacific Islands—in Polynesia, Melanesia, and Micronesia. Coconuts are picked and cut open. The "milk" is drunk. The meat is eaten fresh or is dried into copra. The fiber, called coir, from the husk or shell is used for twine, fishing lines, ropes. The fronds are woven into baskets, used for hats, or for thatching the roofs of huts. In the early days of the coconut trade, copra was collected from island to island, and transported to the middle latitudes. But the small islands could not furnish enough for their own needs plus an exportable surplus. The world had to look elsewhere as a result of the rising demand for coconut oils. Only a few of the "larger" islands contribute small quantities of copra to today's trade—particularly the Samoan Islands, the Fijis, and the Society Islands of French Oceania (Tahiti).

The center of the copra production and trade shifted to the Philippine Islands as the world demand for coconut oil increased. The southern part of the island of Luzon, between Mount Banahao and the sea, is a vast coconut grove; the tree has been planted inland on the plain as well as in coastal locations. And each of the dozens of small islands of the central part of the Philippine archipelago is rimmed by commercial coconut farms. Interisland ships collect the copra and deliver it to Manila and other ports for export.

The Philippine copra industry arose in response to several favorable factors. Before 1946 the islands constituted an American commonwealth. Investment, business, and trade interests with the United States were close. The American market for copra was expanding. Labor was and is plentiful; there were few rubber plantations or other plantations in the Philippines to compete in the labor market. Farmers of the shorelands had always had coconut palms on their holdings. Shipping lines were well organized. And the individual islands are large, compared to the small islands of the Pacific from which copra had been gathered; an exportable surplus was easy to attain. Thus, with the years, the Philippine industry grew to its present size and importance. And, as most of the copra is farm-produced rather than a plantation product in the islands, the sale of copra is a considerable source of income for many.

European-owned coconut plantations were established in what is now Indonesia. Although the plantations of the former Dutch-owned islands are now in the hands of Indonesians with the withdrawal of the Dutch, the industry continues

FIG. 6-1. Palm nuts grow in clusters on the oil palm tree of West Africa. They are gathered both on farms of the natives and from trees growing in the forests. The nuts on this young oil palm are ready for harvest. (British Information Services)

its importance. There are both large and small holdings. Indonesia is second to the Philippines in the world trade in copra.

Malaya and Ceylon contribute copra to world trade. Small quantities come from Mozambique in southeastern Africa.

The United States, the Netherlands, Germany, France, Belgium, and the United Kingdom are the principal importers of copra, and factories in the port cities of these lands process and refine the coconut oils. Oil is both pressed from copra and extracted by boiling and skimming.

The oil palm grows in a 200-mile-wide belt that extends from Gambia and Sierra Leone on the Atlantic eastward along the Gulf of Guinea, a distance of more than 1,600 miles. This belt, where the coast of Africa extends in an east-west direction, lies in the rainy tropics. The inner, or northern, edge of production is at the edge of the savanna grasslands of the interior. To the east, around the Bight of Biafra, the belt widens to include the Congo Basin. Oil palms grow almost to the coast; in early trading days the several mouths of the Niger River were given the name "Oil Rivers."

The growing of oil palms is a widely distributed enterprise in West Africa. There is production of palm nuts and export of palm oil from every country and political unit of the region. Much of the production of the kernels originates on native farms. In this, the palm-oil industry is like the other West African activity of producing cacao beans (see Chapter X). The plantation is not usual. Population density is high, more than 200 a square mile in part of Nigeria, labor is plentiful and inexpensive, collecting systems are well organized (originally under British supervision), and demands of daily routine labor in caring for oil palms or cacao trees are not necessary. Harvest is seasonal. And the forests furnish, also, a source of livelihood for gatherers of palm kernels from wild oil palms, and a place where the enterprising farmer can collect kernels and add to his income.

Nigeria and the southwestern part of Ghana lead in the intensity of African production. In Nigeria, especially, the industry is of utmost significance, Nigeria is the leading world producer, and the export of palm oil and palm kernels accounts for more than a third of the value of all exports; and peanuts are a major crop of the savanna lands of northern Nigeria and total a quarter of the value of exports. Nigeria depends heavily upon the trade in these two vegetable oils and also exports cottonseed from the cotton-growing lands in the northern savanna. And the government has promoted the palm-oil industry, set standards and grades, and conducted educational programs for the farmers. The result has been an increased quality of the oil, and the establishment of refineries to process the crude oil into a more refined product before it is exported.

Palm oil is produced on plantations in the Congo and on plantations in Indonesia to which the oil palm has been introduced. Palm nuts grown in Indonesia have a higher oil content than those from West Africa, and Indonesia is second only to Nigeria in production (but behind all of West Africa regionally).

The palm kernels are pressed mechanically, whether in Africa or Asia. Additional oil is extracted by boiling the fleshy residue and skimming the oils. Export is mainly to western Europe, the chief consumer. Here the major use is for soap. But European factories also produce lubricating greases from the palm oils, which reflects the inadequate home supplies of petroleum.

► COTTONSEED OILS AND PEANUT OILS

The world distribution of cotton is discussed in Chapter VIII. The by-product cottonseeds originates in the same region. In the United States the cottonseed-oil industry is a large one and consumes a large proportion of the yearly supply of cottonseed. Egyptian, African, and Indian cottonseed is shipped to European mills. Mexican seed is both used at home and exported. China has adopted American methods to treat its home supply of seed, and the Soviet Union consumes its supply.

The chief products obtained from cottonseed are the meals, the vegetable oils, and the linters. The meal is the pressed residue, obtained after the oil has been extracted. Cottonseed meal, usually pressed into cake form, is a high-protein feed for cattle. The oils yield a large percentage of cooking and salad oils, and are used in the manufacture of shortenings and margarine. The linters—short fuzzy lint which clings to the seed—supply raw material for guncotton, blotting papers, and paper.

The factories in the United States that process cottonseed are in the South and in California; those of European countries are in the importing ports. The first of the raw materials to be obtained are the linters. The seeds, received from the cotton gins, are ginned a second time to remove the short fuzz. A recently developed process involves a third ginning, from which the very short lint suitable for papermaking is obtained; these lints were wasted formerly. The cleaned seeds are then cracked, and the mass of material is steam-heated and pressed by hydraulic presses for the oil. Most of the residue becomes the raw material for the meals.

The supply of cottonseed and its products is determined by the yearly supply of cotton. In the United States there is an annual supply of from five to six or

FIG. 6-2. A cottonseed oil mill in Texas. The size of this mill, one of many in the cotton lands, reflects the importance of this vegetable oil as a raw material for manufacture and the significance of an industry based upon the processing of cottonseed—once considered worthless and discarded. (Standard Oil Company, N.J.)

more million tons of seed. Texas alone is the source of from one and a half to two million tons. This quantity has attracted many of the oil-and-meal mills to the cotton-growing regions of the state, and to the Gulf Coast industrial area. But mills are widespread elsewhere. Memphis is an important price-quotation and manufacturing center.

The supply of cottonseed products cannot be adjusted to the changing price levels of competing oilseeds. This is because production is at its peak following cotton picking and ginning. Spring and summer is a slack period of year. In contrast, competing oilseeds such as soybeans are stored safely, and the extraction of oil is spread throughout the year. Cottonseed oils, in their use in final manufacture, thus fluctuate with respect to competing materials—except, usually, in the cooking and salad oil field in which they have an advantage.

Peanuts are a field crop of large regions of China and India, of nearly every country of Africa that has any of its area included in the wet-and-dry tropics, of the savanna lands of Brazil and Mexico, and of a few specialized districts in the humid subtropics of the American South. The peanut, native to Brazil, was introduced to Africa and Asia following the early discoveries of South America. The peanut has been an integral part of native agriculture—whether shifting or sedentary—in Africa for 300 to 400 years.

The peanut needs high heat and abundant moisture during its 200-or-more-day growing season. It grows best only on sandy or sandy loam soils, but will yield in any friable, loose soil. This is because of a peculiarity in its development; following flowering, the penducules bend downward and enter the soil, to produce underground stems beneath the above-ground vine. From these stems the peanut, called groundnut in English-speaking countries outside of North America, develops. The peanut is thus an underground "fruit," and is not a root. When harvested the whole vine is commonly pulled up. In the southern United States, where the American acreage is located, the vines are dried and then threshed to obtain the peanuts. Elsewhere in the world the peanuts are usually hand-picked from the vines. The vines are used for hay in the South; the shelled peanuts are fed to cattle or swine, or they become raw material from which peanut butter is ground or oil is extracted. About a fifth of the southern acreage is "hogged-down" —swine are turned into the field to root, and they consume the crop directly.

India, China, and adjacent southeast Asia grow from three-fourths to four-fifths of the world's peanuts. Their crop is used mainly at home to supplement the other local oilseeds in providing edible and industrial oils for the billion and a half inhabitants. Thus Africa, second continent in production, is the major exporter; its peanuts are in demand in Europe, where the oil contained in them is extracted. In fact, as vegetable oils are in short supply in Europe, the nations have fostered and encouraged peanut production in Africa to help meet their needs for fats. The French have been particularly active in this in West Africa.

The savanna interior of West Africa, between the rainy tropical lands of the coastal section and the Sahara Desert, is the chief peanut-growing and -exporting region of the continent. The "peanut belt" stretches, discontinuously, from Gambia on the Atlantic eastward through northern Ghana and northern Nigeria to the vicinity of Lake Chad. The upper course of the Niger is in this region. The Senegal River is in its west. The rail connections between the two navigable streams, and river shipment, are important in the transport of peanuts to the ports. Peanuts from northern Nigeria are shipped southward to ports of the Gulf of Guinea. The other important export crop of this belt is cotton; cottonseed and peanuts, two oilseeds, are principal products of inner West Africa, palm oils of the rainy coastal belt. As noted, Nigeria exports all three. Its trade depends heavily on oilseeds.

Nigeria is the leading exporter of peanuts. The several political units of French West Africa—some now independent—follow. Africa contributes nearly three-fourths of the export trade in peanuts. The great majority of the tonnage originates in West Africa; smaller quantities are from the East African Plateau, and are shipped from ports on the Indian Ocean.

Great Britain and France are the two leading importers of peanuts. The peanut oils are essential for the supplement of home-produced animal fats and oils, and of other imported oilseeds, to enable the nations to meet their overall requirements of edible and industrial oils. The peanut fits this need admirably; it is easily shipped in bags (shelled or in hulls), and it yields from 40 to 50 per cent of oil. Each country has promoted the production of and trade in peanuts in its African possessions—present or former.

Three types of peanuts are grown in the American South. One is an all-purpose peanut. Another is used for oil, peanut butter, and bakery goods. A third type is grown mainly for stock feed. Some of the specialty "southern hams" are from peanut-fed swine.

The discontinuous districts that specialize in the growing of peanuts are all located on the sandy coastal plain. One, wherein peanuts have been grown for more than a hundred years, is in southeastern Virginia and adjacent northeastern North Carolina; a quarter of the United States crop is produced here. A newer peanut district, one which has expanded with the expanding demand for vegetable oils, is centered in southwestern Georgia and southeastern Alabama. This district, extending also for a short distance into Florida, produces just over half of the American crop. Part of east Texas and of central Texas, the two producing an eighth of the output, complete the important districts. But there is some production in every southern state.

The centers for the extraction of peanut oil are in the producing regions. The shelled peanuts are pressed for their oil; some mills use the "waste" hulls for fuel to power the plants. From mills in these areas the oil is shipped to factories where it is used in the manufacture of the final products. But the producing areas contain, also, some of the final manufacturing plants. A third of the American factories making shortening and cooking oils are in the South, with Georgia, Louisiana, and Texas having the chief concentrations of these.

► SESAME AND TUNG OILS

Sesame is an herb indigenous to the tropical highlands of Ethiopia. Sesame seeds yield sesame oil, known also as benne oil. Production is mainly in the wet-and-dry tropics and the humid subtropical lands of the Old World. China and India are the major producers and consumers, but the seed is grown throughout the tropical plateaus of East Africa and in Mexico. Among Western nations only Greece and Turkey have a small production, and France is an importer of the oils for use in its soap-manufacturing industry.

Tung nuts from the tung tree of southern China, introduced to the Gulf Coast of the United States in the 1920's, yield a quick-drying oil, suitable especially for the spray-painting of automobiles. A "tung belt," containing hundreds of tung groves, parallels the Gulf Coast from Louisiana eastward to northern Florida. Tung and linseed oils are the two principal industrial oils used in the United States; but, as noted, some of the edible oils also yield industrial oils in the refining process.

► MIDDLE-LATITUDE VEGETABLE OILS

Soybeans, flax, and sunflowers are the principal oilseed crops of the middle latitudes. These field crops also yield raw materials other than oils.

The rise of the soybean to importance as a crop of the Corn Belt (see Chapter XII) has been striking, and the uses to which the harvested beans are suitable are many. Soybean mills are scattered throughout the western Corn Belt, with a concentration in Iowa and Illinois, where nearly every city of size contains a large mill. Among these centers for primary marketing are Bloomington, Champaign, Decatur, Peoria, Quincy, and Springfield. A great deal of the final manufacture of soybean products and the manufactual use of the soybean oils is located in Chicago and its industrial suburbs.

Flaxseed, the raw material for linseed oil, is a product of the commercial grain-growing areas of the New World and of the Soviet Union. India is also a producer in some quantity. The Spring Wheat Belt of the United States and Canada, and the Pampas of Argentina are important flaxseed regions (see Chapter XI). The American Winter Wheat Belt is a secondary source region. Flaxseed is threshed or combined, like the other small grains. It is shipped from the grain belts to centers to their east, particularly in Minnesota, and especially Minneapolis, for the extraction of the linseed oil. Argentine flaxseed and linseed oil is marketed in western Europe. Surplus flaxseed from India is marketed, also, in Europe.

Linseed oil is quick-drying and is used as the oil in paints and varnishes. It is also a prominent ingredient of linoleum, for when oxidized it becomes partly elastic, and when mixed with cork, resin, and pigments the manufactured result is the various linoleums and certain of the ceiling and wall coverings.

Oilseed Cakes, Shortenings, and Margarines

The by-product meals or cakes from the vegetable-oil industry are important in both domestic use and foreign trade. Mention has been made of the cotton-seed cakes. Soybean meal and linseed meal are equally important as concentrated feeds for cattle. Collectively the various meals or oilseed cakes which enter foreign trade are all directed toward western Europe. The cattle of Britain, Denmark, Norway, Sweden, Finland, Germany, the Netherlands, Belgium, France, and Switzerland are maintained in part upon these concentrated feeds. And western Europe has one of the largest densities of cattle per unit area in the world. The importance of overseas feeds to the maintenance of these cattle was demonstrated during World War II; when supplies of oilseed cakes were cut off, thousands of animals in western Europe had to be slaughtered for lack of feed, and the herds reduced until they came into balance with the supply of home-grown feeds. Argentina is the chief exporter of oilseed cake—linseed meal in this case—and Great Britain and Denmark are the two chief importers among European nations. The United States is about in balance; oilseed cakes are consumed at home, and there is a large domestic trade in them. Some of the manufacturers now add molasses (by-product of sugar cane) to the oilseed cakes and dry the mixture, which is marketed in the form of a bran. Western feeders of beef cattle, beyond the region of local corn production, furnish a leading market for these concentrated feeds.

The manufacturing plants that use the edible vegetable oils in food manufacture are market-oriented in their location in the United States and Canada. In Europe they are located in the port cities. North American manufacturers receive the cottonseed and other oils by railroad tank car, filled at the mills of the primary extractors of the oil.

The larger cities of the northern United States, some few of the South, and the cities of the West Coast are the locations of the factories manufacturing salad oils, shortenings, margarines, and similar products. These cities are the centers of a large consuming market. From them the smaller centers and rural areas are served. The individual "final" factory is large, and commonly corporate-owned; one national company may operate several, each in a different city. The number of factories is few. In the entire United States there are just over 100 factories whose product is shortening, and fewer than 40 that manufacture margarine. In contrast, in a competing field, more than 2,000 factories manufacture butter, and the total annual poundage of butter produced is about the same as the output of margarine.

Margarine is churned from vegetable oils and pasteurized skim milk. In other words, the butterfat of whole milk is replaced by vegetable fats. The chief vegetable fats in use in the United States today in margarine manufacture are soybean oils, which furnish nearly seven-eighths of the total, and cottonseed oils, which furnish nearly one-eighth. Coconut and peanut oils account for the small remainder. Originally, when first introduced in 1874, beef fats were used (hence the American prefix of *oleo*margarine), then there was a shift to imported coco-

Fig. 6-3. Gathering olives in Spain, the leading producer of olives in the world. (Spanish National Tourist Office)

nut oils; now the raw materials in use are mainly of domestic origin in the nation. The manufacturers of shortenings are users today of domestic oils in quantity. Cottonseed oil is important, and is outstanding in the preparation of the salad oils.

There are special concentrations of the margarine and shortening manufacturers near or in the largest urban centers. The New Jersey portion of the New York metropolitan region, the Chicago metropolitan region, and the Los Angeles area contain several major plants. Thus, within the broad market-oriented location, the cities with the greatest total market—because of population—serve as magnets in the selection of sites for the factory.

► OLIVE OIL

The olive tree is indigenous to Mediterranean Europe, Mediterranean North Africa, and to the lands of southwestern Asia at the eastern end of the Mediterranean Sea. It has been cultivated since long before the advent of the Christian era, and is mentioned throughout the Bible. The tree is perfectly adjusted to the warm to hot, but dry summer, and to the mild, rainy winter; it survives the rainless season without being irrigated. Indeed, the distribution of the olive tree is indicative of the extent and distribution of the Mediterranean subtropical climate.

The olive tree requires moderate to high temperatures and abundant sunshine. It survives and thrives during the dry summer; its narrow leaves and thick trunk are factors in reducing the loss of water; its wide-spreading long and narrow roots branch intricately just below the surface and tap any supplies of surface water, such as dews. The mild winter of the climate is usually frostless—an important factor—for the tree will withstand only a few consecutive hours of freezing temperatures. And the moderate rainfall of the Mediterranean subtropical winter—only from 10 to 25 inches—provides enough moisture to carry the tree through the dry summer; in fact, some North African olive groves are in areas with only 8 to 10 inches of winter (and annual) rainfall.

The fruit of the olive tree, the olive itself, is high in oil content. And it is the oil that is the important Mediterranean product—and it might be said "world product"—for the lands of the Mediterranean Basin produce from 90 to 95 per cent of the olives of the world. Only elsewhere, as in Mediterranean subtropical California, is the fruit itself the main end product. And olives are not useable or edible when picked from the tree. They must be marketed as green pickles or ripe fruit soaked in specially prepared brines.

A map of the distribution of the Mediterranean subtropical climate in the Old World and a map of the extent of olive cultivation are essentially the same. From southern Portugal and the southern half of Spain the olive-growing region margins the shores of northeastern Spain and southern France, continues eastward through the French and Italian Rivieras, then around the shorelands of Italy to the Adriatic Coast of Yugoslavia and Albania. Nearly all of Greece is olive country. The shore zones of Turkey and the plains in Lebanon, Syria (United Arab Republic) and Israel carry olive growing to the deserts at the border of Israel and Egypt. And in North Africa all of the area between the Atlas Mountains and the sea is important in olive culture—in Morocco, Algeria, and Tunisia. Cyrenacia in Libya grows olives also. A small section of the Black Sea Coast in northeastern Turkey is Mediterranean subtropical in climatic type and is noted for olive culture.

The one exception on the maps noted is an olive industry in some of the low-altitude south-facing valleys of the Italian Alps. The tree has been introduced to these warm valleys. The valleys lie north of the Po Valley or plain; the Po Valley is continental in climatic type and has too cold a winter for the olive tree to survive this season. The "Alpine Valley" district is separate, thus, in location from the almost continuous major olive-growing region which surrounds the Mediterranean Sea except where the deserts reach to the coast in Egypt and portions of Libya.

It is the Mediterranean peoples who are the producers and consumers of olive oil. Spain produces almost half of the total, and sunny Andalusia in the south is a province wherein extensive olive groves cover large landholdings, and where large factorylike olive-pressing establishments are located. Elsewhere in the Mediterranean the olive groves are usually small and are part of the operation of very small farms, owned or rented by individual peasants. Italy and Greece follow Spain as producers. In Italy there is much interculture—two or three crops at different levels. For example, vegetables may be grown between olive trees in the summer, followed by fall-seeded winter wheat, which grows during the rainy season and is harvested late in the spring. Or—at three levels—the olives highest, the vine trained on trellises built between the rows of olive trees, and vegetables grown at ground level between the rows of the vine. Apulia, the heel of Italy, leads Italian provinces in olive production.

The olives are picked between September and December. High-grade pickling olives are hand-plucked. The olives destined for oil may be picked by hand or may be knocked from the tree. After delivery to the presses, the olive is put through three pressings. The first, gentle squeezing yields table oils, the second and harder one yields the cooking oils—basic to nearly all Mediterranean cookery —and the last and firm pressing yields industrial oils. The Andalusian region of

Fig. 6-4. Presses and vats in a modern, completely electrified olive oil extraction plant in Cordoba, Spain. These factories obtain the maximum of oil and other derivatives from the olive. The olive oil industry is dependent upon abundant labor in the olive groves but is becoming highly mechanized in the mills. (Spanish Embassy)

Spain, with its large groves, has considerable capital investment in modern oil presses; some of the Spanish nobility and certain of the Spanish fortunes are associated with landholdings of olive trees and the extraction and distribution of olive oils.

The foreign trade in olive oil is confined chiefly among Mediterranean countries so far as quantity is concerned, and oil moves from surplus to deficit areas, even though all are producers; this reflects density of population and total of inhabitants. Spain and Tunis, each with "small" population densities by Mediterranean standards, are the chief exporters. France is the major recipient. The other nations are about in balance. The overseas exports are mainly to the United States for reasons already indicated, and the principal consuming centers are the cities of the Eastern Seaboard.

► QUESTIONS

1. What are some of the plants and trees that yield seeds or fruits from which vegetable oils are extracted?
2. What vegetable oils—or the materials from which they are obtained—originate in the tropics of the world? What vegetable and animal fats and oils are from the agriculture of the middle latitudes?
3. From what portions of the world do the industrial countries obtain their principal supplies of copra? of palm oils? peanut oils? tung oils?
4. What manufactures depend upon vegetable oils for raw materials?

VII Coarse Fibers and Rubber

and Their Manufacture

Agriculture produces a great variety of products that serve as raw materials for manufacturing. Certain crops are purely industrial ones; tobacco, cotton, and flax are examples. Animal products such as wool, mohair, and hides and skins are used only in manufacturing industries. And some products of farm, ranch, and plantation serve in part as food, in part as raw materials; corn, potatoes, soybeans, and many others can be cited as in this group. In addition an agricultural product used mainly or entirely for food is processed, and the processing takes place in factories; wheat is from a farm, but flour from a mill, and then flour in itself becomes a raw material for a bakery.

The various agricultural products to be discussed in this chapter are entirely raw materials for manufacturing. The fiber crops are utilized by industry —and the fibers to be dealt with here are those other than the main clothing or textile ones (see Chapter VIII). Rubber is a raw material from tropical plantations.

► FIBERS FROM THE TROPICS

Jute, abaca (manila hemp), henequen and sisal, and kapok are fibers produced only in the tropical portion of the world. Their use is world wide. Jute is the raw material for gunny sacks, the backing of rugs, burlap, and certain twines. Abaca, called manila hemp also, because the city of Manila is a major exporting point, is utilized for twine, ropes, hawsers, and for uses where the manufactured material (as rope, for example) comes into constant contact with salt waters. Henequen and the very similar sisal is the source of binder twine and other coarse cordage; the fiber is strong and durable and is tied easily by machinery without breaking. Kapok, a silky fiber from the inside of the pods of the silk-cotton or kapok tree, is noted for its buoyancy and is devoted to uses in life-saving equipment and rafts.

Each of these fibers competes with others, or with synthetic materials for certain uses. Jute fiber alone is the only one not basically challenged by others of the cheap fibers; its use for cheap, strong sacks and burlap cannot be met by the other inexpensive fibers. Twine and string may be made from cotton; nylon and other synthetics compete for the market too. The fibers used for heavy cordage or hawsers compete with steel roping, metal cables for ships, and other materials. The market for kapok is competitive with rubber, cork, and similar raw materials that are used in life preservers, life rafts, and other buoyant products. And each product may be, or has been, affected by inventions and substitutions; for example, henequen had a monopoly of the market for binder twine during the

FIG. 7-1. Plantation-grown sisal in Haiti loaded for transport to the mill where the fiber will be extracted and processed for export. (Esso Oilways)

period before the middle 1930's, when grain was cut by the binder. The invention of the combine, which cuts and threshes grain in one operation, and the widespread use of combines in the world's commercial grain regions resulted in a decline in the market, consternation in the henequen-growing districts, and the need of the manufacturers to find and develop other uses for this fiber.

► JUTE

Jute is indigenous to and a near monopoly, commercially, of the Ganges-Brahmaputra delta lands of Bengal, a region and a former province of India. In 1947 eastern Bengal, the principal jute-growing area, became East Pakistan, part of the new Moslem nation of Pakistan; West Bengal remained in India, its inhabitants being of the Hindu faith. With the division of 1947, Pakistan became the major producer of jute; this is an example of the continuance of a crop associated with a given regional environment, but a political (and statistical) change. The jute fields are in the same location, but Pakistan has assumed the leadership in production from India.

Calcutta was the center for the preparation of jute fiber for export, and for export itself, when the entire activity was Indian. Chittagong was a less significant manufacturing and export point. The division of 1947 left Calcutta in India. Chittagong was assigned to Pakistan. The jute industry was separated into fragments by the new man-drawn frontier. Naturally the raw jute from the farms of the delta in Pakistan was directed to mills and ports within the country. The phase of the industry in Indian Calcutta declined relatively. But the most efficient and best organized jute mills were Indian, and they continued to compete favorably for a time, using Indian raw jute from West Bengal and imported jute from Pakistan. However, mills and ports in Pakistan were improved and expanded, and new jute mills were erected to utilize the national production.

Today the industry remains in this dual position. The agricultural production is in the same region as it has always been. The manufacturing and exporting activities reflect the relative rise of Pakistan and the relative decline of India in the competition engendered by the partition of 1947. Indian mills have had their supplies lessened, and although they are assured of jute from the Indian portion of the delta, any they obtain from the rest of the delta must be imported. Thus India is both a major importer and exporter.

Jute and rice are the principal crops of the Ganges-Brahmaputra delta. Each is grown in small fields, the jute towering over the rice as maturity is reached. Each is grown as an annual during the hot season of the wet monsoon. Each is grown in flooded fields for much of the period from seeding to harvest.

Jute is planted very close together. The finger-thick stalks grow to heights of fifteen or so feet; the lower portion of the closely spaced jute plants is thus a veritable canelike thicket, almost impossible to traverse, and leafy vegetation is confined to the tops of the plants. When the plant has flowered, and before it develops seeds, the harvest is accomplished. Workers wade in the flooded fields and cut the stalk below the water level; the water may be from a few inches to a couple of feet in depth. In some growing districts the practice is to withdraw the water just prior to harvest.

Jute is retted like flax. Stagnant pools of water, or the fields themselves after reflooding, are used for the retting process. The temperatures of the air are in the high 80's and 90's Farenheit during the retting season, for the delta is in the latitude of the Tropic of Cancer; water temperature of the stagnant waters are almost as high. The result is the rapid completion of the process.

Jute is a bast fiber. Workers separate the six-to-seven-foot-long and silky fibers from the stalk, and the fibers are hung over racks to dry. Following drying, the fibers are shipped to a factory, in which the fiber itself is softened and processed by machinery which separate it completely from the remaining woody portions of the jute plant. Raw jute is baled for export or woven into burlap and other materials in Calcutta, Chittagong, and other cities. Much of the exported raw jute is directed to the jute mills of Dundee, Scotland, an important manufacturing center for jute for more than a hundred years.

The growing of jute is very demanding of hand labor. Inexpensive labor is needed as well to allow this cheap fiber to compete in world markets. India and East Pakistan have been able to furnish an abundant supply of skilled but cheap workers. The agricultural population alone of the delta region is nearly 1,500 per square mile. The labor situation is the fundamental factor in the continuance of the near monopoly of Bengal in jute growing and preparation. Jute will grow well in any wet tropical lowland or delta region, and there are many such in the tropical world. But the labor supply of these potential areas of production is unsatisfactory, either in quality or quantity. A jute industry has been introduced to the Congo and to tropical portions of Brazil, but production is small. Efforts have been made from time to time to establish an industry in southern Florida or in the Mississippi Delta–eastern Gulf Coast region.

Jute imports into the United States are relatively steady in quantity. An interesting sidelight in this country is the use of burlap from almost halfway around the world as the wrapping for cotton bales in an American fiber-growing region.

▶ MANILA HEMP OR ABACA

Skilled workers in the small central islands of the Philippines strip a six-to-ten-foot-long fiber from the leaf stalk of a tree of the banana family. The native name of the tree is abaca. Commercially the fiber is called Manila hemp; it is collected by the owners of coastal steamers, who transport it to Manila, the selling and export point. The outer fiber from the leaf stalk is especially strong and makes fine cordage. Other fibers are woven into native clothing or exported for use in

FIG. 7-2. Mature pods on the kapok or silk-cotton tree. This is one of the few trees of the tropics that sheds its leaves. Notice both the tall ladder placed against the trunk, and the long pole held by the gatherer of the pods. The pods, in which the fiber is compressed tightly, must be knocked down, then collected on the ground. (Netherlands Photo)

the manufacture of such articles as veils or handkerchiefs. Old fibers, even unwound heavy cordage, constitute a raw material for Manila paper.

Abaca will grow throughout the wet tropics, but efforts to introduce its commercial cultivation in several countries have not met with marked success. Thus, as is the case with jute in Bengal, the Philippines retain a near monopoly of the supply. Labor is the explanation. Operators of small farms grow the abaca plant and either strip the fiber themselves or engage professional strippers who earn their livelihood in this way. The cultivation itself is not difficult, the plant sending out new shoots from the root stalk after the leaves have been cut.

► KAPOK

Kapok fiber is contained in a pod which grows on the tree. The floss, or mass of short fibers, is compressed tightly around the seeds within the pod; when the skin is broken a whole room may be filled with the light, fluffy material. Though a fiber compressed into a small space, as cotton is compressed in the cotton boll before it opens, kapok fiber cannot be woven. Its uses, therefore, are other than in the textile or cordage industries.

The kapok tree is found in the wet tropics of the East Indies, the Philippines

Fig. 7-3. A kapok mill in Indonesia. The workers must wear masks over their nostrils and mouths to keep the fine lint from choking or partially suffocating them. The baled kapok fiber will be exported. (Standard Oil Company, N.J.)

and the American tropics of the West Indies, and Central and South America. There is some production in Africa. Labor is not a major factor in the gathering of kapok pods. The tree is one of the few tropical trees that sheds its leaves. The pods then hang exposed on the twigs and branches and can be knocked down easily by the use of poles, or can be gathered from ladders or by climbers, or from the ground after they have fallen naturally. Native farmers have a few trees. Roads and boundary lines may be planted with rows of trees. Commercially the major source region has been Indonesia, where the floss is separated from the seeds and baled for export; the seeds themselves have an oil expressed from them. But other tropical regions also contribute kapok to world markets, the quantities varying with respect to prices and demand.

► SISAL AND HENEQUEN

Two plants of the *Agave* family yield a leaf fiber of commercial importance. The fiber of the henequen plant is yellow, that of the closely related sisal is white. Each of the growing plants looks not unlike the century plant of home conservatories or greenhouses. The two are indigenous to the wet-and-dry tropics of the Yucatán Peninsula in Mexico. The peninsula still has an essential monopoly in the production of henequen, whose environmental requirements are more restrictive than those of sisal and whose peculiar needs are met in the indigenous region; however, production and use of sisal is now far more important than that of henequen, and the near monopoly means far less than it did prior to the 1930's. Sisal, on the other hand (named from Sisal in Yucatán), has been introduced to and is grown commercially in many countries of tropical America, Africa, and Asia. The markets for these fibers are principally in the middle-latitude nations of Europe and in the United States, Canada, and Australia. Henequen fiber is still used for binder twine, for grain binders have not been completely replaced by combines, especially on the small farms of western Europe. Sisal fiber is important for the manufacture of hard cordage such as special types of ropes, lariats, and similar articles, and is used in twine of higher quality than that made from henequen fiber.

Henequen and sisal are xerophytic plants, adapted to dry regions or able to endure prolonged dry spells or seasons. Their indigenous region is one at the "dry" edge of the wet-and-dry tropics, where the dry season is the longer of the two rainfall seasons of the year. Leaves are thick-skinned and waxy, and the bulbous pineapplelike lower stalk acts as a reservoir of moisture. Northern Yucatán, in addition, is a limestone sinkhole or karst country; rainfall sinks into the porous and cavernous bedrock. Even in the rainy season the countryside is relatively dry because of rapid subsurface drainage into the underground channels.

Sisal is more tolerant of "more humid" conditions in the wet-and-dry tropics. It has been introduced to many other areas, including northeastern Mexico. Henequen, in contrast, needs the excellent underdrainage provided by the karst topography of northern Yucatán. Few other world areas meet the special requirements. Commercially, thus, Yucatán has been able to retain about 85 per cent of the production. Nearly all of the remainder of the world's henequen supply is from Cuba, particularly from certain discontinuous and rocky areas scattered along the northern coast of the island.

Commercial production of henequen and sisal involves the cutting of the leaves, one by one, with a machete. New leaves grow higher on the plant, thus successive cuttings add to the length of the "trunk"; after twenty years of cutting, the harvested leaves are six or so feet above the ground, whereas the original cutting was at ground level.

The leaves are dispatched to a mill, or centrale as it is called in Yucatán. Here they are scraped and decorticated to separate the fibers. These are sun-dried on racks, then baled for export and eventual manufacture.

There is considerable regional variation in the henequen and sisal industry. The Mexican land reforms resulted in the division of former plantations in Yucatán. Estate owners were allowed to keep only some 360 acres of henequen; this figure has since been doubled, but the great plantations have disappeared. The rest of the henequen plantings were divided among small farmers. Hand operations, even to carrying the tied-up leaves to the mills by hand or on the backs of animals, prevail in many districts, even in the sisal district of the northeast of Mexico. In contrast, on the efficient British-managed sisal plantations of East Africa, narrow-gauge railroads and trucks are used to transport cut leaves to the mills, and acreages are adjusted to efficient operation of the mill; it requires 5,000 acres of sisal or henequen to keep the machinery unit of a plantation operating. Not the least of Mexico's difficulties in competition with East Africa in sisal has been the present small and inefficient operating unit resulting from the breakup of plantations. The "near monopoly" is retained in henequen only because of the lack of efficient competing regions.

Sisal (sometimes called sisal henequen) is grown on plantations and farms in Mexico, Cuba, Haiti, Brazil, the Philippines, Indonesia, and—in Africa—in Angola, Mozambique, Tanganyika, and Kenya. The sisal plant was transferred in early days to Florida and Cuba; when, at a later time, the Mexican government placed a ban on the export of the plant material for henequen and sisal—fearing competition—enough sisal was being grown in the West Indies so that further spread from there was possible.

Production of sisal from the tropical plateaus of eastern Africa surpassed production from Mexico in the late 1930's. East African output has increased by half again since that period. The continent of Africa, including the British East African lands and Portuguese Africa, now produces about two-thirds of the world's sisal. British-owned and -managed plantations are efficient and employ modern technical methods of production. The fact that the African plantations are within the money area of the British Commonwealth (sterling area) gives them an advantage in price and in marketing. Guaranteed basic prices permit stability and investment in mills and equipment. And the plantations are diversified in that pineapples, cotton, and other products are grown on the same holdings; the operators are not completely dependent upon the world price of a single product.

The sisal plantations of East Africa are on the wet-and-dry tropical upland, at altitudes of 3,000 to 6,000 feet in these latitudes very near the equator. Among the political units, Tanganyika leads in production, followed by Kenya. There is production, too, in Portuguese Mozambique. These three producers ship from an Indian Ocean port. Sisal grown in Portuguese Angola, on the western side of the continent, reaches an Atlantic port.

The specific location of sisal plantations in Africa is determined by railroad access to ports. The plantations of Tanganyika are close to the line leading to the port of Dar-es-Salaam; those in Kenya are served by the line from Nairobi eastward to the port of Mombasa.

Sisal grown in areas other than Africa is from coastal or near coastal locations. Land transport to a seaport is a less significant cost item in the shipment. Brazil's production has expanded rapidly since the late 1930's to a position second only to the African yield. Sisal is Haiti's second export in value. It is grown in the drier portions of the country on plantations—some of which are American-owned— and on hundreds of small native farms, where it supplies a source of cash income for the grower. Haitian production has increased threefold since World War II; in contrast, Indonesia's output has declined since the withdrawal of the Dutch from the islands.

Sisal is grown in Yucatán and in Mexico's other fiber-producing region, in the northeast between the city of Ciudad Victoria and the exporting port of Tampico. This region is more humid than Yucatán but possesses the usual wet-and-dry season of the latitude in the tropics. Sisal is suitable in these "more humid" conditions, but henequen is less satisfactory than that grown in Yucatán and exported from the port of Progreso.

▶ HEMP

Hemp is a fiber from a plant of the cooler middle latitudes. Its use in Europe in the past as a common and cheap fiber resulted in the application of the name "hemp" to some of the tropical fibers, when these became known. Thus we have the terms Manila hemp for abaca, Indian hemp, Bengal hemp, Bombay hemp for certain of the fibers from India, and even the use of the term "sisal hemp." But the "true" hemp is a fiber of a tall annual herb plant of Europe and North America, and grows in cool-summer regions.

Hemp is produced in greatest quantity in Europe in Poland and eastward across European Russia in the same latitudes, for the same reasons that flax fiber is essentially a European product of the identical areas: inexpensive labor is a prime requisite in the industry. And, like flax fiber, hemp must be retted, bleached, and scutched. The plants themselves are planted in very close rows, to discourage branching and encourage a tall stalk, from which the fiber is extracted. The hemp industry was more important in the past, before the introduction of jute from India to Europe and the Americas. Hemp fiber was used, then, for bags, sacks, and canvas, for twine, and, before the nineteenth century, even for coarse clothing.

The established traditions of growing hemp in certain farming regions, and the existence of local hemp mills, have helped continue the activity. Some small regional production continues in a concentrated district in Wisconsin, where immigrant farmers helped found the industry in the past, and where the product is now a cash-crop item on some dairy farms.

► RUBBER

Rubber is today one of the principal raw materials and manufactured products of the industrial world. Its uses are legion. The transportation industry alone is completely dependent upon rubber for certain purposes, not only in the form of tires, but in other multiple uses in the equipment of airplanes, ships, railroad cars, automobiles, and trucks.

The rubber in daily use is of three origins—natural, synthetic, and reclaimed. Natural rubber is derived mainly from the *Hevea braziliensis* tree, or rubber tree. The white liquid, or latex, which oozes from this tree when an incision is made in the trunk becomes the eventual rubber of commerce and manufacture following several processes of treatment. The principal source region of natural rubber is Southeast Asia, the Malayan region, and Indonesia; Africa is a secondary source. Synthetic rubber, a product of the chemical laboratory, is manufactured from several raw materials, the chief of which are products of petroleum refineries or of certain derivatives of coal. The production of synthetic rubber is important in the United States, the Soviet Union, Canada, and Germany. Reclaimed rubber is manufactured from old, formerly used rubber and is important in the fabrication of certain specialized products. The United States, the United Kingdom, and Germany have leading outputs of reclaimed rubber; Australia has a small output.

The Rise of Rubber

Rubber was first described, apparently, by a Spaniard in 1536, who mentioned "Indian rubber balls" used by the South American natives in some of their games. The Indians also used rubber for waterproofing certain items, and used hollowed-out balls of rubber as containers for liquids. In the 1730's a Frenchman introduced to Europe the use of rubber for coating linens to make raincoats.

The uses of rubber during even the nineteenth century were small. Water-

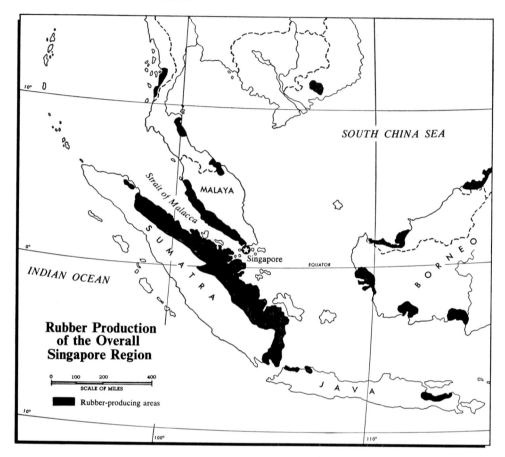

Rubber Production of the Overall Singapore Region

proofed clothing and footwear were the principal manufactured products. The needs of the world were supplied by a wild-rubber industry in the Amazon Basin. Native gatherers tapped wild rubber trees, coagulated the latex over fires, and sold the balls of rubber to traders. The rubber was concentrated at Manaos on the upper river, and at Para (now Belem) near the mouth of the Amazon and shipped to Europe or the United States. The traders from New England brought this "Para rubber" (also known as India rubber) to the docks of Boston, Providence, and New Haven. And, as early as the 1820's, a rubber-manufacturing industry developed in southern New England. Overshoes, rubber boots, "India rubber" shoes, erasers, raincoats, and similar items were manufactured. The Naugatuck Valley of Connecticut retains a rubber industry to this day, one dating from the early trading days.

The use of rubber as a raw material in manufacturing was expanded during the 1820's and 1830's by several inventions. An Englishman developed machinery for processing wild rubber and rolling it into thin sheets. This resulted in an expanded demand, and a great increase in the products made from rubber. Good-year, an American, discovered vulcanization of rubber by cooking rubber compositions with white lead and sulphur on a hot stove. The eventual result was the real rise of rubber industry; rubber in its crude form is actually of little use. Vulcanization and other discoveries and perfections that followed made rubber an important raw material.

The tremendous demand for and use of rubber came toward the end of the nineteenth and the beginning of the twentieth century when the "world went on wheels"—the rise of the automobile industry and the use of rubber tires. During the general period of 1900–1910 the wild-rubber industry of the Amazon Basin could no longer serve the world's needs for rubber. The plantation industry arose. Within a few years the tapping of wild rubber trees was virtually extinct.

The plantation-grown rubber from southern Asia (the Malay Peninsula, Sumatra, and Java) served the world's needs for rubber until the outbreak of World War II. Natural rubber from the Far East plus reclaimed rubber from the manufacturing nations constituted the world supply—natural rubber for tires, tubes, and similar items, reclaimed rubber for kitchen utensils such as dish scrapers, and for many other small but useful items. And the uses of rubber expanded to beltings, insulation materials, composition tiles, use in the telephone industry, and many others.

Synthetic rubber was developed between World War I and World War II. Germany and the Soviet Union had prewar synthetic production, but in the United States the manufacture of synthetic rubber dates from the emergency of World War II. Japanese armies captured almost the entire plantation area of Southeast Asia; Singapore, the great shipping and concentrating point of natural rubber, fell early in 1942. Shipments from nearby areas, such as the Philippines, ceased—in part because of the Japanese capture and Japanese occupation of nearly all of the Pacific area eastward almost to Hawaii, in part because of the diversion of ships to military use. In the emergency the obtaining of tires was virtually impossible in the United States, and federal monies were funneled into the construction of plants for the manufacture of synthetic rubber. Within a year the synthetic industry was in operation.

The period since World War II has witnessed an increased demand for rubber. New uses have been developed. The numbers of automobiles and trucks have increased. In Europe, especially, the automobile output has multiplied rapidly, and the car has become available to families who could not afford it previous to the war. Tractors and even farm wagons now use tires; the airplane industry consumes more rubber. Today, thus, both natural and synthetic rubber are produced and manufactured. The synthetic plants, many of which were closed or placed on a standby basis during the late 1940's, have been sold to the rubber manufacturers and reopened in many places. With a sudden rise in demand the synthetic product can be adjusted rapidly; in contrast, it takes five to seven years for a newly planted rubber tree to come into production. And, today, natural and synthetic rubber are mixed and worked together for certain uses; some manufactured rubber products are said to be superior as a result of the mixing.

Rubber meets competition from other materials. Although the uses of rubber have multiplied with the years, some of the newly developed chemical materials have entered fields formerly held by rubber—garden hoses, for example, are no longer entirely of rubber, and some are made of competing materials. But, to date at least, rubber reigns supreme in the tire and tube field, and in fields for which elasticity and then reversion to original shape is essential. No doubt the world demand for tremendous quantities of rubber will continue and expand as population increases and underdeveloped areas are brought into the modern commercial and industrial scene.

Natural Rubber

Natural rubber is derived from the white liquid known as latex. The outstanding commercial source of latex is the *Hevea braziliensis,* or rubber tree. Native to the Amazon Basin, the tree is now grown widely in the rainy tropics, but the commercial production of latex is confined to a few locations. All plantation trees are descended from seeds smuggled out of Brazil (for the nation had banned the export of seeds or plants) in the late nineteenth century. These seeds, planted in specially heated hothouses in England, produced the seedling trees which, after transplanting in Malaya, became the fountainhead of the plantation stock.

There are other sources of latex in the tropics. Some African trees of the Congo Basin yield latex. In Central America and on the island of Madagascar there are bushes and trees which are tapped for it. And the guayule bush of the hot deserts of northwestern Mexico and the desert border country in the American Southwest produces rubber. But it is the hevea tree which supplies nearly all of the world's natural rubber.

The rubber plantations were established in former British and Dutch possessions in southern Asia. The majority were, and still are, within 100 to 200 miles of the port city of Singapore, a city on an island off the tip of the Malay Peninsula. All shipping rounding Asia must pass Singapore; it is a key focal point on the shipping lanes of that portion of the world. And the investment of British and Dutch capital in the enterprise helped dictate the choice of British colonies and protectorates and the Dutch East Indies as a location, for at that time the areas were possessions, and not independent as some are now.

But the chief factor in the development of the plantation rubber industry in the region of the Malay Straits was and has been the dependable labor supply. This is a very important factor in the production of latex. Daily work at regular hours is required for the tapping of the trees. Each worker cares for some six to seven acres of rubber trees, and taps from 300 to 350 per day. Regularity of work is a necessity. The Malayan, Javanese, and imported Chinese labor of the region is dependable and regular. In contrast, some plantations founded in the Amazon Basin have not been successful because of the paucity of workers; those recruited from tropical coastal Brazil have returned home after a time. In Africa the plantations encountered difficulty, not because of lack of numbers of workers but because daily regularity of work was not part of the culture pattern of the natives; they worked well in "seasonal" activities such as on cacao or palm oils, but on the whole in the early days were not particularly suited to the work in the rubber groves. The Asian planters used local Malay labor and labor from densely peopled Java, and recruited other workers from nearby tropical southern China; the Chinese census records a half million "Overseas Chinese" in the region.

The hevea or rubber tree will grow well in those portions of the rainy tropics that meet its requirements—average temperatures about 80°F during all months, minimum temperatures of 70° or above, about 60 to 100 or more inches of annual rainfall well distributed throughout the year, and friable, well-drained soils. The potential rubber-growing area is large; the producing areas to date have been restricted to the districts of suitable soils near seaports and shipping lanes in regions possessing adequate and dependable labor in numbers.

The gatherer of latex usually taps the trees every other day. An incision is made in the trunk. The latex oozes slowly into a cup hung below the cut. After the output of the trees has been centralized at the plantation headquarters the latex is coagulated by the use of smoke or acids. It is rolled into sheets, is flaked, or is placed in containers as liquid latex. All three forms are exported. An excellent network of roads and railroads in the plantation areas of the Malay Peninsula and on the eastern side of the island of Sumatra, across the straits from Singapore, permits delivery of the product to the ports. Singapore is reached from Malaya by land routes, from Sumatra by ships which cross the Straits.

The success of the Straits region in the growing of natural rubber and its export as latex resulted in the development of native farms engaged in the activity, and in the expansion of the producing area to neighboring countries. Native growers now produce from a third to a half of the output, and the production of latex from plantations and farms has arisen in Ceylon, southern Burma, Thailand, Viet Nam, and in Sarawak and North Borneo on the island of Borneo. Regionally the chief production, however, is still from the Malay Peninsula north of Singapore, and—across the Straits—from islands now in the new country of Indonesia. Export is chiefly from Singapore, but also from other regional ports from Colombo in Ceylon eastward to Saigon.

Tropical Asia and the East Indies surpassed the wild-rubber production of the Amazon during the decade 1901–1910. By the 1910's the plantations and farms were the source of nearly all of the world's crude rubber. The region remains today as the chief source of natural rubber, and produces more than 1.8 million long tons or some 92 per cent of the world's supply. Production in tropical Africa has risen to 6 per cent of the total, and the small remaining tonnage is from tropical America.

The natural rubber from Africa is mainly from the Congo and West Africa. The production from the Congo state and the nearby Cameroons reflects European investments. That from independent Liberia is produced on plantations owned and developed by an American rubber company. In the tropical lowlands of eastern Africa along the Indian Ocean in Tanganyika the British have recently established a rubber industry.

The destination of the exports of crude natural rubber is world wide to the middle-latitude consuming nations. The United States and the nations of western Europe are the chief recipients of the imports. But every nation from Canada through the Soviet Union to China and Japan is an importer, as are Argentina,

Fig. 7-4. Workers on a rubber plantation in Liberia en route from the plantation headquarters to their assigned trees. Each man carries a knife for making the incision, a glass cup into which the latex will flow, and a container into which the latex will be poured at the end of the work day. Each of the workers will tap from 250 to 300 trees during the day. The daily tapping begins shortly after sunrise (note the long shadows). (Firestone Tire and Rubber Company)

the Union of South Africa, Australia, and New Zealand in the Southern Hemisphere. Among countries in the tropics, only Mexico is an importer of consequence and its total receipts are relatively small.

Synthetic Rubber

The detailed analysis of rubber, carried out in chemical laboratories, revealed it to be a hydrocarbon, a polymer of isoprene. Speculation arose as to the types of raw materials which could be used to make a synthetic product, one which contained the same elements of rubber structure. Much of the experimental work was carried out in the United States, Germany, and Russia, and the last two countries had a synthetic industry prior to World War II, one which served many of their needs. The rise of the industry to importance in the United States occurred during the wartime emergency of the early 1940's.

Three or four major types of synthetic rubber are manufactured. One is a general-purpose product used in tiles, flooring, cement, rubber heels, and in tires, where it is used either alone or in mixtures containing natural rubber. Another type possesses resistance to heat of all types, and possesses partial resistance to oil and grease; this synthetic is suited to uses such as for hoses for gasoline pumps, fuel-delivery trucks, and for use as rubber shock-absorbers or undercovering in vehicles. A third type is of significance in the manufacture of inner tubes; it has special qualities of air retention. Each of the types is manufactured by different processes; each of the rubbers is given a special name.

The raw materials for the synthetic rubbers are mainly earth materials; man is still tied to the earth. Principal raw materials for many of the rubbers are products of the petroleum-refining industry. Alcohols and acids are used in some processes, and these are produced by the chemical industries. Certain derivatives from coal can be used. In the United States the products from petroleum refineries are important, and some of the synthetic plants were built near petroleum refineries at the time of the war. In Europe the same types of products are derived from coal, and the synthetic rubber plants, such as those of Germany, are in the coal-mining areas such as the Ruhr. The over-all location of many of the American plants is that of the already established chemical industry, of which the Texas Gulf Coast and West Virginia have a large share.

The synthetic rubber capacity of the industry is very large. During some recent years, owing to relative price situations, the output of synthetic rubber in the United States has exceeded the tonnage of natural rubber used.

Manufacturing

The rubber-manufacturing industry is localized with respect to various factors —historical development and the advantage of an early start, the location of the markets for rubber products, and, in the case of the synthetic industry, the sources of the raw materials. The countries of western Europe are small in area, and the factories are near their markets, no matter where placed; they are usually in or near the importing ports or on the coal fields. In the United States all three of the above general types of location are exemplified.

The rubber industry of southern New England and of New Jersey exemplifies the early start of rubber manufacture near the ports where the wild rubber was landed. These ports handle the imported sheets or flakes of latex and the liquid latex of the present. The rubber industry, rooted in the past, continues at present, and has had a large consuming market grow up around it. For some rubber products the market is the immediate consumer; for many products the market is other manufacturing plants—for example, the shoe-manufacturing industry is a large consumer of rubber heels. The reclaimed rubber industry is associated, also, with urban centers of the Eastern Seaboard; collection of old rubber is from a concentrated area, and the consumer goods manufactured by the industry are sold in sizable local markets.

The development of Akron, Ohio, to its position as the leading rubber-manufacturing center of the country is a result of several factors. The enterprise of local businessmen was important. Local investment, and the residence of some of the pioneers of the industry played a part. And the several factories were well established in Akron at the time of the rise of the automobile industry in not-too-distant Detroit, Toledo, and Lansing. The major market for the Akron factories became the automobile-tire market. And the rooted industry was close enough to the automobile-producing region to serve it; the concentrated tire market was and is the new car—each with five tires—and the widespread, nationwide tire market was and is the replacement market. Akron is well placed to serve the first-named market and to reach the other; and, in time, new tire factories were built in Detroit, at their market; and, as the automobile industry decentralized through the building of assembly plants, so have the tire and tube manufacturers followed it. Thus, today, the Akron companies have established plants in many places; the Pacific Coast plants are in response to both the automobile-assembly industry there and the direct consumer-goods markets in the region. And the aircraft industry of the Coast, concentrated in the Los Angeles region, and at San Diego, Seattle, and Renton, furnishes a large and growing market for rubber products.

The location of rubber factories with respect to the source of raw materials is illustrated by the synthetic industry—not by natural rubber from halfway around the world. The association of many of these plants with petroleum-refining regions and the location of the chemical industry has been mentioned. Some are market oriented. And, for synthetic rubber, the "market regions" in themselves are in part the existing rubber-manufacturing centers where the materials are mixed with natural rubber or manufactured directly into consumer goods.

► QUESTIONS

1. Jute and henequen are two fiber crops in which the producing regions have a near monopoly. What factors, whether natural or cultural, have led to this near monopoly in production?
2. Production of sisal in Africa has increased. What factors help explain this?
3. Comment on the subject: Competition among the fiber crops for the market and competition of the natural fibers with synthetic fibers, rubber, tapes, and other packaging materials.
4. What market factors and demand for rubber were significant in the rapid founding and development of rubber plantations?
5. Explain why the original rubber plantations were established principally in the region near Singapore. What specific sites are occupied by the plantations?
6. There are extensive areas in the wet tropics that are environmentally suitable for the rubber tree. Have plantations been founded in some of these areas? If so, give examples.
7. When a plantation is established in a "new" region what many factors must be considered (in addition to climate and soils) to ensure its success?
8. Obtain recent figures on the output of synthetic rubber.
9. What factors help account for the location and distribution of the rubber-manufacturing industry in the United States.
10. The manufacture of synthetic rubber in the Soviet Union is very large, and the output is believed to be the largest among the countries of the world. Explain why the Union depends almost entirely upon synthetic rubber rather than natural rubber or the combination of the natural and synthetic product.

VIII Textile Fibers, Natural and Synthetic

The fibers from which clothing and many other manufactured products are fabricated are of agricultural or manufactural origin. If agricultural the fibers are of two broad types, either those of animal origin or those of plant origin. If of "manufactural" type the materials are said to be synthetic. The raw materials of the synthetics are various; some are products of the chemical laboratories, but in all cases the original or fundamental materials from which present-day synthetics are derived are natural or earth resources, or are animal or plant materials.

Animal fibers for clothing are such as the wool of sheep, the silk from silk-worms, the mohair of goats, and the hair of camels. Plant fibers are such as cotton from the cotton plant, linen from flax—the flax plant being a small grain—and ramie from the perennial China grass of the subtropics.

There are many synthetic fibers, some of which carry names patented by an individual manufacturer. Certain synthetics are fabricated from such earth materials as coal and limestone. The cellulose of wood is a basic raw material of rayon, and the producers of rayon thread often choose a location in or near an important forest area. Among many names and types of synthetics are the rayons, nylons, Dacron, and Orlon.

The particular fiber in greatest world use has varied regionally and historically. The European peasant, before the Age of Discovery, dressed in home-grown wool or linen, or in leather. A few wealthy lords or nobles were able to obtain silks and cottons through trade with the East, but these were definitely luxury goods. In the Orient, in contrast, cotton was a clothing material of the common man in the cotton-growing districts of India and southern China. Following the discovery of the New World, and its indigenous cottons, Europeans valued their tropical colonies for cotton as well as for sugar, and cotton cloth became common in Europe as plantations were founded in the New World and as trade between Britain and India increased in the Old World.

The rise of cotton as an important fiber in the Western world came with the Industrial Revolution in Britain of the last half of the eighteenth century. Within a short time cotton mills began to compete industrially with woolen mills which had been, until that time, the economic mainstay of England. About a million bales of cotton were produced each year in the world toward the end of the century. But the inventions in England of the spinning frame, spinning mule, and the power loom permitted factories to increase their output of cloth and to place cotton within the reach of masses of people. The demand for raw cotton increased faster than the supply; the bottleneck for the grower was the hand separation of cotton seeds from the lint. This problem was solved by Eli Whitney's invention of the cotton gin in the United States in 1793. An immediate result of this sequence of manufacturing and growing events was the rise of cotton acreage, the increase in manufacture of cotton cloth, and the availability of cotton goods in Western markets. In the southern United States alone, among cotton-growing regions, production rose from 3,000 bales in 1790 to more than half a million by 1825. Following this, each twenty-five years witnessed a doubling of the annual production of raw cotton. This occurred both from an increase of the cotton acreage in the "older" cotton states and the westward movement of cotton growers to the new lands of Mississippi, Arkansas, and Texas. Cotton, as a result of the shifts, competed with wool in certain markets or for certain purposes, became important in warm regions and significant seasonally for clothing in cool areas. Linen declined in use and quantity but advanced in status and became a luxury fabric.

Animal fibers such as wool, mohair, camel's hair and others have been used for clothing materials from the earliest times—the period when man turned from skins to the use of fibers is one which may be surmised, but cannot be known with complete accuracy. And, of course, the dates differed in different parts of the world. The subsistence type of agriculture, which persisted in America even into the early nineteenth century, included a small flock of sheep on nearly every farm and a spinning wheel in the home. One of the wintertime activities was the preparation of home-grown wool, and its home manufacture into garments.

Woolen mills developed as important manufacturing plants during the Industrial Revolution. The widespread distribution of sheep, the development of simple machinery, and the widespread use of small water powers on small streams also permitted enterprising pioneers to set up small woolen mills and blanket factories and sell their product locally. Thus, even though England and New England had many woolen mills following the Industrial Revolution, the local woolen mill was a feature of the frontier lands in what is now the Middle West. The desirable water-power sites were purchased or developed, almost without exception, by the proprietor of a grist mill or a woolen mill—the one using local grains, the other local wool, and each supplying the immediate markets.

Wool has been in continuing use for clothing and fabrics and has not suffered the vagaries of the other animal and plant fibers. It has continued in importance in cool to cold climatic regions. But it has declined, relatively, as a main material in warmer regions of the world. With the present heating of houses and offices, wool meets competition from other materials in its use for certain types of clothing, particularly undergarments. And the annual supply of wool is not completely dependent upon annual production, for wool can be reclaimed and reused.

The synthetic fabrics are relatively recent in appearance upon world markets. Most of the synthetics are developments of this century, and particularly of the period following World War I; some are even more recent. The 1930's and 1940's witnessed the appearance of several, as the research laboratories of chemical organizations developed them, the manufacturing divisions placed them in production, and the sales forces spread them to the markets. The synthetic fibers have obtained increasing percentages of the present markets, both as material which is entirely of synthetic origin and as yarn woven with other materials. Cotton, wool, and other materials have declined *relatively;* they have not declined *absolutely* because the increasing numbers of people in this and other countries use as much or more than did the fewer number of inhabitants of past generations.

Until relatively recent times there was sharp differentiation and specialization of cloth-making factories. A woolen mill worked with woolens, a cotton mill with cotton. Statistics could be gathered on cotton cloth manufacture, woolen goods output, and others with little possibility of overlap.

Today there is increasing mixture of clothing and fabric materials. Some garments are made of mixed cotton and rayon, some of silk and rayon, silk and cotton; some of synthetics woven with cloth of animal or plant origin. Men's lightweight summer suits, at one time fabricated of cotton alone, may be today of a mixed wool and mohair, or of synthetic fibers and mohair, or of silk and wool, and many other combinations. Today the separation, statistically, of cloth-making establishments is not as easy as in the past; what is basically a cotton mill may in fact turn out cloth of mixed fibers as well. A manufacturer of socks may use cotton yarn, silk or rayon yarn, Orlon yarn, or other materials. But woolen mills remain more or less users of wool alone, in part because the market for wool cloth is less widespread areally and is more closely related to temperature and climatic conditions.

► COTTON

The cotton plant is a woody perennial shrub of the warm subtropics and the tropics. All cottons are either of the Asiatic type, indigenous to that continent, or of the American type. All are of the same genus, *Gossypium*. In many regions of commercial production, such as the southern United States, cotton is treated as an annual and replanted yearly; this is because many of the commercial regions, though having the requisite hot growing season for the plant, possess a cool winter season which the cotton shrub fails to survive.

The Asiatic varieties of cotton from India were known to European traders from about the days of the Roman Empire. Cotton is said to have first been received in Europe about 70 B.C. Recent archeological excavations in the Indus Valley, now in Pakistan, have disclosed that cotton cultivation and manufacture existed in this part of the Indian subcontinent as early as 3000 B.C. Indian laws of 800 B.C. refer to cotton. And Asiatic types of cotton were indigenous to China, parts of the Middle East, and Turkestan. From India cotton was introduced to sections of the Middle East, and much later to eastern Africa and the Sudan.

The American species of cotton became known following the discovery of the New World. Columbus found the natives wearing cotton garments; it is said that this was one evidence that led to his conclusion that he had reached the Indies. Cotton was grown by Indians in northern South America, Central America, the West Indies, and Mexico. Of the two native American cottons, the *Gossypium hirsutum* (named from its hairy stem, leaves, and seeds) is the common American upland cotton, believed to have been dispersed from a home region in Mexico; and the other is the long-staple Peruvian cotton, indigenous to the Peruvian area, and the ancestor of the long-staple cottons such as the Yuma and Egyptian cottons.

Environmental Requirements

Cotton requires a hot and humid growing season of six to seven months, and, ideally, a dry picking or harvest season. It will grow in tropical or subtropical dry lands if irrigated. In the tropics the plant may reach a height of ten to twelve feet; in the commercial regions of its production in the subtropics it grows to a height of three to five or six feet.

The rainy tropics, with an all-year hot season, are not satisfactory for commercial production. Cotton grows to the size of a small tree, but the lack of true seasonality permits all stages of cotton to be present at once—buds, flowers, immature bolls, bolls, and ripe cotton. Such conditions are not satisfactory for commercial production. Enough cotton cannot be harvested at any one time to justify expenses, unless labor is extremely inexpensive. In cities of the rainy tropics cotton is used often as an ornamental shrub; in rural areas the commercial output is extremely limited. The world's cotton-producing regions thus lie in other realms, whose environments permit growth of the plant and the harvest of considerable quantities of cotton at more or less the same time of year.

The long and hot growing season must be at least 200 days in length, preferably 230. And at least three months should average about 80°F. The poleward limit of cotton in the subtropics is at approximately the summer, or three-month, isotherm of 77°F and the growing line of 200 frost-free days. This poleward margin has been set through the years by trial and error, and is remarkably sharp; in the southern United States the northern limit of the Cotton Belt is usually within the limit of a county in width.

Frequent rains are necessary for the growth and development of the cotton plant. In the two chief world realms of cotton culture—see later—numerous heavy convectional thundershowers, often as many as two or three a week during the hot growing season, provide the moisture. In a dry region, man supplies water by irrigating the crop. Toward the interior or western edge of the American Cotton Belt in parts of Texas, it has been found through experience that cotton will yield bolls in subhumid regions—but the plant itself in this environment grows to a height of only two to three feet, and no one plant yields a large crop. But large-scale production on extensive acreages per farm, and machine picking, permit the individual producer to grow the crop successively and make a profit.

Two major world realms offer ideal conditions for the commercial production of cotton. Within these extensive realms most of the commercial crop is produced. The humid subtropics offer optimum environments for cotton in their warmer, or equatorward, two-thirds. In this climatic region cotton is planted in the spring; it comes to maturity at approximately the same general period in the autumn with the approach of cooler weather, and it is harvested in middle to late autumn; the crop is treated as an annual and is grown during the long, hot period between killing frosts. The American South exemplifies these conditions. The wet-and-dry tropics produce cotton during the hot, rainy, high-sun period. The crop is planted at the beginning of the rainy season, grows during it, and reaches maturity at the close of the season and the beginning of the dry season. Harvest is early in the dry season. The cotton lands of the Deccan Plateau in India illustrate these conditions. Thirdly, the arid tropics—if man has surplus water for irrigation or is willing to use water upon an inedible crop such as cotton instead of a food crop—is the locale of the long-staple cotton of the world. The Nile Valley and Nile Delta of Egypt are in this realm. In all three areas cotton is treated as an annual rather than a perennial for purposes of commercial production; in the wet-and-dry tropics cotton plants may survive a short dry season, but the general practice is to replant each year.

The total potential cotton area is tremendous. Actual location of the principal areas of production is determined, within the broad climatic framework, by other conditions such as soils of extreme suitability, economic factors, labor supply, access to exporting ports, competition of other crops, and others. The political aspect plays a part; Britain has promoted cotton growing in suitable areas within its Commonwealth of Nations in order to free its mills from complete dependence upon "foreign" imports. And the rise of synthetic materials in world markets and manufacturing has been a factor in forcing marginal cotton areas out of production and increasing concentration of cotton acreage on some of the best lands, where the higher yields per unit area permit the cotton farmer to compete more favorably. Even so, cotton is in surplus production at present, particularly in the United States, in spite of government controls of the acreage. The crop of one year usually does not become a raw material of cotton mills until the second year ensuing.

Cottonseed is planted in rows early in the growing season. In the South this is after all danger of frost has passed, and averages about March 21 along the Gulf Coast (but as early as March 1 in the southernmost parts of Texas), April 1 to 10 in the heart of the southern Cotton Belt, and about April 20 at the pole-ward limits of cotton. Following its appearance above ground, excess plants in each row must be removed by "chopping," usually a hand operation with a hoe. This period is one of the two which requires a peak of human labor—the other being the one-to-two-month picking season.

The cotton plant flowers about five to six weeks after planting. Clean cultivation between the rows of cotton continues—one of the chief factors in cotton being a "soil-eroding" crop. The cotton bolls, or "fruit" containing the lint and seed, develop for some two to three months and burst open when ripe. This exposes the cotton itself, ready to be picked. Each individual boll contains from three to five locks of cotton, and each lock has from seven to nine seeds tightly embedded in the lint. Both the cotton and the seeds are of commercial importance as raw materials of manufacture.

Bolls mature as long as the season is warm to hot and there is adequate moisture. Thus cotton matures during a one-to-two-month period. This necessitates several pickings—usually three—of a given field. The continual maturing of cotton is one of the major handicaps of machine picking the crop. A machine harvesting early-maturing bolls will damage or destroy those not ripe. And the early crop cannot be left on the plants until other bolls have ripened because of spoilage and staining of the cotton lint by rain. But if there is a normally dry autumn the farmer may wait and machine pick; and near the drier edges of a region like the American Cotton Belt it is safe to leave the early-ripened cotton on the plants until all the cotton has matured and pick the entire crop with a mechanical cotton picker. However, in the world cotton regions as a whole hand-picking of cotton is the rule. Thus large amounts of labor are needed twice a year, for the early-season chopping and the late-season harvest. But the demand for labor declines during midseason, and workers are not needed at all in the dormant season.

Cotton is delivered to a gin after it has been picked. The ginning process removes the seeds from the lint. The lint is compressed into bales; these are of different sizes in different producing regions, but the standard American bale is one of about 478 pounds. Government statistics may be given in terms of a 500-pound bale. The warehousing of cotton, its marketing, grading and regrading, compression into more compact bales later, and transportation to market and preparation for sale to manufacturers employ many millions of persons in the world. The work in by-products such as the linters (the fuzz removed from cotton

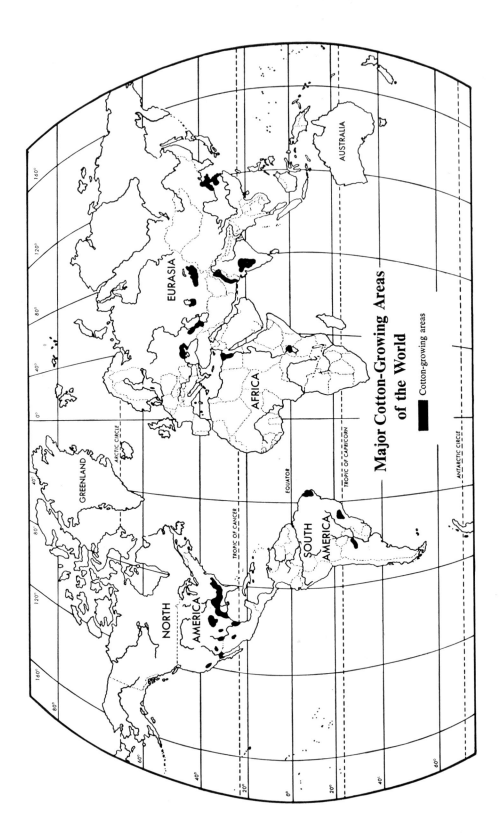

Major Cotton-Growing Areas
of the World

■ Cotton-growing areas

seeds) and the seeds employs many more persons. More than 1,000 major uses of cotton are known. The fact that it is nearly pure cellulose is significant in time of war for use in explosives. And the cottonseed, once a completely waste product except for the seed retained for an ensuing year, is decorticated, heated, and pressed. The cottonseed oils are edible oils used in vegetable shortenings, oleo-margarines, and in cattle feeds such as cottonseed cake. Even the final refuse or residues from the oil-expressing process are useable for candle greases and for such items as waterproofing packing paper.

Cottons are classified by the length of their staple—the length of a stretched-out lock of lint. The cotton grown in the Deccan Plateau of peninsular India is of extremely short staple. Some lengths are as short as three-sixteenths of an inch; most cotton of India is less than seven-eighths of an inch in length. Medium-staple cottons are the product of the Cotton Belt of the American South. Staple length ranges from seven-eighths of an inch to one-and-one-eighth inches; the Yazoo bottomlands, locally called the Delta, of the state of Mississippi produce some cotton with a staple of one-and-a-quarter inches, locally called "long staple" based on the American understanding and practice of considering "long staple" as any cotton with a staple length of one-and-one-eighth inches or more. On the world basis, it is the longest of the medium-staple cottons. Long-staple cotton (more than $1\frac{1}{4}$ inches) is a product of the arid tropical realm and is grown under irrigation in a desert climate. These cottons are the descendants and improvements of the Peruvian cottons and are known often in the trade as Egyptian cottons because Egypt is the largest exporter. Of the three chief countries exporting cotton, India contributes the bulk of the short-staple, the United States the medium, and Egypt the long. Within nations of large size and diverse environment different cottons are produced regionally. Thus the irrigated lands of Arizona and the Imperial Valley of California yield long-staple cotton in the United States, the Cotton Belt of the southeast the medium-staple; the same is true in the Soviet Union, where cotton is grown in irrigated oases of Central Asia in an arid environment, and on the plains north of the Black Sea in a different setting.

▶ REGIONS OF PRODUCTION

More than sixty countries grow cotton. Every nation of the New World except Canada has some production. Nearly every African country or political unit contains cotton acreage in varying amounts. Most Asian nations are producers, northward to include South Korea; Japan's acreage in its south is extremely limited, however. Australia grows a little, but New Zealand lies poleward of the limit of cotton, as does all of Europe except part of the Mediterranean lands and the Black Sea region of Russia. Nearly all commercial production is within (1) the humid subtropics, exemplified by the acreage in the American South and China; (2) the wet-and-dry tropics, as in Brazil, India, Mexico, and the region of the Sudan in Africa, and (3) the arid tropics as in Peru, the American Southwest, and Egypt.

There is cotton production in a few hot valleys and regions of the Mediterranean subtropics, particularly in interior California, and a few valleys of Spain, Italy, and Greece. And in a hot summer (but cold winter) area of the continental lands of the plains of the Soviet Union north and east of the Black Sea there is now a very large cotton acreage and production.

The widespread distribution of cotton culture is reflected in the direction and destination of foreign trade in the fiber crop. The nations of western Europe are the largest importers by far. Japan, with its important textile industries, follows, and receives both Indian and American cotton. India imports medium-staple cottons, and both uses and exports its short-staple crop. In the New World, Canada is the leading importer. The United States, a major exporter, receives some long-staple cotton from elsewhere, but in its net trade is the world's chief exporting nation of raw cotton.

Cotton is grown as one of several crops in all of the world's producing regions; even in the so-called Cotton Belt of the American Southeast its share of the farm acreage, except locally, is usually not as large as that of corn. It reaches its highest percentage of the total cultivated land on the Nile Delta of Egypt, where its growth and sale accounts for about four-fifths of Egypt's total foreign trade. Locally, too, in many oases and irrigated lands of the arid tropics cotton reigns supreme. In Brazil the older cotton area of the northeast is important for sugar cane as well, and the newer cotton area of the Brazilian Plateau is noted also for coffee.

The American cotton production has declined *relatively* in the world scene as other producing regions have engaged in cotton culture. During colonial and early nineteenth-century days the South produced about 90 per cent of the world's commercial crop. The upset economic conditions and the blockades during the American Civil War cut off supplies of raw cotton to European textile mills, then in Britain mainly. A result was the rapid increase of cotton production in Egypt, which had had only a moderate production from the 1830's, when commercial culture began, until this period. As Egypt and other countries entered commercial growing and foreign trade, the American percentage dropped to about two-thirds. Since the 1940's it has dropped further to about one-third. This reflects many factors—the increased acreage in India on the black *regur* soils of the Deccan, the great spread of cotton in Africa, Brazil, and the Soviet Union, the desire of some manufacturing countries to import as much cotton as possible from their political dependencies, cheaper labor in the tropical producing areas, and the acreage-control programs instituted in the United States during the depression of the 1930's. Among present commercial regions and countries Egypt is the most dependent upon the cotton crop for a source of national income and foreign credits. *Absolutely* the United States has not declined, but with the relative decline it has less impact in World Cotton Congresses than formerly.

► THE UNITED STATES COTTON BELT

Traditionally the region known as the Cotton Belt in the South has been the home of cotton, but recently there has been a marked westward shift in cotton acreage and production. California is now the second cotton state, exceeded in production only by Texas. Arizona is fifth, behind Mississippi and Arkansas. The states from Mississippi west are now the heart of the American cotton lands. Traditionally the "Cotton Belt" has been the area from the Atlantic westward to the dry-land border of the humid subtropics in west central Texas. Yet today the "Old Cotton Belt" has experienced a decline in production and a shift to other types of agriculture—even New Mexico's cotton yield has exceeded that of North Carolina in certain years—but the "Old South" still grows large quantities of lint, especially in the Yazoo Basin of Mississippi, the bottomlands locally called the Delta. However, the Cotton Belt as a continuous region has been broken. Introduced pasture grasses and grazing beef cattle now characterize the landscape of many portions of Georgia, Alabama, and adjacent states where "King Cotton" once held almost complete dominance of the economy. What have been the economic and the geographic factors in this westward shift? Why is so much cotton now grown outside the limits of a well-known and long-established Cotton Belt, a

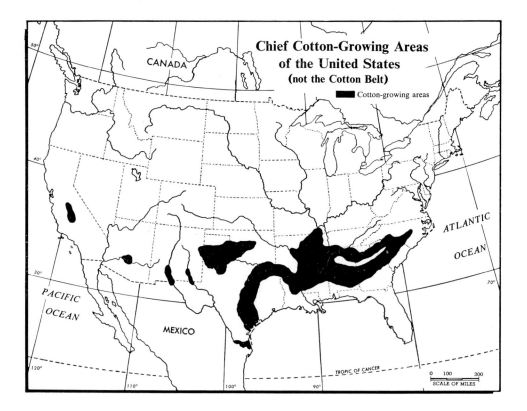

Chief Cotton-Growing Areas
of the United States
(not the Cotton Belt)

■ Cotton-growing areas

Fig. 8-1. A disappearing scene in the American Cotton Belt—cabins of sharecroppers facing a field of young cotton in the Yazoo Basin (known locally as the Delta) of the state of Mississippi. Close inspection will reveal at least two empty cabins. Mechanization of cotton picking began in the 1930's. It accelerated during World War II when many sharecroppers moved to industrial centers for wartime employment, and there was a shortage of labor on the cotton farms. In turn, the increased mechanization—the cotton-cultivating and cotton-picking machines—replaced other croppers. Today this area, the most important cotton-growing region east of the Mississippi River, is nearing complete mechanization. The flat and rich alluvial lands of the Delta have the richest soils "west of the Nile." (Standard Oil Company, N.J.)

traditional agricultural region of the United States which, in total, occupies a sixth of the area of the nation excluding the recently admitted states of Alaska and Hawaii?

A brief history of the cotton agriculture of the South will set the stage and provide a background. As the Industrial Revolution expanded from England to America a market for cotton in the newly founded textile mills grew by leaps and bounds. Plantations in the South, based upon cheap land and slave labor, expanded. Cotton planters engaged in a "westward movement." New plantations and family-operated cotton farms spread into Alabama, Mississippi, and westward into eastern Texas by the 1850's. Production of cotton doubled every twenty-five years, and the mills of New England and England absorbed all the raw cotton grown.

The sharecropping system of cotton production arose following the Civil War and the abolition of slave labor. Former plantations were divided into small operating units, usually forty acres, but the ownership was still held by the original landowner. The landlord provided each cropper with a house, land, seed, power in the form of horses or mules, tools, and credit for the purchase of food. The cropper worked for a share of the crop, usually half. Following picking of the cotton, landlord and sharecropper divided the proceeds, and the landlord deducted from the cropper's share the amounts advanced in the form of capital equipment and food. The owner was certain of obtaining these amounts because all cotton had to be weighed at a central place—the cotton gin. Furthermore, as cotton is inedible, the sharecropper had to market all of it. Originally the majority of sharecroppers were the freed Negroes; in time many white sharecroppers engaged in cotton growing. And, as before the Civil War, white and Negro owners or tenants on small farms engaged also in cotton culture. Sharecropping differs from tenant farming in that the landlord furnishes everything to the cropper, even credit for food; in tenant farming the farm operator supports himself and his family during the year and pays rent in the form of cash or an agreed portion of the crop.

The cotton boll weevil, a beetle, entered the Cotton Belt in southern Texas in 1892. Year by year the weevil spread eastward, ravaging and destroying the immature cotton bolls and depleting or ruining the crop. By 1933 all portions of the cotton lands eastward to the Atlantic had been affected. Two major results of the boll weevil infestation were (1) a gradual diversification of southern agriculture with less dependence upon cotton alone; and (2) the decline of cotton acreage from about Alabama eastward. This eastern portion of the Cotton Belt has a mild, humid winter. The boll weevil survived this, living in trash and old cotton plants. From Mississippi westward lower minimum temperatures are a winter characteristic, even though the entire season is moderate; the cold waves, sweeping down the plains and the Mississippi Valley resulted in the winter-killing of more of the weevils. Also, as the winter is drier than to the east, farmers could burn trash and cotton plants and so destroy a larger percentage of the boll weevils. A present result of the depredations and control is that the eastern portion of the Cotton Belt is the most "broken" part, and is the area now practicing diversified agriculture. Thus the sequence has "left" the western portion as the more important of these two.

The advent of the cotton-picking machine, first developed in the 1930's and improved in later years so that its use became effective in the late 1940's, helped change the cotton picture. Machine picking is most important in the western, drier portion of the Cotton Belt. Here cotton matures at about the same time, and more important, the early-maturing bolls can be left on the plants until later maturing ones burst open; there is little danger of damage and staining from heavy rains. When all of the crop is mature it is machine harvested. A cotton-picking machine is less satisfactory in the eastern portion of the Cotton Belt. Cotton matures over a long period. If the farmer waits for all to be ripe he is certain to suffer losses in the early crop from rain damage; if he machine picks before all the bolls have ripened, he loses the late crop entirely, for the machine is in general principle like a vacuum cleaner; it cannot be selective. Therefore, hand picking still prevails, or the first month's crop may be picked by hand and the later by machine. This poses two economic questions: the cost of hand labor, and whether it is possible to purchase a machine for a part crop. Usually it is not, and consequently the cotton-picking machines in the eastern regions are usually owned by a few, or by custom pickers who perform the work. Again, all want the use of the machine at the same time, posing further problems.

The labor supply in the Cotton Belt has affected many districts. In the past surplus labor was on hand in the summer slack season and the winter dormant

Fig. 8-2. The Delta in the state of Mississippi today. Three men and three machines harvest more cotton in a few hours than several hundred cotton-pickers could pick in many days. Each year the use of the mechanical cotton-picker increases. Note, in this scene and in Fig. 8-1, the flat surface and the woods in the distance; trees remain on the poorly drained areas, such as the ox-bows of former river channels. (Standard Oil Company, N.J.)

Fig. 8-3. Compressing ginned cotton into a bale inside the cotton gin. The cottonseeds have been removed in the ginning process, and piled outside for eventual transport to a cottonseed oil mill. (*Steelways*, published by American Iron and Steel Institute)

period; supply was adjusted to the needs of chopping in the spring and harvest in the fall. After the restriction of immigration in the United States, beginning with 1924, southern workers began to move north in numbers, replacing foreign immigrants in unskilled jobs. The high wartime wages of 1941–1945 caused the northward migration to swell to tidal proportions. The postwar prosperity served to continue the migration. Large areas of the Cotton Belt were depleted of rural laborers; sharecroppers, many of whom had long been tied to this activity, were enabled to leave. School segregation in the South, job opportunities in the northern cities, relief programs of these cities, aid of prior migrants who were relatives, and other factors served to set in motion the tremendous migration of Negroes to the North and West—into the cities of those regions. And many rural laborers moved to the growing industrial cities of the South. Although an equally large migration emanated from the southern mountains, these migrants, not being from cotton areas, did not affect the labor supply for cotton.

What labor adjustments have occurred in the Cotton Belt? Texas has been

FIG. 8-4. Truck load of baled cotton. Burlap, made of jute from India or Pakistan, is used to wrap the bale. Steel bands bind each bale. The building of galvanized iron is very representative of cotton gins in the American South. Note the short fibers and linters from the ginning process clinging to the ventilators and wires. (Standard Oil Company, N.J.)

affected but little; cotton farmers draw upon Mexican itinerant workers or machine pick. The cotton-picking machine has spread through the western part of the Belt. As sharecroppers left the Mississippi Delta (Yazoo Basin) country the farms were consolidated, a neoplantation (but on a different basis than the antebellum plantation) appeared, and the migrants were replaced by tractors, cultivators, and cotton-picking machines. But the eastern "broken belt" could do this less well, for the reasons outlined. Many marginal cotton areas on poor soil, or in eroded country, have ceased production; cotton has been replaced by pastures and beef cattle, which require less labor. Diversification of agriculture, begun with the boll weevil, has continued and accelerated. Better cotton lands continue in cotton as a cash crop, and the variety of adjustments outlined heretofore have taken place. Owners, tenants, and sharecroppers continue to be the major operators of cotton farms.

Governmental programs have had a pronounced effect upon the percentage of cotton acreage. The various cuts in acreage allotments have reduced the total cotton acreage. Each county usually receives an allotment, and the acreage which can be planted is stated. Local committees then make the allotments by farms, using a formula. When a cut in acreage is made it is thus done by percentage; the *pattern* of cotton growing remains the same. A farmer thus plants his cotton on his best land, for he can grow less total acreage; he fertilizes the reduced acreage heavily, and—if there is a shortage of labor—tends to mechanize the cultivation. By doing this he is able to cultivate the young cotton several times. Yields of cotton per acre have increased as a result of all factors, and there has been a resurgence of some of the long-cultivated eastern cotton districts. And the government subsidies in various forms are factors in the farmer's gross income. The land "released" from cotton may be put into nonsupported crops, or into pasture. Thus, indirectly and directly, the governmental programs have led to greater diversification of crops.

Some authorities insist that there is no longer a "Cotton Belt" in the American

FIG. 8-5. The cotton plant grown on the southern Great Plains, as in western Texas, is very short, a reflection of the dry condition. Were it not for mechanical culture the cost of picking would be prohibitive. Because of the dry climate, bolls are allowed to remain on the plants until all have matured. Notice that this type of cotton-picking machine differs from those shown in FIG. 8-2. (Standard Oil Company, N.J.)

South. The answer depends in part upon definitions. In any case there is a large cotton-growing area, an agricultural region covering one-sixth of the nation excluding Alaska and Hawaii. Within this area, or Cotton Belt, cotton is grown on up to 5 or 6 per cent of the land area of nearly all counties. And, within it, seven districts of intensive cotton production stand out; these districts are each of considerable size, and within each 10 per cent or more of the total land area is devoted to cotton. These districts are: (1) the inner coastal plain of Georgia and South Carolina; (2) the upper Piedmont in the same states (separated from [1] by the lower Piedmont); (3) the portion of the Tennessee River Valley in northern Alabama; (4) the broad, rich flood plain of the Mississippi River from the southern tip of Illinois to northern Louisiana—within this are the rich cotton lands of eastern Arkansas and the Delta of the state of Mississippi; (5) the Black Waxy Prairie of Texas, especially its northern half; (6) the coastal plain of south Texas, and (7) the plains of west Texas, particularly the southern part of the Panhandle and southward. This last district extends into southwestern Oklahoma.

Of these intensive cotton districts, the Mississippi flood plain lands lead in the percentage of their area devoted to cotton, followed by the Black Waxy Prairie of Texas.

▶ COTTON IN THE WEST

Two types of cotton are grown in the West—to the west of Texas. One is the long-staple cotton of the irrigated oases of New Mexico, Arizona, and the Imperial Valley of California. The other is the American upland cotton of the San Joaquin Valley—the southern segment of the Central Valley of California. Long-staple is high in value but fairly low in percentage of the total western crop. The upland cotton of the San Joaquin leads in overall acreage and production. None of the western cotton is considered as being from the Cotton Belt—this last refers to only the southeastern United States. All western cotton production is completely mechanized. All is machine picked. Every acre of cotton is irrigated.

The long-staple areas of the arid tropics have an all-year growing season in most districts, such as the Imperial Valley, and a 300-plus-day season in others. The chief production center is the Salt River Valley of Arizona. Land values of irrigated lands are high, water is expensive, and high-value crops are an absolute necessity to repay the capital investments, pay the yearly charges, taxes, the cost of machinery, and other items in the production picture. But the land can produce all year or nearly so. A farmer may choose cotton as a "summer" or hot-season crop and grow hardy vegetables during the winter, shipping them to out-of-season markets. He has a choice of cotton in the hot season, and perhaps the feeding of animals during the cooler period—the cattle being obtained from mountain ranchers and being fed on home-grown alfalfa. He may mix cotton culture with other enterprises, and, incidentally, obtain governmental support prices

Fig. 8-6. Irrigating young cotton plants—a scene in the western cotton-growing districts, west of the so-called Cotton Belt proper. (Standard Oil Company, N.J.)

on the cotton, though he is also subject to governmental acreage controls.

Cotton culture was introduced to the hot San Joaquin Valley about 1910. Its marked expansion occurred following the 1920's. By the 1940's the valley accounted for more than 95 per cent of California's cotton production, and California reached the position of fifth cotton state; by the late 1950's it was second, exceeded only by Texas, and has reached a figure of about one-seventh of the total American yield of lint. The value of the state's cotton crop exceeded that of the better-known California products of citrus fruits and grapes. The state legislature has passed laws limiting plantings to one variety of American upland cotton, with an average staple length of one-and-one-sixth inches. And the "old" cotton region of the South, through its trade organizations, recognized the significance of California by holding a convention of the National Cotton Council there in 1949, the first time outside of the South, and in the late 1950's admitting a California contestant to the Maid of Cotton contest.

The grower in California is not dependent upon rainfall, as is the southern grower. Offsetting this, he has high expenses for irrigation water. Yields per acre of cotton, with controlled water supply, are nearly double that of the old Cotton Belt. Thus the San Joaquin grower receives a higher gross income per acre of cotton to help offset his higher fixed charges. The Californian need not usually worry about rain damage following opening of the bolls; he can wait until all have opened before picking by machine. But, in the San Joaquin Valley, he does have to worry about certain aspects of the weather, such as an early frost, or an earlier-than-usual beginning of the period of winter precipitation.

Governmental acreage controls, as elsewhere, have an effect. But, with higher average yields per acre than in the South, a percentage cut in acreage (applied, as always, nationally) still leaves the individual grower with a larger total crop (on a cotton farm with equivalent acreages in cotton). For example, the acreage allotments of 1954 reduced the acreage of cotton in the San Joaquin Valley by a third (from 1953) but affected the actual production by only one-sixth. And the governmental payments are part of the total income of the grower.

Much of the California production is on large company-owned or individually-owned farms. This reflects the later development of cotton culture in the San Joaquin Valley than in the South; it also reflects the large capital investment needed to place irrigated land under cultivation, no matter whether the water is furnished through a federal irrigation project or a private one. And the company farm is also a California "characteristic" in many of the state's farming areas; in contrast, Arizona's production is mainly on small, intensively cultivated irrigated farms on which cotton is but one of several crops.

United States: Summary

The centers of cotton production have shifted westward, first with the westward movement of the frontier a century and a half ago, then with the expansion of acreage to the dry-land border in western Texas. Thirdly, a further westward expansion has occurred with the advent of long-staple cotton growing in the irrigated lands of the Southwest, and the rise of a significant cotton production in the hot San Joaquin Valley of California. ·

Many factors have been operative in the shifts. Suitable climatic and soil areas, history, economic factors, pests and diseases, labor and machinery, governmental subventions, and others have been operative—not all necessarily at any one period. The center of production for the Cotton Belt proper is in the Delta lands of the state of Mississippi; for overall American cotton production, it is well to the west of the river.

To date there has been no northern shift. Climate, expressed in terms of average summer temperatures and a 200-day growing season, has held the poleward border to a narrow zone, even a "line" in places. This border has remained stationary for essentially one hundred years; the short-time jumping of this border, when cotton was grown in Kentucky during Reconstruction Days in the Deep South, terminated as abruptly as it began.

► COTTON IN EGYPT

Egypt has two contrasting regions of cotton production, each in the arid tropics. One is the narrow flood plain of the Nile in Upper Egypt. The other is the Nile Delta, the center of commercial production for export.

The Nile Valley is densely settled. Landholdings average but two to five acres in size. The economic conditions and population pressure force the fellaheen—the peasants—to concentrate on the production of food crops. The cotton raised in the valley is grown virtually as a garden crop. It is collected, a small quantity only from each village, and shipped by rail or on the river to Cairo.

The large farms of the Nile Delta furnish the bulk of the export cotton. Ten thousand landowners own one-third of Egypt's cultivated land; practically every large farm lies on the Delta. Egypt has instituted a land-reform program to break up large holdings and distribute the land among peasants, but in so doing it faces the problem of less cotton for export as the small farmers concentrate on home supply crops rather than cotton.

The Nile Delta was not placed under general cultivation until the nineteenth century. Drainage and irrigation projects had to be constructed. The Delta is "new" Egypt, in contrast to old Upper Egypt. From the start, Delta landholdings ranged in size from fifty acres upward, and commercial cultivation of cotton was instituted. The local inhabitants can be fed from a small percentage of the land; the rest is available for cotton. Financial and governmental connections with Great Britain were favorable at the time of the beginnings of cotton culture. British mills provide a ready market for Egypt's long-staple cotton, and the port of Alexandria is close to the Delta farms. Cheap labor, imported originally from Upper Egypt, and a dense network of railways and waterways are important factors in the growing and movement of the cotton.

Egypt's money crop is cotton. It alone accounts for 80 per cent or more of the nation's annual income; foreign credits were (and are) based mainly upon cotton alone. In one recent year the government had pledged the future crop of a ten-year period as security for foreign loans. But, since nationalization of the Suez Canal by Egypt in 1956, the canal tolls are an additional source of the total national income; cotton has thus declined in percentage of total value but not in absolute value.

The long-staple cotton of Egypt is recognized as of top quality in the cotton industry. Its staple length is one-and-one-half inches or more. In addition the Delta grows a medium-staple cotton, developed for local conditions by Egyptian agricultural experiment stations. The production of lint in the country has remained fairly constant year after year, and the total yield of the late 1950's showed no essential change from that of twenty years previously—in contrast to the decline in the United States and the rising production in the Soviet Union and China.

► WOOL

Wool is the fiber from the fleece of a sheep or a lamb. Under United States laws enacted by Congress some other fibers can be labeled as wool, particularly those from the alpaca, llama, and vicuna—animals of the Andean Highlands of South America. Wool itself in the trade is restricted to the fresh or unused fiber; reprocessed wool is the name for wool which has been manufactured, but never used by a consumer; reused wool is the name for wool which has been used and reclaimed. Among the fibers wool alone can be reused and remanufactured. Thus the annual production and the annual manufacture may differ considerably.

Wool shorn from a sheep is fleece wool. That pulled from the skins of slaughtered animals is called pulled wool. The grades of each are numerous. Fleece wool differs in type from breed to breed of animal, differs in type in its position of growth on a sheep, and differs from region to region in the world, depending in part upon the environment of the sheep-rearing region, the kind of pastures grazed, and many other factors. Wool within a region differs in its felting quality, color, tensile strength, softness, the length of the wool, and in other ways. The original classifications of wool are made following shearing or pulling, and raw wool is baled by general type. Final and very detailed classifications by type and subtype are made at the wool markets or by warehousemen. The market centers also clean and prepare the raw wool for sale. A fleece may contain as much as 40 per cent by weight foreign material, such as burrs, seeds, dirt, and grease.

Manufacturers purchase special wools. The combing wools are preferred for worsted manufacture, clothing wools for clothing, other wools for the knit-goods industry, for upholsteries, and for carpets. Two broad distinctions in the general grades are those between wools in the apparel class and those in the carpet class.

The production of mutton is a specialty in areas maintaining the mutton breeds of sheep, but in the wool-producing regions, it is a by-product of the wool-growing industry. Mutton is the meat from a mature sheep. In the specialized wool regions the emphasis is upon breeds of sheep noted for their wool, and an individual animal is kept and maintained for several years; meat is a by-product.

There are breeds of sheep noted for the quality of their meat. The regions that specialize in the rearing of these breeds produce lamb for market—as well as mutton—lamb being the meat from a young sheep. All such areas, in addition, yield some wool, for the animal is sheared at least once, but wool production is secondary, or in this case, a by-product of meat production. Very young unshorn lambs, marketed at packing plants, do, however, yield some pulled wool.

Wool Production and Trade

The Southern Hemisphere is pre-eminent in wool production. Australia, New Zealand, Argentina, Uruguay, and the Union of South Africa are the five leading exporting countries. Distant as they are from the wool-consuming countries of North America and Europe, wool serves these producing nations well in the international market. It is durable and compact for shipment and has a high value in proportion to its weight. Wool easily pays its freight rates to markets, even if shipped halfway around the world, as from Australia or New Zealand to Britain.

The United States and the Soviet Union are significant producers of wool. But their production does not equal their consumption, and each is also an importer of wool. During some years wool imports into the United States exceed the total home production; normally they run approximately two-thirds of the amount of the national clip. About half of the imports are usually from Australia and New Zealand, and a quarter to a third from South America.

The nations of western Europe import very large quantities of wool. Great Britain is the chief importer. The total home-grown quantity of wool in western Europe, collectively, exceeds the yield in the United States, but fails by far to satisfy the demands of the European woolen industry. Imports into the United Kingdom alone are often as large as those into the United States. European nations also export some of their fine wools from their sheep, mainly to the United States for the fine-wool market.

The Middle East, Pakistan, and India produce more wool than is used at home, though production is moderate when compared to the Southern Hemisphere, or to Australia alone. The surplus wool from these areas is shipped to European markets. Japan is an importer of wool on a moderate scale for its textile industry.

In the world picture, five nations of the Southern Hemisphere, and the United States and the Soviet Union, are the leading wool-producing countries. Australia, number one among nations in numbers of sheep, produces twice as much wool as the second country, and annually contributes about 40 per cent of the net export trade in the fiber. Two regions on either side of the Atlantic—the northeastern United States and western Europe—are the leading consuming areas where wool is manufactured. World-wide, the chief sources of wool are distant from these chief consuming regions. And, regionally, within the United States and the Soviet Union, wool is produced also in areas quite distant from where it is used in manufacturing.

► WOOL SHEEP

The breeds of sheep developed in Spain are the principal wool sheep of the world. The word Merino is associated usually with the wool breeds; thus there are Spanish Merinos and Australian Merinos, the latter further perfected for Australian conditions. Three types of American Merinos are common in the Intermountain West of the United States. In contrast to the descent of wool sheep from Spain, the commercial mutton breeds are almost entirely of English origin.

Sheep do well in dry lands and in subhumid lands. They are adapted to eating grass which is short, for their mobile lips and incisor teeth permit them to crop it off at practically ground level; a sheep is able to exist on pasturage that is too poor to support cattle. Weeds, untouched by cattle, also provide food for sheep. Sheep are able, likewise, to utilize pastures in rough country, and on rocky elevations. Offsetting this ability to exist in dry and mountainous areas is the fact that overgrazing causes erosion, as the grass is eaten almost to the roots; in the summer grazing of sheep in the National Forest lands of the American West, the number of sheep permitted per unit area is kept at a figure so that erosion will not result. A second factor in the rearing of sheep is that the animal is virtually defenseless. Sheep are preyed upon by wild and by domesticated dogs. Thus in range country a flock of sheep must be under the constant care of a shepherd; in the West sheep are grazed in bands of 1,500 to 3,000 head and are accompanied by the sheepherder. In settled and fenced farm country, where a constant watch is not necessary, "tame" dogs take a large annual toll of sheep.

Sheep possess a natural flocking habit. The flock follows a leader. When a sheep is separate from a flock it is usually ill or injured. In the world's commercial sheep-rearing regions this habit is of utmost importance in management and permits a relatively few workers to care for very large numbers of sheep grazing in open range country.

In regions of open winters and all-year grazing sheep subsist on natural pasturage alone. Introduced grasses and pastures of alfalfa supplement the natural grasses in other areas. In mountainous sheep lands the animals are grazed in lowland areas in the spring and fall, and on the uplands during the summer. They are fed hay and roughages in the valleys in the winter. This migration from valley to mountain is common in the American West; in parts of Europe and Asia it is practiced as transhumance; in the New World only herders, rather than families, accompany the flocks to the mountains.

► WOOL-PRODUCING REGIONS

There is a general correlation between the dry and mountainous lands of the middle latitudes and the rearing of wool sheep. However, in places the existence of inexpensive land and the absence of densely settled farm country permits extensive wool-producing regions to extend into humid areas; in other words, large landholdings in a humid area such as the heart of the Argentine Pampas are used, in part, for sheep pasturage. In time, perhaps, as crops increase in importance and compete for the land in such a setting, the sheep industry will be forced to the drier margin of the Pampas.

The wool of the United States originates mainly in the western half of the nation. Range is in part on drier sections of the Great Plains well west of the 100th meridian, in part throughout the basins and valleys of the Rocky Mountain system, and in part in the dry lands of the Intermountain West between the Rockies and the Sierra Nevada–Cascade system of mountains. Pastures in these mountains, and in other western mountains and high plateaus, are grazed during the summer. The plains at the eastern base of the Rockies, the Snake River plains of southern Idaho, and the irrigated lands of Utah are the locale of intensive concentrations of sheep during the winter. In addition to the aforementioned large areas of the West, the Edwards Plateau of Texas and its adjacent hill country is an area of very important wool production. Numbers of sheep and clip of wool are the most concentrated of any part of the country in this large area of southwest-central Texas. All-year grazing is practiced in the Edwards Plateau; the area is unique in the United States in that sheep and goats are grazed together.

The sheep of the Pampas of Argentina are grazed on native grassland pastures and on alfalfa. Some *estancias* specialize in cattle, some in sheep. In neighboring Uruguay native pastures are the rule. This small nation is one of the most com-

Fig. 8-7. Sheep and goats in a corral on a ranch in the Edwards Plateau of Texas. Note the difference in appearance of the wool on the sheep and the hair (mohair) on the goats. The dry, scrub-tree and grass-covered slopes in the distance and the hilly terrain are characteristic of this important sheep-rearing region of the United States. (Standard Oil Company, N.J.)

pletely pastoral countries in the world. There are three cattle and nearly ten sheep for every inhabitant. All-year grazing is possible in the Pampas and in Uruguay.

Patagonia, the region of southern Argentina, is very dry and continuously cool to cold. The one important economic enterprise is the rearing of sheep and the sale of wool. Very large landholdings, with their central buildings and shelters for sheep located in the canyonlike river valleys, comprise the operating units. The sheep ranches continue, intermittently, southward to the Strait of Magellan and beyond—the southernmost operations being in Chile. And Tierra del Fuego and the Strait area is the chief wool-producing area of Chile. Native moorland-type vegetation, shrubs, and some dry-land grasses furnish the browse in the Patagonia and the Strait region.

South African wool production is mainly from the dry and rough southern portion in the mountains and plateau escarpments to the north and northeast of the Cape, and—on the top of the plateau—on the dry side of the Veld. Large ranches operated by Boer farmers are the rule in both areas. Westward, as the Veld grades into the semiarid and desert lands of Southwest Africa, sheep-rearing continues, but with fewer animal units per square mile. But in Southwest Africa there are many sheep, and this political unit (now annexed by the Union) is the largest world source of Persian lamb skins and wool—the wool of which is very short, closely curled, and almost silky in appearance.

Wool production of New Zealand is from two contrasting types of regions and kinds of sheep. The eastern side of humid and cool North Island and the plains portion of South Island tend, on the whole, to specialize in the English breeds and the production and export of mutton; New Zealand furnishes over half of the mutton in international trade. Wool, however, is an important "by-product" of this specialization. In contrast the drier southern half of the eastern side of South Island—the Otago area—and the eastern or leeward side of the New Zealand Alps is the "High Country Sheep Run" district. Landholdings are exceptionally large, and often extend from the valleys and lowlands well into the mountains. Thus, on a given operation there is lowland pasture, browse at intermediate elevations, and upland summer pasture. Sheep are moved altitudinally with the seasons and yet, on many of the high country runs, remain on the same landholding. This region on South Island is the heart of New Zealand's production of wool from Merino sheep. But wool of this type originates elsewhere in the Dominion as well, and New Zealand is the second wool-producing and wool-exporting country of the world, exceeded in each activity only by neighboring Australia.

► WOOL IN AUSTRALIA

Wool is Australia's most important product. The Commonwealth produces 40 per cent of the world's raw wool. Australia is the leading exporter of Merino wool, and exports more than double the quantity of the second nation. It has been said that Australia would be internationally bankrupt without its sheep, and that the internal economy of the country would be ruined. Not only are sheep the mainstay of the agricultural economy of the plains of eastern and southwestern Australia, but thousands of persons in the port cities of Sydney and Melbourne, and of other ports, are completely dependent upon marketing, warehousing, and shipping of wool.

Australia leads the world in five aspects of its wool industry: There are some 115 million sheep in the Commonwealth, more than in any other country; this is about ten sheep per inhabitant. But more important than numbers are the other aspects. The average weight of Australian fleeces is greater than that elsewhere, a reflection of the fine quality of the sheep. Thirdly, the sheepmen have bred and perfected a type of Merino sheep admirably suited to the Australian environment —they have fitted the animal to Australian conditions. Fourthly, the stockmen have improved the environment, enabling the range to carry more sheep. And all resources have been turned to produce the highest money value for wool; in other words the emphasis of this last aspect has been upon quality at all costs.

The plains of the southeast are the leading wool region. On their east these plains abut against the highlands of the Great Dividing Range, which separates the plains from the narrow and humid eastern coastal strip. From this eastern border the plains stretch westward, becoming increasingly drier; the higher eastern portion is subhumid, and westward there are gradations to semi-arid in the vicinity of the Darling River, and arid to the west—as the plains continue into the desert interior of the continent. The slightly higher, eastern subhumid part of the plains is sheep and wheat country. Wheat disappears westward, and sheep alone constitute the economic base of settlements. Sheep are reared as far into the desert as there is water, but sheep stations in the arid lands are few and far between and are localized either by natural springs (an oasis in the Old World) or by a man-drilled artesian well. The pattern of the sheep country is a great crescent, its horns faced inland, and its body between the Great Dividing Range and the desert interior. From southern Queensland, the crescent swings through interior New South Wales, into western Victoria, and ends near Adelaide in South Australia. The sheep and wool lands, lying across the mountains from the port cities, is the Outback to the urban peoples.

The second, and far smaller—in area and production—wool region of Australia lies in the southwest, in the state of Western Australia. Here, too, the sheep lands are inland; the back slopes and escarpment of the Darling Range is between these plains and the coast. Here, too, is semiarid to subhumid sheep country, aridity increasing inland, or to the east in this region. Perth serves the area; its outport is the exporting point.

Australian sheep are reared on large landholdings which would be called ranches in North America, but are known there as stations. Land is abundant, labor is scarce, rainfall is erratic and unpredictable in quantity and only from ten to twenty inches per year on the "average," but averages are misleading in this subhumid and semiarid country. Droughts every few years are normal. The adjustment to these conditions is the large station, and station sizes increase westward in response to aridity. Originally, too, the lack of competition for the land from the native aborigines of the continent permitted the large holding to develop. Some of the largest stations contain 150,000 to 200,000 acres, or from about 230 to 315 square miles, but this is unusual. The more humid wheat-sheep country has smaller stations—really only large farms. More important than areal size is the size of the flock; the larger stations maintain as many as 50,000 sheep apiece; smaller operations have fewer, but the number may still run into several thousand. The wheat-sheep farms may have a thousand sheep. The critical element of wool sheep to area is not to total area, but is the number of sheep per station or farm that can be carried through a drought year. This reflects the careful management of the sheep pastures, and the adjustment of sheep to the Australian environmental conditions.

Breeding farms for the rearing of high-quality rams were established in Australia as early as the 1850's. Superior stock was imported from Europe. Special

FIG. 8-8. The shearing sheds at the headquarters of an Australian sheep station. Australia leads the world in its sheep industry, in the high quality of its sheep, and in the weight of the individual fleeces. More than 70,000 sheep are shorn in a six-week period at this station. (Australian News and Information Bureau)

strains were developed, all looking to the production of a heavy fleece of fine Merino wool. The results of years of development are shown by a doubling of the weight of the Australian fleece sheared from each sheep. Present wool growers usually do not rear their own rams, but purchase them from specialized stud stations, most of which are located in the Riverina—that part of the Outback or back slopes west of the mountains, and between the westward-flowing Murray and Murrumbidgee rivers. The principal income of the stud stations is derived from the sale of rams, but the income from the sale of wool from the breeding flock is not inconsiderable.

Pasture improvement has been accomplished in several ways. Instead of the early practice of allowing sheep to graze at will on the landholdings, the stations fence pastures of about 1,500 to 2,000 acres each, called paddocks. The enclosures have water within them in the form either of a permanent stream or an artesian well, dominantly the latter. Windmills power the pumps. Some pastures have been improved by fertilization and seeding. With fencing, the native grasses of other pastures have regenerated, for the sheep can be moved from one paddock to another, permitting some pastures to rest. Each pasture has a plowed strip around it, inside the fence. This controls grass fires, a pasture hazard in dry seasons and years, or enables firefighters to direct the fire, if possible, toward the bare ground and so save much of the grass. The bare strips, and the trampled ground near the water supply, also serve to protect the sheep, who retreat—or can be driven—to these non-vegetated areas in the event of a grass fire. Control of fires keeps the pasture in good condition, for a burned-over area may take two to three years before it again provides browse.

Overgrazing is not permitted. This is accomplished by having an animal population not in excess of the feed supply of the expectable drought years. In wet years, when there is excess grass, some enclosures are not grazed, but their grass is cut and baled as hay and stored against the dry season or year. If an individual decides to have these paddocks grazed instead, he keeps animals (to utilize the surplus) that can be liquidated if drought appears—beef cattle, or sheep for mutton. And on each large station some land near the stream or water source is irrigated, and alfalfa is grown and stored for the impending dry year. Hay can be kept in stacks for ten to twelve years in the dry air of the wool country.

Large fires, the depredations of rabbits, competition of kangaroos for the grass, and certain diseases of sheep are difficulties encountered on the stations. Forty rabbits consume as much feed as one sheep, and the rabbit—introduced from England—is Australia's greatest pest. The outer boundaries of all stations are required to have rabbit-proof fences; within the station borders, a crew of men finds year-long employment in the destruction and poisoning of rabbits.

The station headquarters is the working center. The owner, manager (if there is one), and workers live in the houses at the location, the site of which has commonly been determined by the existence of a water supply. The musterers (shepherds), rabbit crews, and other workers fan out daily from the headquarters. Nearby are the sheep pens, shearing sheds, shops, gasoline storage tanks, and other equipment and buildings. Each station is completely mechanized, and the facilities for gasoline storage are large.

Sheep shearing in Australia is performed by specialized crews who do nothing else, and who travel from station to station. Sheep are driven from paddocks into the shearing shed, in which each pen and door leads to an individual shearer. The shearer, using motor-driven shears, removes the fleece—a shearer averages 100 or more sheep each working day. "Picker-uppers" carry the fleece to the wool room or toss it onto the wool-sorting tables, where it is sorted, trimmed or skirted, and classed. A wool classer travels with the shearing teams, and, as a highly skilled worker upon whom the grading depends, is a well-paid individual. After the fleeces have been classed, they are baled by general class. Sheep are sheared for six or seven years, following which the yield of wool usually declines and the animal is sold for mutton.

Wool is forwarded by truck or rail to the warehouse centers and wool markets in the exporting ports. In Western Australia some is shipped to small ports and lightered along the coast to Perth. But the wool-growing region of the southeastern plains is generally tributary to either Sydney or Melbourne, and these two cities contain the largest markets and are the chief exporting ports. Other cities have considerable wool trade, among them Adelaide, Geelong, Brisbane, and Hobart. Regular wool auctions are held at all of the chief wool-marketing centers.

Australian, and other, wool exported to western Europe and the United States passes through well-developed and long-established wool markets. London and Liverpool in England, Antwerp in Belgium, Le Havre in France, and Boston in the United States are major wool-importing centers, and wool-marketing points at or near the chief wool-consuming manufacturing regions.

▶ SILK

Silk is an animal fiber. The silk thread is unwound from the cocoon of the silkworm, which is indigenous to China, Japan, and India.

The silkworm is hatched from an egg laid by a moth. During its life span the worm feeds on several types of leaves, chief of which is the mulberry, and it is the leaf of the white mulberry upon which worms are fed under commercial production. At a certain stage in its life cycle, it spins a cocoon around itself. The fine silk threads of the cocoon are spun from the lower lip of the worm; eventually, as the cocoon is completed, the animal is encased.

Man interferes with nature's normal process at this time. He heats the cocoon by immersing it in a basin of warm water and thus kills the chrysalis inside. The cocoons are then unwound by hand, a long, tedious process—still the practice in parts of China—or are delivered to a factory called a filature. At the filature a girl with deft hands starts the unwinding process, attaching the thread of silk to a machine, and the rest of the silk composing the cocoon is unwound quickly by the machine.

Some cocoons are allowed to continue on the normal life span in order to obtain moth eggs for future production. In this case, in time the chrysalis inside becomes a moth, which emerges from the cocoon. Eventually the eggs laid by the moth, hatched into silkworms, continue the process. In Japan the government has aided and fostered the silk industry, has established hatcheries in which the eggs are hatched, has established experiment stations for silk, and, through stringent laws and practices, has upgraded the quality of silkworms and rid the country of diseased eggs. The hatcheries distribute disease-free eggs to the farmers. All Japanese cocoons are delivered to filatures.

"Raw silk" has two connotations. The baled and unmanufactured silk sent from filature to textile mill, or exported, is said to be raw silk. A second connotation of "raw silk" in the trade is the silk manufactured from wild cocoons, gathered in the forests, spun by wild silkworms that have fed upon oak leaves. The cultivated silks are finer, smoother, and more lustrous than the "raw silks" of the second connotation. The yarn made from the wild "raw silk" is called douppioni, and the fabric manufactured from this (also referred to as raw silk goods) are, in appearance, much like manufactured wool goods; they have become important recently because of their ability to hold color when washed.

The Labor Factor

Abundant, skilled, and cheap labor is necessary in the commercial production of silkworms. Only the crowded Orient and densely peopled Italy have been able to furnish the requisite labor through any period of time, and it is China, Japan, Korea, and Italy which furnish the silk of the world. Manufacturing centers, where the textiles are produced, are near the chief markets—in the Orient itself, in western Europe, and in the United States. Minor silk-producing regions are located in the Middle East. Some silk is produced in the Indian subcontinent. But in India, despite its cheap labor, the Hindu religion forbids the taking of animal life, and so Hindus refuse to kill the chrysalis inside the cocoon. Thus "Indian silk" is produced in small quantities only in Moslem or Christian villages in India, or in neighboring Moslem Pakistan.

The distribution of the mulberry tree, whose leaves are used for feed in all commercial production, does not localize the areas of production. The mulberry grows in all warm temperate realms, and especially thrives in the humid subtropics. Labor is dominant. The daily picking of leaves and the care of silkworms require a twenty-four-hour vigil on the part of the farm family during the rearing and feeding season. Thus, within the warm temperate lands, only a few regions of skilled but inexpensive labor produce silk.

Silk culture has been tried in the American South, and has failed because of the cost of labor. It failed in Virginia with indentured labor in the seventeenth century. It failed using slave labor, which was expensive as the workers had to be maintained, clothed, and fed. The mulberry is widespread, the southern climate is suitable; but the industry has not flourished because of costs. France produced silk for a time until labor costs forced the activity from the scene. A few specialized silkworm establishments have been maintained, outside of the Orient and Italy, only by governmental subventions; thus the one English silk farm at Lullingstone produces home-grown silk for special purposes only, such as coronations of royalty.

Production

The care and rearing of silk worms, as practiced in Japan, illustrates the intensity of the industry in many portions of the Orient. Throughout the southern two-thirds of Japan the industry is, in general, an adjunct to general farming or to specialized production of rice and vegetables. In the mountains of central Honshu—the main island—silk culture is the overwhelming agricultural enterprise, and is not auxiliary to other activities. But in both areas the activity is one which requires the full-time energy of the farm family during the season when the worms are being fed.

The mulberry tree is the chief "commercial" tree of Japan, and mulberry acreage exceeds fruit acreage. The mulberry will grow on land unsuitable for other purposes, and it does not need to be irrigated. It is grown on hard-rock thin-soil foothills, on upland plateaus, on diluvial terraces that lie high and dry above flood plains and delta plains that are devoted to paddy rice, on coarse rocky alluvial fans, and on ash-soil plains. Other less significant, but locally important sites for the mulberry are sandy beach ridges and river levees. In other words, the mulberry—sometimes called "a goat among trees"—thrives on land that is marginal for many uses or that is unsuited for many uses. Competition for the land in densely settled Japan is severe; the mulberry is forced from areas suited for a higher, more productive use. It furnishes hill farmers, who have poor land but ample family labor, with the raw material for the maintenance of silkworms, and the government furnishes him, for a fee, with high-quality eggs from the moth.

The great intensity of sericulture in mountainous central Honshu reflects the need for a labor-using activity in a region where labor is very abundant relative to arable land. The region is relatively inaccessible, yet the final product—silk—is high in value per unit of weight and pays its transportation costs easily. In the basins and valleys of the mountains mulberries occupy foothill situations and extend up the slopes several hundred feet. Villages are at the base, and the mulberry trees are thus accessible. The value of hill land for mulberry growth depends upon the ease of reaching it, usually by walking; as silkworms must have a constant and fresh supply of leaves to feed on, the most distant trees must be within the limits of an hour's round trip, including the time needed for picking the leaves.

Silkworms are kept in special rooms in the farm homes, or in the kitchen, or, recently, in specially built, but small, buildings. Room temperatures must be from 62° to 78°F. Trays of worms are stored in shelves. Members of the family work twenty-four hours a day in order to keep a constant supply of fresh leaves on the trays. Mulberry trees are pruned to bush height in order to facilitate picking and save time during the feeding season; and enough leaves must be picked late in daylight hours to ensure feed for the night.

The sericultural regions of mountainous central Japan obtain only one picking of mulberry leaves, and the tremendous activity of the hatching and feeding season is telescoped into six to eight weeks. Farmers at lower altitudes, and those of southern Honshu and Kyushu, can obtain two to three pickings of leaves. Thus —and it is personal choice—they can rear two or three hatchings of silkworms and extend the season to about four months or more.

The sericulture of Italy is centered in the lower Alpine valleys tributary to the western part of the Po Valley of the north. Silkworm-rearing establishments are the operating units. These are long, low heated buildings. Several long tables extend the length of the rooms and are separated by aisles for the workers. A matting or bed of brush and straw is built up on each table to provide a warm bed, and the room is both heated and ventilated for adequate protection. Groves of mulberry trees surround the buildings. Workers, on a semi-specialized basis, thus cultivate and care for the trees part of the year and engage in the picking activities during the season. Other workers inside the buildings see to the care of the worms, spread the mulberry leaves on the brush-base, and keep the tables covered with a continuous and fresh supply of leaves for the worms, which are voracious feeders. The farm rearing of silkworms is not unknown in the Po Valley, but the factorylike specialization of individuals and companies in the activity provides a scene quite different from that of the usual in the Orient. But Italian labor, hired by the rearing establishments, though more expensive than that of the Orient, is still cheap enough by European standards to permit Italy to be the only important producer of raw silk outside of the Far East.

Silk Trade

Markets of the world have demanded silk since the days of Marco Polo and the development of sea and caravan routes from Europe to China and India. Japan's entrance into the production of raw silk for export dates back only one hundred years. When Perry "opened" Japan in 1853 the nation did not produce enough silk for its own needs.

Japan captured the bulk of the prewar silk trade. The government aid to the industry and the insistence upon high quality were the chief factors in this. China, leading producer in quantity, hardly figured in foreign trade and consumed its silk at home; Japan forced China from the world markets. During the 1930's raw silk accounted for from 40 to 45 per cent of Japan's annual exports. The United States was the major market. In return, American raw cotton moved westward across the Pacific and was one of Japan's chief imports; its cotton-textile industry mushroomed. Cotton brokers in Texas and elsewhere were as interested in the price of cotton in Osaka as they were in prices in Liverpool, England.

Then came two overlapping events. World War II stopped the trade completely. The development of rayon and other synthetic fibers provided silk with severe and increasing competition. Rayon was first exhibited as a silk substitute in 1889; its manufacture began early in the century; but its large-scale production did not develop until the 1920's and early 1930's. Between 1933 and 1936 alone its output in the world increased by 50 per cent, and the industry and the fabric was firmly established before the outbreak of World War II. The war, serving to halt world trade in silk, served indirectly to increase the output of silk substitutes in the world.

Imports of unmanufactured raw silk into the United States from all source regions (but mainly Japan) averaged, in value, more than $100,000,000 per year during the ten-year period of 1931–1940. They dropped during the war years of 1941–1945 to but $12,600,000. Despite inflation and the much lower value of the dollar, the postwar value, during fifteen years, reached only a high of $33 million in one year. This illustrates, in value, one of the results of the war and the competition of silk substitutes for the textile market. It illustrates, also, the trend mentioned earlier of the mixing of fabrics, so that silk and rayon or silk and some other yarn may be woven together.

A second postwar trend in the world silk picture, illustrated by the United States figures, has been an increase in the silk-textile industry of the silk-producing countries themselves. Rather than exporting raw silk Japan and other producers have enlarged their home manufactures, employed home labor, and now export manufactured silks. In value, during recent years, the imported silk dress materials and yarns into the United States have exceeded the value of the raw silk. Thus there has been a definite trend toward a relative increase of silk manufacture in silkworm-producing regions, and a relative decrease of manufactures near the consuming market.

Coupled with the above trends, the world output of silk fabrics (silk alone, and not mixed) has declined by half from prewar days to the present. Yearly figures vary, but the trend has been continuous. Fashion dictates are one of the chief factors in yearly or seasonal variations, for much of the ultimate consumption of silk fabrics is by women. Thus the fashion trend of "the Oriental Look" in women's dresses during the late 1950's resulted in a world-wide increase in the use of silk.

► LINEN

Flax is a small grain—like wheat, rye, barley, and oats. But unlike these other small grains the flax seed is inedible. In commercial agriculture flax for seed is handled like any other small grain; the same type of farm machinery is used in its production.

The flax plant, whose botantical name is *Linum usitatissimum,* is the raw material for linseed oil and for linen fiber. When grown for its oil, which is contained in the flaxseeds (grain) the plant is allowed to mature, is cut and threshed, and the seeds are sold to a linseed-oil mill. Linseed meal, a concentrated feed for cattle, is a by-product of the oil industry. When grown for its fiber the plant is not permitted to mature. Flax fiber, contained in the stalks, is a bast fiber beneath the bark.

Most of the world's flax acreage outside of Europe is for seed. The grain-producing regions of the Pampas of Argentina, the wheat belts of the United States and Canada, and others grow flax for seed alone. The paucity of labor in these areas and the complete mechanization of a large-scale and extensive agriculture preclude the production for the fiber—for this phase of flax culture possesses a large and demanding labor requirement. The flaxseed industry is thus associated almost entirely with the great grain regions of the world. In these regions flax is a secondary crop, but its total production is large.

Fiber flax is produced in Northern Ireland, in Belgium, and in an extensive agricultural region (the Rye-Potato-Flax Belt of Europe) that extends from East Germany eastward across Poland and the north-central portion of the Soviet Union in Europe. Poland and Russia are the chief producers of flax for fiber. During World War II, when fiber from the east was unavailable, new and small fiber-flax regions were developed in Peru and New Zealand. The Irish acreage was increased at this time, as was the Egyptian. Fiber flax has been a small, but important crop in the Nile Valley since antiquity; linen cloth has been preserved in the tombs of Egypt since the early dynasties. Linen is mentioned frequently in the Bible.

Flax grown for fiber is not allowed to seed fully, but workers pull it from the ground before it has matured. From this time until the fiber is sold to buyers for linen mills there is a large hand-labor requirement. The seeds are pulled off by drawing the plant through a comb, care being taken not to damage the straw. The flax straw is dried for a time and then is submerged in water for the retting process—the term retting being a corruption of the word "rotting." During the retting period of late summer and early autumn, the action of bacteria in the water weakens the resin which binds the bast fiber to the straw (or "bark"). When the process is complete, the straw and fiber is removed by hand from the water, and the mass of material is delivered to a scutch mill. These mills prepare the raw flax by removing the woody matter by a machine process, and clean the fiber. After this process, the finished raw flax is ready for market and is sent to spinning mills for its conversion into linen yarn.

The chief flax-fiber-growing regions use different methods of retting; their rural landscape differs during the retting season. In Northern Ireland the straw is immersed in artificial ponds dug on the farms for this purpose, and the straw is weighted down with sod and stones to keep it submerged. In Belgium the slow-moving rivers of the Flanders Plain are used for the retting, and the straw is sunk in weighted crates and boxes. The flax retted in the River Lys is of exceptionally high quality—the Belgians claim this to be the result of the type of water. In Poland and Russia the straw is dew-retted. It is spread out over grassy fields and the moisture from the atmosphere and from almost nightly dews is allowed to react with the straw for a considerable period of time. Polish and Russian flax is apt to be retted unevenly, and sometimes is discolored. Some farmers use the many glacial lakes and ponds of Poland and northwestern Russia for the retting.

Northern Ireland and Belgium are the important linen-manufacturing centers of Europe. The industry is dispersed in lesser concentrations elsewhere. But Irish linens, Belgian laces, and the other products of the linen textile mills of Belfast, Londonderry, Courtrai, and other cities of these lands are well known for quality and are exported to all parts of the world. The United States imports many of its linens; home-manufactured linen cloth is fabricated from imported raw flax, as very little fiber flax is grown in this country except on a few farms in Oregon and Pennsylvania, and on the farms of one or two state prisons. The cost of labor has kept the fiber-flax industry from American farms; the few prison farms that produce fiber do so to aid in the gainful employment of their prison populations.

▶ SYNTHETIC FIBERS

The synthetic fibers are man-made. The rise of synthetic fibers has been the result of many factors. Some have been developed in the search for a substitute for a natural fiber. Many have been first developed or perfected in the chemical laboratories of large manufacturing companies—primarily chemical companies—in the search for new or additional products which might be manufactured by the organization. Some research in the laboratory has been stimulated by a short-age of a natural fiber; for example, the wartime shortage of silk stimulated research for a man-made fiber that might replace silk in such a vital use as the parachute. Some fibers have been developed by an industry looking for a new use for its principal product; the glass companies were interested in marketing their product in a new form, and Fiberglas—used even for some articles of clothing—is an example of a result. Currently much research is being carried forward on "wool substitutes" because recently the world use of wool has been greater than the supply.

The basic and original raw materials of the synthetic fibers are earth resources of one kind or another. Man still lives from the earth. Sand is basic to the manu-facture of glass, a chemical process may involve the use of sulfuric acid and sulfur is dug from the earth, the cellulose of wood or of cotton may be an original material for the manufacture of rayon. Coal, limestone, air, and water are used for certain products.

The manufacture of rayon, whose usual raw material is wood, illustrates how man makes the artificial fibers, though there are differences in the manufacture of each. Thread is produced by driving the cellulose through small aperatures, and the fine filaments are wound together to form thread; the threads themselves are then wound, or combined into yarn for textile mills, use in tire cords, and many other uses.

The source region, or the plant locations, for such synthetic fibers as Nylon 66, Acrilan, Orlon, Dynel, and Dacron are the areas where the chemical industry is located—and the original location was determined by other factors, and the plants were located, for the most part, before the specific fibers became of commercial importance. The two principal regional locations in the United States are the Texas Gulf Coast and West Virginia. The hydrocarbon and chemical raw

FIG. 8-9. A cellulose mill at Prince Rupert, British Columbia, on the western coast of Canada. Wood from the forests is converted into cellulose, from which a legion of additional products is manufactured at other locations. Among these are materials for the synthetic or "artificial" fibers. (Canadian Information Office)

materials used in these two regions are first transformed into chemical inter-mediates, and then these are manufactured or transformed into the specific fibers. The making of the yarn is then carried on in these or other locations.

The markets for synthetic textile fibers and yarns are in the same areas as the markets for animal and plant fibers—namely the textile-manufacturing regions such as the American South and New England.

The uses of the synthetic fibers have been extended. Nylon, which sprang into prominence in the women's hosiery business in the early 1940's, when silk was unobtainable from Japan, has invaded the rope, fishline, toothbrush, broom, tire cord, and many other markets, replacing or competing with former raw materials, such as rayon, hemp, linen cord, bristles, broomcorn, long-staple cotton.

Plastic materials, synthetic fibers and similar products, or combinations are now so usual that countless items are molded or woven from them. Formerly simple statistical separation of the plant and animal fibers are now complicated by the modern chemical or man-made products. Thus government figures of broad-woven fabrics (in addition to cotton, wool, and silk) now must include figures on fabrics composed of rayon, acetate fibers, nylons, glass fibers, and combinations. And, the trends in the world and the United States have been such that the man-made fibers are of increasing relative and absolute importance. They have almost completely replaced natural fibers in a few special uses, and are competing in others.

Synthetics outside of the United States

Rayon manufacture and the production and use of rayon yarn is outstanding in western Europe and Japan. This reflects their dependence upon imported ani-mal or plant fibers from other parts of the world, and, consequently, the desire and even necessity of substitution of rayon and of synthetic fibers in the textile industry. Some of the synthetic fibers, developed and patented in the United States, are not available for use in Europe or Japan unless licensed by the Ameri-can company or unless a foreign subsidiary factory is founded abroad.

Japan follows the United States in the production of rayon staple yarn. West Germany and Britain are important producers, the former using imported and home grown wood as a raw material, Britain depending upon imported wood from Scandinavia. Italy and France also have an important industry. Norway and Sweden use their water power and wood in yarn manufacture but export the yarn to the other countries of the manufacturing regions of Europe, as their home textile industry and market are small, owing to the small totals of the Scan-dinavian population.

The principal textile centers of western Europe are the consumers of rayon and other synthetic fibers. The situation of mixing materials is the same as in the United States. Japan has a very large textile industry, which has been par-ticularly successful in exporting rayon piece goods as well as cotton textiles to world markets. Textile imports into the United States from Japan exceed those from all of western Europe. The low labor costs in Japan are very significant items in permitting the tapping of a world-wide market in the cotton and rayon textile fields, especially.

The Soviet rayon industry is not large, but is increasing in size. Manufacture is chiefly in the textile centers north of Moscow.

► QUESTIONS

1. What are the environmental requirements for the growing of cotton?
2. Cotton from the middle latitudes (such as the humid subtropics of the American South or the Mediterranean lands of Europe or California) competes with cotton grown in tropical lands. Name some other products wherein there is competition for markets between a producing region in the middle latitudes and one in the tropics.
3. What factors have caused American-grown cotton to decline in importance *relatively* in the world?
4. The centers of cotton culture have shifted westward in the United States cotton-growing region. Why?
5. Yields of cotton lint per acre are higher in Arizona, in California, in Egypt than in the Cotton Belt of the American South. Explain why.
6. Why are the principal sheep-rearing lands in the middle-latitude dry climates of the world?
7. What factors have been important in Australia's specialization in wool and its continued dominance of the wool production of the world?
8. Where is wool used as a fiber in manufacturing? Name some of the chief wool-importing and wool-using countries.
9. Discuss the competition which silk must meet in the textile industry.
10. Why is the rearing of silkworms confined essentially to the Orient when many other areas of the world are climatically suitable for the mulberry tree?
11. Linen, a material used for clothing in Europe before the Age of Discovery, is now in the luxury class. What factors and circumstances account for this change?
12. What are some of the synthetic fibers? What industry or industries produce the various synthetic yarns?
13. Briefly discuss the competition (and mixing) among the animal fibers, plant fibers, and synthetic fibers.

IX The Tobacco Industry

Tobacco, native to the New World and unknown to Europeans or Asiatics until the Period of Discovery, is now grown in almost every country on earth. The range of the tobacco plant is practically from the northern limits of important agriculture in the Northern Hemisphere to the southern limits in the Southern. Tobacco is grown on tropical uplands and in the wet-and-dry tropics. The wide range of the plant is one of the principal reasons why foreign trade in tobacco leaf is relatively small, considering the quantity grown; each country tends to grow its own supply. But nations with large populations relative to area import leaf to supplement their home crop; thus western Europe and Egypt are major importers. And the United Kingdom, the chief importer, has always prohibited the growing of tobacco at home, and uses the import duties as a source of governmental revenue.

The type of tobacco leaf, despite the wide extent of its growth, is closely related to soil types and broadly related to the climatic type in which it is produced. Thus tropical tobacco is generally heavy, strong, and dark. Tobacco from the Mediterranean realm is small, narrow-leaf, and aromatic; called Turkish tobacco, the Mediterranean types are in demand for blending. Tobacco from the Southern United States differs from that grown in Wisconsin or New England, and "brown leaf" and "bright yellow leaf" originate in different settings. But the closest relationship of tobacco to the environment in which it is grown is to soils. Tobacco grown in the heavy soils of the southern Piedmont is heavy in body and of a dark color. Tobacco from the sandy soils of the inner Coastal Plain of eastern North Carolina is bright yellow or yellow-brown when cured. And there are soil relationships in the tropically grown tobaccos also. The curing process, and the type of curing, affect tobacco leaf as well. Thus experts in the trade recognize several hundred types of tobacco. Some leaf is classified as cigar leaf, some for use in cigarettes; certain types are used in blending. Cool, northern tobacco districts produce a tough leaf, or binder tobacco which is used beneath the wrapper leaf to hold a cigar together. In contrast, fine wrapper leaf is grown under artificial shade provided by cheesecloth stretched on poles above a tobacco field, and some wrappers are imported into the middle latitudes from tropical growing areas.

Certain features, evident in the landscape, accompany the growing of tobacco. One is the nursery bed, or seed bed, in which tobacco seed is planted. There are 300,000 or more seeds to the ounce. The small seeds, sprouting in the tended seed bed, yield so many plants that thinning by hand is necessary. Following this, when the young plants are of sufficient size for handling, they are transplanted to the fields. A second evident cultural feature is the tobacco barn, a specialized building. Air-tight barns are built for either the flue-curing or fire-curing of leaf. Open and ventilated barns are built for air-curing. In all methods of curing the harvested tobacco is hung in the barn. In flue-curing heat is circulated through flues. In fire-curing a slowly burning wood fire is kept going on the earthern floor of the barn, and a temperature of 90° to 95°F is maintained; smoke escapes by means of vents. In air-curing, which takes a month or more, depending upon weather conditions, the open-slatted barn or a barn with removable boards every few feet is used. The different methods used in curing tobacco leaf, like differences in climate and soils in the producing districts, account for some of the variations and differences in the leaf placed upon the market. And, in the tropical world, where barns for most purposes are almost nonexistent, the presence of tobacco barns in the landscape is a striking feature— one indicative of the growing of tobacco, present even during the period of year when the plants are not evident in the fields.

▶ REGIONS OF PRODUCTION

Tobacco culture is so widespread around the inhabited world that practically every nation contains some acreage. But tobacco, unlike the grain crops, cotton, and the animal industries, does not occupy a large and continuous acreage in the regions where it is grown. Instead, tobacco acreage is concentrated in small districts, of which there may be many disconnected ones in an overall tobacco region. Between these intensive districts of production, tobacco may disappear from the landscape. Thus, the world's tobacco originates mainly in scattered producing areas, which collectively may be called "Tobacco Belts." And, within these belts, one county or minor civil division may contain a large acreage, the next almost none.

Human choice, the availability of labor, the accident of an early start, and the continuance of a rooted activity help explain the location of many districts. The name for quality, the training of generations of farmers, local marketing facilities, and other factors help explain the continuance of the districts in tobacco culture. Yet some tobacco regions of the past have ceased production, usually because a competitive and more profitable enterprise has become available; at one time tobacco was cultivated widely in New York State; with the advent of intensive dairying, the availability of urban markets for fresh milk, and the shortage of farm labor, the cultivation of tobacco virtually ceased. Today there are fewer than a thousand acres of tobacco in the whole state. And other areas with a large supply of family labor—owing to a high local birth rate—have expanded their acreage. And, with changes in the use of tobacco, cigarette-leaf areas have expanded whereas cigar-leaf and chewing-leaf districts have declined or remained stationary.

The United States, mainly in the Upper South, and China grow the world's largest amount of tobacco. The production in India, the Soviet Union, and in western Europe collectively is about the same in poundage. Brazil's crop is not far behind any one of these three last-named. Japan's crop is slightly less in quantity. And in all these nations or areas there exist many specialized tobacco-growing districts.

Canada's chief tobacco districts are two in number, the Old Belt and the New, each in Ontario north of Lake Erie; some tobacco is produced in the St. Lawrence Valley also. The Old Belt production originated and expanded in part, more than a hundred years ago, with the introduction of southern American Negroes, familiar with tobacco, during the days of the "Underground Railroad" before the Civil War, when Negroes were transported to Canada to be freed. This is an example of historical introduction; but the Negro farmer is no longer important in the area, and others engage in the tobacco growing.

Three outlying tobacco regions, not too large in total poundage, are important in tobacco exports and in the growing of "specialty" tobaccos. These are the West Indies, particularly Cuba, the northeastern shorelands of the Mediterranean Sea, and Southern Rhodesia in the Federation of Rhodesia and Nyasaland in southern Africa.

Cuban tobacco, marketed as Havana tobacco, is a cigar leaf. The western province of the island, Pinar del Rio, is the major producing district. Tobacco follows sugar in Cuba's export scene, but, despite its importance, is a poor second in value. The Dominican Republic and Puerto Rico also grow cigar leaf.

Tobacco from the eastern Mediterranean is a small, narrow leaf, is mild, and is in demand for blending in the manufacture of cigarettes. It is called Turkish tobacco, the name dating from the days when the Ottoman Empire ruled the entire area. Present production is divided among several countries, particularly Greece and Bulgaria, but also Turkey and Lebanon.

Southern Rhodesia grows the American-type tobacco, called Virginia tobacco in the Federation. The United Kingdom imports practically the entire production.

World tobacco exports are directed almost completely to western Europe, except for West Indian and Turkish tobacco, which reach the United States as well. But the United States is a net exporter, sending about a quarter of its leaf to Europe. Within Europe only five countries are usual exporters—Greece, Bulgaria, Yugoslavia, Hungary, and Italy. The Italian production illustrates the growing of tobacco in specialty districts, for there are districts in seventeen provinces, and they occur from the base of the Alps in the north southward to Sicily. The leading areas are in the southern one-third of the peninsula, however.

► TOBACCO IN THE UNITED STATES

The tobacco production of the United States is the world's largest—a fifth of the total. Although there is tobacco acreage in twenty-one of the states, a well-defined "Tobacco Belt" (though not called that) lies in the Upper South. The belt, in which there are many tobacco-growing districts, lies in the latitudes between the Corn Belt and the Cotton Belt, and extends east-west from near the Atlantic Ocean almost to the Mississippi River. Five states—Kentucky and Virginia on the north, and Tennessee, North Carolina, and part of South Carolina, form the heart of the tobacco lands and collectively contain four-fifths of the American acreage and production. The Appalachian Mountains divide the acreage of Virginia from that of Kentucky; but southward the cultivation of tobacco extends right across the mountains from Tennessee to North Carolina, and some tobacco is grown at altitudes as high as 3,500 to 4,000 feet in mountain coves.

Southward from the Upper South, tobacco production is important in southern Georgia (the sixth producer) and adjacent northern Florida. And northward from Virginia, the state of Maryland and adjacent southeastern Pennsylvania (particularly Lancaster County) are significant producers.

The principal tobacco-producing districts lie in an overall area characterized by general farming. Tobacco is one of several cash crops or feed crops, but in the specialized districts it is the principal one and usually the only cash crop. If the farm income from the sale of tobacco reaches a defined percentage of the total farm income, the particular farm is classified as a tobacco farm by the Census; thus the specialized districts usually stand out, but by no means does all tobacco originate on "tobacco farms." Much comes from general farms on which other cash crops are sold—some cotton and peanuts in eastern North Carolina, milk in parts of eastern Tennessee, livestock in many Kentucky regions. And, overall, the acreage of corn and hay exceeds the total cultivated land in tobacco by far. But it is the tobacco field or tobacco patch which is of greatest value per acre, and the cured leaf which is the principal source of income for thousands of farmers of the Upper South. In North Carolina alone, the leading tobacco state, almost 200,000 farmers raise the leaf; one county in East Tennessee has more than 4,000 individual growers; many counties have 80 per cent or more of their farms engaged in producing tobacco.

The individual field or patch of tobacco is usually small in size. A twenty-acre field is unusual; ten acres is considered large in most districts. In hilly and mountainous East Tennessee the patch is rarely more than one acre in size, and county averages of tobacco-per-farm are less than one acre for many counties. The federal government, under its crop-control programs, allots acreage to farmers. The original allotments were based on usual acreages grown; with reductions and changes, the field of tobacco has decreased in size proportionally. Thus when an eighth reduction was made one year, a sixteen-acre field became fourteen, a one-acre allotment became seven-eighths of an acre.

Production has increased in spite of acreage-control programs. The smaller field or plot has been fertilized more heavily. New fertilizers and new types of

FIG. 9-1. Air-cured burley tobacco being delivered to the auction floor of a tobacco warehouse in the Tobacco Belt of the southern United States. (Knoxville Journal)

tobacco, such as root-disease-resistant ones, have been developed by Agricultural Experiment Stations. And, to the individual farmer, additional labor and care expended upon a smaller acreage is important in his yearly income. The usual support prices, penalties, and other aspects of the governmental programs have entered the scene, and the government support price, determined annually, is a floor or base beyond which the buyers for the manufacturing companies may bid in the annual auctioning of the crop.

There are several economic, geographic, and even historical factors that have been operative in delimiting and holding the present chief tobacco region to the general location it occupies between the commercial Corn Belt and the commercial Cotton Belt. Among these are the following, not in order of significance in all districts, for a chief factor in one of the growing areas may be of secondary or tertiary importance in another.

(1) The historical development of tobacco culture on colonial plantations in Tidewater Virginia, coupled with inland migration, or the westward movement of persons trained in growing the plant has been important. Many of the original indentured servants moved inland in Virginia, or to North Carolina, when their period of indenture was terminated. Later the tide of migration down the Appalachian valleys from the middle states of the seaboard, then westward through Cumberland Gap into Kentucky, helped spread tobacco cultivation. Furthermore, at this period of self-sufficient agriculture tobacco was grown in the Virginia-Kentucky "migration area" for home use. Some of the estates established in early days by planters who moved to the Kentucky Blue Grass Basin were based upon tobacco and slave labor. All told, the early start has been important in many districts.

(2) The lack of competition from other cash crops has been very significant recently—or, stated otherwise, the inability of the chief tobacco area to grow cotton, as it is poleward of its limit, or to grow corn on a large scale, because of rough terrain or soil types, or both, has led to emphasis on tobacco as a needed source of income.

There is little overlap between cotton and tobacco. The Kentucky and Virginia acreage is north of cotton. The acreage of tobacco in mid-Tennessee is poleward; the eastern Tennessee acreage is both poleward, and altitudinally higher, and tobacco culture extends into many mountain districts. The North Carolina tobacco grown in the Piedmont lies beyond the limit of cotton, and some of the tobacco land of the Coastal Plain of both Carolinas lies east of the principal cotton districts. Only in the recently expanded bright-tobacco district of North Carolina, the source region of much cigarette tobacco (and hence expansion with the rise of cigarettes), is there overlap. Even here, the large grower tends to specialize in one crop or the other; the two are completely competitive for the time and labor of the farmer, the peak labor seasons coinciding.

The portion of the Tobacco Belt west of the Appalachian Highlands is rough, broken country on the whole. Slopes are steep, even if short. Hilly country and true hill lands, narrow V-shaped valleys, and narrow ridge tops preclude large fields. The Corn Belt type of agriculture is difficult to practice over large areas; tobacco fills a need for an intensive crop which can be grown on a small area. Locally, on good soil and flat surfaces, small districts practice a Corn Belt-animal economy, but generally the intensive cash crop of tobacco is better suited to the environmental conditions, and combines with a general farming economy. And, in part through historical development, some of the better areas set among this rough country—such as the Inner Blue Grass of Kentucky—are leading districts of tobacco culture and contain large tobacco fields.

The best soils, which are also heavily fertilized, are chosen for the tobacco field in the rough part of the Belt. Valley flood plains, even if very small, are usual on most farms. Therefore, considering the generally small size of an individual tobacco field, enough area for it is available on the individual farms, and on many the tobacco is grown on a narrow flood plain between the stream and the base of the bordering hills. In contrast, the rough terrain does not permit the large, rectangular field in many areas, and hence mitigates against the existence of the extensive corn field which can be cultivated easily by machine, or the extensive field sowed to a small grain crop. In addition, much of the trans-Appalachian area in Kentucky and Tennessee has soils of only moderate fertility, a second factor hindering the large-scale growing of corn (as in the flattish, rich-soil Corn Belt) without a considerable investment in fertilizer. Both surface configuration and soils are handicaps for the practice of a corn agriculture, except locally.

(3) Tobacco is a labor-demanding crop. This, in part, explains its distribution in the United States. The labor supply on the farms of the principal tobacco-growing region of the southern United States is plentiful, and farm family labor is numerous relative to the capital of the farms, and relative to machinery. The southern highlands area, as in East Tennessee, has one of the highest rural birth rates in the nation. Families are large. The overall tobacco region has been an exporter of people for more than fifty years; thousands of persons from the Carolinas, Kentucky, and Tennessee have moved to eastern and middle western cities in search of industrial employment; the labor that helped man the expanding automobile factories of the 1920's and the wartime industries of the 1940's in Ohio, Michigan, and Indiana was heavily recruited from the Upper South. And the local population has grown in numbers, too, so rural labor on the tobacco farms is plentiful.

The labor in the tobacco enterprise consists of a very large amount of hand labor relative to machines. Tobacco seedbeds must be prepared and planted by hand. Much of the transplanting of seedlings to field is a hand job—even the mechanical transplanter requires two men, one to work with the seedlings while the other drives. The removal of the tobacco worm from the growing leaves is a hand operation. Cutting of the tobacco plant is by hand. The placing of the leaf on sticks, the stacking of the leaf in the barn for curing, the taking down of the cured tobacco, its grading and sorting, and even its arrangement in baskets on the auction floor, are all operations requiring human labor. No other widespread crop of general agriculture left in the United States is so demanding of human labor.

The farms of the principal tobacco region are small in size. Some districts have farm averages of only 50 to 60 acres. When compared to the Corn Belt, with its 160- to 400-acre size units, or the large operating units of the Wheat Belts, the individual tobacco enterprise is small indeed—by American standards. And from a third to as much as half of the total farm in the southern tobacco region is in farm woodlot. Thus, a comparison with the heart of the Illinois or Iowa Corn Belt, where 70 per cent or more of a farm area is in crops and the rest in pasture, is even more out of line, for the 60-acre tobacco farm may contain only 30 acres of cultivated land. Indeed, in some counties the average amount of land under cultivation per farm is less than this figure. Hundreds of southern tobacco farms contain fewer cultivated acres per farm than a Corn Belt farmer might have in a single cornfield. Thus, labor again is an important factor; a large quantity of labor, much of it hand labor, is used on a small quantity of land—the tobacco field or patch. And the labor is invariably family labor.

Returns of tobacco from each acre average about $1,400 gross at present prices. Against this the many costs of growing the crop must be charged. The small grower may not count the hours he and his family have worked, and so not charge it against the gross return. But the acre—or two or three—is the most important one in providing the income on the small tobacco farm. In East Tennessee the average tobacco plot of only seven-eighths of an acre is the chief source of cash income for thousands of hill and mountain farm families.

Tobacco fills a need in the agriculture of the general farming area which lies betwixt and between the best corn country and the poleward limit of cotton. Its introduction to this area was historical. Its present position is economic. Leaf provides the basic cash income of thousands of small farms, farms peopled on the whole by large families and able to provide surplus family labor. And, even where part-time agriculture is the rule, as near an industrial plant, the farmer-factory worker may engage in growing tobacco on a suburban plot of ground if he is the holder of a tobacco allotment.

Northern Tobacco Districts

There are specialized tobacco districts in the northern United States. Thus, although tobacco and cotton are considered by most people to be southern crops, tobacco—like cotton in California—is grown in some quantity outside of the Upper South, as cotton is grown outside of the Deep South.

The Connecticut Valley is noted for its fine cigar wrapper leaf, grown under shade of cheesecloth, principally in the section of the valley between Springfield and Hartford. But Connecticut Valley growers are now competing with rapid suburbanization as the valley is becoming almost a continuous city. Land use problems and the highest and best use of this land, the richest, agriculturally, in New England, now confront the industry and the townships.

Lancaster County, Pennsylvania, although adjacent to Maryland, is not strictly a part of the true Tobacco Belt. Its Pennsylvania Dutch farmers specialize in cigar leaf as part of their general farming operations, and the cigarette and cigar tobaccos of the Upper South are not produced. Like the New England growers, increasing urbanization is affecting this richest agricultural county of the northeastern seaboard region, and one of the richest farming counties in the entire United States.

Tobacco growing was introduced to Rock County, Wisconsin, more than 100 years ago by settlers from the East. By the 1840's many Norwegian immigrants were arriving in this area and adjacent Dane County. Growers hired the Norwegians to perform the hand labor, and as the immigrants obtained capital and were able to purchase their own land, they continued with tobacco culture in their new settlements in adjacent Dane County. From here the industry spread to a separate district in western Wisconsin, in counties bordering the Mississippi River. To this day the two separate tobacco districts in the state are peopled mainly by farmers of Norwegian descent, and the growers are of the third or fourth generation in the United States. The "cultural" factor in this case was obtained in the New World. All Wisconsin tobacco is binder leaf and is grown as a cash crop on dairy farms.

Tobacco marketing of the leaf grown in the northern United States is carried on differently than in the South. All the leaf is air-cured. Buyers visit the farms during the curing season and examine and purchase the tobacco in the barns. The leaf is delivered directly to the storage warehouses; there is no auction. Edgerton is the leading warehouse center in Wisconsin. Large cities serve the eastern growing districts.

The Season

Tobacco growing in the Tobacco Belt is a "thirteen months" project in local parlance. Actually, from planting of seed bed to sale of the crop may take ten to eleven months. It is true in certain districts that a seed bed may be started in January, and the leaf of the preceding year may not pass under the auctioneer's chant until February.

Seed beds are prepared carefully, usually on "new ground." A site in a woodland clearing is used very commonly. The beds are laid out to have a southern exposure toward the low sun of the season, and are placed near water—such as a stream—because the farmer must carry water to the seedlings. The soil of the bed is spaded or plowed, is steamed in some districts, and "burned" in others— slowly burning logs being kept burning on the bed. Tobacco is seeded in the bed in January, February, or March. When the young plants appear, the bed is

Fig. 9-2. Shade-grown cigar-leaf tobacco. The cheesecloth-covered field has been prepared for the transplanting of tobacco from the seed beds to the left. A teaspoon of tobacco seeds will produce enough plants for an acre—tobacco seeds being among the smallest of all seeds. (Standard Oil Company, N.J.)

covered with cheesecloth, which can be rolled back at the time of watering or thinning. Hand thinning of plants is an important operation; there may be 300,000 tobacco seeds to the ounce, and removal of many plants is necessary in order to permit the remaining ones to grow well for eventual transplanting.

Tobacco is transplanted from seed bed to the carefully prepared and abundantly fertilized tobacco field in middle spring. This is late March or early April in southern Georgia, late April and into early May in the heart of the growing region, and June in the northern districts. Cultivation is by mechanical cultivator when the plants are small. But hand hoeing is necessary after the leaves shade the ground; machines may damage them. Again the labor factor of human beings is critical. Dusting, worm removal, and other care of the tobacco plants is a summer operation.

Tobacco is cut by hand in the field, and the harvesters string it on sticks. Five to six individual plants are placed on each four-foot-long stick. Trucks haul the sticks to the tobacco barn, and the tobacco is hung leaves downward. If flue-cured, as in southern Georgia, or fire-cured as in North Carolina and in districts of Middle Tennessee and southwestern Kentucky, the leaf may be ready for market in a few days. The early spring of southern Georgia and the few days of curing permit tobacco auction markets to open in the middle of July. By August—sometimes in July—tobacco sales have begun farther north, in the Carolinas. But in the burley tobacco belt of Kentucky and Tennessee, tobacco is not ready for harvest until late August and during September. Burley is air-cured; depending upon weather, this requires a month or two. Burley sales open throughout the belt on a set date, usually toward the end of November, for not until the winter-type rains, which usually occur about the middle of the month, is it possible to remove the cured tobacco from the barn. Very moist air is needed for handling; this is so-called "casing weather"; handling of the tobacco in dry air—with low relative humidity—causes the leaf to crumble.

The tobacco auction is a feature of the Tobacco Belt. Farmers deliver their crop to warehouses and place tobacco of different grades in different baskets. The ability of the grower to grade his crop well is important in the price he receives for a basket. The auctioners travel from market to market; some start in July in Georgia and end their season in February in Kentucky and eastern Tennessee. Graders for the United States Department of Agriculture also shift northward with the markets. The auctioneer walks along a row of baskets of tobacco; facing him on the opposite side are the buyers for the manufacturers of tobacco products. The entire group proceeds at a steady pace, followed by the growers, who receive their check (which may represent a significant part of their yearly income) from the warehouseman as soon as the crop has been sold and ticketed. And the latitudinal spread of tobacco is such, and the speed of curing (depending upon the method used in the district) is such that the nursery seed bed in Georgia and Florida has been planted for the crop of the ensuing year before the sales of burley tobacco for the preceding year have been completed in Kentucky and the hilly and mountainous portions of eastern Tennessee.

Tobacco is moved to the redrying plants from the warehouse centers; only certain types are redried. This involves removal of the natural moisture, and the steaming of the leaves to add uniform "artificial" moisture. Following this process, the tobacco is packed in oak hogsheads and trucked or sent by rail to the large storage warehouses for aging for several years. In its shipments the leaf has been transported from thousands of farms to hundreds of auction warehouses, to several dozen redrying plants, to a few storage warehouses. If cigarette types of leaf, it will end, for manufacture, at only five locations—Winston-Salem, Durham, and Reidsville in North Carolina, Richmond in Virginia, or Louisville in Kentucky. If cigar leaf, its eventual manufacture is much more widespread, and near the consuming markets, although Tampa and some other locations possess large factories. If for snuff, the manufacturing and consuming locations are generally in the South.

Economic Factors and Competition

Tobacco is the principal remaining "hand-labor" crop in American Agriculture. It is true that certain vegetables require considerable "stoop labor," that fruit must be picked by hand, and that thinning of sugar beets requires human labor. But, in the broad agricultural setting, now that cotton-picking machines are common, it is tobacco that requires much personal labor. This has been a chief factor in holding the crop to small farms in densely inhabited agricultural regions, such as the Upper South. A Corn Belt farmer, or a western wheat grower, who cultivates large acreages by machines cannot afford to "fool" with tobacco; his time is spent in operating machinery; his output per man is great, and he can cultivate many acres in the time he would spend on only one acre of tobacco.

FIG. 9-3. Tobacco plants in early summer. A certain amount of hand labor is necessary early in the season, when the leaves might be damaged by a mechanical cultivator. Tobacco worms must be removed by hand, and harvest requires the hand-cutting of tobacco stalks. This field is in the northern United States, in a district where tobacco is grown as a cash crop on dairy farms. The farm home, dairy barn, and silo are in the right background. The white-roofed barn in the center background and the building at the left of the picture are tobacco barns. (Standard Oil Company, N.J.)

FIG. 9-4. Tobacco in Southern Rhodesia, now the leader in tobacco exports. This is "Virginia-type" tobacco for the British market. Notice the height of the mature plant. The typical savanna landscape of the plateau of southern Africa appears in the distance— tall grasslands, dotted by acacias and other trees singly or in clusters, with patches of low-tree forests. (British Information Services)

The surplus of American tobacco has always been exported, and even in the 1940's about half the tobacco which moved in foreign trade was from the United States. But by the late 1950's American tobacco was down to only between a quarter and a third of the foreign trade. In part this is owing to the rise of new, competing districts, as those in Africa (see next section); in part it is the result of trade agreements between European importing nations and producing countries; and in part it is owing to the competition between "higher" wages or costs in the American scene as opposed to the "cheap" or inexpensive labor in competing tropical regions, such as in Africa and the West Indies.

The result of the increasing world competition, and the loss, or reduction, of the overseas markets has been in research in the United States. The research is aimed at the possibility of greater mechanization in the growing and curing of the crop. As might be expected from the location of tobacco-growing regions, the state and federal experiment stations in states like North Carolina and Georgia have been active in this research. Trial methods of mass curing are under study —in other words, the possible elimination of flue-curing and fire-curing, and the substitution of central "heating stations." A tobacco harvester, power-driven, is another experimental project; the trial ones cut two rows of tobacco and lay the leaves flat. They then can be put into boxes for curing. These projects—and others —all look to less labor and more mass production, and so are in the trend of the type of production for which the United States is noted, agriculturally and in manufacturing.

► TOBACCO IN RHODESIA

The high veld and middle veld of Southern Rhodesia, in the Federation of Rhodesia and Nyasaland in southern Africa has become one of the leading tobacco-growing areas of the world. Salisbury, the capital city of Southern Rhodesia, now claims the world's largest individual tobacco market. Rhodesian bright flue-cured tobacco, suitable for the manufacture of cigarettes, is exported to the United Kingdom. The increase in production and export has been so rapid since World War II that Rhodesia is second now only to the United States as an exporter of tobacco. And, as the Rhodesian crop has increased, and trade agreements have been signed with the United Kingdom, its percentage of tobacco exports in international trade have increased. And the United States percentage of the foreign trade in tobacco dropped from about half (45 to 47 per cent) in the late 1940's to less than a third by the late 1950's; the drop has been both relative and absolute.

The tobacco of Rhodesia, all grown on farms of white farmers (called Europeans, even if African-born), is grown under the most modern methods, uses tobacco planting and cultivating machinery, and is all of United States types of tobacco—called, collectively, Virginia tobacco in the Federation. Rhodesian tobacco farms are large in area, and each farm handles a considerable acreage of tobacco. Needed labor is recruited from the African native inhabitants. In contrast, tobacco grown in the United States is raised on small acreages per farm— acreages under allotment control of the government—and generally by the labor of the farm family.

There are more than 2,500 tobacco farms in Rhodesia—a small number when compared to the approximately 750,000 farms which grow tobacco in the United States. But these farms average some 75 to 100 acres of tobacco per farm, in contrast to less than an acre per farm in some American districts and up to about 20 in others. And some Rhodesian growers produce as much as 1,000 acres— nearly two square miles—of tobacco.

Tobacco in Rhodesia is grown principally on tropical highlands in areas that are between 3,000 and 5,000 feet above sea level—cool uplands suitable for European settlement. The surface of the African Plateau is gently rolling, but two distinct levels are recognized in the Tobacco Belt; a lower "middle veld" level of just over 3,000 feet is the chief area for fire-cured tobacco, and a "high veld" surface area for other leaf. Sandy loam soils, derived residually from granites and sandstones and matured to pink and gray soil types in the climatic setting of the region, are the principal soils of the tobacco region.

The climate is a tropical upland type, and has a wet-and-dry seasonal rainfall regime. The rainy season begins with late September, as the sun's vertical rays advance into the Southern Hemisphere. Seed beds are planted and watered by African workers during the periods between the normal convectional thunder-showers of the season. Many seed beds are faced northward on slopes to take advantage of the warm northern sun in the Southern Hemisphere. By November the hottest period of year has arrived and almost daily thundershowers occur, the water vapor being derived from the monsoonal indraft of moist air from the Indian Ocean. The tobacco plants, transplanted from seed bed to field during late October, obtain a thriving start in the heat and humidity. Evenly distributed rainfall occurs almost daily from November to January (when the sun is directly overhead in Rhodesia). Thunderstorms are less frequent in February and March, but moisture is adequate. The totals during the rainy season of the Tobacco Belt are between 32 and 36 inches, usually.

Tobacco is harvested in Rhodesia at the beginning of the dry season, late "summer" and early "fall," or from March through early May. Harvest labor is recruited in part locally, in part from the many Native Reserves scattered through-out the Federation, and in part from migrant labor recruited from farther north in the Federation, particularly from Nyasaland, and from neighboring Portuguese Mozambique in the lowlands.

The critical factor in the specific location of tobacco farms is access to trans-portation—in this case the railroads of this interior region. Commercial tobacco farms, all of which are in the northeastern portion of Southern Rhodesia, cluster along and near the railroad lines. Only a small percentage of the potential to-bacco-growing area is in the crop today; possibilities for the expansion of acreage are extremely great, both within the outer boundaries of the present tobacco farms, and in areas not now occupied, for the unused areas with suitable soils and climate are very extensive. With improved transportation away from exist-ing rail lines the tobacco acreage could be expanded manyfold—depending upon world market conditions.

Harvested and cured tobacco is shipped by rail and truck to auction centers, of which Salisbury is the most important. The tobacco auction of Rhodesia is modeled on that of the southern United States. During the incipience of the Afri-can industry, warehousemen and auctioneers from the United States were en-gaged to set up and direct the marketing pattern. Following the sale of the crop on the auction floor, the tobacco is packed into wooden hogsheads for shipment by railroad to the exporting ports.

More than 90 per cent of the Rhodesian tobacco leaf is normally exported. Beira, a modern seaport on the Indian Ocean in Portuguese-owned Mozambique, is the chief exporting point. All Rhodesian tobacco is directed to nations of the

British Commonwealth, and chiefly to the United Kingdom itself. Excepting for rail shipments to the neighboring Union of South Africa, the export is by sea.

The British Commonwealth agreements give Rhodesia a tariff preference in the markets of the United Kingdom over non-Commonwealth tobacco, and, in addition, Rhodesia is usually able to undersell its competitors for that market. The demand in England, dating from colonial days in the New World, is for "Virginia-type" tobacco. The fact that Rhodesia has been able to produce and sell this "American type" places the Federation in a competitive position with American export tobacco; and the two supplement the third major exporting region—the Turkish-type tobacco of the eastern Mediterranean lands.

The recent successes of Rhodesia in the international trade in tobacco have caused concern to American tobacco men. The Rhodesian industry is organized for export and is directly concerned with the demands of the European market; in contrast, the overwhelming market for American growers is the domestic one, and the export market—though the United States leads in serving it—has always been incidental, but profitable. This has led to studies of the special de-mands of the European market and the possible improvement of the overseas mar-keting situation for American tobacco. Also, the success of Rhodesian growers in machine-handling of much of their crop, coupled with their advantage of an inexpensive native African labor supply, has resulted in the inauguration of studies in the United States—particularly by experiment stations in North Carolina and Georgia, and by federal experimenters—looking to different handling of the crop than the traditional way, and to the introduction of mass-curing methods as well as to more labor-saving machinery.

► QUESTIONS

1. Tobacco is grown in many climatic settings and on a wide variety of soils. What types of tobacco result? How do the curing processes affect the final type?
2. The growing of tobacco is concentrated, usually, in discontinuous producing districts, each highly specialized. What combination of factors have led to this situation?
3. What is the relationship between the existence of a large supply of labor and the growing of tobacco?
4. Contrast the type of farm operation in the tobacco-growing districts of the American Upper South with the operation of tobacco farms in Southern Rho-desia.
5. The manufacture of cigarettes in the United States is highly concentrated in location; in contrast, the manufacture of cigars is quite widespread and is much closer to the eventual market. Why this difference?

X The Beverage Crops

There are many kinds of beverages in day-to-day use around the world. Coffee, tea, chocolate, wines, milk, and manufactured soft drinks are but a few.

The tree crops or smaller plants from which the raw material is obtained for many of the beverages are distributed regionally, in response to differing environmental conditions for their growth and production. Likewise the markets for the beverages show a distinct regional pattern.

Before the days of rapid transportation the beverage of any given region or country was produced locally. Its type was determined by the home environment and by what particular crop could be grown. Thus the inhabitants of northern France used cider, made from their home-grown apples. Those of the south consumed wine daily for their drink with meals; the Mediterranean environment is one in which the vine flourishes, and wine was pressed from the grapes. The people of the Parana Valley in South America used yerba maté, or Paraguay tea, made from the leaves of a local wild shrub or small tree. The Chinese consumed tea, a plant indigenous to the south of China, Indochina, and neighboring areas of northeastern India, and Burma. The people of southwestern Arabia had coffee, as Arabs had brought the coffee tree from neighboring Ethiopia, where it grows wild in the forests. North Europeans, whose excellent pastures supported dairy cattle, drank milk; from their grains—for example, barley—they brewed beers and ales or distilled beverages which had a high alcoholic content, such as whiskey.

Beverages whose raw material is from a tropical product became widespread shortly after the Age of Discovery, and the development of ocean transportation, originally by sailing vessel. Thus tea was introduced to Britain; although it could not be grown there it became the major beverage of the British people as a result of trade with the Far East. Cocoa, from the cacao tree of South America, spread in use beyond its native region. Coffee, likewise, was introduced to Europe and America. Consequently, today the beverage of largest consumption in a given region may not be grown locally. All of the coffee used in the United States must be imported. All tea and cacao beans are imported. These products, then, function as important ones of world trade. Nevertheless, the present beverage in chief daily use in many of the world's regions still is the one which was in use in antiquity. Habits are hard to change. The Mediterranean peoples of southern France, Spain, and Italy still drink their wine with meals, two or even three times a day; the Chinese still consume nearly all of their home-grown tea. Paraguayans still consume quantities of yerba maté. And those nations with worldwide trade contacts are the chief consuming nations of beverages which were introduced in early days—the British still have their daily cups of tea, the American his coffee.

Several of the beverage crops will be discussed in this chapter. They are grown in different climates. Coffee is a tree crop of uplands and mountains of the tropical world. Tea is grown in both the wet-and-dry tropics and the hot and moist humid subtropics. Cacao originates in wet tropical lowlands, damp and excessively rainy areas. The vine will not withstand moist heat and is indigenous to and grown in the Mediterranean climatic lands, such as the countries around the Mediterranean Sea or in the nonmountainous areas of California, a state with large areas which possess the Mediterranean-type environment of cool winters and warm-to-hot but dry summers. Some few other beverages will be mentioned but briefly. Milk is to be discussed with the animal industries rather than with beverage crops.

▶ COFFEE

The coffee tree grows on tropical uplands and in certain zones on tropical mountains. Coffee is a principal tree crop and export of highlands of Brazil, Colombia, Venezuela, Central America, Mexico, the West Indies, of certain islands in the East Indies, and of eleven political units of Africa. In addition, uplands of southwestern Saudi Arabia and nearby Yemen grow the famous Arabian coffee which is exported for blending with stronger Latin American coffees. Furthermore, India and the Philippine Islands grow coffee for the home market and export modest quantities. Isolated highland islands in the tropical seas have a coffee industry; Hawaii is an example. New Caledonia in the southwest Pacific

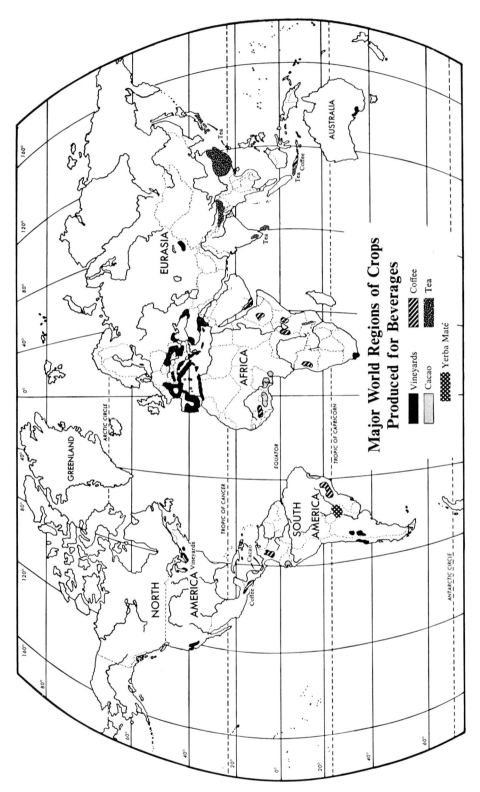

Major World Regions of Crops
Produced for Beverages

Vineyards   Coffee

Cacao   Tea

Yerba Maté

grows coffee for the French market under unique climatic situations which permits the groves to be at sea level—the only such situation in the world.

The nations of Latin America, from southern Mexico and the West Indies to southeastern Brazil, produce from three-quarters to four-fifths of the world's commercial crop. They furnish four-fifths of the coffee which moves in world trade to overseas markets. The United States, principal consuming country of coffee, receives 90 per cent of its supply from Latin America; Brazil alone furnishes over half of this, and in certain years as high as 70 per cent. Thus, in turn, Brazil becomes a principal Latin American market for American manufactured goods. Brazil alone leads all nations in coffee production and export, and is followed by Colombia.

The chief coffee-producing regions of the world have shifted, during the history of the industry, from Arabia (Mocha is a name for coffee associated with this region) to what is now Indonesia (where the name Java became associated with a cup of coffee), to the nations of Latin America, and particularly Brazil. Today the Latin American nations, collectively, are significant enough in the overall production picture to have joined together in an association which attempts to control quantity of production and the amount of exports in order to maintain high prices for coffee.

The consumption of coffee—its use as a beverage—is confined mainly to the United States, Canada, and western Europe. In addition, coffee is consumed in nations which are "descended from" western Europe—Argentina and Uruguay, the Union of South Africa, Australia, and New Zealand, and in the regions of its production. The United States is the leading coffee-consuming nation by far; it uses more than twice the tonnage of coffee used in western Europe, despite its smaller population.

Negatively, coffee is a minor beverage in many parts of the world. Even in western Europe, the use and consumption of coffee varies greatly among the countries. The British people, and the English-speaking nations of the Commonwealth, use far more tea than coffee. The Russian beverage is tea. In the Orient, particularly in Japan, China, India, and Pakistan, tea is the almost universal drink.

Coffee consumption in France is the greatest in Europe. On a per capita basis, however, the Scandinavian peoples in Norway, Sweden, Denmark, and Finland are the chief coffee drinkers. The West German per capita consumption is not far behind. Collectively, despite its far larger total population than the United States, however, the total poundage of coffee consumed in Europe is less than half that of the American. The Canadian use per capita is less. In total, thus, the coffee-exporting countries look to the United States as their major market.

The widespread total use of coffee and its large per capita consumption in the United States are difficult to account for. Originally the colonists were tea drinkers. The English tax on tea provoked them into the Boston Tea Party. The original coffee houses were in London, Paris, and other European cities. German settlers in the colonies apparently consumed coffee in quantity. In any case, later German migrations resulted in the increased use of coffee (as was the case, too, in the increased use of beer in America), importers in New York and elsewhere promoted the use of coffee over tea, and trade contracts with nearby coffee-producing areas in Latin America resulted in the widespread use of what was, at the time, a less expensive beverage.

The American use, in total, of coffee is one of the "wonders of the world." Wherever the American has gone he has taken his coffee habit with him. Servicemen in Italy, the Orient, and Australia during World War II helped create a market for coffee. Since the war the demand for coffee has increased greatly in such countries as Italy. And, since World War II, the advent of the so-called "coffee break" in office and business institutions of America has mushroomed the use of coffee in the United States and resulted in nearly a third increase in per capita consumption.

Environmental Requirements

The coffee tree grows wild on the tropical highlands of the Abyssinian Plateau, in what is now Ethiopia. This is the fountainhead of commercial coffee culture, for Arabs introduced the tree to the highlands of Yemen across the Red Sea. From this area of Arabia coffee culture spread to other world regions. In fact, coffee trees grow wild, too, in some of the highlands of French Equatorial Africa and West Africa, and some of the African production is descended from these areas. But elsewhere, and most important in total, commercial coffee production, as in Brazil, is descended from Ethiopia via the introductions to Arabia.

Coffee grows best in those altitudinal zones of a tropical upland where the temperatures are in the upper 60's Fahrenheit on the average, and in the 70's by day. Near the equator these zones lie at 8,000 to 9,000 feet above sea level, and coffee is a true mountain product. In the latitudes of some of the West Indian islands the coffee zone is at 4,000 to 5,000 feet above sea level. At the Tropic of Capricorn, which crosses the leading coffee-producing area of Brazil, the coffee lands are at about 1,800 to 2,500 feet above sea level, a response to the increasing latitude. Thus, in the great Brazilian area, coffee is a plateau product rather than a true tropical mountain one.

Nighttime temperatures on the tropical plateaus and mountains in the "coffee zone" may drop into the lower 60's, and into the 50's during the period of low sun, or "winter," when the sun's vertical ray is in the opposite hemisphere. This, plus a dry season during the time of low sun, hastens the maturity of the coffee berry. Daytime temperatures rise into the 60's and low 70's. The dry season aids in the harvest of the coffee berries, and in most producing areas permits the outdoor drying of the berry on concrete or tile floors.

The coffee tree will not withstand hot or brilliant sunshine when it is young. Neither will it withstand frost when it is mature. It will not grow in the extreme

F<small>IG</small>. 10-1. The coffee berry, within which are two flat-sided coffee beans, is about the size of a small cherry. (Standard Oil Company, N.J.)

and continuous heat of tropical lowlands. All producing regions the world over possess a tropical mountain or plateau environment, and one comparable to that of the tree's indigenous regions in Africa.

Young coffee trees are planted, usually, among taller, sparsely spaced trees to shade them from the sun until they have become established. In some regions, notably on the highlands of Yemen in the southwestern part of the Arabian Peninsula, and on the Kona (leeward or western) Coast of the island of Hawaii, the shading—or protection—is accomplished by the existence of a fog or mist zone on the mountain slopes rather than by man-planted trees on old coffee lands or remaining forests on newly cleared coffee plantations or farms.

The coffee tree produces its clusters of berries, each berry about the size of a cherry, during the high-sun or rainy season. The berries mature in the low-sun dry season. Like some other highland or subtropical crops, the advent of cooler weather hastens maturity; oranges and cotton are examples, for these, while grown throughout the tropical world, are in chief commercial production toward the margins or even in the subtropics, where maturity is reached within a short period as cooler weather develops. Coffee, thus, does best on those uplands where there is a threat of frost, but not actual frost; its range, unlike cotton or oranges, is not latitudinal but is altitudinal.

Coffee harvests vary in date among producing regions, but are all during the low-sun season or the dry season, which usually correspond. In Brazil the harvest extends from March to September, "winter" in the southern hemisphere. In Mexico and Central America the berries are picked from October through March, the low-sun time of year. Colombia, second coffee country, grows its coffee at high altitudes, and on both sides of the equator; exposure varies greatly. Two harvests are usual, but not from the same region—one from October through December and elsewhere April through June.

The coffee tree grows in many types of soils. Some of the red soils derived from lavas are especially favored in volcanic areas. Red soils of residual origin, derived from underlying crystalline rocks, are noted coffee soils; one such is the well-known terra roxa, or red soil, of the Brazilian Plateau. Some coffee plantings on these excellent soils in São Paulo state have been producing for sixty or more years. On neighboring soils, but in the same climatic environment, a tree will yield berries for only twenty or so years. Plantings made in poor sandy soils have produced for only eight years in some areas. Thus, within the overall climatic environment the soils factor is an important one in production.

Coffee Production and Trade

The coffee tree is a broadleaf evergreen. In commercial production it is pruned to a height of twelve to fourteen or so feet, in order to aid in the picking of the berries. The berries, each about the size of a cherry, grow in clusters, and each berry contains two flat-sided seeds, the flat sides together; the seeds are the coffee beans of commerce. After the picking of the berries, they must be dried and then washed in order to remove the exocarp, or fleshy part; the drying process is conducted differently in different regions. Usually in Latin America the berries are sun-dried on tiles, brick, or concrete floors, raked daily and turned, until the exocarp is loose. Washing then leaves the green coffee beans, which are bagged for export. The brown bean, familiar to the consumer, is the roasted product of middle-latitude coffee-roasting companies.

The United States imports seven times the quantity of coffee imported by France, the second importer, and France uses one-third more coffee than West Germany, third in imports. Italy, Belgium, Sweden, Canada, Great Britain, and the Netherlands are usually the other major importers. Coffee for the American market in recent years has originated as raw or green coffee in more than 40 countries.

The wide sources of imports reflects, in part, the blending of coffees for the retail market. One group of varieties, the Arabians, are considered the best so far as grade of bean is concerned, but the tree is delicate and susceptible to disease and to climatic variations. Another group, the robustas, are hardier, grow at a wider range of elevations, and are less susceptible to weather changes. The practice is to blend Arabian beans with the robustas, the latter forming the bulk or body. Thus, for blending, coffee is imported from Saudi Arabia, Ethiopia, Kenya, and elsewhere in Africa, and blended with the robustas from Brazil. The Kona Coast of the island of Hawaii also furnishes Arabian-type or Kona coffee for American blends. Arabian coffees from Africa, particularly Kenya, are favored in Europe, those from elsewhere in the United States.

A second difference in coffees is that between so-called mountain-grown, the high-altitude coffees, such as those from Colombia, and the Brazilian or "low-altitude" coffees. In general, the trade considers the mountain-grown coffees superior. Some coffee companies, which use mainly the high-altitude beans, so advertise and may mark their retail cans or bags as "mountain-grown" coffees. Nevertheless, in total quantity consumed, it is the Brazilian and other upland-producing regions which furnish the bulk of the coffees, and the body coffee for the various blends.

Coffee is a tree crop and a tree takes from three to five years to come into full bearing. Thus, coffee plantings cannot be adjusted to immediate market demands. At times there has been overproduction with resulting low prices for coffee. At times the demand has been larger than the supply, with resulting high prices in the consuming nations, and active coffee plantings in the producing countries. A serious freeze in a large producing region, such as experienced by part of the Brazilian acreage one year in the late 1950's, resulted in shortages and rising coffee prices in the United States.

The coffee-producing countries, particularly Brazil with its dominant production of coffee, have tried valorization schemes; not only was coffee withheld from the market, but some was used locally in place of coal in the railroads. But Colombian plantings increased as Brazil tried to check production—a good example of regional competition; Colombia's importance in coffee, and increased share of the market, dates from this period. In 1958, when coffee prices fell in the United States, Colombia attempted controls by setting a price below which coffee could not be exported, but by the time the edict was promulgated, the price set was above the quoted New York price. Brazil, in the same year, withheld four million bags from the American market in an attempt to force prices upward, selling the coffee to the Brazilian Coffee Institute.

The above "problems" of the coffee countries are ones which illustrate: (1) the differing economic setting of a tree crop from a planted annual crop; (2) regional competition for markets, geographically, as between Africa and Latin America; (3) competition of individual countries for a market; and (4) competition of producers—the Brazilian plantation owners, for example, and plantation agriculture versus thousands of small farmers in Colombia, where coffee is in general a farm rather than a plantation industry. Finally, the 1958 price situation in the United States resulted in the formation of an International Coffee Organization at a meeting in Rio de Janeiro. An agreement for world organization was drawn up. The basic participants were the nations of tropical Latin America; other countries were included but are overshadowed by the New World producers.

In September 1958 an agreement was signed in Washington among these nations, to promote coffee consumption in the world, lower costs of production if possible, anticipate slumps, and maintain "satisfactory" prices to the producing countries, many of which in Latin America depend heavily upon coffee for their foreign exchange. For example, tiny El Salvador and Colombia received 80 per cent of their export income from coffee.

Sample Coffee Regions

Coffee is grown both on tropical plantations and on small farms. Regionally the situation varies, and all of the producing areas tend to have some of each type of agricultural unit.

The coffee plantation in Brazil is known as a *fazenda*. In Guatemala it is called a *finca*. On the uplands of Africa the British-owned operations are called plantations, the usual overall word in English for the tropical agricultural unit using (1) outside capital, (2) outside or local management, (3) local supplies of day labor, and (4) specializing in one, or at the most two, tropical crops for (5) export to middle-latitude markets which are (6) overseas.

FIG. 10-2. The mountain-grown coffee of Colombia, unlike the plantation coffee of Brazil, is grown on farms, and at very high altitudes. This coffee farm (*finca* in Colombia), like others, is small in area and occupies very steep slopes. (Standard Oil Company, N.J.)

In Colombia, in some other Latin American regions, and over wide areas on the plateaus of East Africa coffee is grown by small farmers, on small landholdings. This is the case, too, in the Hawaiian area. The exporters collect the coffee beans from many farms, bag them at a central spot—a seaport if possible—and ship the green coffee to roasters in the middle latitudes.

▶ THE BRAZILIAN PLATEAU

The uplands of the rolling plateau of southeastern Brazil are the locale of the coffee fazendas. The eastern edge of the plateau is a 2,000-foot escarpment which overlooks the world's leading coffee-exporting port, Santos, located on the Atlantic. More northern portions of this coffee-growing plateau lie in the hinterlands of Rio de Janeiro and export their coffee from that port.

The rolling uplands of São Paulo lead in the coffee industry of Brazil. Southward, coffee plantings extend into the state of Parana, but soon reach the frost zone; in fact, serious freezes have eliminated production from some areas. Northward the coffee region extends some 500 miles (really northeastward) to beyond the latitude of Rio de Janeiro. Inland the coffee fazendas and farms finger farthest along the railroad lines, their lifeline to the ports, and in places lie 250 to 300 miles from the sea.

The altitudes of the Brazilian Plateau decline westward; the crest of the escarpment is the divide. Thus the coffee regions lie on the rolling uplands drained westward to the Parana River. Ridge crests are 1,800 to 2,500 feet above sea level. To date, westward expansion of coffee culture has not reached lower portions of the plateau. But inland there is an altitudinal zone beyond the limit of present settlement, where coffee culture will cease.

Large-scale commercial cultivation of coffee on the plateau dates only from the 1890's, although other regions of the nation possessed a small industry prior to this decade. The westward and northwestward (or inland) expansion of the coffee acreage reflects (1) the expanding North American market in the twentieth century; (2) the coffee boom and high profits received during the 1890–1920 period; (3) the migration of more than two million persons to the coffee area with the early boom—people from elsewhere in Brazil, from Portugal, Spain, and Japan, and especially from Italy—the labor force for the fazendas and the small coffee farmers; and (4) the post-World War II coffee upsurge and continued westward expansion by the sons of the immigrants. The coffee area is served, too, by the best railroad network in Brazil; railroads built to tap coffee areas now, with inland extensions, help to make interior areas accessible for new settlers.

The typical Brazilian coffee fazenda covers several hundred, even thousands, of acres. It extends over several of the rolling ridge crests and has within its boundaries the shallow valleys which interlace the uplands. One fazenda is divided from another along the ridge crests. Roads and railroads also follow the uplands. The home of the owner is usually in one of the shallow valleys; near it are the drying floors, sheds, coffee mills, and bagging equipment, and the homes of the permanent employees. The owner, a Brazilian, may spend more time at his town house in Rio de Janeiro or São Paulo than on his estate, leaving general supervision to a manager.

Continuous plantings of coffee trees, looking like an extensive orchard in the middle latitudes, extend over the uplands in all directions, and down the slopes toward the valleys. But the lower slopes and valley bottoms are in pasture grasses or brush. This is owing to the frost hazard in the lowlands. During calm days in the winter, cold air, being heavier than warm air, drains down the slopes and collects in the valleys. This temperature inversion may result in light frost in the lowlands; air drainage protects the coffee plantings on the slopes and ridges, which are frost-free.

The burst of activity on a fazenda begins with the first picking in March, but the tempo increases as the peak of the harvest is reached from May to August, then tapers off to the last pickings in September. Supplementary labor is employed.

The berries are brought daily to the mill at the headquarters. Here the fleshy exocarp is removed, and the two green beans inside are obtained. After being washed, the beans are spread out on the drying floors, where they are raked daily to expose all surfaces to the sun. When thoroughly dry the beans are bagged for transport to railroad and port.

The landscape of the uplands, as on nearly all Brazilian fazendas, is one of an even skyline of row upon row of coffee trees. No higher shade trees break the pruned uniformity of height of the coffee tree. This is in contrast to all other producing areas. Brazilians have had a "get-rich-quick" philosophy. Young trees are planted in the open. If they die they are replaced. The time and effort to have proper shade protection for infant trees has not as yet been typical of the Brazilian fazenda.

Interspersed among the coffee fazendas of the first (in time) coffee areas are cotton farms; coffee and cotton are the major crops. This reflects the westward movement of coffee lands. As old plantations cease coffee production, and do not replant, cotton is cultivated in place of the former tree crop.

All large regions contain areas within them where the "average" scene, or detail of land use, is not present—and the Brazilian "Coffee Plateau" is no exception. Thus, small farms, instead of fazendas, dominate the coffee scene in certain areas. This is true in parts of northern Parana state, to the south of São Paulo state. Here some virgin lands, suitable for coffee, were purchased by companies whose purpose was to found coffee-growing colonies of small farmers, living on small landholdings. Capital for the enterprise was obtained, in part, from Britain. Settlers were recruited from elsewhere in Brazil, from laborers on the fazendas, and from Europe. As the lands were disposed of, and the coffee plantings came into bearing, a landscape of continuous coffee groves, stretching across the uplands, developed; thus the view is comparable to a fazenda landscape in general.

But, in detail, the more numerous homes, the land boundaries, and the absence of the fazenda headquarters and its buildings provide a different setting. And, in economic practice, the preparation of coffee for the green-coffee market is handled by companies or middlemen rather than by the fazenda.

▶ CACAO

The cacao beans of commerce, product of the wet tropical world at and near the equator, are the material from which cocoa and chocolate is derived.

The cacao tree is a broadleaf evergreen tree, indigenous to the wet tropical lowlands of northwestern South America on the eastern side of the Andes—the upper Amazon Basin in eastern Peru, Colombia, and Brazil. The tree is spoken of as demanding a "hot-house climate"—temperatures always at about 80°F, high humidity, preferably in the 80's, and still air. It thrives in the doldrum belt. The environmental conditions most suitable for the tree are those in which bananas

FIG. 10-3. Cacao is a product of wet tropical lowlands. This scene is in Colombia, as is FIG. 10-2, but in the lowland region. The workers use knives to open the cacao pods, from which the cacao bean is obtained. (Standard Oil Company, N.J.)

also thrive; in fact the products are interchangeable under plantation or farm management—old banana plantations in eastern Central America are now devoted to cacao, and former cacao lands in Ecuador are now the heart region of that country's banana farms.

The cacao tree, after flowering, produces large cucumber-shaped pods from its branches and trunk. The pods are attached directly to the tree, and lack twigs. Inside the pod, when mature, are the many seeds which are the cacao beans (or cocoa beans) of commerce. Handwork is required in the picking and opening of the pods, following which the beans are spread on flat surfaces (tables, floors, or, on plantations drying floors) for drying. During this process, workers stir the beans by hand every hour or so in order to aid the drying process in the damp air. The dried beans, exported to middle-latitude manufacturers in Europe and North America, yield several products. The pliable fatty mass obtained after the beans are ground and roasted is the plain or bitter chocolate of the kitchen. Sweet chocolate and cocoa are obtained through the addition of sugar, milk, and other ingredients. In Europe the chocolate manufacturers often add honey in addition. The candies, ice creams, and other products with a chocolate flavor thus have a distant tropical agricultural product as a basic raw material.

Many companies in Europe and North America process the cacao beans and manufacture the products. Some of the companies date from colonial days and are located at the seaports which were the special trading centers of the past with the tropics (Boston is one such). Other companies, although owning and managing sugar plantations in the tropics (because of their large use of sugar) are buyers only of partially processed beans, and manufacturers of chocolates and various confections.

Regions of Production

West Africa leads the world in the growing of cacao. The coast of northeastern Brazil follows in importance. Northwestern South America produces cacao in the lowlands, and the West Indies, and southern Mexico, Central America, Ceylon, and Java in Indonesia supply cacao beans to the markets as well. American-owned cacao plantations on the island of Hispaniola, particularly on the part in the Dominican Republic rather than in Haiti, give that island the leading position in the product in the realm of Middle America.

► WEST AFRICA

Cacao is suited admirably to the geographic and economic situation of West Africa—that part of the western bulge of the continent where the coastline trends east and west along the shores of the Gulf of Guinea at 5° north latitude. Here is (1) a land of small farms, each operated by native Negro farmers, (2) a region of the greatest density of population in Africa, insuring an abundant labor supply, (3) countries formerly British or French with transportation ties to two of the chief cacao-consuming and -manufacturing countries. Furthermore, and also most important economically, (4) the native operators do not have to engage in day-to-day routine work, as in banana harvest or sugar-cane culture, but harvest their cacao only twice a year during two separate harvest periods; thus the irregular work pattern fits the existing mold of native habits. Every political unit of this coast, from just east of Liberia to Cameroun is significant in the cacao industry. Ghana is the most important of these African exporters, Nigeria is next. Ghana, in fact, leads the world in both the production and export of cacao.

The cacao farms of West Africa parallel the coast but begin some ten to fifteen miles inland, and stretch from this location to varying inner limits. Southern Ghana has the largest concentration, followed by an intensive producing area in south-western Nigeria. The natives dry the beans on tables constructed of local materials, and covered with mats. They deliver the beans to middlemen, whose place of business is in the villages of the region or at the seaports. The buyers see to the

Fig. 10-4. Cacao beans are piled for fermentation and covered with banana leaves for the duration of this process. The logs serve only to keep the leaves in place. This is in the important cacao-producing region of West Africa. (British Information Services)

export and sale. Means of transportation are used in West Africa to get the beans to the buying centers—navigable rivers and railroads where they exist, by bicycle on the trails and roads, and by porter trains of men carrying baskets of cacao beans on their heads, and walking from the inaccessible regions.

West African cacao, on the average, does not command the price obtained by the plantation producers of the West Indies or Central America. This is a reflection of the native agriculture wherein individual producers deliver beans of variable quality. The governments and agricultural schools of the region are engaged in educational programs whose goal is the upgrading of the quality through methods of better care.

► BRAZIL

The tropical coast of northeastern Brazil, in the vicinity of the city of Salvador, is the world's second cacao-producing region. When listed by countries or political units, Brazil follows Ghana in importance. *Regionally,* however, the countries of West Africa combined exceed Brazil in production by far, producing nearly four times the quantity of beans.

Northeast Brazil has a lowland coastal strip some fifty miles wide along the sea; back of this the eastern escarpment of the Brazilian Plateau rises. It is on the plain that the cacao farms are located. Rivers which cross the plain have carved shallow valleys, along the sides of which are dissected bench lands. The centers of cacao production are in the many valleys and on the benches; the pattern is discontinuous, cacao lands extending inland in each of several valleys along a 250-mile stretch of coast. As the locations are generally somewhat inland, the cacao lands are not in the windier coastal sections, and consequently receive the necessary "hothouse" conditions.

The present cacao-producing area is the old center of colonial settlement in Brazil. Portuguese planters imported slaves from Africa to man the sugar plantations of the day. The individual cacao farmers of the present are the descendants of the Negroes, and they own and rent their lands. Thus the collecting of cacao beans, as in West Africa, is one of concentrating the product of many farms at collecting stations, and eventual export, usually from Salvador.

Cacao is subject to a plant disease called witches'-broom. An outbreak of this in the Guayaquil lowland of Ecuador in the early part of this century nearly wiped out the plantings. The rise in importance of the Brazilian industry to its present dominant position in Latin America followed the catastrophe experienced by Ecuador. This illustrates, in another manner, the regional competition among producing regions; it illustrates, also the fact that products which require the *same environment* may shift in location in response to a variety of conditions—sometimes geographical, sometimes purely of an economic nature—provided that access to market, collection and distribution facilities, and costs of transport to

Fɪɢ. 10-5. Hand-picking of tea leaves in one of the important tea-growing districts of Japan. Tea is grown on diluvial terraces and on the lower slopes of hills in order to conserve flat or gently rolling land for rice and vegetable crops. Notice that the tea bushes are separate from one another. Tea leaves are plucked from many parts of the bush. At least two, and occasionally three pickings a year are obtained at this latitude. (Japan Tourist Association)

market are within the same general range, and are not detrimental or prohibitive to the shift; the former cacao lands of Ecuador now are important in banana production.

► TEA

The tea bush, or shrub, possesses a far wider climatic range than the coffee tree or the cacao tree. Unlike these, tea will grow from the warm humid subtropics in the latitudes of the lower and middle 30's to and through the entire tropical world, excepting only the low-latitude deserts and the cooler tropical highlands. Thus the humid subtropics and the wet-and-dry tropics contain most of the producing regions; some even extend into the rainy tropics—or tropical rain-forest climate. Within the regions of production, tea is generally a hill crop—especially so in the Orient.

Economically, tea-producing regions are confined, within the environmentally suitable areas, to regions of dense population and inexpensive labor. The sheer time factor of plucking, by hand, individual tea leaves from the tea bush does not justify high labor costs. It is for this reason that the humid subtropics of the American South do not grow tea; the labor costs are too high. So far as the environment is concerned, tea would thrive; in fact, tea bushes are grown ornamentally in yards and gardens of such states as Florida, Georgia, and South Carolina. Some few tea plantations established near Charleston even in antebellum days found slave labor too expensive for the crop.

Historically and culturally, tea is the drink of the Far East. It is the beverage of Japan, China, Formosa, and India, and has been for untold centuries. In today's

Fig. 10-6. Tea is grown in the trans-Caucasus areas of the Soviet Union, in the warm valleys south of the Caucasus Mountains—the snow-covered range in the distance. Individual farms have been collectivized and mechanized. The use of machinery on tea is completely in contrast to the hand-labor methods of the Orient. Notice that the bushes are planted on low ridges and permitted to grow as if they were a hedge. These machines, developed in Russia, trim the tea to a uniform height. Other machines are in use for other operations. Only the tea of highest quality is hand-picked. (Sovfoto)

economic scene only the Far East is the significant producing region. The abundant labor supply, tradition of cultivation and use, and low rural wages maintain the industry in a noncompetitive regional position. From the Far East the export tea which reaches Western and other world markets is obtained.

The growing of tea outside of the Far East is confined to only two areas, each of which is quite insignificant on a world basis, but important locally. One is in the trans-Caucasian region of the Soviet Union, south of the Cacausus Mountains, and the adjacent portions of northwestern Iran. The other is in warmer areas of the plateau of East Africa.

The trans-Caucasian tea gardens cluster in the valleys at the eastern end of the Black Sea and are protected by the high Caucasus Mountains from the cold waves which sweep the Russian plains to the north of the mountains. The Iranian tea area is on the warm, rainy slopes of the Elburz Mountains at the southern end of the Caspian Sea.

British-founded tea plantations occupy some of the plateau uplands of Kenya and Tanganyika in East Africa. Permanent white settlers manage the operations and Africans perform the labor. Farther south, particularly in Nyasaland, tea is produced in the valleys along Lake Nyasa, and in adjacent Mozambique. The African surplus production is exported to Britain; in contrast, the Russian and Iranian output fails by far to satisfy local needs, and each nation is an importer of tea from the Far East.

Tea Production and Preparation

The tea bush or shrub grows to varying heights. In practice it is pruned to some four or five feet to facilitate picking of the leaves. The yield of leaves, or number of pickings, varies with the latitude and length of season. In central Japan, at the northern limit of tea cultivation, two pickings of the leaves are possible. Farther south farmers obtain three pickings. In southern China, in the border zone of the tropics, four or so gatherings of leaves are possible. India and Ceylon, truly in the tropics, harvest tea leaves in all months, and six to seven pickings of leaves are gathered from the same bush. The longer season in India and Ceylon, plus the investment of British capital in the past, is responsible for plantation agriculture in Indian tea regions. In China, Formosa, and Japan tea is a crop or product of small peasant farms. Indonesia contained Dutch-owned plantations, now expropriated, and peasant enterprises.

The first picking of tea leaves—following a rest period for the plant—is of tender leaves. Successive pluckings are of regrowth which produce stronger teas. This separation is particularly true of the leaves from the humid subtropical climate, where there is a cool and dormant winter season; it is less true in the areas of all-year harvest, but plantation practice in India and Ceylon is to gather for only nine months and allow a three-month rest period.

The kind of tea depends upon the methods used in preparing the leaves for market. The three major types are green tea, black tea, and Oolong. In the preparation of green tea the leaves are withered, rolled, and fired. This is the tea of China and Japan. Preparation of black teas involves the fermenting (or oxidizing) of the plucked leaves before they are fired. This is the practice used in India and Ceylon. Oolong tea is partially oxidized before firing; it originates in parts of Japan and Formosa.

Export and World Consumption

The largest share of the tea production of the Far East is consumed locally. The Japanese use four-fifths of their tea at home; the Chinese are estimated to consume over 95 per cent of their production. India (excluding Ceylon) and Pakistan use two-thirds of their tea output at home. Ceylon, a center of tea plantations, and with a smaller total population, consumes some 10 per cent of its tea and is able to export the rest. Thus, while the total poundage of Ceylon's export tea does not reach that shipped from India, the exports per capita are far larger. Indonesia is in an intermediate position. Consequently, in order, the three major exporters are India, Ceylon, and—with less total quantity—Indonesia. But, it must be remembered, Chinese figures of production and export are only estimates; and the quantity of tea shipped overland from China to the Soviet Union is unknown.

Green teas are those in demand and use in China, Japan, and the Soviet Union. Black teas are those of principal use in the English-speaking world, in large part because of English investment in tea plantations of India and Ceylon, and of their distribution, past and present, by English companies and the nation's merchant shipping. Many of the black teas are sold under trade names such as Pekoe or Orange Pekoe. At one time it was common in the United States for restaurant workers to ask a customer's preference as to black or green tea; today green tea is little used except in some of the nation's urban "Chinatowns." Oolong teas are consumed principally in the regions of their production or in wealthier districts of the large Oriental cities.

The people of the British Isles consume about half of the tea which enters world trade. The daily, midafternoon cup of tea (in addition to the tea drunk with meals) is characteristic of Britain, and a custom in some of the British Commonwealth countries, especially Australia and New Zealand. In western Europe, aside from the United Kingdom, only Ireland and the Netherlands use tea in any quantity. The consumption in central and southern Europe is negligible.

North African lands from Morocco to Egypt, and lands of the Middle East, collectively, are importers of tea. Total use in this wide area is less than a third that of England alone, but the market is extensive. The use of tea exceeds the use of coffee except in Algeria. As these nations are composed of people who adhere to the Moslem faith, wine, the common drink on the northern shores of the Mediterranean is prohibited. The Union of South Africa, in contrast, uses tea in the same ratio as other British Commonwealth nations. Tea and coffee imports are not far different.

Canada, with less than a tenth the total population of the United States, imports and consumes half as much tea. The per-capita consumption is far higher than in the United States. The "English" and the "American" beverage habits mix, or cross, in Canada; currently, on a national basis, the use of coffee exceeds that of tea by a moderate amount.

The United States is noted for its seasonal use of tea. The beverage, as iced tea, is more used during the summer or hot season. Tea sales rise sharply during this period. Overall, on a per capita basis, the total use of tea is not large, considering the total population of the nation. Net imports, on a several-year average, are only twice those of Canada and less than twice those of Australia, with its ten million inhabitants.

Tea is the principal beverage of the Soviet Union. The samovar, in which water is boiled for tea, is a prominent feature of practically every Russian home. Women prize their samovars, which are passed from generation to generation in Russian families. The introduction of tea to the Russian area dates from the days of the overland caravans trails from Cathay (China), through the Jade Gate across the dry lands of Central Asia to the Volga River. The caravans from Asia carried brick tea—green tea leaves pressed in brick form—on the westward journey. Not only is brick tea still distributed, by other means of transportation, from China to Russia, but it is used in the dry lands of inner or western China—the regions of Mongolia, Sinkiang, and others, where its convenience of form permits its transport by the nomads of the area. The extent and quantity of the present China-to-Soviet-Union tea trade is not accurately known.

► TEA IN JAPAN

Tea is a hill crop in Japan. An ideal setting, not always attained on the farms, is to have flat flood plain or delta land for rice and vegetable growing, and hill fields for mulberry trees, whose leaves are fed to silkworms, and tea bushes.

Detailed distribution maps show some 32 separate tea-growing districts on the islands of Kyushu, Shikoku, and the southern half of Honshu, the largest and main island. And these districts do not constitute all, for many small areas of production might be included; also tea is grown in still other "mixed-farming" areas, where it is intercultured with crops which are more important areally. Of the Japanese tea districts, Shizuoka Prefecture, on the Pacific side of Honshu southwest of Tokyo, is by far the most important, followed by an area on the southern shores of Kyushu.

Everywhere in the tea districts the land is divided among thousands of small farms, each of whose operators may cultivate only an acre or less of tea. As the usual farm village is strung out at the base of the hills, where hill meets delta plain, the operator may have rice paddies in one direction from his home, tea fields in another. The land in tea, unlike the other fields, cannot be rotated between rice and vegetables during the march of the seasons, but is permanently in the bush crop.

Labor is provided by the farm family. In Shizuoka two pickings a year are accomplished, in southern Kyushu three. Not only does the family work in the tea harvest, but the initial handling and preparation of the leaves, before delivery to buyers, is a farm enterprise. Income per family is small in the tea regions, considering the amount of labor involved; income per total area is large for the Orient.

► PLANTATIONS OF INDIA AND CEYLON

The long season in the tropics of India and Ceylon, and the obtaining of six to seven or more separate harvests of tea leaves, makes both plantation management and machine handling of the leaves (after they have been delivered to a central point by the pickers) possible. Original investment by British capital when the British controlled India, free access to the world's largest consuming market in the British Isles, and the carry-over following the withdrawal of Britain from India in 1947 have been factors in both the establishment of tea plantations and their continued momentum. Tea production is unique in organization in India, as all other Indian agricultural products originate on small farms rather than on plantations. This is not true of Ceylon, for here many tropical products are grown on plantations; each specializes in one, such as tea, coconuts, rubber, or cacao.

There are two distinct tea plantation regions in India. One is in the northeast in the Brahmaputra River valley of Assam. Tea plantations occupy foothill zones, mantle areas of the Khasi Hills, and, in these latitudes, even occupy valley locations provided the lowlands are well drained; tea will not thrive on poorly drained soils. The other district is that of Ceylon and, on the neighboring Indian Peninsula, the southern portion of the Western Ghat mountain slopes, hill lands facing the Indian Ocean side of the peninsula.

Colombo, the port of Ceylon and a crossroads of ocean traffic rounding India or continuing to the Far East, is the site of many of the tea-exporting companies. Some of these operate world-wide, usually from home offices in London. This city serves both as an importer and re-exporter of tea, and its companies also direct shipments from Colombo to Australian and other markets.

► THE VINE

The grape vine is a member, botanically, of the *Vitis* or *Muscadina* family. The European grape and those of California are of the *Vitis vinifera* species, sometimes called the vinifera type; the clustered fruit of this grapevine—the

Fig. 10-7. Vineyard in the wine-producing area of the Union of South Africa, in the region of Mediterranean-type climate near the Cape of Good Hope. This vineyard has been established for more than 200 years. The Dutch (Boer) architecture of the houses in the distance is characteristic of many parts of the Union. South Africa exports high-quality wines to British markets. (South African Tourist Corporation)

grapes themselves—are hard and firm, have a tight skin, not easily removed, and may be of many colors, depending upon the variety. Black, red, white, light green, and purple are among the colors.

The products of the vine are of three types. One is fluid, in the form of grape juice or wine; another is the dried fruit; a third is fresh table grapes. Small grapes, when dried, are known as currants, a corruption of the word Cornith, for the shores of Greece along the Gulf of Cornith are a center of this activity. Large grapes are dried into raisins. In general, in the world pattern, the grapes of Mediterranean Europe yield wine; in the rest of the grape-growing regions of the world raisins are a significant product. Of course, all regions may and do produce some of each—Greece and Turkey are important producers of raisins; California is outstanding in the production of raisins, but wine is the product of several of the vineyard districts of the state.

There are grape-growing districts of *vinifera* in the Southern Hemisphere. Mainly these serve local or regional markets. The two most important are in the Argentine oases at the eastern base of the Andes, and in central Chile, a region with a Mediterranean-type climate. The wines are consumed in southern South America; the people of Argentina, who are largely of Spanish and Italian ancestry, are important users of wine—a culture trait passed down from their ancestors. Elsewhere in the Southern Hemisphere there are vineyards in South Africa near Capetown and Australia in the area near Adelaide; although the production of wine is not large—at least by European standards—each country exports small quantities to Britain.

Until the discovery and settlement of the lands of eastern North America the vinifera grape was the only type known. But American wild grapes, of two species, grew in profusion. The present "American-type" grape of the humid eastern United States is a development from the wild grapes which still line many country roads and fences. The Concords, Delawares, Catawbas, and other American grapes possess a pulpy, soft interior and have an easily removed purple skin.

FIG. 10-8. Vineyards and ancient castle in Burgundy, an important wine district of France. Grapevines grow on the plains and lowlands here. (French Government Tourist Office)

Commercial production of these is engaged in along the shores of Lake Erie in New York State, Pennsylvania, and Ohio, and along the shores of Lake Michigan in southwestern Michigan, in the Ozarks of Arkansas, and the Finger Lake district of New York. They are marketed mainly as table grapes, but the Lake Erie and Finger Lake districts produce, also, some quantities of wine.

▶ EUROPEAN WINE PRODUCTION

The traveler in Europe witnesses vineyards in practically every lowland which opens to the Mediterranean Sea, from Spain to Istanbul. Terraced vineyards mantle the lower slopes of hills. As he travels eastward, along the shores of Asia Minor, and at the eastern end of the sea in Syria, Lebanon, and Israel, he sees fewer; nevertheless, viticulture is not absent. Westward from Spain the river valleys and small plains of Portugal, opening to the Atlantic, contain sizable vineyards. In a few places, notably in the Douro River Valley of northern Portugal, inland from Oporto, he sees high hillsides above the river, hillsides terraced to the top of the slope, and each terrace supporting a few vines.

A traveler cannot fail but be impressed by the significance of the vine in these sunny-summer Mediterranean lands. Were he on a winter vacation he would see the gnarled stumps of the vines, for workers have pruned them down to this condition. The moderate rains of winter support the plant and provide some ground water. As the vine resumes its growth the deep roots seek out the small amount of moisture left in the deeper layers of soil. The plant, through this ability and its deep tap root, is able to survive the long, hot, and rainless Mediterranean summer. Only in the northern two-thirds of Italy does any significant amount of rain fall in the usual summer.

As the traveler moves northward from the Mediterranean Sea he notices fewer and fewer vineyards. But in striking contrast to the usual Mediterranean scene, those he does see are nearly all on the slopes of hills, except in warmer south-western France in the plains near Bordeaux. The alert viewer is soon aware of the fact that all of a hill is not planted to vines; only the south-facing and west-facing slopes are devoted to this land use. Man has "stretched" the limit of the vine in the poleward direction by facing his vineyards toward the noonday sun and the afternoon sun. Upon inquiry he finds that the more northern vineyards are of higher value per unit of area than those of the Mediterranean lands. He learns that special wines—Champagnes, Burgundys, Rhine and Moselle wines among them—originate in these vineyards. The grape, like some other warm-area products, produces its highest quality wine grapes toward its poleward limit. In Europe this polar boundary, reached through the hillside cultural practices, stretches from near the mouth of the Loire River in France northeastward to the middle Rhine valley of West Germany, thence eastward and southeastward to include Czechoslovakia, Hungary, and Rumania. But within this arc mountain

Fig. 10-9. The poleward limit of the vine is stretched northward and upward in Europe by planting vineyards on the sunny south-facing slopes of hills (compare with Fig. 10-8). These vineyards in Switzerland are at a relatively high elevation for the vine. Notice that certain of the slopes are terraced, and the soil held on them by rock walls. The electrified railroad line, at the base of the slope to the right, is found throughout Switzerland; electric power is generated from Alpine streams. (Standard Oil Company, N.J.)

lands such as the Alps and other cool uplands are excluded. And a poleward limit has been reached on the Iberian Peninsula in even the Douro River Valley of northern Portugal, in which the high-quality port wines are produced.

It is the ordinary wine—the *vin ordinaire*—of the Mediterranean vineyards that is the daily beverage of the inhabitants of the basin of this sea. Only the wealthy can afford the name wines; basically these are for export. But the ordinary wine is used daily on the tables of Greeks, Italians, Spanish, Portuguese, and French people.

The daily use of wine is a natural outgrowth of the Mediterranean environment. Water is at a premium during the dry summers; farm villages cluster around their sole water supply, perhaps a spring, but more often a single well. Water supplies, more so in the past than at present, were often contaminated; the waters carried dangerous bacteria; disease from contaminated waters was rampant. So it was natural for people to turn to wine for their daily beverage. Moreover, wine could be kept in jugs, jars, or bottles and stored against the season of normal drought. Each villager could store his own supply of wine and not be wholly dependent upon the well. Books of antiquity are filled with references to the importance of wine in the Mediterranean lands. The Bible itself, written in this climatic region, contains reference after reference to the wine of the region.

In France a political or national situation enters the picture; *vin ordinaire* is produced in France in quantity only on the narrow plain of the south, the Plain of the Midi along the Mediterranean. Here thousands of small farmers own vineyards of a few acres apiece, but the long narrow plain along the littoral is nearly one solid vineyard. And wine is the daily beverage of nearly all of the French, excepting only those of the extreme north along the English Channel (Normandy

FIG. 10-10. An extreme case of stretching the poleward limit of the vine. Radiated and reflected heat from the rock walls of the terraces on a south-facing slope warm the vineyards. Soil has been carried to each terrace. If it is washed downhill it is shoveled up and carried back to the terrace. In some northern locations in Europe grapes and warm-season fruits are grown on a small scale, the vines or small trees being espaliered against a southern wall. (Standard Oil Company, N.J.)

and Brittany), where it is replaced by cider. Thus, from the Midi (departments of Aude, Herault, and Gard) an enormous outflow of wine occurs. It moves in railroad tank cars and tank trucks. It is distributed throughout the French consuming areas, to the local markets of even the high-quality wine districts. The outflow is supplemented by *vin ordinaire* from Algeria, across the Mediterranean, which ships all of its wine to France. Thus the French obtain their daily beverage. It is used in virtually every home, is served in the schools from the middle grades onward, and is a "must" for the French army units, which are accompanied by fleets of wine-carrying trucks.

The Moslem side of the Mediterranean, despite its favorable environment for viticulture, does not specialize in the vine. Islam forbids the use of alcoholic beverages. Only in Algeria is the acreage large, and all wine is exported to France. A large number of the Algerian vineyards are owned and operated by the *colons*—French farmers who have moved to Algeria or whose ancestors moved there two and even three generations ago, as Algeria has been an integral part of France; the more than a million *colons*, rural and urban, use wine as a beverage, but the native adherents of Islam do not. Turkey, Tunis, and Morocco, Moslem nations, devote their vineyard acreage either to raisins as the product, or to export of wine to Christian nations.

France has the largest production of wine, a fifth larger than Italy, which follows. The Midi alone produces about the same gallonage of wine as Spain and Portugal together, has nearly half the production of all of Italy, and exceeds, in quantity of output, any other wine-growing nation of the world. One of its departments (counties) alone almost reaches the total wine production of the entire United States. And France alone imports more wine (largely the ordinary wines) than all other importing nations together. But the French also obtain foreign credits through the export of their quality wines—not large in gallonage, but of high value per gallon. Exports to the United States are not large; this reflects both the low per-capita consumption in this country and the importance of California and New York State domestic wines in the market.

▶ CALIFORNIA GRAPE INDUSTRY

California, the leading state in the horticultural industry in the United States, grows 90 per cent of the tonnage of American grapes. The entire production is of the vinifera type. Raisins from the Central Valley, particularly from the San Joaquin portion, wine from several coastal and near-coastal valleys not far from San Francisco Bay, and fresh table grapes constitute the output. In addition, small districts in southern California contain vineyards, but these areas—like the citrus lands—are experiencing urban encroachment.

The vine is irrigated in California, except for the acreage in a few of the humid coastal valleys. The irrigation of a drought-resistant Mediterranean product is unlike the situation in Mediterranean Europe. It reflects the fact that, to date, there is ample water for this purpose in the Central Valley, water derived from the Sierra Nevadas, or from the Sacramento River Project, wherein waters from northern California are pumped southward for use in the San Joaquin portion of the valley.

The grapes of the Central Valley are dried into raisins. The clusters of grapes are spread on trays in the vineyards, trays set between the rows of vines, and are sun-dried. There is little likelihood of rain during the dry Mediterranean sub-tropical summer; the Weather Bureau maintains a special warning service for the growers during this period—a "rain-or-dew" warning rather than a "frost" warning, as in California or Florida citrus districts. The vineyards and the raisin industry are quite widespread, but center in the area near Fresno.

The valleys set in the Coast Ranges, and within sixty to seventy-five miles of San Francisco Bay, are the locale of the wine-grape acreage. Each is removed from adjacent wine-producing valleys by hills or low mountains. Each opens into a wider interior valley or toward the great Central Valley of the state rather than seaward. And each individual grape-growing district has specialized production, and so has a product slightly different from its neighbors; the differences in soil, local microclimates, humidity, exposure, source region (in Europe) of the vineyard stock, and specific variety of grape provide a "European-type" special wine district in each valley, prized by connoisseurs. The actual names and types of the bottled wines are the European names. The California wines from these valleys, from some wineries in the Fresno district, and from some in southern California, and the wines of the Finger Lake district of New York and the Lake Erie shore in Ohio (these last-two named districts growing native American grapes) constitute the American output of the beverage. Home production is supplemented by imports from Europe. But wine has never been a principal beverage of the American people; per-capita consumption has been highest among first-generation immigrants, particularly those from southern Europe, and mainly those from Italy.

► OTHER BEVERAGES

There are several beverages in regional use—ones in addition to the principal ones of coffee, cocoa, tea, and wine. Many of these are consumed only by the inhabitants of very restricted areas. In addition, drinks with a low alcoholic content, such as beers and ales, are consumed on occasion, but they are not used as the *principal* daily beverage of the people, as wine is so used in much of the Mediterranean Basin and in France; and wine falls into this category of only occasional use in the parts of the world outside of the Mediterranean Basin and France. Drinks of high alcoholic content do not fall into the category of "principal beverage with meals." The group of manufactured drinks, the soft drinks, and the various colas, though distributed widely throughout the world from their original localization in the United States, are also not the principal mealtime beverage of the majority of people. Over a considerable area, only yerba maté or Paraguayan tea competes with or replaces coffee, cocoa, tea, and wine. And the consumption of yerba maté is restricted to southern Brazil, Paraguay, and large areas in northern Argentina. It is a regional beverage of this part of South America—a region which comprises the basin of the Parana River system.

▶ YERBA MATÉ

The yerba maté tree, which may attain a height of thirty feet, grows in the open, scrubby woodlands of the Chaco, a region in northwestern Argentina and southeastern Bolivia, and in the overall region centering on the area where Paraguay, Brazil, and Argentina meet. Commercially, the leaves are gathered from about a 250-mile radius from this point; there is little commercial gathering in the Chaco. Trees have been planted and cared for in some communities, and the sale of the leaves is an adjunct to farming.

The tea is made from the dried and pulverized leaves. It was the drink of the indigenous inhabitants. Today it is the chief beverage of the same area, plus an area extended eastward into the four southern states of Brazil, and southward in northern Argentina to Buenos Aires. For several million inhabitants of the overall Parana Valley it is virtually the one beverage; in Buenos Aires its consumption is large, but it competes with imported coffees from Brazil, shipped by sea from Santos. Nevertheless, cost, habits, and regional patriotism are factors in its continued use by thousands of the urban inhabitants. Argentina produces and consumes four times more yerba maté than imported coffee.

▶ THE SOFT DRINKS

The soft drinks, originally largely of American origin, are now sold around the world. In some undeveloped countries, especially those with a poor or contaminated water supply, they have found wide daily acceptance as a safe beverage. In the United States, and in Europe, while their consumption is large, they are not usually a principal beverage of the inhabitants, though their per-capita consumption is very high in many regions. Among the soft drinks are the ginger ales, many fruit-flavored drinks, the several colas, and many, many others. The flavoring ingredients are of diverse origins. Some flavorings are actually of tropical-plant origin, such as the ginger root of the tropics or the kola nut from the cola genus of trees, tropical trees indigenous to Africa. The specific flavoring syrup and the combinations of materials are secret formulas of the various manufacturing companies.

► QUESTIONS

1. What are the reciprocal relations in trade between Brazil and the United States?

2. Explain why the coffee tree must be grown at higher elevations in the latitude by Colombia (3° to 8° north) than on the Brazilian Plateau (latitude of the Tropic of Capricorn).

3. What was one of the effects of Brazil's attempts to control the production of coffee? Comment on the subject: Regional competition among areas of the world whose environment and economic setting are suitable for a particular crop. Offer examples of this, using more than one product as an example.

4. Tropical plantations in similar environmental settings may shift their crop to another one suitable for the setting. An example given is the substitution of cacao for bananas (in eastern Central America) or bananas for cacao (in Ecuador). Cite other possible interchanges.

5. Why is the production and export of cacao admirably suited to the geographic and economic conditions of West Africa? Does the palm nut industry satisfy the same conditions? Explain.

6. What conditions in the southern United States have not been satisfactory for a tea industry, despite a suitable climatic environment?

7. Contrast the methods of growing tea as shown by FIGS. 10-5 and 10-6.

8. What market areas consume most of the tea of the world? Explain the reasons for this.

9. What reasons account for (a) the large consumption of wine in Mediterranean Europe, (b) the small consumption in environmentally similar Mediterranean North Africa, and (c) the greater importance in the United States of the use of grapes for raisins and fresh fruit than for wine manufacture?

10. Account for the wide acceptance of soft drinks by the market. In the United States might the bottling of soft drinks be said to be an omnipotent industry?

XI The Small Grains: Production, Use,

and Manufacture

The small grains are those cereal grains that have a small kernel or seed. These many grains are generally members of the various families of grasses. The most widely grown small grains of the middle latitudes are wheat, rye, barley, and oats—considering the areas as a whole. The most widely grown small grain of the hot, humid regions of the tropics and wet subtropics of the world is rice. These five dominate in the world picture. Among these five the "staff of life" in the food supply is provided for millions upon millions of the world's inhabitants. Rice alone is estimated to be the chief food grain of approximately half of the world's people.

Man seeded the small grains and perfected them gradually, in antiquity—so long ago, in fact, that there is still dispute among botanists and agronomists as to the exact regions of origin and domestication of the numerous grains from their wild-grass ancestors. However, the Caucasus Mountain region of southern Russia, the valleys of trans-Caucasia, and the Mesopotamian region of present Iraq, as well as the region between Mesopotamia and the Caucasus (the region presently in eastern Turkey) seem to be the overall area of development and dispersion for the small grains of the middle latitudes. Rice, on the other hand, was indigenous, apparently, to the peninsula of Southeast Asia—the present region of Burma, the Indochina Peninsula, and the Malay Peninsula. Many, many generations of early farmers contributed to the domestication, development, and improvement of the small grains. Research continues, and not a year passes without the introduction of varieties suited to given environmental conditions, to resistance to smuts and plant diseases, or varieties whose yield per acre is greater than even those of twenty or thirty years ago.

Corn is a grain, but not a small grain. Its kernels are large. Some of the millets and sorghums, grains adapted especially to semiarid lands, are small grains; others are not.

Flax is also a small grain of the middle latitudes, but the flax plant does not yield a food. Rather the seed is the source of linseed oil (the Latin name of the flax plant is *Linum usitatissimum*) and the fiber contained in the flax stalk is the raw material woven into linen.

The six small grains of widest world distribution and importance are rice, wheat, rye, barley, oats, and flax. Regionally, in certain parts of the world, one of the millets or one of the sorghums is the chief grain and the source of a local food supply. And there are other local "seed foods" in limited regions; for example, sesame, an herb rather than a grain, is of consequence in eastern Africa and in the Middle East—its seed yields both a food and an oil.

► RICE

Rice is the major small grain of the hot and humid wet-tropical and subtropical portions of the world. It is, to the inhabitants of these regions, the only significant small grain; corn is its only competition. Corn can be, and is, grown in many parts of the wet-and-dry tropical world, and is relatively important as a grain crop and food in the tropical margins and the humid subtropics of the New World; but rice dominates elsewhere. Rice is grown on each of the inhabited continents, but the nations of eastern Asia produce well over nine-tenths of the world's supply. Outside of Asia, among countries, only Brazil, the United States, Italy (the Po Valley), and Egypt have an important production of rice, and the tonnage of each is dwarfed by comparison with that of any single Far Eastern nation. However, some rice is grown in all the tropical nations of Latin America and Africa. Rice is irrigated in the dry lands of the Middle East and along the Nile. A little is grown in Mediterranean Europe, which is warm enough for the crop; more could be raised except for the problem of a generally short water supply for flooding the fields. The Po Valley, not in the Mediterranean realm, has an ample water supply from the Alps, which supplements the natural rainfall for flooding the fields.

Rice reaches its greatest importance—in fact, outstanding importance—in the Orient. From the islands of the East Indies northward through the Philippines, the Indochina Peninsula, Burma, much of India and East Pakistan, and the southern halves of China, Japan, and Korea, rice reigns supreme. Thus, to the outsider, rice is associated with the Oriental or Far Eastern world. The association is true in a general way, but not in all particulars; wheat is the chief grain of dry northwestern India and West Pakistan, certain millets and sorghums the chief grains of the dry portions of inner peninsular India; wheat is the major grain and food of north China and Manchuria, barley and millet comprise the major grains of the dry western provinces of China. Rice is the chief food throughout Japan, but is grown in quantity only in the south; thus Japan stands in contrast to India and China, for the inhabitants of areas which are beyond the limit of rice import it from elsewhere; in the parts of India and China where rice cannot be grown the local grains—usually wheat—are depended upon.

Rice is a high-yielding grain crop. Rice contains a large percentage of starch, but is not satisfactory for breadmaking. Therefore, unlike the bread grains of the

FIG. 11-1. Rice paddies occupy the flat valley floor in the distance, and rice, grown on man-made terraces, stretches up the hillside. The grain has matured and is ready for harvest. The rice on the terrace in the foreground has been cut and is hung across a rack. The virtual impossibility of the use of agricultural machinery is evident from the small size of the individual holdings. (Japan Tourist Association)

middle latitudes, rice is consumed in various direct forms rather than first being processed or manufactured into flours and cereals.

▶ RICE IN THE ORIENT

There are lowland and upland varieties of rice, but the last named are relatively unimportant and are grown only in certain hill and upland areas. Its yields are erratic and generally not high per unit area. Thus it is the lowland rice which dominates and which is the basic food of millions of persons in the Orient.

Lowland rice requires a large water supply, a warm to hot growing season of about 180 to 200 days, and flat land. During the early period of its growth the rice plant must be in standing water; it is this factor which makes it necessary for the farmer to plant the grain on flat surfaces. Ideally, these surfaces are natural ones on old lake beds (lacustrine plains), on river flood plains, and on deltas. It is these landforms in the Orient that constitute the so-called great "rice bowls," such as the Rice Bowl tributary to the middle Yangtze River. But, the combination of population pressure and paucity of flat land in certain parts of the Orient, suitable climatically for rice, has resulted in man's providing the flat surfaces— through the building of terraces on hillsides and the contouring of low slopes to provide steplike fields separated by low embankments. Even on flood plains, which normally have a low pitch in a downstream direction, small embankments are built to provide level land on the flat but pitching surface. Only on lacustrine and delta plains are surfaces normally completely level. Some artificial terracing in the Orient ranks among the "marvels" of the world, especially when the time of their construction by hand in the distant past is considered.

The water on a flooded rice field must circulate slowly; it is not completely stagnant. Under the Oriental system, with very small fields, low banks of earth separate tiny fields. Each field is at a slightly different level—in many cases only an inch or so in difference. The water led onto the upper fields thus circulates slowly downslope, and is controlled by the embankments, small gates, bamboo brush, and other devices. The fragmentation of a large rice-growing area (such as a river delta) into the small *sawahs* (the Javanese name) or *paddies* (China and Japan) is characteristic, and is due to two factors. One is for the control of water under "primitive" methods, but methods in use for thousands of years; the other, equally important today, is separate ownership. Individual paddies in Japan may be no larger in area than a tennis court, but one farmer may own as many as five or ten, each located in a different part of a rice-growing delta plain. Thus, the necessary separation of the past, plus generations of inheritance of separate paddies, results in today's kaleidoscopic landscape.

All conceivable sources of water are used. In parts of the Ganges delta of India and in southern China the normal monsoon rains are heavy enough to keep the paddies flooded. Where this is not the case supplementary water is added.

Canals, ditches, small streams, rivers, ponds both natural and artificial, water draining from cities, and other sources are used. Human labor is pressed into service for the flooding of terraces; water may be carried uphill by men. Some terraces are watered from ditches, which depart from an upstream source and are led on the contour, around hills, many miles to the terraced fields. The dependence upon man-flooded rice paddies increases northward as rainfall decreases and the rains cannot be depended upon to fill the paddies.

Water, in the form of floods, is also a hazard, considering the fact that the majority of rice paddies are located on lowlands near rivers or on deltas. The famines of the Orient, when the rice crop has failed, are owing often to too much rain, and consequent flooding and destruction of the rice bowls, rather than to drought.

Rice is sown in the Orient in prepared beds, comparable to a hothouse situation. It is started as early in the spring as feasible, even before the beginning of the growing season in the fields, and is protected from inclement conditions and tended carefully by hand. Meanwhile the fields are being prepared. The source of power for plowing the low and muddy fields varies. The water buffalo or carabao is usual over wide areas; this beast is suited admirably to the environmental conditions of the low wet lands. Farmers who cannot afford a water buffalo, or the farmers of regions where they are not in general use because of the expense of feeding and maintaining them, spade the paddies by hand. In any case a large amount of human labor is applied to a small quantity of land to prepare the seed bed.

Rice is transplanted to the prepared and flooded paddies by hand. Lines of men, women, and children back across the paddy, carefully setting each individual rice plant in its muddy seed bed. Again the labor factor is dominant. While the rice is growing, and new water is being added as necessary, a second planting of seed may be made, and a "new seedling" crop started in hothouse frames.

Toward the middle and close of its growing and maturing season the rice heads, fills, and yellows; its appearance from a distance is that of wheat or any other small grain as maturity and harvest approaches. Water is withdrawn from the paddies shortly before the rice harvest.

Rice is harvested in the Orient by hand, the sickle being a usual implement. It is tied in bundles by workers and transported to the threshing floor or building. Some threshing here and there is by flail; some is by simple "machines," really a series of sawtooths, through which a worker draws the plant by hand; the rice grains are pulled off, and drop into a bin; the worker places the straw, from which the kernels of rice have been separated, in a pile, and proceeds to pick up more unthreshed plants to repeat the process. Some small threshing machines are in use, particularly in Japan.

Following harvest, the paddy may be plowed again, almost immediately. The second planting of rice is then set out. Through this intensive system, and the seeding and starting of the rice plants in seed beds, two successive crops are squeezed into one year—despite the 180-to-200-day growing season of the grain;

the first part of the period has been accomplished in nurseries, the last part in the paddies. Rice has been double cropped. Actually, the use of double cropping varies with the climatic setting and the latitude, or the possibility of frost. The true tropical settings can yield two crops of rice each year—or, without planting in nurseries, each thirteen to fourteen months. The wet-and-dry tropics of extreme southern China and of Formosa can grow two rice crops with nursery planting. The very south of Japan is able to double-crop rice. Farther north this is not possible, but double cropping is practiced by planting a vegetable crop following the rice harvest. Near, and at the poleward limit of rice only one crop—rice—can be obtained between the last killing frost of spring and the first frost of autumn.

Production and Trade

China and India are the leading rice-growing countries by far. China usually leads. Japan's rice production is third in the world. Regionally, the rice of East Pakistan is part of the Ganges Valley and delta production of the Indian subcontinent.

The chief rice lands of India and East Pakistan are on the flat alluvial plain of the Ganges and Brahmaputra valleys, and the compound delta of these rivers. Discontinuous plains along the rainy western, or Malabar, coast of India and plains and lowlands on the eastern side of the peninsula are important in rice growing. As in all rice areas the existence of flat or flattish lands is a localizing factor. And the rice-growing areas contain the largest densities of rural population of the Indian subcontinent.

The valleys and terraced slopes of southern China, and the Yangtze Valley and delta, are outstanding in China's rice crop. The famous "rice bowl" is in the middle Yangtze Valley, where broad alluvial flats, flood plains, and lake country lie in a basinlike setting. An abundance of water in this lake-lagoon-river country permits extensive and continued flooding of the rice fields. Farther inland the Basin of Szechwan is a leading rice area.

The rice-growing lands of Japan, Formosa, and South Korea are on discontinuous small plains and deltas. Cultivation is intensive and yields per acre are high. All available land is used; even in areas of spreading urbanization near the Japanese cities rice and vegetable production persists as long as possible on lots or vacant spaces in the suburbs. On the island of Formosa two-thirds of all the cultivated land is in rice.

China, India, and Japan are rice-importing countries, despite their home total production of ten million or more tons of the grain annually. This is owing to the total populations of a billion persons to feed. It is to the lands of southeast Asia, between the population centers of China and those of India, that these nations turn. Burma, Thailand, and the several countries of the Indochinese area east of Thailand are the world's principal exporters of rice. Their home inhabitants, though of considerable numbers, are far fewer than in India, China, and Japan, and have a surplus of homegrown rice. They do not press upon all of the rice

FIG. 11-2. The extensive rice field is characteristic of the rice-growing regions of the United States. This field has been contoured, and low embankments hold the water. The rice has been seeded by low-flying airplanes but has not yet grown above the water level. Contrast these fields and methods with the hand-transplanting of rice in the paddies of the Orient. (Standard Oil Company, N.J.)

production of the Irrawaddy Valley of Burma, the Menam Valley of Thailand, and the Mekong in Cambodia. Rice is exported from Rangoon, Bangkok, and Saigon, respectively. Destinations and amounts vary from year to year, but Japan, India, Pakistan, Ceylon, and Indonesia are the usual chief recipients; China is apparently about in balance between production and consumption, but Hong Kong is an importer and re-exporter. During World War II Japan conquered these rice-exporting lands, thus guaranteeing her food supply so long as shipping lanes were open; a corollary of this was a rice shortage in India, unable to import rice during this wartime period.

▶ RICE IN THE UNITED STATES

The growing of rice in the warm temperate regions of the United States is carried on by the use of the most modern machinery. Rice, during its harvest, is treated like any small grain; it is harvested by combines, and a mature rice field looks, from a distance, like a wheat or barley field. Only on closer view do the ditches which thread it, and serve as both sources of water for flooding and for the withdrawal of water later, stand out in the landscape. Low embankments, which separate one huge field from another, and which hold the early season floods, are crossed by the combines easily—in fact, are barely perceptible in a mature field of the grain. In the United States one man handles 100 or more acres of rice; in the Orient one man grows about one acre; total yields in the United States are high per man; in the Orient they are low per worker but high per unit of area. Economically, the completely different settings and population density justify completely different systems of cultivation.

Three small areas are the contributors of the American rice crop. The largest is the Gulf Coastal Prairie of southwestern Louisiana and southeastern Texas. The Grand Prairie of Arkansas, a flat region composed of old alluvium at a slightly higher level than the present flood plain of the Mississippi River, and the Sacramento River delta of northern California are the two other concentrated rice areas.

Rice is seeded with grain drills. Following seeding the large fields are flooded

Fig. 11-3. Rice harvest in the United States. The combines are driven right across the low embankments shown in Fig. 11-2. (Standard Oil Company, N.J.)

for from two to three months. Some few planters flood before seeding, and then seed the grain from airplanes. After the waters have been withdrawn the rice field, for the rest of the period of growth, looks like an extensive wheat field on a flat land surface.

Rice is actually exported from the United States. This reflects the low per-capita consumption at home. Americans have never consumed rice in any large quantity. The entire South is suited to rice, climatically. If demand arose the coastal swamps could be converted into gigantic rice fields; to date only coastal prairies, slightly above the lowland levels, are put in part to this land use—and most of the coastal prairies outside of the existing rice areas are grazed only. The exports of American rice go principally to Europe, in small quantity to Japan. A concentrated home market is in the state of Hawaii, with its predominant population of Oriental ancestry. This is a major market for California growers, who ship rice to Honolulu in bags marked "Grown in California especially for Hawaii." Cuba is another nearby foreign market, the Cuban people being rice-eaters, and the home production not meeting the home demand.

FIG. 11-4. A rice mill in the United States. The general appearance, the storage facilities, and the cleaner and dryer are not unlike mills working with other small grains. (Standard Oil Company, N.J.)

► WHEAT—LEADING GRAIN OF THE MIDDLE LATITUDES

Wheat is the leading grain crop of nearly all of the agriculturally-used portions of the middle latitudes of the entire world. Its production is so widespread that wheat is being seeded and being harvested somewhere in the middle latitudes of the Northern and the Southern Hemispheres every calendar month of the year. Only in two areas *of any size* is the wheat crop exceeded by some other grain. One is the United States as a whole, in which corn is more important. The other is a contiguous area in central Europe, comprising West Germany, East Germany, Poland, Austria, and Czechoslovakia; rye is the major grain of this region. For most persons of the middle latitudes, including the United States, wheat is the so-called "staff of life" or bread grain; however, in Germany, Austria, Poland, and Czechoslovakia rye takes its place.

The wheat production of the United States is second among the nations, exceeded only by the Soviet Union. Wheat is actually extremely important in American agriculture; were it not for the outstanding position of corn, and its use as feed for animals, wheat would be, as elsewhere in the middle latitudes, the leading grain crop.

The wheat acreage and production of the United States is highly regionalized. Wheat is the leading grain crop in the western half of the nation, except in the Central Valley of California, where barley is more important. Corn is the leading grain of the eastern, humid half of the United States—outstandingly so in the so-called Corn Belt, and very important throughout the South, where it leads all grains. Oats dominate among the grain crops grown in the cooler Great Lakes region, in the northeastern part of the country in New York State and New England, and in the Puget Sound lowland of the state of Washington. Despite the extreme regionalization, which is based primarily upon climatic factors, corn dominates on the national basis among the grains; to the non-American the nation and corn are synonymous.

Requirements of Wheat

Wheat (*Triticum vulgare*) is a member of the middle-latitude family of grasses, now, of course, much improved over its original wild-grass ancestor. There are many important species of the wheat plant and innumerable varieties. As a plant of the cooler, middle latitudes of the world, wheat will not yield well under hot, humid conditions, but requires moderate temperatures. It cannot be grown in the wet tropics. Little is grown in the humid subtropics, such as the American South; not only is the combination of heat and humidity detrimental in the wet tropics and humid subtropics, but the plant is susceptible to various rusts and smuts which thrive under the heat and humidity. Wheat will tolerate high temperatures only if the air is dry and the humidity low. Thus, some wheat is grown in dry tropical locations, as under irrigation in the Nile Valley, and in hot but dry areas in subtropical latitudes—as in parts of Australia and Texas.

Wheat requires a cool and fairly moist period following its seeding, a cool period after the plant has become established and is stooling—sending out additional stalks from its base—a warm growing season, and, preferably, a warm and dry harvest season. The world's great wheat belts, though in differing climatic settings in the middle latitudes, all have the requisite environmental conditions for growing the grain. Wheat will grow in many soil types, but does best in loamy soils which possess a high content of lime. The grain does not do well on sandy soils, on which it is replaced by rye, nor on heavy clays with poor subsurface drainage.

The cool temperate marine climates of extreme western Europe, the continental climates of central Europe and the northeastern one-quarter of the United States, and the Mediterranean climates of southern Europe and elsewhere provide excellent conditions for wheat culture. In some of these areas—as will be noted later—the wheat crop is still a dominant one today. In other places, as in the Corn Belt of the United States, wheat has been forced economically into a secondary or tertiary position, for it cannot compete in value per acre with a crop such as corn. Nevertheless, in the world setting, much wheat is produced in the above listed areas, and yields per acre are relatively high.

Dry climatic situations, especially the large world areas of the dry continental climate, were unused for crops until approximately the middle of the nineteenth century. They were grasslands, utilized in part for grazing. Long-grass *prairies* prevailed on the wetter or subhumid side of the dry continental areas; short-grass *steppes* were usual on the semiarid or dry side of the climatic realm. Today these dry continental areas contain, especially on their subhumid sides, the world's great wheat-producing areas. These present wheat belts—to be noted later—in the Great Plains of the United States and Canada, in the Soviet Union, and elsewhere, have been settled for but one hundred or so years. Their soils are rich and black *chernozems* and black-brown *chestnut* soils, and are among the richest in the world. But the rainfall is deficient and subject to wide variation annually. With settlement, it was found that wheat was eminently satisfactory for the environmental conditions. Extensive acreages can be cultivated by the use of modern machinery. Yields of wheat per acre are low, except in unusually wet years, but yields per man are high, owing to the large acreage each farmer can operate. Other crops, such as corn, do not compete with wheat for the land because of the subhumid conditions, which are unfavorable for the corn plant.

In summary, so far as regional settings are concerned, the wheat of the middle latitudes originates (1) in humid regions upon farms, which are generally of small size, but whose wheat yields are high per acre; and (2) in subhumid plains areas, on exceptionally large farms and ranches, whose wheat yields per acre are low, but whose yields per man are high, and each of whose workers produces a large surplus.

▶ WINTER AND SPRING WHEAT

The world's wheat crop is divided between so-called winter wheats and spring wheats. Winter varieties account for three-quarters to four-fifths of the world's wheat. Winter wheat is actually seeded in the late summer or early autumn. Late August and September are the months of seeding in the Winter Wheat Belt of Kansas, for example. The wheat grows to a height of perhaps six to eight inches, and stools during the cool days of fall. It remains more or less dormant during the winter, resumes its growth during early spring, and is harvested during early summer—in June and to about the Fourth of July under the environmental conditions of Kansas, but earlier in Texas, and later in July in Nebraska. In a Mediterranean climatic setting, such as Italy or California, the winter wheat is seeded in October at the start of the winter rainy season, grows more or less all winter because of higher temperatures, and is harvested in May—even in April in some locations. In Australia equivalent months are May and November. Winter wheat is the usual seeding of wheat in areas where the winter is not too severe, or where the young wheat is protected by a deep snow cover from the danger of being winter-killed through the deep penetration of frost.

Spring wheat is seeded during the spring and harvested late in the summer, or early in the autumn. It grows during a continuous growing season (in North Dakota or on the Canadian Prairie)—unlike the winter wheat of Kansas. The stooling is accomplished during the cool period of spring, harvest in the drier seasons.

Most of the world's wheat regions produce winter varieties of wheat. It is advantageous to do so; economically the seeding and harvest periods are not ones of competition with other crops for the time of the farmer; agriculturally the wheat provides a ground cover during the winter, and holds the soil from eroding. But there are two outstanding spring wheat areas among the world's leading regions. These are the Spring Wheat Belt of the Dakotas, Montana, and the Canadian Prairie, and the extensive Spring Wheat Belt of the Soviet Union. In each the growing of winter wheat is not possible: winters are too severe, frost penetration is too deep, and snow cover is too slight for winter wheat to survive the winter period without being killed.

Some few marginally located wheat areas grow both winter and spring wheat. But, usually, the winter varieties are seeded first in the fall. If they survive the winter, they are harvested; if winter-killed the crop is replaced by the seeding of spring wheat. Among these are the wheatlands of the Columbia Plateau (Palouse region) of eastern Washington and nearby northwestern Idaho, and the wheat areas of the part of the Great Plains in Montana to the immediate east of the Rockies and Glacier Park.

► HARD AND SOFT WHEATS

Wheat produced in a humid climate is a soft wheat; wheat grown under subhumid environmental conditions yields a hard wheat. The kernel itself is hard, and the composition of the kernel differs from that of soft wheats. Hard wheats are high-protein wheats, excellent for the making of bread.

One hundred to one hundred and fifty years ago, Europeans and Americans were familiar only with soft wheats. These were grown under the humid conditions of western Europe and the eastern United States.

Settlers pushed on to the subhumid grasslands of the world—the dry continental steppes—during and following the middle of the nineteenth century. The American Great Plains were settled, and the growing of wheat was established in these subhumid lands. Russian settlers occupied the Volga steppes of the southeast, and, in time, the dry continental steppes of western Siberia. Late in the nineteenth and early in the twentieth century the Canadian Prairie was occupied by farm settlers. Similar expansions of farmers to dry continental and other subhumid situations occurred in Australia, in Argentina at the dry edge of the Pampas, in Manchuria, and elsewhere. Soon hard wheats, produced from the transported seeds of soft wheats (from the humid original home areas of the farmers) began to appear on world markets. The kernels, in fact, were so "hard" that new milling machinery had to be perfected for their processing.

Today the terms hard and soft are common. The wheat-growing area of central and western Kansas is named, agriculturally, the Hard Winter Wheat Belt. Agronomists have perfected and developed many strains of wheat, strains suitable for a given regional environment; these are both hard and soft wheats—and seeded in entirely different regions. Millers may use one kind of wheat, or the other, or more commonly a blend of the various types for special flours. Thus, certain bread flours are composed of large percentages of hard wheats; some cake flours may be composed of more soft wheat. "Southern biscuit" flours are commonly of soft wheats; one large southern manufacturer of flour for this purpose uses only soft wheats from Ohio and Michigan.

► WHEAT-PRODUCING REGIONS

Wheat is grown very widely around the world. Its range extends from the cooler edges of the humid subtropical climatic realm well poleward to the margins of the sub-Arctic lands. Nearly every nation and political unit has some wheat production, excepting only those countries entirely in the wet tropics. Even those low-latitude nations that have tropical highland climates within their frontiers have some wheat acreage on the cooler uplands at high elevations.

The great majority of the world's wheat originates in the Northern Hemisphere. Europe, Asia, the Mediterranean lands of north Africa, and North America contribute this to local and world markets. In large part this situation is owing to the wide extent of land areas in the middle latitudes of this hemisphere. The middle latitudes of the Southern Hemisphere, limited in area, are not unimportant in wheat. It is grown in the southern portions of South America, in the Union of South Africa, and in Australia. Because of relatively small total populations in these areas, a large percentage of the Southern Hemisphere production enters world trade.

The wheat production of tropical highlands is small. Only Mexican uplands contain a significant acreage, and the yield does not satisfy the Mexican markets, so that the country is also an importer of the grain. Uplands in Central America, on the Andean plateaus of South America, and on the highlands of East Africa are producers, also, of small quantities.

There are seven great wheat belts in the world, areas specializing in the growing of wheat. In effect, though called "wheat belts," these are actually more properly "small-grain belts" as at least one, and sometimes more than one, other small grain is grown in conjunction with wheat. In each belt, however, the wheat acreage occupies the dominant position in the local agricultural economy. In addition, there are other important wheat-producing areas wherein general agriculture is the rule, but wherein wheat is a leading crop; though outstanding in its production, these areas are less specialized in wheat, and the farmers are less dependent upon wheat sales for their income than is the case in the extensive wheat belts. By and large, "the true" wheat belts are located in subhumid settings, on former grasslands, and are areas of large-scale highly mechanized agriculture, and areas occupied by farmers only for the past one hundred or so years. In contrast, the less specialized, but highly important, wheat areas are older agricultural regions in humid climates, are regions of small family-sized farms, and regions of long occupance, agriculturally. The highly specialized wheat belts are the producers of tremendous quantities of wheat per worker, but are regions of generally low yields of wheat in bushels per acre; and the less specialized, general-farming wheat areas have high yields per acre, lower per farm worker.

The seven great subhumid wheat belts include three in North America, one continuous one extending from southeastern Europe into western Asia, and one each in South America, Africa, and Australia—but the Australian lies in two separate parts of the continent.

The North American belts are all located in subhumid settings on former grasslands at the dry edge of the humid continental climates; each has been pushed, or extended, by man into semiarid lands, where crop failures occur nonperiodically. The bulk of each region, areally, is located, however, on the humid-subhumid transition; even here occasional dry years are expectable. Chernozems are the soils of the regions, except that chestnuts replace them as semiarid lands are reached. The three North American belts are (1) the Hard Winter Wheat Belt; (2) the Spring Wheat Belt; (3) the Palouse wheatlands of the Columbia Plateau in the state of Washington.

The Hard Winter Wheat Belt centers in Kansas, the nation's leading wheat-

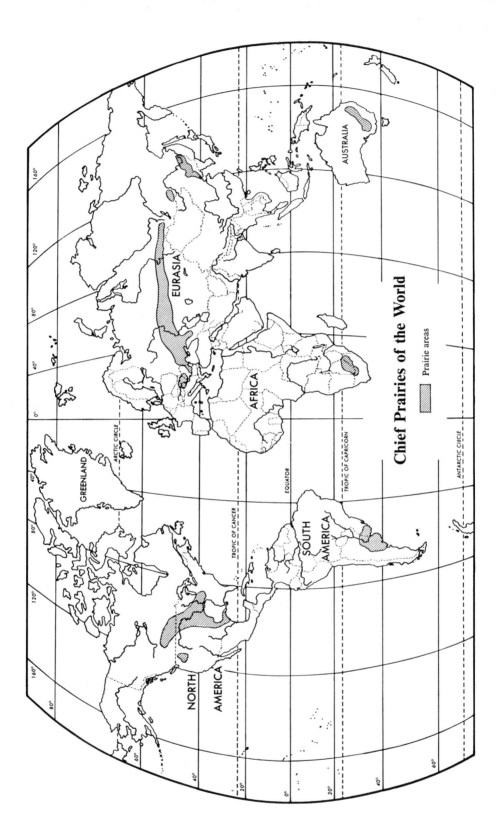

Chief Prairies of the World

Prairie areas

producing state. From this center it spreads southward through western Oklahoma and the Panhandle of Texas to a southern "hot" border at approximately 34° north latitude. Northward from its Kansas core, the belt extends into Nebraska to the Platte River and to the Sand Hills Region of that state. North of the Sand Hills, winter wheat and spring wheat overlap in southwestern South Dakota. Westward from the heart of the belt, winter wheat is grown well into submarginal and even marginal areas, far into the dry steppes of eastern Colorado; its culture ceases, however, before the base of the Rocky Mountains is reached. Eastward, there is a sharp border of the Hard Winter Wheat Belt, despite increasing precipitation. In places it lies against the Flint Hills of eastern Kansas; elsewhere, where the production of corn is more profitable, corn replaces wheat; the latter becomes distinctly secondary.

The North American Spring Wheat Belt lies poleward of the Hard Winter Wheat Belt, and poleward of the Sand Hills. From southern South Dakota the Spring Wheat Belt extends northward and northwestward on the rolling surface of the Interior Lowlands and the northern Great Plains. Within the United States it includes all of North Dakota, the nation's second wheat state, much of northern Montana, and the Red River Valley on the North Dakota–Minnesota border. In Canada, the belt includes all of the agriculturally used portions of the Prairie Provinces of Manitoba, Saskatchewan, and Alberta. On its north (and northeast) the margin of the Spring Wheat Belt is determined by the edge of the forest-park country, beyond the prairie, and by the less desirable, as well as less fertile soils of the grassland-forest transition. Westward, the belt abuts against the dry steppes of Wyoming and southern Montana, but reaches the base of the Rockies in northern Montana—south of the Canadian border—and in Alberta. Throughout the Spring Wheat Belt winters are severe, precluding winter varieties of wheat; however, there are some few exceptions. In some of the basins, among isolated mountains of central Montana (such as the Judith Basin) winter wheat can be, and is, grown; and in a region called the Triangle, east of Glacier Park, on the Montana plains, the warm Chinook winds of winter, descending from the Rockies, keep average temperatures high enough to permit the survival of winter wheat. These "exceptions" help prove "the rule"—if at all possible and feasible, winter varieties of wheat are grown. If, as in these exceptional spots within the Spring Wheat Belt, the winter wheat is winter-killed on occasion, the growers replace it in April with spring-sown varieties.

The Columbia Plateau Wheat Belt is in very rolling, even hilly, country in eastern Washington. Among the world's major wheat regions this area possesses the roughest terrain; old sand dunes, now mantled by wind-deposited loess, account for the irregular, pitching topography. Slopes on and around these old dunes lead in all directions; there is no uniformity in the pattern. Harvesting of wheat is affected by the terrain; on some steep slopes the most modern and largest machinery cannot be used; older, smaller harvesters are necessary. The Palouse region, as it is called, lies between the deserts of central Washington to the west

Fig. 11-5. Oil wells dot many a field of winter wheat in the wheat lands of Kansas, Oklahoma, and the Panhandle of Texas. The grain is almost ready for harvest. The scene is in early June. (Standard Oil Company, N.J.)

and the forested mountains of northern Idaho to the east. Northward it terminates near Spokane, the regional capital of this so-called Inland Empire. Southward, wheat acreage extends to flatter lands in the extreme north of neighboring northeastern Oregon. The wheat belt of the Columbia Plateau is climatically in the border zone between winter and spring wheats. Some farmers seed both; some seed and harvest winter wheat alone, but, in years when it fails to survive the winter, replace it in the spring with spring-sown grain.

Summer fallowing of part of the land is common on the wheat farms of all three of the North American wheat belts. Particularly the practice of the fallowing is followed in the western third to half of the belts, areally, the portions with less than twenty inches of annual precipitation. Summer fallowing involves the plowing and cultivating of the land, but a crop is not seeded. After each rain, the unseeded field is cultivated; weeds are destroyed by this, and the mulch and broken surface left after the cultivation keeps the moisture in the soil. The following year a crop is seeded—in effect summer fallowing results in one year's crop being grown on two years' rainfall. The fallowing of the present is in strips; this results in a distinctive landscape—long narrow fields of wheat, separated from one another by the black or brown soil of the fallow land. Strip-fallowing keeps the soil from blowing severely, for the wind is broken or slowed by the wheat plants of the adjacent field. In the past, severe dust storms often occurred when large blocks of land were in fallow. Dust storms are by no means absent from the North American—and other—great wheat belts, for they are part of the regional environment of the semiarid to subhumid lands; but man has learned how to help "keep his soil at home" through strip-fallowing and other practices. However, in very dry years these practices seem of little avail, as even the seeded wheat lands have topsoil dried to a dusty and powdery consistency. Fallowing as described for the North American belts is usual also on the dry sides of the Russian and other world wheat belts in this type of setting.

The wheat belt of the Soviet Union is the largest and most continuous wheat-

FIG. 11-6. Near the dry edge of the American wheat belts summer fallowing is practiced. The dark strips of land are being fallowed. No grain has been seeded, but the fields are harrowed all summer in order to conserve the moisture in the soil. The following year these fields will be seeded, and those in wheat the present year will be fallowed. The black chernozem soils of the former grasslands are striking features of the landscape. (Standard Oil Company, N.J.)

growing area of the world. From the prairies of the Ukraine, north of the Black Sea, it extends northeastward for 2,500 miles across the steppes of the Don, the Volga steppes, the steppes south of the Urals, and into the western Siberian prairies and steppes. The Don-Volga portion of this extensive grain-producing area, and the Siberian portion, is a spring wheat belt—one of the two chief (with the North American) in the world. The Ukranian part of the European wheat-lands in the Soviet Union, and the part of the wheat belt just north of the Cau-casus Mountains, grows winter wheat. The total wheat production places the Soviet Union as the leading wheat-producing nation of the world. During occa-sional years the Russian production is approximately that of the United States (the second producer) and Canada combined. In "normal" years it does not reach this total because of the large proportion of the Russian belt which lies on steppes, rather than prairies, and which is subject to annual fluctuations of rainfall and occasional droughts, with resulting low yields of wheat per acre. The operating units of the Russian wheat lands are both collective farms and government (or state) farms. In older regions, especially the Ukraine, collectives dominate. These were formed by collectivizing (putting together) former private farms. In newly settled regions government farms dominate.

FIG. 11-7. Harvesting wheat and baling the straw on a Soviet government farm on the steppes east of the Sea of Azov. The line of trees, a planted windbreak, is charac-teristic both of the Russian steppes and of many parts of the American Great Plains. (Sovfoto)

Soviet wheat lands appear in discontinuous prairie and steppe patches to the east of the main wheat belt, and the government has attempted to extend wheat culture southward from western Siberia into the semiarid steppes of Kazakhstan, an area with less than fifteen inches of rainfall, but with a summer warm enough for wheat. This area approximates eastern Wyoming in environmental conditions. Some success has been attained. It is well to remember, in making comparisons, that although the Soviet Union is two and a half times larger than the United States, its high latitude precludes agriculture in its northern areas, and that although its wheat acreage is the largest in the world, its total area of agricultural land does not reach that of North America. Also, since a high proportion of the belt is semiarid rather than subhumid, average yields per acre are not high; in the past, and early in this century, poor farming methods contributed, also, to low yields. What the human effect is at present is unknown, but extensive mechanization has increased yields per man. The Soviet efforts to increase yields per acre are concentrated mainly in the best, or prairie, portion of the wheat belt in the moister and more fertile Ukraine.

The Argentine Wheat Belt, or wheat crescent, is at the dry western edge of the humid Pampas and extends 600 miles in semicircular pattern from its northern edge to the southern or cool edge of the Pampas—also a dry transition. On the average, it lies some 300 to 400 miles in a radius west and south of Buenos Aires, the wheat-exporting port; the southern portion of the wheat belt is nearer to other ports, as it reaches the sea. Only on the northern or hotter edge of the Pampas, does corn replace wheat; as elsewhere, an acre of corn yields a higher gross and net return than an acre of wheat, and, in this northern area, economic competition for the land favors corn. Also, increasing heat and humidity is unfavorable to wheat and produces an environment in which rusts, smuts, and other plant diseases of wheat may thrive.

Australia is the leading wheat producer of the Southern Hemisphere, and, in addition, an exporter of flour as well as of wheat. Winter wheat is the universal seeding in Australia. Export is from the ports of Sydney, Melbourne, Adelaide, and Perth. Australia possesses two separate wheat crescents, or belts, one in the southeast, one in the southwest. The southeastern, much the larger of the two both areally and in production, lies on the inland plains of the eastern portion of the Murray-Darling River Valley, and westward—or beyond—the mountains whose ranges parallel the eastern and southeastern coast. To the coastal citizens the wheat lands (and the sheeplands) across the ranges are the "Black Slopes" or the "Outback." From low plateaus on the western slopes of the mountains the wheat farms stretch westward into dry-land margins. In pattern, from north to southwest, the crescent extends from the Darling Downs of Queensland, across New South Wales and Victoria, to South Australia near the city of Adelaide; the horns of the crescent face westward, partially encircling very dry steppes, semidesert, and desert. The largest wheat acreage is in the eastern, more humid portion of the crescent, against the mountains. Although the majority of the wheat belt, areally, lies in dry continental settings—and, in part, in dry subtropical margins—the western, or southwestern part is in the Mediterranean climate. And, across the continent in the southwest of Australia, is a second wheat crescent, this one with horns facing inland (eastward) toward the interior deserts. These two separate wheat areas are treated as one in the previous classification of seven great world wheat belts located on subhumid former grasslands.

The wheat belt of the Union of South Africa lies on the eastern more humid side of the Veld, the grassy uplands of the high plateau of the Union. Areally and in production it is less important than the Argentine or Australian belts. Unlike these two, also, wheat does not dominate (except in the belt) among the grains of the Union, for corn is far more important.

► HUMID WHEAT-PRODUCING AREAS

The seven great wheat belts, just described, are located on the recently settled grasslands of subhumid to semiarid environmental conditions. The extensive agriculture, large fields of wheat and other small grains stretching to the flat horizon, extensive mechanization, and widely dispersed farmsteads provide a character and flavor to these regions, one described by writers, pictured by illustrators, and romanticized as world breadbaskets. But three vastly different kinds of areas supply much wheat to world markets. These "small" farm, or family-farming lands are more usual in the middle latitudes, less striking in the place of wheat in the landscape, but highly productive wheat-growing areas, both in total quantity of wheat produced and in yield of grain per acre. These three areas—part of the eastern United States, northern China, and nearly all of western and Mediterranean Europe, along with many other small wheat-growing regions, are of extreme importance in supplying wheat to the world. In fact, the total wheat production of all of western and Mediterranean Europe exceeds that of the Soviet Union, the wheat crop of northern China and Manchuria is larger than that of all of the Southern Hemisphere, and the farms in a belt from Missouri eastward to Pennsylvania collectively produce as much wheat as is grown in a single state of the heart of the western belts. Secondly, less is heard, perhaps, of these wheat lands because the production is used rather locally, and little enters world trade, for these three areas are in regions of dense local population. Relatively small flour mills manufacture the local wheat for distribution and sale. The well-publicized long-distance shipment of wheat, by rail or sea, to distant consuming regions, perhaps halfway around the world—so characteristic of the subhumid wheat lands—is not present.

The farms of western Europe, Mediterranean Europe, and North Africa, of Turkey, and of a belt from Iran to West Pakistan and northwestern India produce very large quantities of wheat, as one crop in a general farming program. Winter wheat is the invariable seeding. On a political, or country, basis three nations—France, Italy, and Turkey—of this belt are among the ten chief wheat-growing countries of the world. This is a remarkable situation, and reflects the high yields per acre, for the other seven leading countries are all *large* in area, such as the United States, the Soviet Union, Canada, or Australia; France and Italy are only the size of a state such as Texas. And, within Europe, two small but intensive wheat areas with a local "grain landscape" are portions of the Danube plains in Hungary and Rumania. Modern machine harvesting of wheat is usual in most of western Europe, in parts of Turkey, and in scattered locations elsewhere; hand harvesting with sickles or scythes is common in Mediterranean Europe, the Middle East, and Pakistan and northwestern India.

North China, north of the latitude of the mouth of the Yangtze River is a leading wheat-growing area. Cultivation of wheat extends northward from the North China Plain into the plains of Manchuria, this last a former prairie grassland area of relatively recent intensive settlement, agriculturally. Inland, in China, wheat is grown to the dry land borders of the dry steppes and deserts.

American-grown wheat from farms of moderate size originates in the southern portion of the Corn Belt, and in the general farming agricultural region to its south, sometimes called the Corn and Winter Wheat Belt. Thus soft winter wheats are grown as one crop in the agricultural rotation in a belt of territory from the eastern edge of the Hard Winter Wheat Belt eastward to the Atlantic. Production is from eastern Kansas and eastern Nebraska through Missouri, southern Illinois, Kentucky, and southern Indiana. The wheat acreage then expands northward throughout much of Ohio, and into the southern half of the Lower Peninsula of Michigan, where wheat is an important cash crop sold from dairy farms. Wheat acreage reappears east of the Appalachian Highlands, particularly in southeastern Pennsylvania.

▶ WHEAT TRADE

Wheat is an important commodity in world trade. Moreover, it is moved long distances from the subhumid grainlands of the world to the densely inhabited centers of consumption. Wheat will stand the long shipment. It can be shipped in bulk. It is low in value per unit of weight, is handled easily, and is essentially a nonperishable commodity for a considerable period of time. Wheat can be stored in bulk in grain elevators, loaded mechanically into railroad cars through the use of chutes, unloaded quickly into terminal elevators in the ports, or transferred from car to ship. If not needed immediately for manufacture at its destination it can be stored relatively cheaply.

The United States, Canada, Argentina, and Australia are the four principal exporting countries. And it is the western wheat of the United States and Canada which enters international trade. Western Europe, despite its large home crop, is the destination of most of the exported wheat. Every nation of the western half of the continent, excepting only France, Hungary, and Rumania, are normally the major importers. And India, Japan, and Brazil, among other nations, are usually important in the importation of wheat. The Soviet Union uses most of its crop at home, but exports to the satellite nations in its orbit. Besides western Europe, the principal "deficit" wheat area, and a consequent major market, is the eastern United States. But the supplying of this market, despite distance from western producing regions, is domestic commerce rather than international trade.

The North American wheat from the plains is far removed from Atlantic ports, is separated from Pacific ports by the ranges of the Rockies, and, though the Canadian portion is not too distant from grain-shipping ports on Hudson Bay, the short shipping season in ice-troubled waters precludes more than three months of use of this northern route. But the Great Lakes function in the movement of wheat, both in overseas shipments and in the movement of wheat to and toward markets of the eastern seaboard. In contrast the Argentine and the Australian wheat-producing areas are close to the sea in places and not far removed from it throughout their extent. Consequently, considering the low cost of ocean transport, Australian and Argentine wheat, owing to geographical position and despite long water distances from European markets, can compete with North American wheat in those markets.

Flour, unlike its raw material, wheat, does not enter international trade in any significant quantity. Only Canada, the United States, and Australia export relatively small amounts. Shipping costs for manufactured flour are higher than for wheat. Flour must be packaged or barreled. Also, in order to protect home manufactures many wheat-importing countries impose higher duties upon flour than upon wheat, or admit wheat virtually duty-free. In a large country such as the United States or the Soviet Union flour is shipped long distances, but this is domestic rather than international trade. Flour from milling centers in the interior, such as Minneapolis and Kansas City, reaches markets on both American coasts.

Marketwise the "overproduction" of wheat of the present in North America is essentially a feature of this one continent. It reflects many factors. One has been the inability, in part owing to costs, to sell all the wheat, competitively, on world markets. Lessened per-capita consumption of wheat products in the United States, owing to the rise in competing foods, has been another factor. High yields per acre in given years have added to surpluses. Until the late 1950's the "overproduction" problem was confined to the United States; Canada was able to market her wheat in Britain. Recently the wheat-surplus difficulty has appeared, however, in Canada.

► FROM HARVEST TO MARKET IN NORTH AMERICA

The green and headed fields of wheat begin to yellow as the grain matures. Harvest approaches. Soon, from the southern portion of the Panhandle of Texas northward to the park-forest northern border of the Canadian Prairie the harvest will be in full swing, creeping northward week by week. Beginning in late May in Texas, and continuing until middle September in Canada, the combines will reap the grain. The peak of activity in the wheat lands will move northward, slowly from county to county, and before the combine crews have completed the harvest of spring wheat in Canada the wheat growers of Texas will have prepared and seeded their fields with the winter wheat crop of the ensuing year.

Giant power-driven combines now harvest the wheat. The combine, as its name implies, both cuts and threshes the wheat. The machine cuts a 14- to 16-foot swath through the grain on each round, delivers the threshed wheat to a truck driven alongside (or stores the grain within the combine for a while, then pauses for unloading), and spreads the straw behind it as it proceeds. The combine has replaced the former reaper, the header (which headed the wheat for later thresh-ing), the binder, the threshing machine, and other harvesters of the not-distant past. It has replaced thousands of temporary harvest hands, who once followed the harvest from south to north, shocking the grain as it came from the binders, and so readying it for threshing.

Combine crews are recruited from the wheat belt. In many cases the opera-tion is a family enterprise. The father and sons operate the one, two, or three large combines; mother and daughters serve as cooks and housekeepers during the season—the entourage traveling from farm to farm in the combines them-selves and in an automobile-drawn trailer, which serves as home and kitchen. Other combine crews are composed of men only, one usually serving as provisioner and cook. A combine crew may be away from home and on "the road" for two to three months, starting in Texas and ending their season at the Canadian border. Harvest of Canadian wheat is commonly by separate groups, citizens of Canada, though there is some crossing of the frontier.

Farmers contract for the cutting of their wheat. No longer do most farmers themselves actually engage in the harvest, leaving it to the traveling combine crews. Agents of each crew may precede it, contracting for the harvest, and guar-anteeing certain dates. Once a crew is established, and has made a reputation for performance, the same crew (or its owner and engaged workers) may harvest in the same pattern year after year, and not worry about engagements. Some com-bines are actually farmer-owned; others are village-owned, and many villages of the wheat belts may be partially emptied of their inhabitants during the late May to September harvest season.

The height of the harvest is June in the Texas Panhandle and in much of the Winter Wheat Belt of Kansas; by the Fourth of July the peak has been passed in Kansas. Early July witnesses the clean-up in northern Kansas and the advent of the Nebraska cutting. Usually by the twentieth of July the winter wheat is harvested.

The spring wheat harvest in South Dakota begins from mid-July to late July. Thus there usually is a ten-day to two-week interval of quietus, during which machines may be repaired and serviced. August is the harvest month of spring

FIG. 11-8. Cluster of grain elevators at the port of Duluth, Minnesota, at the western end of Lake Superior. The wheat is shipped eastward as rapidly as possible. That not shipped before the close of navigation is stored in the many elevators. Beyond the bay, on the flatlands in the distance, is Superior, Wisconsin. The port of Duluth-Superior handles much of the iron ore of the Lake Superior iron-mining ranges as well as wheat from the Spring Wheat Belt. (Standard Oil Company, N.J.)

wheat in North Dakota and Montana, and by late in the month and during September combining is in full swing on the Canadian Prairie.

Combines work by day and much of the night during peak seasons. They are equipped with lights for night work. A large crew may operate all night, in shifts. A family crew may be in the fields from 4:00 or 5:00 a.m. until nearly midnight, in rotational turns. The dry periods of harvest aid in this, but schedules are delayed or even interrupted during rains or series of rainy days. As soon as the wheat of one farm has been cut the crew moves to its next engagement, often in a "leap-frog" pattern, as crews keep passing one another on the journey northward. During the movement by road narrow roads may be blocked by the giant combines, some of which reach almost from fence to fence, though the wheel treads are on the highway.

The harvested wheat is transferred from combine to trucks driven alongside.

The truckloads of wheat proceed directly to the country elevators, located on railroad sidings in the villages and towns of the wheat belts. During some years, when the elevators are full, wheat is stored in temporary steel tanklike structures, or even heaped on the ground outdoors. Particularly is this last the case in the Texas-Oklahoma portion of the Hard Winter Wheat Belt where there is less chance of spoilage from rain, and where high daytime temperatures in the 90's, combined with low humidity, permit outdoor storage with some degree of safety.

Wheat is shipped by rail from the country elevators to large terminal elevators at the flour-milling centers, or to elevators at the ports on Lake Superior and Lake Michigan. Rail movements begin as soon as the first wheat has been harvested. Lines of empty box cars have been assembled by the railroads on the sidings of each shipping point. Each car is loaded as it is shoved past a chute, leading from the elevator, and trainloads of wheat are started toward the terminal points, or toward junctions where cars from different branch lines are assembled into longer trains. The peak of this activity on the rail lines lasts from two to three months following harvest; in Canada, with a September start, rail shipments to ports continue at a fast pace until the end of November; by this time, of course, the bulk of the wheat of Kansas has long since been shipped, or is in winter storage in local elevators.

There are many terminal points for rail shipments of wheat. Kansas City, Minneapolis, and Winnipeg are the leading ones just to the east of the principal wheat belts. Kansas City and Minneapolis, both important flour-milling centers, are equipped with giant elevators, capable of storing millions of bushels of wheat for the local mills. Winnipeg, the major railroad center of western Canada, is an assembly point for further shipments to the storage center at Fort William–Port Arthur; its railroad yards are among the largest on the continent. Many, many, other centers likewise serve in the movement; among those not on the Great Lakes, wheat receipts are in the millions of bushels at St. Louis, Omaha, Wichita, and Hutchinson. Some elevators in other cities, such as Lincoln, Nebraska, would be outstanding in size in eastern regions, but are among several "secondary" centers in the picture of wheat movement and storage. Among storage centers, elevator capacity is greatest in Minneapolis, followed by Chicago, Kansas City, Enid, Duluth-Superior, and Buffalo.

A second destination of harvested wheat is a port of the Great Lakes, particularly the two upper lakes. From these ports, wheat is shipped eastward by water. Chicago and Milwaukee function in the winter wheat shipments; all rail lines lead to Chicago, and there are direct connections between Kansas City (and so the Hard Winter Wheat Belt) and Milwaukee. Duluth and Superior, at the head of Lake Superior, receive spring wheat from the plains well to their west, winter wheat from the Triangle of western Montana. North of the Canadian border, the twin ports of Port Arthur and Fort William perform the same function with respect to Canadian wheat.

Some wheat, destined for export, moves in other directions, southward to Texas Gulf Coast ports, westward to Seattle and Portland in the United States, and Vancouver in Canada. A small quantity, as mentioned, is moved northeastward to Churchill on Hudson Bay.

The relatively inexpensive water shipment on the Great Lakes brings the wheat belts "closer" to eastern and export markets, in relation to cost. The ports mentioned are equipped both for rapid loading of ships and for large-scale storage; giant elevators line parts of the waterfront. Grain, especially wheat, is one of the two major items in down-lake shipment, the other being iron ore.

The lake freighters, 500 to 600 or more feet in length, are like giant hollowed-out barges, with engines and crew quarters in the stern, wheelhouse, and officer's quarters in the bow. Between, in the hold, many thousands of bushels of wheat can be carried; or, by segmenting the hold, wheat and other grains can be separated, or different kinds of wheat carried. Loading and unloading is directly from waterside elevators.

American and Canadian traffic divides on the lakes. Ships belonging to com-

Fig. 11-9. Great Lakes freighter being loaded with wheat in the port of Duluth-Superior. Note the water line on the hull of the ship. When fully loaded, the lower (light) part of the vessel will be below water level. (Standard Oil Company, N.J.)

panies of each nation are directed to separate receiving ports. American down-lake shipments are principally to the elevators of Buffalo, at the eastern end of Lake Erie. Canadian ships unload at Port Colborne, Ontario, on the north shore of Lake Erie west of Buffalo, or proceed through the Welland Canal to Lake Ontario and the St. Lawrence. If destined for eastern Canadian flour mills, Port Colborne or Montreal is the terminus; if for export, and a large percentage of the Canadian crop is so directed, Montreal and Quebec are the eventual terminus —directly by water or from Port Colborne by rail.

The waterborne traffic of the Great Lakes operates from early April, when the straits and connecting waterways are free of ice (the lakes themselves do not freeze), until midnight November 30 (but car-ferry traffic across Lake Michigan continues all year). The closing of the shipping season is not because of ice. Rather, the advent of severe winter storms becomes a hazard, and insurance companies do not insure cargoes after the end of November. Shipments of wheat begin during July; all wheat which is to be shipped eastward by water must have been handled by the deadline date. So anxious is the industry to have wheat en route that it is not uncommon for the last cargoes to clear a port, such as Port Arthur, at 11:59 p.m. on November 30.

Buffalo is now the leading flour-milling center of the United States, having surpassed Minneapolis. The waterfront is lined with huge elevators. Wheat for milling during the winter must be on hand. Buffalo has an advantage in being near eastern consuming markets, and a particular advantage, economically, in a freight rate that permits "milling-in-transit." Thus wheat may be stored and manufactured into flour, and then shipped to the eastern seaboard cities as flour at the rate at which it began its journey as wheat.

Export of wheat or of flour from the United States to Europe is through an East Coast port, principally New York. Montreal is the exporting center of eastern Canada. But the lower St. Lawrence is frozen for from three to four months each winter. Canadian wheat which has not been exported before the closing of the lower river is sent by rail to the ice-free ports on the Atlantic—Halifax and St. John in Canada, and to Portland or Boston in the nearby United States.

Domestic movement of wheat and flour to consuming markets is still mainly eastward from the interior wheat belts. However, postwar market changes have resulted in increased movements westward, reflecting the important increments of population in the Pacific states. And, increased prosperity in the South has resulted in a larger per-capita consumption of purchased bread, manufactured in bakeries, and a lessened use of home-baked corn bread, and even of home-cooked biscuits.

► RYE, BARLEY, AND OATS

Rye, barley, and oats constitute the small grains, other than wheat, of chief importance in the middle latitudes. Rye, high in protein, makes a strong flour, and

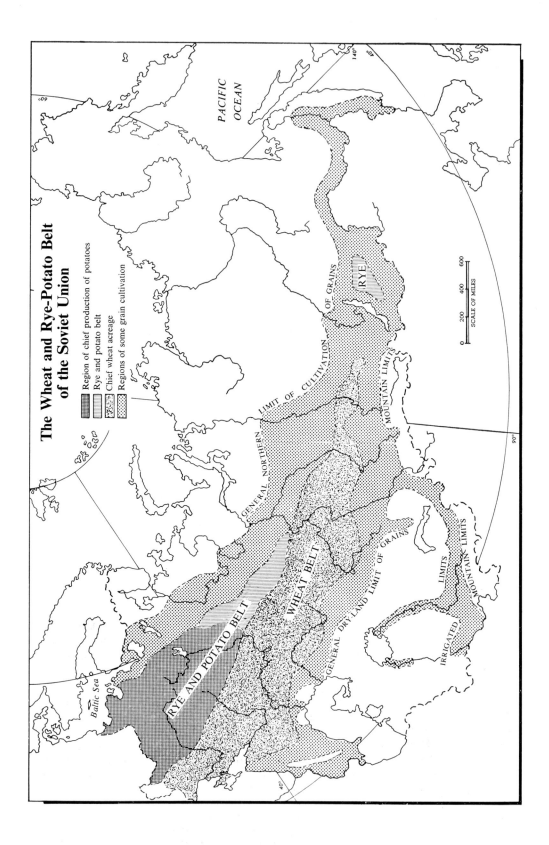

The Wheat and Rye-Potato Belt
of the Soviet Union

Region of chief production of potatoes
Rye and potato belt
Chief wheat acreage
Regions of some grain cultivation

PACIFIC
OCEAN

RYE

SCALE OF MILES
0 200 400 600

LIMIT OF CULTIVATION OF GRAINS

GENERAL NORTHERN

MOUNTAIN LIMITS

RYE AND POTATO BELT

WHEAT BELT

GENERAL DRY LAND LIMIT OF GRAINS

LIMITS

IRRIGATED

MOUNTAIN LIMITS

Baltic Sea

is a leading bread grain in certain regions, particularly in northern and eastern Europe. Barley, whose pattern of overall distribution is not unlike that of wheat, is principally used as a feed grain for animals and in the brewing of ales and beers and distilling of Scotch varieties of whiskey. Oats are significant feed in the animal industries and the ingredient of several cereals.

► RYE

The several attributes of rye, its tolerance of sandy soils and ill-drained soils and its short growing season, are important in the explanation of its world distribution.

Rye is the most tolerant of the small grains to difficult environmental conditions, especially to those of soil. Among the grains it yields relatively the best on sandy or acidic soils; the fact that it has become the chief grain of several sandy regions has given it the name "the poor man's grain."

Rye will withstand a cool summer better than wheat; throughout the plains south of the Baltic Sea, and eastward across central Russia, where the summer averages only in the 60's Fahrenheit, rye is the leading bread grain.

Rye has a shorter growing season than wheat. Thus it is grown farther poleward, as in parts of Scandinavia. Because of the shorter period of growth, rye is used often as a second crop in the subhumid wheat lands, as in the Spring Wheat Belt of the United States and Canada. Rye matures before wheat does, and its harvest thus does not interfere—or compete for labor and machinery—with the wheat harvest.

Rye is hardier than wheat, and will survive a colder winter if fall-sown. In the Spring Wheat Belt winter rye is seeded in the fall—when there is no competition with wheat for the labor and time of the farmer. The virility of rye is illustrated, also, by the fact that it will grow and produce a cover crop on fresh roadcuts, and thus is used by highway commissions as a first planting in many such locations.

Europe grows nearly all of the rye of the world; in some years as much as 95 per cent of the world production is from the continent. Rye is the chief grain of a large agricultural region, the Rye and Potato Belt, which stretches from the North Sea eastward across the cool and sandy plains of northern Germany and Poland, then widens to include the central one-third of the European portion of the Soviet Union. The rolling surface of this region is of glacial origin except in the eastern portion of the Russian plain. Drainage is poor over large areas but excessive on sandy outwash plains; soils are of podzolic type and include many sands and sandy loams.

In Russia the rye-growing areas lie just to the north of the wheat belt of the Ukraine and southern Russia; in western Europe the Rye Belt is north of the Alps. Elsewhere in Europe rye is a grain crop of short-season or poor-soil regions; for

Fig. 11-10. Harvesting rye in the Soviet Union. This view is the northern part of the steppes, not far from the grassland-forest border. (Sovfoto)

example, it is grown on the high Central Upland of France, but the surrounding lowland plains are devoted to wheat.

The servicability of rye as a bread grain gives it importance. Originally used for bread in countries such as Germany, Poland, the Soviet Union, and the Scandinavian lands, this use has spread elsewhere, in part through the emigration of people to the New World. Thus, today, rye bread is of consequence in the United States, more so in some regions than others; and rye is used as human food as well as for feed and for the distillation of beverages.

Rye is not important in international trade, principally because the producing and consuming regions are one and the same. West Germany is the main importer, owing to its large population relative to its agricultural area. Canada, Argentina, and the United States export small quantities to the European market.

► BARLEY

The pattern of the barley acreage of the world is much like that of wheat. Barley is a secondary grain in all of the principal wheat-growing regions and belts. In addition, among the small grains, barley has the shortest growing season.

Thus, in "fringe" areas environmentally, it is the only grain grown; it is grown farthest poleward in the world, farthest into the steppe-desert transition, and at the highest altitudes of cultivation on mountain slopes. These fringe areas, important as barley is to the local inhabitants, are of little consequence, however, in world production. The wide adaptability of barley is owing, partly, to the fact that the name "barley" is applied to species of the grain which are very different —a two-rowed barley which originated in the Middle East, and a six-rowed barley, indigenous to east central Asia.

Barley is an important feed grain. It is devoted to this purpose in large parts of Europe and in much of the Spring Wheat Belt of the United States and Canada. The animal industries of the Spring Wheat Belt depend in large part upon barley, for the season is too short and cool for the growing of corn—the usual feed grain of the New World.

Barley is important in the brewing industry and is the principal grain used in the brewing of ales and beers. Bright barleys from sunny Mediterranean environments are in demand in Britain for light ales. Barleys from the Dakotas and eastern Wisconsin are important in the American brewing industry.

► OATS

In tonnage, the oats production of the world far exceeds that of rye and is somewhat larger than that of barley. But except for a few areas in which part of the crop is used in manufacturing, oats remain on the farm or in the local region of production. This is because of the use of oats for stock feed and its particular importance as a feed for horses. For this reason, oats have retained a high importance in Europe. Mechanization of farms, almost complete in the United States, and the virtual elimination of horses as a source of power on farms have released thousands of acres formerly devoted to oats to other crops or other land uses. Nevertheless the oats crop is large, the grain is used in many prepared feeds— ground locally, or distributed nationally—and in some few, cool-summer areas oats is the leading grain.

Among the small grains, oats is able to yield the best, relatively, under cool-summer, rainy, and cloudy conditions. Thus it is important in the cool and rainy coastal zone of northwestern Europe; its association as a cereal used by the English and the Scottish is well known. In the United States the crop reaches its greatest importance in the cool Great Lakes region from upstate New York to Minnesota, and as a feed grain crop in the Corn Belt. Actually the hot summers of the Corn Belt are not conducive to the best oats crop; local thunderstorms, with strong winds, frequently cause lodging (blowing down) of the grain; and top-quality soils, fine for corn, may force straw at the expense of grain in the growth of oats. But, economically, oats fit the work pattern on a Corn Belt farm. The farmer plows the potential oats field in the late fall, after corn has been harvested; oats are seeded as early in the spring (long before corn is planted) as it is possible to get machinery onto the fields when they have dried; oats are growing during the period of corn cultivation; and oats are ripe and harvested as soon as the period of corn cultivation is over and the corn is tall enough to shade the ground. Thus the oats crop provides home-grown feed and does not at any time compete with corn for the labor of the farmer.

▶ MILLETS AND SORGHUMS

The millets and the sorghums produce well under conditions of deficient moisture. The two groups are composed of a large number of separate kinds of grains, and of a variety of plants, both tall and short. Species and varieties of each are legion; names are numerous, and a single name is not applied over wide areas of the world—thus botanists and agronomists are forced to use the Latin plant names when discussing them. Some are comparable to the usual small grains; some are "large grains" and their plants are not unlike corn in general appearance. One of the canelike grass sorghums, sorgo, yields a syrup and is most important for this purpose; it is the source of the sorghum "molasses" produced in parts of the American South and used locally in place of other syrups.

Some of the millets and certain grain sorghums are of extreme local importance as the leading grain of dry regions. The inhabitants of inner North China, not far from the deserts of Mongolia and the Gobi Desert, depend upon a millet for their bread grain. Grain sorghums are significant elsewhere in dry settings—notably kaoliang in Manchuria, kaffir korn in large areas of Africa, and jowar and ragi in dry interior peninsular India.

Millets and sorghums are relatively important as feed grains in the drier areas of western Texas, western Oklahoma, and southwestern Kansas in the United States. They are seeded annually for feed, and the acreage is expanded in years when winter wheat is affected by drought, and must be replaced in the spring. And since the early 1950's one of the grain sorghums—merely called sorghum—has become of great significance in the Missouri Valley of the United States, where it is used as a feed grain for animals. State agricultural colleges are introducing it widely, even as far east as Iowa; not only does it yield excellent feed, but it can be grown on land released under the federal corn acreage-control programs.

▶ QUESTIONS

1. Contrast the capital, land, and labor in the rice-growing areas of the Orient and the United States. What are the differences in production in these two areas so far as (a) the yields per acre of land and (b) the yields per man-hour of labor input are concerned?

2. Assuming that the population of the Orient and the United States were doubled, how might the rice needs of the two areas be met?

3. Why does the population of Hawaii, whose per capita consumption of rice is fairly high owing to the cultural background of many of the inhabitants, depend upon rice grown in California rather than having a rice industry of Oriental type on the islands or, say, substituting rice for sugar cane? Consider many factors of economic geography in answering this.

4. What is the importance of the region from Burma to Vietnam in the food supply of the Orient?

5. Compare winter and spring wheat, and compare hard and soft wheat. In what kinds of regions does each of the above originate?

6. Comment on: The settlement of the prairie grasslands of the world and the effect, at the time, in increasing the food supply of the well developed portions of the world.

7. How does the wheat belt of the Columbia Plateau differ from the other major wheat belts of the world?

8. What are the collective farms of the Soviet Union? the government farms?

9. In what types of environment are the three important wheat-producing areas of the Southern Hemisphere located? Name these areas.

10. Explain why the international trade in wheat is more important than the international trade in flour.

11. Why are bakeries more widely distributed than flour mills?

12. Rye is the chief bread grain of large parts of northern Europe. Relate this to both geographical and historical factors.

13. What are the major uses of oats?

14. What several factors help explain the eastward spread of sorghum acreage from the subhumid southern part of the Great Plains of the United States?

XII Corn, Soybeans: Production, Use,

and Manufacture

Corn requires a very warm or hot and humid summer for its growth, and is undoubtedly a plant of tropical or subtropical origin. The region to which it was indigenous is still in dispute, but considerable evidence points to southeast Asia; some authorities place it in the broad area including Burma and the Indochina Peninsula. However, the corn plant, *Zea mays*, was unknown to Europeans until the discovery of the New World. It was a staple of Indian gardens and granaries from southern South America northward through Central America and Mexico to the coast of southern New England. And it has been from the Americas, and particularly from North America, that the corn plant has been distributed to other world regions which now engage in its commercial production. Even today, corn is grown most widely in the Americas; the United States alone accounts for about half of the world production, and two states—Illinois and Iowa—usually each produce more corn than is produced in even the second corn-growing country of the world, and between them usually grow almost a third of the corn crop of the nation. To many persons in Europe and elsewhere the United States and corn are synonomous, agriculturally.

There is confusion in the word *corn*. This name is the one used for the corn plant and the grain in the United States and Canada. Elsewhere the word *maize* (from *Zea mays*) is the usual name. There are other local names, too, the South

African being *mealies*. However, the American name "corn" is winning wider acceptance. The reason for the use of the word maize is that many languages or peoples use the word "corn" in a different sense. In the British Isles "corn" refers to the four major home-grown small grains (wheat, rye, barley, oats) collectively. In Germany and Scandinavia *korn* means rye; in some countries the term is used for the most important of the home-grown grains.

Corn in regions of native subsistence agriculture, as in parts of Mexico and Central America, may grow to heights of only three to four feet in some settings, to heights of twelve to fifteen or more feet under ideal environmental conditions and in a soil of top quality. But, today, in nearly all corn-growing regions of the United States, high-yielding hybrid corn plants have been developed by geneticists and agronomists, and the exceptionally tall corn plant is no longer grown; statements such as "where the tall corn grows" are out of date. Instead, corn fields which contain plants of uniform height—around ten feet—are the rule, and the hybrid corn of the present far outyields its recent ancestors in bushels per acre. Also the hybrid corn seed industry has become a major one in this country; certain farmers, partnerships, and corporations specialize in the production of seed corn alone. The individual American farmer now purchases his seed annually rather than growing it himself.

The chief use of corn is as a feed for animals. The crop is marketed mainly in the form of meat "on the hoof." The majority of the corn crop of an individual farmer thus does not leave the farm upon which it has been grown, but is fed to beef cattle, swine, and poultry. A second important use of corn is as a raw material of manufacturing. Industrial alcohol, cereals, corn meals, corn oils and corn syrups, starch, and many other products are made from it.

The use of corn as direct human food is minor, considering the world as a whole. It is important for direct consumption in Mexico and parts of South America, and in Rumania in Europe. In the Union of South Africa corn is the principal food grain of the Negro portion of the population, but not of the white. More corn is used as food in the southern United States than elsewhere in the country; it is consumed as corn bread, hominy grits, and meals. The amount consumed in the United States as fresh corn on the cob, canned or frozen corn, is only a very small per cent of the total production, and is obtained from special varieties of sweet corn rather than from the usual field corns.

The Growing of Corn

The corn plant has a central or main stalk, and a luxuriant growth of long leaves. The tassel on top of the corn plant, after it has reached a certain stage of maturity, contains the pollen. The silks, extending from the immature cob, receive the pollen as it falls; each individual silk must be fertilized by a grain of pollen, for each leads to—or from—the embryo kernel. If one silk is missed, a kernel will be missing on the mature corncob. Winds interfere with pollination, especially if strong winds are prevalent during this season. Growers of hybrid corn must control the pollination; special workers are engaged to hand-pollinate some of the seed corn. The hybrid strains have been developed by the crossing of inbred high-yielding corn. Hybrid corn yields more bushels of corn per acre than the formerly used varieties did, but requires heavier fertilization; the increased yields, however, more than repay the added costs of commercial fertilizers. Because the hybrid varieties are inbred, they tend to become relatively sterile after a generation or two; thus the individual farmer, instead of using seed from his own crop (as in the past) must purchase seed corn from the specialized corn breeders.

The grain of the corn plant is contained on the cob, and, of course, is the kernel or seed. "Native" corn is of many different colors—black, white, red, brown, yellow, purplish, and others. But the usual corn, as perfected and developed in the United States, is white or yellow, and the present hybrid corn yields cobs of uniform size and kernels of almost symmetrical type and uniform quality. Much white corn is still grown in the South for local corn meals and cornbreads, however. Latin American areas, particularly those of subsistence agriculture, still grow many types of corn, and, as a result, corn of color other than white or yellow may be spoken of in the United States as "Mexican corn."

The field corn of the United States is a "dent" corn—the kernel contains a dent, or depression, down its middle (i.e. on the top of the kernel). There are many other types grown elsewhere. Argentine farmers specialize in flint corns—the kernels of which are different in shape and firmness from the dents, and more similar to popcorns. These are in demand among poultry raisers of western Europe, an important destination of exports of corn from Argentina. In contrast little of the American dent corns are exported; they are fed to animals upon the farm of their origin or sold to industrial establishments as a raw material for the manufacture of corn products.

Field corn is the usual type grown and is a major feed for animals, particularly for beef cattle, swine, and chickens. Intensive corn-growing regions, such as the so-called Corn Belt of the midwestern United States, are the centers of intensive animal industries, and the corn and animal enterprises are closely related—in fact, cannot be separated. Field corn accounts for practically all of the world's acreage and production, and in the United States for almost 100 per cent. A second type of corn, for direct human consumption, is sweet corn. There are many varieties. Sweet corn is consumed as corn on the cob or is canned, frozen, or otherwise processed; its total acreage is not great, despite its importance in market gardens, on truck farms, and as a local cash crop in a farming region adjacent to a cannery or freezing establishment.

Corn requires cultivation, and corn fields are clean-tilled. From the time the young plants first appear until the maturing plant is tall enough to shade the ground between corn rows, the field is cultivated; this provides a mulch to keep moisture in the ground and destroys the weeds which come up between the corn rows. Three cultivations are usual; in certain years a fourth may be necessary. Like cotton, also clean-cultivated, and unlike the small grains or a hay crop, corn is thus a "soil-eroding" crop. If cultivated up and down slopes the stirred soil between corn rows becomes a channel for the development of gullies, or for soil washing and sheet erosion. When grown on hilly or sloping fields for many years the erosional problem may become serious. The flat to gently rolling lands of the Corn Belt are less eroded, on the whole, than the southern United States, where long-time cultivation of cotton and corn, coupled with heavy summer thunderstorm rainfall, and bare fields during the winter has led to serious erosion. Even so, present soil conservation measures in the Corn Belt include practices and management based upon corn being an erosion-inducing crop. Ideally the best corn lands are flat or undulating to gently rolling surfaces, and areas of very high quality soil, preferably of grassland (prairie) origin, or soils of alluvial origin.

Environmental Requirements and Regions of Production

The growing season for corn must be warm and humid; at least three summer months must average 70° or higher, and rains must fall every few days. The heat requirements of corn are great, but not so great as required for a crop such as cotton. Hot to warm nights, as well as warm days, are necessary for the best growth; farmers in the Corn Belt speak of "almost being able to hear the corn growing" during the warm nights. The growing season must be 150 days or more; some shorter-season corns have been developed, but at the expense of yield. North, or poleward, of the minimum growing season, and in areas slightly too cool for the maturing of corn, the plant may be grown to only the green or fodder stage, and is cut green and chopped for silage; in such areas, seed corn has to be purchased from growers in warmer areas. Corn is a large user of water. Frequent showers of ample proportions are a must; dry lands are unsuitable, and even the irrigating of corn (except sweet corn) is generally unsatisfactory. Although water is supplied at root level the plant, reaching into arid air, does not do well, its leaves curl, and pollination is not satisfactory.

The best soils for corn are strong soils, high in nitrogen. Ideally the brown to black prairie soils are the best for the crop. Gray-brown woodland soils are eminently satisfactory. The red and yellow soils of the South are not the best for corn, though a large acreage is grown. Yields per acre, however, despite excellent conditions of summer climate, are lower than in the better soil regions of the Corn Belt. The importance of soil is shown, in the South, by vastly different yields on the productive soils of river flood plains, and the lower yields on the uplands; in the Corn Belt there is not this marked differentiation.

Almost two-thirds of the world's corn is grown in North America. Corn is a unique American product, one in which the United States dominates in world production and consumption. And corn is not grown in quantity in all parts of the nation, though every state contains some acreage. Only in the eastern, humid half of the United States is corn a leading crop, and even here the intensity of corn production varies regionally. It reaches its greatest, and dominant, position in the humid continental climate of the American Corn Belt, which region alone produces two-thirds of the United States crop, and is one of the four outstanding agricultural areas of the entire world—as well as containing, within its agricultural borders, an important percentage of America's industrial plants and many manufacturing cities. Corn is important, also, within the humid subtropical climatic realm of the American South, and particularly so in a relative manner in that region's agriculture, for—on the national basis—the entire South, in corn acreage and production, does not have the total of the state of Illinois or of Iowa, each in the Corn Belt proper. The North American scene in corn is completed by Mexico, a moderate producer on the world scene, Central America, and the very small acreage in Canada. Most of Canada has too cool a summer except for silage corn; but peninsular Ontario, to the north of Lake Erie and between Detroit and Buffalo, is warm enough to mature corn for grain.

The humid continental long summer climatic region, or realm, offers the best environment for corn; apparently the conditions are the optimum; certainly it is these regions which contain the several "Corn Belts." And corn reaches its largest relative importance in those level to rolling, prairie and prairie-woodland portions of the realm where the soils are of very high quality. Among these are the Corn Belt of the midwestern United States, the Danubian plains of central Europe in Hungary, Rumania, and Yugoslavia, the Ukraine in the Soviet Union, the Manchurian Plain in China, the northern warm portion of the Pampas of Argentina, and, on the South African Plateau, the Maize Triangle of the Union of South Africa. Also very significant are the corn-growing lands of the humid continental Po Valley in northern Italy (beyond, or north of the region of Mediterranean climate).

The warmer portions of the temperate marine lands of the west coasts of the continents can mature corn. The Aquitanian Basin of southwestern France and the northwestern parts of Spain lie in this setting. Each has a small acreage. But, in general, in the marine realm the summer season is too cool for the production of corn except to silage stage.

The humid subtropics has ideal corn weather, and adequate rainfall, but its red and yellow soils, low in humus, are not the best for corn. Even so the southern United States, northern China, and southeastern Brazil have a large acreage planted to corn. In the South, corn leads cotton in acreage but is generally secondary to cotton and tobacco as a commercial or cash crop, except locally. Soils are fertilized heavily in some of these humid subtropical regions, but overall yields per acre do not average as high as in the corn-growing areas of the world's "Corn Belts."

Corn can be grown in the tropics, excepting the arid tropics. Its temperature and rainfall requirements for the growing season are met all twelve months in the rainy tropics. But the lateritic soils are exceptionally poor. Only Java, with its soils derived from lavas, is an important producer. The wet-and-dry tropics provide a "corn climate" during the rainy season, if it is long enough for corn to mature. There is scattered production in many parts of the world possessing this climate, but no large commercial output. On the plateau of Mexico, however, corn is a major food crop of the inhabitants—with beans and tomatoes it furnishes the base of many Mexican dishes.

▶ WORLD TRADE

The world trade in corn is small when compared to that of wheat and many other agricultural products. This reflects the fact that most corn is used locally as a feed for animals. It reflects, also, a lack of demand for corn in many countries or regions that do not use it for feed because they either possess home-grown grains for feed or use other products as a result of tradition, home supply, or market demand. For example, swine are corn-fed mainly in the United States, but in western Europe they are potato-fed, in the Orient garbage-fed. The swine industry in Germany, Denmark, Poland, and elsewhere depends upon potatoes and other home-grown root crops. Corn is not imported as a feed for several reasons—expense, tradition, and the demands of the European market, perhaps influenced also by tradition. Fat pork is not desired. Lean bacon, pork, and hams command the best prices in the markets, and corn-fed products are considered inferior by the Europeans. The same is true of beef. Europeans demand grass-fed rather than corn-finished beef—the reverse of the situation in the United States. Thus a potentially large market in western Europe for corn is actually a relatively small one. Nevertheless, western Europe is the chief destination of the corn that does enter foreign trade.

The largest demand in Europe is for flint corns for poultry feed. The chief grower and supplier of flint corns is Argentina. The Argentine corn lands are on the hot, northern side of the Pampas, upstream on the Parana River from Buenos Aires. No part of the corn-growing area is far removed from the navigable river. The river city of Rosario in the corn-growing district, reached directly by ocean ships, is the major exporting port. Corn is exported also from Buenos Aires. The feeding of chickens, ducks, and geese, all very important in the western lands of the European continent, depends in considerable part upon these flint corns from the Southern Hemisphere.

The Union of South Africa, the southern states of Brazil, and the United States export small quantities of corn. Europe is the chief destination.

Corn exports from the United States have quadrupled in the years from the early 1940's to the early 1960's. They total, however, only a very small fraction of the production. The increase is attributable to several factors. Among these are the foreign-aid programs of the federal government, the export of corn for use in feeding American military and civilian personnel stationed around the world, and the fact that government export figures include the grain equivalent of corn in exported cornmeals, corn syrups, corn oil, and other manufactured products.

► THE AMERICAN CORN BELT

The American Corn Belt is one of the outstanding and productive agricultural regions of the world. It extends east-west from central Ohio to western Nebraska, and north-south from roughly the latitude of the southern shores of the Great Lakes to the latitudes of the Ohio and lower Missouri rivers. Its specific boundaries will be discussed in a later section.

The Corn Belt occupies less than half of the total area of the humid continental long-summer climatic realm in North America. But it occupies the best half of the soils and of the terrain. As the Corn Belt lies to the west of the Appalachian Highland none of the long-summer lands on the East Coast are included within it; only the plains of southeastern Pennsylvania might be included so far as agricultural emphasis is concerned, but by custom they are not. South of the Corn Belt proper the long summer climate continues across Kentucky and to the Ozarks of Missouri, but these areas are not in the region; soils are poorer, the land surface is hillier, and economically other types of agriculture are relatively more feasible, or more profitable in the environment. Many small districts of flatter topography and better-than-average soils do have a local "Corn Belt economy," but they are few and appear as islands in the broader scene.

The Corn Belt is a region of diverse agricultural systems, and of many crops, but is unified throughout by its emphasis upon corn and the animal industries. Although some hesitate to use the name "Corn Belt" the name itself has been used so long, and is so descriptive, that it is doubtful if it will disappear. Agriculturally, most of the Corn Belt is classified as an animal-specialty region; animals, particularly swine and beef cattle, are the marketed end products. Some portions of the Corn Belt, however, can be classified as areas of grain farming, as corn itself is sold by the farmers. One of the largest of these cash-grain districts is immediately south of Chicago and so is close to the largest market in the country for corn, as Chicago and its industrial suburbs lead in the manufacture of corn products.

The boundaries of the Corn Belt are remarkably sharp. They have been set by various environmental factors; man himself has been unable to shift them to any degree, except slightly on the north owing to the development and perfection of shorter-season corn plants.

The northern border of the Corn Belt approximates the location of the summer (June, July, August) isotherm of 70°F. From southeastern South Dakota on the west, the isotherm extends across southern Minnesota and lies about on the Illinois-Wisconsin border and the Indiana-Michigan and Ohio-Michigan borders. Thus southeastern South Dakota and southwestern Minnesota are definitely within the Corn Belt. Wisconsin and Michigan, on the whole, are not; but the southern two or three tiers of counties of each state are now in the transitional zone into which corn acreage has been expanded. From Minnesota eastward the border zone is a Corn Belt–Dairy Region transition; if environmentally possible, the Corn

Belt agriculture is practiced as it is usually more profitable and is less demanding in daily work than is dairying. In South Dakota the Spring Wheat Belt is to the north of the corn border; the change in agricultural emphasis is quite sharply defined.

The eastern border of the Corn Belt lies against the Appalachian hill lands; it crosses central Ohio from north to south, dividing the state in two. Only the western half of Ohio is in the Corn Belt.

The western border of the Corn Belt is marked by low summer rainfall. The border lies at or near the 100th meridian of west longitude—the approximate beginning of the dry plains lands of the West. But there are two indentations; on the flat flood plains of the Platte and Republican rivers in Nebraska, corn acreage extends west of 100°, owing to a high water table in the underlying porous alluvial material; and in northern Nebraska the Corn Belt extends only to about 98°W. Here its border is sharply defined against the arenaceous soils of the Sand Hills of the state.

The southern border of the Corn Belt is very sharp except in Missouri. This border, as it crosses Ohio, Indiana, and Illinois, is the southern edge of the glacial soils of the last, or Wisconsin, stage of glaciation. The glacial drift deposited by the ice is the parent material of the soils of nearly all of the Corn Belt which

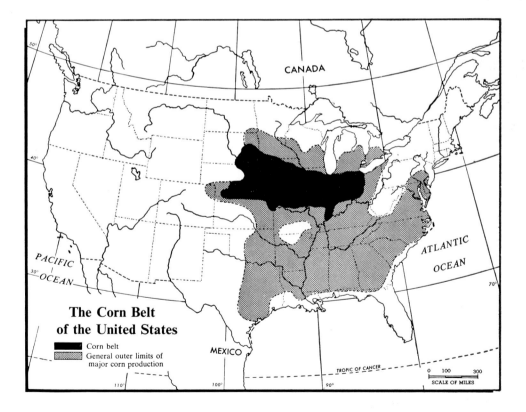

The Corn Belt
of the United States

■ Corn belt
▨ General outer limits of
major corn production

lies east of the Mississippi River and of the Corn Belt in Iowa. From this glacial drift, the interaction of climate and natural vegetation has produced the present gray-brown woodland soils of the Ohio-Indiana portion and the prairie soils of the original grassland-covered areas of Illinois, northwestern Indiana, and Iowa. The southern border of the Corn Belt in Missouri is a zone at about the location of the Missouri River as it flows from west to east across the state. But in Kansas, the southern border becomes sharp again; here it is basically the average northern edge of the hot, arid, searing southwest winds of summer, which blow from the southwestern steppes and deserts, and are detrimental to corn production. This boundary has been set mainly as a result of long-time trial and error.

In summary, the western border of the Corn Belt is climatic as expressed by rainfall (except for the Sand Hills); the northern border is climatic as expressed by temperature and length of growing season; the eastern is topographic with the appearance of rough terrain, and the southern is a soils and, farther west, a climatic boundary. Within the boundaries, the Corn Belt contains large parts of five states—Ohio, Indiana, Illinois, Iowa, and Nebraska—and smaller portions of adjacent states. Iowa, a state with a name for agricultural quality, lies almost entirely in the Corn Belt. A few extensions of a Corn Belt type of agriculture protrude beyond the general borders; chief of these is a long prong southward on the high-quality alluvial soils of the Wabash River flood plain on the Indiana-

FIG. 12-1. Plowing the rich, black prairie soil of the Corn Belt. The nearly-level to very gently rolling surface of much of the Corn Belt permits almost complete agricultural utilization of the region. The prairie portion of the Corn Belt extends westward from about the Indiana-Illinois state line. The eastern Corn Belt was wooded originally, and its soils are forest soils. (Standard Oil Company, N.J.)

FIG. 12-2. A four-row corn planter. Many individual fields of corn in the Corn Belt are more than eighty acres in size, and some exceed this considerably. Farm buildings in the Corn Belt are generally of high quality. (Standard Oil Company, N.J.)

Illinois boundary. Throughout the Corn Belt and its extensions there is remarkably uniform rainfall during the growing season.

The Natural and Cultural Landscape of the Corn Belt

The Corn Belt landscape, generally uniform throughout, locally may be very diverse. Evidences of prosperity are general—fine barns and other buildings, well-kept farmsteads, expensive machinery, top-quality animals, bulging feed-storage units such as silos, corn cribs, and large corn-elevator buildings.

The natural setting is one of an undulating plain. Locally the surface is flat,

locally it becomes rolling to hilly; but throughout the largest extent, broad undulating plains sweep toward a nearby horizon. In the eastern, formerly forested
portion the farm woodlot often marks a nearby horizon; in the extensive view
the woodlots merge to give the impression of a forested skyline. Westward of
the Indiana-Illinois boundary—the approximate beginning of the original prairie
grasslands—the view is generally more distant, and in the undulating to rolling
areas, such as much of Iowa and eastern Nebraska, the distant skyline is traversed
by sweeping fields. Planted woodlots, groves, and lines of windbreaks interrupt
the continuity of the cultivated fields. Soils of glacial parent material, modified
by the original forest vegetation of the east, and the long-grass prairies westward,
exist throughout all save the westernmost portion of the entire belt, which lies
beyond the glacial border.

The rectangular road grid of the American land survey cuts, or blocks, most
of the region into square mile units—roads on all four sides of each section, or
square mile. The original survey stamps the landscape with rectangular farms, the
quarter-section of 160 acres (one-half mile by one-half mile) having been the
usual land settlement unit—the homestead in the "West." Even the fragmentation, or more usually the consolidation, of farms in response to mechanization
does not obliterate the rectangular pattern of field, pasture, and woodland. In
hilly areas, where contour plowing is the rule, the fields may curve, but they do
so within the farm limits, and the curves end abruptly against the line fence or
meet the curved fields of the adjacent farm along a straight line at the border.

The dispersed farmsteads dot the roadsides, three or four to the square mile
—a reflection of the farm size—but fewer westward of the Missouri River, in
response to the 200-acre-or-more average size farm in the Nebraska portion of
the Corn Belt. Each farmstead is usually marked by a small "village" of buildings
of high quality, dominated by the barn and farm home. Four to five acres may
be included in the overall farmstead, a larger area than that of the average-sized
landholding of many portions of the Orient. Surrounding the two principal buildings, one a home, one the "business" center, are the lawns, feedlots, machine sheds,
feed storage buildings, and, if in the western formerly prairie section, a planted
grove or windbreak sheltering this core portion of the farm from the winter winds
and blizzards, the windbreak being on the windward western or northwestern
side. Dominating the whole local scene are the silos, commonly two or more per
farm, though newer installations are likely to be underground trench silos.

Crops

The Corn Belt farmers grow three major feed crops, for direct use on the farm
for the maintenance of animals, and one or two cash crops for direct sale. Over
wide areas of the belt, only three feed crops—corn, oats, and a hay crop—are
usual. Soybeans constitute the principal cash crop of considerable areas and in
some districts are actually the second or third crop in acreage. Winter wheat is

a significant cash crop in portions of the southern and eastern parts of the Corn Belt.

Corn is dominant in acreage in every county of the Corn Belt except for about a dozen counties toward the southern margin or in some hilly settings of northern Missouri. With these few exceptions, corn is everywhere the first-ranking crop. It is exceeded by hay in only a few hilly counties, by soybeans in half a dozen, and by wheat in a few marginal areas. The ever-present corn field of the spring and summer season, the harvesting of corn in the fall, and the corn stubble in the fields during the winter (covered by snow for two months or more in the northern portion of the belt, and intermittently in the southern) are landscape elements and reminders of the region's dominant crop.

The second-ranking crop of the Corn Belt is not as uniform throughout as is corn. But for the northern portion of the western part of the Corn Belt—from Lake Michigan and east-central Illinois to eastern Nebraska—oats are second, and very uniformly so. For example, in Iowa the oats acreage follows that of corn in every county save nine on the Missouri border and one on the Mississippi River. Throughout south-central Illinois and in large parts of Indiana soybeans are second to corn; in southeastern Indiana, and in most of the Corn Belt in Ohio, winter wheat is second. In the rolling lands of northern Missouri hay crops follow corn in acreage.

The third-ranking crop varies regionally. It is a hay crop for much of the western part of the belt and part of the Indiana-Ohio area, soybeans in north-central Illinois and north-central Iowa, and generally oats elsewhere.

The Crop Season

The three principal crops fit into the Corn Belt system of rotation. Oats are spring-sown on fall-plowed ground. They are seeded as soon as the soils have dried out and it is possible to get machinery into the fields. This is during late March in the southern portion of the Corn Belt, but not until about the tenth to the fifteenth of April in the northern areas. Continuing light frosts or light freezes do not damage the seeded oats.

Hay crops for future years are seeded with the oats, at the same time and with the same machinery. When above ground, and growing, the oats furnish a cover or nurse crop for the young grasses and clovers. After oats harvest, the hay crops grow vigorously, taking over the field, and are well established by fall. They will be cut for hay and roughage the following year or the following two or three years. Timothy is a usual seeding, and the main grass crop for hay. But leguminous herbs—the various clovers—are seeded as well, and it is common for mixed timothy or clover to be seeded together. Alfalfa is important, particularly so westward in the Corn Belt; alfalfa may be seeded separately or with a nurse crop. In the Platte River Valley of Nebraska alfalfa is a major cash crop, sold to numerous large alfalfa mills, which prepare it for special feeds.

The farmer turns to the preparation of corn land as soon as the oats are in the ground. The future corn field is spring plowed or disked. Present machinery permits plowing, harrowing, packing, and other preparations for the seed bed to be accomplished in one operation. Corn planting is delayed until all danger of frosts have passed. May is the principal month of corn planting, but it starts in mid-April in the southern portion of the belt, and may not be completed until toward the end of May at the northern edge. Corn cultivation commences as soon as the young plants appear above ground and continues into July, or until the corn is tall enough to shade the ground, at which time cultivation ceases, and the corn is "laid by." During June cultivation will be interrupted for a time when the first cutting and baling of hay occurs.

Oats are ripe and are harvested from early July to the latter portion of the month. Thus the oats harvest fits perfectly into the labor pattern, as the labor of the farmer is no longer needed in the cultivating of corn. The second cutting of a leguminous hay—clover or alfalfa—follows this, again not competing with another crop for the time and labor of the farmer.

Corn ripens and is harvested during the autumn. The denting stage of corn is reached about the middle of September. Usually by the end of the month, unless there are early frosts, the bulk of the crop has passed this stage successfully, and is safe from frost. The harvest begins late in the month if the moisture content of the corn is not too high, for if it is, corn cannot be stored safely. The clear Indian summer weather of October and the light frosts and freezes experienced during the month "dry out" the corn crop, and this month witnesses the peak of corn picking. By mid-October about a third of the corn crop of Iowa and Illinois, in the heart of the belt, has been harvested, and Ohio farmers have gathered about half of the crop. Corn picking continues until all of the production has been cared for, and in most of the Corn Belt the final picking will not have been accomplished until November or later—during certain years not until after the ground is covered by light snowfalls. Corn "picking" today is almost entirely by machine. Some few growers still pick by hand. Formerly corn stalks were cut with a corn binder and shocked by workers in the fields; then, at leisure later, the corn itself was husked. But the "characteristic" field of shocks, looking like a line-up of Indian tepees, has virtually disappeared from the Corn Belt proper, and from all regions of commercial agriculture in the United States—though this landscape feature of autumn remains in some of the districts of near-subsistence farming elsewhere.

Fall plowing of part of the land which has been in corn is accomplished after the harvest; or, if the acreage of corn to be harvested is so large that delays beyond freezing will occur, some of the land from which corn has been gathered will be plowed. The fall plowing is for the oats seeding of the ensuing spring.

The two chief cash crops, distributed regionally, have different calendars of work. The regime for soybeans has essentially the same timetable as for corn. But only one, or at most two, cultivations are necessary before the bean foliage from one drilled row of beans meets that from the adjacent row. Winter wheat, however, is fall-seeded in September or early October. Choice of these fields must be from an early-harvested corn field, or from a field devoted to hay or another small grain.

The usual crop rotation, in summary, is corn, oats, and hay in successive years, with the grass crop occupying the land for two or three years—perhaps two years for hay and the third year as rotation pasture. But variations occur over the belt, and regionally in districts. And, with corn the number one crop in acreage, some fields are in corn for more than a year; heavy use of commercial fertilizers in the modern agricultural systems permit this. Increased yields per acre of hybrid corns usually justify the expense of fertilization. And the introduction of soybeans, which add nitrogen to the soil, and whose vines can be plowed under after the beans have been harvested and threshed by combines, adds fertilizing elements to the soil. Furthermore, the Corn Belt farmer has a supply of animal manures produced on the farm and used to fertilize the corn fields.

FIG. 12-3. A cluster of many buildings is usual on Corn Belt farms. The building to the left is the "corn crib," which, on Corn Belt farms, unlike the usual crib, is in effect a country elevator in which corn is stored. An elevator or inclined-plane is used to lift the corn to the upper level. The silo and other structures are used for the storage of feeds. The field in the foreground is of young oats. (Standard Oil Company, N.J.)

▶ SOYBEANS

Soybeans are a recent addition to the cropping systems of the Corn Belt. This bushy, annual legume of the bean family, indigenous to Manchuria, has become significant in the United States mainly since the 1930's, although a small acreage has been grown for a hundred years.

The Grand Prairie of east-central Illinois contains the largest total soybean acreage. The larger towns of Illinois have the greatest concentration of soybean mills, but mills are located elsewhere in the Corn Belt also. The Chicago Board of Trade, the grain market of the nation, trades in soybeans as well as in corn and the small grains.

The rapid spread of soybean acreage in the Corn Belt, and the expansion of this cash crop, reflects many factors; and the crop is dual-purpose in that the beans are threshed and sold, while the vines may be fed to animals or plowed under for fertilizer; and the growing leguminous plants add nitrogen to the soil. Soybean meal is an important manufactured feed. Soybean oil is used in foods, shortenings, oleomargarine, paints, linoleum, and many other products. Soybean plastic cake is fused into composition material, from which legion products can be stamped. The rapidly expanding plastics industry uses soybeans as an important raw material. Thus, in total, a large manufactural market has arisen for this agricultural raw material. And, in addition, the United States has become an exporter of soybeans to western Europe, opening a market held formerly by China alone.

There have been purely agricultural reasons, in addition, for the rise of soybean acreage. Corn Belt farms became almost completely mechanized during the late 1920's and 1930's—earlier than the almost complete mechanization elsewhere. With the virtual elimination of horses as a source of power, soybeans were planted on land released from the growing of feed for these animals. The crop-control and acreage-allotment programs of the Federal Government initiated in the 1930's and continued in various forms and under various names to the present, have reduced the acreage of corn and of wheat, and imposed restrictions upon some other crops; land "released" under these programs has been available for soybeans.

Soybeans, like other crops of the Corn Belt, are handled entirely by machines. Drills seed the bean seeds. At harvest, the acreage is cut and raked mechanically into rows for machine-threshing or is combined, as the small grains are handled.

Minor and specialty crops are grown here and there in the Corn Belt, in small localized districts. Among these are vegetables for market, corn and tomatoes for canning, broomcorn, peppermint, rye, and orchard products. Of these, only the corn and tomatoes originate on "true" Corn Belt farms; the mints are grown on drained marshlands, the rye in atypical sandy districts, the vegetables on specialized truck farms or market gardens, and the fruits in fruit-growing districts possessing excellent local environments for tree-fruits—an example being the orchard district in the hill lands near the junction of the Illinois and Mississippi rivers.

Grain sorghums have spread into the Corn Belt cropping systems since the middle 1950's, and are increasing in importance. The spread has been from the dry southern plains of Texas and western Kansas northeastward to the Corn Belt in eastern Nebraska. Year by year this feed grain has "crept" eastward, into Iowa, and is now grown even east of the Mississippi. Agricultural Experiment Stations have endorsed the planting of the crop. And to the individual farmer, the reason for planting grain sorghums is partly economic—he can grow the crop on land on which, under government programs, he is unable to sow wheat or plant corn, and thus obtain feed for his animals from otherwise "unavailable" acreage.

Basically, despite local differentiations observable in the landscape, the overall Corn Belt remains a three- (or four-) crop region—corn, oats, and hay almost throughout, with soybeans as a cash crop over many areas and wheat for direct sale in southerly and eastern areas where this winter grain replaces oats in the cropping system.

► THE ANIMAL ECONOMY

The landscape scene in the Corn Belt is not complete without animals. These are mainly beef cattle, swine, and chickens. Dairy cattle are prominent in the eastern, or Ohio-Indiana, portion in response to the milk markets of the numerous cities of these states. Dairying is a secondary activity in districts of Iowa. But the meat-producing animals dominate throughout. They consume the corn, the feed-mixtures of small grains, and the roughage provided by the hay crops.

The Corn Belt is the principal source region in the United States of beef cattle, swine, and eggs. The major meat-packing centers of the nation are all in or adjacent to the Corn Belt. And, from the region as a whole, there is the largest production of eggs in the nation. Other egg centers are market-oriented, as in New Jersey, based on the eastern urban market, or near the urban centers of California. But even these eastern and western egg centers depend heavily upon feeds from the interior of the country, and principally from the Corn Belt. Some California chicken "ranches" are even located along the railroad lines and have sidetrack facilities in order to receive carlot shipments of wheat, corn, millrun, and other feeds from middle western source regions.

The individual Corn Belt farmer has four choices so far as his agricultural enterprises and the animal economy are concerned. He may choose (1) to devote the entire growing season to the raising of crops, and have few or no animals (other than chickens) on the farm. In such a case, he purchases steers from the western cattle ranges in the fall, feeds them during the winter, and markets the fattened and "finished" animals in the spring. He is known as a feeder. Or (2) the farmer may choose to rear his own cattle, keeping them on the farm throughout the year. In this case the calves are born in the spring or early summer, pasture-fed and barnyard-fed, and then fattened for market during the winter on home-grown feeds. Only breeding stock is kept into the ensuing crop-year, the spring calves having been marketed as baby beef—from ten to fifteen months of age. Such a farmer is a rearer of cattle and a feeder; his turnover of beef animals must be rapid—as baby beef—in response to the investment in animals and in the high-priced land upon which they are reared. (3) Thirdly, the farmer may choose to have all-year production of beef cattle and swine, spreading the birth dates of calves so that a relatively uniform number are marketed each month or season. The swine are spring-farrowed for marketing in late summer, and fall-farrowed for winter marketing. Numbers of swine, considering their farrowing, can be adjusted to the factors of feed supply and market prices more easily than can the numbers of cattle. (4) A fourth choice is to rear no animals whatever, and to sell crops alone. In this case, with corn the leading crop, the farmer operates a "cash-grain" enterprise, comparable to that of a wheat grower. Cash-grain districts have developed regionally in the Corn Belt. The principal area lies south of Chicago, in response to the large market in the city for corn for use in manufac-turing. A second cash-grain district is in northwestern Iowa, not so closely related to nearby markets, but determined principally by choice. Even in the cash-grain districts many farms of the first three types of choice exist; they are fewest in the immediate Chicago hinterland, because this part of the Corn Belt is a cash-grain region, and corn is sold in the Chicago market.

The Corn Belt Feedlot

The Corn Belt farmer who engages in feeding alone—the first choice previously listed—purchases some local steers, but mainly purchases steers from the cattlemen of the American West, steers which have been born in the spring, grazed on the ranges during the summer and early fall, and then are shipped to the Corn Belt for feeding and "finishing" for market. To do so the farmer usually must arrange a loan at his local bank. His gain, or income, is derived from the poundage he adds to the animal before it is sold late in the winter or early in the spring; and the specific gain depends upon the differential in the price paid for the animal and the price re-ceived at the stockyards—less, of course, the labor and other factors in the enter-prise. In times of low prices, or a narrow differential (estimated) between the buying and selling price, the banker may urge a small loan and curtailing of the number of animals fed. And the success, or failure, of the individual feeder depends to a considerable degree upon his knowledge of feeds and feeding prac-tices, his home supply of corn and other feeds so that he will not have to purchase additional corn on the open market, and his skill with animals. And, so far as work-load is concerned, feeding helps spread it evenly throughout the year—the warm season is devoted to labor in the fields, the cold season to work in the feedlot.

Cattle feeding although practiced by individual farmers in all parts of the Corn Belt, is most concentrated in the western half. The extreme west of Illinois is feedlot country. From here through northern Missouri, most of Iowa, and eastern Nebraska is the heart of the feeding region. But it extends, too, southward into Kansas and northward into the portions of the Corn Belt in southwestern Minnesota and southeastern South Dakota. The importance of the western part of the Corn Belt in this activity is reflected in the concentration of major stockyards and meat-packing centers in the cities along the Missouri River—Sioux City, Omaha, South St. Joseph, and Kansas City. Chicago, east of the present main feeding region, remains one of the chief meat-packing centers of the nation and is reached by all railroad lines; but Omaha and Kansas City have expanded their receipts of cattle markedly, in large part owing to truck shipments; in certain recent years the receipts of cattle at Omaha have surpassed, in numbers, the receipts at Chicago. Other major marketing centers are at East St. Louis and South St. Paul. And there are many "secondary" centers, each large itself, but overshadowed by the major ones.

The eastern portion of the Corn Belt in Indiana and Ohio, and the environmentally similar district in southeastern Pennsylvania has some feeding of western cattle. But, on the whole, there is relatively more emphasis upon home-reared beef animals. And, as there are numerous cities the individual farmer has many alternatives in his choice of activity—he may engage in "typical Corn Belt agriculture," or, in response to his location close to urban markets, he may practice dairying, be a market gardener, or combine part-time farming with work in the nearby city.

Cattle, swine, and chickens are "run" or fed together in the Corn Belt to best utilize the corn portion of the feeding ration. Not all of the corn is digested by cattle, and some is eliminated. The swine eat, in part, this portion of the corn, and do not digest all. The final "complete" use of this portion of the corn feed is then through the chicken.

Automation has reached the farms of the Corn Belt, long since electrified and mechanized. Many feedlots are so arranged that feed is distributed to feed troughs from a battery of silos or bins merely by the pushing of a button. The feed is mixed automatically in proper proportions and distributed automatically. And the farmer of the region is today a specialist in feeds and feeding—may have a college degree in the subject—and a business specialist in record keeping and in the selection of top animals. The yields per acre and per farm—despite fewer individual farmers than in even the recent past—have been increased greatly through mechanization, fertilization, the keeping of accurate records, the breeding of high-producing animals and plants, and constant attention to the most efficient methods of production. All of this reflects not only the importance of education of the individual, the dissemination of information from the agricultural colleges and experiment stations, the generally top-quality land, but also the economic factor of the expense of a Corn Belt operation. The land is too expensive, the capital investment too great, and the costs too high to justify anything but every effort to repay the costs and have a profit. Even the marginal or poor farmer may

FIG. 12-4. A representative scene in the Maize Triangle on the High Veld of the Union of South Africa, showing Afrikaander cattle, a field of corn (maize) to the right, a grain field in the left distance, pastures, treeless prairie, and rocky flat-topped outliers. The view is in the Orange Free State. (South African Tourist Corporation)

succeed in the area if he has inherited his farm; if he has not, he is likely to fail. The top farmer is usually highly successful. He is working in an area which, on the world basis, is one of the four top agricultural regions, and his human effort is more than rewarded as a businessman agriculturist.

▶ THE MAIZE TRIANGLE OF SOUTH AFRICA

The Union of South Africa, on the High Veld, contains a "Corn Belt," called the Maize Triangle of the nation. Within the Maize Triangle the growing of corn is the dominant crop activity. Like the American Corn Belt, the Maize Triangle is becoming more diversified in its present-day agriculture. And, like the Corn Belt, the Maize Triangle is the outstanding agricultural area of its nation. Despite the small total area of the Triangle it ranks as one of the rich agricultural prairie lands of the world, and its potentialities for the future are great.

The High Veld is a temperate grassland, despite its latitude of 26° to 30° in the Southern Hemisphere. This is owing to its altitude of from 3,000 to 5,000 or more feet above sea level. The climate is continental but lacks a severe winter in contrast to the American Corn Belt, the Danubian plains, or the North China plain. Nevertheless, frost is expectable in the Maize Triangle during a 100-day period from late June to early September, the winter months of the hemisphere. Heavy freezes and snow cover, however, are unlikely and rare, but vegetation ceases to grow with the frost season.

The Maize Triangle includes slightly less than half of the total area of the High Veld in the Union. Within the Triangle is the western half of the southern portion of the state of Transvaal, and the northern half of the Orange Free State. For general purposes of location, the Triangle is said to extend from near the city of Mafeking on its northwest to Carolina on its northeast angle, and to near Bloemfontein on the south. Geographically its northern border zone is the range of hills of the Rand (the gold-mining region), its eastern border is against the rough hill and mountain terrain of the Drakensberg Mountains and the dissected mountain area of Basutoland, and to the south and west the border of the Triangle impinges upon the dry lands of the High Veld. Increasing aridity, most noticeable westward, mitigates against the cultivation of corn.

The rainfall of the Maize Triangle totals between 20 and 30 inches a year. There is a summer maximum as in the Corn Belt, ideal for corn. The summer is warm to hot, despite the altitude, because of the latitudinal and interior position. The soils are dark brown to black prairie soils of the former grassland.

The farmers of the Maize Triangle are whites of Dutch descent—the Boers of South Africa. Farmsteads are neat and attractive and are set on the rolling prairie. Planted trees serve as windbreaks for the home and buildings—the scene is not unlike that of the western part of the American Corn Belt. And the ever-present windmill, as on the Great Plains, pumps the water supply from ground-water sources.

Farms are large, and only part of their area is devoted to corn. Wheat is an additional crop, and there is much land utilized as pasture by the indigenous Afrikaander cattle. Toward the drier western margins kaffir korn, a grain sorghum, becomes important, and is grown along with corn, or used to replace corn if the latter is affected by a spring drought.

Natural hazards of the Maize Triangle are droughts and locusts. Locational difficulties are its interior and high-altitude position in the competition with Argentina for shipment of corn to western Europe. Costs of land transport to the ports are considerable; Argentina's corn is grown near the sea.

The yields per acre of corn in the Maize Triangle are low when compared with the yields in the Corn Belt. This reflects extensive cultivation, lack of much fertilization to date—in part because of unused land to which corn can be rotated —and less efficient farm labor, the laborers usually being Africans who work for the Boers. Mechanization is increasing, however.

The corn of the Maize Triangle supplies the food for African natives of the Union; little is used by the white population or is fed to animals. The surplus, which varies considerably from year to year, is exported. Formerly the export was in bags. Now it is handled in bulk through grain elevators, with Bloemfontein, Bethlehem, and Kroonstad the chief marketing centers for the receipt of corn, and for forwarding it to the seaports several hundred miles distant and a mile lower— below the great escarpments of the African Plateau on which the Maize Triangle of the High Veld lies. The Union is among the ten chief corn-producing countries, and among the three chief exporters of corn, and the Maize Triangle contributes the bulk of the output.

▶ QUESTIONS

1. What is the location of the Corn Belt of the United States? What are its four borders?
2. Corn and cotton are said to be crops which induce the erosion of soils? Why?
3. What is the crop association on Corn Belt farms?
4. What animals are reared or fed on the farms of the Corn Belt? Why the specialization in these?
5. How are the types of corn grown in the United States different from the types grown in quantity in Argentina?
6. Little corn enters world trade in proportion to the corn acreage of the world, yet Argentina is an important exporter of corn. Explain why. What is the destination and use of the exported corn?
7. Fig. 12-4 shows a scene in the Maize Triangle of the Union of South Africa. What elements in this are similar to those of the Corn Belt landscape? What elements differ from a Corn Belt scene? Consider both natural and cultural features of the landscape, of course.
8. Account for the location of the large meat-packing centers of the United States.
9. What are some of the products manufactured from corn?
10. Why are soybeans called an all-purpose crop?

XIII The Animal Industries and Associated

Manufacturing

There are many domesticated animals. The distribution of some of them is almost world-wide, and these are found in regions of commercial agriculture, of subsistence farming, and in areas of nomadic herding. The rearing of certain other domesticated animals is highly regional, and the particular animal is known only in a limited district.

Beef and dairy cattle, swine, sheep, and chickens are found throughout the world. But their numbers and specific distribution are regionalized within the broad areas in which they are reared; for example, swine are absent in the world of Islam for religious reasons, beef and dairy cattle are few in China and Japan for reasons both of the culture of the Orient and of the pressure of population upon the arable land—the land is used directly for the growing of food for humans. And commercially certain regions have developed a specialization in the animal industries or in the rearing of one or two animals—thus there are intensive dairy regions, beef-cattle regions, and areas which specialize in the sheep and wool industry.

The animals whose distribution is within a limited district—environmentally or in geographical location—are many. These animals are essentially unknown in the agriculture of large portions of the world. Among these are the llama, alpaca, and vicuna of Andean South America, the yak of the high plateaus of

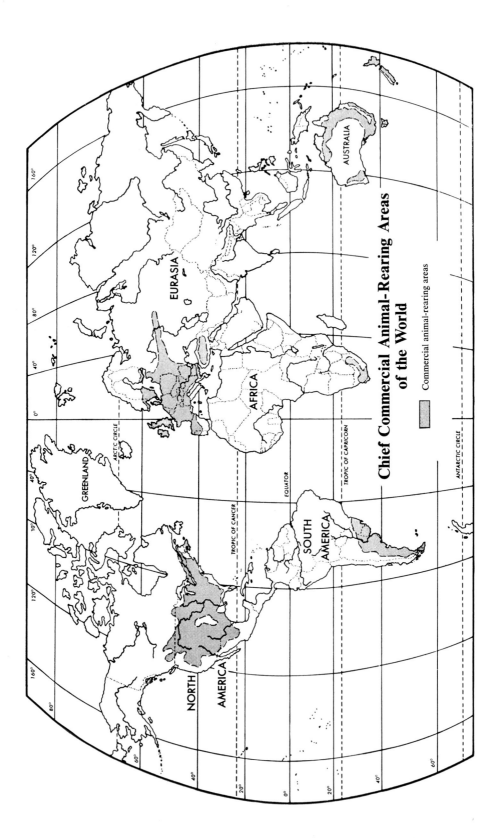

**Chief Commercial Animal-Rearing Areas
of the World**

☐ Commercial animal-rearing areas

inner Asia, and the two types of camel of the deserts of the Old World—the one-humped dromedary camel of Arabia and northern Africa, and the two-humped Bactrian camel of inner Asia. Certain other animals or birds are reared commercially in only a very few places; an example is the ostrich industry of a few ranches in the Union of South Africa.

Ducks, geese, rabbits, pigeons, and goats are specialty animals of a few regions. Wild animals, such as the fur-bearing mink and fox are maintained in fenced enclosures on fur farms, particularly in northern cool or cold regions where the quality of the pelt is enhanced by the severity of the winter.

The larger animals, such as beef cattle, are reared in pastoral regions in parts of the world, and on farms in other portions. In a pastoral region the animals are maintained by grazing extensive areas—these may be fenced or may be open ranges; on farms animals are grazed in small pastures on the farms but are maintained in large part by being fed the crops and roughages that are grown on the farm.

Certain animals are associated in parts of the world with regions of very dense habitation. The poultry (including the pigeons) and the rabbits of western Europe are raised on very small landholdings, and even in the back yards of city dwellers as a supplementary source of home meat. But the feed for these animals is purchased from abroad; some of the poultry of western Europe are maintained, actually, by land areas in Argentina and South Africa, as flint corns grown in these countries are imported for feed. In densely peopled China pigs and chickens are the only significant animals; swine are garbage-fed and consume the waste materials from the kitchen and the crops, such as hulls from the rice. On densely inhabited Oahu in Hawaii swine are garbage-fed likewise, and dairy cattle are maintained in large part by feed shipped from the middle latitudes to tropical Oahu.

The rearing of animals is a two-cycle activity in agriculture. Land is used for crops, and the feed crops are then fed to animals. In one-cycle agriculture, common in the Orient, the land is devoted to crops which are for direct human consumption. In very densely inhabited areas, where there is pressure of population upon the land resource, a one-cycle agriculture is a necessity. The peoples of the Western world are accustomed to meat in their diet, and animals are part of the scene. But many of these animals, particularly in western Europe, are fed only in part from the land of the home area, and are actually being fed on feeds imported from land areas elsewhere in the Western world, in some cases half a hemisphere away.

► CATTLE

Cattle are distributed throughout the settled portions of the world. Nearly every agricultural region has some production of meat, but, as is the case in modern agriculture, there is marked regionalization in the numbers of cattle and in the occurrence of specialized animal-rearing regions. Four areas of major concentrations of cattle in the world are: (1) in all of Europe, excluding only the very northern nonagricultural areas and the Mediterranean lands; (2) in the Pampas of Argentina, throughout adjacent Uruguay and into the very southern-most states of Brazil; (3) in the Indian subcontinent (India and Pakistan); and (4) in North America in (a) the Corn Belt, (b) the Dairy Region of the United States and Canada, and (c) in the north-south strip of territory of the Interior Plains of the continent from southern Saskatchewan and North Dakota southward to and including Texas. Of these four, the Indian region is not comparable to the other three—except in numbers of cattle; the reasons for this will be noted later.

The cattle of the world are of many different types and breeds. But, in commercial agriculture, the fundamental difference is that between cattle developed and reared primarily for their beef, and cattle breeds developed and maintained for the production of milk. In addition, there are some so-called dual-purpose breeds which yield moderate quantities of milk and are satisfactory beef animals.

In some parts of the world the principal use of cattle is as draft animals. This is the case in some of the so-called underdeveloped areas, and is also the case in India, where the adherents of the Hindu religion consider cattle to be holy and will not slaughter them. A few small districts of subsistence agriculture elsewhere use cattle as draft animals; but in general draft cattle, like the oxen of the past in the United States, have disappeared from the Western world.

A second broad distinction among cattle is that between the middle-latitude cattle and those of the tropics. The cattle originating in Europe, and now the most widely distributed in the cooler regions of commercial agriculture, belong to the family *Bos taurus,* whether of a breed developed for beef, for dairying, or for the dual purpose. Many cattle of the tropics, and particularly those of India, belong to the family *Bos indicus.* Breeds developed within this family withstand great heat; in a pasture stocked with mixed cattle, the Indian breeds will graze in the sun on days when taurine cattle languish and seek shelter in the shade of trees. The *Bos indicus* cattle are humped. There are several Indian breeds of these zebu cattle. In the hotter subtropical portions of the United States to which they have been introduced—particularly in Florida, the Gulf Coast, and south Texas —they are all called Brahman cattle; the most common of the introduced breeds is the Guzerat.

The principal breeds of beef cattle and of dairy cattle in all the major commercial livestock regions of the world are members of the *Bos taurus* family. Beef and dairy animals are very unlike one another, and are bred and developed for very different purposes. The beef animals are rectangular when viewed from above. The breeds have been developed for rapid growth of individuals, the ability to gain weight, and to yield meat of high quality. Beef cattle are shipped to market at an early age, invariably at two years or less, and increasingly at an age of only a year because of the present emphasis upon "baby beef" and the present knowledge of scientific feeding. Only the breeding stock is maintained for longer than two or three years. In contrast, the ideal dairy animal is triangular in shape when viewed from above. A dairy cow does not yield milk as a heifer; production starts when the animal is about two years of age. They are then maintained and milked as long as they are productive—as long as the income received from the sale of milk exceeds the costs of keeping and feeding the animal, the labor costs, and the capital costs of its replacement. This is ordinarily for eight or ten years, and some individual cattle have been productive for as many as eighteen.

Beef and milk production differ in many other ways. All beef calves are reared for meat, the male calves as steers. In the dairy industry only the heifers are reared to become milk cows; bull calves, except the few kept for breeding, are sold for veal.

The principal breeds of beef cattle in the middle latitudes are of British origin. It is in England and Scotland that these cattle were developed and perfected. The white-faced Hereford, the black Aberdeen-Angus, and the red-and-white or roan-and-white Shorthorns are the most widely distributed breeds in the British Isles, the United States and Canada, Australia, New Zealand, and the Pampas— all important beef-producing areas. These breeds, as well as locally developed ones, such as the Charolaise of France, are significant in continental Europe too.

The principal breeds of dairy cattle are of both British and western European origin. The white, or red, or white-and-red Ayrshire is from one of the southwestern counties of Scotland. The English-owned islands of Guernsey and Jersey in the English Channel have each contributed a dairy breed—the fawn-and-white Guernsey, and the fawn to gray-colored Jersey. The Holstein-Frisian, large blackand-white dairy cattle, originated in the low, coastal lands of northwest Europe— the region included in the Netherlands and northwest Germany. The Brown Swiss, one of the first-developed specialized dairy breeds, is from the Alpine pastures and Alpine Foreland countryside of Switzerland. The dairy regions of northern France and of the Central Upland have local breeds, such as the Salers; unlike the aforementioned dairy breeds, those of French and other origin are not widely distributed in the world; some are locally important in the French-speaking portion of eastern Canada. Danish Red cattle are important in Denmark, an outstanding dairy country.

Dairy cows do not do well in the hot, humid subtropical or tropical regions of the world. Among the breeds the Jersey withstands heat the best and is the most usual dairy cow of the American South; but in the major dairy regions, such as that of the region in the latitudes from New England to Minnesota, other breeds are much more numerous.

Middle-latitude taurine cattle are not the best for the wet tropics because of their inability to withstand continuous heat, especially when it is associated with high humidity. The British and other peoples have introduced them to hot regions; experience indicates that both beef and milk production decline under the environmental conditions. Experiment station researchers, such as those in the tropical northern portion of South Africa, have decided it is better to work toward improvement of native humped Afrikaander cattle (related to Indian animals) than to continue to attempt introductions.

The tropics, except for India, are not noted for particular breeds of cattle. Animals tend to be nondescript. They do not produce quality beef, and their yield of milk is low. Nevertheless, they are important to tropical peoples, especially those who live on the savanna grasslands such as the Sudan of North Africa or the Campos of southern Brazil. Native tribes and individuals of large areas of the Sudan count their wealth in cattle; gifts of animals are made at the time of marriage. The Afrikaander cattle of the Veld of South Africa, descendants of the indigenous cattle, are reared by many Boer (whites of Dutch descent) farmers in the Union, and have been improved through selection and breeding; enough improvement has been made so that some American farmers and ranchers have imported the Afrikaander. The native cattle of northern Africa are usually long-horned. Similar cattle from Spain and Morocco were brought to Mexico by the Spanish. They spread northward, and a type was the now-extinct Texas Longhorn.

There are several breeds of the humped *Bos indicus* cattle of India; collectively they may be spoken of as Zebu cattle, and—in the United States only—as Brahmans. As these animals are revered and worshiped by people of the Hindu faith they are not slaughtered for meat. When their use as work animals is terminated they continue to be fed and maintained until their death, or are allowed to roam the fields and wander in city streets, unmolested. They die a natural death or perish from starvation. Upon death, the hide is removed, and India is one of the chief sources in the world for hides for "heavy leather." During their lives the animals furnish the cow dung, the chief fuel of India. Production of beef in the Indian subcontinent is from non-Hindu areas such as Christian villages, or from the Moslem nation of Pakistan. The tremendous numbers of holy cattle in India account for the country being one of the four major cattle areas of the world—but India is not comparable to the other regions of dense concentrations, all of which are areas of commercial livestock farming or ranching.

All cattle, for whatever purpose they are reared and maintained, yield valuable by-products upon their slaughter. Chief among these are the hides from mature animals and the skins from calves and heifers. The world's leather industry depends upon a constant supply. There are also many other by-products used in manufacturing. Among these are the hair, horns and hoofs, blood, and edible fleshings used in the production of gelatins. Factories whose raw materials are obtained from slaughterhouses and meat-packing plants often cluster in their vicinity.

Factors in Beef Production

The great majority of the world's beef originates in two kinds of regions, regions where commercial and highly developed agriculture is oriented toward the livestock enterprise. One type of region is on middle-latitude grasslands, generally in subhumid or even semiarid settings, and far removed from the markets for meat. The individual operating unit of this type of area is the extensive livestock ranch. The second type is in a highly developed and well-cultivated farming area, such as the Corn Belt of the United States, where beef cattle are born, raised, and fattened on the farms and are fed roughages and grain as well as maintained upon pastures. The animals turn low-value grain and hay crops into high-value beef. These areas are generally close to, or at least not far removed from, meat-consuming centers. The operating unit of this type is the livestock farm.

Three additional types of region produce beef, but only the first is strictly commercial, and beef production is, in fact, a by-product. This type is a dairy region, and its location is related to the conditions suitable for intensive dairying. But old dairy cows are marketed for beef when their maintenance as milk producers is no longer profitable; collectively, a considerable amount of meat originates in these regions, but, as might be expected, much of it does not yield high-quality beef. Also, an additional by-product of dairying is veal, the meat of young calves; all male calves born on a dairy farm, save only a few raised for breeding purposes, are marketed within a month or two of their birth as veal calves. The two other types of regions are not important commercially; one is the area of subsistence agriculture, the other the extensive Old World dry lands of nomadic herding. Locally produced meat helps feed local inhabitants. Particularly, the nomad is utterly dependent upon his animals for his food supply, but he contributes no surplus to the world.

The development and perfection of mechanical refrigeration in the 1870's revolutionized the world's trade in meat. Prior to this all beef and other meat had to be produced locally. Range cattle, such as the Texas Longhorns or the cattle of the Argentine Pampas, were slaughtered only for their hides and tallow; some meat was salted and became so-called jerked beef. The carcass and most of the meat was left upon the range.

Refrigerated railroad cars and ships permitted the expansion of livestock ranching to grasslands far removed from the world's markets, or permitted existing cattle regions (such as the Texas Plains and the Pampas) to shift to a commercial livestock industry. Within a relatively short period of time the unproductive Texas Longhorn was replaced on the range by white-faced Herefords, and the scrub cattle of the Pampas were replaced by the English Shorthorn. The world's beef supply expanded enormously. Chilled beef from halfway around the world could be shipped to European markets and could compete with the home-grown product.

Beef produced in the distant regions of the world is produced on land which is relatively cheap. But transportation charges to market are an important cost factor. Beef produced on expensive land, as in the Corn Belt or in western Europe, is nearer consuming centers. But rapid turnover is necessary; cattle cannot be carried on expensive land too long. Production and feeding must be efficient. This, as well as other factors, has been important in the marketing of cattle at an early age—the trend to "baby beef."

Modern research has resulted in an increase in the supply of beef per unit area. The research has been on many aspects—the improvement of beef animals, methods of feeding, the feeds and their storage for a winter dormant season or for a dry period of year, the quality of pasture grasses, and many other factors in production. The present purebred beef animal is a more efficient supplier of meat than its ancestors.

Regional Differences

The world's beef-producing regions differ among themselves in local environmental conditions and practices. Though the subhumid to semiarid settings of the grassland regions are generally alike, they differ in detail. And the markets of the world differ in their demands as to what constitutes quality meat.

The basic feed in the United States for fattening beef animals and "finishing" them for market is corn. Many other feeds are used as supplementary ones in the nation, too. Cattle from the western ranges, or from the southwest, are shipped to the Corn Belt for finishing. From the feedlot they are shipped to the meat-packing centers, the great majority of which are in or very adjacent to the Corn Belt. Corn-finished meat is "marbleized"—there are thin streaks of fat throughout the beef. And American grades of meat are based in large part upon the marbleization and other factors associated with corn-finished animals. The South, with corn, finishes many animals upon this, but in some of the South, and in large parts of the West, cattle called "grassers" are grass-finished. Under American standards these cattle command lower prices and a considerable portion of the meat is not graded as top grades. Thus, it comes as a surprise to Americans to find that the reverse is true in western Europe, which is too cool for corn. The demand is for "grasser" beef; American corn-fed beef is graded as low in quality, and Argentina alfalfa-finished beef as top. Australian and New Zealand beef, Uruguayan beef (generally produced from pasture feeding) and other areas thus have an advantage over the United States in many world markets. The presence or absence of certain feeds—owing to environmental conditions—the tastes and demands of markets, the traditions of what is "good," trade contacts, and similar factors are significant in the foreign trade in beef.

The Pampas of Argentina are a grazing land in their humid portions. The wheat belt is on their dry western margin; Argentine corn lands lie on their hot northern border. Large estancias, really cattle ranches, date from the days of the earliest Spanish land grants, when favored people received land by the square league. The Argentine cattle industry is thus in an area environmentally like the Corn Belt, except that winter in the Pampas is not cold, and average temperatures are in the 50's; all-year grazing is possible and practiced. Cattle are pastured both on native Pampa grasses and on introduced alfalfa. And—witness the reversal in practice from that of the United States—Argentine corn is exported and alfalfa, used as a hay crop in the United States, is pastured. Many beef cattle are continuously on alfalfa pasture and are used to it; in the Corn Belt, cattle, unused to fresh alfalfa, often bloat when they break through a fence and feed on it.

Fɪɢ. 13-1. The beef cattle industry of Australia centers in the northern portion of the continent, in a wet-and-dry tropical climatic setting. More than a million cattle are pastured on very large landholdings. Here cattle are being herded toward water in the dry season (note the dust). The Australian government aids ranchers in the drilling of artesian wells so that the numbers of cattle and the exports of beef can be expanded. (Australian News and Information Bureau)

Argentina's chief exports, meat and corn, are in demand in Europe, the flint corn as poultry feed; with the setting, steady market, and established trade with Europe, there is no economic pressure to grow and feed the dent corns used in cattle feeding in the United States. And the best land of the Pampas continues to be used for a livestock ranching economy, in large part because of the size of the individual estancia, lack of population pressure at home, and the lack of rural labor supply—this last in part related to the history and size of the landholdings. Tradition continues this—wealth and prestige in Argentina is measured in terms of land ownership.

More than half of Australia's beef cattle are reared in the northern subtropical and tropical state of Queensland. These cattle represent the largest single group of cattle of European breeds in the entire tropical world. The cattle stations (ranches) are in savanna grasslands and savanna-woodland country. The grass is not extremely nutritious, and the cattle are slow-growing and tend to become muscular. They rove over the stations, some of which include more than a million acres; some station headquarters are as much as a hundred miles apart. Overland cattle drives to coastal slaughtering and packing centers, or long hauls by truck, are necessary. The remaining beef cattle of the continent are clustered on stations inland from Brisbane and in nearby northeastern New South Wales, and—removed from these areas—the humid and cool coastlands of southern Victoria, in excellent pasture country.

Foreign Trade

Nearly all nations have a production of beef. In the Orient both production and consumption, however, is small. And, in net trade, it remains for one region to be the chief importer of beef, and some half dozen to furnish the surplus.

The major importing area is western Europe. Within this realm, Britain is the major importer by far, and the major world importer of beef. The other West European nations import more moderate quantities, but three small countries are net exporters—the Republic of Ireland, Denmark, and the Netherlands. The United Kingdom is the destination of this beef.

The chief sources of beef exports are Argentina, Uruguay, Australia, New Zealand, and Canada. Trade of all is directed toward Europe. The United States, owing to its large population and high per-capita consumption of beef, is usually a small importer, despite the size of its home production. Most imports are of canned beef from American-owned packing plants in Argentina, Uruguay, and extreme southern Brazil.

▶ THE UNITED STATES CATTLE INDUSTRY

The beef-cattle industry of the United States, the major world producer of beef, is diverse, to be expected considering the size of the nation. But, in general, three broad patterns stand out. These are: (1) the livestock ranching economy of large areas of the western dry lands—the dry western side of the Great Plains, the plains of Wyoming, and the dry intermontane lands between the Rockies and the Sierra Nevada–Cascade range; (2) cattle rearing and cattle finishing in the Corn Belt and in the environmentally similar lowlands of southeastern Pennsylvania; and (3) a rising, and considerable, beef-cattle industry in the American South, of importance now for some twenty to thirty years.

Livestock Ranching

The livestock ranching of the West covers a very large area. It extends into many of the mountain lands, either as upland ranches or with the utilization of humid highland areas for the summer pasturing of stock. But the largest area lies in subhumid, semiarid, or arid lower lands (although these are high above sea level), lands which are steppes and deserts. The carrying capacity of the western ranges is low per unit area—the lowest in some of the deserts, and higher on the steppes. In Nevada, as a whole, it takes 75 acres or more to support one steer. As a result of the low quantity of rainfall, there is little alternative use of the land; large ranches occupy the bulk of the dry-land area, the small irrigated district interrupting the livestock ranching economy only occasionally, where there is a source of water for irrigated farms. Cattle ranching lies in these western lands today by default—the major early American ranching country was on the Great Plains in the areas of the present wheat belts.

The cattle densities of the West are related to environmental conditions—especially the rainfall and resulting carrying capacity of the range. In response to increasing humidity and lower evaporation northward, the density of cattle in the intermontane area increases in this direction. But, on the plains to the east of the Rockies much of the northern area is suitable for wheat—the Spring Wheat Belt bends well westward into Montana—and the cattle numbers and densities are greatest southward, in western and southern Texas. Sheep, rather than cattle, utilize the driest areas. But the individual rancher has a personal choice over most areas; he may be a cattleman or a sheepman.

FIG. 13-2. The American-developed Santa Gertrudis breed of beef cattle. This breed was developed on the King Ranch in South Texas for the semi-tropical dry land conditions of the region. These steers are in a feedlot. (Mrs. Helen C. Kleberg)

Fɪɢ. 13-3. Hereford steers being assembled on a western ranch for shipment to feedlots in the Corn Belt. (Standard Oil Company, N.J.)

The livestock ranch is the operating unit. The name "ranch" is used throughout the western area; but locally a regional term may be used—a cattle "spread" is common in Montana. The ranch is owned and operated by an individual or by a company. The home site, or headquarters, is localized by the existence of a suitable water supply. The ranch lands, large in area, must include some hay land, for hay is necessary for the maintenance of the cattle during the winter. Commonly the hay field is irrigated unless the ranch contains upland grassy meadows within its borders. The other lands are fenced into large pastures, each with a water supply pumped from a well by a windmill if there is no flowing stream; some areas, with no ground or surface water supply, are unsuitable for cattle ranching.

Western range cattle are almost entirely of the Hereford breed, the best of the rustlers. The Aberdeen-Angus is not unknown, but it is most common in farming regions and is apparently less suited to range conditions. In South Texas the American-developed Santa Gertrudis breed (a cross of Brahmans and Shorthorns) and Brahman cattle stock many of the ranches.

The breeding stock is kept on the ranch during the winter. They are fed at the ranch headquarters or driven to the haystacks in the fields. At the eastern base of the Northern Rockies in Montana, the warm, descending chinook winds keep the plains free of snow intermittently, and there is some winter grazing during these warm periods. But hay must be available as supplementary feed and for the intermittent periods of snow cover.

The spring "crop" of calves is branded before the advent of the pasture season; all calves are kept to rear for beef, the male calves as steers. Branding is necessary if some of the cattle are to be pastured in nearby mountains, or if they are to graze far from headquarters. The cattle kept on a well-fenced home ranch may not be branded; the practice is not as necessary as it was during the past days of unrestricted grazing on unfenced range, much of it part of the public domain.

The summer season is one of relative quiet. Fences are mended, hay is cut, the pastures are visited to ensure the rancher that the cattle are safe, the water supply is adequate, and for salting of the animals.

The fall roundup brings the cattle to or near the headquarters. One of the purposes is to "cut out" the animals that are to be marketed. Cattle are sold as feeders, and trainloads or truckloads are shipped eastward to Corn Belt feedlots, or are sold to farmers of the irrigated areas, where sugar beet pulp and molasses, pea vines, cull potatoes, and hay and other feeds (except corn) are available. Some large-scale feeders purchase their cattle directly; middlemen between the rancher and the farmer operate this activity also.

Feeding and Meat-Packing Centers

The Corn Belt is the chief region in which range cattle are fattened for market and in which beef animals are reared on livestock farms for sale to slaughtering centers (see Chapter XII).

The major meat-packing centers, except for three, are in or near the Corn Belt, and the eventual sale of the cattle is to the stockyards and meat-packing plants at such locations as Sioux Falls, South Dakota; Sioux City, Ottumwa, and other centers in Iowa; Albert Lea and South St. Paul, Minnesota; South Omaha, Nebraska; South St. Joseph, Missouri; Kansas City, Kansas; East St. Louis and Chicago, Illinois; Cudahy and Madison, Wisconsin; Indianapolis, Indiana; and many others. The long-time pattern of cattle-to-meat-packer-to-market has been from west to east; but recently the pattern has been modified by the growth of population on the West Coast, and much beef now is shipped to Pacific Coast markets from midwestern meat-packing centers. In the West (and also in parts of the South) the advertising sign "Kansas City steaks" means Corn Belt beef; this and similar signs are used by restaurants to distinguish corn-fattened beef from local grasser beef.

Three large meat-packing centers are not in the Corn Belt—Fort Worth, Texas; Denver, Colorado; and Jersey City, New Jersey. Corn-finished and many other animals reach these centers; Jersey City, among these, is market-oriented to the New York metropolitan market. Lubbock, Texas, Lancaster, Pennsylvania, and many other meat-packing centers of some size are in animal-rearing regions not included in the Corn Belt.

There are feeding districts elsewhere. Although many cattle are finished in the western irrigated valleys, the winter-feeding of sheep is relatively more important in them. California farmers are now engaging in winter-feeding in certain districts.

The South

Many factors help explain the recent rise of the Deep South—the cotton country—in the beef-cattle industry. The change is part of the overall scene in which much cotton acreage has shifted westward, and the former emphasis in the South upon cotton has been replaced by the diversification of agriculture.

The ravages of the cotton boll weevil, the cotton acreage-control programs, serious soil erosion on sloping fields, and the establishment of conservation programs to aid in the checking of erosion have been background factors. Subtropical and tropical grasses and legumes, some of African origin, have been introduced to the region; seeded pastures have replaced cotton acreage, both because of erosion and because of the governmental control programs, and the cutting of cotton quotas; much of the land removed from growing cotton is now in grass. The rural South has been affected by the out-migration of its Negro and white labor to northern and western cities, and to the growing industries within the section itself. Beef cattle require less labor than cotton; mechanization has replaced the lost workers, and some former cotton "plantations" which had many workers are now family-operated cattle farms. Even the levees along the lower Mississippi are now grazed by Herefords and Aberdeen-Angus cattle. Georgia and Mississippi have become major cattle-rearing states. And Florida, always important for its numbers of cattle, has upgraded its herds, had Brahman cattle introduced in numbers, and today, in a few districts, contains a range cattle industry comparable to that of the West. All-year grazing is possible in Florida and along the Gulf Coast; little shelter in the way of barns is necessary in most of the Deep South. Thus the costs of production are, on the whole, less than in many other established cattle regions, and this, in itself, is a factor attracting additional entrepreneurs to shift to a beef enterprise. By the late 1950's nearly ten million beef cattle grazed in the states from South Carolina westward to Louisiana and Arkansas, not the numbers per unit area in the Corn Belt or in Texas, but a significant and revolutionary change in the American pattern of meat production.

The farmers of the South grow a great deal of corn. Cattle feeding has developed in certain districts. Many cattle from the pasture areas of the Deep South are now being fed and finished in the Upper South, in the limestone lands of the Central Basin of Tennessee and the limestone valleys of East Tennessee. And, like the Corn Belt, some of the farmers of the South are both rearing and feeding beef cattle for market on a single farm. The slaughtering and meat-packing industry has increased and expanded in the region.

► THE DAIRY INDUSTRY

Dairying is an intensive type of agriculture. A dairy farm carries a large herd of cows per unit of land or farm. The farmer has a relatively even input of labor throughout the year; he works with the raising of feed crops and the milking in the summer, and with the barn work, feeding, and milking in the winter. Every day in the year there is the twice-a-day milking of the cows in production, and a daily routine in the preparation of the milk for delivery to a city distributor or a dairy-products manufacturing plant.

Dairying, unlike most other types of agriculture, yields a steady, year-round income; the farmer is paid for the milk every two weeks or every month. Merchants and bankers operating in a village or city in a dairy region experience a relatively even flow of sales or deposits, and business activity is more or less uniform during all months of the year. This is quite unlike the situation in a wheat, cotton, or tobacco area where crops are sold but once a year.

The dairy enterprise is oriented around the sale of milk and associated live-stock products such as veal calves, and the growing of feed crops, maintenance of pastures, and—usually—the production of one cash crop for direct sale. The major portion of a dairy farmer's income is derived from the sale of milk; the feed crops are "marketed" in this form, just as the corn of the Corn Belt is marketed as meat.

Dairying requires lush pastures, an ample supply of fresh water for the cows, and a climate whose summer is cool, preferably with average temperatures not above the lower 70's Fahrenheit, and ideally in the 60's. The dairy cow, a highly bred animal, will not withstand too great heat for any lengthy period; milk production declines during prolonged hot spells. Only the Jersey is best adjusted to warm-to-hot summers, such as those of the American Southeast.

Rolling to rough topography of glacial origin characterizes many of the world's leading dairy regions. Rough glacial moraines, rolling plains of glacial drift, drumlins, marshes (used as lowland pasture) of glacial origin, and similar landforms are usual in the chief dairy regions of the northern United States, southern Canada, and northern Europe. There are many stony and bouldery districts, also; these areas are used for pasture. Yet, set among the rougher glacial terrain, there are small outwash plains, smooth till plains, and other glacial landforms that are eminently suitable for the crop land of the dairy farms. In part, of course, the fact that the cool-summer northern lands are important dairy areas, and that these lands were glaciated during the last or Wisconsin stage of glaciation, is responsible for this correlation. But, in addition, the dairy enterprise can utilize this type of terrain much better than can crop farming.

Certain mountainous areas are characterized by dairying; the Alps offer an example. The slopes furnish both pasture and hay land, the valley bottoms provide the crop land. Many of the cool, high-altitude valleys of the Rockies, particularly

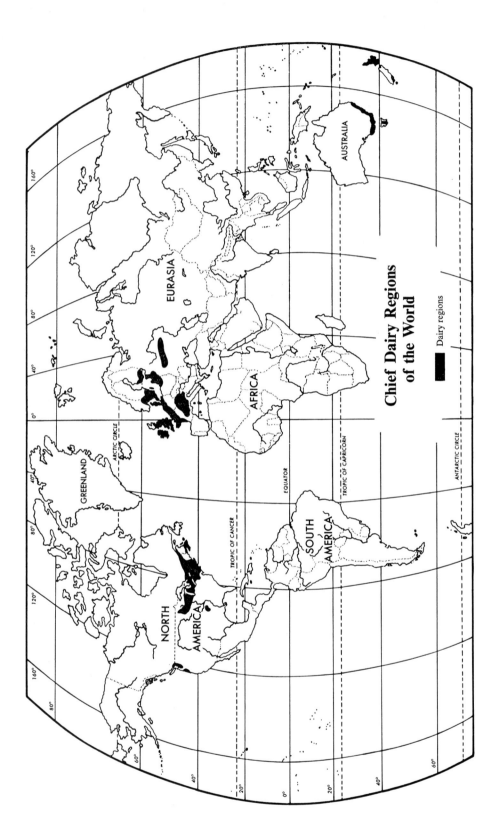

**Chief Dairy Regions
of the World**

Dairy regions

in western Montana, also have important dairy districts interspersed among the more usual cattle-ranching economy of these highlands.

Flat, poorly drained surfaces in a cool climatic setting are used for a dairy economy. Important dairy districts in the Netherlands and along the North Sea coast of Germany, and in the Waikato and Thames River valleys south of Auckland in New Zealand, are on ill-drained plains. Lush pastures in the Dutch polders, the diked meadows of Germany, and in the Waikato Valley support more than one cow per acre; only hay and oats can be raised locally but they thrive in the environment, and supplementary feeds can be purchased.

▶ PRINCIPAL DAIRY REGIONS

There are six principal dairy regions, and several minor ones, in the world. Two are in Europe, two are in North America, and there is one each in New Zealand and Australia.

The European regions are (1) in the cooler northwest of the continent, along the shorelands of the English Channel, North and Baltic Seas, and throughout much of the British Isles; and (2) the Alps and Alpine Foreland countryside. On the continent the first-named dairy region extends from Brittany and Normandy in northern France, through Belgium, the Netherlands, northwestern Germany, all of Denmark, and into southern Norway, Sweden, and Finland. The Alpine Foreland region extends from eastern France through Switzerland, southern Germany, and much of Austria, and—on the southern slopes of the Alps—into the valleys of the Italian Alps and the Piedmont and Lombardy portions of the Po Valley of Italy. Among European countries, the Netherlands, Denmark, and Switzerland possess a particular fame for their high-quality dairy products.

The main North American dairy region, both in area covered and in milk production, includes the east-west strip of territory in southern Canada and the northern states of the United States from the Atlantic Ocean westward to the prairie-plains border. The Maritime Provinces of Canada—Prince Edward Island, Nova Scotia, and New Brunswick—are dairy lands where lands are utilized agriculturally rather than for forests, and the entire plain of the St. Lawrence Valley in Quebec is an almost continuous region of dairy farms. And, south of these areas, dairying extends from the six New England states westward across New York State, peninsular Ontario (north of Lakes Ontario and Erie, east of Lake Huron), to Michigan, and reappears west of Lake Michigan throughout Wisconsin and into west-central Minnesota, where it meets the plains border— drier prairie lands of rich soil, utilized for the less-demanding (in labor) activity of grain production—the Spring Wheat Belt. This principal North American region, on its south to the west of the Appalachian Highlands, meets the Corn Belt along a transitional dairy-Corn Belt border zone.

The second North American dairy region is in the cool valleys and basins of western British Columbia in Canada, and the Pacific Northwest of the United States. The farmers of the Puget Sound Lowland of Washington, and of the coastal valleys of Oregon (such as the Tillamook) and northern coastal California engage in the dairy enterprise. There is also considerable dairying in the flat-floored Willamette Valley of Oregon.

North Island of New Zealand is outstanding in dairying. The plains south of Auckland and the Taranaki area surrounding Mount Egmont on the west coast of the island have long been famous for their milk cows and dairy products.

Australian dairying is located on the island-state of Tasmania and on the southeastern and eastern shores of the continent. The dairy lands of the south shore are in Victoria; those of the east shore lie in the narrow strip of rough terrain between the sea and the Australian Alps or Dividing Range. Nowhere is this strip wide, but it is long, as emphasis upon dairying extends from Brisbane southward to the southeastern tip of the continent.

Fig. 13-4. Farm, Holstein dairy cows, canal, and canal boat in the Netherlands. Much of the agriculture of the lowlands of northwestern Europe is organized around the dairy industry. Thousands of Dutch families live on their canal boats (note the laundry hung out to dry) and transport products of all sorts on the canals. (Standard Oil Company, N.J.)

Fig. 13-5. Danish Red dairy cows staked out for pasture. Land is scarce in Denmark; labor is plentiful. Therefore labor is used to stake the cattle so that they graze only in a limited area on any given day and do not trample the grass in the entire pasture. Labor is used to transport water to the cows—the vehicle is a waterwagon. (Danish Information Office)

Two world climatic realms, each eminently suitable for lush pastures, each with cool summers and adequate water—many flowing streams in the pastures and abundant ground water supply for pumping to the drinking cups in the barns —offer the best natural environment for dairying. One, and probably the better of the two overall because of milder winters and year-round drizzly type of precipitation, is the temperate marine realm. Its location is on the western sides of the middle-latitude continents poleward of 37°–40°F north and south. The dairy regions of northwestern Europe, of the Pacific Northwest and British Columbia, of New Zealand, and of much of Australia are in this realm. The other realm is that of the humid continental medium-summer climate. The spring, summer, and fall of this realm are not unlike the same seasons in the temperate marine lands. But the winter is cold and characterized by a continuous snow cover. Cattle must be housed and fed in substantial basement barns. The barn itself is a considerable capital investment for the farmer; it is also a prominent landscape feature of these dairy regions. And, in addition, the pasture season of the realm is not as long, necessitating more winter-feeding of cows, and the growing and storage of more feed per farm. The dairy regions of the United States and Canada from the Atlantic to Minnesota, and of the Alpine Foreland of Europe are in the medium summer realm.

The northern portion of the Australian dairy region, among the principal areas, alone extends into a climatic realm other than the two chief ones. It extends into the humid subtropical lands of the northern coast of New South Wales.

Kinds of Dairy Products

There are two types of primary markets in the dairy enterprise. One is the direct sale of fresh milk to the city milk bottler and distributor. This product from the dairy farm is known as market milk. The other is the sale of milk to factories. This product is called manufactured milk. The factory may be a creamery which makes butter, a cheese factory, an evaporating plant, a condensed milk plant, a plant producing dried milk or ice cream mix; or it may be a modern multiple-purpose plant equipped to manufacture any of the dairy products. In the multiple-purpose dairy factory the particular output of a given period is determined by the market conditions.

The sale of market milk is characteristic of those portions of a dairy region that are close to cities. The area producing this milk is said to be the milkshed of the city. A small city possesses a small milkshed; that of New York City extends over much of New York State and into adjacent states. Nearly all of the agriculturally used areas of Great Britain are in the milksheds of the numerous British cities.

The sale of manufactured milk and the existence of dairy-manufacturing plants is characteristic of those portions of a dairy region that are far removed from urban markets. Milk is bulky and is low in value per unit of weight; it is turned into a more concentrated product, one higher in value per unit of weight and thus able to pay its transportation charges to distant markets. Consequently, while in market milk 100 pounds of milk is transported to the city as 100 pounds of weight, only 45 of the original 100 is marketed as condensed or evaporated milk, only 10 of the 100 as cheese, and only 4 to 5 as butter. Theoretically a dairy region is zoned with respect to city markets, with condenseries in the zone beyond market milk production, cheese factories farther removed in the dairy region, and creameries most distant from the cities. The theoretical zones have developed, in general form, in the American Dairy Region. The dairy farms of the New England states and New York State produce market milk for the numerous cities of the East; Wisconsin (except for its southeast near Chicago and Milwaukee) is the chief cheese-manufacturing state; and Minnesota, farthest from the principal urban markets, leads in butter output. On the world scale, the principal product of the dairy farms of northwestern continental Europe and the British Isles is market milk, and Australia and New Zealand, halfway around the world from this market, are producers of butter and cheese for it.

The international boundary between the United States and Canada cuts through part of the North American dairy regions. This has an effect upon the disposition of milk. No market milk can be imported into the United States unless it passes through a milk-import station, and few of these have been established. Therefore the Canadian side of the border is one where milk is sold for manufacture, except near the Montreal urban market, and the United States side one of market milk. The Detroit milkshed extends a hundred or more miles around the city in a semicircle on the Michigan side of the city; east of Detroit there are dairy-manufacturing plants in Canada. Canada is an exporter of butter and cheese to the British market.

Dairying for market milk, and for some manufacture, exists outside of the principal dairy regions of the Western world. Every city is surrounded by a milkshed, in proportionate size to the demand for milk in the city; if there is a temporary deficit, milk must be purchased from the Dairy Region. The presence

FIG. 13-6. Barrels and cartons of butter on the docks at Esbjerg in western Denmark for shipment to Hull in England. Denmark exports butter, bacon, and eggs to the English market. (Danish Information Office)

of the metropolitan city markets of Philadelphia, Baltimore, and Washington results in neighboring milk production well southward from the major dairy region as far as northern Virginia. Dairying is a secondary activity in parts of the Corn Belt, and in the medium-summer lands of central Russia and western Siberia. Local dairy districts have developed in hilly lands in warmer climatic settings, one such in the United States being in southwestern Missouri in and near the Ozarks.

The presence of large urban markets for milk in portions of the Western world not located in "natural" dairy regions results in the production of local market milk. Thus, Mediterranean lands of southern California possess dairy farms in response to the city markets. Cows are kept on small areas, and their feed is shipped from irrigated valleys or from the Middle West. They are milked and fed on a "factory-type basis," as machines, and are replaced by cows purchased at a distance when their productivity declines. Or, as in central California, in part of the lower San Joaquin Valley, dairy farms occupy irrigated land in response to the present of the not-too-distant San Francisco market. But, in one part of the Western world, Mediterranean Europe, there are few dairy cows. Pastures are poor during the dry summer, and cattle are not maintained on irrigated land, unlike the situation in Mediterranean California. Traditionally, the peoples are not consumers of milk from cows; milk needs are furnished by sheep and goats, and some of the types of south Italian and Greek cheeses are manufactured from ewe's milk; needs of fats and oils are furnished by the home-grown olive. Only the Italians are consumers of cheese in their soups and other cookery and these cheeses are manufactured mainly in non-Mediterranean northern Italy.

Foreign Trade

Manufactured dairy products are imported by some of the nations of western Europe. As is expectable from the knowledge of the principles of production, there is little foreign trade in market milk; some milk is shipped across the Irish Sea from the Republic of Ireland to cities of the United Kingdom, and milk from Denmark reaches nearby cities in Germany. The Orient receives only powdered or canned milk; Oriental peoples are not accustomed to dairy products in their diet, although the Japanese are attempting to change this, and a small dairy industry has been established in cool Hokkaido and near the northern, cool tip of Honshu. The Caribbean islands are importers of powdered milk; foreign citizens of tropical lands consume canned butter from Denmark.

New Zealand and Australia are the major contributors of butter and cheese in foreign trade, and their markets for these products are halfway around the world. Canada exports cheese likewise, and only very moderate quantities of butter and cheese are now shipped from the United States. In contrast, during the early days of this country it was the major source of exported dairy products. For a time after World War II American dairy manufactures were included in

FIG. 13-7. Summer grazing of dairy cows on the upland meadows of the Alps in Switzerland. Cows belonging to farmers in the lower valleys are driven to the Alpine pastures under the care of herders. Each farmer has inherited rights as to the number of cows he is permitted to send. The herds usually total from 50 to 100 cows. Cheese is manufactured during the summer, the cheesemaker being the most important individual with each herd. (Swiss National Tourist Office)

the foreign-aid programs, as they were in surplus supply. But by the end of the 1950's the dairy surplus had declined to a virtual balance within the nation, and exports consisted principally of powdered and condensed milk.

Within Europe itself, a few small countries are exporters; these nations contain an intensive dairy enterprise whose output exceeds the demands at home. The Netherlands and Denmark ship both butter and cheese, Switzerland mainly cheese, and Norway and Sweden butter. Some few specialties of an individual district are shipped widely around the Western world; thus Roquefort cheese, a ewe's-milk cheese from southern France, and some Italian varieties of cheese from northern Italy and a small district in Argentina reach wide areas—the Roquefort being used both as cheese and in salad dressings, and the Italian varieties being sold in Italian settlements in the Americas.

► SWINE

Four different areas in the world are outstanding in the rearing and feeding of swine. Each is a region wherein hogs are maintained on farms where the animals are kept in relatively small enclosures, fed concentrated feeds, and allowed only limited pasturage. The pig is associated, thus, with sedentary agriculture, despite the original roaming and rooting habits of its wild ancestors or of the present wild swine found in a few parts of the world.

The four major regions of swine-rearing are: (1) the eastern, humid half of the United States, east of the 100th meridian, but within this broad area the Corn Belt is outstanding in numbers of animals and production of pork and associated products; (2) western and central Europe, north of the Mediterranean lands, and eastward into central European Russia; (3) all regions of dense habitation and intensive agriculture in China—from the eastern coasts of the country westward to the dry lands of inner Asia; and (4) southern Brazil. Many different feeds are utilized for the maintenance of swine in each region, but one or two major ones characterize each: thus there are the corn-fed swine of the United States, the potato-fed swine of Europe, garbage-fed animals of China, and corn-fed ones in Brazil. Among supplementary feeds of regional importance are skim-milk in the western part of the Dairy Region of the United States (where only cream is sold for butter manufacture) and in Denmark; various root crops—such as rutabagas and turnips—in Europe; and several in Brazil. And the term "garbage" for China includes not only kitchen wastes but gleanings from the fields such as rice hulls and weeds and waste grasses and water plants gathered laboriously from fields, canal banks, and rivers and canals.

The close relationship between corn as a feed and numbers of swine in the United States is shown by the sectional variation in swine rearing. An average number of nearly 44 million hogs are recorded on the farms of the North in an enumeration taken on January 1. About 12 million is the usual number on the same date on the farms of the South. In contrast, in the Western states— all of them west of the 100th meridian and not in the chief corn-growing regions—there are usually fewer than a million and a half. The five states in the heart of the Corn Belt, from Ohio westward to Nebraska, contain nearly 30 million swine, more than half of the total in the entire nation, and Iowa alone usually has a fifth of the swine in the entire United States.

Swine farrow twice a year. Therefore their actual numbers depend upon the date of a census enumeration. Spring farrowing in the Northern Hemisphere regions of production results in shipment of hogs to market late in the summer or during the early autumn. Fall-farrowed litters are fed during the winter and marketed in the spring or early summer. Many farmers in the commercial regions spread the farrowing dates throughout the year now; this is possible when the animals are housed in tightly built, heated, and ventilated hog houses. The animal responds to cleanliness and care, and its reputation for rooting in filthy hogyards, perhaps deserved in the past, is no longer valid in most of the Corn Belt or in Europe. In fact, in Denmark, swine are reared entirely indoors on many farms, and labor is plentiful enough to permit daily washing of the animals and hog houses, and the carrying of feed to the hogpens. In the United States considerable pasturage, tightly fenced, is provided on many farms, and portable feed troughs are moved to the pastures for supplementary feeding. And, on the large farms, where several hundred or more hogs are maintained after the farrowing, automation is used for the mixing and distribution of the feeds in order to save labor.

Swine, whether in the Corn Belt or elsewhere, can be adjusted in numbers relative to market prices and feed conditions quite easily, and much more easily than the numbers of cattle. Thus if a farmer is short of home-grown corn one year he can reduce the size of the swine drove and still feed as many cattle as formerly. The same is true in other important regions, except China. In China, between farrowing periods, the number of swine is only one or two per family and the industry is almost "subsistence"; the pig is kept for a home food supply, and in many parts of the country is comparable to the situation wherein an American family maintains and feeds a dog as a pet. Dogs are kept by some householders in China, too, but as meat dogs rather than pets—the chow is an example of a meat dog of the Orient.

There are many breeds of swine in the world. Some breeds are classified as fat hogs, certain ones as the bacon type, others as dual-purpose. The bacon type or "leaner" hog is more common in Europe than elsewhere, and is common in dairy regions where skim milk constitutes an important ingredient in the feed mixture. The fat hog was in the past most usual in the Corn Belt. Today, however, the dual-purpose breeds are numerous and are increasing in response to market conditions. Lard was and is a significant product of the fat hog; the competition of lard with vegetable fats manufactured from several oils—among them coconut oils, peanut oils, cottonseed oils—and the wide market acceptance of vegetable shortenings by housewives, has resulted in the shift of Corn Belt farmers to the dual-purpose breeds which yield relatively more meat with respect to fat.

Intensive swine-rearing districts have developed within the principal regions. All of the Corn Belt except the cash-grain district near Chicago contains many swine. Southeastern Iowa has the largest proportion of hogs to area in the United States. Denmark, the Baltic Plain of northern Germany, and Poland are outstanding in Europe. These areas, and particularly the Baltic Plain, are in the Rye-Potato Belt of Europe agriculturally. A large and rather flavorless potato is grown for feeding the animals. Storage buildings, instead of corn cribs, are potato and other root cellars. And there are other specialty areas. Certain of the "Virginia hams" and some from southern Georgia are from peanut-fed hogs. Denmark, with its skim-milk-and-grain-fed pigs, is a producer of special bacons, exported to the United Kingdom.

Marketing and Trade

Meat-packing plants purchase the ready-for-market hogs and prepare the pork, bacon, and hams for market. There remains, too, even in the United States, a very large home-slaughtering activity. The meat from this which is not consumed fresh or smoked is packaged and stored in home freezers or in commercial freezing plants in frozen-food lockers rented by individuals.

The major meat-packing centers in and near the American Corn Belt are the principal packers of pork products as they are of beef. Their relative importance in the two differs, however. In recent years East St. Louis, Omaha, and South St. Paul have each exceeded Chicago in the receipt of hogs at their stockyards; the receipts at Sioux City have approached those of Chicago. This reflects not only the significance of the western part of the Corn Belt in feeding, but the increasing delivery by truck. A farmer can receive the morning's price quotations by radio, and, if the price is satisfactory, can market a truckload of swine in the afternoon or early the following morning after a night drive. Nearly all of the major packing centers, however, receive large annual shipments of swine; those relatively the lowest are Denver and Fort Worth, beyond the major corn-producing and swine-feeding regions.

Bacon and ham are the two principal meats from the hog which enter foreign trade. Denmark, with its important exports of bacon to England, leads in this by far. Poland and the Netherlands follow with much less tonnage. Exports from the United States are small. These four nations and Canada supply nearly all of the trade, the importing nations being the United Kingdom and Germany mainly. The United States, although a net exporter, is an importer of quality canned hams from all three of the European exporting countries, and of Canadian bacon (prepared differently from American) from Canada.

► SHEEP

The lamb and mutton production and trade has been discussed elsewhere (see Chapter VIII). For comparison with the beef and pork industry, however, the differing regionalism of the meat-packing industry will be discussed here. Because the principal sheep-rearing regions of the United States are in the West, and many of the winter-feeding regions for sheep are in the western irrigated valleys, the pattern is different. Some western sheep are fed in the Dairy Region, as in Wisconsin and Minnesota, where pea vines from the pea-canning industry constitute an important part of the feed; a relatively small number of sheep, compared to western steers, are fed in the Corn Belt.

Seven of the nine major meat-packing centers are in or near the Corn Belt; only Denver and Fort Worth are removed from it. The seven, during a recent year, received 95 per cent of the total number of hogs shipped to these nine centers for slaughter. They received 88 per cent of the cattle shipped to the nine. But the seven were the destination of only 61 per cent of the sheep sent to the nine, and Denver and Fort Worth received 39 per cent. Denver is the largest lamb- and mutton-packing center by far, followed by Fort Worth. Each is nearer the sheep-raising and -feeding regions, and there is less loss in weight —or in the lives of sheep—in the relatively shorter shipment distance. Trainloads of western-fed sheep still reach Chicago and other centers, but Kansas City, Omaha, and South St. Paul, more than a day closer in travel time to the western districts, now each exceed Chicago and farther eastern packing centers in this activity. And there are several "secondary" (in size) sheep-packing centers in the West itself.

► GOATS

The goat is a native of the Eastern Hemisphere, descended from and domesticated in the Middle East. It is now distributed throughout the world, but its numbers in the New World are few compared to those in Mediterranean Europe, Mediterranean North Africa, the Middle East, the Indian subcontinent, and even the plateau lands of East Africa.

The goat is adapted to rough, rocky highland country and to dry-land rocky pastures such as those of the Mediterranean lands with their dry summers. Goats crop the grass and weeds down to the ground level and are "erosion-inducing" animals. They destroy small bushes and seedling trees. For this reason they are not desired as grazing animals on the federally owned mountainous lands of the American West, and no doubt some of the serious erosion in the Apennines of Italy and the Greek mountains is owing to centuries of overgrazing by goats and sheep.

The long, silky fleece of the goat is mohair, used in the clothing, fabric, and upholstery industries. Special breeds of goats, such as the Angora, have been developed for their prime fleece. Dairy breeds of goats, such as the Toggenburg of the Alps, yield milk, relatively small in quantity but high in quality. Norwegian gjetost cheese is made from goat's milk. And, throughout the Mediterranean area of Europe and Africa the goat as well as the sheep is the "dairy animal." The meat of the goat, chevon, is consumed in the Mediterranean area and the Middle East but has never gained popularity elsewhere. Goatskins are raw material for fine leather and are used in the manufacture of kid gloves and similar articles.

The largest numbers of goats reared commercially are in the area from Greece eastward through Turkey and in the Middle East. Turkey has long been a principal exporter of mohair.

FIG. 13-8. The Edwards Plateau of Texas is the only important mohair-producing region in the United States. Angora goats provide the clip. Boston is the major market to which the baled mohair is shipped. (Standard Oil Company, N.J.)

The dry lands of the Edwards Plateau of southwest Texas and of the Rio Grande Plain to its south contain nearly all the goats reared commercially in the United States. Goats are grazed on ranches which also have some sheep and cattle, and the animals are grazed together in the same fenced enclosures. The goat grazes on the foliage of the small live oak and of other trees and brush of the Edwards Plateau, sheep in the same pastures consume the weeds, and the two animals thus supplement the grass-eating cattle as well as serving as "land clearers" for cattle.

All Texas goats are of the Angora breed, introduced to its dry southwest in 1849. The areally highly concentrated Texas industry now usually meets the American demand for mohair. Annual production has increased from a million pounds in 1900 to 15 or so million, and in some recent years has exceeded 20 million pounds. The entire emphasis is upon mohair, but in the last few years a small meat industry producing chevon and cabrito (the meat from kids) has developed in response to a Spanish-American market in Texas.

► QUESTIONS

1. What factors help explain why certain farm or ranch animals that are of commercial importance in some parts of the world are virtually absent from other agricultural regions?
2. Western Europe has a dense animal population; how are these numerous animals maintained?
3. Where are the four regions which contain the largest numbers and greatest density of cattle?
4. What is the general world distribution of cattle of the *Bos taurus* family? of the *Bos indicus* family?
5. Why have breeds of *Bos indicus* cattle been introduced to some parts of the extreme southern United States?
6. How does India differ in its use of cattle from the other cattle-rearing regions of the world?
7. What kinds of regions, so far as agricultural organization is concerned, contribute most of the beef to world markets?
8. What countries are leading exporters of beef? What region is the chief importer?
9. What are the leading cattle-regions of the United States? The leading feeding regions? Why?
10. What is the pattern of the location of the major meat-packing centers of the United States? Explain why.
11. What kind of "agricultural revolution" is going on in the American South, particularly that portion in the Cotton Belt?
12. How does dairying differ economically from the growing of crops for sale?
13. Describe the capital, the land, and the labor input of the dairy enterprise.
14. In what form, and where, does New Zealand market its large output of milk?
15. Explain why districts in a dairy region specialize in either market milk or manufactured milk?
16. Where are the four principal swine-rearing regions of the world?
17. Upon what principal feed is the rearing of swine dependent in the United States?
18. Explain why the meat-packing centers that slaughter the greatest numbers of sheep differ in location from the chief cattle-slaughtering centers.

XIV Commercial Fishing

Commercial fishing is not distributed evenly over the oceans of the world. It is highly regionalized. The four greatest fishing regions lie on either side of the North Atlantic and North Pacific Oceans, in the waters off of western Europe, northeastern North America, northwestern North America, and eastern and northeastern Asia. More than 95 per cent of the world's fish are captured in the waters of the Northern Hemisphere. On a world basis it is estimated that essentially all of the commercial industry is concentrated in not more than 7 per cent of the area of the world's seas and oceans, and mainly in the shallower waters of the immediate inshore areas, in the waters of continental shelves, and of banks some distance from the land.

The catch of fish, as measured by landings at fishing ports, is unevenly spread among the continents. Although the tonnage varies from year to year, the pattern, or relative position, has remained somewhat the same through a considerable period. Figures for a recent year, as estimated by one of the working subdivisions of the United Nations, depict the pattern. Of some 55,000,000 pounds of fish, more than 26 million, or nearly half, were landed in Asia, excluding the Soviet lands. Japan alone is the leading fishing nation by far in the world; more than two million Japanese are dependent upon the industry for a livelihood. European landings total some 13 million pounds, about a quarter of the world catch. Norway, the leading fishing nation of Europe, has a catch of only a little over a third that of Japan. The estimated poundage of fish in North America is somewhat over 8 million. Soviet fisheries, divided between those in European waters and in Soviet Asian waters, total half of the poundage of North America. Africa accounts for about a million and a half pounds, South America only a little over one million, and all of Oceania—the Pacific Islands and Australia and New Zealand—but 300,000 pounds.

Reasons for the Unequal Distribution

There are many reasons, both geographic and economic, for the unequal distribution of the world's fisheries. These reasons are not all of equal importance in the various fishing areas, nor are all of them operative in any single region.

Fish are distributed, basically, in relationship to the physical geography of the oceans (see later section). The geographic conditions of the North Pacific and the North Atlantic are the most favorable for large populations of fish, and particularly for the existence of large schools of edible fish. Environmentally the inshore waters, poleward of latitude 40°N, thus contain quantities of fish, and the very existence of this resource is a factor in its utilization.

The presence of large populations in eastern Asia and western Europe and of "medium" populations in North America is a significant factor in the fishing industry. The inhabitants of these areas offer a concentrated market for the sale of fish. Before the days of the canning of fish, and later of the quick-freezing, fish had to be either consumed within a day or two of their capture, or else dried. Thus the densely peopled shores of Asia and Europe offered an immediate market; this in itself helped the early development and increase of nearby fisheries.

The perfection of mechanical refrigeration during the 1870's increased the area of the market. The crates of fish, packed in ice (and ice at the time had to be cut from northern lakes and rivers in the winter), could not be shipped far. As the market expanded in area the commercial fisheries increased; in fact, each grew together. But the market was still mainly the densely settled areas not far from the coastlines.

Developments of many types increased the range of a fishing fleet. New types of nets, steam and oil-powered vessels, mechanical refrigeration on the ships themselves, and other changes occurred. But, as these modern fishing methods were introduced, so was the market expanding with the increase of population. And, basically, no new fishing regions came into production. The four principal world regions continued, but increased their output. Rapid rail transport on land widened the area of the market.

Minor fishing areas served only a local market. This situation continued until World War II; for example, South African fisheries were small in response to the limited home market. New Zealand fish were marketed in the Dominion. Marked postwar changes have occurred, as will be noted later, and some formerly minor regions have increased in importance—not because the numbers of fish have increased, but because present methods of access to distant centers of population and their markets have increased so much in rapidity.

The Market

The market for and consumption of fish is of differing intensities in different parts of the world. The largest total markets are on the western and eastern littorals of the Eurasian continent. This reflects the long-time dominance of fishing in the adjacent seas and the eating habits of many generations of people. The British, the Dutch, the Scandinavians, the Chinese living near the coast, and the Japanese consume large quantities of fish. A fish course is a standard part of an English meal; fish and chips are served in public houses, in restaurants, and at sporting events. Fresh or dried fish are consumed daily by the Japanese; rice, vegetables, and fish are the foundations of the food supply.

The Far Eastern use of fish provides protein to the diet of the inhabitants of lands where meat is generally absent, or extremely expensive. Land cannot be used for pastures in densely inhabited coastal China, Korea, and Japan; moreover their Oriental civilization is one without dependence upon meat animals. On a *total* basis the millions of people depend upon the sea for an important part of their daily food, but owing to the standard of living the per-capita consumption is moderate or low. In western Europe meat and dairy products are the chief protein sources; thus, although the *total* dependence upon fish is less than in, say, Japan, the per-capita consumption of fish is higher.

Another factor in the regionalized market for fish is the fact that, despite modern methods of preservation and transportation, inhabitants of coastal areas consume larger quantities of fish than do persons in the continental interiors. The people of New England eat more fish, on a total or per-capita basis, than do an equivalent number of inhabitants of the Mississippi Valley. Particularly is this true in the case of fresh fish, quick-frozen fish or fish filets, and seafood such as lobster or crab. The market for canned fish is not so sharply regionalized. In large part the coastal consumption is owing to such factors as immediate availability, eating habits, the continuance of pride in important regional dishes (New England clam chowder or Maine lobster, for example), and, negatively, to unfamiliarity of many housewives of the inland regions with varieties of fish or with recipes for their preparation. The present nation-wide distribution of precooked and frozen fish filets, coupled with national advertising, may change this. But quick-freezing dates only from the late 1930's, its widespread use only from the 1940's; eating habits, once fixed, are slow in changing.

Religious factors are significant also. The serving of fish or of other substitutes for meat in the homes of Roman Catholics on Fridays and on other fast days is a case. Originally, in the dry-summer Mediterranean lands, with their brown and barren pastures, meat was a deficit item. Fish from the sea helped supplement the food supply, even to conserve it. As persons of the Catholic faith settled other areas, as in the New World, a weekly demand for fish arose. In much of the United States, Thursday is the day on which most fish are sold. Fish trains, carrying solid cargoes of fish, leave certain seaports on Tuesdays or Wednesdays, and the fish reach market counters in time for the weekly rise in sales. There is also a large north-south trade in fish between the surplus countries of northern Europe (as Norway) and the fish-deficit countries of southern Europe (as Italy) in response to the Catholic market of the south; in return, olive oil is exported northward, and Norwegian sardines are canned in this ingredient. The nations of South America and the West Indies, whose inhabitants are largely Catholics, are major importers of fish; local fisheries are poor and do not supply the demand. These nations thus offer markets for the fish captured in the waters off northeastern North America.

▶ GEOGRAPHY OF FISH DISTRIBUTION

The world's chief fisheries are concentrated in the shallower waters of continental shelves and shallow waters over banks in the Northern Hemisphere. These are the centers of fish population for reasons of the physical geography of the oceans. Fish must have food, and the numbers in any area depend upon the food supply; the shelves and banks of the higher middle latitudes offer the best food supply.

Minute floating forms of plant life, floating in the ocean, constitute the base of the so-called biotic pyramid for the support of fish. These microscopic plants, called plankton collectively, are so numerous in certain middle- and high-latitude waters as to discolor the water, and so small as to pass unnoticed through a fine mesh; several hundred may occupy the space of a cubic centimeter. Microscopic animals of several families, but of which the crustaceans called copepods are most important, feed upon the plankton. The copepods (a few species of which reach somewhat over a quarter inch in length) are the chief food of small fish. The small fish in turn are eaten by still larger fish, and these are the food of bigger fish. The largest fish and sea mammals thus have a wide variety of potential food in the seas about them. The biotic pyramid thus is based upon plankton, is continued by the copepods, and is culminated by the larger fish of the ocean.

Plankton are apparently most numerous relatively in the warmer waters of the oceans, copepods relatively most numerous in the cooler waters. Locations where ocean currents mix the waters of differing origin are those areas offering the best food supply, and hence the greatest number of fish; where these areas of mixing currents are located over shallows or banks, such as the Grand Bank of Newfoundland, the conditions are ideal.

The "shallow water" situation is important. Light penetrates below the ocean surface; the depth of important penetration is to about 600 feet. Plants require light for their growth. Therefore the top 600 feet of ocean water contains nearly all the plant life, such as the plankton, which are floating forms. Attached plants must be in water of this depth or less. Because plants are in this upper zone, the copepods are also, most of the fish are, and so the pyramid peaks; commercial fishing thus is in the upper waters, even though the industry may speak of "deep-sea fishing" in contrast to inshore fishing. Continental shelves extend outward (where they exist at all) to a general depth of 600 feet below sea level, so it is over these that fish are most abundant. Where banks way out at sea exist, the waters above them are less than 600 feet deep, and in most banks less than 200; some portions of the banks east of North America are covered only by 60 feet of water.

One of the ideal overall combinations is to have mixing currents over banks or continental shelves. This is exhibited in the Gulf of Maine and the banks off of Nova Scotia and Newfoundland. The waters of the warm Gulf Stream (now more properly the North Atlantic Drift) mix with the cold waters brought southward from the Arctic through Davis Strait and past Newfoundland by the Labrador Current. The mixing, over the banks, provides an ideal environment for the support of tremendous schools of fish. A fishing fleet based upon ports in Newfoundland, Labrador, Quebec, Nova Scotia, Maine, and Massachusetts engages in the banks fisheries. It is joined during the summer by French fisherman from Brittany; three small islands south of Newfoundland, retained by France when she lost Canada to Great Britain, serve as the base for this fleet. Portuguese fishermen cross the Atlantic for the season but have to return home periodically; ships of other nations, even the Soviet Union, are observed occasionally in this area. The fishing vessels face a hazard; the very conditions of mixing water which make for good fishing are conducive to fog, as the warm air moves over cold water and is chilled and condensed. The Grand Bank is one of the foggiest regions in the world.

There are other well known and productive banks. Several lie off of northern Japan, the Kurile Islands, and Kamchatka in the northwest Pacific. Dogger Bank, a shallows in the North Sea, has long been known for its productivity of fish. Dutch from the east, Norwegians from the north, and British swarm over it. The importance of Dogger Bank and the North Sea in general in the industry is reflected in the fact that out of 28 major fishing ports in Britain, 17 are on the eastern, or North Sea coast of England and Scotland. The two largest, in total landings, are the closest to the Dogger Bank—Hull and Grimsby.

The geography, or the regional distribution, of fish discloses a significant difference from area to area. The colder waters of the oceans contain relatively few species of fish when compared to the tropical waters. Thousands of fish of one kind travel in schools, feeding as they move. A net brought up in colder, northern waters usually contains, principally, the fish being sought after, for the commercial fishermen must know the habits of the fish; when captured they are landed in quantity—of 100 fish in the net, well over 90 per cent, sometimes all, are of one species. Thus there are salmon fishermen, herring fishermen, those seeking cod, or mackerel, or halibut, or others. This characteristic of northern waters—fish in one species in large schools—enables commercial fishing to be conducted on a firm economic basis, enables the use of special equipment designed for capture of the particular fish, and is the foundation of the sale of the fish, as to a salmon cannery, a cod-drying establishment, or a herring or sardine cannery.

The tropical seas are different. Hundreds of species of fish swarm in the shoals around islands and coasts, hide in the coral reefs, or maintain themselves some distance at sea. Of 100 fish in a net there may be fish of 30 or 40 species. Not only does this handicap the processing of fish in the tropics, but it tends to keep simple equipment in operation, forces overall prices downward as many tropical fish are inedible and useful only for fertilizer, and the type of equipment precludes much refrigeration. Thus, unless landed immediately, even some of the edible fish spoil in the heat of the area. All told, despite the fact that island and coastal dwellers in the tropics depend heavily upon fish for food, commercial fishing is a small and very local activity. The landings of fish on some of the West Indian islands does not even total that from the individual lakes of the Great Lakes chain. The tropical lands even import fish to supplement the small local catch, especially true of those lands with a large population of the Catholic faith. Even a modern, well-equipped area like Hawaii does not supply itself with fish, but imports some kinds from the American mainland and from New Zealand. Yet in the days of Captain Cook the estimated 300,000 Hawaiians depended greatly upon fish for food, and lived in alongshore locations; today twice that number of people (but only some 15,000 of pure Hawaiian blood) do not produce enough for local markets—even with a declining consumption of fish per capita as a result of the heavy American migration to the islands.

Classification of Fisheries

There is no hard and fast classification of fish or of fisheries to which all scientists or commercial fishermen will agree. Nevertheless, based upon the habits and life cycle of fish, there are four major groupings. Fishing is based upon the habits of each of the anadromous, demersal, pelagic, and sedentary types.

Anadromous fish are those which spawn in fresh water but spend most of their life in salt water. The salmon of the Pacific Northwest, British Columbia, Alaska, and eastern Siberia are examples. After the young fish swim downstream to the ocean the salmon spends its life well at sea and is not caught—or sought after—until it reappears in coastal waters after a three- or four-year interval. The eel reverses this process, spawning in salt water and living in the lower reaches of fresh water emptying into the sea.

Demersal fish spend their lives near shore on the continental shelves or over banks. The halibut of the Atlantic and Pacific waters of the United States and Canada, and the cod (different varieties) of all four of the great fishing regions are examples.

Pelagic fish swim the open seas, far from land. If seeking after these fish, the fisherman must range far and wide. Among the most important of pelagic fish, commercially, is the tuna, a warm-water fish. It is caught in the Pacific, commercially by North American (mainly United States) fishermen in waters from the equator off South America to Oregon; Japanese fishermen seek tuna from south of their home islands to and beyond the equator, and eastward into Hawaiian waters. The tuna, too, is an exception to the general rule about fish in tropical waters or warm subtropical waters. It travels in large schools. The problem of the fisherman is to locate the school, then fish by hand line and pole from the deck of the ship.

Sedentary "fish" (so called commercially) are really not fish but are the forms of marine life which spend their entire life in a very limited area; in contrast to true fish they stay put. Among the sedentary fisheries are those seeking clams, oysters, shrimp, crabs, and lobsters. Of these, the oyster, once attached to an object early in its life cycle, is truly sedentary.

Chief Fishing Regions

Space precludes mention of the vast array of fishing types and fish caught. A brief summary will depict the world setting in its broad outlines.

► NORTHWESTERN ATLANTIC (NORTH AMERICAN) REGION

The northwestern Atlantic, in the New England–Grand Bank–Newfoundland–Labrador region, is noted for its cod fishing. Cod are dried and packed in salt for home use or for export. But mackerel, menhaden, halibut, rosefish, and others are products of these fisheries. Swordfish have become of increasing importance in the market. Nearshore sedentary fisheries include the lobster, crab, and clam fisheries.

The fisherman of the region live in several coastal towns of Newfoundland, in the Maritime Provinces of Canada, where Lunenburg, Nova Scotia, is a principal fishing port, and, on the United States shore, in Maine and Massachusetts. The Maine fishermen engage in sardine and lobster fishing as well as banks fishing, although overfishing in the past has seriously depleted the lobster grounds today. Small fishing towns dot the Maine shore. Portland is the principal center here for the banks fishing.

Boston and Gloucester, Massachusetts, are leading fishing ports. The state of Massachusetts is second only to California in the poundage of fish landed. *Regionally,* of course, it is far ahead, as Massachusetts landings are along the short coastline of the state. California shores account for more than half of the total Pacific Coast of the country in the section between Canada and Mexico. Gloucester, as a small city, has the "flavor" of a fishing center. In Boston, more important today, the fishermen and fishing "flavor" is scattered and lost within the confines of a large urban region; only near the docks themselves is the importance of the activity evident in the landscape.

Southward beyond the main fishing region of the northwestern Atlantic, as the waters become warmer from Long Island Sound to the great bays or sounds of North Carolina are the centers of oystering. Oyster beds are private property in many of the bays, the boundary corners being marked by poles in the shallow waters. From Cape Hatteras southward the chief fishing in the Gulf Stream and adjacent warm waters is for menhaden, manufactured into fertilizer. The United States usually leads the world in the fish-fertilizer industry. Species of fish increase south of the cape, too; more than 70 are considered of some com-

FIG. 14-1. Vessels of the fishing fleet at Gloucester, Massachusetts. (Standard Oil Company, N.J.)

mercial value. Florida waters partake of the characteristics of the tropical seas.

Off western Florida, in the Gulf of Mexico, are the shrimp grounds and the fishing (really diving from fishing boats) for sponges. The gulf shrimp are captured in two areas, one near Key West, the other farther northward. In numbers they are landed, also, farther west, where Biloxi, Mississippi, is a canning center, and in newly discovered shrimp grounds, partly in American and partly in Mexican waters, off Brownsville, Texas. Tarpon Springs, Florida, is the home of the sponge fleet. The gulf oyster, smaller than its Atlantic counterpart, is produced commerically in the shallow bays and lagoons along the entire coast except where the Mississippi Delta interrupts the activity.

► THE NORTHEASTERN ATLANTIC (EUROPEAN) REGION

The waters of the northeastern Atlantic, including the seas such as the North and the Baltic, and the Gulf of Finland, are one of the world's richest fishing regions. Westward the fisheries extend to the waters of Iceland and Greenland. Northward they reach the Arctic, especially along the Finmark coast of northern Norway. Cold and warm waters mix. The cold currents originate in the Arctic and in the East Greenland current and from the Barents Sea. The warm water is supplied by the North Atlantic Drift, continuation of the Gulf Stream of North American waters. Many banks and a very wide continental shelf provide ideal conditions. The entire North Sea is shallow, and the British Isles are above-water projections from a wide continental platform.

Cod, herring, haddock, sardines, and many, many other species of fish are caught. One of the world's greatest cod runs is west of Norway. In the West Fiord, between the mainland of Norway and the Lofoten Islands, more than 40,000 fishermen gather for the February-to-May cod fishing. Cod are the principal fish caught off the Finmark coast during the summer. Herring runs in the fall in the North Sea and over the banks west of southern Norway attract thousands of commercial fishermen. Vessels from all surrounding nations engage in the regional fisheries. Norway is the leading fishing nation of the area, followed by the United Kingdom with its access to Dogger Bank, and by West Germany. But every nation has a large fishing fleet and important fishing centers. Many Norwegian fishermen are able to combine this activity with farming; they engage in the late winter cod fishing of the Lofotens, farm during the summer, then engage in the fall herring fisheries.

Southward in Europe, particularly in the Mediterranean, the catch is far less than in northern Europe. However, in the Atlantic, Portuguese, Spanish, and French fishing fleets engage in sardine fishing. Bordeaux is an important center for this in France, and Portuguese canneries have an exportable surplus.

Mediterranean waters exhibit a profound difference between the large number of fishermen and the small number of fish caught. The shores are lined

with fishing villages and fishing is an occupation of thousands; the total catch
is low. This has given the sea a reputation of being "fishless," which, of course,
it is not. But on a North European basis the landings are small; even tiny
Netherlands exceeds Italy in tonnage. Because of the large population and the
religion a nation such as Italy thus becomes an importer of fish.

Eastward lie the world's largest sponge grounds. Sponges are pulled by hand
from the Adriatic, from nearly all of the inshore waters which surround the Greek
archipelago, and along the shores of Libya and Egypt. The Greeks, as well as
other Mediterranean fishermen, retain fish not considered worth keeping in
the major fishing regions, and capture and sell "fish" such as the octopus not
generally considered of commercial importance elsewhere.

The new nation of Israel at the eastern end of the Mediterranean has introduced "revolutionary" methods (at least for Mediterranean fishermen) into
the industry in the sea. Oil-burning and steam trawlers, modern equipment,
and modern fishing methods are used; this introduction reflects the western
European background of many of the Jewish people of the new state. The modern industry is in contrast to the rather primitive methods of neighboring Arab,
Greek, and other Mediterranean fishermen. The larger catches have been wel-
come additions to the food supply of Israel; they have elicited, also, complaints
and jealousies from neighboring nations whose fishing fleets adhere to former
methods.

► THE NORTHWESTERN PACIFIC (ASIATIC) REGION

The warm Japanese current, or Kuro Siwo, brings abundant plankton northward from tropical seas. Cold, southward-moving currents pass Kamchatka
and other cold waters leave the Sea of Okhotsk. The meeting zone and a wide
surrounding area is one of the rich fishing grounds of the world. The dense
populations of Japan, southern Korea, and coastal China provide an almost
bottomless market for fish.

Japanese fishermen ply their occupation in inshore waters, in the surrounding waters, and in the Inland Sea of Japan. They fish northward in international
waters but are barred from Soviet waters in Siberia. Southward a large Japanese
fleet seeks tuna in the tropical Pacific. Eastward, Japanese ships, fitted out as
floating canneries, invade Alaskan waters beyond the territorial limits of the
United States and Canada. The bulk of the catch is consumed raw in Japan—
the Japanese eat fish in this form. The canned salmon, canned tuna, and
canned crabmeat are destined for export to build up foreign credits. In 1958
the Japanese even sent a fishing fleet through the Panama Canal to fish in Atlantic waters.

In China, Japan, and elsewhere the "entire" fish is used as food. Fish heads
are sold separately and cut up for soup stock. Any waste is used for fertilizer.

Fɪɢ. 14-2. A fishing village in Japan. (Japan Tourist Association)

Many species of commercial fish are caught in the area. Cod, bonito, sardines, sharks, and others are important. Salmon, unless caught some distance at sea, are primarily in Soviet waters where they ascend the Siberian rivers to spawn; thus salmon are of principal importance in the Russian fisheries. Vegetation, not generally sought after elsewhere—such as various types of seaweed—are a product of Oriental fisheries. The seaweed is used for food and fodder.

► THE NORTHEASTERN PACIFIC (NORTH AMERICAN) REGION

The fisheries of the northeastern Pacific extend from Alaska to California. The cold California current "carries" northern-type fishing well into more southerly latitudes than usual. Of the two important regional fish—salmon in the north and tuna farther south—the original salmon area extended from somewhat north of San Francisco to Alaska, and tuna were the principal product of California fisheries. Overfishing and the capture of salmon ascending the rivers to spawn has eliminated this fish commercially from northern California; its range now is northward from southern Oregon. In contrast, a gradual warming of the waters throughout a period of several years now permits tuna to range into Oregon waters. Thus the canneries at the mouth of the Columbia River now pack both salmon and tuna.

Salmon and halibut are the principal commercially caught fish of the Oregon to Alaska shores, salmon being well distributed but halibut being principally a product of the fisheries of British Columbia in Canada. In the Puget Sound region the adjacent markets of the large cities has been a factor in the widening interests of the fishing industry; diversification has increased, and cod, ling cod, sole, rockfish and other species are now marketed in Seattle and other cities.

The Pacific fish which are not canned or marketed locally are frozen for shipment eastward. The Pacific now exceeds the Atlantic in its halibut catch, but the main market is still on the east coast in response to long-established habit. Thus trainloads of fish are dispatched from British Columbia and elsewhere to New England and New York distributors of halibut. Oysters, a product of Washington bays and Puget Sound, were introduced from Japan; the waters are too cold for the Atlantic oyster of the east coast, and the small native oyster was depleted through overfishing.

California fisheries depend heavily upon the tuna. Los Angeles and San Diego are important canning centers. The tuna fleet now ranges into Mexican waters and as far south as the Galapagos Islands on the equator west of Ecuador. A crab fleet is based on San Francisco. Mackerel are caught in southern California waters and canned during the off season for tuna. Abalone, a large mollusk, is an important product. Monterey, once the largest sardine-canning center of the United States, has declined in importance owing to the depletion of the fisheries and small catches during recent years.

► AFRICA

African fisheries have increased greatly in importance in recent years. The Union of South Africa has attained eighth position among the nations in fishing. It has had a fourfold increase since 1948. Much of the increase is attributable to the development of a pilchard industry, which is based at Helena Bay and Walvis Bay, and extends from the latter city of southwest Africa to the southern tip of the continent. Waters are cold, as the area is bathed by the northward-flowing Benguela Current. The pilchard, captured at night, is manufactured into fishmeal, of which the Union is now the world's largest exporter, and is second only to the United States in total production. Edible fish are all consumed at home.

A second commercial industry in Africa is the capture and export of a giant crayfish in West Africa. This crustacean is marketed as lobster in the Northern Hemisphere. The rise in importance of the industry resulted from the decline of the Maine–Nova Scotia lobster catch. Unlike the Maine "true" lobster, much of which is edible, only the tail of the African lobster is consumed—hence the present emphasis upon lobster tails in restaurants and hotels.

► OTHER FISHERIES

Space precludes the discussion of the varied fisheries of the fishing regions of lesser importance. In some cases a particular product of these furnishes one major item to world markets. The fur seal industry of the Pribilof Islands in the Bering Sea off Alaska, the whaling industry, now concentrated in Antarctic seas south of South America, Africa, and Australia, and the turtle fisheries of the Caribbean Sea are each an example of the varied and specialized location of a particular fishing activity—for even the whale, though a mammal, is considered as a product of the fishing economy, as are many other forms of plant or animal life taken from the oceans and seas. And, as demands have expanded in parts of the world a fishing industry has arisen to supply the market; thus the fishing in New Zealand and Australia has expanded in response to the increasing population.

► THE SALMON FISHERIES OF THE PACIFIC NORTHWEST

The salmon fisheries of the Pacific Northwest, British Columbia, and those of Alaska reflect all of the adjustments that commercial fishermen must make in order to gain their livelihood. Capital, sometimes as much as $75,000, must be invested in a fishing boat, in nets, refrigerating units, radar, food, and other equipment. The crew of from seven to ten individuals must be paid, either from accumulated assets or from a share of the catch. Licenses must be obtained. Knowledge of both the habits of the salmon and the waters to be fished in is essential. The kind of run expected—hence the life cycle of the particular fish due to spawn—is a prime requisite; the habits of and the timing of the runs of sockeye salmon, spring salmon, chinook salmon, and others differ. Some runs start in June. Near other streams or over reefs and banks the run of another species may be late—as late as August 20. Fishermen without capital may have to choose other, and less expensive, forms of commercial fishing such as reef netting or gill netting, where the investment in money is less but the investment in time may be more.

The habits of the salmon and the life cycle of this fish are such that not only is the commercial fishing closely adjusted to them, but conservation measures must be drawn and enforced with respect to them. The salmon is one of the most easily "eliminated" fish; the disappearance of the Atlantic salmon from the waters of Maine, New Brunswick, and Nova Scotia, and the virtual elimination of Pacific salmon from the waters of northern California and southern Oregon, is owing not only to overfishing in the past, but to the ease by which man can prevent the young fish from being hatched—through his greed for profits.

The salmon spawns in fast-flowing fresh-water streams. Following the spawning the parent fish die and drift downstream; their life cycle is completed. The young fish, after a period in the cold-water creeks, descend downstream to the ocean. For a period of three or four years this is their home. The specific locale in the North Pacific in which the salmon live is unknown. Following this portion of their lives the fish return to the fresh-water rivers to spawn. They swim upstream to the headwater brooks and creeks, where the spawning takes place. In the process of swimming upstream they surmount innumerable obstacles—swift currents, eddies and rapids, waterfalls of moderate height, predatory animals (such as bears) seeking them for food, and man. Man, so long as he was not numerous in the salmon-fishing regions, never caught all the fish, but some seeped through the array of obstacles to reach the spawning grounds. As man's technology advanced it became possible for all, or nearly all of the fish to be captured before they were able to reproduce. Fish traps were built at the mouths of the streams and rivers. Fish traps in the rivers themselves, placed at locations toward which the fish were directed by the vagaries of the current, eliminated others. Where salmon were forced, by nature, to jump from pool to pool in order to surmount waterfalls, skillfully handled hand nets plucked them from pool or air. When long, mechanically handled nets were developed, a stream could be barricaded; or a narrows between two islands offshore, a natural passageway for the fish, could be blocked also by the net. When high dams were built, they were insurmountable during the upstream migration, and the fish thrashed themselves to death or died of exhaustion—to drift downstream without reproducing. Furthermore, although not one hundred per cent true, a very high proportion of the mature fish return to ascend the stream of their birth. Thus, as obstacles appeared and salmon disappeared from stream after stream the salmon run ceased eventually, not to return.

The management of the salmon fisheries in the Puget Sound–San Juan Island–Strait of Georgia region of Washington and British Columbia illustrates the modern conservational practices agreed upon and enforced vigorously—practices presumed to maintain salmon fishing as an indefinite regional occupation of the period of year between about June 15 and September 30. But, in effect, even these conservational measures, successful though they have been and are, cannot overcome the building of a high dam on a tributary river, with resulting closure of the spawning grounds of the fish.

First, international agreement is necessary. The fishing fleet of American ownership, based upon Gig Harbor, Friday Harbor, Bellingham, Seattle, and other fishing bases, must operate under the same rules as the Canadian fleet. Commercial fishing is restricted to certain set hours (which may be changed from year to year as conditions warrant). More important, all commercial fishing must cease promptly at 5:00 p.m. on Friday. There is no commercial fishing permitted on Saturday or Sunday. Early Monday, at a standard hour, fishing is resumed. Thus the period of time between 5:00 on Friday and 6:00 a.m. on Monday is the one wherein those salmon fortunate enough to appear from the outer ocean are not molested by man's modern appliances. Gill netting, reef netting, and trawling for salmon cease. The salmon enter the tributary streams, and, at present, the larger salmon runs are those which follow the period of commercial quiescence. Furthermore, in these waters fish traps are banned; only a very few remain, small in size, relics of the Indian treaties of 150 years ago wherein the Indians were given permission to fish in their accustomed manner at their accustomed locations in perpetuity. (It is these Indian treaties which, still in force, are the chief anticonservation practices in some areas; and in practice, government-raised hatchery fish, released to help maintain the commercial industry, may themselves be the present unwitting victims of the ancient treaties.)

There are three principal methods of commercial fishing for salmon in Puget Sound–San Juan Island waters—reef netting, gill netting, and purse seining. These are named in order from the simplest and least costly to the most expensive in investment and equipment.

Reef netting is a two-man operation; equipment is simple and investment small. Flat-bottomed oar-propelled boats are anchored from fifty to a hundred or more feet apart, over a reef of known productivity. A horizontally placed net lies in the clear water between the boats. Each fisherman sits on a platform, mounted on a ladder on the boat. When a salmon enters the space between the boats, the reef netters signal for the instant to raise the net and extract the fish.

Gill netters usually operate at night. One, or at the most two, men in an outboard motor-powered boat float (with the motor off) over a known bank of high productivity. Stretching from the stern of the boat for 1,500 or more feet is the net, the top of which is held at the surface by floats, lighted at night. As the net sways with the currents it entraps swimming salmon; its mesh and grain is such that it is an almost invisible barrier-screen in the darkened waters, and the gills of the fish become emmeshed.

Purse seining is the modern and scientific fishing; reef netting is really only a present adaption of Indian methods, and gill netting is a hit-or-miss activity, with a large element of chance. A purse seiner is powered by modern engines and can dash to the location of a school of salmon which has been sighted by the lookout. It lets out its long net, which opens in baglike form as it reaches and passes over the school. When the run has been made, the opening of the net is closed by machinery and a large "purse" is formed, from which the salmon cannot escape. The net, drawn in by machinery, is unloaded by the crew, and preparations are made for another run. The catch is high; if in very productive waters the purse seine can be kept open for a long time—theoretically until the net is completely filled—for the salmon already entrapped cannot escape while the seine is being pulled behind the moving vessel. The vast majority of salmon delivered to the canneries at Friday Harbor, Bellingham, and elsewhere in the region of Puget Sound are captured by the purse seiners. Many of the recently introduced conservation measures, such as the closure of fishing on week-ends, have been the result of the increase of purse seining.

Federal fish hatcheries help maintain the supply of salmon. These are placed at strategic spots on the rivers, locations where the salmon roe can be collected easily. Some are near fish ladders, others near fish elevators.

The fish ladder is a man-made device to enable salmon to pass a dam. It is a series of watery steps from base to top of dam, up which the fish proceed, jumping from step to step as they would jump a natural, low waterfall. The fish elevator is an opening in the dam, into which the salmon swim. The door, or gate, is closed when the elevator is "full" and the entire mass of fish and water is then lifted to the top of the dam, where the salmon are discharged into the slack waters above the barricade. The roe is extracted by fisheries employees stationed at these strategic spots and then transported to the hatchery.

Man's efforts to maintain a salmon-fishing industry with a sustained yield over the years have met with general success. A considerable amount of money is invested in and spent yearly in the effort. International cooperation with Canada has been necessary. Agreements with Japan as to territorial (or surface-water) fishing have been drawn up in order to apply a degree of conservation to the problem of the floating fishing-canneries manned by Japanese offshore, outside the limits of American waters. But always there is the problem of nature and of man; a landslide in British Columbia some years ago blocked the salmon run for several years, or until the life cycle of the fish which could not ascend the stream had ended, and few other fish appeared later; and man's construction of giant Grand Coulee Dam on the Columbia River has forever blocked the salmon run to all upstream main and tributary rivers and creeks—those above Grand Coulee Dam.

► QUESTIONS

1. What are the reasons for the uneven distribution of the fisheries of the world?
2. Why is the market for fish unevenly distributed?
3. What is the biotic pyramid?

4. Why are the banks off of Newfoundland, Nova Scotia, and New England the location of some of the most productive fisheries of the world?
5. Comment on: The economic and the food importance of commercial fishing to Japan.
6. How do the habits of fish affect the type of fishing?
7. Why are conservational measures necessary to maintain commercial fisheries? Name some fisheries which were depleted owing to the lack of conservation of fish resources in the past.

XV Forests and Woodworking Industries

Forests and woodlands are estimated to cover about 30 per cent of the world's land area, a percentage about the same as that of the world's agricultural land. But, unlike farm land, the largest areas of present forests are in environments that are not the most hospitable for man—(1) the cold, northern subarctic regions of North America and Eurasia; (2) the hot tropical rainy areas of South America, Africa, and parts of the East Indies; and (3) in humid mountains. Consequently, today the chief sources of wood and wood products are some distance removed from the consuming markets, which are in the highly industrialized portions of the world. In the past, before man cleared the more hospitable lands of their trees to make way for his farms, forest products were obtained and consumed locally.

A forest is the natural vegetation of a region which possesses a humid climate. All months must have adequate precipitation for tree growth; no normally dry season can prevail—in such climatic environments grasslands replace forests as the natural vegetation. However, in some portions of the monsoon lands of Southeast Asia the wet summer monsoon provides so much moisture that ground water is enabled to carry a forest through the dry season, or dry monsoon period. But it is the humid climates of the world wherein forests are found in the main. And it is these climatic settings, especially those of the

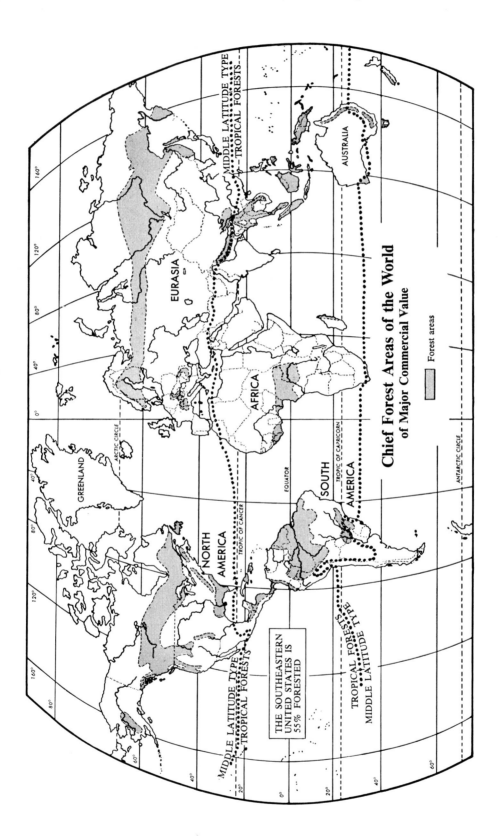

Chief Forest Areas of the World
of Major Commercial Value

Forest areas

THE SOUTHEASTERN
UNITED STATES IS
55% FORESTED

GREENLAND

NORTH
AMERICA

SOUTH
AMERICA

EURASIA

AFRICA

AUSTRALIA

ARCTIC CIRCLE

TROPIC OF CANCER

EQUATOR

TROPIC OF CAPRICORN

ANTARCTIC CIRCLE

MIDDLE LATITUDE TYPE
TROPICAL FORESTS

TROPICAL FORESTS
MIDDLE LATITUDE TYPE

MIDDLE LATITUDE TYPE
TROPICAL FORESTS

humid continental climates and the temperate marine lands that are of great value for agriculture. Thus, through the years, the world regions of these climatic realms have been cleared of their trees, and the land has been devoted to the higher land use of agricultural crops. Only where the soil is poor or rocky, the terrain rough, broken, or mountainous, or the surface ill drained has man permitted forests or woodlands to remain in these settings. But for economic reasons and the desirability of a home supply of firewood, many farmers even of the best agricultural areas still retain a small farm woodlot for home use.

The three great forest regions of the world remain because the areas they occupy have not been in demand for another, or more productive, land use. The great Northern Forest, which girdles the world through northern North America and northern Eurasia, is in a region which is submarginal for agriculture; the growing season of less than one hundred days is too short for most crops, and too cool for even the shortest-season crops; poor soils of podzolic character are unproductive; in North America and northern Europe the continental glaciers deposited a boulder-strewn surface, or where glacial erosion was dominant they removed the topsoil and left an ice-polished bedrock surface. The second region, the mountain forests, remain in terrain which is too steep for agricultural use, too cool in many mountains, or—as in the middle latitudes—both too steep and too cool; only pastoral pursuits can compete with forest use, except in occasional broad and sheltered warm valleys. And the third great forest region, the wet tropics, has to date not been in demand for other uses, except locally, and this particularly in parts of Southeast Asia. The dense vegetative growth and the insect infestation have made them undesirable for settlement, and the small local populations have not pressed upon forest land. Native gatherers harvest nuts and berries, native villagers find ample room for their shifting agriculture and commercial plantations choose accessible island and shore locations for their clearings. On the whole the lateritic soils are poor. But it has been chiefly the local lack of population pressure which has permitted the forests to remain; in Java and some other areas there are exceptions—much tropical forest has been cleared for farming. With increasing population in the tropics— the "population explosion" coincident with changing birth and death rates (the last the result of modern medicine transported to the tropics) the area of tropical forests will probably decrease.

There are extensive areas of remaining virgin forests in both the Northern Forest and the tropics, fewer such areas in accessible mountains. The accessible portions of all forests, especially those reached by adequate rail or water transportation, have been logged. The regrowth of trees following lumbering (if fire and insects have been controlled) or the replanting of trees (reforestation) have resulted in the continuance of the forest, and the sustained yield of forest products; again, regrowth or reforestation has been allowed, permitted, encouraged, or promoted only because the land occupied has not been in demand for an alternative use.

Woodlands and woodlots, rather than "true" forests are common in many agricultural regions—provided that the environment of the area is suitable for tree growth. Thus the farming regions of western Europe and the eastern portion of the United States have many farm woodlots contained within the farm boundaries. But the originally treeless prairie and steppe lands—the extensive present regions of commercial grain farming—are without woodlands; the environment of the Great Plains, the Russian steppes, the Canadian Prairie, and similar regions is not suitable for tree growth. Collectively the agricultural regions with woodlots provide a considerable supply of wood, but they are not the major source regions of wood as a raw material for manufacture, with a few exceptions, such as the hardwoods of the southern Appalachians. Farm woodlots furnish large quantities of fuel wood, however, and, in certain areas, superior hardwoods for the furniture industry.

Much of the present farm land of the world was in forests in the past. The land was cleared of timber for use in the growing of crops. Eastern China has been denuded of its forests for centuries. In western Europe there were extensive forests in what is now Germany and England even in Roman times, but today less than 6 per cent of the British Isles is wooded. The settlers of what is now the United States cleared the finest hardwood forest in the world to make way for their farms; at the time the trees were "weeds" in the path of settlement. Now, many years later, the remaining hardwood woodlots, of second or third growth, are one of the principal sources of hardwoods for the American furniture industry, and these valuable woods originate almost entirely on farmlands in the rough country associated with the Appalachians and the Ozarks. Kentucky, Tennessee, and nearby areas provide the oak, cherry, and other hardwoods in use. Former northern furniture manufacturing centers have lost their relative importance of the past, and the furniture industry has shifted southward. North Carolina now is one of the chief centers of this industry; Memphis, Tennessee, is the oak flooring center. Former furniture centers of Michigan, Wisconsin, and New York now find other industries more important locally than the portion of the furniture industry which remains.

Some land devoted to farming in the past has reverted to forest use. This is the case in many upland districts of New England. Land was cleared for agricultural use because it lay in the path of settlement. The agriculture it supported was largely of a self-sufficient or subsistence type in the eigtheenth and early nineteenth centuries. When the interior plains were settled grain from what is now western New York State and the Middle West could be grown more cheaply and the yields were higher. With the opening of the Erie Canal "western" grain, shipped eastward on the Great Lakes and the canal, virtually eliminated New England farmers from the market. Farms were abandoned. Farming moved downhill to the valleys and lowlands—or, more correctly, only these better lands were able to compete. The upland districts, marginal in their agriculture, became definitely submarginal. In time they became forested by nature; later, man helped with the advent of the conservation movement (about

1900) and reforestation. And today good second-growth forests mantle many portions of upland New England. The stone walls built by past generations to enclose fields and pastures now thread many of the present forests.

▶ FOREST TYPES

There are two major types of forests or woodlands, types based upon the association of trees. Trees are either of hardwood type—the trees with leaves, or broadleaf trees, or of softwood type—the needle or coniferous trees. Thus there are broadleaf forests and coniferous forests; where there is overlap in certain settings the forest is said to be a mixed forest. In general pattern the hardwoods occupy the better lands, whether these be the more moderate regions climatically or the regions of better soils, and the coniferous forests occupy the poorer lands—those with the shortest growing season or those with poor, sandy soils or thin, rocky soils. In mountainous terrain the coniferous forests are usually at higher altitudes than the hardwood forests, and in less favorable areas for trees.

Trees that shed their leaves are deciduous trees; trees that retain them are evergreen. In the latitudes of most of the United States the hardwoods are deciduous, most of the conifers are evergreen. Hence many Americans associate a needle tree with "evergreen." Such is not the case. Some hardwoods retain their leaves and are evergreen—the live oak and magnolia are examples; some softwoods shed their needles in the winter—the tamarack and larch are examples. And in the tropics the hardwood forests, which dominate throughout, are evergreen; only some species lose leaves—the teak tree of Southeast Asia is an example, and it sheds its leaves during a dry season.

The broad distinctions in forest types and the different climatic settings account for the present kinds of world forests—the Northern Coniferous or Boreal Forest, the Tropical Hardwood Forests, and the Mountain Forests, which generally are of coniferous trees at present. Subgroupings and subtypes, beyond these, are recognized by botanists, foresters, and others. And, locally, the climatic and edaphic (soil) setting, the exposure, and many other factors account for the wide array of tree associations.

In general, in the middle latitudes the forest is dominated by only a few species of trees in a given area. Thus it may be said that an area has an oak forest, an oak-hickory forest, one of pine, or of maple; in the tropical world, in contrast, the forest is composed of hundreds of species of trees. This difference in type is of tremendous importance in the commercial logging industry. In the middle latitudes the entire forest may be logged—with due regard at present to conservational practices; in the tropics logging involves the problem of the removal, say, of only three or four mahogany, or rosewood, or ebony trees. Tropical lumbering, despite cheap local labor, is thus usually more expensive than lumbering in the middle latitudes.

FIG. 15-1. Sawmill and lumber mill in a forest region. If the mill is not located on a river, an artificial pond is dug in order to get the logs into the sawmill easily. Note that the logs are directed and floated toward the conveyor into the mill. See FIG. 15-4 also. (Standard Oil Company, N.J.)

▶ NORTHERN CONIFEROUS FOREST

The Northern Coniferous Forest extends from Alaska eastward across much of Canada, reappears in southeastern Norway, in much of Sweden, the majority of Finland, and then extends from west to east across the northern Soviet Union to the Pacific. It girdles the world in the latitudes of the upper 50's and much of the 60's. This is the forest of the cool-temperate or very short-summer lands. The poleward limit of the forest is the "tree zone" (comparable to the timber line on a mountain) that lies at about the location of 50°F for the warmest month. The equatorward limits grade into mixed forests in the latitudes of north-central European Russia, and the latitudes of northern New England, northern New York State, Michigan, Wisconsin, and Minnesota—thence northwestward at the border of the Canadian prairie. The white and Norway pine and hemlock are important trees in the southern portions; the balsam, spruce, and others dominate poleward. In the mixed forest hard maple and birch are usually the chief hardwoods.

The Northern Coniferous Forest was logged originally for its white pine and hemlock, and so only the southern portions were of interest to the lumbermen. These woods were used for construction purposes. Lumbering in the United States swept westward from Maine to Minnesota between the 1840's and 1910. Production today from this zone is from reforested areas, or is of less valuable species of trees used for pulpwood.

The Northern Forest is the chief source of pulpwood, wood pulp, and newsprint. Pulpwood is the wood itself; when processed the wood pulp is produced; this is the final raw material of newsprint. Canadian forests are the outstanding sources of these materials in North America; as more northerly portions of the forest are logged, the trees are suitable only for the paper industry. The equivalent production of pulpwood, wood pulp, and newsprint for Europe is centered in Norway, Sweden, and Finland. The Soviet Union supplies its needs and exports when it is desired to do so.

► TROPICAL HARDWOOD FORESTS

The tropical hardwood forests are centered in the northern half of South America, particularly the Amazon Basin; along the coast of West Africa and the Congo Basin; and in the peninsulas of Southeast Asia and the islands of the East Indies and the southern Philippines. There are other areas of forests in scattered locations, as in eastern Central America. The forest is limited to frost-free areas, to regions of heavy rainfall, and of temperatures continuously in the 70's and 80's; in places the outer borders extend to localities where the coolest month has an average temperature in the higher 60's. Basically this is the forest of the rainy tropics and the wetter portion of the wet-and-dry tropics. Marginal areas, as in Cuba and part of southern Brazil, contain coniferous trees, but these are not present in the true areas with a rainy tropical climate.

Commercial logging and export is confined to accessible coastal districts. Central American and West African logs are shipped to the United States for veneering. The Philippines export lumber. Teak from the forests of Thailand and Burma is in demand for use in the decks of ships, and other places where salt water comes into contact with wood. African woods reach Europe. And some very large mills have been erected recently in the outer Congo area for manufacture of the wood locally, and its export as lumber. Home industries in the more developed areas produce handicrafts of wood for export; many of these items reach American markets from Haiti, from Java and elsewhere in the East Indies, and from the Philippines.

▶ MOUNTAIN FORESTS

The most important of the present forests associated with mountains is the coniferous forest of the Pacific Northwest of the United States and of neighboring British Columbia, and the forest extension into coastal Alaska. But the many small mountain ranges of Europe are clothed in forests—in Germany some mountains are called "forests," as the Black Forest, Thuringian Forest, or Bavarian Forest. The European forests have been maintained through rigorous conservation methods, and the planting of a new tree for every one cut down; the profession of forester is an honored one in the continent.

The forests of the Pacific Northwest contain the Douglas fir, the Western hemlock, the Western red cedar, the Englemann spruce, and other important lumber-producing trees. In the Coast Ranges of California there are districts in which the redwood is the major product; California accounts for almost all of the production of this wood. The Douglas fir is the important tree of the Coast Ranges and the Cascades of Oregon and Washington. The western pines are more important inland, in the northern Rocky Mountains of Idaho and Montana. The Pacific Northwest, including northern California, became a leading lumber-producing region following the depletion of the forests of the Great Lakes area. Many of the same sawmill companies and lumber companies that operated in Wisconsin and Minnesota in the 1890's and early 1900's are now centered in Washington and Oregon. In broad pattern the lumber industry became important in Washington first, then shifted southward to Oregon. But, learning from the experiences of the Northern Forest in the United States, and with the advent of a strong conservation movement about the time of the inception of western logging, the forests of the region have been maintained and protected. The wood resource is a continuing one in the region. Both government-owned national forests and privately owned forests are protected from fire, insects, and other depradations; and reforestation, selective cutting, natural reseeding of trees, and other important aspects of forest management are standard practices.

▶ LUMBER AREAS OF THE UNITED STATES

There are sources of wood in the United States other than from the Northern Forest and the Pacific Northwest. One has been mentioned—the hardwood production from the rougher lands of the eastern part of the country, from woodlot remnants of the original Central Hardwood Forest. The other two chief regions are the Rocky Mountains (excluding the densely wooded Northern Rockies of Montana, regionally like the Pacific Northwest), and the Southern Coastal Plain. Each of these two regions possesses a coniferous forest.

The forests of the Rockies are less extensive and more open than the forests of the West Coast. Rainfall is less. Lower slopes are often unforested when south-facing toward the sun, and bear trees only on northern slopes. But the logging industry is important throughout the wooded areas of the Rockies and in the Black Hills.

The Southern Coastal Plain, from southern New Jersey to eastern Texas, is sandy. A southern coniferous forest, broken by farms, is very extensive. And, in total area, forest land dominates over agricultural land; the most usual landscape element of the Atlantic South and the Deep South is not the cotton or peanut field, but is a coniferous woodland. Wet lowlands have a growth of cypress, a hardwood tree.

The Southern Coniferous Forest contains different species of conifers than the Northern Forest. This is the region of the yellow pine, the loblolly and slash pines, and other resinous conifers. From these lumber and wallboard are ob-

FIG. 15-2. The tapping of southern pines for turpentine is a subsidiary industry in the coastal plain forests of southeastern Alabama, south Georgia, and northern Florida. See FIG. 16-7 also. (Milwaukee Journal Photo)

tained, naval stores (turpentine, resin, and tar) are produced, and pulpwood is cut for raw material for the kraft paper (brown wrapping paper) industry. The poor soils are reflected in the density of the forest stand—trees are widely spaced, an automobile or jeep may usually be driven through the woodlands.

The lumber industry developed to a national commercial importance in the South at about the same time as in the Pacific Northwest, following the end of the first phase of logging from Maine to Minnesota. Some lumber companies moved south—the payrolls of some mills are still made out at headquarters in Wisconsin or elsewhere in the former lumber areas; other companies began operations in the South with the expanding market.

The South, including both the hardwood production of the Upper South and the softwoods of the Deep South, and the Pacific Northwest now lead in the output of lumber. The South as a whole is slightly more important in production, but its output extends over the extensive area from Virginia to eastern Texas. The Pacific Northwest, with its large trees, dense stands, and many board-feet of lumber per acre, is the most concentrated of the lumber producers.

FIG. 15-3. Transporting logs on the Gulf Intracoastal Canal. Very large log rafts are transported in other regions—as the Pacific Northwest, Alaska, and across Lake Superior from the Canadian to the American shore. (Standard Oil Company, N.J.)

Oregon is the leading state in national production, followed by Washington. The two leading regions are thus not really comparable; in one the industry is widespread over a large area, in the other it is so concentrated and dominant between the Cascades and the Pacific that it is evident everywhere. Even the agricultural valleys, such as the Willamette of Oregon, are the sites of dozens of lumber mills, the logs being trucked in from the forested mountains.

The Pacific Northwest illustrates the modern development of lumbering. Sawmills, lumber mills, paper mills, and peeler or plywood mills are characteristic of almost every community in the Coast Ranges and the foothills of the Cascades. There are mills in the ports on the Pacific and Puget Sound, and on the rivers such as the Columbia. Specially built and maintained logging roads thread the mountainous forest lands. Trucks deliver the logs from forest to mill. Sawmills now saw lumber from small logs only; they trade the large logs to peeler or plywood mills, and, instead of burning sawdust and waste wood, ship these to the manufacturers of compressed wood. Odd pieces of wood, such as "squares," are exported overseas or sold to manufacturers of small knick-knacks of wood. And the large integrated mill is present; this type of mill produces all of the products. The region originates rail shipments of lumber to all parts of the United States. From its ports newsprint and lumber is shipped to California markets and, by way of the Panama Canal, to East Coast and European ports. Lumber is exported as well to Japan. The lumber shipments are but one of many types of products handled in the large ports such as Seattle or Portland, but the smaller ports—an example is Coos Bay, Oregon— are essentially lumber and wood-products handlers alone.

The forests of New England, New York, the Great Lakes area, and those of the Pacific Northwest are the present leading sources of pulpwood, woodpulp, and newsprint. Even so the United States depends heavily upon imports of these materials from Canada. Southern forests are significant in woods from which kraft paper is made; the South thus has a paper industry, mainly of papers other than newsprint. But new processes have been developed, and white papers can now be manufactured from southern raw materials. A newsprint industry has arisen recently. A major newsprint manufacturer, centered in Newfoundland in Canada, has built paper mills in Alabama and Tennessee; newsprint is made for sale locally and is exported from the port of Charleston, South Carolina, to England. An advantage the industry has in the South is the rapidity of tree growth; pulpwood can be "turned over" every twenty years in managed forests compared to a longer period of time in the North or Canada.

▶ THE WOOD-USING INDUSTRIES

The softwood forests of the world are the source regions of more than half of the world's wood. In part this is owing to the suitability of softwoods for industrial use. In part it reflects the depletion of the hardwood sources of the middle latitudes, the principal consuming areas of wood and wood products.

The simplest use of wood is for fuel. In this aspect the Soviet Union is the chief producer and consumer. Western Europe and the United States are about equal in this use. The actual American consumption can only be estimated because of the home-to-home sale of firewood by many farmers. Much of the American use of fuelwood today is of the luxury rather than the necessity type. Wood is burned in home fireplaces basically for reasons other than heating the room or house. But many sawmills and lumber mills are powered by the burning of sawdust and waste wood; the practice is becoming less common since the development of processes whereby the material can be compressed into wallboard and pressed wood.

Sawmills receive the cut trees in the form of logs and manufacture lumber in boards or other forms, or veneer the logs. A lumber mill carries on the processing—but today the large integrated sawmill–lumber mill engages in the entire process, and turns out a great variety of basic products. The mill is located centrally in the forest district or near it, and logs are delivered to it. In Scandinavia and part of Canada the logs are floated down the rivers to the mill. In the Pacific Northwest and the South the logs are received by truck, and the building and maintenance of logging roads is a considerable expense, especially in the mountainous terrain of the Pacific Northwest.

Newsprint is a major product of the wood from the Northern Forest. Norway, Sweden, Finland, and Canada are outstanding in its manufacture. Originally these nations exported the pulpwood; they still do, but in lesser amounts. Then they erected pulp mills, which grind the pulpwood and manufacture wood pulp. Large quantities of water are needed for this; before being dried the wood pulp mixture is 95 per cent fluid. A pulp mill is always on a stream or lake; some individual mills use as much water in a day as used by a small city. Finally, in response to the employment of local labor, the producing areas or countries entered the manufacture of newsprint. Eastern newspapers depend heavily upon imported Canadian newsprint from eastern Canada. Newspapers in California depend upon Washington or Oregon newsprint, shipped southward by ship and rail. Western European papers purchase newsprint from Norwegian, Swedish, and Finnish mills. Great Britain imports, too, from Canada. The Soviet Union has begun the export of wood pulp and newsprint. Its forest, logged only in accessible areas, contains the largest stands of untouched timber in the middle latitudes. Besides Norway, Sweden, Finland, and Russia only Austria is a surplus producer and exporter of wood in Europe.

The United States, in large part because of its size and commercial development, and because of its demand for wood products and large use of these products per capita, is the chief consumer of wood among the nations. The total consumption in western Europe, despite more inhabitants, is only about half. Soviet consumption is about the same as western Europe. On a per-capita basis no other world area approaches the United States. The greatest total dif-

Fig. 15-4. The layout of a large pulp and paper mill in the Northern Forest of Canada. The river is filled with logs, the raw material. Piles of logs are evident, also. The dam furnishes power for the mill. Inlets to the mill funnel the water needed in the manufacturing process into the buildings. See Fig. 8-9 also. (Canadian Information Office)

ference in wood consumption is in paper products; American newspapers publish "mountainous" editions, European ones hold to a few pages, in part because of the cost of their imported newsprint. Europeans are amazed at the American consumption of paper in all forms; the American housewife has the perennial problem of the disposal of old newsprint and the avalanche of packaging materials. (Not all packaging materials, nor the high-grade linen or cotton bond papers, are made from wood, however.)

The United States is also a major producer of wood and wood products. It leads in the production of hardwoods and is second among the nations in its output of softwoods. The country leads in wood pulp, though some of this is manufactured from imported pulpwood. It has an important rayon industry whose raw material is wood. And the United States also is usually first or second in the import of wood products, a large item in this being the newsprint from Canada. Secondary products are important as well—the boxboard and carton industry uses waste paper as part of its raw material; this is collected mainly in the larger urban centers where the supplies are concentrated in quantity and collection costs are consequently less. It is estimated, however, that only some 28 to 30 per cent of old newspapers are ever returned to mills in the United States; in Europe, some of Latin America, Japan, and elsewhere there is almost complete collection and return, a reflection of the shortage of the primary materials. Overruns of American newspapers are generally shredded for packing materials after they have been kept for a time.

The various wood-products industries of the United States are both concentrated and dispersed in their location, depending upon their type and need for access to either raw materials or markets. The sawmills and lumber mills are near or in the forests. The manufacture of rayon fiber and yarn is mainly in the Appalachians from Pennsylvania southward. Mills in or near the forests use local wood in the production of acetate fibers for the textile industry, plastic materials, explosives, and for the manufacture of transparent packaging films. Wood is a partial raw material for some of the missile fuels. Furniture manufacture, originally in the hardwood regions of the East and Middle West, has shifted to the Upper South, a shift to or toward the present chief sources of hardwoods. Chicago and Grand Rapids are still the centers of the semiannual furniture markets, but a competing southern center and market has been founded at High Point, North Carolina. The wood pulp and newsprint centers are in the northern tier of states, reflecting their original establishment in the Northern Forest. And the mills remain in these locations because of the continued local production of pulpwood and the accessibility of Canadian wood pulp, plus the adjacency of the large urban markets just to their south in the manufacturing belt. The mills are concentrated along major rivers from Maine to Minnesota; the rivers furnish part or all of the power and the large quantities of water needed for use in the mills. Among these concentrations are the paper mills of the Penobscot and other valleys in Maine; the Black River Valley of New York; the rivers issuing from the Adirondacks; the Fox, Wisconsin, and Chippewa rivers in Wisconsin; and the upper Mississippi River in Minnesota. And the Pacific Northwest has a separate concentration. The kraft paper industry is mainly in the South; Georgia and Florida centers are important, among many. The secondary industries using waste paper and the manufacturers of high-grade bond papers of part linen or part cotton content are most concentrated in or near the major cities. Holyoke, Massachusetts, was one of the early centers of the manufacture of bond papers, but now there are many more. And with decreasing local supplies of pulp and increasing Canadian competition, some of the original newsprint mills of the northern border states now have entered the bond paper and "slick paper" field, or have added specialty papers to their lines of manufacture—papers such as Christmas wrapping papers, paper cups and plates, napkins, towels, tissues, handkerchiefs; some of these are entirely of pulp, others partially so.

► SUBSIDIARY PRODUCTS FROM FORESTS

There are subsidiary activities localized by many of the world's forest lands. Some of these, such as the trapping of fur-bearing animals, are commercial; others, such as hunting and fishing for sport, are seasonal and recreational. However, a recreational industry based upon lakeshore or mountain locations in forested regions is of commercial consequence in several parts of the world, such as in the "North Woods" of Minnesota, Wisconsin, Michigan, Maine, the Adirondack Mountains of New York State, and in eastern Canada, Sweden, and elsewhere near densely peopled regions.

Furs

The gathering of pelts from fur-bearing animals is now located mainly in the Northern Coniferous Forests of the world. The Soviet Union and Canada are leading suppliers. Although this forested area has yielded pelts for hundreds of years, its percentage of the world's supply has increased as a result of the clearing of more southerly areas for agriculture during the last two hundred years. The St. Lawrence Lowland and the region tributary to the Great Lakes were the principal source areas of furs during the 1700's. French and Indian trappers and fur traders ranged the waterways, and canoe-loads of furs were concentrated at Quebec and Montreal for export to European markets. At a later date the Ohio, upper Mississippi, and Missouri Valleys supplied pelts. St. Louis, at a central position near the junctions of these waterways, became a leading fur center; the city retains its importance in fur manufacture, but the pelts now originate in distant regions. The central portions of European Russia, now mainly agricultural, were suppliers of pelts to western Europe, and large fur fairs were held at several cities, notably Nizhni Novgorod (now Gor'kiy).

The opening and mapping of many of the waterways of the Northern Forest was accomplished by fur traders and fur-trading companies. The Hudson's Bay Company was significant in western and northern Canada; its trading posts were at significant sites at or near junctions of waterways, sites to which the trappers brought their catch, and at which they obtained supplies. Some trading posts still operate, and the pelts are shipped to fur markets by airplane. The north of European Russia, and Siberia were dotted with fur-trading posts. The industry is now operated under the control of the Soviet government.

Today the pelts of fur-bearing animals trapped in the Northern Forest are concentrated for market at cities to the south of the forest. Montreal, Toronto, Moscow, Leningrad, and other centers in Canada and the Soviet Union are among these. One of the major fur markets of the world is at Leningrad. The

Soviet government concentrates its prime furs at this market, and attracts buyers from the United States and western Europe to it.

Fur-farming has become an important activity in northern lands, a response to the increasing market for furs and to the costs of collecting and transporting pelts from the forests of northern Canada and of Siberia. There are many such farms in the Maritime Provinces of Canada, in the Scandinavian countries, and in the Upper Great Lakes region of the United States. The fur-bearing animals are reared under conditions which simulate their natural habitat so far as possible. The kind of animal maintained and reared reflects the style fashion of the moment; silver-fox farms were once paramount. Shifts in styles to mink and other furs resulted in their decline. Thus the specialist in rearing one animal gambles upon the continuance of demand for the particular fur and may find himself with a lessened market as the demand shifts in response to changes in the market, for the eventual market is mainly in the women's clothing and luxury field, one subject to rapid style changes.

Some furs originate in non-forest areas. The marshlands of the delta of the Mississippi River are the major trapping region for muskrats. Australia is the principal source of rabbit skins and rabbit fur—used both in the fur industry and in hatmaking for felt hats.

The fur-manufacturing industry is located in the chief styling centers of the world, such as New York, Paris, Rome, and Moscow. It is also widely spread in the major cities of countries such as Canada and the Soviet Union, where the furs are prepared for marketing, and where furs for the home market are made into coats and neck pieces. Some fur centers, such as St. Louis, retain the industry from the past through the momentum of an early start and the continuance of important firms in the trade.

► QUESTIONS

1. Where are the present major forest regions of the world located?
2. Do you think that competition for the land now occupied by the Northern Forest will develop in the forseeable future? Why or why not?
3. Why are coniferous forests more extensive in area today in the middle latitudes than hardwood forests—which were extensive at one time?
4. Why are the logging and lumbering industries less developed in the tropical forests than in the forests of the middle latitudes?
5. Why are many mountains likely to remain in forests? Has man aided this likelihood? Explain.
6. The lumber industry of the Pacific Northwest claims that it can be self-sustaining in the region. Explain.
7. What forests, regions, and countries are the major suppliers of newsprint to the world?

8. What factors have caused a shift southward of the furniture-manufacturing industry of the United States?

9. Explain why certain of the industries depending upon wood for a raw material are concentrated in location while others are dispersed widely.

10. Account for the fact that the United States is both a principal producer and a principal importer of wood and wood products.

XVI Energy Resources: Coal, Petroleum,

and Natural Gas

Power is the basis of industrialization. The important manufacturing nations of the world are the largest users and consumers of power in all of its forms. The primitive and undeveloped portions of the world use very little energy. The importance of power increased with the Industrial Revolution. Today it is so important that no significant commerce, commercial agriculture, or manufacturing can exist without adequate energy resources and the continued development of these regions requires constantly increasing power.

The sources of power are several. Among these are coal, petroleum, natural gas, water power, nuclear fuels such as uranium and thorium, fuelwood, the wind, peat, and waste plant and animal materials. Future resources are probably the increased use of nuclear energy (now restricted by governments mainly to military and defense purposes) and the use of solar energy, derived from the sun in climates with suitable clear weather and low percentage of cloud-cover. The French are using some solar-developed energy in Algeria, focusing the sun's rays into solar furnaces.

The modern industrial regions and nations of the world obtain their power today from the mineral fuels—coal, petroleum, and natural gas—from water power, and, in a few districts, from recently built nuclear power plants built for peacetime use. The energy actually reaches the factories and homes in the form of electricity. During the period from the advent of the Industrial Revolution to the late nineteenth century, factories were built immediately at the source of water power, or their power was furnished by steam engines in the plant, engines run through the burning of coal and the transforming of water to steam. However, today the energy of falling water, or of burning coal or petroleum, is transformed to electrical energy; this can be sent by wire for distances up to 350 to 400 miles. No longer must a factory be confined, say, to a site beside a dam or adjacent to a coal-burning power plant. Factories have been freed of restricted sites, and can be built at favorable locations within the overall region of the power resource.

The undeveloped or underdeveloped portions of the world use relatively little power. But these parts of the world are so extensive in area that it is estimated that perhaps 15 per cent of the world's energy supplies are produced in them; a large proportion of these supplies are from human muscles, from animal power, from primitive equipment such as windlasses turned by driven animals, from the burning of dung, fuelwood, small quantities of coal (compared to the developed regions), and other sources. In fact, the outside aid and development brought to these regions is partly in the form of better energy sources; the changes taking place in India are examples. And, with the modern aid programs, electricity is being brought to the undeveloped lands.

► WORLD PATTERN OF DEVELOPED ENERGY

The largest energy consumption of the world is centered in two locations. One is the United States and southern Canada. The other is western Europe and the Soviet Union. The two face each other across the North Atlantic Ocean, with the North American region extending westward to the Pacific, the European region extending eastward to include the Russian lands of the Soviet Union. Removed from these two larger areas are smaller concentrations which are important in the use of energy; these are Australia, New Zealand, the Union of South Africa, Japan, Venezuela, and the belt of territory in South America including part of southern Brazil, Uruguay, and the Pampa region of Argentina. Lesser areas of moderate consumption, but ones above that of "undeveloped areas," are Chile, Mexico, and Cuba. In effect, just the above listing of the important users of power is also mainly a listing of the outstanding manufacturing and commercial-agricultural regions or nations of the world.

The daily lives of the people of the United States, Canada, western Europe, Australia, New Zealand, and the Union of South Africa is almost completely dependent upon the energy resource and its continued and uninterrupted availability. Commerce, manufacturing, agriculture, transportation, and the heating or air-conditioning of homes all depend upon electricity, coal-burning equipment, or petroleum (in its many refined forms such as gasoline, diesel fuel, or other liquids) for power and heat. Although Japan still uses a large amount of human power in its agriculture, it depends heavily upon electrical energy generated by its water power. But in the United States, Canada, Australia, and parts of Europe the agriculture is so mechanized that food production would be seriously affected—would even cease—if gasoline were not available; not enough horse power remains to cultivate the land. Thus, in highly industrialized and mechanized parts of the world the power plants and the oil refineries are the most vulnerable targets for enemy attack, for their destruction would cause nearly all of "modern activity," both urban and rural, to cease.

The highly industrialized portions of the world have become so completely dependent upon the energy resources that even a slight breakdown of the flow of electricity causes economic difficulties. A broken power line, or power lines downed by ice storms, fallen trees, or other causes may result in the shutting of factories. Electrically heated homes have no heat; gas furnaces or oil-burning furnaces cease to function because their thermostats fail because of the lack of electricity. Elevator service in office buildings and apartments is terminated; subway trains come to a stop. Severe blizzards or ice storms may cause the stoppage of highway or airplane traffic, and, on fewer occasions, of railroads. In fact the discomfort and economic costs of such factors as power failures and severe storms are far greater in today's complex mechanized economy than they are in undeveloped lands, or were in the days of subsistence agriculture; the discomfort and closing of industry are more likely today, too, than even in the last century when homes were heated entirely by the burning of wood or coal, transportation was powered by steam locomotives which carried their coal and water with them, and factories were powered by a steam engine, with its stockpile of coal beside it, or by power transmitted by belts and pulleys from an adjacent dam. Even highway traffic usually kept moving in the past through the use of horses and sleighs in the winter. Thus, despite man's technical advances, he is more harassed than in the past during periods of power (energy) failure. And, if isolated by flood or storm, his present supplies of food at home are less than his ancestors stored in a subsistence economy.

The four important present sources of power for the industrial centers of the world will be discussed in this chapter and in Chapter XVII. Coal, petroleum, water power, and natural gas are not distributed equally throughout the world. Some nations are "haves," some are "have nots." Some very important countries of the ancient world and of the Middle Ages have been by-passed, and they are not leaders of the present economic scene. Their relative decline began with the Industrial Revolution elsewhere, and they failed to catch up mainly because of a lack at home of energy resources—no coal, for example, and few or no home products which could enter foreign trade in exchange for coal. Some nations, such as China, failed to develop local sources of energy, and are just now doing so, two hundred years after the beginning of the Industrial Revolution. And, in order of time, among the regions which experienced the Industrial Revolution, the energy resources were first from coal and from small water powers, then petroleum and large water powers were added, finally natural gas entered the power picture in a few regions and countries. Now the world stands at the threshhold of the peaceful use of nuclear energy, and the probable future development of solar energy.

▶ THE COAL RESOURCE

More than half of the world's industrial energy requirements are from coal. In the United States and Canada the total energy obtained from petroleum has surpassed that obtained from coal. In Europe, however, more than four-fifths of the total is from coal, although the use of oil is increasing. As in agriculture, forestry, and all other activities the scene is regionalized, not uniform throughout the world. Thus, to use the United States as an example, there are regions wherein energy obtained from water power exceeds all other forms, regions where the coal-burning power plant is dominant in the production of electrical energy, regions where the natural gas or oil-powered plant is significant. But in the world as a whole coal is dominant, and it is still of major consequence in the industrial scene in the United States.

Coal is important both because of the heat it produces when it is burned and because it is a source of raw materials for the chemical and other industries. It is the first-listed use which is significant in the production of power. It is the second-listed use which is becoming increasingly important; more and more in the way of raw materials for industry are being furnished by coal.

Historical Development

Coal was known to the ancient world, but was little used. By about A.D. 1300 the use of coal for heating buildings and its use by blacksmiths for the forging of iron became of some consequence. But it was not until the Industrial Revolution of the eighteenth century that coal became a leading fuel.

The Industrial Revolution, beginning in England in the early 1700's, brought the position of coal into prominence. Then, for more than 150 years it was the chief source of energy—competing only with wood, the power generated by wind, by water, and human and animal power. Coal held sway until the discovery and development of competing fuels (such as petroleum) late in the nineteenth century. And, as noted, even today coal generates more than half of the world's total energy.

The earliest small factories in the Midlands and the north of England were powered by water wheels. Coal soon came into the power scene; England had and has abundant supplies of coal, and, equally important at the time, Englishmen developed a series of inventions between 1705 and 1781, inventions and perfections of the coal-burning steam engines. Thus the factories of England became associated with the coal fields, the coal-mining industry developed in response to the factory market, and in turn the number of factories increased in response to available cheap coal as well as to the world markets.

The Industrial Revolution reached other countries later. In fact, it is just now beginning in some of the so-called undeveloped countries. But in Europe it was established in the western part of the continent by the early to middle 1800's. In the United States the factories of New England became important after the 1820's, but these were based on the use of water power. By the 1840's the use of coal in New England and Pennsylvania factories had increased, and the anthracite coal fields of eastern Pennsylvania were developed and operating. In a few years the Appalachian coal fields of western Pennsylvania were in operation on a large scale, and the Pittsburgh manufacturing centers had started. Thus, at the time of the outbreak of the Civil War the northeast was well industrialized, and coal was the source of the power in nearly all centers except in certain valleys of New England, where water power furnished the energy for manufacturing.

World Pattern of the Coal Resource

There are three major kinds of coal—anthracite or hard coal, bituminous or soft coal, and lignite or brown coal.

Anthracite, a high-carbon coal, is low in its gas and volatile content and is very high in its heat value. It is an almost smokeless coal when burned. The world supply of anthracite is small. The United States has only some 475 square miles underlain by anthracite in four basins in eastern Pennsylvania, and a very small anthracite field in Colorado. Anthracite is the most expensive of the coals. This is in response to several factors—the heat value, the quality, the quantity, and the difficulty of mining, for the coal lies in folded layers of rock and is, as a result, at different levels in the mine. The dip and pitch of the coal seams necessitate removal of much valueless rock in order to obtain the coal.

Bituminous or soft coal is the chief of the coals of the world and is mined in every inhabited continent. The grades are many and are based, in general, upon carbon and gas content. The ranges of these are great within the bituminous coals. Certain grades, or kinds, are used for special purposes—thus there are steam coals, bunker coals, and many others. The most important, industrially, is "coking" coal—a grade of bituminous that can be made into coke; coke is the basic fuel of the blast furnace in the iron and steel industry, the fuel used in the smelting of iron ore. Coke, the residue obtained when coal is subjected to destructive distillation, holds up or supports the masses of iron ore and limestone with which the blast furnace is charged, permits the blast of air to circulate in the furnace, and still burns fiercely. Bituminous coal is not satisfactory as it compresses and clinkers. Anthracite can be used, but is a fuel only in the part of the iron and steel industry located near the anthracite basins.

North America, Asia, and Europe have the largest quantity of bituminous coal, and the chief coal fields both in production and in potential production. The continents of the Southern Hemisphere have much less coal. They are not "coalless," however; considering their present state of economic development they have surplus coal. But if coal were mined at the rate of that of the United States or western Europe, the resources of the Southern Hemisphere are small indeed. Thus, in the future, it is still the coal of the Northern Hemisphere upon which the major future energy development from this resource is dependent. Within the Northern Hemisphere, in postwar years, the United States has mined about 30 per cent of the annually produced coal (both anthracite and bituminous), the Soviet Union has contributed almost 20 per cent, Britain 16, and Germany about 10. These four nations are the so-called "big four" in coal. Within immediately recent years, coal production in West Germany has surpassed that from Great Britain. And there has been a spectacular rise in the coal production of Communist China. Substantial efforts have been made in that country to develop and increase its supplies of energy, and to industrialize. Although China has chosen to cut itself off in many ways from the rest of the world, statistics released by the Chinese, as well as some from the United Nations, indicate that China became the fifth largest coal producer in 1957, possibly the third in 1960, and, if plans are realized, will considerably surpass West Germany and Great Britain in output in the early 1960's. In any case, all are agreed that with recent increases China has become one of the foremost coal countries of the world.

During some years of the 1930's Germany mined more coal than Britain. Economic conditions such as the state of business, the recovery or lack of recovery from depressions, wars, the cost of labor, strikes, and other factors result often in "changed positions" of Britain and Germany in coal production, and of "changed positions" among China, Poland, and France. The coal mined in all of the leading producing countries is mainly bituminous.

Lignite coal or brown coal, the lowest grade, is softer and of higher volatile content than bituminous coal. It contains other impurities and considerable water or moisture. Because of its low value, lignite is usually mined only where it is possible to strip the coal from near the surface, and is not mined from underground mines. Special equipment is needed for its burning. It is used principally for heating and for the raising of steam. It cannot be made into coke, and so cannot be used in the basic industries such as the iron and steel industry. Germany, including both West and East Germany, produces half the lignite mined annually. The Soviet Union mines a quarter of the total. The other quarter is scattered among several nations, nearly all on the European continent. Only small quantities of lignite are mined in the United States, mainly in western North Dakota and in eastern Texas.

Peat is a brown tobaccolike spongy substance of swamps and marshes in temperate lands. It is the predecessor of coal geologically—peat to lignite, bituminous, and anthracite coal in the geological sequence. The United States, Canada, Sweden, Finland, and the Soviet Union have extensive but generally unused deposits. Only in Ireland is peat important as a fuel. It is dug from bogs, dried and briquetted, and used in steam plants to generate electricity and in home fireplaces for heating. In Scotland and Ireland some peat is used as fuel in the processes of preparing whiskey.

Coal Reserves

The coal reserves are calculated from informed estimates of the amount of coal remaining in the ground. The estimators formerly projected the rate of annual mining and arrived at a date when the resource would be exhausted or seriously depleted. Such is rarely the case in present estimates because of many uncertainties. For example, coal production in the United States declined following World War II, reached a "low" figure in 1954, then turned upward. Merely using the 1940–1944 average, then the 1950–1954, results in different estimates for this country alone. Future demands for coal will increase *if* a competing source of energy, such as petroleum, becomes less plentiful and more expensive, or they will decrease if nuclear energy becomes universal. Moreover, the future needs for coal as a raw material in industry are unknown. Synthetic rubber, for example, may be made from coal products in the future rather than the petroleum derivatives of the present.

World coal reserves are estimated at about four and a half million million tons of anthracite and bituminous, and more than one billion tons of lignite. The reserve picture is different from the picture of past and present mining. Asia is estimated to contain nearly half (46%) of the total reserves of the three kinds of coal, North America nearly 40 per cent, Europe some 13 per cent, and the southern continents only a small quantity. China alone is said to possess a fifth of the world's coal reserves, the United States a third, the Soviet Union a quarter. If just anthracite and bituminous are included, the same three nations contain the bulk of the reserves—about the same percentages as listed when lignite is included. With these figures in mind, and with Europe (excluding the U.S.S.R.) low in reserves and without much oil, the reason for the interest of European nations in peacetime development of nuclear energy for the future is evident.

► COAL PRODUCTION OUTSIDE OF NORTH AMERICA

Coal is mined in more than forty countries. However, about ten account for nearly all of the output, and four of these mine nearly three-quarters of the world total.

Europe and the United States have been the principal producers of coal to date. Until the rise of Soviet coal mining to importance following the 1920's, most of the coal which had been used in the world had been mined in Great Britain, Germany, Belgium, France, and in the Appalachian and Eastern Interior coal fields of the United States, fields east of the Mississippi River. The Industrial Revolution and the existence of coal in northern Europe were factors in the rise of the nations of the north to world importance industrially, and to the relative decline of the countries surrounding the Mediterranean Sea. The centers of European power shifted from the Mediterranean Basin to the lands surrounding the North Sea. The rise of the United States, industrially, paralleled the rising energy resources obtained from coal. The Soviet Union has repeated the process in this century. Eliminating other energy sources for the moment, the industrial potential of China, when its coal fields are more highly developed, is very large.

Great Britain has the most concentrated coal fields for its area of any part of the world. The Midlands of England, the North of England, the Scottish Lowland, and southern Wales are the locations of several separate fields. The coal fields are either at or very near the sea. Some coal is mined from beneath the North Sea. Practically every major industrial city on the island is on a coal field, or within a very few miles of one. These cities grew with the Industrial Revolution; in fact, some did not exist prior to it. London, not near a coal field, receives its coal both by rail from distances of only a hundred to 150 miles, or by sea from the Newcastle area of northeastern England. The coal-carrying ships proceed up the Thames to London, and the lower river is lined with coal-burning power plants.

The coal mines of Britain are becoming more difficult to work. Many mines are inheritances from the past and cannot be mechanized easily, and some not at all. Other mines have reached exceptionally deep levels for coal mines; the costs of raising the coal to the surface are high. Wages have risen and represent a considerable portion of the ultimate cost of the coal. The British miner produces less coal per day than the American miner—not because he works less hard, but because the American is now working in almost completely mechanized mines. Nevertheless, the British industry continues to operate even marginal mines because of the nation's needs of coal. Nearly seven-eighths of all the energy requirements in Britain are still obtained directly or indirectly, as manufactured gas, from coal, but the use of petroleum is increasing. The same situation as regards old and uneconomic mines is true in the western part of the neighboring continent in France and Belgium. Despite these conditions, the mines of western Europe follow those of the United States and the Soviet Union in the amount of mechanization.

The Ruhr coal field of West Germany is the leading coal producer of western Europe. The Ruhr is a long, narrow field in the valley of the Ruhr River, a right bank, or eastern, tributary of the Rhine. The field is well placed for water as well as land transport. The navigable Rhine is at its western edge. The river port of Duisburg-Ruhrort is the busiest river port of Europe. Downstream fifty miles the Rhine enters the Netherlands. Ruhr coal reaches the Dutch ports, such as Rotterdam near the mouth of the Rhine, and by canal system can be distributed by water to nearly every place in the Netherlands and to parts of Belgium. Within the Ruhr Basin itself is the industrial heart of Germany. An almost continuous series of manufacturing cities lie on the coal field. Essen is the largest, but Dortmund and others form a continuous urban area, or megalopolis. Germany's heavy industry is concentrated in the Ruhr. The Basin accounts for nearly three-quarters of the nation's steel output and more than a quarter of the production of electrical energy. During a few pre-World War II years, when Germany under Hitler was rearming, the Ruhr alone produced more coal than all of Great Britain, and Germany became the second coal country of the world. During recent years the industrial revival of Germany has been based in large part upon the coal resources of the Ruhr, utilized for power. The significance of the Ruhr is illustrated by the immediate post-World War II situation; the Allies began the dismantling of Ruhr factories, and the coal production dropped as a result of the loss of a home market; soon Europe was importing coal, even from across the Atlantic. It became apparent that the economy of the free world in the western part of the continent was so dependent upon Ruhr coal and West German industry that the policies were reversed. Foreign aid, principally from the United States, poured into the Ruhr to help rebuild the German economy.

The northwest of Europe contains several coal fields. The Saar field of Germany is important for coal used in heating, for the generation of steam on transport systems, and for use in the generation of electricity. The Saar continues into France, where it is known as the Moselle field, now the most productive in the nation. Saar coal, unlike that of the Ruhr, is not a principal coking coal. The coal fields of the Aachen region of Germany, of the Netherlands, and of Belgium lie west of the Rhine River but continue the strike (trend) of the Ruhr deposits. The Belgian fields are contiguous to the coal field of the extreme north of France.

The Silesian coal field is now almost entirely in Poland; there is a small extension into Czechoslovakia. Production of coal in this nation has surpassed that of France, and Poland has assumed fifth or sixth position, usually, but one well below the "Big Four." A unique feature of the field is that a metal, zinc, is mined from different levels in many of the coal mines. Silesia was in Germany before World War I, was divided among Germany, Poland, and Czechoslovakia between the World Wars, then passed to Poland. The original development of the field was by German capital and management; in prewar Germany the coal production was second only to the Ruhr. The increase in output is in part the result of the existence of the Iron Curtain—Polish coal powers not only the industry of Poland, but is used in the industry of East Germany; the coal is shipped also to other countries in the Soviet sphere, and is used in the nearby parts of the Soviet Union, for its coal fields are distant from the western border. No doubt the increased output has been in part the result of Soviet economic control, although ostensibly the region is under complete Polish control.

The coal fields of the U.S.S.R. lie in both Europe and Asia. Soviet coal production has doubled since the late 1930's. The development of an important coal industry began in the early 1920's; at that time Russian production was low by any measure, and amounted to less than 16 million tons of coal a year; and this figure, ten years later, was the increased production of just one year—1934 over 1933. The "Industrial Revolution" in the Soviet Union has occurred since the days of World War I.

The principal coal fields of the Soviet Union are the Donets Basin (or Donbas), located in the plains north of the Black Sea, the Kuznets Basin (or Kuzbas), in Siberia some 1,300 miles east of the Ural Mountains, and the Karaganda coal field, a thousand miles southeast of the Urals, in the Kazakh S.S.R. north of Lake Balkash. Karaganda is some 700 miles southwest of the Kuznetsk Basin, and midway between Kuznetsk and the Aral Sea. These three fields supply most of the coal of the Soviet Union. In addition to these there are coal fields in the Urals, in the Pechora region of European Russia north of the Arctic Circle; in the vicinity of Lake Baikal in eastern Siberia; and in the far east, north of the boundary with Manchuria. And a small and long-worked field, that of Tula, lies south of Moscow. Throughout northern European Russia lignite is worked and is burned in power plants at or near the mines for the generation of electricity. Other lignite-powered plants generate energy for cities such as Petrograd.

The pre-1920 and post-1930–1940 scenes are quite different. Tula and the Donbas supplied the coal for czarist Russia. The Soviet government developed the Donbas further, but the area was captured by the Germans during World War II. Factories were moved to the Urals and to Siberia. The large-scale development of the Kuznets Basin commenced in the 1930's, accelerated during this emergency. Engineers and workers were shifted from the Donbas to open the Kuznets mines; now the basin contains many cities. The Karaganda field, opened in the late 1930's (like Kuznets) did not experience its rapid rise until the last fifteen to twenty years.

China, with about a fifth of the estimated coal reserves of the world, initiated a program of industrialization early in the 1950's. Coal is the basic energy resource in the country, and the expansion of mining is a prime factor in the industrial effort. Manchuria has been the leading producer among Chinese areas—in large measure because of its head start—obtained when the province was under Japanese control and occupation, 1932–1945. At Fushun in Manchuria an open-cut mine operates in the thickest-known bed of coal in the world. Fusin, nearby, produces the same quantity of coal, and the total output from Manchuria has been the chief factor in raising China to its present significant position in coal production. The Kailan Basin in Hopei province, as well as fields scattered from north to south in China proper, contribute the remainder. New fields have been discovered recently in the western portion of the country. A large percentage of Chinese coal is suitable for coking. Total output of coal has doubled between the middle 1940's and the early 1960's.

India's development program involves the coal fields of the northeast, not far from Calcutta. The Damodar field contributes most of India's supply. The new iron and steel industry draws its coke from this area.

The Union of South Africa is the leading coal producer of the Southern Hemisphere. Coal is mined in Natal and Transvaal; the Transvaal fields lie just south of the gold-mining district of the Rand, and furnish the coal for the complete electrification of the mines, the entire Rand, and the city of Johannesburg. Australian coal, mined chiefly near Newcastle, is the energy base for the rapid postwar industrialization of southeastern Australia.

► COAL IN THE UNITED STATES AND CANADA

A generalization about American coal is that it declines in quality from east to west. The anthracite basins of eastern Pennsylvania are farthest to the east. The extensive Appalachian bituminous field, presumably the greatest in the world, contains high-grade bituminous coal. Toward the eastern edge of this

FIG. 16-1. Mechanized mining with a coal-cutter in the Kailan coal mines of Hopei Province of the People's Republic of China (Red China). (Eastfoto)

FIG. 16-2. Many coal mines in the valleys of the Appalachian bituminous field are drift mines, and extend back under the hill. Miners go "up" to the mines from their homes in the valley bottoms. The mined coal descends by gravity or belt to the tipple where it is screened and sorted. Railroad cars are loaded by gravity from the building. (Chesapeake and Ohio Railway Company)

field the highest-grade coals are mined; these are usually marketed under a special name; and there are larger areas underlain by coal of coking quality in the Appalachian Field. The interior field centering on Illinois, and extending into southwestern Indiana and western Kentucky contains good grades of coal; some of these coals can be coked. These three fields—Pennsylvania anthracite, Appalachian bituminous, and Eastern Interior—supply over 95 per cent of the coal mined and used in the United States, and exported overseas or to Canada.

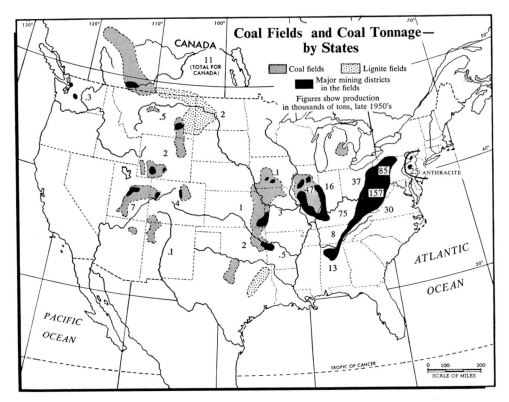

Thus the coal used in the nation originates mainly between the east coast and the Mississippi River—the region of the most concentrated market, by population and by industry.

The coal fields west of the Mississippi are the Western Interior Field of Iowa, Missouri, Kansas, Oklahoma, and Arkansas; the several fields of the Rocky Mountains, their basins and plains border country; and a few small coal fields in the state of Washington. Some of the fields of the Rockies contain very high-grade coal. Coking coal for the regional steel industry is obtained locally (Colorado, Wyoming, and Utah), coking coal for the West Coast steel industry is mined in and shipped from Utah. The coking coal used by the steel industry of Texas is mined in Oklahoma.

Lignite is little used in the United States. North Dakota has a small production. That mined in eastern Texas is used by certain industrial plants of the Gulf Coast.

A second generalization about the coal fields of the United States is that they have not localized industrial regions on the fields themselves. This is in contrast to the situation in western Europe and the Soviet Union. There are exceptions—Scranton and Wilkes-Barre in the Pennsylvania anthracite basins, the Pittsburgh region, the chemical centers along the Kanawha and Ohio rivers in

West Virginia, the Birmingham area of Alabama. But in general the coal of the United States is mined elsewhere than where it is used. Coal is a chief item moved by rail from mine to consumer. It is a prominent cargo on the Great Lakes; Toledo is a major coal-forwarding port, receiving coal by rail from the northern Appalachians, and shipping it to ports on Lakes Huron, Superior, and Michigan. Coal is a principal cargo on the navigable Mononga-hela and Ohio rivers, moving by barge. Coal accounts for over half of the water shipments on the Tennessee River. Coal is shipped by rail to ports on the Delaware River, Chesapeake Bay, and the Hampton Roads area for transport to industrial centers via coastwise shipping, or for export overseas.

The reasons for the non-localization of industry on American coal fields are several. The anthracite fields and the Appalachian Field are in hilly or mountainous country. Valleys and ridges are narrow, slopes are steep. And, when mines were first opened, the Pennsylvania coal was shipped easily to East Coast cities, already established as manufacturing centers. Coastwise trade developed, ships transporting the coal from Philadelphia to New England factory towns by water. Railroads promulgated special rates. As mining spread to West Virginia and Kentucky it entered country even more dissected and rough than western Pennsylvania. There were few sites for manufacturing plants in the narrow valleys, many valleys were subject to floods, and markets for manufactured products were at the time distant. The Eastern Interior Field, centered on Illinois, in level to gently rolling country, was not opened until after the cities on the Great Lakes and the Mississippi and the Ohio rivers were well established industrially. And, to compete in Great Lakes markets, Illinois coal had to meet and undersell Appalachian coal, brought to the lake ports by water. Until coking processes were developed for Illinois coal it could not be marketed at the steel centers on Lake Michigan, which were at the time bound to Appalachian coking coal. Furthermore, overall the interior position of the Illinois field did not offer the advantageous location for manufacturing plants in competition with a site on the shores of Lake Michigan, or on the waterways of the navigable Ohio and Mississippi rivers. Thus, in general, American coal fields furnish fuel and energy for distant industries, European ones localize the manufacturing establishments.

Canada's coal is not well placed with respect to the population and industrial centers of the country. The coal lies in the far east, on the Atlantic in Nova Scotia, and on the western prairies at the base of the Rockies in Alberta. The coal of Cape Breton Island in Nova Scotia is used at Sydney in the iron and steel industry of eastern Canada, the iron ore being shipped by water from Newfoundland. But the industrial heart of Canada—the region from Montreal southwest through Toronto, Hamilton, London, and Windsor—is an importer of coal from the United States; however, some coal from Nova Scotia does reach this area by ship on the St. Lawrence Seaway during the navigation season.

American Coal Fields

The four Pennsylvania anthracite basins lie in the folded sedimentary rocks of the Folded Appalachians. The coal has been preserved from erosion in the downfolds, or synclines. Mining is difficult, as the seams are at different levels, and dip strongly—in contrast to most other mining areas of the country, where the coal lies in nearly horizontal beds at any given locality; of course, it is the extreme pressure put upon the coal by the folding which has been responsible for the anthracite or hard coal.

The anthracite coal industry has suffered severe economic competition from petroleum and natural gas. Anthracite was the paramount fuel for the heating of American homes during the latter part of the nineteenth and the early twentieth centuries. As a nearly smokeless fuel it had no competitor for this purpose; so important was it that a seven-month coal strike in 1902 resulted in a fuel shortage during the ensuing winter in the cities of the Atlantic Seaboard and Great Lakes shores. The introduction of the oil-burning furnace after World War I and the advent of pipelines transmitting natural gas from the southwest began to cut into the home-heating market for anthracite. Many householders prized the ease of heating by oil or gas, the ability to turn a thermostat rather than fire up the furnace or bank the fire, and did not bother to compare b.t.u's or relative prices at their specific location. A result has been the serious drop of the market for anthracite and the resulting economic dislocation of the mining regions. Production dropped from nearly 70 million tons annually in the 1930's to 50 million in the mid-1940's, to 44 million tons by 1950, and dropped below 20 million by the end of the decade. The number of men employed in anthracite mining has dropped from an average of 151,000 in the early 1930's to only 30,000 at present. The anthracite basins have been classed as "economically depressed" areas by the government, and have become labor surplus areas and "exporters" of labor to other portions of the nation. The plight of the industry reflects the competitive situation among the mineral fuels in the competition for the market, and in market acceptance. All of the market has not been lost, of course, and anthracite is a leading regional fuel in the generation of electricity in the power plants of eastern Pennsylvania.

The Appalachian bituminous field is nearly co-extensive with the rough, hilly Appalachian Plateau (or Hill Country). It includes western Pennsylvania, eastern Ohio, nearly all of West Virginia, eastern Kentucky, a small portion of the extreme west of Virginia, and parts of Tennessee and Alabama.

The Appalachian Field is the leading producer of coal. It lies between the industrial centers of the East and the Middle West. It is crossed by numerous transportation lines; the northern portion in Pennsylvania and Ohio is especially well served by main-line railroad routes, as it lies between the cities of the East Coast and those of the Great Lakes and Ohio Valley. Mining developed earliest in the northern Appalachians in response to position, accessibility, and the market. Pennsylvania was long the leading state in coal mining; it is now second, as the centers of production have shifted southward into West Virginia. But in this northern portion of the field—Pennsylvania, eastern Ohio, and West Virginia—is the leading *region* of overall production. By states the five leaders in coal production are West Virginia, Pennsylvania, Kentucky, Illinois, and Ohio; of these only Illinois and the western part of Kentucky lie in the Eastern Interior Field rather than the Appalachian; the five states produce nearly four-fifths of the nation's coal.

The central portion of the Appalachian Field includes all of eastern Kentucky and adjacent portions of southern West Virginia and Virginia to the east. This is a mountainous one-industry country; its economy depends upon the coal industry and the out-shipment of coal. Mining development is irregular. Some valleys have continuous coal-mining villages and successions of mines; other valleys, not reached by rail transportation, are occupied only by subsistence farmers living on small plots, and by woodsmen. When new mines or mining areas are opened, the opening is preceded by the advent of rail lines built only for the purpose of coal shipping. Serious depression has been prevalent in the region since World War II and the falling demand for coal; large mechanized mines and small truck mines operated by from two to six men are the present chief operating units. Employment has fallen because of a complex set of factors—mechanization, automation, market factors, rising costs of mine labor, and others. Marginal mines, or those with high transportation costs, have closed; large mines have completely mechanized. More coal is produced per man hour, and the total employment has fallen. In West Virginia the coal produced in the early 1960's was mined by 50,000 men, 75,000 fewer than ten years previously. In the Kentucky fields the proportions are about the same.

The southern portion of the Appalachian Field is in Tennessee and Alabama. Mining in Tennessee is most concentrated in two sections—near the Kentucky border, where the coal is shipped northward to market (comparable to the pattern in eastern Kentucky) and near the Alabama border, where nearby cities furnish part of the market. In addition much Tennessee-mined coal finds a market in the steam plants operated by the Tennessee Valley Authority, which has long since outgrown its original dependence upon the water-power resource and now generates two-thirds of its electricity from coal. The T.V.A. claims to be the largest single buyer of coal in the nation, and has recently taken options on coal lands in southeastern Kentucky. But the largest coal production in the southern field is from the Black Warrior portion of the Appalachian Field in Alabama, the supplier of coking coal for the Birmingham iron and steel district.

The Eastern Interior Field, south of Chicago, covers much of Illinois, southwestern Indiana, and western Kentucky. The largest production is from southern Illinois. But other portions of the field, particularly toward its outer margins, contribute much coal; thus western Kentucky (southern margin), southwestern

FIG. 16-3. A shaft mine in Colorado, with the high ranges of the Rockies in the background. Note that the entrance to the tipple is inclined, and that the coal must be raised to the building, beneath which the railroad cars are loaded. (*Steelways,* published by American Iron and Steel Institute)

Indiana (eastern margin), and scattered districts in western and northern Illinois are producers. There are coal mines within forty miles of Chicago—closer to this industrial center than coal fields are to the East Coast cities, and the highly concentrated mining districts of southern Illinois are less than a hundred miles from St. Louis.

Coal Mining in the United States

Coal is mined by shaft mining, drift mining, strip mining, and auger mining —this last a very recent development. A new system, called punch mining, is used in a few places.

Shaft mines, as in any mining operation, are sunk vertically or at an angle to the coal seam or seams. Some shaft mines are deep, some relatively shallow. Although there are a few deep coal mines in the world, coal mining, on the whole, is "shallow mining" by comparison with metal mining; problems of gas and adequate ventilation, and the possibility of explosion, are greater in coal mines than in so-called hard-rock metal mines. The number of openings off the principal shaft into the coal seams are determined by the seams, the structures, and other technological factors. The Ruhr Basin, for example, contains more than a hundred workable seams; others have fewer than a dozen; in some Appalachian areas only two principal seams are worked.

Drift mines are possible only in hilly terrain. They are common in the Appalachian Field. The mine mouth, or adit, is the opening to a horizontal, or nearly horizontal, tunnel that extends under the hill or mountain. The coal is handled by gravity after it reaches the adit; it is dumped into tipples below the mine mouth, proceeds through the building for washing and sorting, and then is loaded into cars at the base of the tipple; the tipple is staggered, often, against the hillside. Hundreds of Appalachian mining towns are in the valley bottoms, below the mine mouth; miners go "up" into the mines instead of "down" into them.

Underground mines, both shaft and drift, have produced 73 per cent of the coal of the United States in recent years. Nearly a quarter is now from strip mines, the remaining percentage from auger operations.

A strip mine is an open cut or pit. Shovels remove the overburden of soil, subsoil, and rock to expose the coal seams. One consideration in the decision to strip-mine coal is the cost of removing the overburden relative to the price of the coal to be removed and the quantity available. Furthermore, if a second seam lies beneath the top one, the costs of removing the intervening shale or slate must be estimated with respect to the value of the lower seam. Thin seams can be stripped when it would be too costly to mine them underground, although depths of stripping and water problems in the pits are other factors which must be taken into account.

Strip mining was originally a feature of the Eastern Interior Coal Field and its level to gently sloping terrain. Stripping was confined to the margins of the field, where the coal was near the surface; in the center of the coal syncline (downwarp) the seams are too far from the surface for economical stripping. Illinois, Indiana, and western Kentucky are marred by the remains of strip pits; the countryside has been turned upside down, the soil and subsoil underneath the rock fragments piled up in "spoil banks" as the shovels moved through the pits. Some states now require strippers to replace the soil and smooth the surface after mining operations; Indiana has turned some strip pits into parks and fishing lakes. In other places the pits remain as rocky "deserts" surrounded by farm land. Stripping continues to be an important method of mining in the Eastern Interior Field.

Strip mining began in the rough and hilly Appalachian Field much later— in fact not many years ago. This is in response, in part, to more efficient machines which can work on hillsides, and to the competitive costs of stripping versus underground mining—important because of increasing labor costs and the competitive situation of coal with respect to oil and natural gas. Stripping in the anthracite basins and the Appalachian Field is on the contour. The coal outcrops on a hillside. To reach it roads must be built from the valley bottom, and preliminary grading must be completed at the outcrop for the installation of the machinery. The overburden is removed from the upslope, higher on the hill than the coal, and is dumped on the downslope. A triangular-shaped over-burden, back into the hill and upward, is removed. The actual coal removal is along the contour, around promontories on the hill, into valleys cut in it by streams—but the machines remain at the same level, the contour of the coal. It is feasible to strip back into the hill some 200 to 300 feet or more, depending upon the slope and the amount of material to be removed as overburden. As might be expected, stripping in rough terrain often results in severe erosion of the stripped areas and the downhill dumps, marring of the hillsides and the silting of flood plains in the valleys below. Some states now require conserva-tional measures, others have not as yet attacked the problem—costs enter be-cause the replacement of overburden or replanting of trees raises the cost of the coal to the stripper, who is operating in a highly competitive market.

Average production of coal by stripping is about 5,000 tons per acre, or more than three million tons per square mile. It is estimated that approximately 136,000 acres or about 212 square miles are in strip pits in the Eastern Interior Field; some districts have as much as nine to ten contiguous square miles of entirely stripped land—as near Morris, Illinois, and Pittsburg, Kansas. Some 150,000 acres or 238 square miles of strip scars exist on the hillslopes of the northern Appalachians in Ohio, Pennsylvania, and West Virginia. Stripping is now common, in the central and southern Appalachians, and in the western coal fields.

Auger mining is a recent development in use in hilly terrain such as that of the Appalachian coal field. Like stripping, it is on the contour of the outcrop. Large augers, some with diameters up to five feet, are bored into the horizontal coal seams that underlie the hill or mountain. Augers penetrate 200 to 300 feet into the seam and recover three-quarters or more of the coal. A rounded hill can be bored in a circular pattern; a valleyside is bored from the slope above the valley bottom. Some augers are used underground in large rooms where there is space, and the coal beyond the "end" of the mining is thus obtained.

Punch mining is used on outcrops or the walls of strip mines when the over-burden thickens. The seam is mined through undercutting. In effect, the method is not different from auger mining, but the machinery differs, and blocks of coal instead of rounded cores are obtained.

The mechanization of American mines has more than doubled the output of coal per day per miner since World War II; it is now eleven to twelve tons a day. Pick-and-shovel mining is virtually extinct. A machine named the "under-ground miner" cuts into the coal and loads it on belts which transport it to the mine mouth. Automation in the mines has reduced the working force of coal miners by more than half; those who remain are receiving higher wages. In fact, the constantly increasing wage scales, granted following World War II, were a major factor helping lead to mechanization.

Wages, costs, and competition have been factors leading to the increase of strip mining and auger mining. In some of these mines output per man averages twenty-five tons of coal a day.

► FOREIGN TRADE

England used to be the major exporter of coal. The export, originating principally in the South Wales field, was a necessity to help balance trade, and to provide cargo for ships which reached British ports with bulky imports—

FIG. 16-4. The triangular-shaped railroad yards and the piers fitted with mechanical loaders are associated with the export of coal in the Hampton Roads area—the port of Hampton Roads includes Newport News, Norfolk, and Portsmouth, all in Virginia. Port facilities shown in the airview include merchandise and other piers as well. (Chesapeake and Ohio Railway Company)

raw materials and foods. English bunker coal, stored at the ports of the ocean seaways, powered the ships of the world.

The situation has changed. Although England is second in coal exports its tonnage shipped overseas has dropped by more than half. This reflects several factors. Ships are now powered by oil. Home supplies of coal have declined and have become more expensive. And American coal is now shipped to many countries—even, at times, to Britain itself. The export of United States coal is owing to search for overseas markets, to (especially following the war) the need for coal in industrial countries whose mines had been damaged by war, and to the foreign-aid programs. The tonnage exported began to decline in the late 1950's, and the coal industry renewed its search for foreign markets.

The Norfolk-Newport News area is the major port region for the export of coal. The Delaware River ports follow. Several of the chief coal-carrying railroads lead from the West Virginia fields to tidewater at Norfolk and Newport News, and operate facilities for the loading of ships at their terminus. One railroad, Norfolk to Toledo, carries coal in two directions, from West Virginia to Norfolk and Newport News for export or for coastwise shipment to New York and New England, and from West Virginia to its Great Lakes docks and facilities at Toledo for shipment to markets on the lakes.

Coal crosses many boundaries in the small-area nations of northwestern Europe. German coal moves to French and Belgian iron ore, French coal to Belgium and Germany, and so on. Hence these countries are both exporters and importers. The establishment of the European Common Market has changed this so far as tariffs or duties are concerned, but the interchange of coal continues within its framework.

► PETROLEUM

Petroleum, like coal and natural gas, is one of the mineral fuels. The refined products yield fuels in several forms and yield raw materials for manufacturing.

Oil seepages were known to and used by the ancients, as records from India, the Middle East, and the Far East testify. Seepages were in use, too, in Europe and the United States for lamp fuel, pitch for ships, and other purposes, but the oil was expensive.

The modern petroleum industry began in 1859 with the drilling of a well near Titusville, Pennsylvania, by Edwin L. Drake. The idea was conceived that oil might be tapped in underground reservoirs (or the present so-called oil pools) and the supply increased. The shallow Drake well, only 69 feet deep, was the forerunner of the revolutionary changes which have occurred during the last one hundred years—the advent of an "Oil Age."

The first gusher, or well in which the oil was under such pressure that it was forced out as a fountain, was drilled in coastal Texas in 1900. The open-ing of many southwestern fields occurred during the years immediately follow-ing. The growth of the oil industry mushroomed, and paralleled in time the years of the principal introduction and expansion of the automobile. Gasoline came into demand, and the expanding use of automobiles provided an increas-ing annual market; in fact, the gasoline-powered car soon replaced the early steam-driven automobile. And, with the increased tremendous use of machines of all types, petroleum products assumed the critical position they now oc-cupy—the lubricating, maintenance, and powering of millions of machines in the industrial world.

Petroleum as crude oil or in most of its refined forms is easily movable by pipeline. Considering the facts that its major use did not develop until this century, and that the general pattern of the industrial regions had been de-termined previously, the oil fields, on the whole, have not localized industry. Instead, crude oil and refined products are shipped by pipeline and other methods of transportation to the regions of greatest use and most concentrated markets. Thus, on the whole, the location of oil fields has not been a major factor in site determination of industry; this is unlike the localization of Euro-pean and much other world industry on or near coal fields. There are excep-tions, of course; part of the chemical industry has been drawn to or established in coastal Texas near the sources of petroleum; the glass-making industry has sought sites near oil and natural gas fields. But in the United States, the states or regions producing the petroleum are not the major manufacturing centers. Neither are the European, Asian, or Middle Eastern oil fields the centers of industry.

Pipelines have become so important that they now constitute one of the leading methods of transportation. They are regulated by federal agencies in the United States as part of interstate commerce, as most pipelines cross state boundaries in transporting petroleum products to or toward markets. Pipelines in the Middle East and elsewhere cross international boundaries. Pipelines from Canadian oil fields deliver petroleum products and natural gas to portions of both the northwestern and north central United States. Even at the time of the Pennsylvania discoveries, simple pipelines of wood were constructed to carry the oil to rail or water shipment points; these pipelines did not last long because teamsters, thrown out of work by the new innovation, either chopped them up or burned them; but these were the forerunners of the mod-ern pipeline system.

Oil Fields

An oil field is not continuously underlain by petroleum. Rather it consists of a cluster or group of oil-producing pools, or of a single isolated pool. Thus, within the outer boundary of a so-called oil field, the production is irregularly

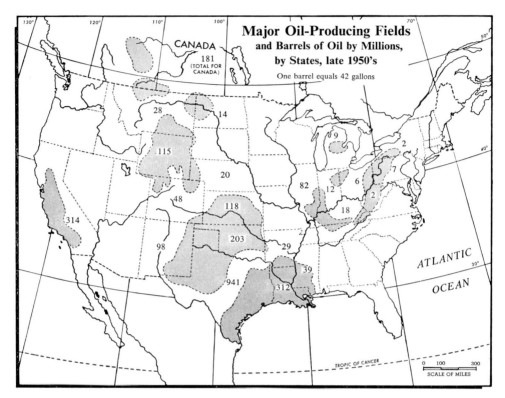

Major Oil-Producing Fields
and Barrels of Oil by Millions,
by States, late 1950's

One barrel equals 42 gallons

CANADA
181
(TOTAL FOR
CANADA)

distributed; and the outer boundaries of many fields have been extended through geological exploration, geophysical work, electric logging, neutron and sonic logging, technological advances in the study of underground structures, and by other methods. Thus the "original" Mid-Continent Field of the United States in Kansas, Oklahoma, and Texas has been extended into Arkansas; the Gulf Coast Field of Texas and Louisiana now has been extended eastward into Mississippi and seaward into the Gulf of Mexico. And existing oil fields, particularly in the United States, have had their production increased through the deepening of oil wells; in other words, new oil pools have been "discovered" at levels far below the original depth of the production. Some oil wells are now drilled to depths of 26,000 to 30,000 feet.

The areas underlain by petroleum in an oil field are variable in the quantity of oil they contain. A map may show several square miles or more in an individual pool, and yet production is not large. Another pool of only two or three square miles—just a dot on the map of the oil field—may be characterized by gushers (now capped and controlled when completed), and have a very large production per well or pool. It is not unusual for producing wells to be on the land of only a few farms in an oil-producing region, and for adjacent farms to be beyond the limit of the oil-bearing strata.

Oil fields, and even pools within the fields, vary widely in their character-istics as well as in their size. In some cases the oil is recovered by oil wells spaced a half mile to a mile apart; in others the wells may be spaced only a few hundred feet apart. And land ownership and the leasing of mineral rights to competing oil companies plays a part. If one company has the leases to several farms they space the wells with respect with what is believed to be the best recovery; if farms are leased to many different producers, each farm is the site of oil wells. In a few cases, where oil has been discovered beneath cities, city lots are leased and "forests" of oil derricks appear, some even on adjacent lots. Such is the case in parts of the Los Angeles region, and in some parts of Oklahoma City. Even the state leased its subsurface rights, and there are pro-ducing oil wells on the grounds of the Oklahoma capitol. The leasing of private lands, just described, is not usual outside of the United States, Canada, and some other countries—for, in general, in much of Europe and elsewhere the subsurface materials are reserved to the state, and the landowner of the sur-face does not receive royalties. In the Middle East the oil concessions and leases are thus with the government rather than the farmer, rancher, or lot owner. The American oil companies, now operating in Venezuela, Colombia, the Mid-dle Eastern countries, and elsewhere have to be familiar with and work under the local laws of the nation in which exploration and production are being prosecuted. And some countries, such as Iran and Mexico, have nationalized their petroleum resource.

Petroleum production and patterns have changed with the years—the re-source is exhaustible and many former pools, even fields, have declined in production or have ceased to yield. There is no reason to believe that this situa-tion will not continue in the future; in fact, it is expectable. Hence the con-stant search for new oil fields, and the constant research for better and more efficient methods to extract as much petroleum as possible from existing wells. There have been many changes in production; for example, Mexico was at one time the second petroleum producer but is now low on the list; the early developed Lima-Indiana field of Ohio and Indiana retains but a small yield; Michigan fields have dropped by half in output in the last twenty years. Even in the major fields some pools have been exhausted and their wells capped. New pools have been discovered. Others have had their life extended through the deepening of wells, and the use of more efficient methods of recovering the oil contained in the oil sands.

The search for petroleum continues. Large fields have been discovered and developed within this generation in western Canada. North Dakota and Ne-braska have been added to the list of states producing oil since the beginning of the 1950's. The Middle East is relatively "new" in the petroleum picture. And in 1959 the French discovered oil in the Sahara Desert, well inland from coastal Algeria; equipment for the drilling of oil wells has to be flown in, as does food, water, and other supplies. Seekers after oil in the Libyan Desert discovered a downed American plane, intact in the desert for seventeen years; the fact that it could have been missing so long in the barren desert, and then was discovered by an oil "prospector" is significant; it shows how oil is being sought after in the world. Oil-searching parties explore the jungles of inner Africa, the Niger Delta in West Africa, the tropical lowlands of the Amazon Basin, the interior highlands of New Zealand, the Pampas of Argentina.

The worldwide search for petroleum is by no means confined to American companies, although these were early in the activity—reflecting the early start of the petroleum industry in this country, and the familiarity or know-how accumulated from experience in Pennsylvania, Texas, California, and elsewhere in the oil fields of the United States. The British and Dutch possess worldwide oil interests, the British originally having operated in Iran and nearby areas, the Dutch in South America and the Netherlands Indies, now the new nation of Indonesia. The Soviet Union is active within the one-sixth of the world's land area within its home borders. French companies operate in the Sahara. And one of the two largest of the world oil companies is a British-Dutch one;

FIG. 16-5. Oil derricks in the shallow waters of Lake Maracaibo in Venezuela. See FIG. 11-5 also. Limestone for the manufacture of cement is being unloaded from the barge. (Standard Oil Company, N.J.)

this company not only seeks oil in nearly all continents, but produces it from wells in nearly thirty nations, transports it in tankers to the markets, and operates even in the United States through American-formed companies. In Europe this combine maintains petrochemical plants, and so engages in the manufacture and distribution of subsidiary products whose raw materials are petroleum derivatives.

Every undeveloped or underdeveloped country wants its own oil fields—the riches in royalties accumulated by the sheiks and rulers of the Middle Eastern nations, and the governments of some Latin American countries, have proved powerful spurs to the granting of concessions to the oil companies of the middle-latitude nations. The concessions usually require that the company drill in favorable areas—the concession-granting country hoping to become oil-rich, and to build up its foreign credits. When oil is found and produced, money flows into the country and can be used for internal improvements. The undeveloped country is able, in time, to place its inhabitants "on wheels," to industrialize in part, and to proceed on the road to development; Venezuela and Saudi Arabia are examples. On the other side of the ledger, the "developed" countries with oil fields and an export trade in petroleum products experience a loss of exports and some economic problems in the home industry; the loss of some of the petroleum exports of the United States, and the slowing-down of production in some states (such as Texas) is owing in part to the competition of imported petroleum, which, in the early 1960's, was at the rate of a million barrels a day. Some of the imports are produced by American companies. Some are from foreign operatives.

Informed estimates place the known world petroleum supply, now in proven producing fields, at forty years or more, based on present consumption plus a 75 per cent rise in demand in the United States by the mid-1970's, and a threefold increase in demand from the rest of the non-Communist world. Soviet estimates are unknown.

The general opinion of specialists is: (1) that the major present or potential oil-bearing regions of the middle latitudes are reasonably well known—increased production, if any, will have to come as a result of better recovery; (2) that the Middle East contains the largest-known reserves, nearly two-thirds of the total, and will be the oil center of the future; (3) and that large areas of South America and Africa, not known in geological detail, offer perhaps the best possibility for the addition of petroleum reserves to those known. And (4) the petroleum possibilities on the below-water continental shelves are bright in many areas; oil is being pumped from offshore Texas, California, Louisiana, and Venezuela. The Russians have wells in the Caspian Sea. Oil is being pumped from below the floor of the Persian Gulf. Today the oil-seekers are just beginning to explore and map the structures of the continental shelves. (See FIG. 18–15.)

Producing Areas

More than forty countries produce petroleum from oil fields within their boundaries. But some dozen of these account for the major share of the world's crude oil of the present. In many nations the yield is very insignificant, and does not meet even the most modest of home needs.

The leading countries in petroleum at the start of the decade of the 1960's were the United States, Venezuela, the Soviet Union, Kuwait, Saudi Arabia, Iran, Iraq, Canada, and Indonesia. Barring any major new discovery (and development) elsewhere there is no reason to believe that there will be a notable change in the immediate future.

The major *regions* of the petroleum production currently are: (1) the United States west of the Mississippi—and particularly the part centering upon Texas, Louisiana, and Oklahoma—and upon the southern half of California; (2) the Middle East, centering in that part of the region surrounding the Persian Gulf and continuing up the valleys of the Tigris and Euphrates to include the oil fields of Iraq; (3) northern South America, mainly Venezuela; and (4) the regions between the Black and Caspian Seas, and the upper Volga to Urals area, in the Soviet Union.

Twenty-one states of the United States produce appreciable quantities of petroleum; twelve of these are west of the Mississippi River, and these contribute more than 90 per cent of the total, Texas alone nearly 40 per cent. The situation is the complete reverse of that in coal. The chief energy resources based upon petroleum are west of the river, those based upon coal are east of it.

The leading fields in production are the Mid-Continent, the Gulf Coast, and the California field, this last entirely in the one state. But several fields collectively named the Rocky Mountain Field are important, particularly in Wyoming, Colorado, and New Mexico. Fields on the northern plains are located in Montana, and non-contiguous ones straddle the Montana–North Dakota border. To the north of Montana, in Canada, the province of Alberta is a leading oil producer; Edmonton is a center of the Canadian industry.

The Illinois field east of the Mississippi, the Lima-Indiana, fields in Kentucky and Michigan and the Appalachian Field, mainly in Pennsylvania and West Virginia, contribute the oil pumped from the eastern third of the nation. The Appalachian Field in western Pennsylvania has been unique for its light crude oils, from which a large percentage of high-grade lubricating oils are obtained, and for its long life as a field of more than a hundred years. However, Pennsylvania production has declined by a half from 1940 to the present, and by nearly 40 per cent since 1950.

Western Venezuela and eastern Venezuela contain the chief producing oil fields of that nation. Production is near the seacoast; some wells are in Lake Maracaibo, an arm of the sea. American capital is prominent. Nearby fields in northern South America lie in Colombia and on the offshore island of Trinidad.

FIG. 16-6. The cracking unit in an oil refinery at Sarnia, Ontario, Canada—a city at the outlet of Lake Huron. (Standard Oil Company, N.J.)

Crude oil from Venezuela is exported to refineries in the United States. There are refineries, also, offshore on the islands of Aruba and Curacao, owned by the Netherlands. The investment in this enterprise was made on the Dutch-owned islands rather than in Venezuela because it was felt that the government, at the time, would be more stable—an example of a manufactural location determined primarily by political and governmental considerations.

Western Europe contains a few small oil fields; Austria and West Germany have a modest yield. Romania, the leading European producer after the Soviet Union, was at one time in fourth position in the world, but its production has declined relatively. The Mediterranean lands have little oil—their sources of home energy from oil, as from coal, are negligible.

Petroleum production of the Soviet Union, as mentioned, is from the Black-

Caspian Sea country and from the Volga-Ural Field. Baku is well placed for water shipments—the oil fields are on a peninsula extending into the Caspian Sea; crude oil and refined products are shipped on the sea, thence up the Volga to the Russian industrial districts. Important industry has developed on Second Baku, the name for a recently discovered oil field in the Molotov region, west of the central portion of the Ural Mountains in European Russia. This field now produces half of the petroleum of the Union. There are Soviet fields also in central Asia and on the island of Sakhalin in the Pacific.

The Middle Eastern oil-producing region is significant both in present output and in reserves, in which it is unsurpassed. The several producing fields are (1) on the western shores of the Persian Gulf, (2) on islands in the gulf, (3) at the head of the gulf and thence to and near its northeastern shores, and (4) inland—in the valley of the Tigris in the vicinity of both Mosul and Kirkuk. The fields of the first three-named locations are at or very close to the sea. Pipelines make all very accessible to shipment points. The Mosul and Kirkuk fields are about equidistant by pipeline from either the ports at the head of the Persian Gulf or the ports at the eastern end of the Mediterranean Sea. Both crude oil and refined products are shipped from the Middle East; there are very large refineries in both Saudi Arabia and Iran.

The Middle East is second in oil production only to the United States as a *region;* but the Middle East is so fragmented politically that no one country is second when the listing is by nations—Venezuela and the Soviet Union follow the United States when listed in this way. However, as noted, Kuwait, Saudi Arabia, Iran, and Iraq are among the first eight countries in annual production; collectively the Middle East exceeds Venezuela in output. Among other oil-producing political units in the Middle East are the Bahrein Islands in the Gulf, the shiekdom of Qatar, and the Neutral Territory between Saudi Arabia and Kuwait.

The oil fields and the royalties paid to the governments have resulted in many changes in this age-old region. Shipping has been drawn to the Persian Gulf, previously a side sea with little traffic. The tonnage through the Suez Canal has increased and now exceeds that passing through the Soo, formerly the world leader in this respect. Pipelines cross the deserts. The first railroad in Saudi Arabia has been constructed from the port region of Manama and Dharan to the inland capital of Riyadh. Air bases have been built. And the Middle East has been drawn into the strategic position it now occupies in the world—the supplier of petroleum to run the machines of western Europe. The oil of the Middle East is needed by the West; since the Soviet sphere of influence is not far from the Middle East the Western nations are constantly apprehensive. The oil fields at the head of the Persian Gulf are but 800 airline miles from the Soviet oil fields at Baku—a distance exactly the same as the airline (and pipeline) distance from these Middle Eastern fields to the eastern shore of the Mediterranean Sea.

Indonesia is the principal oil producer of the Far East, and its output places the new nation among the top ten producers of the world. Market orientation is toward Asia.

Oil Refining

An oil refinery receives crude oil and from it obtains gasoline, diesel fuels, lubricating oils, kerosene, raw materials for manufacturing, and a host of other products—even a small refinery usually produces two dozen or more items.

There are basically two types of locations—the market refinery, and the field refinery. The market refineries are at or very near the major markets for petroleum products; among these are the refineries in or near such cities as Los Angeles, St. Louis, Chicago, Philadelphia, and New York. The actual site of the refinery is usually on the fringe of the metropolitan region, and was originally, in most cases, beyond the heavily populated districts; but now communities of workers have grown up around them. Thus Wood River, Illinois, near St. Louis; Whiting and East Chicago, Indiana; and Perth Amboy, New Jersey contain refineries localized by the urban markets. Market refineries receive their crude oil by pipeline, by oil tanker (ship), or by rail—mainly by pipeline or tanker. Thus a market refinery depending in part upon ocean receipts of crude oil is at the water's edge in a port. Practically every western European refinery is of the market type, and is located in a port city. The Thames estuary below London and the route of the Manchester Ship Canal are important in England. Refined products are distributed inland by rail and truck. But European market refineries, like their counterparts in the United States and Canada, are now using pipelines for some of the distribution. A pipeline leads from the refineries at Rotterdam in the Netherlands to the Ruhr Industrial Region of West Germany; another pipeline connects the refinery at Marseilles in France with industrial centers of southern West Germany—Karlsruhe and its vicinity.

A field refinery is in or near the oil fields. It receives its crude oil by pipeline, and ships most of its products by the same form of transportation. The refineries in Oklahoma, such as at Tulsa, and Texas are principally of this type of localization. Some recently built ones have been placed on navigable waterways near the fields; refined products can then be shipped by barge as well as by pipeline, rail, and truck. The refining center at Baton Rouge, Louisiana, occupies a site of this type on the Mississippi.

Some refining centers, originally of the field type of localization, have had extensive local and regional markets develop around them. The refineries of southern California and of the Texas Gulf Coast occupy, today, this intermediate position. The early refineries in the vicinity of Houston were field refineries. The construction of the Houston Ship Canal, opened in 1914, and the growth of industry along it, and on the shores of Galveston Bay, and the

FIG. 16-7. A tank farm for storage of petroleum products. The coastal plain forests appear in the distance. Trees and other vegetation have been cleared from the area occupied by the tank farm because of the hazards of fire. (Standard Oil Company, N.J.)

growth of Houston itself (78,000 in 1910 to nearly a million at present) have resulted in the development of a large local market for energy sources, and expanded and new refineries serve the region.

The petroleum of the Middle East is both refined locally and exported to refineries at the port cities of western Europe. Large refineries at Abadan in Iran, Ras Tanura in Saudi Arabia, and elsewhere receive crude oil from several producing fields by pipeline, and export refined products.

Transportation of Petroleum

The pipeline carries the largest quantity of petroleum and its liquid products on land. Specially designed oil tankers transport crude oil and its refined products on the seas. Rail movement and distribution by tanker truck are also important in some regions. Final distribution to retail markets, such as gasoline stations, are by truck.

The pipeline pattern of the United States is generally from southwest to northeast—from the producing areas of the Mid-continent and Gulf Coast to the concentrated markets and market refineries of the northeastern quarter of the country. California pipeline patterns are from interior to coastal districts. But there are other pipeline networks, as from the Wyoming fields to their markets, and from the Alberta fields of Canada southwest to market refineries in the United States (such as Ferndale, Washington), and southeast to the shores of the Great Lakes. When refined products are shipped by pipelines, each pipeline is separated from the next by water. Pumping stations, spaced twenty-five or more miles apart, depending upon the terrain, keep the products flowing at a speed of about four miles an hour. Diameters of the pipes are not large, for the pipe must be completely filled at all times. The use of large-diameter pipe (such as of the type used for sewers) is not feasible because materials become mixed. Pipelines in cold climates, or in areas of severe winters, are buried; pipelines in some areas are above ground, laid on supports. Rivers are crossed by the use of specially built bridges, by allowing the pipe to lie on

Fig. 16-8. Pipes leading from an oil refinery to the docks where oil tankers are loaded. Each pipe has a label to indicate the product it carries—such as motor fuel or aviation gasoline. See Fig. 22-11 for picture of an oil tanker. (Standard Oil Company, N.J.)

the river bed, or by running the pipe along the side of an existing bridge, away from the roadway.

Some of the petroleum of the Middle East is moved across the deserts to the ports at the eastern end of the Mediterranean Sea by pipeline. From these ports the oil is shipped to Europe. These pipelines cross the deserts and reach the sea in Syria, Lebanon, and Israel. The unsettled political conditions in this part of the world, and the conflict of interests between the Arab countries and Israel, have exposed and continue to expose these pipelines to sabotage, and place them in a precarious situation in times of stress; therefore some of the companies prefer shipments all the way to Europe by sea, or combine the two methods of transportation for reasons of security and certainty.

The oil tanker is a specialized ship built for the transport of crude oil and refined products on the seas. Oil tankers are in use, also, on the Great Lakes. Most of the ocean transport of petroleum and its products is overseas or foreign commerce between two countries, the producing nation and the consuming nation. But in the United States there is a large coastwise and inter-coastal shipment of petroleum. One important segment of this domestic trade

Fig. 16-9. The beginning of a pipeline—the location where the pipe enters the ground. (Standard Oil Company, N.J.)

is the shipment from the Texas Gulf Coast to the cities of the Atlantic Seaboard. Another is from southern California northward to the ports of the Pacific Northwest and Alaska, and from southern California to Atlantic ports of the nation. Petroleum is one of the principal products moving through the Panama Canal from its Pacific entrance to the Caribbean and the Atlantic. The oil tankers on the Texas-to-Northeastern-Seaboard route compete with pipelines. However, some refined products from northeastern cities, made from the crude received by tanker, are also distributed inland by pipeline.

The oil tanker is the principal means by which petroleum reaches western Europe. It is also the form of transportation for the import of petroleum to the United States from Venezuela and elsewhere. One of the large European oil companies alone operates more than 550 tankers.

There are two major present water routes by which the petroleum of the Middle East is transported to western Europe by tank ship. One is by pipeline from the Persian Gulf–Mesopotamian producing area to the ports on the eastern shore of the Mediterranean, thence by tanker to Europe; this route, of course, avoids the Suez Canal. The second, and all-sea, route is from the Persian Gulf, around the south of the Arabian Peninsula, thence through the Red Sea and the Suez Canal to the Mediterranean Sea and Europe. Suez, once the "lifeline of the British Empire" to India and the Far East, has become an important "oilline" to western Europe.

Egypt nationalized the Suez Canal in 1956. Because of the fighting and the deliberate sinking of ships by the Egyptians to block the canal, traffic ceased until salvage operations were completed the following year. At present, with Egypt a member of the United Arab Republic, the final settlement of the "Suez controversy" is in the jurisdiction of the International Court so far as differences (payments, etc.) between the former private company and the Republic are concerned. Only the shipping of Israel is barred from using the canal.

The Suez crisis had one temporary and two profound effects on the petroleum industry and the dependence of Europe upon Middle Eastern oil. Temporarily some tankers were diverted to the long route around Africa, and the trans-desert pipelines to the Mediterranean were used to capacity; even so Europe faced oil shortages. And the pipelines were subject to closure—in fact, some were shut off in certain countries—because of the Israeli-Arab hostility. The permanent effects have been the building of giant tankers, of 80,000 tons, to transport Middle Eastern oil on the Cape of Good Hope route around the southern tip of Africa; and increased drilling for oil west of Suez in Libya and Algeria, to avoid dependence upon the canal. A few of the giant tankers, too large to navigate the Suez Canal, were on the ways before the crisis. European companies speeded up their construction, even negotiated contacts with German and Japanese shipyards at Hamburg and Yokohama for additional giant tankers not contemplated previously. And the search for oil west of Suez resulted in

Fig. 16-10. A pumping station on a pipeline. (Standard Oil Company, N.J.)

the oil discoveries in Algeria and in the exploration throughout the Sahara and elsewhere in Africa. Needless to say, the developments west of Suez have caused concern to the Arab sheiks and rulers of the Middle East so far as their royalties are concerned and have, at times, become a matter of difficulty between the government of the United Arab Republic and the rulers of the Arab states near the Persian Gulf.

► NATURAL GAS

Natural gas is produced both from fields which contain gas alone and from certain petroleum fields. In the former, wells are sunk for the recovery of the gas, and it is piped to distant markets. In the latter the gas is above the oil of the oil pool, as it is lighter, and is trapped between the oil and the impervious rock layer that seals the materials. In this case a well is sunk to the oil; as the gas above the petroleum is under pressure its expansion helps force the petroleum out; in fact, gushers may result from this situation. In this type of oil-and-gas field the petroleum is extracted first, and then the same well may yield the natural gas. Thus much natural gas originates in "pure" gas fields—just as much crude oil is the only product of many oil fields—and the rest of the natural-gas production is from fields that yield two materials of the energy resource.

The United States is the chief producer and consumer of natural gas. Texas, Louisiana, Oklahoma, and New Mexico are the leading states in output, but some gas is produced in more than twenty of the states. The four above states and Kansas are estimated to contain the largest reserves of natural gas. Production in the Pacific area is principally from California, while gas fields in West Virginia are outstanding in the output from the Appalachian Oil Field.

Natural gas is used in the producing regions and is also shipped by gas pipelines to distant consuming markets.

Electricity is generated in the power plants of Oklahoma and Texas through the burning of the natural gas as a fuel. The generation is thermal; steam produced through the heating by gas powers the generators. Some industries have been attracted to the gas regions—the glass industry, in particular, is one admirably suited to the use of gas as a fuel. If local supplies of glass sand are available, as they are in several districts of Oklahoma, the energy and raw materials are at hand, and the industry is established locally. Other glass plants, newly founded ones of national organizations, have been built near the gas fields, and the state now contains several glass-manufacturing centers. These and some other activities are often associated with this fuel. In the case of the Texas-Oklahoma locations some of the capital used in the founding of a manufactural enterprise has been accumulated within the area from profits made in the petroleum industry.

Gas pipelines extend from the producing fields to distant markets for the fuel. The original market was mainly the home. As pipelines reached cities as distant as southern Minnesota and eastward of the Mississippi to the eastern portion of the Middle West, and were extended to the eastern part of the South and around the Appalachians to the Carolinas, home owner after home owner converted from heating with coal to heating with fuel oil from the oil pipelines or with natural gas. Owing to competitive prices some cities witnessed conversion from fuel oil to gas when the latter became available (these competitive prices differ from place to place and time to time—there have been reconversions, also). From its original domestic use the use of natural gas has expanded to other markets. Some cities have witnessed the closure of the plant manufacturing gas from coal, and the purchase and distribution of natural gas by the local gas company. Certain factories now use gas for heating purposes and in some manufacturing operations. Thus the mineral fuels (coal, petroleum, natural gas) are competitive and yet supplement one another; power plants using gas in the Southwest have standby diesel-oil units for use in emergency; factories often have standby equipment powered by another fuel; some city gas distributors pipe both natural gas and home-manufactured gas into their gas mains.

The use of natural gas outside of the United States is not large. Monterrey, the important industrial city of northern Mexico, receives natural gas from fields near Tampico. But wherever gas is present in many world oil fields, it is usually wasted because of the location of the fields overseas from industrial markets, and difficulty of transporting it. However, technologists have found ways to compress methane, a major component of natural gas, to 1/6000 of its volume, and the British have developed methane tankers. The first tank ships transporting the compressed gas discharged their cargo in the Thames River estuary below London in 1959, and the gas was used by the local gas boards for distribution in its mains.

▶ OTHER MINERAL FUELS

Oil shales and tar sands exist in quantity in the western United States, in parts of Brazil, in many areas of the Soviet Union, and in Canada. Retorting of oil shales and special treatment of tar sands results in the extraction of the oil. To date pilot plants work on the processes, but costs and the competition of existing fuels and other sources of energy have held these resources from development. The extent of Soviet work on oil shales is considerable. Some oil is actually distilled from the oil shales of Scotland.

▶ QUESTIONS

1. Where were factories located when water power was used directly to supply energy through mechanical transfer? What shifts occurred in location when steam power was developed?
2. How has electrical energy freed factories from restricted sites?
3. What are the mineral fuels?
4. Compare the highly developed regions of the world with the "underdeveloped" or "undeveloped" portions of the world in the use of, and dependence upon, energy resources.
5. What is the world pattern of the coal resource?
6. What is the difference between a developed resource (say, coal) and a potential resource? What country or countries contain large reserves of coal?
7. Why are the manufacturing regions and transportation systems of western Europe relatively more dependent upon coal as a fuel and a source of energy than the manufacturing regions of the United States?
8. What is the importance of coking coal from the Ruhr to the economy of West Germany and nearby countries of western Europe?
9. Which of the coal fields of the United States have contributed, and continue to contribute, the largest quantity of coal? Explain why.
10. Explain why most of the industrial districts of the United States are not directly on the coal fields—the reverse of the situation in much of Europe.
11. Where are the coal fields of Canada located?

12. How does the stripping of coal in the Appalachian Field differ from strip mining in the Eastern Interior Field? What several factors have been operative in the increase of strip mining in rough terrain—as in the Appalachian Field?

13. Compare the type of mining of Fushun in Manchuria with that of Kailan in Hopei Province (see FIG. 16-1).

14. Explain the type of mining shown in FIG. 16-2. Comment on its relationships to the environment.

15. Compare, briefly, the world pattern of petroleum production with the world pattern of coal mining.

16. Compare the pattern of oil fields in the United States with that of coal fields.

17. Account for the rapid rise of the petroleum industry, an event principally of this century.

18. Why, in general, have oil fields not localized industrial areas? Consider all factors in this.

19. Why is the Middle East of such strategic importance in the world today?

20. So far as the foreseeable future is concerned, what is the position of the United States in regard to (a) the domestic petroleum resource, and (b) the domestic coal resource?

21. What fuels are used in thermal power plants for the production of electricity? Comment on their regionalization, competition, and their supplementing one another.

XVII Energy Resources: Water Power, Interconnected Power Systems, and the Nuclear Fuels

The production of energy from water power, from solar energy in desert climates, and from the nuclear fuels is conservational. These sources of power save the mineral fuels. The mineral fuels, exhaustible resources, thus have their life or period of use extended into the future. The metals used for the generation of nuclear power are minerals, of course, but very small quantities are needed in comparison with the use of coal, petroleum, or natural gas; and the chain reaction continues in the nuclear fuel, whereas the mineral fuels are destroyed and gone as soon as they have been burned. Perhaps, in the future, the saving of mineral fuels and the extension of the period of their use will be most important in the field of their supplying raw materials rather than power —assuming, in this case, the substitution of nuclear energy for the energy derived from the fuels. One does not know what the future holds in this. In any case water power and nuclear power are inexhaustible when compared with the mineral fuels.

► WATER POWER

Man's use of the power of falling water or swiftly flowing water to generate energy dates from ancient times, and has been in use in China and Egypt for

FIG. 17-1. A thermal power plant, burning natural gas for the generation of electricity. A site at a water source is essential for the production of steam and for cooling and condensing purposes. This thermal plant is equipped with standby units in which diesel oil is the fuel. The majority of thermal plants in the world are powered by coal. Note that there are no coal piles at a gas-powered or oil-powered thermal power plant. (Oklahoma Gas and Electric Company)

centuries. Some simple water wheels, turned by the flow of streams, still exist in primitive areas of the world.

The undershot and overshot water wheels, operated in mills at dams built on small streams were common in Europe and North America before the Industrial Revolution. The mills ground grain for surrounding farmers and manufactured local wool into articles such as blankets. Local coarse millstones were used for grinding grain; one of the bedrock formations of northern England is named the Millstone Grit. Small water powers were used for the earliest manufacturing in England and later in New England. With the Westward Movement in the United States, the small power site was always among the first of the lands to be entered, claimed, or speculated in; even Daniel Webster, who never went West, had interests in potential power sites on streams in Wisconsin.

Advancing technology permitted the harnessing of larger rivers; the power sites developed at Lowell, Massachusetts, on the Merrimack River and at Holyoke, Massachusetts, on the Connecticut River, were among the first large waterpowers in the United States. Soon, with the Industrial Revolution in New England, the Merrimack became the most harnessed river in America. Water was diverted right through the mills; the energy of the falling water turned wheels. Belts and pulleys attached to the shafts turned the machines of the factories. The mill buildings, of necessity, had to be directly beside the dam site. The early developed mill towns of New England, most of which still exist, were crowded into narrow valleys. Today, of course, supplementary power is needed for their energy requirements.

Water-powered factories continued in Europe and the United States even after the widespread introduction of the steam engine and the use of coal. The first cotton mills, "moved" from New England to the Southern Piedmont of the Carolinas in the period of 1890–1910, were still generally beside the water power and in the narrow valleys.

The development of the electric generator and of transmission lines released the factory from the dam site. The cotton textile mills of the Southern Piedmont founded during the early 1900's are on the level to rolling uplands—the divides between the streams—even if originally dependent upon water power. And the advancing technology of the early part of this century permitted power developments on very large rivers, shipment of hydroelectric energy by high-voltage transmission lines, and its interconnection with electricity produced by thermal plants burning coal, oil, or natural gas. Modern turbines have long since replaced water wheels.

Today the exceptionally large water-power development is feasible, something unheard of even fifty years ago. Hydraulic cement permits the construction of large dams, and modern turbines receive the water from the bottom of the reservoir; thus the pressure of the water provides the head. High-voltage transmission lines permit the development of remote power sites. Among these "great powers" are such as Grand Coulee Dam, Bonneville Dam, and others on the Columbia, Hoover Dam on the Colorado, the dams in Hells Canyon on the Snake, Hungry Horse Dam in western Montana, Dneproprestroi on the Dnepr in the Soviet Union, Aswan Dam on the Nile, several dams in the French, Swiss, and Italian Alps, Bhakra Dam on the Sutlej in India, and Okutadami on the Tadami in Japan. Rivers like the Tennessee have been turned into a series of lakes by multipurpose (navigation, flood control, and power) dams, and the upper Missouri has been harnessed, with the largest reservoir being above Fort Peck Dam on the plains of eastern Montana. Unfortunately—as some of the above listing indicates—some of the largest power sites and developments are located at a distance from present immediate manufactural regions. The power developed has to be "exported" to find a market, but the high-voltage lines of the present permit the shipment—within the limits set by the losses in transit owing to the resistance of copper wire and other factors.

Factors in Development of Water Power

Early water-power developments were small, and a six-to-ten-foot drop in a stream was usual at the power site. These small drops are no longer harnessed, so far as new developments are concerned. The emphasis today is on the large power site, and many of the world's recently built power dams are from 100 to 400 feet or more in height. A very large percentage of the present dams have been built as multiple-purpose dams and combine the functions of flood control, irrigation, maintenance of a navigable channel, and the development of power in the form of electrical energy. Of course, very few dams serve all four purposes, but combinations of two or three are quite usual; some of the present major developments built by the power companies function as producers of power alone.

There are two extremes in the serviceability of a power site. On the one hand a large flow of water in a major river and a relatively small drop (head) of thirty to seventy or so feet yields a great quantity of power; on the other hand there is the small or moderate-sized mountain stream or torrent, with a large drop—this may yield the same amount of power. In one case the quantity of water is the major factor; in the other, the head developed. The world's longest dams and largest above-dam reservoirs are usually at the first-listed type of site. The world's highest dams are at the second type, at the other extreme. Some few locations combine the advantages of the extremes—Niagara Falls is an example. The total drop in the large Niagara River between Lakes Erie and Ontario is 327 feet, of which about half is in the natural falls proper. The other half lies in the rapids above the falls and especially in the Whirlpool Rapids below the cataract.

Water power is classified as developed or potential. Among the continents Europe has the highest percentage of presently developed power; Africa has the largest amount of potential water power—power that can be harnessed in the future. The Congo River alone, descending from the African Plateau in a series of falls and rapids, is estimated to have the largest water-power potential of any world river. In contrast, the Amazon of South America, the world's *? volume* largest river, and one draining a broad area of heavy tropical rainfall, has little power potential except in its Andean tributary headwaters. The main Amazon is but twenty-three feet above sea level at Manaos, 2,000 miles above its mouth.

About half of Europe's water power is developed. North America follows, with somewhat over 40 per cent developed. But, if broken down regionally, the water power of western Europe is nearly completely harnessed—the figures for Switzerland, Italy, Germany, and France are essentially 100 per cent; no potential power remains. Nearly all of the water power of the British Isles is developed. Thus the potential power remains only in part of Scandinavia and in the Soviet Union, though Norway and Sweden have large developed powers and even export electricity by cable under the straits to Denmark. In North America the eastern half of the United States and southeastern Canada has a very high percentage of developed power; the northern Rockies of the United

FIG. 17-2. Dam and hydroelectric power plant on the Volga River in the Soviet Union. This is Kuybyshev Dam, which furnishes part of the electrical energy for the new industrial regions west of the central Ural Mountains. (Sovfoto)

States and Canada, and the Canadian north and Alaska the greatest percentage of water power still to be harnessed.

The Soviet Union has made rapid strides in its development of water power for hydroelectric purposes. Much of the Russian plain is flat to gently rolling, and large power sites are not usual. However, the size of the rivers compensates for the low heads at power sites, and, as noted, the development on the Dnepr was one of the first undertaken before World War II. The northern, glaciated half of the Russian plain contains the chief potential and developed powers in the European portion of the Union. Much of this area is removed from markets, but power stations in the northwest, near Leningrad, help supply energy for that city, and some in the outer industrial zone north of Moscow are important. New power plants have been constructed on the Volga near Kuybyshev, and on rivers north of the Black Sea.

The hilly and mountainous portions of the Soviet Union are the Urals between Europe and Asia, the Caucasus south of the Russian plain, and, in Asia, the whole Far East of Siberia and the Soviet-China border mountains. It is in these regions, and on the large north-flowing rivers of Siberia, that there is the greatest potential. The Lena River in the northeast of Siberia is estimated to possess the largest potential, but is very distant from population centers. The Angara, draining Lake Baikal, the deepest fresh-water lake in the world, has great potential powers. The late 1950's and the early 1960's witnessed the construction of what is said to be the largest dam in the world—at Bratsk on the Angara, 200 miles north of the Trans-Siberian Railroad. Its electric power output is scheduled to be more than double that of Grand Coulee on the Columbia and more than triple that of Hoover Dam on the Colorado. There are other new water-power developments in Siberia on the upper Yenisei.

The utilization of available water power is small in southeast Asia, and negligible in the steppe and desert southwest (the Middle East). Both the Indian government and that of Communist China are planning and building hydroelectric power plants. Taiwan, the island seat of Free China, has had nearly all of its potential harnessed into useable energy in recent years. Japan is an exception to the usual present Asian scene. The nation has developed nearly all of its hydroelectric power; short, swift-gradient streams descend from the rainy mountains of Japan to the sea. These generate electricity at very numerous dams. No part of Japan is far from a hydroelectric installation, and the energy is thus near the market. Even the farms of Japan were electrified long before complete electrification was attained in American farming districts and homes.

The water power of the Southern Hemisphere remains in the potential classification. Australia, in the southeast and in Tasmania, and New Zealand have installed dams and generating capacity for about a quarter of their estimated total. South American installed capacity is only 2 or 3 per cent of their total; Africa's power development is less than 1 per cent—among the continents, Africa's potential water-power resource is larger than the total of developed and potential power in Europe and North America combined. A start has been made where there are markets for electricity, especially near the Katanga mining region of the southeastern Congo, and in 1959 a major dam on the lower Zambesi River was completed and put into operation. The Union of South Africa has few water-power developments; its high percentage of electrification depends upon its coal resource.

The developed water-power resources of the world are mainly in the commercial and industrial regions and nations. The close relationship is striking, and is evident from the foregoing paragraphs. It is western Europe, the United States, the southern portions of Canada, and the Soviet Union that are the chief users of energy from water power—as they are, too, the major consumers of energy from the mineral and nuclear fuels. It must be remembered, though, that even so the total energy derived from water power in these commercial and industrial areas is but a small percentage of the energy used. Far more energy is in use today in the United States than could be derived from water power, even if completely developed in this country.

► ELECTRICITY

Electricity is the useful way of distributing energy for use as heat or power —the electrical energy may have been derived from the energy of burning coal, the energy of burning oil or natural gas, the energy of falling water, or from nuclear particles. Electrical energy is "produced" by an electric generator and is capable of driving electric motors. The generator is any machine by which mechanical energy is changed into electrical energy.

The chief power plants of the present are thermal (carboelectric) plants or hydroelectric installations. In the thermal plant the heat from the combustion of coal, oil, or natural gas is used to turn water into steam. The steam drives the electric generators. In the hydroelectric plant the turbines are driven by the water, and the water turbines drive the generators. The specific localization of either type of plant is determined by the location of water—water for steam and for cooling and condensing purposes in the one case, water for power in the other. Thus thermal plants are all on rivers, lakes, or canals. Their concentration on certain rivers in cities has been a factor in the rising temperature of some of the streams—rivers that used to freeze over now rarely freeze within the confines of many northern cities.

Thermal plants receive their oil or natural gas by pipelines; some on navigable waterways receive oil by barge. They receive coal by rail, barge, and in some locations by ships on the Great Lakes or the ocean. A recent development has been the introduction of pipelines for the transport of coal; one such extends from coal mines in southeastern Ohio to a thermal power plant near Cleveland. The coal is pulverized, mixed with water, and pumped through the pipeline. Upon its emergence at the terminus the mass of material is dried, and the powdered coal is piled for its eventual feeding into the boilers.

The thermal production of electricity is far more important than hydro-electric generation. In the United States the latter accounts for only about 20 per cent of the total electrical energy. The percentage will decrease because the easily reached power sites have been developed and the rising demand for electricity is principally in the densely inhabited areas, where there is little water power and where that available has been developed. Even areas "noted" for hydroelectric power, such as that served by the Tennessee Valley Authority, now receive their energy chiefly from coal, nearly all dam sites are occupied by power plants, and the TVA is busy constructing coal-burning plants to add to its power. For the world as a whole thermally produced electricity adds up to more than three-fifths of the total, and is increasing in the industrial regions. Hydroelectric energy is increasing at the fastest rate in remote areas, where formerly potential power is being developed.

The actual relative importance of thermal and hydro electricity is regional-ized, as are the fuels. In the United States and Canada important regions of hydroelectric energy are (1) the Laurentian Plateau north of the St. Lawrence River; (2) the power on the St. Lawrence between Lake Ontario and Montreal, and the power at Niagara Falls, now being increased by new construction; (3) the southern Appalachians and Tennessee Valley; and (4) the Sierra Nevada and Cascade Mountains and the adjacent Columbia River system in the North-west and upper Sacramento River in northern California. In Europe the im-portance of hydroelectricity is greatest in and near the Alps, Pyrenees, and in Scandinavia. In Japan it outranks thermal electricity. The regions of dominant energy from fuels are the entire eastern half of the United States and southern California, and in western Europe the British Isles, the Low Countries, Ger-many, Poland, and northern France, plus Mediterranean Europe south of the Alps. Even the relative importance of the fuels is regionalized. In the eastern United States coal (and fuel oil) heats the water for the steam-driven generators. In the north Texas-Oklahoma area it is natural gas, in coastal Texas and southern California it is oil. And all areas have standby plants based on other fuels. An electric company depending on water generation has emergency coal-burning plants to carry a load during low water or drought. And the modern systems of transmission are interconnected; electrical energy is trans-ferred in emergencies. The transmission lines of the power companies serving many northern, glaciated regions where there are moderate-sized power dams interconnect the hydro and thermal plants. In West Germany hydroelectricity is fed into interconnected systems in quantity in the spring and summer, when alpine snows and glaciers are melting and the streams are full-flowing; during the fall and winter the coal-burning power plants of the Ruhr Basin supply the chief electrical energy to the systems. In northern Italy hydro plants in the Alps feed the systems in the summer, those in the northern Apennines during the winter.

► THE ELECTRICAL INDUSTRY

The rise of electricity to importance—about 1900—produced profound mining and manufactural changes. The demand for copper expanded because of its conductivity. Copper mining increased to its present significance all over the industrial world. New factories were founded to produce the legion of electrical equipment—light bulbs, wire, armatures, dynamos, generators, transformers, switchyards, and hundreds of other items. Invention and perfection of electrical machines, from tools and kitchen utensils to transportation equipment, resulted in the rise of new industries. Zinc, tungsten, and other metals received new impetus as their use in electrical equipment became prominent. Certain cities became noted for their manufacture of electrical goods. Giant corporations developed.

Recently the overall electrical industry has entered a new phase, broadly called electronics. Radio and television manufacture is included in this field. Originally the term electronics was applied to those parts of the electrical industry wherein vacuum tubes were used in the equipment or products; today there is no sharp distinction in the border zone, and many complicated computers and instruments are said to be products in this field. New centers of industry have arisen, some in formerly nonindustrial centers such as inner Florida and in suburban communities of California and elsewhere, based on the electronics field. A principal reason for the emergence of these new electronics centers in these areas is living conditions; many companies in the field have deliberately selected sites where they believed there was "good living" for the educated and highly skilled professional people—engineers, mathematicians, physicists, and others—employed in the industry, and also to which they could attract the skilled personnel needed in the manufacturing operation. Another important locational factor has been the selection of a site near a major university, from which professional personnel could be recruited and technical advice obtained. The end products of the industry are high in value per unit of weight, are of value chiefly because of the skilled workmanship in the manufacture rather than for the intrinsic value of the raw materials used, and will bear the costs of long-distance shipments to market, even by air. Electronics plants have also sprung up in all principal industrial centers, and have been a major factor in the rapid rise of some formerly "moderate"-manufacturing centers to national and world-market importance; an example is Dallas, Texas. Patent rights and assignments have been significant in the location of specific products of the electronics industry; for example, electrical computers and many other complex machines can only be manufactured by a company or companies holding rights for the life of the patent; if a particular product is made in only one or two plants, it is, of course, the city in which the plant is located that is the manufacturing center.

FIG. 17-3. The Dresden Nuclear Power Station near Dresden, Illinois. This power plant, following a testing period, entered the production of electrical energy from nuclear fuels in July, 1960. Power from the station is distributed to a wide area in northern Illinois. (Commonwealth Edison Company)

► POWER FROM RADIOACTIVE SOURCES

The expansion, and probable rapid expansion, of power produced from nuclear fission is a virtual certainty. The question is when. The broad pattern of the location of nuclear fuels, particularly uranium and thorium, is fairly well known in the Free World, and is undoubtedly known to the nations of the Communist World. Great Britain contains several nuclear power plants for the generation of electrical energy for peacetime or industrial and home use, the first at Calder Hall having been placed in operation in 1954. The first plant in the United States was put into operation in 1958 at Shippingport, Pennsylvania. Poland and East Germany have plants, and the nations of the European Common Market have signed an agreement for development. The extent of the use of atomic energy for nonmilitary purposes is unknown in the Soviet Union and Communist China.

The world may be divided into three broad categories so far as industrial (i.e. nonmilitary) use of atomic power is concerned. The interest and economic development reflects in each area: (1) the extent to which atomic development for power has been released from strict governmental or military control, and (2) the competition—or really the need—of atomic power within the area, with respect to the abundance or the costs of the usual sources of power.

The first category, or broad group of nations, consists of the industrial countries wherein inexpensive usual sources of energy are lacking, are in short supply, are partially exhausted, must be imported, or are relatively expensive. This category includes western Europe and Japan. In these areas the water power is nearly all developed, there is little or no home petroleum, and coal is increasingly difficult to mine cheaply, for reasons heretofore explained. Britain leads the world in industrial production of electricity from nuclear reactors; more than a dozen large nuclear power plants were in operation by the beginning of the 1960's.

The second category includes the United States and Canada. In these countries there is no real present shortage of power. Coal, petroleum, and natural gas are abundant, relatively inexpensive, and easily transported. Potential water power remains. As for cost, the nuclear plant (to date at least) is relatively more expensive. Competitively, for industrial purposes, the emphasis has been upon the conventional sources of power. The situation may change with the increasing efficiency of nuclear plants and the rising costs of fuels, owing to increasing costs of labor and to other factors. Furthermore, the control of the energy of the atom by federal agencies and the emphasis upon the Defense function and upon military fuels and purposes have been factors in the relatively slower advent of the industrial nuclear power plant than has been the case in western Europe. There has not been the pressure or need for peacetime atomic energy; the needs for additional power have been supplied by domestic coal, petroleum, natural gas, and water power.

The third category is nations which are interested in atomic power plants, and which have few present "conventional" power plants. India and some of the Latin American countries are examples. With little coal, and few existing power plants, the feeling in these countries is that power can be provided most quickly from scratch by the atomic reactor. However, most of these countries are in the talk stage rather than in the action one.

A fourth category, an unknown, is the extent of development of the atomic power plant back of the Iron Curtain and the Bamboo Curtain.

The nuclear power plant thus is feasible and is in operation in many places. If and when it enters the commercial field it may come with a rush. The disposal of waste materials—as well as economic and military factors—have slowed its advent below the forecasts made immediately following World War II.

Uranium is the most important source of atomic fuel. The original sources of the ores from which the uranium was extracted were two—the Katanga region of the southeast Congo in inner Africa, and one mine near Great Bear Lake in northwest Canada, close to the Arctic Circle. From these distant localities the uranium used in the chain process of the atomic bombs of World War II was obtained. Sources of the uranium ore for the Soviet developments were undoubtedly in the mineralized regions of the Erzgebirge Mountains on the border of Czechoslovakia and East Germany. Radium has been produced from the Erzgebirge for some time, and the region has long been closed by the Soviet authorities to outside travel or scrutiny.

A worldwide search for uranium ores characterized the immediate postwar years. Prospectors from all walks of life swarmed over the United States and Canada. They were equipped with Geiger counters and other modern instruments for the detection of radioactive materials. The United States Atomic Energy Commission promoted and encouraged the explorations by studying and purchasing the samples of ore; it built installations for study and research, built pilot plants, and negotiated contracts with universities and other agencies for field work, study, analysis, and research on possible sources of ore.

Uranium is a constituent of more than a hundred types of minerals; it is widely disseminated in many rocks. But only the rocks which contain more than 1 per cent of uranium are considered commercially valuable as ores. The two original sources in the Congo and northwest Canada contain between 1 and 4 per cent of uranium. The chief commercial ores are pitchblende, davidite, uraninite, and a few others.

The exploration for uranium resulted in widespread discoveries, but few are of a richness to justify the expensive and complex processes of extracting the valued mineral. Ores of suitable richness are known now in the United States, Canada, France, Portugal, and Australia; in addition the gold mines of the Union of South Africa yield uranium as a by-product of the refining. The extent of the resource in the Soviet-bloc countries is unknown to the rest of the world.

The principal mining districts in the early 1960's are in North America. Canada has production from Great Bear Lake and Beaverlodge in its northwest, and from Blind River and Bancroft north of Lakes Huron and Ontario. The Colorado Plateau is the source region for the ore mined in the United States; western Colorado, southeastern Utah, northwestern New Mexico, and northeastern Arizona were the "gold-rush type boom areas" during the uranium explorations and are the areas of present production. Small processing mills for preliminary concentration are located near the mines; sites are in small towns such as Rifle and Grand Junction, Colorado; Moab and Monticello, Utah; Shiprock and Grants, New Mexico; and Tuba City, Arizona—all in the Colorado Plateau. The end product of the mills is sold to the government. Final refining plants are in Missouri and Illinois, but the final use is in the dozens or more installations of the Atomic Energy Commission, each devoted more or less to specific purposes. About 85 per cent of the known (or released for public knowledge) reserves are in the Colorado Plateau; New Mexico contains two-thirds of the total.

The uranium ore of the western part of Europe is from the Massif Central, or upland, of France, and from Portugal and Sweden. France and England have the processing plants.

The distribution of the Soviet processing plants and refineries is not known. Among the ore deposits that are known, in addition to the ore bodies of the Erzgebirge in Czechoslovakia, are those of Fergana in Soviet Central Asia, Pervomisky north of the Black Sea, and several in the Lake Baikal district of Siberia.

Thorium, another nuclear material, is scattered in several localities of eastern and southeastern Asia, parts of Africa, the Urals in the Soviet Union, and in coastal Brazil. There are ores from which thorium is extracted or can be extracted in California and South Carolina.

► ENERGY SUMMARY

The mineral fuels, water power, and nuclear energy are supplementary and competitive. Electricity developed by one source of energy can be fed into

FIG. 17-4. Uranium mine in the Colorado Plateau of the western United States, one of many small mines now producing uranium ore. (Standard Oil Company, N.J.)

interconnected systems. Any one of the energy-producing materials can be substituted for one of the others. Cost and accessibility are important factors in their distribution.

A hydroelectric plant is expensive to construct. Capital investment is very great in the modern installations. The dam itself is expensive. The costs of the flowage lands—to be covered by the reservoir—are significant items in the investment. But once constructed and in operation, the plant is operated by only a few men and the continuing costs are lower. The water is a "free" item.

The thermal plant is less costly to build. But its continuance and operation depends upon continuing outlays of money for the purchase of fuel.

The nuclear power plant (to date) is expensive and the cost of electricity generated by it is high when compared to that from conventional power plants. The production of energy from nuclear reactors is an accomplished fact—not only are there the well-known governmental and private installations, but the atomic-powered submarine has become a reality. A nuclear power plant providing power for a large section of northern Illinois was placed in operation in mid-1960; it is said to be the first one in the nation to serve an extensive rather than a limited and local area.

The total need for power has increased in the industrial countries. It continues to do so at mounting rates. Estimates made of the needs by 1975 are in excess of the present generation by far. Thermal and nuclear generation is not fixed and can be expanded rapidly as needs arise or are anticipated. In contrast, the total energy available from water power is a fixed item, terminated when all available potential power sites are developed, and variable because the power produced at low-water flow is different in amount from that during full flow. Water power is conservational, too, in that it does not drain the fuel resources of a country. However, with expanding demand in the industrial countries for power, the percentage of electricity developed by hydro plants declines each decade. Thus the modern trend is toward interconnected power systems and toward increased dependence, nationwide in a country like the United States, upon thermal power plants, with nuclear plants increasing in importance and feeding into the interconnected systems. Even this may not completely release man from the use of all available sources of energy to promote, continue, and expand his economy and to provide power for the increasing populations of the world.

► QUESTIONS

1. Explain how man's advancing technology permitted the increased use of water power during the period from the Industrial Revolution to the early twentieth century.

2. What major sources of water power have been developed in this century?

3. Make a list of ten or a dozen of the present large hydroelectric developments in the world. List these in order, and by country and continent.

4. Explain why the Congo River Basin contains the largest potential water power in the world.

5. Western Europe, the United States, southern Canada, the Soviet Union, and Japan are the major consumers of hydroelectric energy, as they are of energy generated from other sources. Explain why.

6. Could the energy resources of the United States today be provided entirely by water power? What of the future—if all hydroelectric power is developed?

7. Why is the water supply a critical item in the determination of the specific site of a power plant?

8. The electronics industries, relatively new, have generally been able to locate without consideration of the past (i.e. the inheritance of a location as a result of the historical development of a predecessor industry). What various kinds of locations have been chosen?

9. What is the present situation with respect to the industrial and civilian development of the nuclear power plant? Check the latest data.

XVIII The Mineral Raw Materials and Industries

Based upon Them: Iron and Steel Manufacture

Earth materials in the form of minerals are among the most important raw materials of the modern industrial regions of the world. Manufacturing plants use large quantities of minerals as they do of agricultural and forest products; but it is the mineral base—and especially those minerals which are metals—that supplies the world with the ingredients from which modern machines are manufactured. The quarrying and mining industry itself provides employment for thousands of workers; the mechanical concentration of mineral materials and the refining of ores is a source of gainful employment for others; and the legion of finished products made from metals—both producer goods and consumer goods—supports both great capital investment in plants and machines and millions of industrial workers in the world.

Industry and the industrial nations have become increasingly dependent upon the mineral resource in general and upon the metals in particular. So dependent have the manufacturing regions and nations become for these raw materials that all modern industrial countries must either have adequate supplies of metals within their borders, have access to worldwide supplies (necessitating a continual flow of transportation), or must stockpile essential ones for use in an emergency. The dependence upon and use of metals has become so great in this century that it is estimated that half of all mined to date were mined in the long period from the dawn of their use to about 1900, and the other half have been mined between about 1900 and 1960.

Minerals are an exhaustible resource. Therefore the wise and efficient use of them is a necessity. Individual deposits of metals have been worked out. The mining community, dependent upon the ore of the mine, is ephemeral; many ghost towns dot the mountainous regions of the West, abandoned when the lode or vein which supported it was exhausted. But man has increased his supply of necessary metals through new discoveries, better and scientific methods of prospecting and exploration, and with improved technology—the ability to extract the desired mineral from ores of lower grade. Nevertheless, all ore bodies have a limit beyond which it is unprofitable to work them. And the question as to when an ore body is marginal is related, too, to the economic and price conditions of the moment—usually the world price in the case of the metals. During peacetime a country may import a metal, despite supplies at home, because of the cost differentials and, in some cases, the desire to conserve the home resource.

▶ INDUSTRIAL CLASSIFICATIONS OF MINERALS

The mineral resources of the world may be divided into metals and nonmetals. The distinctions are not always clear and definite. Further subdivisions or groupings are usually based upon their use in industry—but these groups are merely conveniences for economic purposes and are different from the recognitions and classifications of mineralogy. Thus we have the mineral fuels, the ferrous metals, the ferroalloys, the nonferrous metals, the precious metals, the fertilizer minerals, the earth materials used in manufacturing, the gemstones, and others.

The mineral fuels, discussed in the previous chapter, are the chief sources of energy for manufacturing. They comprise both organic and inorganic earth materials. The fuels of organic origin are coal, petroleum, and natural gas. Recently, as noted, some metals, particularly uranium and thorium, inorganic materials, have been added because their use is mainly as nuclear fuel.

The metals comprise those mineral substances of particular luster. On the whole they are good conductors of electricity, and they are malleable. There are dozens of useful metals, each normally in solid form at usual temperatures, except for mercury. Upon heating the metals become molten or fused, and they can be worked or rolled into many shapes and forms. They can be alloyed with another metal to produce a different metallic substance; bronze is an alloy of copper and tin, brass is an alloy of copper and zinc, steel is an alloy of iron, manganese, and other materials. Gold, too soft to be used in its pure form (except as bullion) is alloyed with small amounts of other metals when used in coins or for industrial purposes.

The metals can be subdivided on the basis of their use into those used mainly for industrial purposes, and those classed as precious metals—gold, silver, and platinum. Yet there is no hard and fast border zone. Silver is used in many manufactured products. Gold, the reserves of which are basic to the value of most coinage in the world, is released for certain purposes.

The ferrous metal is iron itself, found in nature in three or four major types of iron ore, and the basis of what some call the present—the Steel Age. The ferroalloy metals are those whose principal use is that of being alloyed with iron to make steel, or alloyed with steel to produce the special steels. The manufacture of iron and steel is considered a basic industry of the present. The daily, weekly, monthly, and annual steel output is an economic barometer of the industrial activity of a country.

The ferroalloy metals occupy a special and strategic position in the steel industry and its production of steels for special purposes. Among the ferroalloys are chromium, cobalt, manganese, molybdenum, nickel, tungsten, and vanadium. All steel contains a small amount of manganese. Additional amounts of this and the other ferroalloys impart certain special qualities to the steel. From these are obtained the stainless steels for household use, kitchen trim, and construction trim; the steels which are resistant to high heat and from which engines, machinery parts, jet engines and missiles, and similar items are fabricated; the steels for the manufacture of high-speed cutting tools; the alloy steels for ball bearings, armor plate, and projectiles; and the many other special-purpose products.

The ferroalloy metals are used by the steel industry. But the eventual user of the special steels are the engine and machine industries, the automobile, aircraft, and shipbuilding industries, and the manufacturers of machine tools—to name a few. Machine tools, capital goods of modern manufacturing plants, are in turn used to produce the thousands of products—producer goods and consumer goods—of the present. Even the working and shaping of ordinary steel is accomplished by machine tools composed of the ferroalloys which impart hardness and cutting ability to the steels. The development and use of ferroalloys cannot be overestimated; they have made modern machines such as jet engines possible. Though the special steels constitute but a small part of the total production of steel, they occupy a special place, and give the ferroalloys a highly strategic importance.

Copper, lead, zinc, tin, antimony, aluminum, and several others are the important nonferrous metals used in manufacturing. Copper, one of the metals used by early man because it is ductile and was found in pure form at that time, continued in moderate use for brass and bronze for centuries; but the present large-scale use of copper, now smelted from ores, is owing to the rise of the electrical industry. Lead and zinc, important for many uses, are mined individually, or in some places in the same district. But commonly these metals are found in silver-lead-zinc ores. Thus much of the silver production of the present is a by-product of a mining operation wherein lead and zinc are the metals in demand and sought for. The rise of the light metal aluminum to its present importance dates only from the beginning of this century. Now it is one of the leaders in the metal industries. Magnesium and other light metals became important when uses were found for them; magnesium plants extract the material from sea water in several locations. No doubt other "new" minerals will enter the scene as industrial raw materials; hundreds are known to mineralogists, but until metallurgists and others find important uses for them they are of little value. The picture of the value of uranium as between "before and after" the discovery and development of the nuclear chain reaction is a case in point.

Nitrate, phosphate, and potash constitute the chief fertilizer minerals, and support a large manufacture of commercial fertilizers. Acids, explosives, and other industrial uses are important as well. Man now extracts nitrogen from the air at several large hydroelectric powers in the world, and manufactures artificial nitrates that compete with the natural nitrates, and have actually replaced them in certain markets.

Earth materials such as sulphur and salt occur in rocks in some parts of the world but are uncommon in others. As each is of low value per unit of weight, they are not shipped farther than necessary. Deposits of each have localized important chemical centers. Sulphuric acid is an important raw material, and the most widely used of all chemicals; thus its consumption is a rough index of the activity of the chemical industry. Salt is used widely in many industries. Salt, mined as a rock in many regions, is extracted also from salt brines, salt lakes, and from the evaporation of sea water in some countries. The Gulf Coast of Louisiana and Texas is the world leader in sulphur production, the sulphur being obtained from native sulphur; wells are drilled to the sulphur beds, and water forced down them dissolves the sulphur. The water is then pumped up; the brine runs into vats for evaporation. Since the middle of 1960 some of the sulphur wells have been on man-made platforms out in the Gulf of Mexico (comparable to the oil wells in the Gulf). Sulphur is mined in Sicily and Japan. In addition, sulphur for industry is obtained from pyrites in Europe and at a few locations in the United States as a by-product of smelting operations. Tank cars on the railroads may today contain various acids, alkalis, and other chemical materials, for certain of the ingredients used in the over-all industry are prepared in bulk form at the source region of the earth material from which they are prepared.

Diamonds and many other gemstones, mined from the earth, occupy a particular position in the minds of the public because of their relative scarcity and resulting value. But new and large diamond discoveries in Africa, such as those of the Congo, Angola, and especially Sierra Leone, have resulted in the closure or the slowing of digging in the diamond mines of South Africa; the "Diamond Trust" regulates the supply of gem diamonds to the demand. Industrial diamonds, small stones, are in considerable use in industry as cutting tools in the producer goods field, and in certain consumer goods items, such as phonograph needles. (See Fig. 18–14.)

Building stones, sand and gravel, limestone for the cement industry, clay for ceramics, and other earth materials are generally abundant, but are not equally distributed. Special marbles, limestones, granites, and other rocks command good prices and are marketed widely. Glass sand is far more valuable than common sand; kaolin, or china clay, for the high-grade potteries is exported by some countries, imported by others. In general, however, the ordinary stones, sands, and clays are considered to be "inexhaustible" materials. There are exceptions; islands may be short of sand for construction purposes—the island of Oahu (the location of Honolulu) in Hawaii has to barge in sand from other islands both for the construction industry and to maintain sand on several of its beaches.

Finally—not in the usual classification—water is a mineral resource. It is probably the "most valuable" in urban and industrial regions, but the public and industrial plants take it for granted until shortages develop, or until exploding populations and expanding cities more than press upon the local supply of this earth resource, and the city is forced to import water from a considerable distance. Western Europe has long been aware of the importance of water. Recent shortages here and there in the United States, and chronic short supplies in some areas, are provoking the American public to the importance of water for industrial use as well as for potable water.

► THE IRON AND STEEL INDUSTRY

Iron and aluminum are the most widely distributed of the metals, but occur as ores rather than in metallic form in nature. Iron has been in use since earliest times; pieces of iron have been found in the Pyramids, constructed about 4000 B.C.; excavations in buried cities in Assyria and Greece have resulted in the finding of pieces of iron used by these peoples. The Romans encouraged an iron industry. By 1400 shaft furnaces for the smelting of iron ore were in use in England. But the modern industry dates really from the hundred years before the major Industrial Revolution. For example, forty-foot-high blast furnaces, using wood or charcoal as a fuel, were in use in southern England by the late 1600's. Similar furnaces, smelting local bog ores (limonite) from the marshes were in use in the eighteenth century in New England. During these early stages a small furnace depleted the supplies of neighboring timber. Laws— early examples of conservation practices—were passed to help maintain the wood supply. Some fine charcoal steel is still made in a few localities, particularly in Sweden, and is exported to Britain for use in special purposes.

The date of the discovery of steel is unknown. It was probably very early, for a blacksmith or iron forger, working with iron, and pounding and shaping it on a bed of charcoal fuel, undoubtedly ended up with the iron and carbon material we now call steel.

Gross Distribution

The present important manufacture of iron and steel is associated with the leading industrial regions and nations of the world. Thus the leading *regions* are (1) the northeastern quarter of the United States and adjacent southeastern Canada, with steel production elsewhere in the United States at scattered localities in the South and West; (2) northwestern Europe from the island of Great Britain eastward to Silesia in Poland, and including parts of England, Scotland, Wales, France, Belgium, Luxembourg, West and East Germany, Poland, and Czechoslovakia; (3) four separate regions in the Soviet Union, two which are in Russian Europe, one in and near the Urals, and one in central Siberia; and (4) in Japan.

There are several minor steel-producing regions, minor on the world scale, but of extreme importance to the economy of the country in which they are located. These likewise are in industrial regions of some importance. Among these are the steel industries of (1) southeastern Australia, at and near Newcastle; (2) the Union of South Africa at Pretoria; (3) southeastern Brazil between Rio de Janeiro and São Paulo—the Volta Redonda development; (4) northeastern India; (5) Italy; and (6) Monterrey and a couple of other centers in Mexico.

The situation in China is difficult to compare with the established regions. Anshan in Manchuria has long been important, and ranks with the secondary centers. However, the Five-Year Plans of the Communist government place extreme emphasis upon industrialization and the promoting and development of the iron and steel industry, basic to this premise. Capital to support this planned economy has had to come from agriculture and an increase in farm production, and from channeling surpluses into the hands of the government. Thus the Chinese people have been forced to accept severe economic austerity. Widely distributed small home furnaces have been built, almost backyard furnaces. New steel mills have been constructed. An increase of steel manufacture has resulted, and China—in part because of its areal size alone—has surpassed some of the smaller countries (in area) in output of iron and steel. If the paper plans are all accomplished China expects to become the third producer among countries, following only the United States and the Soviet Union, by the late 1960's. Even so, Chinese production will not affect the world markets, for all of the output will be needed at home, and China has never been a major market owing to its agricultural hand-powered emphasis in the past at home. Its modest needs in the past were supplied from Anshan and elsewhere, and a small surplus was exported to Japan. The fact that some steel was exported emphasizes the lack of industrialization, even in the recent past.

Iron and Steel Manufacture

The iron and steel industry uses three basic raw materials from the earth in its manufacturing process. Iron ore is smelted in a blast furnace, a tall silo-like structure through which a continuous blast of air is forced. The furnace is loaded from the top with layers of the iron ore, with the fuel, and with limestone. The fuel is coke, manufactured from bituminous coal of coking quality. In a few districts anthracite coal is used. The function of the limestone is to unite with the nonferrous material in the ore to form a slag.

Coke is the fuel of a blast furnace because the layers of coke are able to hold up the weight above them and still permit the circulation of the blast. Bituminous coal itself is unsatisfactory because it compacts, and it clinkers. The manufacture of coke for the steel industry results in many by-products— gases, coal-tar products and many others. The present by-product coke ovens obtain the coke and permit the by-products to be reclaimed. In the past only the coke was obtained and the gases escaped into the air or were burned in the coking process. By-product industries are numerous. Gas may be sold for home use; glass-manufacturing plants are attracted to steel districts because of the abundance of gas, a favored fuel in this industry. Chemical and other industrial plants based upon derivatives of coal are common.

FIG. 18-1. The coke-manufacturing plant and coke ovens at Krivoi Rog in the Ukrainian S.S.R. of the Soviet Union. (Sovfoto)

The limestone in the blast furnace functions as a fluxing agent. The slag drawn from the furnace is composed of the material formed by the uniting of the limestone and the impurities in the ore. As a result the slag is high in lime content and is often of such a quality as to be suitable as a raw material for cement manufacture. Large cement mills in many steel districts are based upon the use of the slag. Certain iron ores are self-fluxing because of their composition; in this case limestone is not added to the mixture.

The end product of a blast furnace is pig iron. The molten material was in the past all directed into channels from which side channels extended; presumably this looked like a suckling pig, hence the name pig iron. When the cast iron had hardened it was broken off, piled up, and useable to the manufactures of products made from cast iron—stoves, furnace shakers, grates, and many, many others. With additional working the material from the blast furnace was wrought iron. Pig iron is still cast into molds and hardened. But today, in the steel mill, much of the molten iron drawn from the blast furnace is moved directly in molten form, in giant ladles, to the steel mill to become a raw material of steel. However, statistics of blast-furnace output are still in terms of tons of pig iron, whether or not it has been cast into pigs.

The raw materials of the steel mill are pig iron, manganese and the other ferroalloys if special steels are produced, and often scrap iron and scrap steel. The steel mill around the world is usually associated with the blast furnace operations—the whole is an integrated industry, starting with the ore, coke, and limestone and turning out the finished products of the mill, which in turn become the raw materials of the metal-working industries. But a development of the twentieth century, the electric furnace, permits some steel plants to be in market locations and completely independent of the blast furnace; these purchase their materials from the operators of blast furnaces and other mills and also use large quantities of scrap iron and scrap steel.

The iron and steel mill is the assembly point where the raw materials are concentrated. In some steel regions of the world the mills are at the coal fields; those of the Ruhr of Germany and many of the British mills are directly on the fields. The Pittsburgh region lies on the Appalachian coal field. Some few steel districts, those of northeastern France, Luxembourg, and southeastern Belgium are on or very adjacent to the iron ore fields; but these, too, are within 150 miles of the sources of the coal used. Many steel districts are, however, pure assembly points to which the coke, iron ore, and limestone are transported. These assembly points, which are near the markets for the steel, are usually nearer the source regions of the coal than of the iron ore, for it takes nearly two tons of coal (manufactured into coke) to smelt one ton of iron ore. Transport costs of the materials are thus also significant factors of location. The steel regions on the south shore of Lake Erie and at or near the southern tip of Lake Michigan are of this type. In a few favored locations all of the major raw materials are in the same region; the coal, iron ore, and limestone for the steel mills of Birmingham, Alabama, is all mined or quarried locally.

Thorough study is made before a new steel mill is built. Transport costs, the richness of the iron ore to be shipped (by weight and time it is as costly to transport a 40 per cent ore as a 60 per cent one), the availability and cost of coking coal, and many other factors are taken into account. Once built the capital investment is so great that the plant is rarely dismantled or moved unless changed sources of raw materials make the location distinctly submarginal. Many mills which have become marginal in location have continued operations as long as possible until forced from markets by competitive situations.

The specific site of a steel mill is at a water supply, as the industry is a large user of water for many purposes. Ideally, as on the shores of the Great Lakes, the water body is used for transport of the materials (in this case the iron ore and the limestone) by vessel, and as a source of industrial water. Most steel mills of the world are built on rivers. Those mills not at a large and dependable supply of water have to cool and recirculate their water, using it many, many times. One steel mill in southern California, through an elaborate and expensive system of treatment and the use of cooling towers, recirculates its water from forty to fifty times before it is "used up" through vaporization, and through evaporation in cooling ponds. The steel mills at Birmingham, Alabama, use ten times more water daily than is used in the city. The steel mills near Baltimore use the entire flow of the city's sewage water in their plants. The Mahoning River in northeastern Ohio, along which the steel mills of the Youngstown district are located, is said to be the "hottest river in the world"; its average temperature, from used water discharged into it, is twenty degrees higher than the air temperature, and has reached a temperature of 140°F in stretches even during the winter.

Iron Ores

The chief iron ores are hematite or the red ores, limonite or the yellow or yellow-brown ores, magnetite, and siderite. Hematite is the most important in use.

The iron ores of the world vary greatly in per cent of richness or the metallic content of the ore. The ores of northern Sweden and of Magnitogorsk in Russia at the south end of the Urals—(and the originally mined ores of the Lake Superior District of the United States)—contain nearly 70 per cent of recoverable iron. Other rich ore bodies have iron contents in the 50's and 60's. The average of presently mined ores of the Lake Superior area are in the low 50's. The ores of Lorraine in France are 30 per cent ores. Ores of this "low grade" in the United States are used only at Birmingham, where the coking coal and limestone, and the ore, are all mined or quarried within a few miles of the steel mills. Thus whether or not an ore is a useable ore depends upon its grade, its location with respect to coal, its location with respect to inexpensive transportation—preferably water transport—cost of mining, and other factors. The east-coast steel industry of the United States is importing rich iron ores from

Venezuela to its tidewater-located plants, and at the same time low-grade Appalachian ores, used in early days, are now essentially unused and are listed as reserves. Whether or not these home ores come back into use depends upon a web of economic circumstances impossible to forecast. As long as foreign ores mined near the sea and transported at cheap ocean freight rates to the docks of steel plants are available the low-grade ores cannot compete in our setting. Other nations, without access or foreign credits to purchase rich ores use their home low-grade ores. In other words, the question as to "when is an ore not an ore" depends upon economic conditions as well as upon its mineral composition. Two ore bodies, one easy to smelt, the other difficult, are very different in their use at any given time.

(1) Iron ore, in general, moves to or toward coking coal. Transfer costs are leading factors in this; a larger tonnage of coal than of iron ore is needed in the smelting process. The Lake Superior ores are shipped on the Great Lakes to Lake Erie ports such as Cleveland, Ashtabula, and Conneaut (all in Ohio), from which they are moved by rail the 50 to 125 miles to the steel mills of the Pittsburgh region; the Mahoning Valley of northeastern Ohio (Youngstown district); or the mills scattered along the upper Ohio River in Pennsylvania, Ohio, and West Virginia. The rich ores of northern Sweden, mined north of the Arctic Circle, are shipped by sea from Narvik, Norway, and Lulea, Sweden, to German and British coal. The Spanish ores are shipped from Bilbao on the north coast to England. In part this movement reflects two other factors—lack of coking coal in these above-mentioned iron-mining regions, and lack of a market for iron and steel products in these areas because of sparse population and location far from major industrial centers.

(2) The movement of iron ore toward coking coal is to convenient assembly points for the raw materials. The steel mills on Lakes Erie and Michigan receive their iron ore and limestone by Great Lakes vessels, the coking coal is shipped by rail from the Appalachian and Eastern Interior coal fields. The site of the mill is that of an assembly point of the materials. Tidewater-located steel mills on the east coast of the United States, in Europe, and in Japan exemplify this principle as well.

(3) Where iron ore and coking coal are located within a few hundred miles of each other via land transport the materials are interchanged via the same carrier. There is interchange in the industrial region of northwestern Europe; it may increase now that several countries on the continent have formed a European Common Market. There is much interchange by rail in the Soviet Union. There is a small return of coking coal on the Great Lakes, the ore carriers taking the coal to a steel industry near Duluth; this plant is not large, owing to market factors in the region it serves.

(4) Defense reasons, market factors, or government-controlled situations frequently depart from the normal movements. A steel mill was constructed sixty miles inland from the southern California coast during World War II to

serve emergency needs for steel in the area; transport of steel from Atlantic Coast plants, via the Panama Canal to California, was virtually impossible because of the submarine menace in the Atlantic. The plant, after the war, is market-oriented to the expanding West Coast market. Coking coal and iron ore for this operation was and is brought in by rail from Utah, each being moved as one-way traffic for from 500 to 750 miles, but most of the iron ore comes from Eagle Mountain, California. The outstanding long-distance movement of raw materials by land is in the Siberian portion of the Soviet Union. Coking coal from the Kuznetsk Basin is taken by the train load 1,300 miles west to the iron ore of Magnitogorsk in the Urals; on the return trip ore is brought to Kuznetsk. There are large steel mills at each end of the line. This movement would be comparable to the interchange of the heavy and bulky raw materials between New York City and Denver. The development of iron ore deposits near Kuznetsk and the increased output of coking coal from Karaganda (600 miles closer to Magnitogorsk) has lessened the amount of interchange between Kuznetsk and Magnitogorsk during recent years. The Shoria Mountains near the Kuznetsk Basin supply iron ore to the steel mills of Stalinsk and other cities of the Basin.

► THE IRON AND STEEL INDUSTRY OF THE UNITED STATES

The American steel industry is the largest in the world. Its capacity is about 40 per cent of the world steel capacity. Its production is roughly the same figure. Its growth from pre-World War II to the present has been phenomenal and has increased absolutely as well as relatively, for the prewar output was slightly over a quarter of the world total. This relative position has been attained despite the great growth of certain foreign steel centers.

Seventy-five per cent of the steel ingot capacity of the United States is in the American Industrial Region, or Manufacturing Belt, of the northeastern quarter of the country. Many factors help explain this. Among these are the access to iron ores and coking coals, the market factor—important because of the numbers of people alone and because of the industries which are buyers of steel and serve this market—the transportation network by rail and water, the labor supply, the capital, the advantages of an early start, industrial inertia because of the fixed capital tied up in plants and equipment, and others.

The steel industry of the United States is mainly market-oriented today. Some of the early locations were raw-material-oriented, but the markets for steel products have grown up around them. Recently built integrated mills, which carry on the entire process from the manufacture of coke, the blast furnace operations, and the manufacture of steel, are at planned locations, and are principally market-oriented at convenient points for the assembly of raw materials. New mills have been built in the West with the rise of that market. New mills on the East Coast, depending upon imported iron ore, have been placed at tidewater or on navigable waterways in the centers of the largest market regions of the Atlantic Seaboard.

The steel-making districts are concentrated in well-defined areas within the American Manufacturing Belt. From east to west these include: (1) the Atlantic Seaboard and southeastern Pennsylvania; (2) the overall Pittsburgh region of western Pennsylvania, west of the crests of the Appalachian highlands; (3) northeastern inland Ohio, especially the Mahoning River Valley—the overall Youngstown district; (4) the upper Ohio River Valley, from Pennsylvania southwestward through Wheeling, West Virginia to Ashland, Kentucky at the northeastern corner of that state; (5) the steel industry of the Great Lakes shores, particularly Lakes Erie and Michigan; (6) the Miami Valley of southwestern Ohio. The nearby Canadian centers of steel manufacture have a location on the Great Lakes and rim the western end of Lake Ontario, and are also at Sault Ste. Marie at the Soo.

FIG. 18-2. Steel mills beside the Monongahela and Ohio rivers in the Pittsburgh district use the rivers both for water supplies and for transportation. Coke, coking coal, and manufactured products are moved in part by barge. Partially manufactured and semi-finished steel products are shifted by water from mill to mill for further manufacture or assembly. (Standard Oil Company, N.J.)

Many cities, large and small, contain important iron and steel centers. A few, listed by the above-named districts, are as follows: (1) Sparrows Point, Maryland and Morrisville, Pennsylvania are important sea-oriented centers, using imported ore; the first is outside of Baltimore and near the head of Chesapeake Bay, the latter is at the head of navigation on the Delaware River, nearly opposite Trenton, New Jersey. There are other mills on the Delaware. South Bethlehem, Coatesville, Steelton, and other inland localities in southeastern Pennsylvania are steel "towns." (2) The steel industry of the Pittsburgh region lines the Ohio and Monongahela rivers, uses much water transportation to shuttle materials from mill to mill and coke from riverside by-product ovens to the mills. This explains the heaviest concentration of river traffic in the nation, that on the upper Ohio and lower Monongahela. The mills themselves are in cities or towns politically separate from Pittsburgh—Alequippa, Turtle Creek, and many, many others. Pittsburgh itself contains but one primary steel mill. Johnstown, east of Pittsburgh on the Conemaugh, lies in the district but is not on a navigable waterway. (3) Youngstown, Ohio, and the "state-line" town of Sharon, Pennsylvania, and other steel centers are on the non-navigable Mahoning and Shenango rivers; Canton, Massillon, and nearby cities are in the region. (4) Steel mill centers, more widely spaced than near Pittsburgh, dot the Ohio as it flows between Ohio and West Virginia. Wheeling, Weirton, Steubenville, and Ashland (Kentucky) are among them. (5) There are many large steel mills on the Great Lakes. The industry is important on Lake Erie at Buffalo, Cleveland, Huron, Lorain; is market-oriented to the automobile industry at Detroit, on the Detroit River inlet of the lake; and rims part of the head of Lake Michigan—in the southern part of the city of Chicago, and in adjacent Indiana at Indiana Harbor and Gary. A Canadian center is Hamilton at the western end of Lake Ontario. Newly opened Canadian iron ores, mined in Quebec and Labrador, are shipped by rail to the St. Lawrence River and now reach lakeshore steel centers by way of the St. Lawrence Seaway. But the lakeshore industry depends principally upon ore from the Lake Superior District. (6) Hamilton, Middletown, and neighboring places in the Miami Valley have steel industries.

The steel centers not in the principal manufacturing belt possess a fifth to a fourth of the American capacity. Birmingham, Alabama, accounts for about a tenth itself, and is the center of industry in the southern United States, a rapidly expanding market. The city is not on a river, but has the advantages of a "water-rate" because the railroad operating between the mills and a river port on the navigable Black Warrior River operates, as to rates, as if it were an extension of the waterway. Mills at Longview and Houston, Texas use east Texas limonite and imported ores. Pueblo, Colorado is the steel center of the area between the Mississippi River and the western slopes of the Rockies. Two new, completely integrated mills, built with government funds or loans during World War II, and now operated by private industry, serve the western

Fig. 18-3. Open-pit mining of hematite iron ore on the Mesabi Range of northern Minnesota. The ores loaded into these flat cars by power shovel are then transferred to larger cars, and trainloads of ore cars are assembled for the downhill haul to Duluth or Superior. Very long trains are handled; the return trip, upgrade, is of empty cars. (Standard Oil Company, N.J.)

market. One is at Geneva, Utah, and the other at Fontana, California. Prior to their construction there was no major steel industry west of Pueblo; the West Coast steel was shipped to the market from mills on the Atlantic or manufactured from partly-fabricated shipped-in materials at mills in the San Francisco region, or produced in electric furnaces from "imported" materials and scrap.

Sources of Iron Ore Used in the United States

Until recently the American iron and steel industry depended entirely upon home supplies of ores. Today there is a significant import of ore from Chile and Venezuela, particularly the latter, and moderate imports from Liberia in Africa, Newfoundland in Canada, Brazil, and Cuba. Imports from the new operations in Quebec and Labrador will undoubtedly increase, as the Lake Superior ores are declining in quality. Imported ore is used mainly only in the mills of the

East Coast and southeastern Pennsylvania. The steel mill at Morrisville was built to work upon the ores of Venezuela, mined in its southeastern interior, and transported to a deepwater port on the Orinoco River, from which they are shipped directly by sea to the docks of the plant.

The original ores used in the United States with the advent a century or more ago of the large-scale iron and steel industry were hematites from the Appalachian valleys. These were low grade, 30 to 40 per cent, but were widely distributed. The ores in central and eastern Pennsylvania and the anthracite coal mined in the anthracite basins helped localize an important steel industry in several cities of the Philadelphia hinterland. Anthracite can be used directly in the blast furnace. The Appalachian ores are now mined only at Cornwall, Pennsylvania, and Morgantown, West Virginia, but, except where exhausted lo-

FIG. 18-4. The top of an ore dock on Lake Superior (also see FIG. 18-5). Trainloads of ore are run into the dock, and the ore is dumped from the car into the pockets—their openings are shown. When the train left the Mesabi or other iron ore range, a sample of the ore contained in each car was taken. The sample was analyzed as to its iron content while the train was en route to the dock and reported upon before its arrival. Thus it is possible to unload ore of a uniform content into the same part of the dock, and load a ship with ore of similar quality throughout. (Standard Oil Company, N.J.)

cally, remain as reserves. Their general disuse came with the discovery and development of the richer ores of the upper lakes region.

The Lake Superior iron ores, which have supported the ore needs of the United States for a hundred years, were discovered in the 1850's. These high-grade hematites originally contained ore of as much as 70 per cent iron content; so much high-grade ore has been mined that the averages are now in the lower 50's.

The Lake Superior iron ranges are six in number. The Mesabi Range, northwest of Duluth, Minnesota, is by far the most important and in many years has contributed two-thirds of the nation's iron ore. The Vermilion and Cuyuna Ranges of Minnesota are, like the Mesabi, tributary by rail to the ore-shipping twin-port of Duluth, Minnesota and Superior, Wisconsin at the head of Lake Superior. Ore from the Vermilion also moves through the port of Two Harbors, Minnesota. The Gogebic Range in Wisconsin and the Upper Peninsula of Michigan ships its ore from Ashland, Wisconsin; the Marquette Range of Michigan ships through Marquette. Thus all of the ore from the above five iron-mining areas is shipped by water from a Lake Superior port, and is moved down-

FIG. 18-5. Two Great Lakes ore carriers being loaded at an ore dock on Lake Superior. The pilot house is at the fore of the ship, the engine room and crew quarters are aft. Between is the hold for the iron ore (or coal, or grain). The hold can be filled as a unit or divided into segments containing ore of different iron contents. (Standard Oil Company, N.J.)

FIG. 18-6. Unloading iron ore from a Great Lakes ship in River Rouge, near its mouth in the Detroit River. The stacks of an automobile factory are visible at the left. (Standard Oil Company, N.J.)

lakes to or toward the coking coal. The Menominee Range, in the Upper Peninsula, is tributary to a Lake Michigan port, Escanaba.

The Soo Canals at Sault Ste. Marie, Michigan, and Sault Ste. Marie, Ontario, carry shipping past the rapids of the St. Mary's River, the outlet of Lake Superior. The original Soo Canal was opened in 1855. Thus, two fortunate circumstances, the discoveries and the canal, in the 1850's combined to make the rich Lake Superior ores available to the growing steel industry. Pittsburgh was, in part, a result. Today the three Soo Canals, open only from early April to December, carry some of the largest tonnage in the world. They led all world canals in tonnage until passed by Suez in the 1950's as a result of the twelve-month oil movement through the latter. During some wartime years a hundred million tons of iron ore were transported down the lakes through the Soo.

The steel industry in the Pittsburgh region arose with the development of

FIG. 18-7. Entrance to an under-the-sea iron mine in eastern Canada. The beds of iron ore are 800 feet below sea level. This is at Conception Bay in Newfoundland. (Canadian Information Office)

the Connellsville coking coals. The Pittsburgh seam was once mined locally, but now is most used in the counties of southwestern Pennsylvania, south of Pittsburgh. The original iron ores used in the developing Pittsburgh industry were mined down the Ohio River or were transported across the Appalachians from eastern Pennsylvania. But it was the combination of the advent of Lake Superior ore, unloaded at ports on the shores of Lake Erie, only 125 miles from Pittsburgh and the locally manufactured coke, that rooted and expanded this steel center. Capital, management, and other factors, of course, played an important part. And the Civil War, during which Pittsburgh became one of the armament centers of the Union, was significant in its industrial growth.

The steel centers expanded toward and eventually to the lake shores as new plants were built. The first expansion was along the route that the ores were shipped from the lake ports to Pittsburgh—the Mahoning Valley of Ohio. Eventually the mills were built at the lake edge. Gary, Indiana was the first of the deliberately planned and scientifically located steel centers. Its site was selected in 1906 and the output was oriented to the Chicago and Middle Western markets. Otherwise the lakeshore plants were built in existing cities, such as Cleveland, Buffalo, and Chicago. Transport of coking coal or of coke to the lakeshore mills "replaced" the transport of the iron ore to inland cities in this phase of the location of the industry.

The ore for Birmingham is mined within a few miles of the mills. It is Appalachian hematite, low-grade ore, yielding only half or so the iron content of the Mesabi per ton of ore. It is the juxtaposition of coking coal, iron ore, and limestone at Birmingham that makes the industry feasible. The city did not exist during the Civil War, but, like Gary, grew with the advent of the steel mills.

Iron ore is mined in the western United States in Colorado, California, Idaho, and Utah. The production in Utah is especially important. Utah ore is that used mainly in the integrated mills at Geneva, Utah and Fontana, California, and is shipped eastward to Pueblo, Colorado. Limonite ore, strip-mined in East Texas, is shipped to the steel mills at Houston and Longview.

The Adirondack Mountains of New York are the source region of American-

Fig. 18-8. Open-pit mining of magnetite iron ore on a mountainside of Vancouver Island, British Columbia, Canada. The ore is concentrated in Canada, then exported to Japan. (Canadian Information Office)

mined magnetite ores. The Adirondack ores are shipped mainly to eastern steel centers. The mining centers are both in the eastern and the northern portions of the mountains.

The grades of the Lake Superior ores have been declining for some time as the open pit and shaft mines expand into ore bodies less rich than those mined originally. The mammoth appetite for iron ore during World War II ate heavily into the ore deposits and reserves. The ores are transported inexpensively down-grade 100 or so miles by rail to the ports, and cheaply by the Great Lakes ships. But additional transport by land to the Eastern Seaboard forces costs to the competitive situation with foreign imports. And the import of ore by an all-water route to the Great Lakes by way of the St. Lawrence Seaway is increasing. The impending situation, not serious at present, has resulted in stock-taking, study of, and research on the tremendous reserves of iron-bearing rock in the region—taconite.

Taconite is an extremely hard rock. It is the mother lode of wide extent from which the present hematite has been leached and concentrated through the geologic ages. It is so hard that special equipment of the hardest alloy steels had to be developed to work with it. Even the containers and railroad cars handling it had to be built especially. The machinery in the original pilot plants was perfected for the purpose.

The taconite is ground to the fineness of flour, for the iron-bearing particles are so thoroughly dispersed in the rock that they must be concentrated and separated through the use of a variety of processes. The end product of the operation is the manufacture of pellets or small chunks of iron, suitable for transport down the lakes to the steel mills, and suitable in quality for feeding into the blast furnaces. Beaver Bay, Minnesota, a newly built port on the north shore of Lake Superior, handles the shipments. The taconite-processing plant at Silver Bay is now being expanded.

The hope of the mining operators in the Lake Superior District is that the production of taconite will take up the slack as the hematites decline, and that cost factors of production will become such that the output of taconite can continue the mining area indefinitely. The world economic situation, the costs of mining and of labor in competition with foreign mining districts, the costs of ocean transport and the wages of foreign crews (as compared to American crews on the lake ships), and similar factors are beyond their control but nevertheless play a part in the over-all situation.

The United States has long been an exporter of steel, and recently has become an importer of iron ore. But a significant change, maybe only a trend, began in the last few years of the 1950's; steel imports arose. By the end of the decade a million and a half tons of steel were exported in a year, a drop of 80 per cent in two years from 1957 through 1959, and imports rose in the period from a million tons to 4,500,000 tons. West Germany and Japan, through post-war aid, newly built postwar plants, and less expensive labor, were able to capture certain American markets. Nearly all barbed wire was imported and could be manufactured abroad and landed at Great Lakes ports, via the St. Lawrence Seaway, more cheaply or as cheaply as it could be made at home. Some steel was imported even from Australia. The trend is disturbing to the American industry, which has estimated that the result was about 10,000 fewer jobs in the industry at home. Many factors have contributed to the trend; two of the chief are the costs of American labor in comparison to foreign labor costs, and the inflation of the dollar. One result of the imports has been the building of American-owned factories abroad—on paper only, to date, in steel, but accomplished in the automobile and other industries. The manufactured products are then shipped to the United States. The whole situation illustrates the economic interdependence of the commercial world in a continuously "shrinking" world, and the manufactural similarity in products (but not in size) in the chief manufacturing regions of the world—the United States, western Europe, the Soviet Union, and Japan.

► THE IRON AND STEEL INDUSTRY OF EUROPE AND ASIA

The steel industry of western Europe, collectively, accounts for a quarter of the world production, that of the Soviet Union for 17 to 18 per cent. Thus, with the United States, these three major industrial centers manufacture nearly 85 per cent of the steel of the world. Japan, with 3 to 4 per cent, completes the picture of major production. The situation of China has been mentioned. The rest of the world, including India and the producers of the Southern Hemisphere, contribute the small remainder.

The United Kingdom and West Germany are the major iron and steel producers of western Europe, followed by France, Belgium, Luxembourg, and Czechoslovakia. The United Kingdom is mainly an importer of rich ores from Sweden, Spain, North Africa, and Newfoundland. The countries on the continent, in contrast, (except for West Germany) use the Lorraine lean ores, or local home-produced lean ores, and are not major importers of ores from overseas or from Sweden or Spain. West Germany imports much Swedish ore; many of the blast furnaces of the Ruhr are designed for use of this rich ore rather than the lean ores of Lorraine. But there is foreign trade in iron ore from France and Luxembourg to Germany and Belgium; thus the steel producers import ores, but mainly from regional rather than distant sources. Now that the European Common Market of several of the continental countries has been accomplished the ore still moves across boundaries, but has freedom of movement so far as tariffs and duties are concerned.

The British industry is dispersed in inland and coastal locations, but all have easy access to good coking coals; distances are not great. The inland mills are on the coal fields of the Scottish Lowland, the fields of Lancashire and

Yorkshire in northern England, and the Birmingham area. The coal fields around Newcastle in the northeast of England are at the sea; the steel industry is in this area, and south of it at Middlesborough, a port near the iron ores of the Cleveland Hills. The South Wales coal field localizes steel mills and is close to the ports of Cardiff and Swansea, where mills are at tidewater. The steel industry is thus in the Midlands and North of England, southern Scotland, and South Wales—the same general areas that contain much of the rest of British heavy industry.

The Ruhr of West Germany is the steel center of the nation, and one of the major industrial centers of the world. Lorraine of northeastern France is the metallurgical center of that country, and, from four separate basins, the major iron-mining region of western Europe. The iron-bearing formations extend into Luxembourg and provide that small country with a steel industry and a dependable source of income, despite its only 999 square miles of area. Belgium has coking coal fields north of the Ardennes; the field extends into the extreme north of France on the west and into Germany on the east. Thus the overall north-

FIG. 18-9. The world search for iron ore has resulted in the opening of many newly-found deposits. This processing mill at an iron ore mine in Sierra Leone, West Africa, concentrates the ore for export. (British Information Services)

western European region on the continent, through the exchange of raw materials, contains the base for the major iron and steel center it has long been. Moreover, the Rhine, Meuse, and Scheldt rivers provide excellent water transportation, the entire area is tied together by man-made canals, and the railroad network is superb. Not all coal or iron-mining centers are on waterways, but all have excellent and dependable transportation. With the advent of the European Economic Union the Benelux countries, France, West Germany, and Italy profit from the interchange without duties and tariffs.

The principal economic dependence is upon Ruhr coal and Lorraine iron ore, though there are other coals and imported ores in use. The Lorraine ore averages from 30 to 37 per cent, depending upon the basin it is mined in. Some of the ores contain enough lime content (oolitic ores, or minette ores) to be self-fluxing. Phosphorus is an impurity which must be removed. The reserves of ore are tremendous, estimates running as high as six billion tons. There is possibility of extending the field to the south and west, as the beds dip southwest; but, to date, there has been no need to do so, as the near-surface ores have been adequate, and mining varies in depth from 900 to 1,800 or so feet. Despite the low grade, the Lorraine ores seem destined to provide a base for the regional iron and steel industry for a long time to come. And newly found and developed extensions of the Saar coal field of West Germany into French territory, plus improved technology, permits the coking of nearby coal, not formerly thought possible—and increasing the "within France" portion of this northwestern European metallurgical center.

The Soviet iron and steel districts are widely spaced. Materials are moved long distances to and from some of the centers, but they are highly concentrated in production in one—the Donbas.

(1) The Donetz Basin or Donbas north of the Black Sea contains coking coals. Nearby in the Krivoy Rog district iron ore is mined in approximately the same quantity as in Lorraine. Manganese is mined within the region, in the Nikopol district. Southeast, across the Black Sea in Georgia (south of the Caucasus Mountains), accessible by Black Sea shipping, lies another major manganese mining region. The Soviet Union produces, from these two manganese districts, half of the world total of this necessary ferroalloy. The Donbas region (extended slightly from the strict Donetz coal field) contains all three major raw materials, and has adequate limestone sources. There are many steel-manufacturing centers, Stalino, Zhdanov, Zaporozh'ye among them.

(2) The southern Urals and the portions of Siberia immediately to their east constitute a second steel district. The Urals have long been famous for the variety of metals mined in them. The development of their iron ores is recent, however; some of the mining dates only from World War II, when the German armies captured the Donbas, and much of the Russian industry was moved to the Urals and to Kuznetsk, 1,300 miles farther east in Siberia.

The rich ores of Magnitogorsk, and major iron-mining centers in Nizhni

Fig. 18-10. View of part of the Kuznetsk steel works in the Siberian portion of the Soviet Union. (Sovfoto)

Tagil, farther north, support the steel industry. Coal, as mentioned previously, is transported now mainly from Karaganda rather than Kuznetsk. Magnitogorsk itself, Chelyabinsk, and Sverdlovsk are among the principal steel-mill centers.

(3) The Kuznetsk Basin or Kuzbas is a coal field in Siberia, north of the hills and mountains which extend to the Chinese border. Iron ore is mined nearby at Abakan, is mined also several hundred miles south, near Lake Balkash, and is transported from Magnitogorsk. The city of Stalinsk is a major steel center. Other newly founded cities engage in the industry. The actual size and magnitude of the industry is not known to the rest of the world, and the location of the region, deep in the heart of Siberia, protects it from non-Soviet visitors. Its industry is being expanded continuously.

(4) A market-oriented steel-producing region is located north of the Donbas, in the vicinity of Moscow and in surrounding cities, particularly to the south of the capital. Ore is mined locally, is available from the Urals to the east and from the mining district of Ivdel in the northern Urals, to the northeast of Moscow. Coal is mined in several small fields and is shipped from the Donbas. No single steel center is as large in production as those named in the preceding

paragraphs, nor does any reach the output of two districts back of the Iron Curtain in satellite countries—that of Polish Silesia, and that of Czechoslovakia.

► JAPAN

Japan's post-World War II recovery in manufacturing in general and in iron and steel in particular has been rapid, even sensational. The Yawata district at the northern shore of the island of Kyushu, on the Strait of Shimenoseki, is one of the early steel centers developed originally by the Japanese government. The industry of the Kobe district and that of the environs of Tokyo, both on the main island, Honshu, have expanded. A new steel industry, completely integrated, has been built on a protected harbor on the northern island of Hokkaido, at Muroran. Two large mills at this location now make it one of Japan's leading steel centers, and employ more than three-fourths of the industrial workers of the city. All Japanese iron and steel mills are at tidewater. All use Japanese coal and some Japanese ore, but the ore particularly is supplemented by heavy imports of iron ore and of scrap iron.

► THE FERROALLOY METALS

The ferroalloy metals, taken collectively, are not mined in the chief industrial and manufacturing nations of the world. Thus the iron and steel industries of the highly developed countries are dependent upon distant sources of ferroalloys. The transportation routes must be kept open at all times to ensure a supply, even though the tonnage involved is small when compared to that of iron ore, copper, and other ores of the metals. Consequently the ferroalloys assume a very strategic place. Wars, strikes, and interruption of a normal flow through other events (such as embargoes on exports from Iron Curtain countries) affect the consumers. The alternative is stockpiling of these essential metals, a practice used by nations for defense purposes and by industries for protective and insurance purposes, and to maintain continuity of production.

Africa, Asia, and South America are important source regions of several of the ferroalloy metals. The Soviet Union and India contain the major deposits of manganese, and the Soviet Union is the best off among industrial nations in its home supplies of the ferroalloys, taken collectively. Canada is a significant producer of nickel. The United States, from within its boundaries, yields only two of the ferroalloys in quantity. A corollary of the above situation is that it is the United States, the United Kingdom, West Germany, and France that are the principal importers of the ores or the concentrates of the various ferroalloys. In times of emergency, as during a war, a few can be obtained at considerable expense from by-products in other ores; for example, considerable manganese can be produced from the iron ores of the Cuyuna Range of Minnesota. But, dur-

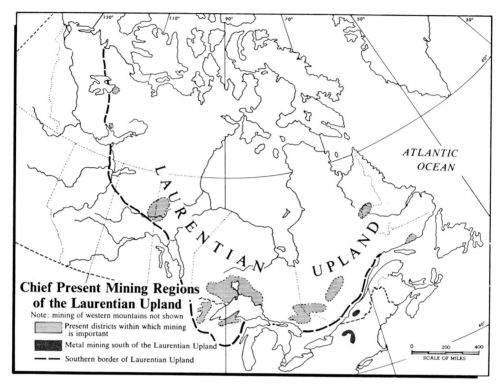

**Chief Present Mining Regions
of the Laurentian Upland**
Note: mining of western mountains not shown

▭ Present districts within which mining
is important

▮ Metal mining south of the Laurentian Upland

— — Southern border of Laurentian Upland

*ATLANTIC
OCEAN*

ing usual times, only about a fifth of the ferroalloys used in the United States are produced at home.

The automobile, machine tool, machinery, aircraft, and engineering industries are the principal users of ferroalloy steels. Therefore, although the steel industry consumes the metals, it is these other industries that determine the demand for the product, and the resulting use of the metals at any given period.

The Soviet Union, with half the world's production, and India, with an eighth, are the leading sources of manganese ores. Deposits in Ghana and in the Union of South Africa contribute much of the remainder. Other deposits are scattered in South America, southern Europe, Asia, and Africa. The Free World industries have had to shift to non-Russian sources since the advent of the Iron Curtain. Exploration has been pushed vigorously. Money loaned by the Export-Import Bank of the United States to an American-Brazilian company and resources of the company have been used to open new manganese mines in Brazil and construct a 120-mile-long railroad to the new manganese port of Santana. The United States is turning more and more to Latin American sources of this and other ferroalloys. Within this country there is only a very small production of manganese from mines in the West and the iron ranges (some of which, like Cuyuna, yield the ore as incidental to another), and from mines in the mountains of Tennessee and Georgia.

Turkey, the Philippines, South Africa, and Rhodesia are the main exporters of chrome ore to the Free World. The Soviet Union is one of the largest producers; its trade is principally with the satellite countries.

The Katanga mining region of the southeastern Congo, one of the great mining regions of the world, yields three-quarters of the cobalt and is the world's major source, chief producer, and exporter. The Katanga, noted as a major copper-mining area, produces tungsten as well as manganese among the ferroalloys, and mines silver and zinc. The Sudbury mining district north of Lake Huron–Georgian Bay in Canada produces cobalt. Kellogg, Idaho, some mines in Missouri, Pennsylvania, and Vermont, and a recently opened mine near the Salmon River Canyon in Idaho account for the small American output.

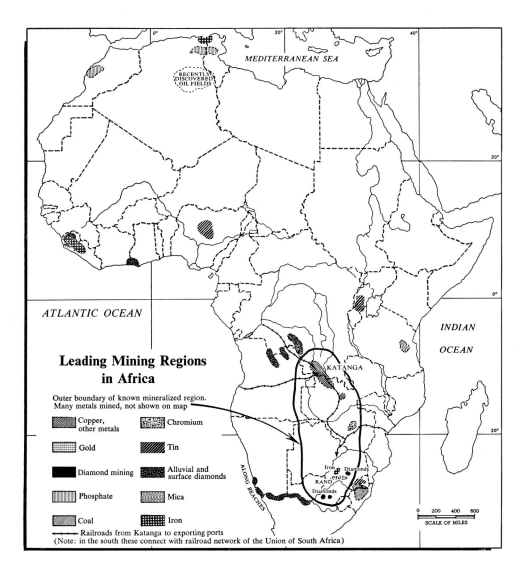

Leading Mining Regions in Africa

Outer boundary of known mineralized region.
Many metals mined, not shown on map

Copper, other metals
Chromium
Gold
Tin
Diamond mining
Alluvial and surface diamonds
Phosphate
Mica
Coal
Iron

Railroads from Katanga to exporting ports
(Note: in the south these connect with railroad network of the Union of South Africa)

The Sudbury district of Canada leads the world in nickel production, with two-thirds of the total. This metal is thus easily available to American industry. New Caledonia in the southwest Pacific mines and exports nickel as well as chrome. Mines in what was northern Finland are now in Soviet territory.

American industry is more fortunate in its home needs of molybdenum, vanadium, and tungsten. More than 80 per cent of the first is mined in the United States, originally at one mine at Climax, Colorado, 11,500 feet above sea level, where only one square mile is underlain by the ores; now other mines have been opened in the West. The western United States, with four-fifths of the world total, and Peru contribute most of the world's vanadium; the Peruvian mines are high in the Andes, above timber line, and at more than 15,000 feet above sea level. China is the chief source of tungsten, the western United States is second, with an eighth of the total. Because the Chinese mines are in Communist China the Free World has had to draw on widely scattered sources.

► NONFERROUS METALS

Lead, zinc, tin, copper, and others of the nonferrous metals are used widely in industry. Of those just listed, tin alone is mined in regions distant from manufacturing regions on the world basis, it being mined mainly in the Malay region near Singapore, in Indonesia, in Bolivia, and in Nigeria in Africa. Singapore is the smelting and exporting center of the Far East. Prior to World War II tin ores from Bolivia were shipped to England for smelting, then the tin was exported to manufacturing centers or used in Britain. A tin smelter was built on the Gulf Coast of Texas during World War II to ensure an American supply from imported ores, and to save on needed shipping from South America to England. Two-fifths of the final use is in tin plate for cans and containers, even though an individual can contains less than 1 per cent of tin, and is really a "steel can."

Copper follows iron ore in tonnage as the most important metal mined in the United States. Butte, Bingham, Bisbee, Globe, Ely, and other western centers are the chief copper-mining centers. Half of the nation's production is from Arizona; Utah, Montana, and Nevada are leading sources. Canada, Andean South America, the Katanga, and many areas of the Soviet Union are other outstanding producers. The copper mined in the West and in other localities in the world is obtained from ores which must be smelted. Bingham's production is entirely from a huge open pit. Even underground mining centers of long standing, like Butte, are now stripping such ores as they can, to save on production costs.

The principal copper-mining regions in the eastern half of the United States are those of Ducktown, Tennessee and the Keweenaw Range of the Upper Peninsula of Michigan. The smelting at Ducktown yields iron pyrites in the slag,

Fig. 18-11. Copper mining in the Katanga mining region of Africa. This mine, concentrating plant, and village occupied by the native workers is just across the boundary of the Congo area and is located in Northern Rhodesia. (British Information Services)

and this district is the chief producer of the pyrites in the country. Pyrites are used widely in the chemical industry. Some of the concentrates of iron are shipped to blast furnaces and refractories in Tennessee and Alabama, and used in the iron and steel industry. The Keweenaw Range, earliest American major producer in point of time, is unique in that native copper rather than ore is obtained. Some of the mines are now among the deepest in the nation. During early days, boulders of native copper, swept southward from the range by the glacier, were gathered in the glacial drift of Wisconsin and sold to users of copper.

The Katanga is an important copper region. Discoveries of even larger deposits about thirty years ago to the south of the original mining area, and across the border between the Congo and Northern Rhodesia, and the opening of mining operations have resulted in Northern Rhodesia assuming third to fourth position in production. British and Belgian capital is invested there.

Copper's chief industrial use is in the electrical industry. Roughly a quarter of the world output is used in generators, switchboards, motors, apparatus of all kinds, and nearly an eighth is used in transmission of electricity. The telephone, radio, and television manufacturing industry consumes considerable quantities. It is also a major alloying metal, used in the manufacture of brass and bronze.

Lead and zinc are mined widely in North America and Europe. The United States leads in the output of each, with Missouri leading in lead mining, Tennessee in zinc. The island of Sardinia in Italy leads among European zinc-mining areas; the rest of the zinc ores and the lead ores are mined widely, nearly every country having some production. The Soviet Union and Australia are leading producers, also. Zinc is used in many alloys, is galvanized with steel into wire nettings and fencings and for use in bolts, nuts, pipes, screws, and many other manufactured products. Lead has many uses, among them solder, type metal, and uses in gasolines and in the chemical industries.

Movement to Market

Many of the metal-mining districts are distant from regional markets, but not so far removed as tin ores are. The mining districts of the American West

Fig. 18-12. Copper smelter at La Oroya, Peru. (Standard Oil Company, N.J.)

and of the Laurentian Shield of Canada, dependent upon land (rail) transportation thus first concentrate or reduce their ore in bulk to save on shipping costs. Copper ores, for example, are first concentrated to remove as much of the worthless rock material as possible, then are smelted. These operations localize these types of manufacturing at or near the mine. The material which emerges as the end product of the smelting operation is then shipped to market regions for refining. In other words, (1) the ore is reduced in bulk at or near the mine; (2) the smelting is near the mine if there is a source of power, or, in any case, is accomplished at some point on the way to the final market, but closer to the mine than to the market; (3) the reduced bulk of purer material is shipped to the market region; and is (4) finally refined at the market. Copper ore from Bingham, Utah, is transported to Magna and Arthur for the first processes, then moved to Garfield for smelting, then shipped to the market regions for final refining. This takes place principally in the Baltimore region and in New Jersey. Zinc ore from Mascot and Jefferson City, Tennessee, is concentrated mechanically (not chemically, as in smelting) near the mines, then is shipped to Columbus, Ohio, and Franklin Furnace, New Jersey, for the final processes. The factories using the refined metals thus receive these raw materials of their operations from nearby locations.

Metal-mining districts near navigable waterways, or the oceans, with cheaper freight rates available, and with ships handling materials in bulk, may ship the entire ore, particularly if it is (1) rich enough to pay the cost of transport, or (2) there is no local source of inexpensive power. As noted, the Lake Superior iron ore is routed in bulk on the Great Lakes; Venezuelan iron ore is shipped to the steel mills of the East Coast; Bolivian tin and some of the tin of Malaya moves in the form of ore; but Singapore itself is also a center of smelting.

Inland mining regions far from world markets reduce their ores in bulk if they have sources of power. The Katanga has some local coal, and access by rail to South African coal. New hydroelectric plants provide electrical power. The ores, depending upon type, can thus be smelted or reduced by certain electrical processes and then moved by rail to exporting ports in Angola on the Atlantic and Mozambique on the Indian Ocean for final shipments to market-oriented refining centers in the United States and Europe. The silver-lead-zinc ores of Broken Hill, Australia, at the edge of the desert, are transported by rail to Port Pirie on the coast for preliminary processing, then by sea to the island state of Tasmania, where there is abundant hydroelectric power, and thence by sea to Australian and European manufacturing regions.

► THE ALUMINUM INDUSTRY

The aluminum industry has risen to its present importance in this century. The metal is light in weight, and aluminum alloys are extremely strong. Uses are many. The airplane industry consumes large amounts in the construction of planes. Lightweight railroad passenger cars, buses, sheathing for buildings, interior trim, foil for wrappings, kitchenware, and other uses are important.

Bauxite, the ore of aluminum, is a soft, earthy material formed very commonly under rainy tropical conditions by the decomposition of clays or of rocks of high aluminum mineral content. The United States industry draws mainly upon bauxite from British Guiana and Surinam (Dutch Guiana) in tropical northern South America, and upon ores mined near Little Rock, Arkansas, and in Georgia. The industry of Europe uses ores from southern Europe—southern France, Italy, and Yugoslavia—ores of different origins. Soviet-mined ores are in the Urals.

The reserves of low-grade ores are large in the rainy tropical world. The clays of the tropics have a high aluminum content, but usually not enough to be considered as ores under present economic conditions and in competition with present ore bodies. Locations of higher than average grade can be worked if located on or very near the seacoast. Jamaica and the coast of West Africa supply some ore, and reserves are large.

Bauxite ore is concentrated near the mines, and the concentrates shipped by sea from the mining districts of the Guianas, by rail from the American mines, and by rail and inland waterways in Europe to alumina plants. These produce the alumina (Al_2O_3), which in turn is shipped to the final aluminum plants, the reduction works that turn out the aluminum sheets, rolls, and similar products. Cryolite, a mineral needed for use in one stage of the process between ore and finished aluminum, is mined only at Evigtok in West Greenland; it is now manufactured, too, artificially for use in the industry. The manufacturers using aluminum as a raw material in their product are commonly at market-oriented locations in the world's manufacturing belts.

The mills producing alumina are at, or very near, the importing ports. Mobile, where much of the American-destined bauxite is landed after the sea journey from the Guianas, has alumina works. Baton Rouge, Louisiana, on the Mississippi, and Arvida, Quebec, near the St. Lawrence in Canada, are other water-oriented centers. Alumina works at East St. Louis, Illinois, handle ore from Arkansas. Lister Hill, Alabama, is another center.

The alumina is transported to the aluminum plants. The manufacture of aluminum is the phase of the industry that "seeks" hydroelectric power in large quantity. Many aluminum plants are right at the sources of this, the industry having developed many of the power sites itself. In this phase of the manufacture, a very large electric charge is needed irregularly; it can be provided at least cost by hydroelectric energy. The turbines can be shut off or started automatically as power needs fluctuate. Thermal power, while it is used at some locations, cannot be adjusted as quickly to the variations in electrical load, for the boilers must be kept operating.

Mention of a few locations of aluminum plants illustrates this seeking of large-waterpower sites. Among these are: Massena, New York, on the St. Lawrence River power project; Longview, Vancouver (Washington), and Trout-dale near the Columbia River powers; Spokane, near the water powers of the Idaho mountains and the Spokane River of Washington; Shawnigan Falls and the powers on the Saguenay River, both in Quebec; and Alcoa, Tennessee. The dams in the Smoky Mountains, above Alcoa, were built before the advent of the Tennessee Valley Authority. This governmental agency took over their opera-tion, placed their output in the electric power pool, and, through arrangements, provides the aluminum plants with an equivalent amount of power—but not necessarily that generated at the so-called "aluminum dams."

Foreign production of aluminum also seeks and is localized at large hydro-electric powers. European plants are concentrated heavily in the French, Swiss, Italian, and Austrian Alps, the Pyrenees Mountains, and at Norwegian and Swedish power sites. Russian plants use power from the Ural streams, and are at Zaporozh'ye near the major water power on the Dnepr. Some Canadian sites have been mentioned. A large new one, involving the diversion of a river by tunneling through a divide, is at Kitimat in British Columbia.

Some new aluminum plants have been built in or near gas fields, and are powered by natural gas generating thermal electricity. In countries without large water powers, or where all water power has long since been developed, this "new" industry is at the ports. Britain is a case for some of this; but the industry has located also at recently harnessed water powers in the Highlands of Scotland, distant (as the North American industry is) from the final manu-factural use of the aluminum.

The manufacture of aluminum sheeting, of consumer goods of aluminum, and of similar items is generally market-oriented. The Pittsburgh region, Los Angeles, and eastern Wisconsin are among important manufacturing centers of aluminum products. The British, French, and West German industrial cen-ters are important final consumers of aluminum.

▶ PRECIOUS METALS

The average yearly production of silver is about seven times that of gold. In part this is because silver is a by-product of silver-lead-zinc ores, and its production continues because of the need of the industrial metals, whereas gold mines can be shut down if there is danger of an oversupply and a drop in price. Silver is mined, also, from ores which yield only silver—the case in many mines of Mexico, the leading world producer, with about a quarter of the total produc-tion. Silver has become increasingly important in industry. It is used in many manufactured goods, in jewelry, in photography, the motion-picture industry, and in the electrical industry; its use as coinage has declined relatively. The

Fig. 18-13. A gold mine in the Orange Free State, Union of South Africa. This gold-mining region is more recent in development than the better-known Rand. (South African Tourist Corporation)

leading silver-mining area is the entire western cordillera of North and South America—the mountain and plateau country of the western United States, Mexico, and the Andes of South America. Potosi, Bolivia, has mined silver commercially since 1545, and the Spanish explorers found silver to be a common metal in use among the Aztecs of Mexico and Incas of Peru; it had been mined for local use for generations. Cerro de Pasco, Peru, and Broken Hill, Australia, are leading centers; and there are numerous important silver districts in Mexico.

Gold was a scarce and valuable metal from antiquity. News of discoveries of the metal in gravels caused gold rushes to California, to Colorado, to Australia, to Alaska. Some prospectors became rich, some found little gold but helped settle the areas to which they went, some returned penniless. The discovery of the Witwatersrand (or Rand) gold field of South Africa in 1884 (opened in 1887) changed the entire world situation in gold. Every prospector in the ensuing gold rush returned empty-handed; instead of "native gold" the gold of the Rand is finely dispersed through an ore body. Its grade is low. It has to be refined. A ton of rock is lifted from 2,000 to 9,000 feet from below ground to be refined, and yields but half an ounce of gold. The modern mines of the Rand have produced half of all the total gold in the world; they produce half of the annual world output. With their development the "silver standard versus gold standard" basis of coinage in the world was settled in favor of gold, and ceased to be a political issue, as it was in the United States in the 1890's.

The Black Hills of South Dakota lead in the gold production of the United States. Canada and Australia are important producers. The Soviet Union, whose total output is unknown, has many gold-mining areas, and placer-gold dredging (as in Alaska), in the mountainous eastern third of Siberia, especially in the Lena River Valley. Angaraland, an old region geologically, like the Laurentian Upland of Canada, is an important metal-mining area of the Union; it includes much of the Lake Baikal area and the Lena Valley.

Platinum, mined in the Sudbury district of Canada, in the Urals, in Alaska, South Africa, Colombia in South America, and at two locations in California, has declined in importance in the manufacture of jewelry, but increased in importance in heavy industry. Its uses now include the metallurgical and engineering industries and use in oil refineries.

► THE MINERAL FERTILIZERS

The principal fertilizer in world use is animal dung; the exception is India, where dung is used as fuel. With the development of commercial agriculture, the depletion of soils, and the scientific knowledge accumulated about the maintenance of the soil, the mineral fertilizers came into use. The present intensive agriculture of northwestern Europe and of large parts of the United States is maintained both through the complete use of the animal wastes and the liberal use of the prepared and manufactured commercial fertilizers.

The three mineral fertilizers are nitrate, phosphate, and potash. Commercial fertilizers with numbers like 10-10-5, or others, upon the containers indicate, in order, the percentage of each of the above. Thus the 10 represents 200 pounds, each, of nitrogen and of phosphoric acid in each ton of the manufactured mixture. There are many other minerals in use in special fertilizers. And lime, crushed limestone, marl, and other materials with a calcium carbonate content are spread upon the land in fields or regions wherein the soil is acid.

The world's natural source of nitrates was (and is) from the Atacama Desert of northern Chile. But Chile attempted to "live" from the exports, and raised money from export duties, increased with regularity. Particularly the use of nitrates in the manufacture of explosives, and World War I, with shortages, resulted in the shift from natural to artificial nitrates in the commercial countries. The processes for making these had been developed during the late nineteenth century. The shift was gradual as technology was improved and costs were lowered. But today nearly all of the nitrates are produced by man. The raw material is the nitrogen contained in the air, or the nitrogen (as sulphate of ammonia first) obtained as a by-product of the manufacture of coke and of coal gas. Large quantities of power, preferably hydroelectric, are needed for the extraction of nitrogen from the air, and for the processes of producing nitrates.

The industry is a very important one in Norway which uses its water power and "free" air. A large source in the United States is from the operation on the Tennessee River at Muscle Shoals, Alabama.

The potash mining of the world centers in Germany (both West and East)

FIG. 18-14. Diamonds are now obtained from several parts of Africa, and the diamond mines of the Union of South Africa supply only part of the African production. Alluvial diamonds are found in river gravels in several African countries. One of the diamond workings is on the beaches at the mouth of the Orange River in South Africa. This operation removes 70 feet of sand and piles it in "dunes" in order to obtain diamonds from the sands and gravels of old beaches. (South African Information Service)

and France, these three having nearly half of the production. A quarter of the world supply is from the United States, at Carlsbad, New Mexico, the major region, and from the salts of Searles Lake, California. Spain and the Soviet Union have mines, and Israel obtains salts from the waters of the Dead Sea. Despite its large home production, the United States is an importer, a fact reflecting the tremendous use, not only in fertilizers, but in the chemical and glassware industries, and in soap manufacture.

Phosphate rock is widely distributed. Deposits in Florida and middle Tennessee, strip-mined by the use of power shovels, provide this country with more than half of the world production. Morocco, Algeria, and Tunisia in North Africa are important producers. Nauru Island (with 5 per cent of the world output), Ocean Island—each in the Pacific—and Christmas Island, south of Java, supply the not inconsiderable needs of Australia and New Zealand, each a lavish user of fertilizers, New Zealand especially. In addition to natural sources, phosphates are extracted from the slags of some blast-furnace districts in the industrial centers.

The manufacture of commercial fertilizers is market-oriented. The southeastern United States, the earliest large user of commercial fertilizer in the country (because of its worn-out soils, cotton culture, and climatic conditions leading to heavy leaching) contains a considerable part of the industry. But with the spread of the use of fertilizer to the better soils of the Corn Belt and elsewhere the industry has dispersed. Savannah, Charleston, Jacksonville, and other southern cities are important centers of the mixing and preparation of fertilizers.

► SUMMARY

Space precludes the discussion of all of the minerals, gemstones, earth materials, and building stones in world use and demand. The general principles heretofore brought out in discussion of individual metals, or in the mineral industries collectively, hold true in practically all aspects of the production and consumption of these natural resources.

The various mineral products—metals, mineral fertilizers, fuels, and the others—are raw materials of modern industry, of modern farming, of transportation equipment, and of a multitude of basic materials in use in the developed portions of the world. The industrial nations have an insatiable appetite for minerals. The representatives of the manufacturing and mining companies search the world for new supplies. Pressure upon certain minerals is great. It will increase, not only in the industrial nations, but in present undeveloped countries as they develop themselves or are aided from the outside. New deposits will be found—are found annually; and yet minerals, an exhaustible resource, are being used, and in some cases are being used up at an alarming rate. Minerals

F<small>IG</small>. 18-15. Man-made "steel islands" in the Gulf of Mexico. These are for the location of the sulphur wells for the extraction of sulphur from the bedrock beneath the waters of the Gulf. Similar installations are in use for the many oil wells obtaining oil from the continental shelf. (*Steelways,* published by American Iron and Steel Institute)

not now in use will undoubtedly have uses developed for which they are suitable. Ore bodies not now considered as economic will come into use. Metals are the materials of the world's machines, machines which do increasing amounts of the world's work in agriculture, in commerce, in transportation, in manufacturing, and in the mining industry itself.

► QUESTIONS

1. What are the classifications of minerals?
2. Why are the metals and the mineral fuels so significant to the world in general and to the present industrial nations in particular?
3. Why is the activity and capacity of the iron and steel industry used as an "industrial barometer" of business and manufacturing?
4. Where are the principal iron and steel districts of the world located?

5. What raw materials and fuels must be assembled for the smelting of iron ores?

6. What are the ingredients for the manufacture of steel?

7. Why do the ferroalloy metals occupy such an important place in the steel industry? What is the situation of the United States and of western Europe with regard to domestic sources and supplies of the ferroalloy metals?

8. Name the source region or regions from which the following steel centers obtain iron ore and coking coal: (a) the steel industry on the shores of Lake Michigan; (b) the steel industry on the shores of Lake Erie; (c) the Pittsburgh–Mahoning Valley steel centers; (d) the Ruhr of West Germany; (e) English steel mills; (f) mills on or near the Atlantic Seaboard of the United States; (g) Magnitogorsk; (h) Kuznetsk; (i) the Donbas.

9. Describe the carriers and routes followed in the transport of iron ore from the Mesabi Range to Pittsburgh.

10. Why, in general, is iron ore shipped to or toward coking coal, or to assembly points that are closer (in distance) to the source of coking coal than to the iron-mining region?

11. What is taconite?

12. Where are the newly opened iron ore districts of eastern Canada located?

13. Comment on the following, bringing in various principles of economic geography: The possible future competition between the iron ores of eastern Canada and the taconite of the Lake Superior District at the steel mills located on the Great Lakes. Indicate the carriers and routes each would be transported on to the docks of the mills.

14. Why has the production and consumption of copper risen so markedly during the last one hundred years?

15. What is the significance of the Katanga to western Europe and the United States? Which of the two would be more affected by the inability to receive ores or concentrates from the Katanga? Why?

16. Why is tin, as well as some of the ferroalloys, stockpiled in the industrial nations?

17. What is the pattern followed by nearly all of the ores of metals (so far as manufacture is concerned) between the mine mouth and the final consumer?

18. Why is aluminum transported relatively long distances from the bauxite ore bodies to the final consumer? What source of power is very important in localizing one stage of the refining process?

19. What are the mineral fertilizers? Why is the manufacture of nitrates now not completely dependent upon a mineral raw material?

20. Why is the pressure upon the mineral resources of the world likely to increase—and at expanding rates?

21. Minerals are an exhaustible resource. What practices of a conservational nature have been established (and are practiced) to assure their continued availability. (Note: Conservation of natural resources does not mean non-use of the resource, but wise use.)

XIX Manufacturing: General Features

The chief manufacturing nations of the world are the United States and Canada, the nations of western Europe, the Soviet Union, and Japan. Within southern Europe the northern portion of Italy belongs, manufacturally, to the scene in western Europe and southern Scandinavia. In addition there are manufacturing cities and regions in other parts of the world, but, except for local districts, the intensity and quantity of industry is not as great as in the major manufacturing nations.

The industrial societies of North America and Europe have developed within the last two centuries. Timing differed from country to country. The Industrial Revolution, beginning in England during the eighteenth century, spread to the northeastern United States early in the nineteenth. Germany and other states of the western part of Europe became industrial nations toward the middle of the past century. Japan's industrialization dates only from the beginning of the twentieth century. The rise of the Soviet Union industrially is a feature of the last forty to fifty years.

Manufacturing, originally dependent upon small water powers or human power, received its spur to development two hundred years ago with the use of coal and the introduction of steam power. Coal became the basis of power in industrialization. The rapid perfection of machines and the inventions and technical changes during the period from the beginnings of the Industrial Revolution to the present have been astounding. The list is too long to detail. In the field of power alone the shifts involving steam engines, internal combustion engines, the gasoline engine, diesel-electric engines, steam, gas, and water turbines, electricity, interconnected power systems, electric motors, the harnessing of energy from the atom, give some indication of the technical advances. And, with inventions and perfections, other natural resources—petroleum, natural gas, large water powers—became of value. In the actual fabrication of manufactured goods, the development of and changes in machines and the changing sources and kinds of raw materials have been equally astounding. The metals became most significant raw materials of manufacture. Coal is now important as a raw material as well as a fuel. The chemical products, dating mainly only from this century, the synthetic materials manufactured by industry, and thousands of other products are among the present manufactured materials which are the result of a two hundred-year sequence of events, inventions, perfections, developments, and trends in industry. And changes and developments will continue.

► THE GROWTH OF MANUFACTURING

Industrial growth has been made possible by many factors. Capital has been accumulated and reinvested in industry. Markets have arisen as population has grown in numbers. The increased industrial output of labor, made possible by the introduction of machines, has resulted in a rising productivity per worker. New industries have absorbed labor and created jobs—for example, the many primary and secondary occupations which are the result of the automobile far exceed the employment in the livery stables and care of horses. Workers have been released by machines, and new industries have absorbed not only these, but also the labor furnished by population increase. The laborer of the industrial countries has received higher wages and has attained a constantly rising standard of living. This, in turn, increases the market for consumer goods—the family automobile and the kitchen and household equipment of the homes of factory workers as well as of the other components of the population are examples. Increasing amounts of leisure time has created demands for recreational equipment; the markets for the factory production of sporting goods, boats, and similar products is many times what it was even a decade ago.

It is impossible to evaluate all factors. They vary, too, from industry to industry. But among other things the growth in capital, the increased productivity of labor, the expanding markets—both in total numbers of people and the higher buying power of the population of the industrial nations—have created and continue to create an economic climate most favorable for the expansion of manufacturing. And urbanization, which has accompanied the development of manufacturing, has resulted in the increase of persons employed in transportation, in the service and professional activities, and in specialized occupations; thus the overall market has expanded, and the local or city market offers a concentrated location for the use or consumption of factory-made goods as well as for the products of the food industry.

Today, in the favorable settings of the industrial countries with their important manufacturing, the recent introduction and use of automatic and electronic controls and equipment opens the possibility of manufactural expansion at an accelerated rate.

▶ SPREAD FROM THE TRADITIONAL CENTERS

The industrial nations of North America, of western and eastern Europe, and Japan have been, with some exceptions, the world leaders and the nations whose inhabitants have been the best off economically. There are differences among the industrial countries. Standards vary; some have relatively inexpensive labor compared to others, some have chosen a state-controlled system of production; but all are high or relatively high compared to the undeveloped portions of the world.

The success of the manufacturing countries in the establishment of a high standard of living for their inhabitants has stimulated "copying," or the desire to copy—and so to industrialize—on the part of the non-industrial countries of the world. But the non-industrial countries, at least before World War II, could be divided into (1) five highly developed nations, engaged in commercial agriculture and marketing their output in world markets, and (2) the "undeveloped" lands. The division continues at present.

The five highly developed countries, distant from the traditional manufacturing centers on either side of the North Atlantic Ocean, are Australia, New Zealand, Argentina, Uruguay, and the Union of South Africa. These countries, with the exception of Uruguay, have witnessed marked industrial expansion during and since World War II. The spread or increase of manufacturing within them was hastened by the war.

Australia and New Zealand, even when they were almost entirely dependent upon agricultural products, reached and maintained standards of living comparable to the United States and western Europe. Australia had some important prewar industries manufacturing both producer and consumer goods; New Zealand's manufactures were mainly the processing of agricultural raw materials and the making of consumer goods for the home market.

The Union of South Africa, with capital accumulated from both agricultural and mineral production, likewise contained prewar industry. It has expanded since the war. Like Australia, it now exports some steel. Unlike Australia and

New Zealand, the labor element in the population—native African—does not enjoy as much of the fruits of their efforts as in the Antipodes, but the standard of living of the European-descended inhabitants is high.

In summary, the above three members of the British Commonwealth now are outlying locations of manufactural importance. Their industries received an impetus during the war, when the traditional industrial nations, except for Switzerland and Sweden, were engaged in the "war effort" and their factories were geared to armaments. The inhabitants of these three outlying nations were able to provide the management, the know-how, the capital, and labor.

Manufacturing in Argentina has followed the same pattern, but more slowly. There was not the wartime incentive to arm at home or to replace imported materials, as in the British dominions. Governmentally the industrial climate was not as favorable during the immediate postwar years. Nevertheless, Argentina is a developed country with important home manufactures.

The industrialization of the second group of countries—the so-called underdeveloped or "undeveloped" lands—is another matter. Capital is lacking, or, if present, it is in insufficient quantity. Technical skill and know-how is lacking. Although large labor pools exist, labor is, in general, unskilled and poorly educated. It is these lands which need (and are getting, in places) both agricultural and technical assistance from the outside.

India is the best off, and contains some industrial districts. An educated and trained managerial group reflects the "early" establishment of education during the period of British control. China is engaged in the attempt to industrialize under the system of rigid state control. Some generally undeveloped lands, such as Brazil, contain highly developed industrial regions of small extent, such as the manufactural districts of São Paulo.

The spread of industry, thus, from the early established and so-called traditional centers has been, to date, mainly to distant but high-standard developed countries. India is intermediate; China is unknown. Forecasts about worldwide spreads to undeveloped lands, or growth of industry in these lands, are subject to so many imponderables and qualifications that they are merely educated guesses. For some time to come these areas will no doubt remain markets for manufactured goods—markets large so far as total population is concerned, but small on a per capita basis or buying-power basis.

► MODERN MANUFACTURING

Modern manufacturing is descended from the Industrial Revolution which began in England in the eighteenth century. But truly "modern" manufacturing, with its large use of many raw materials, of abundant power, and of quantities of labor dates only from the period near the close of the nineteenth century. And "very modern" manufacturing, with assembly-line techniques, standardization of many products and parts, and mass-production methods, is a development of the period since 1910; the mass production of standard automobiles, introduced by Henry Ford in Detroit, is credited as being the fountainhead of this presently continuing phase of manufacturing. The assembly line, the mass production of products, and the "continuous-flow" methods of the fabrication within the manufacturing plant, introduced in the United States and once considered to be "typically American," have spread to other countries, particularly since World War II. Thus the same kind of long, low modern factory buildings, the assembly line, the use of large quantities of power, and the substitution of machines for hand workers is as characteristic today of the new factories of western Europe and of Japan as it is of the United States and Canada.

Land, labor, capital, management, raw materials, power, markets, and transportation are needed for the successful prosecution of manufacturing. In these ingredients manufacturing is no different from commercial agriculture or commercial fishing, but the proportions of the ingredients differ. Land, used extensively in agriculture, is used in far smaller quantity in manufacturing. Power is used in exceptionally large amounts in many industries—witness the situation in the manufacture of aluminum. Capital equipment in the form of buildings and machines requires a large and continuing investment and replacement factor in industry. Management must be highly trained to be effective.

The various ingredients necessary to manufacturing are rarely, if ever, all in the same place, at the same site. The location of certain industries is decided upon commonly by two or three factors—raw materials, power source, and market. Land is rarely a determining factor because a favorable region offers a selection of several suitable sites, on existing transportation lines, or to which highways and railroad spurs can be built. Sources of labor may be important considerations, but within limits the labor force is mobile and can be attracted to a location by exceptional wage offers, if necessary. The more skilled the labor or the more inexpensive the workers—two extremes—the more likely is the labor supply to be a partly determining factor. Capital was originally site-bound, often in the community in which the founder of the enterprise resided. Today, with corporate management in the Western countries and government planning in the Soviet world, capital is collected from wide areas and may be used in places distant from where it was accumulated. Management is mobile. In original industries it was usually local in residence, and is so today in family firms. But in the great majority of present industry the highly trained and educated managerial staff is recruited from all parts of a country, trained in the operations by industry itself, and—in nationwide or worldwide concerns—subject to transfer and promotion from plant to plant. Thus, since the essentials of industry are not all at one site, the location of the factory is oriented toward one, two, or three of them. The plant is staffed by local or recruited labor and management (or labor and management assigned to a plant in the countries of the Soviet bloc), and is able to obtain its capital from wide sources.

Modern manufacturing, like agriculture and other forms of human economic activity, is not spread evenly around the world; it is not evenly distributed within the highly industrialized nations. It is highly regionalized. Manufacturing regions have evolved, and districts within the regions. The factors which have led to the regionalization of manufacturing within the industrial nations are numerous. In some cases the plants were established under the conditions of the past. Other factories making the same product were attracted to or founded in the same region. A regional name for quality was attained. Or the conditions proved so advantageous that competing firms were drawn to it. Thus there are cotton-textile manufacturing regions, steel-producing regions, and many others of noted specialization. Certain cities have become highly specialized in the manufacture of a product—thus there are rubber centers, steel cities, ones noted for automobile manufacture and assembly, furniture-manufacturing centers, clothing centers. Individuals of marked managerial ability, who founded successful industries in the past, have had much to do with the attraction and continuance of a special industry in a city; thus, within the United States, there are cities with a high degree of specialization in a product—Detroit, Akron, Muncie, and Rochester, New York, are examples in the United States. Other cities are noted for the diversification of their manufactured products. No single type of industry dominates, and diversification is as characteristic of these cities as specialization is of others. Philadelphia is noted especially for its diversification of industry.

Certain concentrations of a given type of manufacture are raw-material oriented. Industry in the Pacific Northwest, in northern Sweden, in the upper Great Lakes region is associated with wood from the nearby forests as a raw material. Agricultural raw materials are outstanding elsewhere. Large cities offer a favorable location for the manufacture of goods sold directly to consumers.

The present and recent past has witnessed the planning of industrial locations. Experts engage in the field. Large companies maintain staffs of persons to study future expansion. If a manufacturing plant—say, a branch plant—is being located today, scientific studies by these experts precede the choosing of the site, and many factors are weighed and balanced against one another—not only the raw material, power, and market situations, but such man-made factors as tax rates, freight rates, costs of power, rentals, accessibility and cost of industrial water, community attitudes, school and recreational facilities for employees and their families, and many others. At the other extreme, states, cities, countries, chambers of commerce, railroad companies, and other agencies assemble figures and describe the industrial assets of their localities and service areas in the attempt to attract new industry. And governmental units often offer concessions or subventions to obtain industrial plants. These may include temporary exemption from taxation, special utility rates, the rent-free use of existing build-ings, even the construction of a small factory building, and other inducements.

► LOCATION BY ASSOCIATION WITH CERTAIN FACTORS

A brief résumé of industrial location associated with one of the ingredients of industry will be given. It must be remembered, however, that while one in-gredient may be dominant, the market and other factors are of importance as well. Also, in preceding chapters, several manufacturing industries have been discussed in association with a raw material; among these are the iron and steel industry, the manufacture of electrical goods, vegetable oils, aluminum, and other industries.

(1) The number and kinds of raw materials are very great. Raw materials may be of direct origin from the earth (sand, ores, coal); a natural resource growing from the soil and in a climatic setting (hardwoods, softwoods, tropical woods); an agricultural product produced by man; an already partially manu-factured product; or they may be of other origins. The basic raw materials of manufacture come from the earth; man is still earth-bound. The partially manu-factured products have been fabricated from original raw materials.

The mineral, agricultural, forest, animal, and fish materials are direct raw materials. The partially manufactured products become raw materials for further manufacture; they may be thought of, for this purpose, as secondary. To illus-trate: iron ore is the raw material from which pig iron is produced. This is the finished product for many purposes. But pig iron is one of the raw materials from which steel is made. The finished product of the steel mill is steel in various forms, shapes, and sizes. A manufacturer of machine tools purchases steel; this is his raw material. Other illustrations might be given: cotton to yarn, yarn to cloth, cloth to clothing; bauxite to alumina to aluminum, aluminum to the manufacture of airframes; or wheat to flour, flour in turn to the bakery.

The processes just illustrated add value from step to step. Pig iron has a value greater than iron ore; value is added when pig iron is made into steel; the machine-tool manufacturer adds greatly to the value of the material by producing a lathe or some other machine. *Value added by manufacture* is re-corded in industrial and other censuses (such as the U.S. Census). Obviously there are duplications as a material moves from simple to complex uses. Some industries add relatively low values to their raw material; others add substantial values. The cost of a watch is barely related to the intrinsic value of the gold or steel in it; the skilled labor, precision workmanship, and time expended upon its manufacture result in a high value added by manufacture. Thus watches, in-struments, lenses, and many similar items have a high value added to the original raw material; cast iron, cotton cloth, twine, and other similar products have only moderate values added through the manufactural process.

The location of a factory oriented to raw materials may be (1) near or at the direct source of the natural resource, or (2) near or at the location of the partially manufactured material; the choosing of a site depends, consequently, upon the product of the factory. A paper and pulp mill is near the forests which supply it with wood, but a sawmill is directly at the source of its supply. The large users of steel tend to cluster near the steel mills. Slaughterhouses and meat-packing plants are within the regions wherein the rearing of animals is an outstanding agricultural enterprise. The factories using by-products of the packing plants (hides, skins, hair, blood, horns and hoofs, fleshings for gelatin) cluster near the sources of these, their raw materials; many such are in an outer ring surrounding the slaughtering and meat-packing industry of the Chicago stockyards district. The factories using perishable raw materials—fruit, milk, vegetables—are in the source regions of these; canneries, creameries, vegetable-freezing establishments are widely dispersed, and in the specialized farming regions; citrus-juice extracting plants are in the villages and towns of the citrus-growing districts.

(2) The quantity and cost of power localizes the industries which are exceptional users of power. Niagara Falls is the locale of many major metallurgical plants. The dispersion of aluminum manufacture at large powers has been noted. The two uranium-reduction works founded by the Atomic Energy Commission during World War II were placed at Hanford, Washington, near the power pools along the Columbia River (Grand Coulee, Bonneville, and other dams) and at Oak Ridge, Tennessee, in the heart of the upper area of the Tennessee Valley Authority. Today, with interconnected electric power systems, the factory is freed from certain restricted sites. When atomic power is a peacetime reality the factory can be freed from consideration of the power factor by having its own reactor.

(3) Labor may or may not be a localizing factor. The situation varies with different industries. Users of highly skilled labor are held to these pools of workers; such workers are home owners, tied to communities, proud of their traditions and skills, and rarely mobile. Diamond-cutting centers in Amsterdam, Antwerp, and Rotterdam have existed for generations; only when German occupation resulted in the fleeing of some of the workers did a diamond-cutting industry of some size originate in New York and in Israel, in part through the migration of the skilled cutters to these areas. The American jewelry industry has long been related or tied to skilled workers in the jewelry centers of southeastern Massachusetts and Rhode Island. Unskilled labor is usually not a determining factor, but large numbers of semi-skilled and inexpensive workers may be. Puerto Rico offers an example. Following its attainance of commonwealth status, and its passage of tax laws which were especially favorable to industry, American companies built branch factories on the densely peopled island. Raw materials of all sorts are now shipped to Puerto Rico, fabricated there, and returned duty-free to the United States. Products range from textiles to radio

tubes and electronic equipment. These materials and products are light in weight and high in value, a concession to transport costs. More than 1,000 factories have been established on the island since the early 1950's.

Certain industries add only a low value in the manufactural process. These seek large supplies of semi-skilled workers, or regions of dense population and little manufacturing, where workers can be trained. By the very nature of the activity and value of the product the worker operating machines in a cotton mill cannot be as productive *per hour* or *per day* as the builder of, say, machine tools. The cotton-textile industry has moved and continues to move to supplies of inexpensive labor as a result. In the United States, New England contained nearly all of the cotton-textile industry before 1890. Between 1900 and 1930 the mills shifted their locale to the southern Piedmont in southern Virginia, North and South Carolina, Georgia, and eastern Alabama. Since the 1930's the South has had nearly 90 per cent of the industry. The shifts continue. Many mills within the South have moved from the cities to the less expensive labor of small towns and villages. Others have shifted westward into previously non-industrial Mississippi, and into small towns in Texas. Japan, with its inexpensive labor, has taken over much of the percentage of the cotton industry held at one time by Europe. Theoretically the cotton-textile industry should "end up" in the tropics; such will probably not be the actual case. Nevertheless some of the first factories in the tropical countries today are new cotton mills.

(4) Capital, as noted, is generally mobile today. A large capital investment in buildings, equipment, machines, docks, sidings, and land—as in a steel mill—may, however, tie the industry to the site even if economic conditions change and the original favorable location becomes marginal. The industry continues; costs, management, and other savings are effected or are improved. If, however, the situation becomes submarginal the capital investment may be abandoned and the particular industry liquidated or moved. In many industries the capital investment is such that a new site may be chosen without severe loss; machines and other equipment can be moved. Buildings are abandoned or sold to other manufacturers.

(5) The market-oriented industries are legion. Mention has been made of several in preceding chapters. The food-manufacturing industry of New York City is generally oriented to the market furnished by the 20,000,000 people in the metropolitan area. Shoes, clothing, and many other consumer goods are market-oriented in many countries. In the United States a company reaching a national market may do so from its original location, from the establishment of regional branch factories, or—after weighing all factors, from materials to taxes and freight rates—it may build a new plant at the most favorable overall location. In the early 1960's this has been the western Ohio-Indiana region. To take advantage of being near this central location, and yet be located in a major city and labor market, one of the largest of home appliance manufacturers for the national market, after extensive surveys, built its plant just outside of Louis-

ville, Kentucky, across the Ohio River from the western Ohio-Indiana area.

(6) Transportation is absolutely essential to industry, both for the receipt of raw materials and the shipment of the finished product.

Ocean transport is the cheapest of all forms among the major carriers. Those industries working with imported raw materials are mainly in the port cities. Every major port city of western Europe is an important manufacturing center. Japanese industry is almost entirely at the sea—in part, of course, because of the narrowness of the islands. Japan is an importer of raw materials; it fabricates them and exports much of the finished product. Raw cotton from the United States is made into cloth and clothing in Japanese factories, and the cloth is shipped in many cases back to the cities of the American cotton region, where it competes favorably with home-manufactured materials. Japan is able to do this, despite the length of transport and the expense of duties, because of the costs or differentials in costs of labor. The recently built steel mills in the eastern United States, as on the Delaware at Morrisville, Pennsylvania, have been so placed to receive Venezuelan and African ore at their docks.

A variety of forms of transportation is advantageous to manufacturing. The factory at the seacoast can choose among ocean or coastwise shipping, rail, and truck. The cities of the Great Lakes offer water, rail, and truck transport. Cities on navigable rivers, such as the Ohio, Rhine, and others, offer transport by barge, rail, or truck. In an inland manufacturing center, such as Indianapolis, the factory has access to railroad or truck transport. Factories in small towns not on railroads have no choice of transport and no competition of rates among types of carriers, but are bound to the truck.

There are types of transfer mediums other than those in usual use by industry. The pipeline is the most important after the seaways, waterways, and landways listed in the above paragraph. The pipeline, as noted in previous chapters, is outstanding in certain manufactural industries—refineries, for example —both for the receipt of raw materials and for the shipment of the manufactured product. Belts, cables, and aerial conveyors are in use here and there. The airplane is important for goods of high value per unit of weight, for which speed is an essential factor in delivery. Airplanes can be and are used for transport of heavy, low-value goods in emergencies, or for delivery of manufactured products to inaccessbile places—for example, mine equipment to a mine being opened in northern Canada; the advantage of the air route is the low capital cost of the development of the route. Once the mine is in operation, however, its ore is shipped by newly built railways or highways.

(7) Management is an extremely important part of industry. The success of individual factories is often tied up with the quality, vision, and decisions of management; failure of even the best located plant may be attributable to poor management. And management is responsible for the evaluation of the many man-made rules, laws, and regulations—rates, costs, tax differentials, and others—which figure in the industrial scene.

► FAVORABLE AND PERMISSIVE REGIONS

The distribution of industry within the manufacturing nations of the world —to be discussed in the next chapters—is in part the result of its long-time historical growth, in part related to man-made or modified factors, and in part owing to recent planning and establishment at the most advantageous locations. In other words, some present industrial districts are related to the past, but continue at present; some are of modern origin.

Industrial or potential industrial districts may be divided into (1) favorable, (2) permissive, and (3) unfavorable. The conditions have to be evaluated for each individual industry; a region presently favorable to the manufacture of cotton textiles may be unfavorable for a heavy industry such as iron and steel.

A favorable region is one wherein, all factors considered, the industry is well located. In the planning and establishment of branch factories the favorable areas of the time are sought. Maximum returns to industry are theoretically possible in the favorable area; assuming good management there is an excellent chance of their realization.

A permissive region is one whose location permits reasonable return, even though all factors are not necessarily the best. In fact, a permissive region of today is usually an inheritance from past industrialization. During the past growth the region offered favorable conditions. Changed sources of raw materials, power, changes in the labor pattern, changes in freight rates, the competition of new producers located in favorable areas, and many other factors have resulted in the first region being forced into a permissive situation. An organization planning new branch factories will weigh all factors seriously before moving into a permissive region, and may not even consider it.

An unfavorable region offers little or no advantage to industrial development. Its population may be too small to merit establishment of a branch factory for consumer goods. Its raw material, transport, and other ingredients may be unsatisfactory. If such a region contains existing extractive industries, such as mines, the ore is reduced in bulk for shipment elsewhere for final processing.

There are many illustrations. One or two will suffice. Suppose one of the early developers of the automobile had happened to live in a small village in the dry-land area of Nevada instead of in the Toledo-Detroit-Lansing area. His opportunities for obtaining local backing or capital at home *at that time* would have been negligible. Either his inventions would have gone unnoticed, or he would have had to move to attract capital and start manufacture. Patent offices are full of grants which have not materialized. The early developers of the automobile (so far as the United States is concerned) happened to be residents of a region which, *at that time,* was favorable. The demise of the lumber industry in Michigan was releasing capital seeking investment. Many other factors, too, helped contribute to the rise of Detroit. Whether the automobile centers of Michigan *today* are favorable or permissive is beside the point; in other words, *if* the industry were to be relocated, would it center where it now does? The fact is debatable, but the rapid founding of assembly plants in many parts of the United States helps point up the question. Another example is California, a magnet for industrialization today. Conditions in population and in other ways, fifty to sixty years ago, did not attract or develop much manufacturing; the market was served from the East and Middle West. Today the situation on the West Coast is quite the reverse. Conditions have changed. Change is a characteristic of the commercial and industrial world. Some regions are left behind, relatively, with the changes; others profit by them. Within the United States, extensive as it is in area, the changes are within the framework of the national boundary. Within the smaller-area countries of western Europe the changes are within smaller districts, or are from one country to another so far as a given industry is concerned.

A great many industries and industrial regions lie, today, in regions which are permissive. Industries are rooted to the region in which they were founded and grew. They persist in their original location. Their name, tied to the city or region, may have a value of association. They enjoy the advantage of an early start and a good name built up through the years. Although their location may have become even marginal, the various attributes of good will, expert management, cost cuts in production, and perhaps adjustments in other ways, permits continuance. If, however, the location becomes submarginal and competitors have a disproportionate advantage as a result of better locations and newer buildings and layouts, the location may become untenable. Despite all the efforts of management, the business declines in the competitive situation. If concessions are granted—say, a voluntary reduction of wages by employees, who would otherwise lose their jobs—the factory may be able to continue operations for a while; such was the case when New England was losing the bulk of its cotton-textile industry. Measures of this sort are usually only temporary stopgaps. Other measures may "save" the industry for a while, such as an increase in efficiency, but competitors in better locations can do likewise and restore the differential. The factory may be faced with either relocation or liquidation. The empty factory building results. In turn, however, this building may become, with renovation, a magnet for another type of industry, suited to the area. The buildings of one of the largest cotton mills in New England were occupied, within a few years' time, by several dozen light industries. When a region loses a particular industry, it may find itself, following a period of adjustment, with as much manufacturing as previously, but manufacturing of a different nature, using different raw materials and reaching a totally different market.

An industry relocates in various manners. The whole operation may be moved to another city or region and relocate in a newer, more modern building. In this case the workers are offered the opportunity to change their residence. Or a new, more favorable region competitively, develops. The relocating industry enters this region; management and superintendents move, but new workers are recruited. This is the case if the move is to a region of inexpensive workers. Few of the textile workers of New England moved to the South during this thirty-year shift. Thirdly, and most commonly, the "shift or relocation of an industry" does not involve movement at all; new producers in the developing region capture the production and markets, and, during a period of time obtain the dominant position—the industry has developed, literally, in a new and favorable region rather than undergoing a shift from one area to another.

A location may change from favorable to permissive and back to favorable through a period of time and the reorientation of raw materials and markets. The original steel manufacture in the United States was near the anthracite coal of Pennsylvania and Appalachian ore (excluding the colonial bog ore period). Many mills were at tidewater. The shifts to Pittsburgh and the shores of the Great Lakes followed. Early in this century a new eastern mill was built at tidewater near Baltimore to use imported ore. Recently built plants are at tidewater, as imported ore becomes more significant owing to the depletion of the high-grade Lake Superior District ores. Now, with the deepened Great Lakes–St. Lawrence Seaway the mills on the lakes also have access, at least seasonally, to ore imported by water routes.

Many industries in a country find their major competition for the home market from an overseas manufacturer or manufacturing region. The industry asks for tariff or other protection, which may or may not be granted. The increase of efficiency may enable competition to continue; but the foreign efficiency of operation today (and plant machinery and labor) is usually just as efficient. The home manufacturing industry, as a result, will be hard pressed. This has occurred many times; manufacturers have gone out of business. The American pottery industry has suffered economic consequences recently as a result of competition from Japan. In other cases, instead of closing, the home manufacturer may start operations in the competing country, partaking of the advantage —cost of labor, or whatever it may be. American automobile companies, for example, maintain foreign plants, not only to build cars for the foreign markets, but in some cases for shipment back to the United States.

The large nationwide, or even worldwide, corporation, so characteristic of certain types of industry in the Western world, faces the same problems which have been outlined. But the problems can be met in a different way. If, for example, a concern with twenty manufacturing units scattered throughout the United States finds two or three in a submarginal situation, they may be combined with other producing units—ones in better locations. A site is abandoned or sold, true—but the economic consequences to the industry are not as severe as if each unit were a separately owned plant, operated by an individual producer. This is not to say that there are no economic dislocations; these are severe for the community in which the plant was located, and for the workers who are not transferred.

Management of the nationwide company in the United States must decide, too, on the number of its manufacturing plants. Are all regional markets to be served by a regional plant? Is the market to be reached from a single center? Obviously the problems differ from industry to industry and are very different as between the producer-goods industries (machines for manufacturers, say) and the consumer-goods industries. For the latter, to date at least, it is generally agreed that: (1) the original plant is in the Eastern or Middle Western manufacturing region, from which a large share of the market is reached; (2) the first branch manufacturing unit is placed on the Pacific slope to serve the western market; through the sheer weight of numbers of people this has meant, recently, the general region of Southern California; and (3) the third manufacturing unit to be placed in the South. The South is generally "delayed" till after a Pacific Coast plant is built because it can be reached more easily and cheaply from the Northeastern Manufacturing Belt than can the Coast.

► SUMMARY

Finally, in summary, a few trends are evident. (1) The large size of the United States, and the differential growths of population from region to region, makes for widespread manufacturing, and the tendency for industry to follow the consumer; marked shifts, relatively, have occurred toward the southwest (Texas Gulf Coast) and the Far West. New England, the original industrial region, contains as much industry as it ever had, but has declined relatively. (2) Soviet manufacturing, under a completely different economic system, likewise shows regional dispersal as a trend of the present. (3) The countries of western Europe, small in area, cannot have the dispersal enjoyed by the larger nations; a "shift" of 300 miles carries across most international boundaries. (4) There has been local development of manufacturing, hastened by World War II, in the highly developed nations far removed from the traditional industrial areas on either side of the North Atlantic Ocean. (5) Japan has reassumed its importance as an industrial nation since the war. And (6) the undeveloped countries all hope to industrialize. If and when this is accomplished the effects on the present industrial regions of the world will be enormous, and can, at present, only be surmised.

There are marked trends in the specific location of new factories in all countries. The trend began before World War II, was continued by the founding of plants during the war, and has been accelerated since the war. Factories are becoming suburban rather than urban.

The suburban location has been the result of the automobile, and indirectly the result of the congestion of the central city. But there are other considerations, too. The need for a large land area is more pressing than in the past. Factories are now long and low buildings. The need for space for the parking of automobiles of workers adds to the needs for a large land area. Needs, subject to lower taxes, exist only beyond the built-up city. The automobile and paved highways have made the land accessible. The superhighway, the highway belt line around a city, the high-speed toll road, and other factors are involved, some so recent that their impact is not fully understood. Some bypass roads, to speed traffic around a city, have now become congested twice a day by factory employees en route to plants located near the highway exits.

Manufacturing is ever-changing within regional, national, and world frameworks. The basic patterns remain, but are being modified in the present world by dispersal—dispersal of manufacturing within the overall industrial countries, and dispersal of plant location from central city to suburban sites.

► QUESTIONS

1. What is the pattern of distribution of the major manufacturing regions of the world? Where are some of the outlying and smaller centers of industry?
2. What are some of the handicaps within the non-manufactural countries that make it difficult to establish important industries?
3. List the chief ingredients for the establishment and prosecution of manufacturing. Discuss one or two of these in some detail.
4. Cite examples of present industries that are oriented (in more than usual degree) toward one or two of the ingredients necessary for manufacture.
5. Why do very large cities tend to develop considerable manufacturing which is related to the existence of the city market itself?
6. Bakeries, machine shops, and printing are types of industry that are said to be ubiquitous and present in almost all towns or cities. Why is this the case?
7. What are the chief industries of your home region? Can you suggest reasons for their existence in the town, city, or region?
8. Many, many countries and regions are interested in the development of manufacturing at present. China and India are developing factories; formerly nonindustrial portions of Europe and the United States are developing industry. In fact, various Chambers of Commerce, boards, and commissions in several states are engaged in seeking factories. What are the effects of this in the existing manufactural regions? Will the advent of nuclear power plant aid this trend? Read the advertisements for "new industry" in the nationally circulated magazines. What inducements are offered?

XX The Chief Manufacturing Regions:

The United States and Canada

The chief manufacturing regions of the world are the entire regions of western Europe and the broad manufactural region of the eastern half of the United States and adjacent southeastern Canada. Eastward from western Europe important manufacturing is carried on in the extensive lands of the Soviet Union, particularly the western—or Russian—portion of the country. Westward from the core region of North American manufacturing, industry is a significant feature of the Pacific Coast area of the United States and southwestern Canada.

The important manufacturing *countries* of the world are the several nations of western Europe, Italy in southern Europe, the United States and Canada in North America, the Soviet Union, and Japan. There is significant manufacturing in many other countries of the developed world, but these outlying industrial centers are smaller in area and less intensive in overall production than the major centers.

The four principal manufacturing countries are the United States, the Soviet Union, the United Kingdom, and West Germany. The order of their significance differs from industry to industry. The first two named are large in area and contain many manufacturing regions within their boundaries. The other two are small to medium in size, and are much more intensively developed in manufacturing per unit of area. Other individual countries of western

Europe—France or Belgium, for example—are very important in manufacturing and rank among the major manufacturing nations of the world.

Western Europe and the northeastern United States constitute the so-called traditional regions of manufacturing. Industry has been a feature of the United Kingdom and nearby parts of the continent of Europe for two hundred years. Manufacturing of importance has been in the scene of New England and of southeastern Pennsylvania for 150 years. From these traditional regions, manufacturing has spread to other countries of Europe and other parts of the United States, or has developed separately in these other areas—but often with capital and experience gained, in the traditional areas, by the founders.

Japan, the Soviet Union, Italy, the western and southeastern United States are among the newer manufacturing areas. Within them manufacturing of major importance has been a feature only of the last fifty to sixty years. In fact, although Russia under the czars contained industrial centers, the rapid industrialization of the Soviet Union has occurred only since the late 1920's and early 1930's.

There are four major *regions*, in summary, of manufacturing. (1) Western Europe, collectively, is the most important, and contains several nations. (2) The northeastern quarter of the United States is the core of the American Manufactural Belt, and contains roughly two-thirds of this country's manufacturing. (3) The manufacturing region of the Soviet Union and (4) Japan constitute the two others. The four principal industrial *nations* consist of two very large ones—the United States and the Soviet Union—and two which are small in area, but which are very highly industrialized by any measure used—the United Kingdom and West Germany.

► MEASUREMENT OF MANUFACTURING

Manufacturing in the world's industrial regions or countries is based upon the various ingredients of industry discussed in the preceding chapter. The intensity or amount of any one differs from region to region, or industry to industry. Great Britain, for example, imports very large quantities of raw materials, applies home fuel and power (coal), home labor and capital, processes the raw materials, and exports large quantities of the manufactured products to overseas markets. Other manufacturing regions are concerned chiefly with the use of local or regional raw materials. Certain regions expend large quantities of labor in the manufacturing process, others utilize tremendous amounts of locally developed power. And, within any manufacturing region the various industries differ in their relative use of the ingredients.

The complexity of the industrial scene in the chief manufacturing regions of the world makes the relative intensity of manufacturing from district to district within the region difficult to measure and to compare. It is not like a world measurement of tons of coal, kilowatts of electricity, acres of wheat, bushels of potatoes. True, the manufacturing regions can be compared by (1) total numbers of persons engaged in manufacturing and (2) the production workers actually in the factories, excluding in this case the managerial and office staffs. But the output per worker differs from industry to industry in the same region. Manufacturing can be compared by (3) the value added by manufacturing, another basis. Here the difficulty of obtaining comparable world figures is encountered not only because of many differing statistical bases used from country to country, but also because of the differing (and fluctuating) values of the currency; hence it is virtually impossible to develop a standard unit of measurement. However, within one country the value added is expressed in a uniform manner. Two of the significant items about manufacturing recorded in the United States Census, national statistical abstracts, and other records are the two labor items and the value added by manufacture.

Economic geographers, economists, industrial engineers, and others have worked out various formulas to help measure relative intensity of manufacturing. Some use one item only—workers, value added, fixed capital, all salaries and wages, and others. Some use two or more items, develop a formula (certain ones simple, others complex) and assign relative weights to the results—certain figures express high intensity, others medium or low. Industrial cities, metropolitan districts (which include suburban factories), and manufacturing regions are compared in this way—particularly within one country to date because of the difficulty of obtaining a standard world unit. Other formulas attempt to eliminate the ubiquitous industries—those found everywhere, such as bakeries, printing establishments, machine shops—and thus measure only the "surplus manufacturing," the goods which enter a regional or national or world market. There are other categories of measurement attempts—ratios between two or more units in the same area, and ratios between the same unit in different areas.

The difficulties of measuring manufacturing intensity from region to region are apparent from the preceding paragraphs. But no completely satisfactory method, acceptable to all—even within one country—has been developed. The difficulties are many. An industry employing a large number of workers may add low values; it rates "intense" on the worker basis. An oil refinery or chemical plant, adding large value to the raw material, may be operated by as few as 200 workers, owing to its automatic operation. The textile industries rate "high" when measured by labor employed, the refining centers "low." The reverse is the case when measured by value added. Thus it is virtually impossible to compare the "intensity" of the industrial scene in the textile region of the southeastern United States with the scene in the refining and chemical districts of the Texas Gulf Coast. Even the manufactural landscape differs; in the one region hundreds of small manufacturing towns focus around the many textile mills, each a building of moderate size; in the other region large and complex buildings and refineries, many of them open to the weather, mount skyward and, with their adjacent storage tanks, cover extensive areas. Even the period prior to operation—the construction period—differed. Relatively few construction workers are or were required to build the textile mills; once built and in operation the industry employs more people than were required to erect the building. Many construction workers are employed to erect the modern, complex refineries and chemical plants; once built and in operation, fewer people are employed than were in the construction stage.

In summary, the difficulties encountered in measuring manufactural intensity within the United States, a nation with excellent statistics to work with, become complex in the attempt to measure world industrial intensity. Therefore, in the succeeding sections on the world's manufactural regions only the most general of comparisons can be made on the *regional basis;* accurate comparisons of the total production of goods can, however, be made among the industrial *countries.*

Finally, as in all economic activities of man, the manufactural scene is ever shifting, both within the traditional regions and to new areas. New power supplies, labor factors, the growth of regional markets, new sources of raw materials, political and governmental situations, taxes, and other items may be governing factors, singly or in combination. The growth and dispersal of population—the market factor—has been one of the strongest recently. Thus manufacturing is dispersing from its traditional regions. Its movement has been southward and westward in the United States, eastward in Europe. This does not mean that the traditional regions of manufacture have lost importance. In fact, on the *absolute base* they are more important now than in the past; manufacturing is more extensive within them, and output of manufactured goods is greater. But the traditional regions have *declined relatively* as a result of the more widespread dispersal of manufacturing. England and New England were two of the world's greatest manufacturing centers a hundred years ago; they accounted for a considerable percentage of the world's manufactured products. Today their production is far in excess of that of a hundred years ago. But this output of today constitutes a far lower percentage of the world's present manufactures.

► MANUFACTURING IN THE UNITED STATES

There are about 300,000 separate manufacturing establishments, or factories, in the United States. These employ more than 17 million persons, about 13 million of whom are production workers in the plants. The value added by manufacture is about 150,000 million dollars based on the currency value of the early 1960's. More than twenty categories of manufacturing are recognized for statistical purposes. The largest number of manufacturing plants are those engaged in the food industry. Other categories of industry in which there are more than 20,000 separate factories are the clothing and apparel industry, lumber and wood products, printing and publishing, metal products, and the manufacture of machinery, except electrical machinery. The three categories in which the number of establishments is fewest are petroleum refining, rubber manufacture, and tobacco manufacture, industries characterized by very large plants.

The states including the six of New England, the Middle Atlantic states, and the five which lie between the Appalachians and the Mississippi River–Great Lakes (Ohio, Indiana, Illinois, Michigan, and Wisconsin) contain nearly 60 per cent of the total number of factories, slightly more than this per cent of the workers in plants, and not quite two-thirds of the national total in value added by manufacture. This northeastern quarter of the nation is the heart or core region of American manufacturing.

► THE AMERICAN MANUFACTURAL BELT

The Manufactural Belt of the northeastern portion of the United States stretches westward from the great port cities on the Atlantic to the approximate location of the Mississippi River. Manufacturing, unlike agriculture or forestry,

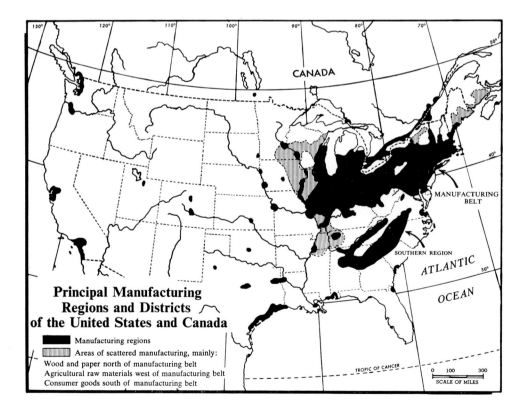

FIG. 20-1. A portion of the industrial area in New Jersey, across the Hudson River from New York City. Note the numerous stacks of power plants and factories toward the skyline in the distance. The elevated road (Pulaski Skyway) crosses industrial districts and, at the left, rises above the New Jersey meadows, tidal marshes, and the rivers within them. The meadows, nearly all of which are within a dozen miles of the center of Manhattan Island, provide present and potential sites for heavy industry; first, however, artificial fills are necessary. This is proceeding piece by piece. The lower Hackensack and Passaic Rivers provide water transportation from the sea to factory sites; note that the bridge on the lower road (to the left of the gas tank) is equipped with machinery for its being opened to permit the passage of ocean ships. The meadows are one of the only large areas of present and potential industrial land this close in location to a major city of the United States. Beyond them, to the west, are numerous New Jersey residential suburbs of New York City. (Standard Oil Company, N.J.)

is not continuously developed over extensive areas; it is localized at the favorable locations within a broad region. Thus there is no continuous industrial landscape for hundreds of miles, as there may be an agricultural landscape. The eastern portion of the American belt, in addition to industry, is characterized by farms and forests in the interstices between nodes of manufacturing. The western portion of the belt, in addition to its many industrial towns and cities, is one of the most productive agricultural portions of the nation.

There is no sharp line of demarcation between the eastern and the western portions of the American Manufactural Belt. In a general way the highlands of the Appalachians separate them. Industry east of the highlands is oriented toward the cities on the Atlantic for its regional markets, but includes also many industries oriented toward the nationwide market. Industry westward of the highlands is heavily localized—in site—toward or on the Great Lakes, or on the navigable Ohio River. But there are industrial centers within the Appalachians themselves, though more widely spaced than on either side; and three major centers—Pittsburgh, Buffalo, and Erie—though in so-called Eastern states, lie west of the "divide" and are "Middle Western" in many of their industrial aspects and types of industry. And the western portion of the belt is the locale of many of the factories which serve and look to a national market.

The simplest outline of the Manufacturing Belt, one delineated fifty or more years ago, is that of a quadrangle. The four corners of this are Portland, Maine on the northeast; Milwaukee, Wisconsin on the northwest; St. Louis, Missouri on the southwest, and Baltimore, Maryland on the southeast. Three sides are thus "straight," the eastern side follows the irregularities of the Atlantic coast. Actually, the "corner" demarcations are principal cities, from each of which manufacturing is important outward to neighboring districts.

There are many refined and detailed classifications of the Manufactural Belt. Their general outer boundaries coincide in broad aspect with the simplified concept of the Quadrangle. And, regionally rather than by states, some cities not in the aforementioned census-grouping of states lie in the belt; among these are Baltimore, and the cities on the south bank of the Ohio, some in West Virginia, some in Kentucky, such as Louisville.

The principal subregions or districts of the manufactural region each possess a regional personality; they differ from one another. The differences reflect different source regions of raw materials, differences in the type and time of manufactural development, power and labor situations, the traditions of early location combined with industrial inertia and the persistence of rooted industries. These districts collectively constitute the highly varied manufacturing region of the northeastern quarter of the United States.

The New England Manufacturing Region

The people of New England have had experience with manufacturing for 170 or more years—longer than that if the ubiquitous spinning wheel and home-grown wool of the seventeenth and eighteenth centuries are included.

The New England region, and especially Boston, was the earliest North American center for the accumulation of capital. Ships of the Boston merchants sailed the seas of the world. Goods transported and traded, services rendered, and home-manufactured trinkets sold abroad helped enrich the merchants. Investments in home industries helped found an economy based upon manufacturing. Some of the early-founded industries still persist; the important processing and manufacture of cocoa and chocolate in the Boston area dates from the days of colonial trade. The manufacture of high-quality cotton goods, still an activity, persists from the days of an important coastwise trade between New England and the South, when bales of cotton were received from southern ports; but the bulk of the cotton-textile industry has been lost.

The Industrial Revolution, transported to the New World, reached New England earliest. The abundance of small, easily harnessed water powers provided the mechanical energy (water wheels, belts, pulleys) to power the small mills and factories. Capital was invested in new enterprises; for example, Lowell, Massachusetts, on the Merrimack at a "large" power site for the time, was the first deliberately founded factory town in America, established by Boston capitalists. Labor to man the factories was abundant. It was recruited from the large families of New England farms. The difficulties encountered by New England agriculture, in its competition with the newly settled lands of the West (upstate New York and Ohio at the time), resulted in large-scale abandonment of the hilly, upland farms. History emphasizes the westward movement of New England farmers to new lands. Of almost equal importance was the farm-to-factory or mill town movement of other rural inhabitants to the growing manufacturing towns.

New England became the "traditional" center of manufacturing in the United States. Not until the middle of the last century did immigrants from Europe begin flocking to its factory towns to sell their labor in the well-established and important industries of the region.

Manufacturing in New England, except for the forested regions of the north (especially Maine) has always depended upon the import of raw materials from elsewhere in the United States or from overseas. The home water-power resources have long since been outgrown; even a hundred years ago coal was received by ship from the ports on the Delaware, and steam-powered cotton mills were built at the seacoast—Fall River, Pawtucket, Providence, New Bedford, and other points. Today the receipt of coal by rail and ship, the thermal power plant, and interconnected electrical transmission lines supply the bulk of the power for manufacturing. The industries of New England, thus, on the whole apply large quantities of skilled or semi-skilled labor to generally high-value raw materials, and produce surplus high-value goods for markets only part of which are within the region. The setting of New England has changed radically in relation to the market. As the traditional center of manufacturing it tapped the national market of the time. With the westward expansion of population in the nation the location deteriorated; New York, Philadelphia, Pittsburgh, and later Chicago became more centrally placed. New England manufacturers met the changing times, and continue to meet it, by continuing shifts to higher value materials and goods, able to pay their way in freight and distribution charges. With the almost complete demise of the cotton-textile industry (but not woolens) the region, speaking generally, now depends upon metals as raw materials. The sources of the metals are the iron and steel districts, metal-refining areas, and partial processors of metal goods, nearly all of which are located outside of New England.

The manufacturing region of New England includes all of the industrial portions of the six states except for southwestern Connecticut. This part is oriented toward New York, and is now experiencing industrial overflow from that metropolitan center. The New England manufacturing is oriented toward Boston in regard to capital, or is related to the national scene. Vermont is the least important in manufacturing, the most important relatively in the regional agriculture.

Massachusetts is the leading manufacturing state of New England. Within it are nearly half of the factories and production workers; the Boston metropolitan district alone has more production workers than any of the other states except Connecticut, and two-fifths of those of the state.

Regionally, there are several districts or nodes of manufactural intensity. These center (1) around the regional centers of Boston, Providence, and Worcester; (2) in the Connecticut River Valley from southern Vermont, southward through Holyoke, Springfield, and Hartford to New Haven; (3) in many smaller river valleys—the Merrimack (Manchester, Lowell, Lawrence); the Naugatuck, and (4) along the shores of Long Island Sound in Connecticut. Outlying manufacturing towns are scattered from southwestern Maine (Portland, Auburn, and others) to western Massachusetts (Pittsfield). The stream-orientation, more prominent overall in New England than in other American regions, reflects both the early start and the use of many separate water powers. If the industries were founded today they might be at one large power, a single dam taking the place of the many of the past; such is the case in the wood-products and paper-mill plants of northern Maine.

Boston, like any large manufacturing center, contains a wide diversity of industry. But the metropolitan region is noted for its leather goods and its woolens and worsteds. The port of Boston is one of the principal ones in the nation for the import of hides, skins, and wool. The city is a leading market center for domestic wool from the western United States. It ranks high in world wool markets. Shoe manufacture is located in Boston, in the towns to its north and south, and continues into southwestern Maine. The centers in the country for the manufacture of shoe machinery are in the metropolitan district. Woolens and worsteds are manufactured in the region; Lawrence, on the Merrimack, is a noted woolen center. Boston factories use other domestic and imported raw materials, such as cacao beans, vegetable oils, and rubber. The rubber-manufacturing industry, dominantly concerned with footware in New England, extends beyond the Boston area to industrial centers in the Connecticut and Naugatuck Valleys.

New England contains many specialized manufactures based on metals and gem stones. In most cases these reflect an early start, the development and continuance of a pool of skilled labor, and the pride of tradition and quality-market acceptance. North Attleboro and Providence are jewelry centers. Silverware and silver industries center in Meriden and nearby cities in Connecticut. Copperware near Boston dates from the days of Paul Revere. Bridgeport and the Naugatuck Valley are brass-manufacturing locations. Subsidiary industries cluster around their markets; for example, the ear-wire industry of Rhode Island is associated with its market—the jewelry and earring manufacturers. The few remaining American companies making clocks and watches are still in their New England location.

The use of metals is important in New England. Manufactured items are many; a large number are grouped under the term "hardware industry," a noted one in western Connecticut. Firearms factories are in Springfield, New Haven, and other cities. Worcester is a machine-tool center. Ball-bearings, metal parts and products, rifles, pistols, armaments, and other goods of metal are prominent; New Haven advertises that more than 200 kinds of metal products flow from its factories. Shipbuilding is a leading industry at Quincy in the Boston area.

New industries have been established. The manufacture of helicopters is centered at Stratford, Connecticut. Airplane engines and parts are fabricated in many recently founded modern plants. The manufacture of submarines—an assembly industry—at New London uses many of the regionally manufactured products, made from distant raw materials.

The Metropolitan Manufacturing Region

The Metropolitan Manufacturing Region fronts the Atlantic seacoast from New York to Baltimore. It includes the port and manufacturing cities of New York, Philadelphia, Wilmington, and Baltimore, and extends inland to include (1) northeastern New Jersey, tributary to New York; (2) the Delaware Valley in New Jersey and Pennsylvania, oriented to Philadelphia; and (3) the plains of southeastern Pennsylvania, in which there are numerous separate manufacturing cities of importance. A northeast-southwest axis from southwestern Connecticut, through New York and Philadelphia, to Baltimore and Washington is so urbanized today that a "Megalopolis," or very large, continuous city can be recognized; it lies along the line of the Pennsylvania Railroad between New York and Washington, parallels the lower Delaware for a stretch, and crosses from the head of Delaware Bay to the head of Chesapeake Bay. Only one or two "open gaps" of non-urban land remain—one between Newark, Delaware, and Baltimore, the other a short stretch near Princeton, New Jersey. The axis is the core of this manufacturing region; it does not reach the sea in southern New Jersey, but lies along the navigable Delaware River. Within the megalopolis are many cities of size, separate from the major cities politically; among these are Newark, New Jersey; Jersey City; Trenton; Camden; and others.

Washington, D.C. may or may not be included in the manufacturing region. It is part of the megalopolis. But as a capital city, zoned against heavy industry, there is relatively little manufacturing except of consumer goods for direct consumption (bakeries, breweries, and some light durable goods). Much of the manufacturing which might be expected in a market the size of Washington is located in Baltimore, forty miles northeast. Furthermore, economically, industry is not attracted to this market, even if permitted; the competition with the federal government for labor is too severe, both as to wage rates and security and fringe costs.

The Metropolitan Manufacturing Region contains every type of industry, from the most skilled-worker activities to the heaviest of industries—cement, iron and steel, smelting of ores, refining of petroleum, and others. Within the overall region two important types of goods reflect the geographical location— the manufacture of consumer goods within this most-concentrated large-market region of the nation, and the manufactures based upon sea-borne raw materials, whether ores or industrial crops from overseas or petroleum and other raw materials delivered by the ships operating in coastwise trade. Even some of the coal used for thermal energy is received by ship from ports such as Newport News and Norfolk.

The principal port cities are major commercial centers as well as manufacturing centers. Much of the activity of New York City, for example, is associated with commerce, but the sheer weight of numbers of inhabitants (market) and the raw materials delivered by the ocean portion of the commerce provide a milieu favorable to industry. Thus the New York Metropolitan District (New York–northeastern New Jersey) is first in the nation in manufacturing, both in workers employed, and in value added by manufacture. Each port city, however, differs in the relative emphasis of given industries, despite their general similarity. New York City is the outstanding clothing-manufacturing center (particularly women's clothing) of the nation, has an important food-processing industry, manufactures cosmetics and perfumes, and is an important printing and publishing center. Philadelphia contains these same industries on a lesser extent; is, like Boston, a leather and wool center; and, in addition, is one of the most highly diversified manufacturing cities of the nation. Wilmington is a chemical center, and the headquarters of a major national company in the chemical, synthetic fiber, and related fields. Baltimore, with iron and steel, airplane manufacture, sugar refining, and food processing, contains also a vast array of factories engaged in varied industries.

New York City is dominantly a commercial city. Its rise to eminence, following the opening of the Erie Canal in 1825 through the water-level route of the Mohawk Valley to the Great Lakes, was owing largely to commerce. New York became the inlet and outlet for the productive interior. Its commodious harbor became the North American focal point of the sea route to Europe. But, with the development of the city to a major position on the East Coast, there arose the conditions favorable to manufacturing (Boston and Philadelphia were the major cities, and centers of capital of early America). Among the continuing factors favoring manufacture the following have been of great significance. (1) The concentration of population provides a large local market; during some years as much as half of the cities manufactured goods have been sold within the New York metropolitan area. (2) A large, and—in the past—cheap labor supply was furnished by the continuing wave of immigrants from Europe, nearly all of whom entered the United States at Ellis Island in the harbor, and large numbers of whom remained in the city. Today the majority of workers in the needle trades and some other industries are descendants of the immigrants; many are first generation; and Puerto Ricans and migrants from the American South now provide a continuing source of supply. With national minimum-wage laws, and the abolition of home piece work (sweat shops) in the clothing and home furnishing industries, the factor of inexpensive labor is no longer operative. (3) The prestige value of New York is significant in many products—products affected by fashion, style changes, art objects, cosmetics, and others. These goods, originally imported through New York by the wealthy, had, at one time, prestige value from Europe; New York manufacturers supplanted the European manufacturers as the nation grew. (4) The fact that New York was the chief port brought seaborne commerce to the city. Hence these raw materials were processed or manufactured at the port—coffee roasting, manufacture of soaps, varnishes, drying oils, paints; and, later, minerals and petroleum, smelted or refined not in the city proper but on cheaper and more extensive sites on the New Jersey shore of New York harbor.

Today the extensive manufacturing region of New York–northeastern New Jersey occupies more than the 22 square miles of Manhattan Island, or the 314 square miles within the five boroughs which constitute New York City. In fact, much of the manufacturing is in New Jersey, and the heavy industry associated with the port is mainly on the New Jersey rather than the New York side. The Manhattan portion of the port is dominantly passenger traffic rather than commodity flow. Nevertheless, the manufacturing of the city proper is very high in labor employed—reflecting the large number of operatives in the garment industry—and is very high in value added by manufacture, reflecting the clothing, printing and publishing, and the luxury-goods manufacture. New York leads in both measures.

The overall metropolitan region (southwestern counties of Connecticut, lower Hudson Valley, northeastern New Jersey, and the western half of Long Island) illustrates several principles of industrial location, despite its fragmentation by rivers, channels, the upper and lower bay, Raritan and Newark bays, peninsulas, and islands. Manhattan Island, the core of the region, is dominantly commercial and residential, but contains much manufacturing of the type that can use space vertically. The garment industry, fur manufacture, lace manufacture, and similar activities occupy "loft" buildings in concentrated clusters, buildings which are tall in themselves, but dwarfed by the skyscrapers. The printing and publishing industry, some divisions of food processing, pattern-making, and such can accommodate themselves to this type of space. No modern assembly-type industry, such as an aircraft plant, automobile plant, iron and steel mill, or aluminum plant could afford the land values and taxes of Manhattan Island. In fact, some such existing plants in the United States, *if* on Manhattan Island, would occupy *one-seventh* of the entire land area.

The factories processing imported raw materials are at or very near the docks of the port. The freight portion is the Brooklyn waterfront, Staten Island, and much of the New Jersey side, some of it across the Hudson, some as far removed as Newark Bay and Raritan Bay, this last twenty airline miles from the southern tip of Manhattan Island. Some few of these plants remain in their original location on Manhattan, coffee roasters, for example. Many, originally on the island, have moved owing to economic pressure.

Manufacturing plants needing large areas of land, but working with imported raw materials or bulky goods received by coastwise trade, are located on distant portions of the harbor, where land is less expensive. The Staten Island shores, Raritan and Newark bays localize these plants. Thus there are petroleum refineries, metal smelters, and other heavy industries, as well as automobile assembly plants, shipbuilding yards at localities in New Jersey such as Perth Amboy, Elizabeth, Harrison, Kearny, and other centers. Some few, dating from an earlier day, are on the Brooklyn waterfront.

Recently built factories using domestic raw materials received by rail are mainly in New Jersey, accessible easily from southwest, west, and northwest. Factories in Brooklyn, such as its extensive food-processing plants, can receive only part of their material by direct rail shipment. To reach a Long Island location (except from the north or northeast via bridges) railroad freight cars are loaded on car-floats (barges propelled by tugs) at the terminal piers on the New Jersey side of the Hudson, and moved south of the tip of Manhattan Island to a Brooklyn pier. This increases freight costs and consumes time. To-day it provides New Jersey with an advantage when new sites are under consideration.

At present an outer "new" ring of industrial expansion is developing. Many of the new plants are based on light manufacture, on "air and space," and on accessibility to their employees by automobile. Some are in Connecticut, some in New Jersey as distant as Morristown and Princeton. Some have been located on Long Island, east of the presently urbanized area. Certain ones are new industries such as the assembly of airplanes and automobiles, the manufacture of airplane engines, the electronics industry; some are branch plants of national industries centered elsewhere; and some are relocated factories—moved from New York City itself in response to many factors. In any case, all reflect the trend mentioned in the preceding chapter—the suburbanization of manufacturing.

The garment and clothing industry illustrates the type of manufacturing held to New York by the exigencies of style change. There is definite advantage to each manufacturer in being together, not only in the same district but even many in the same loft building, although each is a competitor of every other one. A "new style" created by one can be copied within a matter of a day—even hours—when it is placed on the market. If a plant continues with some style which has "gone out-of-date" for even a working week, it may find itself in serious economic difficulty. Before the days of rapid communication and television the out-of-date goods could be marketed in distant localities; today this is virtually an impossibility. Because the style changes affect women's clothing principally, it is this division of the garment industry which is held to New York. Although other clothing is manufactured, the men's clothing industry, children's wear, knit goods, house dresses, and other divisions are widely scattered in the principal cities of the American Manufactural Quadrangle. But women's clothing, shoes, accessories, hats, furs, are held to a central and prestige manufacturing district. Another factor leading to continuance of the concentrated center is the marketing pattern; buyers come to the manufacturing location, in contrast to the usual pattern of the salesman visiting the retailer. There is advantage to both buyer and seller in this; the buyer can compare goods, materials, and styles, and the seller has lower marketing costs. New York newspapers carry daily lists of buyer registrations, and buyers are from all parts of the country. The New York clothing industry is not without competition. As noted, it is severe in the men's clothing field. Hollywood (part of Los Angeles) developed a women's clothing industry, based originally upon the prestige of the name, the ability to "show" (advertise) the manufactured results in the movie industry, and on a specialization in outdoor and casual wear. Recently Dallas has followed suit, and now has a significant manufacture of women's clothing and accessories.

The food-processing industry of New York was originally market-oriented entirely. It has become "surplus" in packaged products. Thus flour from Minneapolis, Kansas City, or Buffalo may be shipped to a Brooklyn factory manufacturing standard crackers. The packaged crackers not destined for the metropolitan market then are shipped to distant markets, necessitating a haul "back" through the congested district, or by car-float to a New Jersey pier, and then loaded for shipment by rail or truck. Today many of these plants are owned by national organizations in the food industry. The result is a tendency to disperse the manufacture, and locate a new plant nearer the eventual market. Some of the recently constructed food-processing factories, serving both the metropolitan and the "surplus" market, have been located in New Jersey or in southwestern Connecticut in the outer ring of manufacturing.

The manufacturing in the Delaware Valley is remarkably diversified. Philadelphia itself is principally a producer of consumer goods. The manufacture of capital goods is located on the river both upstream and downstream, chiefly the latter. A sixty-mile stretch of the Delaware from the mouth of the river to the head of navigation at Trenton is important in shipping, is lined with industry, and constitutes one of the leading port regions of the world. Open spaces are still available. The new steel mill at Morrisville, Pennsylvania, nearly opposite Trenton, is near the head of navigation and roughly halfway by land between the Philadelphia and New York markets.

Philadelphia and Camden, across the river, manufacture the entire array of household goods and appliances, radios, and television sets, and have a knit goods and clothing industry, a leading woolen manufacture, and food industry. Camden is the packing and canning center for the vegetables grown in the truck-farming districts of southern New Jersey. Philadelphia has a wide variety of factories, many of modest size. Wool and leather products are notable.

The steel mills, wire and cable plants, oil refineries, smelters, machine manufactures, chemical plants, and shipyards are on the Delaware; some, not in the "heart" of the urbanized centers, are in political Philadelphia, however, because the city and the county are coextensive. Others are in separate cities (boroughs in Pennsylvania) such as Chester, or on the New Jersey banks. The products of these plants are marketed over wide areas. New York is the destination of many of them—the Delaware region having an advantage over the New York region in its accessibility to steel, cement, and other heavy, bulky materials; it is closer to the iron and steel centers of southeastern Pennslyvania, and the factories are also at or very near the steel mills on the Delaware River which use imported Venezuelan iron ore.

The Baltimore waterfront localizes the heavy industry of the city, and the factories dependent upon imported raw materials—steel mills, sugar refineries, plants using copper, fertilizer factories. The port of Baltimore is third in the nation in tonnage of imports, and much of the material is processed or manufactured at or near the harbor. Other plants, scattered throughout the city, produce diversified products, mainly consumer goods. There is an important clothing industry. New, assembly-type factories, such as the airplane industry, have suburban or fringe locations.

The manufacturing cities not at or near the ports of the Metropolitan Region—but inland—are principally in southeastern Pennsylvania. These include the steel centers such as Bethlehem, Coatesville, Harrisburg (Steelton), and others; the cities specializing in knit goods, of which Reading is the outstanding center; diversified manufacturing cities such as Lancaster with its meat-packing plants and cork, linoleum, and floor-covering manufactures; York, important in consumer goods and in the manufacture of refrigeration and air-conditioning equipment; and smaller cities with leading food industries.

Southeastern Pennsylvania experienced an early start in manufacturing. Some of the colonial Germans (Pennsylvania Dutch) were artisans in the Palatinate before their migration. The manufacture of paper was introduced by these people. The region contained local Appalachian ores; an iron industry was developed. With the introduction of nearby anthracite coal (about 1800) and accessible local iron ores and limestone, the blast furnaces were enlarged, and eventually a steel industry resulted and still persists. German skilled workers founded home industries and small factories, some the antecedents of present industries. Today the region depends upon metals, steel, yarns, and some imported raw materials (cork, ores) for the basis of its manufacturing economy, and contains a supply of labor which is highly skilled, thrifty, and takes pride in its work.

Mohawk Valley and Appalachian Manufacturing

The Hudson-Mohawk Valley provides the historic water-level route from the Atlantic at New York to the Great Lakes. The Hudson-Champlain Valley provides a similar route, New York to Montreal. Of the two, the Hudson-Mohawk is the more important because traffic in this part of the United States is oriented east-west.

Manufacturing centers dot the Mohawk like beads on a string. This district of American manufacturing is explained by transportation. There are few local raw materials; the forest products north of the valley, in the Adirondack Mountains, furnished some wood in the early days. Only Syracuse, with its underlying salt beds, had a local material suitable for the development of an industrial center.

The water-level route from New York extends up the Hudson for approximately 150 miles to the Mohawk junction. Here and there on the Hudson there are small manufacturing centers. Clustered near the Mohawk-Hudson junction are Albany, Schenectady, Troy, and Cohoes.

The Mohawk Valley proper extends from Rome to the mouth of the river at the Hudson. Rome, Utica, Little Falls, and Amsterdam, and some smaller cities, lie in the valley. Johnstown and Gloversville (each glove centers) are in the broader, eastern part of the valley, but not on the historic Erie Canal route, or the present main-line railroad, or the New York State Barge Canal (replacement of the Erie).

The water-level route emerges upon the Lake Ontario Plain west of Rome. Syracuse is at the eastern end of the plain, toward the "funneling" of the plain into the constricted valley. Rochester, at the falls of the Genesee, has grown northward ten miles, since its inception, to Lake Ontario. Buffalo, at the eastern tip of Lake Erie, is where the land and lake routes meet.

Early industries of the Mohawk routeway (using the term in its broader sense) were based upon the raw materials of agriculture, and their processing and transport on the Erie Canal to the Hudson and New York for export. Cheese, manufactured in the valley, was moved eastward; at the time Herkimer County led in this manufacture, Little Falls was the marketing center. It still retains industry manufacturing cheesemaking equipment, and rennet. The rich Genesee country of the Lake Ontario Plain led the nation in wheat until the prairies were settled; Rochester was the flour-milling center of the country, utilizing the falls for power.

The development of the present industries can be traced to the transportation advantages between East and Middle West—as the latter became settled. Albany is a transshipment point, and has light and varied industry; Troy is a clothing center, specializing in various articles of men's attire—and during the days of detachable collars was the collar-manufacturing center of the nation; Schenectady is the home city of one of the largest of the electrical-goods manufacturing firms of the country, and also a machinery and locomotive center. The three nearby cities, taken as a unit, thus contain a balanced economy.

The manufacture of very diverse articles characterizes the Mohawk Valley cities. Tanneries, leather goods, food products, office equipment, knit goods, carpets and rugs, chains and cables are specialties in various ones.

The industries of Syracuse are diverse and range from chemicals through light durable goods to postwar-founded electrical and electronics manufacture. The salt industry, the original one, dominated until after the Civil War; at one time Syracuse supplied nearly all of the salt used in the United States. Rochester, through the invention made by Eastman—and financed by local capital—has become the photographic, camera, film, and optical center it is noted as today. Precision instruments, optical materials, lenses, meteorological and aviation instruments, manufactured in Rochester, are products too of cities in southern New York, Corning and Binghamton. Cameras and photographic equipment are made in Binghamton. The rise of the optical industry in Rochester and elsewhere was helped immeasurably by the invention of the movie camera, the demands for film, and the shift of the home-camera market from a luxury one to an ubiquitous one. As might be expected from the type of industry in Rochester, the value added figure is high in porportion to the number of workers.

Manufacturing in the Appalachian highlands is in scattered locations. The manufacture of business machines and electronic computers is outstanding in Binghamton. The anthracite towns, Scranton, Wilkes-Barre, and others had parastic manufacturing, particularly silk; today the mines are not operating at capacity and the silk manufacture has suffered from the inroads made by rayon and other synthetic fibers. Rayon-fiber plants dot many sections from Pennsylvania southward, using local wood as a raw material. There are pulp and paper plants in the highlands and surrounding the Adirondack Mountains in northern New York. Iron and steel communities—as Johnstown, Pennsylvania—are located in some of the valleys. The Kanawha Valley of West Virginia is one of the leading chemical centers of the nation, plants lining the river for many miles. But, in general, the Appalachians furnish fuels and raw materials to the manufacturing cities eastward in the Metropolitan Manufacturing Region or westward to the industries of Pittsburgh and the Great Lakes shorelines. And the railroads crossing the highlands, unlike the lines in the water-route depression of the Mohawk, do not run through successions of manufacturing towns.

Pittsburgh–Mahoning Valley–Lake Erie Iron and Steel Region

The western portions of Pennsylvania, in the valley of the Ohio River and its tributaries, and adjacent northeastern Ohio is the most concentrated district of the iron and steel industry in the United States. Pennsylvania (the whole state) and Ohio produce 40 per cent of all the pig iron manufactured in the nation, and their furnaces yield somewhat more than half of the total production of the special ferroalloy steels. The Monongahela Valley, the upper Ohio downstream into West Virginia and Ohio, the Shenango Valley in western Pennsylvania, the Mahoning Valley in northeastern Ohio, and the southern shore of Lake Erie constitute the intensive segments of the region. Eastward, on the Conemaugh in the Appalachians, is Johnstown. West of the Mahoning Valley several cities on the plain of northeastern Ohio are steel manufacturing centers. The Pittsburgh district and its nearby satellite cities and the cities of Youngstown and Cleveland are the principal large cities.

The economic geography of the steel industry has been discussed elsewhere (see pages 395–411) and will not be repeated here.

The steel region is characterized by hundreds of factories whose raw material is iron, steel, or the ferroalloys. These manufacture a vast array of both capital and consumer goods. The foundries, machine-tool plants, manufacturers of structural materials, heating and plumbing equipment, wire and cables, the metal stamping and coating plants, and many divisions of the machinery industry cluster near their raw materials.

Other industries are present, also. Pittsburgh is the headquarters of one of the large aluminum companies. Some of the final fabrication of aluminum into capital and consumer goods is accomplished at factories whose sites are comparable to those of the steel mills, but in towns on the Allegheny. A major electrical industry is located in the Pittsburgh area. And, queer as it may seem to some, the city is the headquarters of one of the major food preserving and canning and pickling companies of the nation, and contains its home plant; local residence of the founder explains this; all of the specialized branch plants are elsewhere in agricultural areas.

Western Pennsylvania and eastern Ohio—in this case southeastern rather than northeastern—is the American center of the ceramics industry. Factories producing clay products characterize nearly every town of size. The manufacture of drain tile, small-diameter tile-pipe, flower pots, roofing tile, sanitary pottery for bathrooms, and other clay products draws upon local pottery clays. Tableware for the low-priced market is manufactured, but, in general, not the high-grade tableware. This phase of the American pottery industry is in Cincinnati and a few other locations, and meets strong competition in the domestic market from the imported English, French, and other European tableware. Since the recovery of Japan from the effects of the war, the Pennsylvania-Ohio tableware portion of the industry has met strong competition from the Orient;

plants in the United States have closed, unable to compete with the wage differential. The heavy, low-value products, such as tiles and drain pipe, have not been affected; they take too much space to be shipped long distances cheaply. East Liverpool, Ohio and nearby cities are in the heart of the pottery "region," but it extends far beyond them. Both Ohio State University and the Pennsylvania State University recognize the importance of this regional industry with teaching, experimental, and research work in departments of ceramics.

The Great Lakes Manufactural Region

The manufacturing regions of the western portion of the manufactural belt are in the Ohio Valley, the Great Lakes shorelands, and in an inland location between the two above-mentioned waterways. Their location by states is thus Ohio, Indiana, Illinois, Michigan, and Wisconsin—the census-defined East North Central states. Extensions of these middle-western industrial regions continue into Kentucky (Louisville, Lexington) and the St. Louis Metropolitan district in Missouri.

It is these regions that have received the largest impact of expenditures for new plant and equipment since World War II. This has been added to the already large prewar manufactural base, which has accounted for half of the manufactures of the whole manufactural quadrangle of the United States. The large expenditures for new plants reflect the favorable geographic location (as well as other factors) for industry in the East North Central states; from a location in this group, a manufacturer can reach the largest potential market in the nation—East, South, West or Far West. Within these states the total expenditures for new factories and additions, and for new machinery and equipment, were 33 per cent and 31 per cent of the national expenditures in 1954 and 1957, respectively. The magnet attracting a considerable part of the expenditures was the shorelands of the Great Lakes; rail, truck, air, Great Lakes ships, and ocean ships provide a variety and a choice of transportation, as well as competitive rates. And, for those industries requiring large quantities of water in their operations, only the Ohio River or one of the lakes can meet the requirement.

The manfacturing cities of the Great Lakes are on Lake Michigan, Lake Erie, or the St. Clair and Detroit rivers, connecting Lakes Huron and Erie. Only near the head of Saginaw Bay are there two industrial centers on Lake Huron, which is mainly a "transit route" for ships. If Canada is included in the regional setting the core area, or main line of its manufacturing, lies on the shores of Lake Ontario. Lake Superior, as noted elsewhere (wheat, iron ore), is very important in shipping. Duluth-Superior is one of the chief ports in tonnage of the United States, but it and other ports on the lake are chiefly shipping points for raw materials forwarded to the manufacturing cities of the lower lakes.

The manufacturing centers on Lake Erie are at both eastern and western "ends" of the lake, and on the southern or United States shore. The Canadian shore is, in contrast, dominantly rural. Buffalo is at the eastern tip of the lake. Although in New York State, its manufacturers are of the "Middle Western" or Great Lakes type, with heavy emphasis on flour milling and the iron and steel industry, based upon ore from the Lake Superior region. Niagara Falls to the northwest of Buffalo is a metallurgical center; electric power is shipped to wide areas. From east to west on the south shore, important cities are Erie in Pennsylvania, and, in Ohio, the cities of Conneaut, Ashtabula, Cleveland, Lorain, Sandusky, and Toledo. Cleveland dominates in size and in manufactures. Its steel, machine tool, and electrical industries are among the largest in the country. Toledo occupies a strategic location at the southwest corner of the lake. Besides being the leading coal port, the city is one of the leaders in the manufacture of glass. It is also a manufacturer of motor vehicles. Manufacturing centers on the west shore are in Michigan, south of Detroit. Monroe is the largest center. Lake commerce is important at all ports, outstandingly so at Buffalo, Cleveland, and Toledo. Every city has interests in iron and steel products, and Buffalo, Cleveland, Lorain, and Monroe have steel mills.

Detroit and Port Huron are on the natural waterways connecting Lakes Huron and Erie. The growth of Detroit has been associated largely with the accidental establishment of the automobile industry there. This has attracted an iron and steel industry to the city. Port facilities, originally on the city waterfront where ships were berthed against the shore, have been added to and improved by dredging the lower courses of small rivers tributary to the Detroit, notably the River Rouge.

Saginaw and Bay City, originally lumber ports, are the industrial cities on Lake Huron.

The head (southern end) of Lake Michigan is surrounded by one of the leading manufacturing regions of the United States, the Chicago–northwestern Indiana metropolitan region, second only to New York–northeastern New Jersey in all employees in manufacturing, in production workers in the factories, and in value added by manufacture. Gary, the steel center, is at the very head of the lake. Westward and in the crescent northwest (following the curving lake shore) is the complex of heavy industries comparable to part of the New Jersey shore in the New York region. These include several large petroleum refineries, steel mills, cement mills, manufacturers of heavy goods fabricated from steel, chemical plants, soap factories, and others. Giant thermal power plants are at the lake shore. The complex is in several contiguous cities in Indiana—East Chicago, Whiting, Hammond—and extends into the southern part of the city of Chicago—the south Chicago (not a separate city) steel district, the heavy industries on the Calumet River (the Calumet Industrial District), and the industries of the Pullman area (the original Pullman railroad-car center). Vegetable-oil mills, corn-products refining, soybean mills, flour mills, malting plants, and other very large establishments diversify the scene somewhat. All are large

Fig. 20-2. One of the heavy industrial districts near Chicago stretches southeastward along the shore of Lake Michigan, from the southern part of the city well into Indiana. Oil refineries, steel mills, cement mills, and other space-using plants characterize this area. This view shows the very southern rim of Lake Michigan and the steel mills at Gary, Indiana. This site, until 1905, was occupied by blowing sand dunes and by scrub-oak covered old sand dunes separated by marshy swales, through which the Calumet River flowed. A steel company purchased the land and laid out an industrial city, which has now grown far beyond the original site. The steel mills lie between the lake and the Calumet River (to the right). The railroads (lower right) are main lines between Chicago and major cities to its east, including New York and Boston. The residential area of Gary is farther inland (to the right). Iron ore and limestone are unloaded from lake freighters at the docks of the mill. The docks are on the slip (a dredged channel), the entrance to which is protected by a breakwater built out into the lake. Coal and coke are received by rail. This steel mill is one of the largest in the nation. Note that additional industrial land has been obtained by filling in the beach and the near-shore areas. In the distance the wide beaches and the active sand dunes (white areas) are visible; currently this land is "in dispute" between organizations wishing to expand lakeshore industrial areas and organizations wishing to preserve the beach-and-dune areas for recreational use. (United States Steel Corporation and Chicago Aerial Industries, Inc.)

users of land. Toward the western margin of this industrial complex the city has established the overseas port, concentrating it on Lake Calumet, reached from Lake Michigan by the Calumet River. New factories, using imported raw materials, are rising in the vicinity.

Manufacturing of both light and heavy nature is widespread throughout the rest of Chicago. It is localized chiefly along the railroad lines. There is no impediment to the construction of these, and no paucity of flat land for the plants themselves; the city lies on an almost featureless plain, most of its surface less than twenty feet above the level of Lake Michigan.

A manufactural ring surrounds Chicago. New automobile factories, diesel-locomotive manufacturing plants, processors of agricultural products, and electronics plants are important.

The meat-packing industry and the centers of the manufacture of agricultural machinery and implements, two notable industries in Chicago, and the main plants of national electrical manufacturers are within the older parts of the city, and, in the case of the electrical manufacture, in the nearest (and earliest developed) industrial suburb.

The manufacturing region which swings around the head of Lake Michigan continues northward, where it culminates in Milwaukee. Waukegan and North Chicago, each in Illinois, are manufacturing cities—pharmaceuticals, roofing and asbestos materials, and varied light industries. Kenosha, in Wisconsin, is an automobile-manufacturing city, sharing with South Bend, Indiana, the "distinction" of having the major plants of companies not of the so-called Big Three in the industry. Racine is an agricultural-machinery, lithographing and publishing, and tanning center.

Milwaukee is a highly diversified manufacturing city. The use of iron and steel, received from elsewhere, dominates among materials. The city is a leading machine-tool manufacturer and foundry center; its factories also produce electrical and water-power machinery, turbines, pipe for pipelines, automobile frames and parts, spark plugs, agricultural machinery, and earth-moving machines. The brewing of beer is important. Reflecting this, the city is the largest malting-barley market and manufacturer of malt in the country. The tanning industry was localized in the past. Shoe manufacture is a leading industry.

Sheboygan, Manitowoc, and Green Bay are on Lake Michigan north of Milwaukee. The first two have important manufacture of aluminumware. Manitowoc is one of the leading ship-building centers on the lakes, the more concentrated region, however, being the Cleveland-to-Toledo region on Lake Erie, which is much closer to the sources of steel.

The eastern shore of Lake Michigan is far less industrialized than the southern and western. Cities are smaller and more widely spaced. This side of the lake is on the "wrong side" so far as a large hinterland is concerned; and the hinterland in Michigan focuses eastward toward Detroit rather than to Lake Michigan. Muskegon, the largest city, is a machinery center. Much of its production of parts is directed toward a market in the automobile industry of the Detroit-Flint area. Holland is a furniture-manufacturing city, has factories manufacturing furnaces and heating equipment, and is the location of the chief pickle factory of one of the national food companies.

There are inland cities not far removed from the Great Lakes that are sites of manufacturing of consequence. The Fox River Valley of Wisconsin, between Lake Winnebago and Green Bay, is a major paper-manufacturing district, based originally on abundant and even waterpower, and access to the northern forest. The mills now produce specialty papers; tissues, napkins, cleansing papers, and sanitary papers are the principal products, marketed nationally. Southeastern Wisconsin towns invariably have a shoe factory—an overflow from Milwaukee—or an aluminumware industry. The aluminumware industry dates from shortly after the World's Fair at Chicago in 1893. A resident of Manitowoc, interested in the "new" metal from which souvenir coins of the Fair were fabricated, established a factory to work with the metal. From this center the industry spread to other towns. Some of the factories now specialize and manufacture restaurant and kitchen trim equipment using other metals as well as aluminum.

Grand Rapids, Michigan, originally a major furniture-manufacturing city, still retains part of the industry, but much of it has shifted to the South. An annual furniture market is still held, following the major Chicago market. The factories of the city now use steel as a major material, and market automobile parts. The manufacture of parts is significant in the other cities of southern Michigan—Battle Creek, Kalamazoo, Jackson, and Lansing. The parts manufacturers cluster around their market, the Detroit-Pontiac-Flint automobile center. Battle Creek, in addition, has a leading food industry, the manufacture of cereals, established in the past by an individual whose name is still associated with the company.

South Bend, Indiana, localized by an early-developed water power, now outgrown, is an automobile and machinery center, some of the machines being manufactured for markets in the aviation industry.

The automobile industry lies within the manufactural region of the Great Lakes, but was not associated with transport of materials or cars on lake ships for many years. Its axis is slightly northwest from Detroit; the Detroit-Pontiac-Flint line of cities is the heart region. Two of the so-called Big Three in the industry have their major factories in Detroit or its suburbs (Dearborn); one has its major operation in Flint, a city in which 80 per cent of the gainfully employed workers labor in automobile factories. All companies now have plants and headquarters in Detroit. All companies now operate widely dispersed assembly plants from coast to coast, some in the South at locations near Atlanta, Memphis, and Dallas–Fort Worth. European, Australian, and New Zealand plants are operated. The Canadian portion of the industry is mainly within a few miles of the center of Detroit and across the river.

A location on the lake shipping routes (River Rouge) was established by one of the manufacturers. Materials and coal were received by water. But the use of the lakes by the industry is principally in the shipment of new cars, and this is minor and seasonal as compared to other methods of delivery to the salesrooms of the nation. Nevertheless, new automobiles and trucks are the fourth item of traffic on the lakes, following the major commodities moved— iron ore, coal, and grain. Driveaway points are at the extremities of the lakes— Chicago, Milwaukee, Duluth, and Buffalo; from them the ship-delivered cars are forwarded by other means of transportation.

The Detroit-Pontiac-Flint automobile center, the traditional region, is (like New England) becoming *relatively* less significant in automobile manufacture (but not *absolutely*) with the widespread dispersal of assembly plants in response to the widespread national market. The factor of market-orientation is of paramount importance in the continuing dispersal of the industry. The traditional region, however, retains all the engineering, styling, and management phases of the industry.

The Ohio Valley Manufacturing Region

The Ohio River flows generally southwestward from Pittsburgh, through hilly country in much of its course, to its mouth in the Mississippi River. The river provided a water route westward during the early days of the Westward Movement; pioneers reached it from the road which led to the Forks of the Ohio (Pittsburgh) or from the Wilderness Road, Cumberland Gap to the river. Only at the site of present-day Louisville was navigation interrupted by falls and rapids. This location became a break-of-bulk point for the transfer of goods around the falls by land.

The advent of railroads during the 1830's and 1840's changed the relative importance of the Ohio. Traffic was oriented east-west, from the cities of the Atlantic Coast to the growing cities of Chicago and St. Louis. The cities on the Great Lakes and the railroad-served interior cities between the Great Lakes and the Ohio waterway become important in manufacturing. A few important manufacturing centers developed on the river—Cincinnati, Louisville, and Evansville being the chief ones. But the greatest number of manufacturing centers grew either on the shores of the Great Lakes or in inland Ohio and Indiana.

Today the manufactural position of the Ohio River vicinity has shifted again —very favorably. River locations have drawn large water-using plants to their banks (the inland cities cannot compete in attracting these). The growing markets of the South, markets which have increased rapidly both in total income of the population and per-capita income of the inhabitants, lie from the "front door" of the region southward to the Gulf of Mexico. Good railroads and highways lead southward to these markets; bulky, low-value goods can be placed in many markets by the use of water transportation down the Ohio and Mississippi (Memphis, New Orleans) or down the Ohio and up the Tennessee and Cumberland to the "heart" of the southern market (Chattanooga, Knoxville, Nashville, and, by short land haul from river ports in northern Alabama, to Birmingham). Pipelines and river barges transport fuels and raw materials to the region. Steel is received, in part by water, from the steel districts upstream (Pittsburgh, Wheeling, Ashland); coal is delivered in part by water. The Monongahela and the upper Ohio, Pittsburgh to Cincinnati, carry the largest tonnages of materials of any inland waterway in the nation, excluding the Great Lakes. There are other factors leading to increased industrial development. One important one is the location of the middle portion of the river near the "freight-rate center" from which a national market can be reached at relatively low cost; the location of the home appliance plant of a major manufacturer at Louisville has been mentioned in the last chapter.

Cincinnati has long been the leading manufacturing center and chief city on the Ohio below Pittsburgh. It is one of three cities at angles of a triangle, the sides of which are each about 100 miles long; Cincinnati and Louisville are on the Ohio, Indianapolis is inland. And, north of Cincinnati, a chain of manufacturing centers in the Miami Valley of Ohio supply iron and steel (blast furnaces at Hamilton, continuous-strip sheet mills at Middletown) and partially processed materials to the factories of the city. The foresight of past citizens has been of importance in access to raw materials from the South and access to southern markets; the city built and owns the railroad line southward to Chattanooga; it is now leased to a railroad company. This railroad route to the South—one of the earliest in point of time—was important in helping Cincinnati obtain a head start over competing river cities.

The manufacture of machine tools, a major soap and detergent industry, potteries, musical instruments, radio and television, breweries, and the assembly of automobiles are among the manufactures of this diversified center. From the waterfront, bargeloads of new cars are dispatched to markets on the Ohio and Mississippi.

Louisville is another diversified center of manufacture. The appliance industry, breweries, the glass industry, synthetic rubber, and the distilling of whiskey are outstanding. The city is also the location of a large manufacture of cigarettes; the other cigarette centers are all in either North Carolina or Virginia. Before the passage of national minimum-wage laws, Louisville was able to attract industry to this Ohio River location at the wage rates of the South, whereas nearby cities on the north bank such as Cincinnati and Evansville (and Evansville is farther south than Louisville) had the northern wage scales.

The Inland Ohio-Indiana-Illinois Manufactural Region

Manufacturing is widespread in interior Ohio, Indiana, and Illinois. It decreases in regional intensity westward, and the manufacturing cities of the Illinois portion are more widely spaced than those of Ohio and east-central and northern Indiana. And, in the region, all cities are surrounded by some of the most productive farmland of the nation.

The manufacturing centers are based on land transportation, and are on the numerous railroad lines. Several of the north-south chains of cities in Ohio grew along the several canals built from Lake Erie to the Ohio, or to south-flowing tributaries of the river. Although the canals, long since abandoned, were significant in the location of the present cities, these cities' growth and development came after the east-west railroads were built.

Akron, Lima, Mansfield, Ashland, Marion, Columbus, Dayton, and Springfield are among the many cities. The Dayton area, with its metal, business-machine, and airplane industries has the largest number of production workers in factories. Columbus, a larger city, has governmental functions in addition to considerable manufacturing. Akron, the rubber-manufacturing center of the nation, is tied closely to Detroit and the automobile industry there and elsewhere; were it not for the early start of the industry in the city—long before the development of the automobile—the tire-manufacturing center probably would have emerged in Detroit or nearby. Tire manufacture is now dispersing in response to the dispersal of the assembly of automobiles and trucks, and the widespread national market for replacement tires.

This Ohio industrial region, the steel towns of the northeastern part of the state, Cleveland, Toledo, and other lake-shore cities, Cincinnati and the Miami Valley, and other centers and regions collectively place the state fifth among the states in numbers of manufacturing establishments, and third in total payrolls, numbers of production workers, and value added by manufacture.

Indianapolis, with leading pharmaceutical, machine-manufacture, stock-yard, meat-packing, and other diversified industries, is the chief industrial city of the interior of Indiana. A group of smaller cities east and northeast—Richmond, Anderson, Muncie, and others—have specialty production: school buses, machines, glass containers. Some of the plants were founded when the Lima-Indiana Oil Field was developed. Kokomo, north of Indianapolis, has metal industries and a major automobile plant. Lafayette has become industrialized relatively recently; prefabricated buildings are among the products. Fort Wayne is highly industrial; South Bend, almost at the northern state line, is, as noted, more oriented toward the automobile region and the Chicago manufactural area.

Soybean mills are located in nearly every city of Illinois. The manufacture of agricultural machines and processing of farm products is significant—reflecting the increasing importance, relatively, of agriculture and the farm market westward. But other raw materials and products are within the manufactural scene. Peoria is important in the manufacture of earth-moving machines, Rockford is a machine-tool and furniture center. The cities near St. Louis engage in oil refining, smelting, the electrical industries, iron and steel manufacture, and shoe manufacture.

The Western Fringe and St. Louis

The western "boundary" of the Manufactural Belt is nowhere clearly defined. Though it is cornered rather abruptly at St. Louis, one of the largest and most diversified of the manufacturing centers of the United States, elsewhere it merely grades westward through a broad zone. The chain of cities on the Rock River in Wisconsin and Illinois, from Janesville through Beloit to Rockford, have large and important manufactures—for example, automobiles, pens, office products in Janesville; the manufacture of scales, pumps, and other valuable items in Beloit; and the just-mentioned interests of Rockford. Beyond these cities there is industry in the cities of Moline, Rock Island (the Rock flows into the Mississippi at these two neighboring places), and Davenport, opposite on the Iowa bank. Cedar Rapids and Des Moines in Iowa, Madison in Wisconsin, La Crosse, Eau Claire, and others are outlying centers. Some industries—air conditioning, for example, at La Crosse—manufacture with a national market in mind. But most of the factory production in the transitional zone is either related to the use of agricultural raw materials or manufacture of products for the agricultural market, such as farm equipment.

St. Louis is a major and concentrated manufactural city. Its industries are highly diversified. The heavy industries are not in the city, but in the industrial suburbs and satellite cities across the Mississippi, in Illinois. Shoe manufacturing and brewing are two important industries in the city. Fur manufacture dates from the early trading days, when the small settlement—centrally located on the waterways, and accessible by canoe or boat from the upper and lower Mississippi, the Ohio, and the Missouri—was a fur market. The trading function of early St. Louis, and its position as an outfitting point for journeys west, was important; descendant activities of the present are an important wholesale trade within the same broad region, and the manufacture of consumer goods in the city, and their distribution both nationally and in the city itself and in the same original broad trade territory. The manufactural importance today is reflected in the facts that the St. Louis Metropolitan District (in both Missouri and Illinois) ranks ninth among all such districts in the nation in number of production workers and eighth in value added by manufacture. By any measure St. Louis is one of the ten leading manufacturing centers of the United States.

► MANUFACTURING OUTSIDE OF THE MANUFACTURAL QUADRANGLE

One-third of the manufacturing in the United States is in the South (including Texas), the Pacific States, and in the several cities between the Manufactural Belt and the West Coast. These cities are the commercial centers of wide areas, and the interests of their citizens are associated mainly with commerce;

but the size of each is such that there is a local market of importance, and the trade territory of each is extensive enough to provide a regional market. Among these cities are Minneapolis, St. Paul, Omaha, Kansas City, Dallas, Denver, Salt Lake City, and Spokane. Manufacturing elsewhere than in the South, the Pacific Coast, and the commercial cities is very local and scattered. Much of it is associated with the processing of local agricultural raw materials or the smelting and concentrating of ores.

Manufacturing Regions of the South

Manufacturing has attained importance in the South (essentially the southeastern quarter of the United States) since the early years of this century. The South now contains a preponderant percentage of the cotton textile industry, a high percentage of the synthetic and other textile industries except woolens, nearly all of the manufacture of cigarettes, a large percentage of the furniture manufacture of the nation, an important knit-goods industry, and large chemical industries. The manufacture of fertilizers is important. And, during recent years, other manufacturers have developed or show a trend toward a southward shift. Among these are shoe manufacture, certain divisions of the hardware industry, and the pulpwood and paper industry.

The various industries of the South are regionalized. Thus textile-manufacturing regions, regions whose industries are associated with wood as a major raw material, and shoe-manufacturing regions have developed. Considering the size of the South—much larger in area than the American Manufactural Belt—the overall intensity of manufacturing is less than in the traditional manufacturing centers; within some districts, however, it is just as concentrated. Considering the recency of establishment of manufacturing, and the continued growth, the southern states show a higher *percentage* increase in manufacturing than the northern ones. And the continued rise of industry has resulted in profound changes in the South; several southern states have passed from dominantly agricultural states—the traditional concept of the South—into the situation where more than half of the state's gainfully employed workers are in activities other than farming.

There are many reasons for the development of manufacturing in the South, many assets that the section offers industry. Not all are operative in any one type of manufacturing. Among these are the raw materials of farms and forests —cotton, tobacco, peanuts, meat animals, hardwoods and softwoods; the mineral fuels and waterpower; mineral raw materials within the section; about 50 million people who constitute both a large market and a source of capital, management, and labor; lower costs of land than in the major industrial regions; a varied and efficient transportation network; a mild climate, with resultant lower costs of heating factory buildings and permitting workers to reside on small farms and commute to their jobs without weather hazards or the possibility of highway blockage by blizzards or drifting; the location near the Manufactural Belt, resulting in the ability to deliver products in the East or Middle West within 24 to 48 hours—the heart of the cotton-textile region in Piedmont South Carolina is closer to both its New York and Chicago markets than New York and Chicago are to each other. Finally, and so intertwined today with other factors that it is difficult to assess and evaluate so far as relative importance is concerned, is the question of market. The market for both capital goods and consumer goods has increased enormously in the South itself. Incomes have risen. Demands have increased. The southern market in itself has drawn many industries to it. And the existence of factories results in the establishment of subsidiary industries whose market or source of materials is the original factory or industry. Following the southward shift of cotton-textile mills the bleaching and dyeing plants moved southward, to their sources of cloth. The manufacturers of mill machinery established repair and replacement centers; later they built factories in which parts were made, and finally plants for the manufacture of machines, spindles, and other equipment.

The South has always been able to furnish an adequate supply of labor to factories. The section has the highest birth-rate in the nation; it has always contained a large number of people relative to the economic opportunities—therefore it has long been an exporter of people to other parts of the country; and it has not been a section to which foreign immigrants, who usually have only their labor to sell, have been drawn. Despite the export of people the region's growth of population has been such that workers are numerous for the jobs—the result is relatively inexpensive labor except in the nationally unionized industries. The lower costs of living, of heating, and the large percentage of workers who live on small farms and grow part of their food supply, the generally lower taxes than elsewhere, make real wages higher in proportion to actual ones.

The original shifts and developments in the South, from the 1890's to the 1910's and 1920's, were basically toward less expensive supplies of labor. Today, no doubt, many of the shifts and developments are associated with the regional market. The South has ceased to be a "colonial" supplier of raw materials to the Manufactural Belt and has become a manufacturer itself, and supplier of products to its own markets and of partially processed or finished goods to national markets. Within it are more than 90 per cent of the spindles, turning out cotton and mixed-fiber materials for the United States markets.

There has been some manufacturing in the South since colonial days. There were cotton mills in the 1830's. But until the close of the nineteenth century, the basic economy, in the Deep South or Cotton Belt, especially, was associated with agriculture. Toward the end of this century manufacturing began to develop, originally mainly with the use of non-regional capital. The steel center of Birmingham—the only major southeastern city which was "not present" during the Civil War—was founded during the 1870's; the cotton-textile industry began to attain importance during the 1890's.

The southward shift of the cotton-textile industry attained momentum about 1900; by the 1920's the South surpassed New England; by the depression years of the 1930's the shift was virtually complete. As explained earlier (page 438) it was in response to the search for regions with non-competitive manufactures and for a supply of inexpensive labor, considering the low productivity per hour of a textile worker. In 1900 New England factories contained two-thirds of the cotton spindles of the nation, the cotton-growing states had about a quarter, and all other states (mainly New York and Pennsylvania in this case) less than a tenth. The South surpassed New England shortly after 1925 in spindles, earlier in spindle-hours. By 1940 the cotton-growing states contained three-quarters of the spindles. At present they have 92 per cent of the cotton spindles (regardless now of the fiber spun, because of the mixing of cotton, rayon, and synthetic yarns), New England retains but 7 per cent, and all other states do not have even 1 per cent. Obviously nearly all clothing or household materials in which cotton is a fabric now originate principally in mills in the South.

The textile region of the South is on the Piedmont, inland from the Fall Line (where the rivers flow onto the Coastal Plain) and seaward from the Southern Appalachians; thus it is between the mountains and the Fall Line. Its core is the northeast-southwest-trending Piedmont, from southern Virginia, across North and South Carolina into Georgia, then curving westward across the Piedmont of Georgia into east-central Alabama—the western end of the Piedmont. The falls and rapids of the numerous rivers were harnessed, and furnished the power originally; these sources of power have long since been outgrown. The additional sources of power from thermal power plants have released the industry from constriction within the Piedmont proper; today some mill towns are eastward, on the Coastal Plain; and westward from eastern Alabama, new mills are now in other parts of the state, are scattered in Mississippi, and the industry is growing in eastern Texas. Some mills in towns near San Antonio draw in part upon Spanish-American labor.

The most concentrated district of textile manufacture is in the upper Piedmont of southern North Carolina and South Carolina—a district within which there are several hundred mills and many mill towns, and the cities of Charlotte and Gastonia, North Carolina, and Spartanburg, Greenville, and Anderson, South Carolina.

Labor for the mills, when they were established, was recruited from the farms of the Piedmont and from the mountain areas of the southern Appalachians. Some was recruited even from across the mountains, in the Tennessee Valley. Labor was, always has been, and still is composed almost exclusively of white persons. To understand this, the setting of the mills and the *time* of their original establishment are important. The original mill areas in the western part of the Carolinas had few Negro inhabitants to start with; the farms of the Piedmont were not plantations but small farms operated by white families. *At the time,* by custom in the South, various occupations were filled by members of the two races, separately. The "upper class" whites were merchants, bankers, businessmen; customary trades filled by Negroes were those of brick-

layer, barber, and service occupations. Locomotive engineers were white, locomotive firemen Negro. The small-farmer white and the growing town groups
had no capital and little education to enter the "upper group" and were barred
by custom from other occupations. It was this large supply of potential workers who manned the mills and filled the mill towns, recruited from Piedmont
farm, small towns, and the adjacent mountains. Today the older southern
manufacturing regions have their own labor force; recruitment is no longer
necessary. The factories of the newer regions receive applications from potential workers, the result of economic pressure or of the desire to shift from the
rural to semi-urban or urban scene. Time after time a factory being built in the
post-World War II period has had applications from as many as 4,000 persons
—before it opened its doors—for 1,000 or so jobs available.

Locally grown (Piedmont) cotton has never been of great importance in the
textile region. Cotton has been received by rail through cotton markets farther
west, today mainly from Mississippi through Texas. The southern, or Georgia
and Alabama, portion of the region is in large cotton-growing areas; even here
the local supply fails by far to meet the demand. The industry, not originally
shifting to sources of raw materials, has always depended upon distant sources.
However, the presence of the textile region today, and the mixing of materials,
has attracted manufacturers of rayon and of synthetic yarns. There is important
rayon yarn production in the adjacent mountains, the wood being from the highlands. Eastern Tennessee contains several large rayon plants; Elizabethton, Lowland (near Morristown), and others, and Asheville, North Carolina, are important production centers. Through licensing, some of the plants produce the
various synthetic-fiber yarns for the textile industry. Other supplies of yarn are
purchased from more distant producers.

The Southern Textile Region manufactures cotton and mixed-fiber goods
for national markets. Quantities of these are shipped to the clothing centers.
Every major manufacturing company maintains a New York office. Chicago,
New York, and the most concentrated of the textile districts form a triangle; it
is about 600 miles from the core of the manufacturing district to either market.
Many divisions of the clothing industry are today, too, in the region or in
nearby parts of the South. The manufacture of underwear, shirts, blouses, house
dresses, sweat shirts, athletic jerseys, and light-weight summer suits for men
are significant southern industries. Certain southern cities are the sites of factories making "western wear"—blue jeans, "western" shirts, and other clothing
marketed in the ranching areas of the western United States. Cotton goods are
shipped to California and Hawaii for use in the local clothing industries. The
textile region contains, also, many new—or modernized—mills that perform
the entire process from raw material to finished clothing or household goods
(towels, sheets); cotton bales are unloaded at one end of the mill, yarn is manufactured and woven into cloth which is bleached, dyed, and sewn into finished
products.

The Piedmont contains manufactures other than textiles. The portion in North Carolina is more diversified than the neighboring states—in South Carolina, for example, about 85 per cent of the manufactures are textiles and the associated industries. North Carolina has a greater number of production workers than any other southern state (though Texas is approaching it), and is second only to Texas in value added by manufacturing. High Point and neighboring cities are furniture-manufacturing centers; recently a furniture market has been established, adding High Point to the Chicago and Grand Rapids markets; the retailers assemble at these three centers semi-annually to buy from the manufacturers. Hardwoods for the furniture industry are obtained now chiefly from the mountains and from farm woodlots in Kentucky and Tennessee. Durham, Winston-Salem, and Reidsville, North Carolina—with Richmond, Virginia, and Louisville, Kentucky—dominate the national manufacture of cigarettes. Food and tobacco-processing plants are numerous.

Atlanta, the major commercial city of the southeast, has attracted manufacturing in addition. The consumer goods are distributed within Atlanta's trade territory. Also, in recent years, airplane manufacture, the assembly of automobiles and trucks, and similar industries have been founded in the metropolitan region surrounding Atlanta.

The fertilizer industry of the port cities has been mentioned.

Shipbuilding is an outstanding activity in the port cities of Newport News and Norfolk, Virginia, and in Pascagoula, Mississippi. New Orleans also has shipyards. The Virginia centers obtain steel and fittings from Baltimore and the Manufactural Belt. Birmingham and its steel industry supplies the others, and, through a freight-rate situation, the mills at Birmingham supply steel to most of the South without severe competition from the mills north of the Potomac and Ohio.

The Tennessee River Valley west of the southern Appalachians is industrialized. However, unlike the Piedmont (and like the American Manufactural Belt) manufacturing is associated dominantly with larger cities—or the cities have grown as the result of manufacturing; whereas the mill towns of the Piedmont have remained generally small and oriented to the few local mills. Bristol, Kingsport, Johnson City, Knoxville, and Chattanooga are the principal manufacturing cities of the valley. The knit-goods industry is the main one, overall, and small towns as well as the cities usually have a knit-goods factory; the manufacture of women's hose (nylons) and of children's socks are especially important. The aluminum industry at Alcoa, the nuclear center at Oak Ridge (each in the Knoxville Metropolitan area), the chemical industries in Chattanooga, Knoxville, and Kingsport are large. The printing of books is a major industry in Kingsport, and has attracted the paper-manufacturing industry to this market for paper.

Nashville and Memphis are diversified in their manufactures. The shoe industry of Nashville (and of St. Louis, not too far away), has spread into almost all of the small towns of western Tennessee and western Kentucky (as well as neighboring southern Illinois). Memphis, in addition to its regionally oriented industries—cottonseed oils, soybean oils, and cotton—is an important location in the mid-South for the southern manufacturing plants of many of the national industries of the Manufactural Belt.

New Orleans and the cities of the Texas Gulf Coast process imported raw materials, such as raw sugar, and use the local and regional petroleum and natural gas for fuels and raw materials in the petrochemical industries. Salt and sulphur are mineral products of this coast as well; needs of lime are obtained from oyster shells. The extreme southeast of Texas—the cluster of Beaumont, Port Arthur, Orange, and Port Neches—is probably the most concentrated petrochemical center in the nation. The port of Houston now handles more *coastwise* (domestic) shipments in tonnage than any American port except New York and the Delaware River ports (combined); much of this is outgoing petroleum and petroleum manufactures destined for the New York and Philadelphia regions. The manufacture of oil-drilling equipment is very important. The size of the Houston market localizes a large manufacture of consumer goods. The cities located on Galveston Bay, and ports like Corpus Christi, are petroleum, petrochemical, and refining centers for imported oil and ores—bauxite, tin ores, and others. The Texas Gulf Coast is the site of the extraction of magnesium from sea water, and the production of the metal for industry.

Dallas and Fort Worth, thirty miles apart, constitute a leading manufacturing district. The cities are very different. Dallas is the principal commercial city of the southwest and has national interests as a result; it has contacts with all parts of the main Manufactural Belt, and is a distribution and wholesaling point for its products. Dallas also has an important manufacture of women's clothing and is one of the principal electronics-manufacturing centers of the country; the production of electronics instruments is outstanding. Fort Worth, in contrast, is a leading user of regional materials; the flour mills, slaughtering, and meat-packing industries exemplify this. The "countryside" between these two cities is now urbanized, in several suburban industrial towns. Here is the automobile assembly, the important aircraft industry, and others. Taken collectively —the Metropolitan Region of Dallas–Fort Worth—is very diversified, and, at the beginning of the 1960's, had more production workers in industry than any other southern metropolitan region. In value added by manufacture, however, the Houston Metropolitan Region, with its petrochemical manufactures, outranks it.

Manufacturing in the Commercial Cities, the Great Plains, and the Mountain West

A series of large commercial cities stretch from north to south in the interior lowlands of the United States. They are located west of the American Manufactural Belt, and toward the plains border. Their trade territory extends long distances to their west; each territory is large in area, relatively small in population density. These cities are: Minneapolis and St. Paul—the Twin Cities—in the north; Omaha in the central stretch; Kansas City; and Dallas. The trade area of the Twin Cities stretches westward to the Rockies in western Montana; Omaha serves the north-central area, but competes westward with Denver, the commercial center of the inter-mountain country and part of the plains. Kansas City's territory lies in Kansas, and southwestward also through Oklahoma and the panhandle of Texas. Dallas serves the southwest. As noted (page 471) St. Louis competes in the central area, in some functions, but the city is definitely within the American Manufactural Belt. And some wholesaling services for the entire interior and West are performed in Chicago.

Each of these major commercial cities contains manufacturing. Dominantly it is associated with the processing of raw materials from the agricultural hinterlands to their west—flour milling and the manufacture of cereals in Minneapolis, Kansas City, and others, meat-packing in St. Paul, Omaha, Denver, Kansas City (Kansas City, Kansas, rather than the contiguous part in Missouri in this case), and the Dallas–Fort Worth Metropolitan region—and other industries associated with the regional materials (linseed-oil mills, for example). But the organizations for the distribution of materials is a magnet for the location of factories producing consumer goods. These are sold within the cities, and in the trade territories; some plants are local in their founding and management, others are branch plants of national companies.

There are a few manufactural centers in the plains area. Wichita, formerly engaged in regional industries, became a major American aircraft center (as did Fort Worth) during World War II when the federal government insisted upon new plants being located inland, rather than in the existing aircraft centers on the Pacific Coast. And there are many cities with petroleum refineries or with manufactures of materials and machines for the petroleum industry—Tulsa and Oklahoma City, for example. Near Denver, the iron and steel center of Pueblo is the most highly industrialized city, by percentage, of any city between the American Manufacturing Belt and the Pacific Coast.

Manufacture in the Mountain and intermontane West is largely the smelting and the preliminary processing of minerals. Most of the smelters are near the mines. But a large smelting industry in El Paso, Texas, dates from the period when ores from much of Mexico were shipped there; at present the industry draws mainly upon ores from the American side of the border. Even a regional commercial center like Salt Lake City has many smelters in its suburban areas. Spokane, however, in the wheat belt of eastern Washington and nearby Idaho, is a flour-milling and agricultural-processing center. And, on the western plains and throughout the irrigated basins and valleys of this extensive region, the sugar-beet mill is present, manufacturing this important western crop into beet sugar.

Manufacturing on the Pacific Coast

The rapid growth of population on the Pacific Coast of the United States has been paralleled by a rapid growth in manufacturing. The region, with its distance from the main manufacturing centers combined with the higher-than-average incomes, per capita and per family, of its inhabitants offers a large market for consumer goods. The capital-goods industries are now developing, and in time the Pacific Coast will no doubt furnish its machines and other capital goods for its regional factories. The large market is concentrated in a few major cities; elsewhere it is scattered over less-peopled agricultural and forest areas. In total, however, the bulk of the market is in the urbanized regions surrounding San Diego, Los Angeles, the cities of the San Francisco Bay area, Portland, and the Seattle-Tacoma district.

The large urban area (Metropolitan Region) of the Los Angeles conurbation contained in the late 1950's well over a third of the total market of the Pacific Coast. This fact alone has resulted in the development of manufacturing in the Metropolitan Region and the establishment of western manufacturing plants of national companies in Los Angeles and its suburbs and satellite cities. Every type of manufacturing activity and product is represented; the basic iron and steel industry at Fontana, near San Bernardino, was founded in the 1940's.

Los Angeles, dominantly because of its market size and potential, has become the leading manufacturing city on the West Coast—this despite the fact that it is off-center geographically, and well to the south of the central position on the Coast. Marketing, and much of the distribution of goods, is in and from the Los Angeles area. The influx of people to southern California—several thousand per month during certain recent years—has had two effects, manufacturally; it expands and continues to expand the local and regional market, and it furnishes labor to the factories, for all migrants expect to stay and are seeking jobs; if a position in a service occupation or in some field in which the breadwinner was familiar, is not available, he finds employment in a factory.

Transfer costs of goods manufactured in the Los Angeles area permit its manufacturers to reach the entire market of California, Oregon, and Washington. In the northern area, particularly eastern Washington—east of the Cascades—this is not always the case with certain commodities. But the markets of the Puget Sound Lowland, the most-peopled area of the state, are available to Los Angeles, by land or sea, and thus in nearly all of the Pacific area, Los Angeles products have a competitive advantage in transfer costs over those from the American Manufactural Belt. This is one of the chief reasons why a company centered in the northeastern United States, and planning branch factories, establishes one on the Pacific Coast before considering the founding of a branch in the South. In total, the Los Angeles and San Francisco districts comprise a little over half of the market.

The total market of the Pacific states, measured in numbers of people, does not reach that of the metropolitan regions of New York and Philadelphia. But it is a very different kind of market. Luxury items, goods for "outdoor living," sporting goods, boats, and similar items are purchased by a larger per cent of the population. The per-capita ownership of motor vehicles is higher. On the other hand—and especially in the California markets—woolen clothing, over-coats, heating equipment, insulation materials, and similar products are in less demand.

The manufacturing region of the Pacific Coast can be divided into two sub-regions. The southern half, from San Francisco southward is very diversified, but oriented toward the variety of consumer goods, the aircraft industry, and petroleum refining. The northern half—California north of the San Francisco Bay area, western Oregon, and western Washington—is concerned principally with the processing of wood, the local raw material; this is the region of saw-mills, lumber mills, veneer plants, and pulp and papermills; only Seattle, with an important airplane manufacture and diversified manufacturing, departs somewhat from the average. Inland, in the Central Valley of California, the food industry leads; it is important as well in the Willamette–Puget Sound Low-land. On the coast itself in smaller as well as larger cities the canning and freezing of fish is very important.

The aircraft industry is centered in southern California, where San Diego, Los Angeles, and several suburbs of Los Angeles (Burbank, Santa Monica) are among the principal manufacturing centers of the entire nation. The airplane industry in Seattle dates from the early days when wood was used in planes, and where the founder of the company obtained an international airmail con-tract to fly the mail to Vancouver, B.C. Renton, a suburb of Seattle, is also a major center.

The Los Angeles Metropolitan Region now has more than three-quarters of a million employees in manufacturing, of whom over half a million are pro-duction workers in factories; it is third in the nation in total employees and workers (exceeded only by the New York and Chicago areas) and third in value added by manufacture. The discrepancy, or wide spread, between total em-ployees and production workers—larger than in most other manufacturing centers—reflects the "peculiar" character of certain manufactures; for example the end product of the Hollywood movie industry is a roll of film. To make this there are many employees, but few classed statistically as laborers in a factory.

San Francisco proper is mainly a commercial center. There is little space at the tip of the hilly peninsula for manufacturing. The Bay cities, such as Oakland, Richmond, Crockett, and others on the eastern shore of San Francisco Bay are the manufacturing centers. Here are most of the processors of imported raw materials (coffee, raw sugar), the industries using materials from the hinterland, and the market-oriented factories. South of San Francisco, through Palo Alto to San Jose, light manufacturing is dominant; the electronics industry is es-pecially important.

FIG. 20-3. The major manufacturing district of Los Angeles, in the foreground, covers an extensive area—one deliberately planned and zoned for manufacturing. There are several other manufacturing districts as well as "isolated" aircraft factories in the city and its suburbs. The city, being "newer" than most others in the United States so far as manufactural growth is concerned, planned and set aside manufacturing districts prior to its expansion to these areas. (Spence Air Photos)

Portland is a lumber and papermill center, a processor of food, and, in satellite cities the aluminum industry has been established. The electrical power from the many dams on the Columbia River has drawn this industry; its major market for sheet and fabricated aluminum is the aircraft industry of the Pacific Coast. The wood products reflect the regional raw material from the mountains. The flour mills, meat-packing plants, and food processing reflect Portland's command of the agricultural Willamette Valley and its access by way of the Columbia Gorge through the Cascade Mountains to the agricultural interior of southeastern Washington and northeastern Oregon. In addition, the city's maritime interests are many; shipbuilding is important.

Wood products, fish canning and freezing are important in the cities on Puget Sound. In addition, Tacoma and Seattle are importing centers for tropical products and products from Asia. Tacoma is an important smelting center, manufacturer of explosives, and lumber-mill city.

Seattle is a leading port, and its factories process some of the imported raw materials. The aircraft industry is outstanding. Diversified manufacturing plants supply goods to regional markets and to Alaska. Canadian oil received by pipeline is refined in nearby centers. The commercial interests of Seattle are very significant. On the whole, many activities look seaward and Alaskaward rather than toward the agricultural interior across the Cascade Mountains.

In total, in the entire Pacific Coast, the production workers in all industry, in all centers other than metropolitan Los Angeles, do not reach the figures of Los Angeles alone. Not only is this city dominant in manufacture and in market, but it becomes increasingly so with the years.

► MANUFACTURING IN CANADA

The manufacturing axis of Canada is from Montreal southwest to Windsor. It lies along the St. Lawrence River, the north shore of Lake Ontario and inland Ontario between the western end of Lake Ontario and the Detroit River.

The eastern part of this axis is not contiguous with the American Manufactural Belt. The Adirondack Mountains of New York separate the two. The New York side of the St. Lawrence is "off-center" in the United States scene, although now developing industry, as at Massena. In contrast, the Canadian side of the river is the "main line" of Canada between Montreal and Toronto. The western part of the Canadian Belt meets the United States region at Windsor-Detroit and Sarnia–Port Huron.

The Canadian Manufactural Belt contains the same variety of industry as that of the United States. Montreal is highly diversified. As a great port, it processes imported raw materials, manufactures flour for export, engages in the manufacture of consumer goods fabricated from Canadian and imported materials. Petroleum is refined.

The cities on Lake Ontario from Oshawa and Toronto on the north shore, through Hamilton at the western end of the lake, to Niagara Falls at the United States border display great industrial diversity. Here is the manufactural heart of Canada. Nearly 7,000 factories in the belt between Oshawa and Niagara Falls contribute nearly one-third of the nation's manufactures. One-seventh of the Canadian population lives in this belt and provides a large local market; incomes are high, and a third of Canada's income taxes are collected from the region. Manufactured products are distributed nationally from the region and are exported overseas as well. Toronto, the largest city of this so-called "Golden Horseshoe" by far, is a diversified manufacturing center. Hamilton is an iron and steel center, Welland is important in the machine tool and ferroalloy industries, and Oshawa contains large automobile factories. New automotive plants have been built in the region in response to the Canadian and the export market.

London is the leading manufacturing city of inland peninsular Ontario (the "peninsula" among Lakes Ontario, Erie, and Huron). Farm machinery for the Canadian and export market is important in this and other cities. Windsor contains many automobile factories, some of them the Canadian plants of the companies centered across the river in Detroit, Michigan. Walkerville is a distilling center; Sarnia, at the outlet of Lake Huron, has important petroleum refining.

Iron and steel for the varied Canadian industries is manufactured at Hamilton at the western end of Lake Ontario, Sault Ste. Marie, and, in the Atlantic Provinces, at Sydney, Nova Scotia. The industry at Hamilton imports Lake Superior ore (via the lakes and the Welland Canal) and Appalachian coal which is coked at the plant. Its market is over 60 per cent south of a line from Oshawa to Sarnia, and 20 per cent in Montreal—the Canadian Manufacturing Region. The industry has been active in promoting the use of taconite; it has a plant for this at Aurora, Minnesota, and also has interest in iron mines in the iron ranges of Minnesota and Michigan. The orientation of the Hamilton steel center, and of Sault Ste. Marie, to the Great Lakes and to materials from the United States (and the Michipicoten iron range in Canada, north of Lake Superior) is evident. The steel industry at Sydney uses Nova Scotian coal, and iron ore and limestone both brought by ship from Newfoundland; the iron ore is moved to the coal. The market for the steel is mainly Montreal, and is reached by ship during the navigation season on the St. Lawrence, by rail in the ice-season.

The new iron-ore developments on the Quebec-Labrador boundary, with rail shipment to the water route on the St. Lawrence, will change the dependence of Canada on percentages of ore from the United States. The deepened St. Lawrence Seaway undoubtedly will result, too, in increased imports from overseas. The market-orientation of the steel industry to the Canadian industrial axis may not change; in fact, new construction is expectable on Lake Ontario.

Winnipeg is a flour milling center, and the dominant wholesaling point for the Canadian Prairie. Calgary, Saskatoon, Edmonton, and other prairie cities process farm products, and Edmonton, in addition, has a steel industry based on scrap and is the petroleum center of the oil fields of Alberta.

Vancouver is the great port of western Canada. Its regional market is small, but growing.

Two Canadian industries of importance are dispersed rather than concentrated in the industrial (and market) axis. These are the pulp and paper industry and the smelting and refining of metals. The Laurentian Upland and the Rocky Mountains are the major sources of both pulpwood and metals. The more accessible parts of the Laurentian Upland, north of the St. Lawrence and north of Lake Superior—particularly the former—are the areas of paper manufacture. Many mills are on the north bank of the St. Lawrence below Quebec. Three Rivers (Trois Rivières) is said to be one of the largest manufacturing centers of newsprint in the world; Canada is the world's largest producer and exporter. The smelting of metals is near the mines, the final processing in the manufactural axis. And, as discussed elsewhere (pages 421–423) the aluminum industry is localized at many large hydroelectric developments in Canada.

Manufacturing in Canada is now "excess"; the nation not only supplies itself with varied items but exports manufactured products.

▶ AFTERVIEW

The many factors, or ingredients, necessary for successful manufacturing are all operative within the United States. One or two may be more important in a given manufacturing enterprise, or in a certain industry, than others. All are taken into account and weighed by experts when a new or branch plant is being established. Factories processing primary raw materials are usually near or at the source of these. Further (secondary) fabricators of these materials are footloose, are between the first factory and the eventual market for their end product, and an important factor in their location is usually the transfer cost. The "final" factory—user of the partially fabricated materials— tends to be market-oriented. These simplified principles are operative on a broad and generalized scale in the manufacturing scene of the United States and Canada.

The American Manufactural Belt is the core region of manufacturing in the United States. This is true no matter what the variety and explanation of the reasons for its development—whether or not the reasons are mainly geographic, economic, or historical—or a complex combination of all three and others. Two-thirds or more of all materials used by factories have been processed in part or in whole; only one-third or less are basic raw materials from the farms, forests, sea, or earth. Therefore the "final" factories and assembly plants of the Manufactural Region are the *main market* for the secondary factories—those whose end product is sold to another manufacturer. Thus the secondary manufacturer tends to locate near or in his *market*—the American Manufactural Belt. This alone tends to keep the existing major manufacturing region the important one; it is estimated that more than one-half of the entire American market for all products—primary, partially processed, finally manufactured, and retail— lies within the confines of the industrial quadrangle of the northeastern quarter of the United States. The momentum of the early start and the inertia of the present are, then, potent factors in the ability of the Manufactural Belt to retain its importance.

Dispersal in response to the widely flung markets of a country the size of the United States is normal. Therefore markets which reflect the pattern of population distribution have evolved. Shifts of industry to these markets is expectable.

Therefore sub-manufacturing districts develop—in response to many factors—but again the market situation is extremely significant. In time other manufacturing districts, even regions or belts may develop. The Los Angeles Basin may be in the evolutionary stage of this development now, the reasons for which are complex, but again the regional market of the Pacific Coast is a potent factor, combined with the transfer costs—wherein a regional manufacturing center has a cost advantage over the principal manufactural centers in reaching and serving that market.

The same general principles are evident in Canada. A manufactural axis, Montreal to Windsor, has evolved in response to many factors, not the least of which is its location with respect to the population distribution and density. This region has attained momentum, and will continue and grow as the core region of Canadian manufacturing. *If* the boundary between the United States and Canada did not exist, much of the present market of the area *might* have been served from the existing American Manufactural Belt; this is academic; the boundary *does* exist. An axis oriented to different markets has developed (even if, on a broad scale, the Niagara Falls–Hamilton–Toronto region and the Canadian side of the Detroit River are considered as contiguous parts of a *North American* Manufactural Belt). Therefore, two parallel core regions of industry, of markedly different size in response to differential population totals, themselves form a market for many other primary and secondary manufactural enterprises.

► QUESTIONS

1. Why is it more difficult to measure the intensity of regional (or national) manufacturing than to measure regional agricultural production?
2. How do various man-made factors, such as laws or taxes, sometimes have a marked effect on the manufacturing scene?
3. What is the extent of the American Manufactural Belt? Does the delimitation of this region imply that manufacturing is spread equally throughout it? About what proportion of this country's manufactures are produced in the factories of this belt?
4. Relate the location of the chief manufacturing centers of Canada to the location of the nearby American Manufactural Belt.
5. Where, outside the Manufactural Belt, is manufacturing important? What percentage of this country's manufactures are now produced "outside" of the Manufactural Belt?
6. Comment on the subject (either for or against): Manufacturing will continue to grow at a rapid rate in the sections of the nation not now in the principal American Manufactural Belt. Support your answer with as many facts as possible.

7. What advantages to certain kinds of manufacturing (name them) are offered by a location (a) on or near the Atlantic Seaboard, (b) on the Great Lakes, (c) on the Ohio or Mississippi Rivers?

8. What changes in kinds of manufacturing and its products have occurred in New England from the inception of industry in the region to the present?

9. Why is every type of manufacturing found somewhere in the urban region between New York and Baltimore-Washington?

10. Approximately two-thirds of the manufacture of women's clothing is concentrated in a twenty-block area on Manhattan Island in New York City. Why do various factors tend to "hold" this industry in this location?

11. How did the transportation advantage enjoyed by the Mohawk Valley enable it to develop manufacturing?

12. What many advantages are there for manufacture in the Pittsburgh region —despite the difficulties of hilly terrain?

13. Why were (and are) the shores of the Great Lakes a magnet for industry? Why is water for industrial use of increasing importance in attracting industry to a lakeshore site—when this item was usually not considered in the early development?

14. The Ohio Valley developed industry quite early, declined *relatively* for a time, and now is undergoing vigorous industrial expansion. What various situations (whether within or without the immediate valley) help account for these regional trends?

15. What are some of the major manufacturing cities in inland Ohio, Indiana, and Illinois between the Great Lakes and the Ohio and Mississippi waterways? What are inland centers, not on the lakes, in Michigan? Explain their development.

16. What are some of the assets of the southeastern United States for manufacturing?

17. For what types of manufactured goods is the southern Piedmont noted? Explain the reasons for the regional specialization in the three or four "Piedmont industries."

18. Account for the types of manufacturing that have developed in Texas. What raw materials on the Gulf Coast region have been significant attractions for certain industries?

19. What various factors have been important in aiding the growth of manufacturing on the Pacific Coast? How does the type of manufactural emphasis differ in the Pacific Northwest from that of the southern two-thirds of California? Explain.

20. Explain why much of Canada's manufacturing is concentrated in the belt from Montreal through Toronto and Hamilton to Windsor.

21. Why does the existence of manufacturing regions, like the American or Canadian Manufacturing Belts, tend to hold or retain large numbers of "secondary" manufactures?

XXI The Chief Manufacturing Regions:

Other Regions throughout the World

This chapter will deal with the manufactural scene in the world outside of the United States and Canada. These regions will be discussed in less detail than those of Anglo-America have been. The usual person resident in the United States will have his life-time contacts, perhaps livelihood, in some aspect of the commerce and industry of this country. The principles and regions of manufacture will affect his daily life. But foreign-made goods enter the United States in quantity, also, and economic conditions in other manufacturing centers, the ability or inability to compete in world markets, affect the American citizen, too—perhaps indirectly, perhaps very directly. He should be aware of the worldwide distribution of industry and the advantages and disadvantages the various manufactural regions may face. And, the industrialized portions of the world are themselves markets for American and Canadian manufactured products. Our foreign trade has shifted from being concerned basically with the exports of foods and raw materials—characteristic of the young, developing country—to a large export of manufactured goods.

Western Europe, the Soviet Union, and Japan are the principal manufacturing areas outside of North America. The western European industrial region centers approximately in Belgium, and includes the areas within a 500-mile radius of this center. Soviet industry is regionalized within its extensive area—

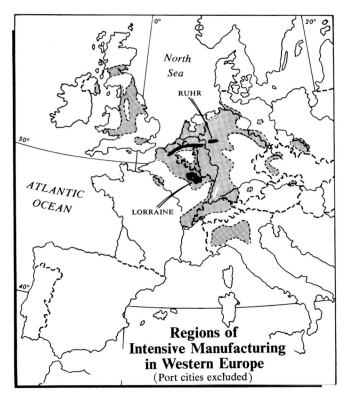

one-sixth of the land surface of the world. Japan's manufacturing centers lie within a part of that nation. The industry of most of the countries of western Europe and of Japan is organized on the same principles as that of North America—the free enterprise system. That of the Soviet Union is under the control of the state, and capital investment, capital accumulation, and the decisions as to its type of product (whether steel is to be used for producer goods or consumer goods at any given time) is the function of officials of the government.

► THE WESTERN EUROPEAN MANUFACTURING REGION

The important industrial nations in western Europe are the United Kingdom, West Germany, the Netherlands, Belgium, France, Switzerland, and Luxembourg. Manufacturing is significant in many districts of these countries; in addition, it will be remembered that agriculture is highly productive in nearly all of the same territory.

Industry extends beyond the borders of the seven countries named. Northward it is significant in the south of Sweden, in small districts of Norway, and in the city of Copenhagen in Denmark. Southward manufacturing is important in the Po Valley of northern Italy; there is also an "outlying" textile district at Barcelona in Spain. Eastward from the important industrial countries manufacturing is actually more concentrated than it is to the north or south; this eastward extension, now in East Germany, Poland, and Czechoslovakia, lies back of the Iron Curtain and is in the Soviet sphere of influence at present. The development of manufacturing in these "eastward areas" occurred long before they fell under the control of the Soviet Union; manufacturing was then west European in type and organization. In fact, Germany's great industrial strength between the 1880's and 1940's was owing to the inclusion of what are now the resources and industries of West and East Germany and part of what is now western Poland within a single national unit.

The basic pattern of industrial location in western Europe as a whole is its distribution on or very near the sources of energy—in Europe's case, principally coal—or, secondly, in the port cities of the maritime nations. The first-named localization reflects the fact that Europe's coal fields are near the population centers, and on plains; factories at the coal fields thus have a level site at the source of fuel or electrical energy and near markets; the very fact that industry tends to follow the coal field (as in Belgium or the Ruhr of West Germany) has resulted in the growth of densely-peopled industrial areas; the inhabitants themselves furnish a market for goods, and the primary industries attract secondary ones, and factories whose product they use in their own plants. The coal fields and their dense concentrations of population stand out on a detailed map of the population density of the western part of the continent. Secondly, the importance of manufacturing in the port cities reflects the dependence of many European industries upon imported raw materials; it reflects, also, the importance of the overseas or export markets, for there is a surplus of manufactured goods over and above the amount which can be marketed at home, even though the home market collectively exceeds that of the United States in numbers—although not in buying power per capita.

The consumer-goods industries, oriented to the home markets of European industrial countries, are usually most numerous in the capital city or its industrial suburbs. The capital city is the chief city of most of the countries. Here is the major market in buying power, and the concentrated market for luxury items. Here is the center of the transportation system; products are directed to all parts of the country from the central transport point. And the outlying parts of an individual country are not far. The small areal size of the western European nations means—unlike the United States or the Soviet Union—that the customer is not far in miles, in hours, or in transport costs from the producer. England proper is the size of Wisconsin or of Illinois; the United Kingdom has the total area only of Oregon; France is smaller than Texas; Switzerland, Belgium, the Netherlands, and Luxembourg together are smaller in area than Virginia. Thus London, Paris, Vienna, Brussels, Stockholm, Copenhagen, and other capitals are centers of consumer-goods manufacture. Berlin was the

Fig. 21-1. One of the new, post-War constructed factories of Europe, laid out on the "American-type" or horizontal use of space. Notice that this factory uses more land than is included in any of the individual fields in the distance, and that the area included in the factory building, its yards, and parking lots is such that several farms have been purchased and the farm families displaced. This is a more serious problem in western Europe, where land is a shortage item relative to population, than in the United States or the Soviet Union. The factory manufactures electrical equipment. It is in Northern Ireland, part of the United Kingdom. The sea cliff at the right margins North Channel, separating Ireland and Scotland. The rural area is dominantly in hay and pasture, and specializes in dairying. (British Information Services)

German center before the division of the country; its remaining manufactures are still principally of this type.

The factor of planned locations of strategic industries, placing them away from the frontiers—important in the Soviet Union and in the relocation (expansion) of the aircraft plants in the United States during World War II—is hardly operative in western Europe since the development of the airplane. No place in the British Isles is as far as 75 miles from the seacoast; an industry cannot be inland, or even far removed from a port. London and the Ruhr of West Germany are only a little over 300 miles apart by air—and part of the

North Sea and the Netherlands lies between, in a distance the same as Chicago to Cleveland, or from Washington through Baltimore, Philadelphia, and New York to Hartford, Connecticut.

Labor is plentiful in Europe. It is trained, skilled, and available at all manufacturing centers. Labor is not then, on the whole, a localizing factor of manufacturing, except in the highly skilled trades, ones requiring long training and apprenticeship, such as the diamond-cutting experts of the Netherlands and Belgium or the watchmakers of Switzerland. Furthermore, in many European nations youths were (and still are in some) separated in schooling at teen-age, and directed through a trade-school education to become technicians, laboratory workers, or skilled mechanics for "blue-collar jobs" in manufacturing; others were schooled through the universities for management and governmental positions. A great deal of Germany's pre-World War success in industry was attributable to the large pool of skilled and technical personnel available to her industry. One of the human factors responsible for West Germany's resurgence to manufacturing importance in the 1950's was the enormous pool of refugees with skills from East Germany who fled the communist regime, and, after a period of economic stress (for themselves, the government, and foreign-aid programs) were absorbed into industry, where their talents and skills were utilized.

A temporary shortage of labor may develop in Europe from time to time, owing to war or to unusual circumstances—or even the rapid growth of an industrial district. A rise of wages to attract people from a distance is not necessary; the overpopulated parts of Italy and (in the past) of agricultural central Europe are drawn upon. The general practice has been the temporary recruitment of Italians, who then return home after the conditions have resumed normalcy. The Slavic workers, attracted in the past, have tended to remain; many of the coal miners of the Ruhr are of Polish descent; the industrial and mining districts of northern France contain many Polish workers. In recent years, the refugees without skills have been a reserve or pool of low-cost labor.

European nations have always furnished their own supply of unskilled or semi-skilled workers. In fact, the supply often outran the demand, and many migrated to the New World. Today some districts or industries—coal mining areas in England—are facing the problem of an oversupply of labor. And, since World War II, in addition to the refugee problem, some countries are receiving immigrants for the first time—Algerians in France, Jamaicans and Africans in England—who compete with Europeans for the unskilled and semi-skilled jobs; resulting economic bitterness has erupted in a few districts.

The labor situation in Europe, as outlined, thus differs from that of the United States. Europe uses land more sparingly (even in manufacturing), labor somewhat more abundantly. Land is a shortage and expensive item; labor is surplus and relatively inexpensive. The land and labor factors thus are the reverse, in general, of the situation in the United States. In some countries, mechanization has proceeded recently as fast as it has in this country. European workers of high skill, in modern postwar factories, are as just as productive per man or per hour as Americans. The recent successes of European manufacturers in tapping the rich American market is owing to many factors, but one of the significant ones is the relative cost of European labor, now working, in many industries, in as modern, mechanized, and up-to-date factories as in North America.

Capital to finance the industries of western Europe has been accumulated in different ways, and in different manners from country to country. Britain, historically and at present, imports raw materials and food, manufactures, processes, and consumes them by the use of home coal and home labor, and pays for the needed materials through exports and services. The services—invisible exports —include transport of commodities in British ships, world-wide insurance and banking services, and the tourist industry to the home islands. The Empire, later the Commonwealth, and the colonies and possessions helped in the building of a favorable balance of trade, and the accumulation of capital which was invested in industrial enterprises. But, as during World War II, much of the fixed capital investment in plants and machines was destroyed, and liquid assets were used in the building and maintenance of the armed forces. Thus the foreign aid and loan programs and other projects initiated by the United States, some as gifts, some as loans, have been important in the recovery programs, not only of the United Kingdom, but of other western European nations. Certain of these aids have been used in western Europe in the rebuilding of the industrial plants and in equipping them with machine tools and other appurtenances —not always directly, it is true, but often indirectly through the bolstering of the overall economy of a particular country. The European peoples were also asked (or forced) to accept severe shortages for a time in consumer goods in order to conserve resources and rebuild or refurbish the capital goods industries; high taxes were the rule. Without unraveling the complex circumstances of the past fifteen or more years, it is now fair to say that the West European industrial regions are back in operation, are manufacturing products which are marketed around the world, and are generally being financed by the normal methods.

The transportation system of western Europe is one of the finest in the world. Railroads, paved roads, and airways connect all important cities and manufacturing districts. In addition the north of France, the Low Countries, and West Germany are interconnected by a canal system which transports heavy, bulky materials of low value; the navigable rivers are connected by canals. And the northwest of the continent possesses the Rhine and its navigable tributaries and distributaries; the Rhine flows through one of the most concentrated industrial centers of the world and carries the greatest tonnage of any river in the Western world. And the Rhine Valley is connected to Berlin by the Mittelland Canal, which provides the city with a water route to the Rhine and the ports of the Netherlands at its mouths.

The manufacturing regions of western Europe lie, also, at the European terminus of the North Atlantic Seaway, busiest shipping route in the world because it connects manufactural Europe with manufactural North America. Many other sealanes extend to Europe—from the Mediterranean, South America, and elsewhere. Merely the number of ships, the frequency of sailings, the shipping services available in the port cities, and the world-wide destination of the carriers provides manufacturers in western Europe with transport service at competitive rates to overseas markets enjoyed by few other manufacturing regions of the world.

Foreign or international trade zones have been established in several European port cities. These help increase home manufacture. Raw materials landed in these specially set aside (and fenced) areas are partially processed or completely manufactured within their limits. The semi-processed or finished manufactures are then shipped to markets overseas or in adjacent countries; the imported materials have not had duties paid upon them nor are duties collected on the exports (there are, of course, some charges for services). The advantage of these to the country and port city is not only the employment of home labor and management, but an increased income from shipping and other services.

The most concentrated manufacturing region of Europe—the "workshop" —includes the Central Lowland of Scotland, southern Wales, nearly all of England except the extreme south, and—on the continent—the strip of territory from the Dutch and Belgian ports eastward across Belgium and northern France, to the industrial centers of West Germany. The British manufacturing regions are somewhat scattered in location, but are most concentrated in London and its industrial suburbs, in the Midlands and the northeast of England, in South Wales and in the Central Lowland of Scotland, and at Belfast in Northern Ireland (part of the United Kingdom rather than the Republic of Ireland). The continental counterpart is more continuous. From near Lille in the very north of France, almost contiguous manufacturing cities stretch eastward on the coal fields of Belgium to the West German border near Aachen. East of the Rhine this conurbation is continued by the compact coal-mining and manufactural cities of the Ruhr. It then widens into many portions of West Germany. And a north-south industrial string of cities lie on the banks of the Rhine, united to the Ruhr center by excellent rail, water, and highway transportation. And, in northeast France, only a hundred miles removed from the continuous industrial region, is the iron ore and metallurgical center of Lorraine.

Every conceivable kind of manufactured product is produced in the British and continental core region of European industry. Here are the coal-mining districts which supply fuel and raw materials. Here is the iron ore of Lorraine. Here is the heavy industry—iron and steel, locomotives and railroad equipment, cement, and others. Here are the automobile and airplane factories, the chemical and associated manufactures, the machine and electrical industries, much of the consumer-goods manufacture. In short, to repeat the varied list of industries and products from country to country would involve the same general listing of manufactures in each, with only different centers of localization as boundaries are crossed.

Six European nations have formed a European Common Market recently to permit the interchange and free flow of raw materials and goods among them, and to enter world markets as an economic unit. Three had joined previously in a customs union—the Benelux countries of Belgium, the Netherlands, and Luxembourg. West Germany, France, and Italy have joined these three in the European Community. The community has problems to solve. Production costs in both manufacturing and agriculture, consumer prices, and government aids to farming and industry differ among the six countries. The United Kingdom chose to remain outside, but its manufacturers are watching the experiment, both as to its workability and the possibility of strong competition in European and world markets.

► THE UNITED KINGDOM

The coal fields of the Midlands and Northeast of England constitute the core region of British manufactures. Northward in Scotland the coal fields of the Central Lowland localize industry. The coal field of South Wales lies in hilly country; the industrial district using this coal is nearby on the Welsh shore of the Bristol Channel. The heavy industries, the lighter industries using steel in quantity, and many associated manufactures are within or very near the coal-mining areas. The textile industries, dating from the Industrial Revolution, also are mainly on or near the coal fields.

The manufacture of locomotives and railroad cars, of which Britain is the major exporter, and the shipbuilding industry are examples of the heavy industry of the Midlands and North.

Crewe, Manchester, Derby, Doncaster, and Glasgow are but a few of the cities in which the manufacture of railroad equipment is important. Both diesel and steam locomotives are produced. All types of railroad cars are built, reflecting the wide market. British investment in or building of railroads in South America, Africa, the Middle East, and India is reflected in the persistence of these world-wide markets for equipment, partly because of the use of the British gauge, and partly because of continued financial interests in the lines. Most of the steam locomotives are destined for export, because the British railroad system is now being dieselized. When this is accomplished the fuel for their operation will have to be imported.

The shipbuilding industry is concentrated in the ports near the steel mills and machinery centers of the North of England; it is a leading industry of the Glasgow district of Scotland, also, and of Belfast in Northern Ireland (part of the United Kingdom). Newcastle and neighboring cities at the mouth of the

River Tyne (Tyneside), Middlesbrough, and other cities on the Tees constitute the leading shipbuilding centers in the northeast of England. The Liverpool area (Merseyside) is important in the northwest. The Clyde River industrial complex, from Glasgow to the sea, is dotted with shipyards. Belfast receives its steel, machinery, and other equipment that is not manufactured in the city, and its coal for power, from the Scottish industrial centers across the Channel. All types of ships are constructed; the building of oil tankers is important at present. Also there is some shipbuilding in every British port of prominence, and all are equipped for the repair of ships.

British manufacturing centers specializing in automobile production, the manufacture of machine tools, heavy and light machines, electrical equipment and machinery, and similar "newer" industries are somewhat more widespread in location than the basic iron and steel industries, or the traditional woolen and cotton textiles dating from the Industrial Revolution. Although located in part in the iron and steel centers and the port cities, the machinery centers have evolved, or been located, in cities which were not highly industrialized during the last century. Coventry is an example. It is one of the automobile-assembly centers. As such—and with its wartime manufacture shifted to armaments, radar, projectiles, precision equipment, and similar items for the military— Coventry was bombed severely by the German air force. Other automobile centers in England are Kingston, Wolverhampton, and Oxford (originally only a university community) among smaller cities, and Birmingham and the Greater London area among larger.

British manufacturers have been very successful recently in the invasion of the machinery and automobile market of the United States, as well as other markets of the world. Electrical equipment, pumps, hydraulic machinery, transformers, and similar complex products are now in use in many American cities. Recently the United Kingdom and West Germany (together) have supplanted the United States as the chief exporters of automobiles. In part this was owing to aggressive salesmanship, in part to the small and compact European automobile offered to the American public. The small car of Europe reflects the high cost there of imported crude petroleum or refined gasoline, the existence of paved roads nearly everywhere in the western part of the continent and the British Isles, and the short distances to be traversed. The import of British, West German, French, and Italian cars to the United States and Canada became large enough by the late 1950's to result in the introduction of the American "compact car" in 1960 to meet the competition. Some American automobile companies have long had European manufacturing facilities or assembly plants; certain of these have been exporters of their European models as well, in part to the United States.

The cotton textile and the woolen and worsted industry of England were the first large-scale manufactures to develop with the Industrial Revolution. Each industry has been rooted to its original area for 200 or more years, the result of historical development. Originally many of the early factories were located at small dams, but the advent of steam power freed them from the dependence upon water power. Streams flowing from the Pennine Hills—a low range of hills extending north to south in the northern half of England—furnished the early powers, and then coal fields which lie on either side of the Pennines and at their southern terminus were drawn upon. Cotton textiles became localized on the western side of the Pennines, particularly in the region surrounding Manchester—the region of Lancashire. The woolen and worsted industry became centered east of the Pennines, in Yorkshire and adjacent counties. Cotton for Lancashire was imported through the nearby port of Liverpool. Two further reasons often cited for the cotton concentration on the damper western side of England were the need—at the time—for spinning cotton in damp air to prevent breakage of the thread, and the pure water from certain bedrock formations of the Pennines for perfect bleaching of the cloth. Air conditioning has made the former requirement a non-operative factor (there are modern cotton mills in desert-air Egypt) and modern technology permits treatment of water and the removal of harmful substances. The woolen and worsted industries, east of the Pennines, obtained wool from these highlands, from upland pastures, and from the important lowland sheep lands; today the local clip is supplemented by large imports of wool from the Southern Hemisphere. Woolens are important Scottish industries (many of the names in the trade are Scottish—tweeds, for example, from the River Tweed); wool from the Highlands of Scotland, the Southern Upland, and imported raw wool supply the raw materials. All raw cotton for the British industry is imported, principally through Liverpool, and, since the opening of the Manchester Ship Canal in 1894, through Manchester itself as well as Liverpool. Recently, the Lancashire Cotton-Textile District has suffered a large decline. Competition with Indian, Japanese, and other newer textile districts has been severe; markets in former British colonies have been lost to the evolving textile industries of countries with less expensive labor. As in New England, the English mills now stress mainly the high-value goods. These are exported to other industrial centers whose markets can absorb them; long-staple Egyptian cotton is imported for manufacture of quality cottons. And many of the mills—as in the United States —are no longer cotton mills alone, but work with other fibers and with British-made synthetic fibers.

The Manchester Ship Canal, 35½ miles long, has proved a magnet for the construction of new industrial plants along its banks. There was industry along it before World War II, but many war-founded plants were constructed on the Canal, as it was "farthest" from German bombing planes and yet near the coal fields for power. Recently, the rapidly-expanding chemical industry of the country, the petroleum-refining industry, the petrochemical industry, and others depending in whole or in part upon imported raw materials have chosen this location.

The potteries of Staffordshire are located in the area between the Liverpool-Manchester industrial areas on the north and the steel and machinery centers to their south in the "Black Country" around Birmingham. Many small to medium-sized towns constitute the pottery-manufacturing centers. Originally local China clays were used. Clays are now received from Cornwall, in the southwest of England, and from elsewhere. The market acceptance and the high quality of the British product, marketed throughout the world, has given Staffordshire fame and prestige. Sanitary pottery for the household market at home is manufactured also.

South Wales is an important manufacturing center. The industrial cities are mainly port cities on the Bristol Channel; they are very near the coal field. Other cities are on the fields themselves, but large parts of this coal field—in contrast to the usual situation in Europe—are in very rugged country, unsuitable for large urban development; some of the cities are crowded into narrow valleys, as in parts of the American Appalachian coal fields. Shipbuilding and the iron and steel industry are important in the port cities, such as Cardiff and Swansea, where there are many smelters and refineries which use Welsh coal in the smelting or processing of imported ores. Paper and rubber-goods are manufactured from imported materials, and Swansea is the tin-plate center of the United Kingdom. Such coal as is exported from Britain is usually from the South Wales field; before the days of oil-burning ships, the steaming coal from this field was shipped in quantity to coaling stations on the world's seaways for use as bunker coal.

Greater London is one of the largest manufacturing centers of present-day Britain, but is not one of the cities known for heavy industry. Manufacturing in London is characterized by its great diversification, its emphasis upon the consumer-goods industries in response to the local markets, its important food-processing industries associated with the importance of London as a major port and market as well as distribution center (in this respect much like New York), and as a men's clothing center. In addition, the Thames estuary, downstream from London, has developed, and continues to develop, as an important manufacturing district for the location of those industries using seaborne materials; some of these industries are in the East End of London, newer ones are between the city and the mouth of the Thames. Among these are petroleum refining, the chemical industries, and the power plants producing electricity from coal shipped southward on the North Sea from the Newcastle coal area of northeastern England.

Every type of manufacturing is engaged in somewhere in the United Kingdom, from heavy to light, from capital goods through consumer goods to specialty items, and even to some remaining handicraft industries dependent upon highly skilled labor. The nation is one of the major manufacturing countries of the world, and its wide array of manufactures is within a compact total area—the size only of an American state such as Oregon.

► THE INDUSTRIAL HEART OF WESTERN EUROPE

The Ruhr is the core of the intensive manufacturing region of the western part of the continent of Europe. Ruhr coal, iron and steel, and capital goods are so important to the industrial complex that the victorious powers in World War II, after first embarking on a project to dismantle the factories of the Ruhr, found it necessary to rebuild or refurbish them in order to keep the economy of the industrial area operating and prevent an economic collapse in the overall manufacturing region from Belgium to West Germany and in Luxembourg and northern France. The Ruhr alone produces half of the coal and a third of the steel of the new European Common Market (Netherlands, Belgium, Luxembourg, West Germany, France, and Italy). The Ruhr plus the industrial regions of Belgium, Luxembourg, and northern France mine as much coal as all of the United Kingdom and produce nearly twice the quantity of steel as Britain. Steel from the region even is exported, some to the United States. Essen is the best known of the cities of the Ruhr because it is the center of activity of one of the largest (both pre-World War II and postwar) of the German companies— one engaged in the manufacture of armaments, of iron and steel and their secondary products; one owning many of the most productive coal mines of the country and engaged in shipbuilding (at Kiel) and the construction of factories, steel mills, and refineries in several parts of the world. But Dortmund, Mulheim, Duisburg and a host of other cities dot the manufactural Ruhr. Duisburg-Ruhrort, at the junction of the Ruhr and the Rhine, is one of the busiest river ports of the world, crowded with barges. Dusseldorf, on the Rhine a short distance from the Ruhr proper, is the banking and financial center for the heavy industrial area. In addition to the Ruhr, the Saar of West Germany, Lorraine in France, and the industrial belt through central Belgium are leading steel centers and suppliers of capital goods in western Europe.

The centers of manufacture in western Europe are inland, on or near the coal fields. Electrical energy is supplied mainly by thermal plants; there are also hydroelectric plants, this region having essentially all of its water power developed. Additional energy is transmitted from the Alpine dams of Switzerland and Austria by wire, and is generated from imported petroleum.

Antwerp, Rotterdam, and Amsterdam are the principal ports which serve the continental manufactural region. They have direct rail and water connections with many of the industrial centers. Hamburg, Bremen, and Emden on the North Sea in West Germany and LeHavre in France perform certain services in the import and export trade engendered by the industrial centers.

The continental manufacturing region is an outstanding center of heavy industry and of the engineering, metallurgical, and machinery industries. It is also the center of the chemical and petrochemical manufactures of western Europe, and of automobile and aircraft manufacture. Its secondary and tertiary manufactures are numerous, and produce thousands of items made from steel and metals; steel (see pages 411–413) is a basic material of much of the manufacturing.

West Germany, France, and Belgium together produce the same quantity of locomotives and railway equipment as Britain. Barges, tugs, and small canal boats are an important regional industry, reflecting the significance of the Rhine and Scheldt rivers and the canal systems.

Automobile manufacture is important at Wolfsburg (near Hanover) in West Germany—the plant is one of the largest in the world; Nuremberg, Cologne, Dusseldorf, Stuttgart, and Bremen are other automobile centers of the country. The French portion of the industry is in part of the northern industrial centers, in part in industrial suburbs of Paris.

The chemical centers are located within the industrial region, and in the port cities—this last the result of the import of certain low-value, bulky raw materials, such as sulphur; potash is a regional raw material (pages 426–427). Germany has long been known for its varied chemical manufactures. The Netherlands has risen as a petrochemical center, the port cities of Amsterdam and Rotterdam, and inland cities in the Province of Limburg (in the extreme southeast, and on the small extension of the "Belgian" coal area into the Netherlands) now having leading chemical manufactures. Liége is an important Belgian center of industry. The Ruhr, and a string of river-located chemical plants on the Rhine, dominate the West German scene, but there is a chemical industry in practically every major manufacturing district of the country; Cologne, Wiesbaden, and Ludwigshaven are among the centers on the upper Rhine in West Germany. Frankfort on the Main is a diversified manufacturing city; some of the large chemical companies and the prewar combine were directed and managed from Frankfort; certain of their office buildings were taken over by the American Armed Forces for headquarters buildings of the American Zone of Occupation. Two or three large companies now dominate the German portion of the industry; these are post-World War II successors to the prewar chemical giant, the I. G. Farben, which controlled the German manufacture and had world-wide trade and interests.

The chemical industry of France is in three major districts. One is in the northern industrial region, part of the regional scene just discussed. The two other districts are near large sources of electrical energy developed by hydroelectric installations. One district uses the power from the streams of the French Alps, the other draws on power from the Pyrenees Mountains. Lyon and the Rhone Valley and its tributary Isère Valley are the sites of the plants oriented to the Alps; Bordeaux and several towns at the French base of the Pyrenees contain the plants of this district.

The machine and metallurgical centers, too numerous to mention, are generally in all of the manufacturing towns and cities of the West European industrial region. There are a few regional specialities; Belgium, for example, has long been important in the smelting of zinc. The smelting or the refining of other ores increased as the mining development of the Katanga of Africa expanded.

Textile industries are widespread within the industrial region. Lille in the extreme north of France is a significant center; labor is drawn in part from Belgium, the workers commuting daily. The linen and lace industries are noted manufactures of the Flanders Plain of western Belgium; Antwerp, Ghent, and Brussels are leading centers of this industry.

Amsterdam, Rotterdam, and Antwerp (see page 437) are the world centers of diamond cutting.

There is a scattered, but important manufacturing beyond the continuous industrial region. Several cities of southern West Germany are the location of the manufacture of machinery. A large chemical industry has been established in Munich. The coal field of Le Creusot in central France localizes industry; one of the important products of this region is armaments and military supplies, the French wishing to have this type of manufacture relatively far from their northeastern and northern frontier.

Shipbuilding in France is mainly an industry of the western peninsula—Brittany—and of the lower Loire River estuary. Brest is the major center. Other important shipyards are on the shore of the English Channel and North Sea—Dunkirk in France, Rotterdam and Amsterdam in the Netherlands, and Hamburg, Bremen, and Kiel in West Germany, Kiel being on a bay of the Baltic Sea but connected with the North Sea by the Kiel Canal which crosses the isthmus.

Paris in ringed by industrial suburbs. Paris proper is the center of consumer-goods manufacture of France, and of the women's clothing industry. The textiles originate in the mills of the north of France, or in the silk-manufacturing district in and around Lyon. Although the silk industry has declined relatively, the textile centers of the Lyon area continue as important producers of fabrics made of synthetic yarns. The position of Paris as the center of women's fashions for the Western world has been challenged recently by an Italian fashion industry in Rome. The growth of the women's-wear industry in the latter city has been phenomenal in recent years, and has been promoted by wide-scale advertising campaigns in Europe and the New World.

Manufacturing centers and districts of the Mediterranean coast of France and of Italy are in the two port cities of Marseilles and Genoa, and in the Po Valley of the north of Italy.

Marseilles is the chief port of the French trade with the tropics, and with North Africa and the Middle East. The cacao, cotton, peanuts, palm nuts, and other agricultural products of the French Community in tropical Africa are processed. Olive oils and wines, as well as wheat and mineral raw materials (phosphates) from the south shore of the Mediterranean are handled and processed. Oil from the Middle East is refined and distributed northward by pipeline. Marseilles, as a result of its trade, is a chocolate and vegetable-oil center, has a large soap industry, and is a distributing point for the French perfumes manufactured at Grasse and nearby towns in the flower-growing region of Mediterranean France.

The Po Valley or plain of North Italy has only two major assets for manufacturing—hydroelectric power from the Alps and inexpensive labor; peninsular Italy has the labor in quantity but lacks abundant power resources, and has to import the mineral fuels, Italy being deficient in all. Milan, Turin, and Genoa are the chief manufacturing cities. Steel for the automobile, railway equipment, shipbuilding, and machinery manufactures is imported by rail from north of the Alps or by sea from northwestern Europe; also there are small steel mills, working with imported ores and fuels, and with Italian iron ore from Elba, at all three cities. Milan, the leading manufacturing city of the country, has highly diversified industries; recently it has become the leading chemical center of the nation. Turin is the chief location of the Italian automobile industry. Genoa, the port, processes imported raw materials, is the major location of shipbuilding in Italy, and, with Turin, manufactures heavy equipment, locomotives, and railroad rolling stock. The Italian manufacture of silk, rooted in the Po Valley from the early days of trade with the Orient, is located in several Po cities. It depends upon imported raw silk as well as upon the Po Valley production.

Peninsular Italy contains many recently founded chemical industries, especially in its northern half. Naples and other cities have electrical manufacture, and a great deal of small-shop handicraft manufacture; Italian-made articles of leather are examples.

Switzerland and Austria differ from the chief manufactural regions of western Europe in their type of industry. The emphasis is upon skilled labor and high-value products, whose value is owing mainly to the labor expended upon them rather than the intrinsic value of the materials. Of the two, Switzerland is far more industrialized.

Switzerland has few local raw materials. Milk for the manufacture of cheese and milk chocolate is the only one in surplus supply that can be used in manufacturing. All other materials are imported in whole or in part. High-grade steel, cloth, machine parts, gold, and similar materials are imported for use and further manufacture. Many hours of expert labor are expended upon these to produce watches, watch movements, scientific apparatus, precision articles, hydraulic machinery, turbines, electrical apparatus, sewing machines, and other specialty products for export. Geneva and the French-speaking portion of Switzerland is the watch-manufacturing district; La-Chaux-de-Fonds and Le Locle are other important centers of this industry. Zurich is important in the manufacture of electrical equipment and hydroelectric machinery; many American companies in this field have Swiss engineers on their staffs. Textiles are manufactured in eastern Switzerland. Large-scale manufacture, however, is not unknown; Basel, on the Rhine at the head of navigation, is a chemical center. Hydroelectric power from Alpine streams is used in Swiss industry and is exported to Germany; and electricity powers the Swiss railroad system.

The manufacturing districts east of the Iron Curtain are in East Germany, Poland, Czechoslovakia, and Hungary—countries now in the Soviet sphere of influence. Manufactured products from these countries are marketed within them, are shipped to the Soviet Union, or are exported under various trade agreements or barter arrangements of the Union. For example, machine tools from Czechoslovakia, steel from Poland, and buses from Hungary are in use in many parts of the world wherein trade agreements or other exchange arrangements have been negotiated. There are lignite and bituminous coal fields in East Germany, several steel centers, a significant chemical industry in the Zwickau-Chemnitz region, and diversified manufacturing in large cities such as Leipzig and Dresden. The Bohemian portion of western Czechoslovakia has long had highly developed industry. There are steel and armament factories at Pilsen, a large manufacture of heavy machinery, machine tools and metals, and an important glass industry—pre-War Czechoslovakia was world famous for its glass. In Silesia, now chiefly in Poland but partly in Czechoslovakia, the coal fields supply fuel and coke for one of the important steel districts of Europe; it will be remembered that zinc is mined in Silesia, too, and helps supply raw materials for varied industries using metals—other metals being mined nearby in the Erzgebirge Mountains on the border of Czechoslovakia and East Germany. Lodz in Poland is a leading textile center, and textiles and shoes are important manufactures of Czechoslovakia. Hungary is less industrialized than its satellite neighbors. Meat-packing and the milling of flour reflect the home agricultural materials. Assembly-type industries have been introduced; of these the manufacture of buses and trucks is especially important. Some of the parts and the engines are manufactured in neighboring Czechoslovakia and East Germany, and sheet steel is received from these countries and Poland. Industries based on agricultural raw materials, such as sugar-beet refining, are present in all of the satellite countries, and Poland and East Germany manufacture starch, flour, alcohol, and other products from the ever-present potato—so dominant in the agriculture of the Baltic Plain. Poland exports canned ham to the United States and other countries from its own ports of Gdansk (former Danzig), Gdynia, and Szczecin (former German city of Stettin) and has a shipbuilding industry in each of these ports.

The Scandinavian countries contain less intensive industry than the main manufacturing regions of the European continent. Sweden is especially important among the three. Its industry in the south is associated with the manufacture of machines, tools, and specialty steels for export. The wood-products industries of the north lie beyond the major manufacturing region. Norway is important for the use of its abundant hydroelectric energy for the manufacture of nitrates from the air and for various metallurgical industries requiring large amounts of power. Final use of these products is in the continental or British industrial centers. Copenhagen in Denmark is noted for its chinaware industry, the clay originating on the Baltic island of Bornholm. Finland has leading wood-working industries, and shares with Sweden and Norway the export of home-manufactured wood pulp and newsprint.

► MANUFACTURING IN THE SOVIET UNION

The Soviet Union ranks among the top four manufacturing countries of the world. Its position from one industry to another varies when compared to the United States, the United Kingdom, and West Germany. It is second only to the United States in certain manufactural activities, and follows the three nations in others.

Soviet manufactural regions are widespread. Districts within the broad regions are developed intensively. But, on the whole, no single Soviet district has the concentrated industrial continuity of the core area of manufacturing in western Europe.

Contained within the Soviet sphere of influence are the manufactural regions of East Germany, Poland, and Czechoslovakia, and the oil fields of Rumania. The fuels, raw materials, and manufactured goods of these satellite countries are directed to and consumed in the Soviet sphere—many of them in the Soviet Union proper, adding to the industrial strength of the nation.

There was manufacturing in the Russian Empire of the last century and the early twentieth century; the Tula area near Moscow, the St. Petersburg (now Leningrad) district, the Donbas and other areas were suppliers of goods to Russia. But the particular and spectacular rise of the country to its present manufactural importance has occurred since the 1920's, and was initiated on a planned scale with the First Five Year Plan of 1928–1932. The fact that governmental authorities could decide on where power plants and industries were to be established, could dictate what end products were to be supplied (capital goods were emphasized above consumer goods), and could move labor at will from place to place provided a milieu for industrial development unlike that of the Western world or of Japan. New power sources and industries were established under later Five Year Plans. Old industrial regions were expanded; for example, the Donbas supplied 25 million tons of coal in 1915, but this constituted seven-eighths of the entire Russian production; by 1940 the mines of the Donbas yielded nearly 85 million tons of coal, but this was only half of the coal production of the Soviet Union. And, with the opening of new coal fields elsewhere not only was capital directed to the enterprise, but labor was uprooted and moved to the new area to man it.

The rise in manufactures has been accomplished in several ways under a regime foreign to the Western world. Government-appointed managers have had quotas to reach, at the threat of removal. Labor has been given quotas and the speed-up has been introduced. Workers who have met or exceeded the quotas may be rewarded with better housing; or, recently, incentive pay has been given them.

FIG. 21-2. A chemical plant, manufacturing synthetic fibers for the textile industry of the Soviet Union. The plant is in Trans-Caucasia, south of the Caucasus Mountains. (Sovfoto)

F<small>IG</small>. 21-3. Factory near the Baku Oil Field of the Soviet Union where plastics are manufactured. (Sovfoto)

To date the products of Soviet industry have only a small impact on world markets—everything produced has been needed at home to develop the country. This is not to say that "dumping" of goods to upset western markets, barter arrangements, and outright gifts of products to receive favors in return have not occurred. They have. But the building of heavy industry, railways, metallurgical centers, a textile industry, and the entire industrial complex has required the use of nearly all of the products of manufacturing within the Soviet area, and since the late 1940's and early 1950's a very large but unknown quan-

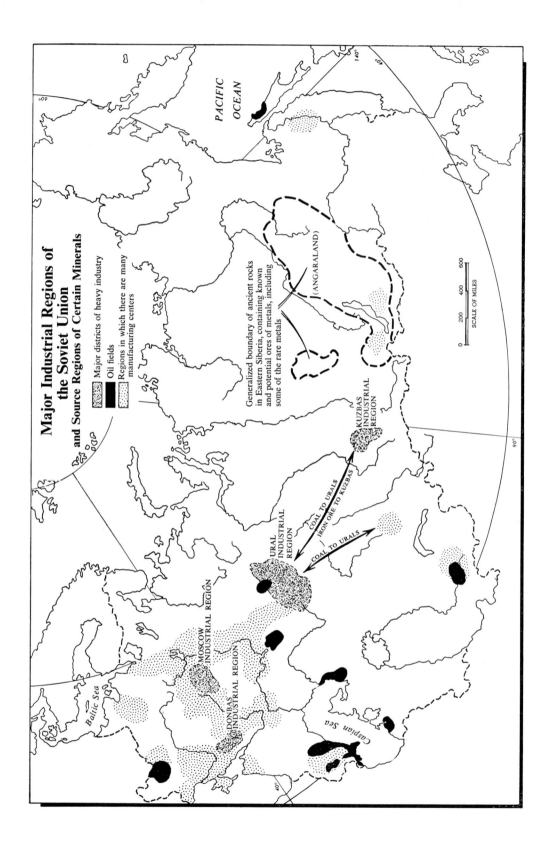

Major Industrial Regions of the Soviet Union and Source Regions of Certain Minerals

Major districts of heavy industry

Oil fields

Regions in which there are many manufacturing centers

Generalized boundary of ancient rocks in Eastern Siberia, containing known and potential ores of metals, including some of the rare metals

(ANGARALAND)

PACIFIC OCEAN

KUZBAS INDUSTRIAL REGION

URAL INDUSTRIAL REGION

COAL TO URALS

IRON ORE TO KUZBAS

COAL TO URALS

MOSCOW INDUSTRIAL REGION

DONBAS INDUSTRIAL REGION

Baltic Sea

Caspian Sea

SCALE OF MILES

0   200   400   600

tity of capital goods, ranging from mining machinery to tools for factories, has been poured into the development of the People's Republic of China (Red China). During the last few years somewhat of a change in industrial output has occurred within the Union, the consumer-goods industries having been expanded in response to increasing pressure from the Russian people for household appliances and other goods so usual in the Western world.

There are three major iron and steel regions in the Soviet Union, several of lesser relative importance, and some now under development. The major ones are on and near the coal fields of the Donbas in southern European Russia, on and near the coal fields of the Kuznetsk Basin (Kuzbas) in central Siberia, and in the region of the Ural Mountains (see pages 413–415). In addition there are iron and steel districts north of the Sea of Azov and on the Kerch Peninsula between this sea and the Black Sea, districts in central Russia in a broad arc south and east of Moscow (and steel is made in the environs of Moscow), mills in Leningrad and its suburbs, the so-called Molotov group of steel mills west of the central Urals, a large and new steel mill at Temir-Tau in Kazakhstan, and a steel industry in Siberia near Lake Baikal and at Komsomolsk on the Amur River in the Soviet Far East near the Pacific Ocean. Iron and steel for the Central Asian lands is provided by a mill in the vicinity of Tashkent. Furthermore, in addition to the widespread dispersion of the steel industry in the home territory described above, the Soviet Union either controls or has access to the production of the steel districts of Silesia in Poland and Czechoslovakia, of Pilsen and other Czech centers, and of East Germany.

Much of the basic heavy industry of the Soviet Union is associated with the three major steel-producing regions or with the steel-producing regions in the broad vicinity of Moscow. These regions have the advantage of location in and near the "heartland" of the Soviet Union, and hence in an area which has experienced, and continues to experience, the rapid development of industry through government planning and determination of the sites of secondary and tertiary industries (in effect, thus, near markets). Among these industries associated in general with the principal steel-producing regions are the metallurgical industries, the manufacture of transportation equipment (except airplanes), and the manufacture of heavy machinery and mining machinery. The largest of the chemical centers are likewise in the same general regions, reflecting in this case the use of coal as one of the raw materials. The manufacture of synthetic rubber, for example, upon which the Soviet Union is almost completely dependent, is based upon coal as the primary raw material—rather than petroleum, as in the United States.

The "outlying" steel centers—those of Kazakhstan, those near Lake Baikal, and those of Komsomolsk—serve their regions. As these regions develop, the steel industries are expanded, and the metallurgical and other industries are introduced. Thus it is to be expected that heavy industry will increase in these outlying centers as regions such as Kazakhstan, Central Asia, the Lake Baikal

Fig. 21-4. Workers entering the main gate of the steel mill at Stalinsk in the Kuznetsk Basin of Siberia. (Sovfoto)

area, and the Soviet Far East develop. But, to date, the principal of the heavy industrial centers are associated with the Donbas, the Kuzbas, the Urals, or the broad Moscow region.

The machine-tool industry, the manufacture of automobile, truck, and airplane engines and other special engineering products, and the manufacture of other special machines is more widespread. Many of these are made in the broad region of Moscow-Tula-Gor'kiy and nearby cities. Tractors and other agricultural machinery are produced at many centers in the agricultural belt of the southern half of European Russia, and in the towns of the steppe lands of the wheat belt of western Siberia. Stalingrad, on the lower Volga River, centrally placed in the extensive wheat lands of the Volga steppes, claims the largest tractor factory in the world. Saratov, farther north on the lower Volga, is another of the major centers for the production of tractors. Automobiles are made in Moscow itself, and Moscow and its satellite cities are the location of the manufacture of precision machines, for the production of which highly skilled workers are essential.

The manufacture of consumer goods in which steel or metals are part of the material, and of other consumer goods—clothing, leather products, and so on—is widespread within the southern half of European Russia, the area with the largest and most evenly spread population of the country. Within this area there are local concentrations in the major cities, and a particular concentration in Moscow and the circle of cities surrounding it at a distance of 100 to 200 miles. Electric power for this area is generated in thermal plants which use lignite coal from the Moscow Lignite Field; some thermal plants burn peat. The Leningrad market, 400 miles northwest of Moscow, is served by consumer-goods industries in the city.

The cities of the Moscow region contain much of the textile industry of the Soviet Union. Ivanovo is the leading textile center, followed by Moscow itself. The textile plants use wool from Soviet sources; silk is received from China and is from the silk-producing valleys south of the Caucasus Mountains—the valleys between the Black and Caspian Seas; cotton is obtained from the cotton lands of the steppes north of the Black Sea and from the government and collectivized cotton farms of Soviet Central Asia; the synthetic yarns are products of the chemical industry. The textile region is basically oriented to the markets. The manufacture of textile machinery is most important in several cities north of Moscow and is related to the market for these machines.

Recent Five-Year Plans have envisaged a dispersal of textile manufacture. New cotton mills have been established in the cotton-growing area of Central Asia. Other mills have been built between this chief source region of cotton and the present major textile centers.

New industrial regions have been developed in the Soviet Union as a result of several of the Five-Year Plans. These regions are now having industries expanded within them, and even the manufacture of consumer goods for regional use is being introduced. This is to be expected in a country the size of the Soviet Union. Among the several relatively recent industrial areas are the region west of the central Urals (the Molotov area), the region in the same latitude but east of the Urals, the region around Novosibirsk in western Siberia, the Irkutsk area near Lake Baikal, the Soviet Far East, and Soviet Central Asia near Tashkent. These areas have been added to the "older" regions of the Donbas, the Moscow-Tula-Gor'kiy area, Leningrad, the middle Volga area, the older region of the Urals, and the Kuznetsk Basin—of course, with a few exceptions, the "older regions" are relatively new in the manufactural scene of the world.

The Molotov area contains some coal fields and lies in the broad region of the Second Baku Oil Field. Both thermal and hydroelectric installations provide power. According to Soviet figures the Second Baku now provides half of the petroleum of the Union. Iron and other metals from the Urals are used in the region. On a broad scale the two new regions of industry on either side of the central Urals might be considered a part of a "greater Urals" district; they lie, however, somewhat farther north than the Sverdlovsk-Chelyabinsk-Magnitorgorsk centers in and near the Urals.

The Novosibirsk industrial region is west of the Kuznetsk Basin. The city contains plants which manufacture tractors and other agricultural machines for the government farms of the Siberian steppes. Electrical equipment is made. The manufacture of railway equipment reflects the position of the city as a major center on the Trans-Siberian Railroad (see Fig. 22-2).

A coal field now being developed lies near Irkutsk. The metals of Angaraland are obtained in the trade territory of the city. Large water power dams are being developed—one to be the largest in the world (see page 381). Transportation equipment is manufactured for use on the Trans-Siberian Railroad, and on the lines of Outer Mongolia and China. Other industries are being expanded.

The Bureya coal field and coal from the island of Sakhalin supplies the Soviet Far East. Komsomolsk, with its steel and metallurgical industries is the industrial center.

The steel, chemical, and machine industries of Soviet Central Asia supply the regional market. Tashkent has been developed as the major industrial center. The textile industry, as mentioned, is of national as well as regional importance.

Pulp and paper manufacture, the sawmill and lumber industry, and other factories using wood are located in the broad areas of the wooded lands of northern European Russia and in accessible sites in northern Siberia. Wood pulp and newsprint are two of the principal exports of the Union. Archangelsk, on the Northern Dvina River near its mouth in the White Sea, claims to be one of the largest sawmill centers in the world.

Shipbuilding is an important industry of Leningrad on the Gulf of Finland, and of Nikolayev on the Black Sea. There is a modest construction of commercial ships at Vladivostok on the Pacific. The construction of ships for the navy, particularly the submarine phase of the industry, is unknown.

The Soviet Union lacks tropical raw materials. These it must purchase, obtain in barter agreements, or else use substitutes. The beet sugar industry is fostered at home; occasional arrangements result in the obtaining of cane sugar, such as the exchange in 1960 of Soviet oil for Cuban sugar. Many plants from which rubber can be obtained (guayule bushes and others) are the subject of experimentation; there has been some success in adapting them to the Russian environment. Nevertheless, natural rubber is imported, and, to ensure home supplies of rubber a very large synthetic-rubber industry has been developed. The production of synthetic rubber is believed to be the largest in the world.

The locative factors, even the location of production, of many Soviet industries are unknown or known only to the degree that the government chooses to release. Airplane production in total is second only to the United States but the locations of many producing centers are not known. The atomic and other nuclear installations, the missile-manufacturing centers, and similar "strategic" manufactured locations are closely guarded secrets; the general broad region of production can only be surmised. The Soviet Union is able to withhold facts of this sort because of its size. Places in inner Siberia are 2,000 miles from the western frontiers or from the Pacific, and (by polar route) that far or farther from inhabited areas of the Western Hemisphere. Foreigners are barred from visiting large parts of the country. Thus the output of certain products or industries cannot be compared accurately with the production of other industrial regions of the world. For others complete figures are released and published.

► MANUFACTURING IN JAPAN

Japan now leads all countries in the building of ships and has an important manufacture of locomotives and railroad equipment and a large textile industry. It produces more cameras than any other nation, and has developed an automobile industry of moderate size. The chemical industries are important and have grown rapidly during the last few years. The manufacture of agricultural machinery has been established. The manufactural importance of Japan not only has resumed its significance of the days prior to World War II, but has exceeded it; total production during the decade of the 1950's rose by 70 per cent.

The basic manufacturing activity of present-day Japan is associated principally with the same types of industry that characterizes the United States, western Europe, and the Soviet Union. In addition Japanese products include the many goods associated with the Orient and marketed around the world in luxury markets or as exotic material, and the novelty items of inexpensive manufacture which flood the tourist centers and compete in the seasonal markets.

Manufacturing in Japan—other than the handicraft and small-shop industries—dates only from the very end of the nineteenth and the beginning of the twentieth centuries. During this period the country embarked on a course designed to emulate the United States and western Europe. Japanese manufacturers at the time looked to China as a source of cotton and other raw materials, and to China as a market for goods produced in Japan. The economic penetration of Manchuria followed some years later, and the fuels, mineral materials, and soybeans of Manchuria supplied further bases for industry. In the 1920's and 1930's the markets of the East Indies, and even of India and eastern Africa, were penetrated, and the exports of manufactured cotton goods to the United States was considerable. A large import of raw cotton from India and the United States arose, the expanding exports paying for these. The textile industries— in line with economic theory—became the most important original industry. Now the nation has moved beyond this state to a more varied industry and to more complex manufactures.

Japanese manufacturers possess a cost advantage over industries in the traditional manufacturing nations. Labor costs have always been low. Prior to World War II, industry, on a western standard so far as production was concerned, remained on an Oriental standard in wage scales and the living level of the workers. Wage rates and standards have risen since the conflict, but the differential remains and provides Japan with a competitive advantage in many world markets. Furthermore a fact of importance to industry is the large size of the Japanese merchant fleet and the relatively low transfer costs (including wages of seamen) in the overseas shipments of manufactured goods. This permits manufacture and export of some items of remarkably low value. Examples of these—exported to the United States—are cotton rags for use in filling stations for the attendant to wipe windshields, Easter bunnies and "cotton" chickens, souvenirs for tourist centers from coast to coast, low-value cotton materials, and novelties of all sorts. The merchant fleet, in turn, returns with raw materials for Japanese industry—raw cotton, scrap iron, ores, and other materials (see FIG. 18-8). The fishing fleet ranges into the eastern and southwestern Pacific, returns with tuna for Japanese canneries, and some of the canned fish are exported across the Pacific to United States markets; the distances traversed in these operations are tremendous.

The Japanese manufactures (and exports) based upon their Oriental heritage form a different category. The silk brocades and art objects are in demand in luxury markets of the Western world, reflecting the difference in types of product owing to different cultures. These and other "Oriental goods" of high quality are manufactured today chiefly in Japan or in the British crown colony of Hong Kong, near the coast of southern China. The two compete; labor in crowded Hong Kong—now even more crowded with refugees from Communist China—is even less costly than in Japan. There is some specialization in these two centers; for example, the carving of ivory from African elephants into art objects is a virtual monopoly of Hong Kong. Competition is strongest in the high-quality textile field, and Oriental brocades are manufactures of importance in both Hong Kong and the textile centers of Japan.

The industrial region of Japan lies on the Pacific side of Honshu, the main island, and extends to the northern shores of Kyushu, the southernmost of the large islands. In its mid-section the region lies on the "inland sea of Japan"— the channels and waterways which separate Honshu from the island of Shikoku. Its overall extent is from the Tokyo-Yokohama conurbation to Nagasaki. Between these extremities are the manufacturing cities of Nagoya, Osaka, Kobe, and Hiroshima, as well as smaller industrial clusters. Within this region all types of industry are present, but it is the manufactures based upon iron and steel, metals, chemical materials, and the textile industries which provide Japan with its present importance as a principal industrial center—rather than the novelty and exotic (for the Western world) items. The steel (see page 415), metal, and chemical industries provide many of the materials which are used in the region.

The shipbuilding industry is most concentrated in the Tokyo-Yokohama area, and in Osaka and Nagasaki, but there is some construction of ships—particularly fishing vessels—in every port of consequence. The concentrated and major region, however, specializes in liners, merchant vessels, oil tankers and other major types of carriers. Japanese shipyards now construct and launch more vessels for registration in the merchant fleets of the world than are built in any other country; collectively the countries of western Europe build more ships, but no single one now reaches the total of new registered tonnage from Japan. Japanese-built tonnage surpassed that of Britain during the decade of the 1950's; between 1950 and 1960 the countries' output of world-registered tonnage advanced from 10 per cent to about 30 per cent of the total. Not all Japanese-built ships are for the nation's merchant marine; European shipyards have contracted for the construction of many oil tankers; American shipyards have had merchant vessels, ore carriers, and tankers built in Japan—officials of the companies have then flown to the Orient for the launching ceremony. The main advantage enjoyed by Japan is its skilled workers in the industry and its far lower costs of labor, whether skilled or semi-skilled.

Tokyo, Nagoya, Osaka, and Kobe are the leading centers for the manufacture of railway cars and locomotives. Several suburbs and satellite cities of Tokyo contain automobile factories. Tokyo itself is a major center of the industry. There are plants, too, in Yokohama, Osaka, and Hiroshima.

Tractor factories are a very recent addition to the Japanese manufactural scene. The demand, resulting from the very small size of farm, is for the hand tractor—comparable to a power mower. The home market for these has expanded enormously during the 1950's. Thus Japanese agriculture is becoming mechanized to this degree.

The chemical industries of Japan are located mainly in the southern half of Honshu in smaller cities, although Tokyo, Nagoya, and Osaka are important centers. Sunagawa, in inland Hokkaido (the northern island) has a large industry. The widespread waterpower, developed on the many steep-gradient streams descending from the interior mountains, has been a localizing factor for many plants.

The Osaka area has long been a principal cotton-textile center. The manufacture of silk is inland, in part, in the towns of the mountain valleys and tectonic basins, near the principal silkworm-rearing regions.

The many products of the consumer-goods industries which are marketed in Japan and are exported in quantity—transistor radios, standard radios, cameras, photographic equipment, pottery and chinaware—are manufactured within the industrial region; Tokyo is a leading center. In contrast some of the novelty items are produced in small and scattered factories or even on farms during the off-season in agriculture.

The market-orientation of Japan's manufactures has changed with the years. The Chinese market has been lost; it now lies within the Communist world. China is engaged in the development of manufacturing. Raw materials are no longer available to Japan. With the years beginning even before World War II, Japanese manufactures for export were directed to world markets rather than the nearby Asian mainland. The reorientation is virtually complete. The question of the reopening of a market in mainland China depends upon circumstances beyond the control of Japan.

► OUTLYING MANUFACTURAL DISTRICTS

The highly developed self-governing nations of the British Commonwealth of Nations contain small manufacturing regions. These supply home markets and produce surpluses for export. The post-World War II rise of manufacturing in Australia has been especially prominent. Both Australia and the Union of South Africa now export small quantities of steel and some capital goods. Australia, New Zealand, and the Union have food-processing industries, and they manufacture many consumer goods for home markets. Smelting of ores is important in Australia and prominent in the Union of South Africa.

There are local manufacturing districts in the nations of Latin America. The food industries of Argentina, Uruguay, and southern (non-tropical) Brazil are associated mainly with meat packing and—in Argentina—flour milling and the manufacture of cheese. São Paulo in Brazil has become the major industrial center of the country. Its growth has been rapid. Industry is varied. Iron and steel from nearby Volta Redonda is used in manufactures of capital and consumer goods. The textile industry is important. Monterrey in Mexico is the leading industrial center of that country. An expanding textile industry in and near Mexico City is probably the vanguard of increasing diversification of manufacture.

India is expanding its industries. Basic manufactures, such as steel and cement, are well established there in certain districts. Communist China is following the Soviet Union in efforts to industrialize.

The impact of manufacturing on world trade varies among these outlying districts. Australia, New Zealand, and the Union of South Africa supply certain products to world markets, produce some of their own needs of capital goods, and produce more of their needs of consumer goods. They offer, however, large home markets for the manufactured products of the major manufacturing regions of the Northern Hemisphere. Thus the reciprocal trade is in all varieties of goods. In contrast the manufactural output of Brazil, Mexico, and India is needed at home (except, say, for mineral concentrates) and is so used; imports of manufactured goods from the traditional industrial centers is large, by percentage. In further contrast, the developing industrial output of China is all needed at home and has made little impact on overseas trade; interchange and aid is within the Communist world, and the extent of this is unknown as it is with the Soviet Union. Neither is the amount of aid in the shipment of capital goods from the Soviet Union to China—to help establish industry—known. If history repeats itself, and China is able to develop a large output of manufactures, it will be many years—even decades—before the home needs of the teeming and expanding population (some estimates forecast a billion Chinese by the year 2000) will be met.

► QUESTIONS

1. Where are the important manufacturing districts of western Europe? Where are those of central Europe, now back of the Iron Curtain but not in the Soviet Union proper? What have been the major factors in the localization of these districts?
2. What advantages, besides the momentum of an early start, does the United Kingdom possess for manufacturing?
3. It has been noted (in the sections on agriculture) that land is in relatively short supply relative to population in western Europe. What is the situation regarding land and labor in the manufacturing activity of western Europe?
4. What land, water, and sea transport routes serve the industries of western Europe?
5. The Ruhr of West Germany is very significant to the industrial scene in several neighboring countries as well as in West Germany. Why?
6. Explain why much of Belgium, the Rhine Valley, and the north of France constitute the "core region" of manufacturing in the western part of the continent.
7. Why are the Rhine River and the ports of the Netherlands among the largest handlers of waterway traffic in the world?
8. London is one of the most important manufacturing cities of Europe, but it is not noted for the kind of products made in the Midlands of England, in the Ruhr, or in Lorraine. What is the differentiation in manufacturing between London on the one hand and the others collectively?
9. Has the development of large hydroelectric powers in the Scottish Highlands, the Alps, and the Pyrenees been a factor in the location of "new" industries? Explain, and give examples.
10. The manufactures of Marseilles are oriented toward Middle Eastern and African raw materials. Explain.
11. Why is there a great deal of manufacturing in the chief port cities of western Europe? How do international trade zones aid this, in part? Why are imported ores usually smelted or refined in a port city?
12. What assets does the Po Valley possess for manufacturing?
13. Characterize the types of manufacturing of Switzerland.
14. Compare the types of industry of the Scandinavian countries with those of Canada that are found north of the St. Lawrence Valley–Ontario peninsula.
15. Which iron and steel districts of the Soviet Union are basically located with respect to raw materials, and which are related, at least in part, to the population centers (and hence markets)?

16. What are some of the industries associated with Moscow and the ring of outlying cities some one hundred to two hundred miles from the capital?

17. Why has Soviet emphasis been upon the primary and capital goods industries rather than upon consumer goods (although production of the latter has increased recently)?

18. The Soviet Union has a long coast line, but much of it lies on the Arctic Ocean. Excluding this, where are the ports and the shipbuilding industry located?

19. What mining, power, and manufactural developments are associated with Angaraland, the Irkutsk region, and the Soviet Far East?

20. How has the distance and size (not to mention censorship and travel restrictions) of the Soviet Union aided the government in withholding information from the Western world—or releasing only the information it wishes?

21. What enables Japanese industry to import raw materials, fabricate them, and export manufactured products successfully to distant world markets?

XXII Commerce, Transportation, Service,

and Recreation

Commerce includes the wide range of activities associated with buying and selling, with the handling and transport of goods, and with the financing of the economic system. In its many forms it is part of and basic to the modern agricultural and industrial world. The service occupations have increased by percentage as manufacturing and commerce have developed to their present significance. As machines have replaced and aided men in the manufactural centers, and as hours of labor have been shortened, an important recreational industry has expanded. Thus the activities of commerce, the serving of others, and the provision of recreational facilities employ large numbers of people. These in turn furnish markets for the agricultural and manufactural products. These markets are not only domestic but often are international as well, forming ties among nations the world over. The interdependence of peoples the world over, and the complex web of interdependence in the industrial nations, in the countries engaged in commercial agriculture, in the business centers and market places, and in governmental activities is astounding. It is characteristic of the developed portions of the modern world. The interconnections are more simple in the less developed areas.

The business center of a city is its commercial core. Here are the retail establishments, the banks, insurance offices, stockbrokers, and the headquarters of other commercial activities. Nearby, or in outlying locations, are the wholesaling establishments and warehouses. Business districts in other portions of a city are also commercial centers, usually, in this case, serving the surrounding neighborhood. Shopping centers and suburban commercial districts to which the customer transports himself by automobile have arisen, especially in the United States and Canada. And, as a result of suburbanization many wholesaling and warehousing activities have shifted their location from a crowded commercial core to an outlying site offering more space and lower taxes; this last is mainly a shift occurring in Anglo-America alone—in response to the automobile.

Commerce is an important function of all port cities, and is outstanding in the great ports of the world. The merchant ships transport the varied products on the oceans. Landways and airways are routes of commerce. And other "transporters" of commerce are the telephone lines, cables, telegraph systems, wireless and radio systems—for commerce involves the buying and selling of promises as well as goods; the purchaser of an insurance policy receives only a piece of paper which is a contract or a promise.

Commerce, like other forms of human activity, tends to become regionalized; it is not spread evenly throughout a country. Thus, not only have specialized commercial districts developed in every city, but individual cities—usually those possessing a commanding geographical location—have become commercial centers. Both a large number and a high percentage of the gainfully employed workers of such a city are engaged in commercial activities. These cities stand out from other cities because their commercial specialization is above the average. All cities, large or small, have a generally uniform percentage of their workers employed in commercial work, such as retail stores; even the small rural village is basically a commercial village serving the surrounding territory. But the cities whose economic life is oriented heavily to commerce may be termed commercial cities, just as other cities are definitely centers of manufacturing, of government, or are educational centers such as college towns.

► COMMERCIAL CITIES

Every industrial or commercial nation contains a city or cities whose business activities transcend manufacturing alone, and a large percentage of whose inhabitants are engaged in commerce. The commercial functions of these cities serve the entire country, or, in the case of a nation with a large area, serve a considerable region or even a section. The commercial cities are the dominant national or regional banking and financial centers, the market place for stocks and bonds, the quotation centers for prices of commodities, the warehousing centers, and the places where goods are stored for distribution to the retail merchants of the territory served by the city.

The great commercial cities of Europe are usually either the major port city or the capital of the country, commonly the latter. The small area of most countries, the dominant position of the capital as the center of the government, of the transportation system, and of finance, has resulted in the centralization of many branches of commerce at this location; the port cities handle the imports and exports, but the capital furnishes nearly all other services.

London is the transportation and banking center of the United Kingdom. Its financial services extend beyond the nation itself to many countries of the British Commonwealth. Certain aspects of its commerce are world-wide. Paris not only performs many commercial functions for all of France, but contains highly centralized activities; farm produce from all over the country, for example, is transported to Paris, sold there in wholesale lots, then distributed to retailers all over France. Garden produce from the Riviera thus is shipped to Paris, wholesaled, and may be returned for retailing to the nearby city of Marseilles. The payrolls of many companies and the drawing of checks in payment —even the payrolls of the French university system—are made out in Paris rather than locally. Berlin lost many of its commercial functions when it became an outlier of West Germany; Bonn, the new capital, has assumed only a few. Dusseldorf is the commercial center for the nearby Ruhr industrial area.

Tokyo, Buenos Aires, Rio de Janeiro and other capitals are major commercial cities.

In contrast to the non-American and the non-Canadian scene, the principal commercial cities of the United States and Canada are elsewhere than in Washington or Ottawa. However, as more power has been centered in the federal government recently than was the case in the early days of the Republic, and as many decisions affecting the money market particularly are made in Washington, its effect on financial and banking affairs is now considerable. Montreal, Toronto, Winnipeg, and Vancouver are the principal cities of Canada with leading commercial functions of all sorts.

The commercial cities of the United States—those with very important regional commercial activities—have developed at locations that have proved exceptionally favorable for the command of large surrounding regions. They have become the centers for the national or regional distribution of goods and commercial services such as banking and insurance. Their site may be at a natural focal point of land traffic, a well-located and commodious harbor from which there are easy routes to a productive hinterland, the gateway to a pass through which traffic is funneled, at or near the end of a natural barrier around which land transport is directed (Lake Michigan and Chicago—southern terminus of the higher Appalachians—Atlanta), or at a focal point on navigable river systems (St. Louis in the past, and then, with the advent of railroads, becoming a rail center). In all cases the strategic site has become a regional center for the railroad and highway systems, later of the airways. Man has made the focal point accessible from the surrounding region, and in turn the surrounding region is accessible from the commercial center.

The commercial cities of the United States differ in size. They serve regions of different types of markets and densities of population. They receive manufactured products from many places; and they wholesale and distribute these in their trade territories. The distribution of consumer goods, of processed foods, and of machine parts is of significance in all. Some are so large and complex that they are important manufactural as well as commercial centers, New York and Chicago being examples. Some—particularly two, New York and Chicago—are national distribution centers for individual products or of national retailing organizations. Some are oriented to their region almost entirely; they receive goods from the Manufacturing Belt and distribute them entirely within their regional trade territory. Atlanta dominates the southeast in this, Dallas dominates the Texas and southwestern region. The locations of the headquarters of the Federal Reserve (Bank) districts of the United States is in effect a listing of the important commercial centers, with one or two exceptions; and some regional centers in addition are not included as headquarters cities. The list, however, is revealing of the regional centers, not only in the types of commerce discussed heretofore, but regional centers for shopping, to which people of the region "go to (the master) town" where they are able to find a broad selection of stores and goods. The list is: Boston, New York, Philadelphia, Cleveland, Richmond, Atlanta, Chicago, St. Louis, Minneapolis, Kansas City, Dallas, and San Francisco.

The warehousing of goods by national organizations is commonly located at the major commercial centers; from this location the goods are distributed. Not all companies have branch facilities in every city. A company distributing nationwide from a single location usually is at New York and Chicago; if from two distribution points it usually is at each of these cities. A firm distributing from three points commonly has facilities at New York, Chicago, and San Francisco. When a fourth is added it is commonly Atlanta to serve the southern market, heretofore reached from New York and Chicago. If more than four facilities are maintained the pattern varies considerably.

New York and Chicago, and their metropolitan districts, are so large that manufacturing as well as commerce is outstanding. But Manhattan Island in New York and the Loop in Chicago are major commercial districts whose functions extend far beyond their limits. And the shipping and port facilities of each city lie beyond the business centers. Warehouses and wholesaling establishments are characteristic of many fringes of the commercial core (or cores, as the two—uptown commercial and downtown financial—of Manhattan) and of railroad-oriented or waterway-oriented sites in outlying parts of each metropolitan district. New York is the financial center of the nation, the site of the principal stock exchanges, the bond market, the buying headquarters of many national manufacturing companies and wholesale and retail organizations, and the location of firms engaged in national advertising. The skyscrapers of Manhattan Island are occupied principally by the offices of commercial organizations, and of professional people such as lawyers or doctors. Chicago, the railroad and air center of the country, commands the large and productive upper Mississippi Valley and much of the Great Lakes area; its commercial functions extend south to and beyond the Ohio River. Like New York, Chicago's commercial services of certain types are nationwide. It is the home or buying location of large retail-chain organizations and the distribution point for their goods. And the Chicago Board of Trade is the market center of the nation for grains and soybeans. Prices of these and other commodities are determined by the daily results of trading on the Board of Trade just as nationwide stock prices are the result of trading in New York. The skyscrapers of Chicago contain mainly the offices of commerce and of professional people.

Memphis, Denver, and Los Angeles are regional commercial centers of importance—not in the aforementioned list as they are not headquarters of Federal Reserve districts. The lower Mid-South comprises the territory of Memphis, whose commercial functions have increased coincident with the economic expansion of the area. Memphis competes with Atlanta to the east, Dallas to the west, and its services are expanding into the transitional zone between these two major distributing centers. Denver's trade area is large, the population small. Nevertheless it is the regional capital for the mountain and intermontane West.

Los Angeles, through sheer size and market potential, and favorable transfer costs to the entire Pacific slope of the United States (page 479), is challenging San Francisco's long-time dominance in commerce. San Francisco has a superior harbor, is the financial center of the Pacific coast, has the advantage of an early start through its sea connections, and is the Pacific terminus of the first transcontinental railroad. The rapid development of manufacturing in the Los Angeles region to its present output of nearly half of the total production on the Pacific Coast is another factor weighing toward the increasing distribution of goods from the location in which they are manufactured; as consumer goods for the retail markets are so prominent among its manufactures the economic advantage of their distribution directly from the same center is an important factor in the expansion of the city's commercial functions.

► TRANSPORTATION

Landways, waterways, seaways, and airways constitute the transport routes of the world. The carriers moving on them handle not only the vast multitude of raw materials and finished products, but transport millions of persons.

Landways include the railroad and highway systems, the pipelines, and, in certain cities, the subway routes for both passengers and freight. Waterways, as distinguished from seaways, include the navigable rivers and the man-con-

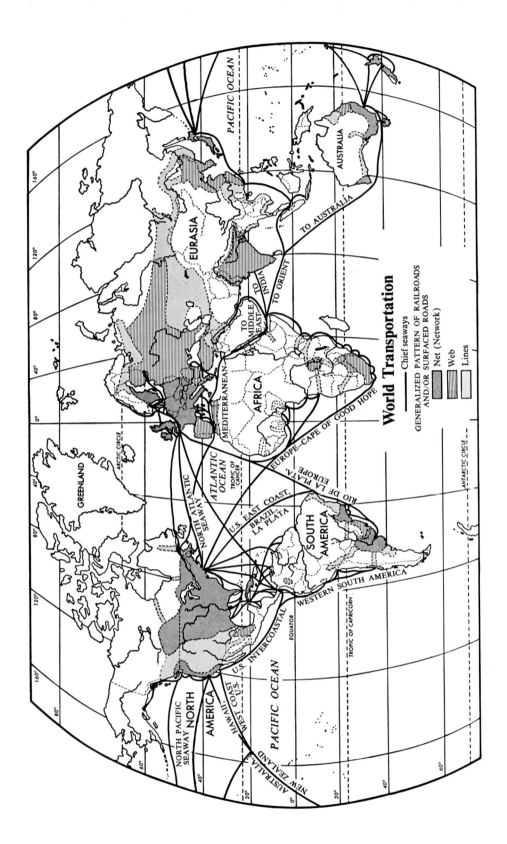

World Transportation
— — — Chief seaways
GENERALIZED PATTERN OF RAILROADS
AND/OR SURFACED ROADS

Net (Network)
Web
Lines

structed canal systems. The seaway is the broad path in the oceans used by ships with some degree of regularity; the North Atlantic Seaway, connecting the ports of eastern North America with those of northwestern Europe, is the busiest. The airway is the route followed by commercial air traffic.

The railroad and highway routes are obvious and observable features of the landscape. Their *network* is densest over considerable areas only in the four highly developed industrial regions of the world, and in outlying developed regions which specialize in commercial agriculture, such as the Pampas of Argentina, the Veld of South Africa, the coffee-producing area of Brazil, and a few others. In less developed areas the network deteriorates to an open *web*, in sparsely settled areas or underdeveloped lands the single *line* of road or rail replaces the pattern of a *web* or the dense *net*. The pipeline and the pipeline pattern is less obvious from the ground (although often it may be observed from the air) because the pipes are usually buried. But the pumping stations, the bridges on which pipelines are carried across rivers, and the terminals are observable signs of its existence.

The navigable river or canal is observable, and the channel is marked and maintained in all highly developed regions.

The seaway—at least in the open ocean—is not marked or maintained; the mariner navigates in broad bands of water, aided now by radar, radio signals and other electronic devices. On busy seaways "channels" are marked off on charts, and separated lanes are provided for ships sailing in opposite directions. Passing ships may thus sight only the upper portion of each other where the lanes are wide. But near the shore buoys, lightships, lighthouses, and other signs either mark locations of the seaway or serve as guides and warnings to the mariner. Nantucket Lightship, off the coast of Massachusetts, is a focal point at the United States "end" of the North Atlantic Seaway; the entrances to the English Channel, such as the lighthouses of Bishop's Rock, Land's End, and the Lizard are key landmarks toward the European terminus.

The commercial airway is marked at intervals on the ground by the airports themselves and the various other markings between. Today's technology also permits "marking" of the route in the air itself through the controls exerted by airport towers and check points, the reports to control points, and the separation of planes into "lanes" at even-numbered or odd-numbered altitudes, depending upon the direction of flight.

There are other transport systems of great importance locally in commercial and industrial areas. Among these are the endless belts, which now carry materials such as coal for distances of up to 100 miles from mine to market (Fig. 22-7). The elevator is important in the movement of both passengers and freight. In fact, it is said that elevators on Manhattan Island move more passengers each working day than any other kind of carrier. Underground tubes in which mail and light freight is transported under pressure systems are significant in some large cities.

Fɪɢ. 22-1. Railroad division point and railroad yards. The crews of trains change at division points. The two tracks in the foreground are the through ones for passenger service and freight trains (which stop only for a change of crews). A "railroad town" or a railroad community in a larger city often grows up at a division point. (Standard Oil Company, N.J.)

The Great Lakes may be placed either with the inland waterways—the classification of navigable rivers—or with the oceans so far as their navigability, problems, types of ships, and bulk handling of large cargoes are concerned. Their connecting rivers and canals are constrictors and concentrators of traffic from one lake to another.

If "transportation" is enlarged in definition to include communications, the telephone and telegraph lines, commercial radio and short-wave messages, code signals, and mail service are forms of communication absolutely essential to the commercial and industrial world; in fact many messages may be transmitted for every shipment of materials or goods, whether by rail, truck, pipe, barge, ship, or airplane.

Landways

Landways reflect man's efforts in the development of a region. Economically important districts are connected by them; there is reason for trade and interchange of goods. If rough terrain intervenes between these districts, man will construct routes through it—the Alpine passes have been the sites of trails and roads for centuries because there was reason for trade between the areas to the north and the south of the mountains. If, on the other hand, there is a flat plain on which it is easy to construct highways or railroads, but the plain is not developed economically, there will be few or no landways upon it, despite the surface of the plain, since there is little reason for trade—the dry plains of the western Sahara, the plains of Arctic Canada and Arctic Siberia have few landways. The flattish surface of the interior plateau of Africa have few at present, reflecting the underdevelopment of many parts of the area. The density of landways thus reflects the economic importance of a region. The landways connecting one region with another and the density of traffic upon them reflect the interregional trade and connections. The landways of the world thus are generally related to economic development. In some cases, however, from time immemorial to the present important landways have been built for military reasons instead of economic factors.

FIG. 22-2. The railroad station and three transcontinental passenger trains at Novosibirsk on the Trans-Siberian Railroad. (Sovfoto)

The routes on the surface of the land are affected by the surface configuration or topography. A level or gently rolling plain offers no barrier to the construction of straight railroad lines or highways. Distances are covered easily and rapidly; two industrial cities many miles apart are closer together in terms of shipment than they would be if in hilly terrain.

Hill country or mountainous terrain is traversed with more difficulty. Railroads and highways follow winding river valleys. The airline distance between two industrial centers thus is shorter than the surface distance.

Gateways or valleys through hilly terrain funnel traffic. The Hudson-Mohawk trough, the combination of the two "water level" valleys in New York State, is one of the best known and the most used traffic throughways: the Erie Canal, and later the railroads through the Mohawk Valley, provided New York City,

Fig. 22-3. Extensive switching and storage yards on a transcontinental railroad in eastern Kansas, with grain elevators between the principal yards. The size of these yards and the number of tracks in part reflect the important seasonal movement of wheat from the Winter Wheat Belt to Kansas City and other points. Also, through freight trains from California—with produce and perishables—are broken up here; the cars are reassembled in other trains for dispatch to the urban markets to the northeast, east, and southeast—in effect the cities from the east of the longitude of Kansas City to the Atlantic. (Standard Oil Company, N.J.)

FIG. 22-4. A valley providing a route to a mountain pass. Railroads frequently tunnel beneath the pass itself, while highways cross it. At present, some highway tunnels are being driven under the passes of the Alps. (Note the landslide. These may block landways.) (Standard Oil Company, N.J.)

at the mouth of the Hudson, with easier access to the developing interior of the United States than was enjoyed by any other Atlantic port. In turn the products of the interior reached New York by the same route. The Mohawk access to a rich hinterland was of inestimable importance to New York, and one of the major factors in its growth to the primate city of the country. Today the Mohawk routeway is of less *relative* importance than formerly; modern locomotives and trucks now cross the Pennsylvania Appalachians with relative ease. Modern turnpikes tunnel the mountains in several places. The principal railroad routes across the northern Appalachians, aside from the Mohawk Route, follow valleys of the eastern slopes—the Juniata and the Potomac— cross or tunnel the divide and descend the valleys of the westward drainage. Buffalo, Pittsburgh, and Cincinnati are the focal points west of the uplands; farther west, Chicago is a major terminal for the so-called eastern lines, St. Louis a second one.

Europeans make much of their gateways—relatively broad lowlands be-

Fig. 22-5. A parkway—the Merritt Parkway in Connecticut. This by-passes all of the shore towns on Long Island Sound but has many exits, so that each town can be reached. Truck traffic is not permitted on most parkways. The areas within the right-of-way of parkways are landscaped and maintained. During the time of year when foliage is out, it is virtually impossible to see beyond the planted trees, and travel is within what has been called a "green tunnel." (Standard Oil Company, N.J.)

tween the various low mountain ranges in Germany, France, Belgium, and other countries north of the Alps. The Lorraine Gate, the Burgundy Gate and others concentrate the rail, highway and canal systems. The Rhine and the Marne, the Rhine and the Rhone, among many rivers, are connected by canals through the gateways.

Railroads and highways cross mountain ranges through passes. Access to a mountain pass is by way of a valley, preferably a naturally well-graded valley. In fact, a pass higher in altitude than a neighboring one may be selected for the route if the valley leading to it has an easier grade than the valley leading to the lower pass. The landways may be built through the pass; they may tunnel beneath it, or the road may go through the pass and the railroad be tunneled.

The Alpine passes have been used for centuries. The Mediterranean lands to their south and the north European lands yield different products. Therefore there was demand for the exotic materials and reason for trade. Except for the Brenner, the major Alpine passes are now tunneled by the railroads. A vehicular tunnel is now under construction in the Alps to permit direct automobile and truck traffic from the northern side to the Po Valley of Italy; heretofore, because of heavy snow on the passes in winter, these vehicles have usually been put on railroad flatcars for transport "through" the Alps; the alternative has been the long journey around, by way of the French Riviera on the Mediterranean coast.

The several passes through the mountain ranges of the western United States were used first (commercially) by the transcontinental railroads. The highways, built later, follow the same general routes and use the same passes. The pattern of transportation in much of the area is one of lines rather than a net; raw materials, goods, and passengers are being transported across the mountains from or to settled areas on either side—or on the broad scale, across the Rockies, the intermontane West, and the Sierra Nevada–Cascade Range from the densely-

FIG. 22-6. Toll gate on a toll road or turnpike. The driver receives a ticket, and pays at the gate at which he leaves the road. Truck traffic is permitted and encouraged. Turnpikes have few exits, these chiefly near the larger cities. The long mileage of turnpikes is too great for the costs of landscaping, and the type of country traversed—whether farm area, forests, or urban—is visible and evident. (Standard Oil Company, N.J.)

settled eastern half of the United States to the well-settled Pacific Coast—or vice versa. Only some ten to a dozen passes are important so far as the total volume of traffic is concerned. These thus funnel land traffic into them; each major pass is used by one of the transcontinental railroad systems and by a U.S. highway.

Chicago is the eastern terminal of the transcontinental railroads, St. Louis and New Orleans are others. The western terminals of the lines are Los Angeles, San Francisco, Portland, and Seattle; one reaches Tacoma by way of Seattle. The term "transcontinental," as used in railroad transportation, means Lake Michigan and the Mississippi River to the West Coast—it reflects the fact that the first so-called "transcontinental line" connected the then thickly settled "edge" of the nation with California. Airlines, more recent in origin, are truly transcontinental as they extend from coast to coast.

Fig. 22-7. Belt conveyors carrying coal which has been washed and screened at the plant in the valley below to a steel mill many miles away. Some coal-conveying belts now transport coal for distances of more than 100 miles. The entire setting is characteristic of the coal-mining industry in the rough Appalachian Coal Field—narrow valleys, mining towns in the valley bottoms and on the lower slopes, space in the valley bottoms only for roads and railroads, drift mines on the slopes above, wooded mountains. Flooding is a hazard in many of these narrow valleys. (*Steelways*, published by American Iron and Steel Institute)

Fig. 22-8. Belt conveyors at the site of Bhakra Dam in India. The belts move concrete aggregate over very rugged terrain for five miles and deliver the aggregate to a concrete plant at the site of the dam. (*Steelways*, publishd by American Iron and Steel Institute)

The Rocky Mountains are bypassed on their south by the transcontinental railroads and highways, which skirt them by way of Albuquerque. The central lines cross either the mountains or utilize the broad, high plains of Wyoming between the Northern Rockies and the Southern Rockies. Despite this easier grade, the plains are more than 7,000 feet above sea level for long stretches, and are reached after a short climb to more than 8,000 feet over a low portion of the Rockies; the original route passed north of this, remaining on the plains, as did the Oregon and California trails; the railroad and highway now follow a cutoff that saves distance through the relatively low additional ascent. Farther west the central lines cross the Sierra Nevadas before the Central Valley of California is reached. The northern transcontinental railroads, after crossing the Northern Rockies in Montana, all meet at Spokane, then fan out to different ascents and routes across the Cascades.

Important cities may develop where the pass routes debouche upon plains or low plateaus. Munich is at the northern, lowland end of the Brenner Route. The three great trans-Alpine routes in Switzerland merge southward at Milan on the Po plain. Turin lies at the Italian end of an Alpine pass route from France to Italy. The same is true of some American routes; Reno and Sacramento lie at either end of the route across the Sierra Nevadas by way of Donner Pass. Snoqualmie Pass, the only "all-year" highway pass in Washington, points directly at Seattle. The original transcontinental railroads terminated at several towns on Puget Sound; eventually Seattle's combination of waterfront and easy access to the interior by way of low Snoqualmie Pass gave it an advantage over nearby towns; the railroads which had terminated at other ports extended their lines to Seattle.

The turnpike, toll road, thruway, freeway, or parkway in the United States, the Autobahnen of Germany, and other superhighways are the latest additions to the landways of some highly developed nations. The Federal Interstate Highway System of the United States is under construction. Not all of these modern roads are open to the trucks of industry and commerce; they are generally barred from the parkways but sought after by the turnpikes and toll roads. Several states have passed enabling legislation permitting "state corporations" or "authorities" to be formed. These build the highways and amortize the bonds from the tolls collected. To date the turnpikes have been most successful either in densely inhabited regions, such as the New York and Chicago urban and suburban regions, or where they connect major cities between which there is heavy passenger and truck traffic—the series of connecting state turnpikes (Indiana names its a toll road) between New York and Chicago—or the New Jersey Turnpike, which connects the New York Metropolitan region with the Philadelphia area (not directly, but through exits in New Jersey) and southward.

The Autobahnen were built for military reasons. Their ordinary traffic at present is composed of passenger and commercial vehicles. The U.S. Interstate System has a strategic and military background—bridge heights are determined by the size of military vehicles—but it will function principally in commerce except during periods of emergency.

Waterways

The river and canal systems of western Europe, of the Russian portion of the Soviet Union, and of China are used far more than are the inland waterways of the United States, except for the Great Lakes. Use of the waterways is increasing, however, in this country. The Mississippi system connects manufactural regions with raw-material areas in the South; the Gulf Intracoastal Canal, especially that part between the Mississippi and the Houston-Galveston Bay district, extends the water route into the heart of the sulphur, salt, and petroleum region. This permits an all-water transport of low-value bulky materials such as salt and sulphur from the producing areas to such distant points as Minneapolis, Omaha, Pittsburgh, or Knoxville. Petroleum moves on the

Mississippi system in some quantity as well, as has been noted. The largest and most concentrated traffic movement on the overall Mississippi system is on the upper Ohio and lower Monongahela. These stretches of waterway flow through the heart of the Pittsburgh steel district, and of a coal-mining and heavy industrial area. Tonnage moved is large, distances are relatively short—in many cases from steel mill to steel mill or metal-fabricating plant to a metal-using plant.

Waterways have the disadvantage of circuitousness (and ice in certain latitudes in the winter), the advantage of low rates, and the ability of one diesel-powered towboat (still called towboat even though the modern ones push from behind) to handle a fleet of ten to a dozen barges, lashed together in pairs. Bottlenecks are the locks, where the tow has to be taken through in sections. A disadvantage of the inland waterway, from the standpoint of the businessman or manufacturer, is the length of time involved in delivery. This does not affect low-value materials. High-value materials, which carry high insurance rates,

FIG. 22-9. Barges of sulphur on the Mississippi River at New Orleans. These have been towed to the Mississippi from the southwest Louisiana, southeast Texas sulphur area on the Gulf Intracoastal Canal. See FIGS. 11-9, 13-4, 15-3, 18-2, 18-5, 18-6 for additional scenes of waterway traffic. (Standard Oil Company, N.J.)

Fig. 22-10. Denmark, the Puget Sound region of the state of Washington, and many other areas of the world have extensive ferry systems connecting mainland, islands, and the peninsulas. This is one of many ferries in Denmark. It crosses the Great Belt, the channel between the islands of Funen and Zealand. Through trains from Germany to Copenhagen or to cities in Sweden are transported from island to island here. The Danish ferry system carries more than 4,000,000 passengers a year, half a million vehicles, and nearly 100,000 bicycles. (Standard Oil Company, N.J.)

generally are not shipped on American waterways; the insurance costs and the time factor involved may add up to more than the transfer cost of the shipment of the same material by rail or truck.

The Chicago Sanitary and Ship Canal connects Lake Michigan with the Mississippi River system by way of the Des Plaines and the navigable Illinois rivers. A connecting canal, the Calumet Sag Channel, leads from the Calumet Industrial District to the Sanitary and Ship Canal. Chicago, Calumet harbor in South Chicago, and the Gary region thus have an all-water route to Gulf markets. Steel shapes, bars, and structural steels are important items shipped from the Chicago area to river ports. The New York State Barge Canal, replacement of the Erie Canal, from Buffalo on Lake Erie to the Hudson, carries relatively little traffic in contrast to the Chicago "outlet."

The Rhine and other waterways, their importance, and the products moved upon them have been discussed elsewhere in connection with specific industries.

The Great Lakes—inland freshwater seas without peer in the world—have heavy traffic for eight months of the year until their connecting waterways are closed by ice. Carferry traffic across Lake Michigan continues all year. The Great Lakes traffic and its commodities have been discussed elsewhere. The Soo Canals at Sault Ste. Marie (Michigan and Ontario) carried the heaviest tonnage of any canal in the world until surpassed recently by all-year Suez; during some years of World War II, 90 million tons of iron ore passed through the locks each eight-month year. The lakes have three water connections to other waterways; the connections at Chicago and Buffalo cannot be used by lake ships, and transfer of cargo is necessary. The enlarged and deepened St. Lawrence Seaway permits direct passage to the Atlantic Ocean.

Seaways

The seaway shortens the distance between two ports by following a Great Circle Route, the arc of the circle being the shortest distance on a curved surface.

The North Atlantic Seaway is the route of manufactured goods—it connects the world's two leading industrial regions. Raw materials for Europe are moved on it, too, but by percentage in larger quantity from Canada (wheat, ores) than from the United States. The European ports are the many of the United Kingdom, the Low Countries, West Germany, and Scandinavia. Canada's chief ports are Montreal and Quebec; Halifax, and Portland, Maine serve as winter ports when the St. Lawrence Seaway is closed by ice. The ports of the Atlantic Seaboard constitute the American terminals. By extension, the Baltic ports are reached eastward in Europe, the Gulf ports "westward" in the United States.

The Europe-Mediterranean-Orient or Australia Seaway carries manufactured goods eastward, mainly raw materials and petroleum to Europe. Straits funnel the route in many places; only small segments can follow Great Circles; the straits on a seaway function like mountain passes in their control and focusing of traffic. Among the constrictions, and consequent concentrations of ship traffic, are eight-mile-wide Gibraltar at the western entrance to the Mediterranean, the narrows between Sicily and Tunisia, the man-made Suez Canal, the Strait of Bab-el-Mandeb at the southern entrance of the Red Sea, and the Strait of Malacca between Sumatra and the Asian mainland. Britain guards the straits. Respectively, in the order of the above list, the British bases are at Gibraltar, Malta, Cyprus (since the withdrawal from Suez), Aden, and Singapore.

Traffic flows into side routes at many points on the Europe to Orient and Australia seaway. The Italian ports are reached from this route. The Straits (Dardanelles and Bosporus) provide natural water routes to Black Sea ports.

The oil tankers sail into the Persian Gulf for their cargoes. Bombay in India draws traffic. At Colombo, an important port of call, ships diverge—northward into the Bay of Bengal to Calcutta, eastward to the Strait of Malacca and Singapore, and via a Great Circle southeastward to Australia. From these divergences, on the Europe-bound journey the cargoes entering the seaway may contain jute from India and Pakistan, rubber and tin from Singapore, wheat, raw wool, and dairy products from Australia and New Zealand.

The Europe–River Plate (or Rio de la Plata) Seaway is one on which diverse products are shipped for a reciprocal trade—manufactured goods from Europe, foods (meat, wheat, flour, corn, cheese) from Argentina and Uruguay. The two regions supplement one another, providing basis for trade. The ships from the United States enter this seaway near Cape San Roque—the bulge of Brazil. Their destination is usually Rio de Janeiro and Santos with cargoes of manufactured goods; coffee, sugar, cacao, and other tropical products are return cargoes. The United States and Brazil have a basis for trade owing to the difference in their products—Brazil because of its tropical climate produces materials in demand in this country. In contrast, Argentinian and Uruguayan exports are competitive with foods produced in the United States, and are not in demand.

The Cape of Good Hope Seaway connects Europe and South Africa. The principal traffic terminates at Capetown. African ports on both the Indian and the Atlantic oceans export the ores of the Katanga and the Rhodesias; Capetown handles the ores, wheat, wool, and gold bullion of the Union.

The North Pacific Seaway follows the Great Circle Route from San Francisco, Portland, Seattle, or Vancouver to Yokohama, almost reaching the Aleutian Islands of Alaska at its northernmost arc. It carries less shipping than the North Atlantic route by far. Japan is reached also by a longer route, the arc of a circle to Honolulu, then another to Yokohama. The presence of an intermediate port—Honolulu—draws shipping this way; cargo can be loaded or discharged en route, except that trade between Honolulu and the United States mainland must be carried in American flagships.

The Pacific seaway to Australia diverges at Honolulu, proceeding then to the Fiji Islands, and Auckland or Sydney. Passenger lines using this route are mainly British ships sailing from Vancouver. If the passengers from Australia are continuing to England a single ticket takes them across Canada by transcontinental railroad, and across the Atlantic by ship.

The seaway from the East Coast or the Gulf Coast of the United States to western South America utilizes the Panama Canal. Manufactured goods are shipped southward. The ores and concentrates of ores are returned—copper, iron, tin, vanadium, and other metals. The important traffic with the West Indies (sugar) and Venezuela (oil, iron ore), and the Guianas (bauxite) utilizes various passages between Caribbean islands.

The Panama Canal functions in the large intercoastal traffic of the United

Fig. 22-11. An oil tanker passing Gaillard Cut in the Panama Canal. (Standard Oil Company, N.J.)

States. A variety of manufactured goods and considerable steel moves on the ships traversing the canal from the Atlantic to the Pacific ports of the nation. Lumber products from the Pacific Northwest and oil from California are important in the Pacific-to-Atlantic intercoastal traffic. Its large use in this trade was not foreseen at the time of its opening in 1914; it was thought of as a naval canal, and a canal making the west coast of South America accessible. Little traffic from Australia or New Zealand passes through Panama. The bulk of their exports are shipped to Europe by way of Suez.

Airways

Airways girdle the earth. They bring peoples closer together in point of time. All major places are now easily accessible from other centers in a relatively few hours provided the traveler has the necessary credentials for a journey outside of his own country, and the fare.

Airplanes can operate without regard to the topography of the land: in actuality this is subject to some qualification; for reasons of safety, commercial airlanes are laid out in many places with "doglegs" or other deviations to avoid unusual hazards. But on many routes the true Great Circle can be followed; the ship cannot embark on a Great Circle route until it is out at sea—at Nantucket Lightship in the case of the North Atlantic Seaway. The Great Circle from New York to England lies over land in part of New England and Nova Scotia, crosses Newfoundland, and then the Atlantic. The airplane uses this route, one that is shorter than the seaway. And airplanes can fly trans-polar routes, or on Great Circle routes which take them into very high latitudes; an example is the Los Angeles-to-Stockholm route, which crosses Greenland.

The airplane must operate from a base. This is an airport, or possibly, in the case of planes of the armed forces, an airplane carrier at sea. Although the planes of the Armed Forces can be and are refueled while in flight, the commercial airlines of the world, flying under strict safety regulations and anxious to retain the confidence and good will of the public, do not engage in this practice. In other words, though free to travel in almost any direction, the commercial airlines must operate from suitable bases and land only at airports qualified by their size, length of runways, and facilities to handle the type of plane in use. Many airports at one time on airlines now have no scheduled service, usually because the increasing size of planes has outgrown these airports.

Airplanes carry freight and express in some quantity; some lines operate cargo planes on regular schedules. The general type of materials carried are either high in value per unit of weight, are perishable products shipped long distances (orchids from Hawaii), or are items for which speed of delivery is essential. The airplane is adapted to the delivery of heavy, bulky, and even low-value articles if exigencies warrant paying the freight charges, or if the point of delivery is inaccessible to the usual carriers of this type of product. Coal was flown to Berlin during the abnormal period of the Berlin Airlift when the Soviet Union refused to allow the railroads, trucks, and canal barges to cross East German territory to reach West Berlin. Mining machinery is flown to mine-construction work in the high Andes and in northern Canada, and oil-drilling equipment is flown from France to the Sahara. Many places in inner Alaska and northwest Canada are accessible only by air during much of the year. But concurrently with, say, the construction period of a new mine, railroads or highways are being built to it, for transport of the bulky ores to concentrating plants or ports for export when the mine is in operation.

Airlines may be classified in different ways. Some are trans-world. In the United States a classification is into transcontinental, regional, and feeder lines. The first is coast to coast, the second serves a large region, the third is a local line, feeding its passengers and cargo into the regional systems. Several regional systems are pie-shaped, fanning out from an apex at Chicago.

The pattern of airways in the world parallels the patterns of railroads and highways; nets, webs, and lines characterize the pattern. The densest network of airways, and the largest traffic, is in the highly developed manufactural regions of the northeastern quarter of the United States and of western Europe. The net opens somewhat in the southeastern United States and eastern and part of southern Europe, but is still dense by comparison with most other portions of the world; in part, the wider spacing is the result of the more widely spaced major cities in the southeast than in the northeastern quarter of the United States.

The airway pattern in the western half of the United States—west of the 100th meridian—parallels the landway pattern in that the through routes appear as lines on a map, lines leading to the major cities of the Pacific Coast. The denser network reappears, as in landways, in a north-south direction paralleling the coast.

The web pattern in airline density is in much the same broad regions as the webs of landways—India, Spain, much of the Soviet Union. The heart regions of the Soviet Union in Russian Europe have a net; the outlying regions of importance a web; the far northern areas, the dry lands of central Asia, and eastern Siberia have a line pattern. One of the important lines connects the two centers of power of the Communist world, Moscow and Peiping; it crosses the dry lands of the northwest of China. It will be remembered that a new railroad branches from the trans-Siberian and connects with the Chinese system and Peiping. This carries the goods and passengers between the two countries; the airplane apparently carries mainly the officials and the technicians, and undoubtedly some high-value materials.

The Canadian system is east-west, like the railroads, in the peopled areas of southern Canada. From cities in the south, scheduled lines extend north, mainly to northern mining centers in the Laurentian Upland. In addition, the bush pilot of northern Canada and of Alaska, flying a small plane on non-scheduled operations, is extremely important in serving mining camps, isolated and small new settlements, and hunting and fishing centers reached only by air. The "bush" planes usually are equipped to land only on water during the summer, and with skis on ice or packed snow during the winter. In periods of the spring break-up and fall freeze-up they are unable to operate.

The overseas airlines—to name a beginning point—extend from the highly developed region of western Europe, and of the United States and Canada to the areas where there is business and passenger travel. All international flights are concentrated at airports where there are customs and immigration officials.

The heaviest air traffic, in number of flights and in passengers carried, is over the North Atlantic, connecting the highly developed areas of western Europe and of the United States and Canada. The pattern of density thus parallels that of the North Atlantic Seaway. Two basic routes are followed by the planes—the Great Circle Route between New York or the East to the European destination, and the route by way of the Azores Islands to Lisbon, Portugal. On the first-named route the destination may be London, Paris, or some other city. Two major airports lie on this route between the starting point and the terminal. One is Gander in Newfoundland, the other Shannon in western Ireland; the "over-the-Atlantic" portion of this airway is between these two airports. A stop may or may not be made at Gander or Shannon; originally all planes landed, but longer-range aircraft has made this unnecessary. The route via the Azores usually includes a brief stop there. The "front door" of Europe, on this route, is Lisbon; all other "front doors," or entrances whether by sea or air, are in the British Isles or the continental industrial countries.

The overseas or long-distance air routes from Europe to South American or African centers extend southward from the point of origin. If a French carrier it is Paris; if British, London; if Belgian, Brussels; and so on. The route to eastern South America or to western Africa is essentially the same as far as Dakar, on the bulge of Africa. Then the 1,700 mile over-the-Atlantic flight to the bulge of Brazil is accomplished. Terminals are usually in Buenos Aires, because of the trade and business connections between Europe and Argentina. Stops may be made at Rio de Janeiro, São Paulo, and Montevideo. The airway to further-Africa from Dakar proceeds southeastward, usually to the two business centers of the Congo region—Leopoldville, the capital, and Elisabethville in the Katanga mining region. Connections continue to Johannesburg.

The second (and usually British-line) entrance to Africa is the air route from London to Cairo. The airway crosses the desert by following the Nile (not all of its meanderings, of course) to Khartoum in Sudan. Thence Nairobi, Entebbe, and Salisbury are the usual landings, and finally Johannesburg in the Union of South Africa—the business and mining center and leading city. Connections continue to Capetown. Note that inland Johannesburg is the "air entrance" to South Africa on each route. Capetown is the sea entrance. The airplane has changed the position of Johannesburg relative to Capetown.

Unlike the North America to Australia route, the important Europe to Australia and New Zealand air route lies almost entirely over land except for short stretches. Principal landing places which mark the route are Baghdad, Karachi, Calcutta, Singapore, then Darwin on the north coast of Australia, finally Sydney or Melbourne. Passengers, mail, and light freight can be picked up or discharged at many airports on this halfway-round-the-world air route, again in contrast to a trans-Pacific flight.

International flights from the United States proceed southeastward to the West Indies and Venezuela, thence to Brazil or southward to the Panama Canal

Zone, thence along the coast of western South America. Mining interests are prominent among those of businessmen passengers on the flights to Peru and Chile; the iron ore and oil fields of Venezuela are business interests of persons bound for there.

The trans-Pacific air routes are two; and one of these divides at Hawaii. The northern air route is the Great Circle across the North Pacific, from Seattle to Yokohama. It is almost the exact route of the seaway. Signals and weather reports are received from Alaska en route, and emergency stops can be made at airports on the Aleutians if necessary.

The southern trans-Pacific route has the same first segment—the 2,400 miles from the United States mainland to Honolulu, a Pacific crossroads by air as well as by sea. A Coast Guard ship stationed at the halfway point in the Pacific is a "safety valve" on this long over-water flight with no islands. This segment is the busiest part of the whole route; on it there is the heavy air traffic to Honolulu; in fact the majority of aircraft shuttle back and forth between San Francisco or Los Angeles and Honolulu.

The true trans-Pacific "southern route" divides at Honolulu. One branch proceeds to Australia by way of island stepping-stones—Wake Island, Suva in the Fiji Islands, New Caledonia, thence either Sydney in Australia or Auckland in New Zealand. The westward-extending branch makes long hops from island airport to island airport—Honolulu to Wake, Guam, thence Manila; from here airlanes extend to airports in Asia, such as Bangkok and Hong Kong (these two are also reached by coming the other way around the world—New York, London, the Middle East, India, and Singapore) or Tokyo.

The third branch from Honolulu is northwestward to Tokyo. Long-range planes make this possible now; originally this was Honolulu-Wake-Tokyo, a route still in use.

It will be noted that United States–owned Wake Island is actually the usual division point. Wake consists of three small islets surrounding a lagoon, the total land area being but three square miles. Wake was uninhabited until the mid-1930's when it was chosen as a base and repair center by an American airline company. A government installation was constructed later. Every person living on Wake is connected with airline traffic—from servicing the planes to serving meals. Aside from reading, recreational games, or fishing in the lagoon, the only thing to do on Wake is watch the planes come and go. Wake is an example of the complete orientation of every aspect of life to one commercial activity. All food and materials of any kind reach the island only by air.

Midway Island, 1,300 miles northwest of Honolulu, was an early stepping-stone—Honolulu to Midway, thence Wake. The advent of long-range airplanes resulted in its being bypassed by commercial planes. It remained a base for American armed forces planes. But in 1958 commercial and military air traffic (the latter to American bases in the Philippines and Okinawa, and to Japan) had become so heavy that federal aviation authorities divided the route, except for emergencies. Commercial traffic was routed as stated above—Honolulu, Wake, thence westward; military traffic was routed Honolulu-Midway-Kwajalein (an air base built during World War II in the Marshall Islands west of Wake) —thence westward. This ability to realign or change routes illustrates the flexibility of the airplane over the constructed landway, provided there is an airport.

There are hundreds of other air routes of local or regional importance in the world. Bush planes in Alaska, Canada, and elsewhere fly—when there is business—to otherwise inaccessible places. The same sort of flights, usually of small planes, reach small airports in inner Africa and the Amazon Basin of South America, tying these localities into traffic centers of airlines, railroads, or paved highways. And there is the non-scheduled airplane here and there, flying when a load is obtained; one of the heavy passenger movements of this type is the "commuting" of Puerto Rican labor in New York City back home at intervals, mainly for tax purposes.

The military airplanes of the world lie outside the realm of commerce. They may be said to fly anywhere. Some governments use cargo planes for transport of food, materiel, material for the stores maintained for the armed forces, and military personnel and their families in much the same manner as a commercial line operates—the Military Air Transport Service (MATS) of the United States is an example.

The impact of the military planes of the world (whether, as in the United States, Army, Navy, Air Force, or Marine Corps planes) is the maintenance of a demand for airplanes which keeps the aircraft manufacturing industry of the world far larger than it would be otherwise. Estimates of its size otherwise—if the market were only civilian—vary considerably; most run in the neighborhood of less than half. In some countries figures are withheld. Figures published for Great Britain for a recent five-year period indicate that during this time 5,500 military planes were manufactured, and 2,486 civilian planes. The demand for civilian planes varies more from year to year than the military demand. To even the work load many aircraft plants engage also in the manufacture of guided missiles. However, with the rapid rise of the "missile industry" during the last ten years, the electronics industry and the manufacturers of instruments are now very important producers of the various guided missiles.

▶ SERVICE INDUSTRIES

The service occupations range through a wide variety of activities, and provide the livelihood for millions of people the world over. Persons performing a service may engage in an unskilled or semi-skilled work or be among the world's most professional workers. Many service activities are ubiquitous, others are regionalized in intensity.

Workers in the service occupations are paid for the services they render; they do not earn their living in commerce, manufacturing, mining, forestry, or agriculture. The service may be a relatively simple one, such as that of a maid, bootblack, or doorman; it may be classed as a semi-skilled type of work such as that of cook or barber; and it may range to occupations requiring a highly specialized education and years of training, such as that required of lawyers and doctors. Thus some people serve others by selling their labors, others are selling their knowledge. Many workers in the service field are self-employed. Others are on the payrolls of industrial or commercial organizations; still others are paid by various governmental units (teachers, policemen, firemen) in some countries.

The sellers and purveyors of their services cluster near the market for their services. The largest markets are the urbanized portions of the developed world. Thus the large cities contain the principal concentrations of lawyers and doctors, of janitors, repairmen, laundry and restaurant workers, and many others. A business selling its services is located near the buyers; a laundry and its pick-up stations, or a barber shop, is near its customers and is located on or very near the streets which have the largest pedestrian traffic or an arterial street used by its customers, or it is in a shopping center with off-street parking; negatively it is not in an isolated site, away from traffic flow.

The service occupations, quite general throughout the highly developed portions of the world, are of greatest relative concentration and variety in the large cities. Merely the numbers of inhabitants within the city and its suburbs is a factor in the concentration; services are purchased, when in a small town or village they are performed by the family itself—yardmen, janitors, gardeners, for example. The office buildings, stores, and apartments, and many home-owners employ professional window-washers, an occupation almost unknown in small cities and rural communities. And the feeding of thousands of commuters at noon in the large cities, the staffing of the many hotels, the workers in the amusement industry, and scores of other activities are all operative in making the service occupations of greater relative significance by percentage among the gainfully employed workers in the large centers of population than in smaller communities.

The sellers of certain services find it to their advantage to cluster together. Thus an entire office building may be occupied by doctors' offices; other office buildings may have a concentration of lawyers among its tenants. Even when a doctor builds an office building in a commercial district not part of the commercial core, surplus space is commonly rented to other doctors or dentists.

Some people market a special talent they possess. In this case the major market is usually in the primate city or the principal cities of a country, ordinarily the former. Those persons wishing to market a talent for acting, art, or music must therefore move to the primate city and hope to sell their special abilities. Thus the would-be actor or actress moves to London, to Paris, or in the United States to New York or Los Angeles (Hollywood). The ballerinas in the Soviet Union, the toreadors in Spain or Mexico, hope to attain the prestige and financial rewards of employment in Moscow, Madrid, or Mexico City. Although there are musicians and dance bands in every locality there is a much larger than normal concentration in New York, Chicago, and Los Angeles, where outlets such as broadcasting companies, the makers of television and movie films, and recording companies are potential markets for their services.

The primate city and the large cities contain the concentrations of specialists in particular fields. Thus, while doctors are distributed generally in some relationship to the population pattern, the highly specialized practictioners are principally in the major cities; their customers travel to them or are referred to them by other doctors. In a few cases specialized medical centers have developed in smaller towns, largely because of the fame of a particular doctor originally, and through his influence a noted medical center has developed.

Higher education, wherein the student is the buyer of the professional services and knowledge of the instructional staff and the knowledge stored in the library of a college or university, is—in the United States—both near its customers and in sites (college towns) to which the students move temporarily. The present trend in the establishments of junior colleges and the establishment in large cities of branches of well-known universities takes the professional service to the consumer; the college town and the nationally known private or state university attract the student to their sites.

Collectively, the service workers of the world—whether semi-skilled or highly professional—form a large total market. Certain manufacturers cater to the specialized markets offered principally by the numbers and incomes of the professional personnel and their families.

► RECREATION

The provision of recreational facilities and activities has become an important industry, employing many. It may be considered a service industry because large numbers of persons in it are actually paid for services they provide. It extends beyond this, however, in that intangibles are "sold"—scenery, swimming in lakes or in the ocean, cool summer weather, warm winter weather, cruises on lakes or ocean, snow cover suitable for skiing, fishing excursions, golf courses. An important part of Switzerland's national income is derived from the selling of scenery—an invisible export; the money left in the country by tourists is just as valuable for purchasing needed imports as if it had been obtained from the selling and exports of electrical equipment, milk chocolate, watches, or cheese. The money spent by the tourist is, of course, actually paid to commercial enterprises, to transportation companies, and to the hotels, restaurants, guides, and the host of service employees who have performed services for the visitors.

The recreational industry has grown to its present importance only during the last thirty to forty years, and much of the growth has occurred since World War II. Increased leisure time, shorter hours of work, longer vacations, the increase of family incomes, and the rapidity of transportation enabling tourists to reach a distant recreational center in a short time have been factors in the growth of the industry. The five-day week of many businesses has boomed the types of recreation that may be pursued on a week-end—golf and boating, for example. Investments by entrepreneurs in recreational establishments are thus local—near the week-end markets—and at distant scenic locations. The recent growth does not mean that recreational facilities are entirely new; there was in the past the summer hotel accessible by railroad, the summer cottage and camp, the beach resort. The automobile has permitted the spread of hotels and cottages to areas not accessible easily to public transportation. And the automobile has changed the character of the summer hotel or resort business from the all-summer stay of many in the past to the relatively short stay and mobility of the present. It has brought in the motel business among many others. The damming of rivers—for power or irrigation reservoirs—in areas previously without natural lakes has resulted in intensive recreational development; reservoirs in Kansas, Oklahoma, and Texas are now centers of boating and water skiing.

The large increase in numbers of tourists is owing to additional factors than those just listed; there is a widening tourist base to draw from. Before World War I travelers were drawn mainly from the more wealthy members of society; this is still the case in much of Europe, Asia, and Latin America. But the base has been broadened in the United States and Canada to include office personnel, factory workers, students, and persons from many walks of life—groups which, in the past, rarely traveled far for vacations; this is true in the week-end market as well. Golf was considered only a "rich-man's game" before World War I, but witness its broad base of participants today.

The recreational industry, and particularly the "distant" portion of the industry has the disadvantage of depending upon the prosperity of another region —the source region of visitors. The depression of the 1930's, the restrictions on travel imposed during World War II, and short "recessions" resulted in serious effects in the tourist centers of Switzerland, Florida, and elsewhere. And the cities depending upon the visitor trade often have no other economic base to serve as a cushion when the number of tourists drops.

Recreation is the market for a host of manufacturing industries. The building of boats, outboard motors, the production of the array of sporting goods, the divisions of the clothing industry making sportswear are only a few of the many manufactures oriented toward this market.

The number of regions or districts wherein recreation is a significant enterprise are too numerous to mention. A few, illustrating certain geographic principles of localization, will be listed. Some are winter resorts, some operate only in the summer, some are all-year tourist centers, although even these usually have seasonal ebbs and flows.

The densely inhabited urban centers and the principal industrial regions of the Western world are the chief source regions of tourists. Mountainous or hilly terrain, lakes, beaches, and parks—or a combination such as lakes in a mountain setting—within a day-or-two drive, or an overnight trip by rail, are the major centers of the recreational industry. The French, Swiss, Austrian, German, and Italian Alps are within 600 miles of all parts of the densely inhabited areas of southern Great Britain and the western portions of the continent of Europe. They are accessible from all directions in a few hours—even from England by train to a Channel port, ship, and train from the port of debarkation on the continent. The Catskill and Adirondack Mountains of New York State, the Berkshires of Massachusetts, the White Mountains of New Hampshire, and the Poconos of Pennsylvania, north of Philadelphia, are leading recreational areas. The Maine coast and the beaches of Cape Cod, Long Island, New Jersey, and Delaware are well developed; the resort community of Atlantic City, with its clusters of hotels, specializes as well in conventions. Tourism in the Middle West is most concentrated in the northern tier of states—the lakes and North Woods of Michigan, Wisconsin, and Minnesota (comparable in all three states to the North Woods of Maine in the East), and on the sand dune-backed beaches of the eastern or leeward shore of Lake Michigan.

Attractions further afield, but still within an easy two-day drive of the densely inhabited Manufactural Belt, lie in Canada to the north or in the high Southern Appalachians to the south. The Great Smoky Mountain National Park in North Carolina and Tennessee receives more visitors annually than any other national park, largely because of its accessibility to many million people living within a 600-mile radius. Yosemite National Park in the Sierra Nevadas of California is easily accessible to the densely inhabited portions of that state.

The mild-winter French and Italian Riviera draws heavily from European countries. The similar region in the Soviet Union, on the south shore of the Crimean Peninsula in the Black Sea, is the Russian winter resort. Climatically similar southern California had a heavy tourist industry until the urban expansion of the region affected seasonal housing and tourist motels, many of which became all-year residences. But shore resorts are still very important, drawing now more on the local populations. The winter-tourist industry of Florida is well known—the Atlantic beach resort towns, including Miami and Miami Beach; the interior lakes; and the west or Gulf coast recreational centers. The Florida industry expanded rapidly after 1946, the normal growth plus the added accessibility to the East and Middle West being factors, and also the "diversion" of tourists and retired people to the area who might otherwise have gone to California. Greater Miami claims to be the largest of the recreational cities in the United States; of course, it has many other activities too.

The Rocky Mountains and other western mountains contain important recreational centers. The Rocky Mountain National Park area is one of the most concentrated. It is the closest of the high-mountain areas to the broad area of the lowlands and plains stretching from Chicago to Texas, and westward to the Rockies. Yellowstone, Glacier, Grand Canyon, and other parks draw heavily. On the whole the total number of visitors falls far short of the eastern recreational areas, however, despite the scenic wonders. Many of these areas are just "too far" from peopled centers, considering driving distance, for the family with a two- or three-week vacation; the West may be visited once, and inertia, time, or accessibility determine the return to the "closer" place in other vacation periods.

Recreational areas attempt to stretch their season for economic reasons. The winter resort of New England and of Michigan and Wisconsin is based on the winter sports, especially skiing. Ski trains are dispatched northward from New York, Chicago, and other centers. The "warm-winter" resort areas, such as Florida, promote summer tourism and offer inducements such as special rates to attract customers. The Swiss tourist industry stresses winter sports as well; as the Alps are surrounded by densely-peopled lowlands which have only a short, and intermittent snow cover, the Swiss have been particularly successful.

Some favored areas climatically, in transitional locations, have an all-year recreational activity because of their position. The Southern Appalachians in western North Carolina is a fall, winter, and spring resort center for people from the northern United States, and a most important summer resort for people from the hot and humid lowlands of the South.

A recreational industry has become important recently in Japan. Golf courses, summer resorts, and winter skiing in the mountains have been introduced. The extent of the Soviet development is not well known. Alaska, Hawaii, and Norway find that tourism is an important contributor to their economies.

There is competition among regions for tourists, very severe competition, as witness the advertising and promotional campaigns—not only in the United States, but including European travel bureaus, Mexican, Canadian, West Indian, and state and regional organizations. As formerly well-known centers to the wealthier people become "filled" these persons tend to go further afield. As rates are lowered, air service to distant places is introduced. During several recent years as many as 1,500,000 to 2,000,000 tourists from the United States have traveled each year in Europe—a vital economic asset to the European economy, and from the standpoint of the American recreational centers, a "loss" to the American economy.

▶ QUESTIONS

1. List some of the important activities carried on in a commercial city.
2. What kinds of locations that are focal points for large surrounding regions are the sites of some of the leading commercial cities of the United States?
3. Why have many capital and port cities become the leading commercial cities of Europe and of Japan?

4. What does the density of landways indicate about the economic development of a region? Differentiate among the following patterns of landways: net, web, line.

5. What inland waterways connect the Great Lakes with navigable rivers?

6. Explain why two or three of the world's seaways (name these) are the routes on which the bulk of ocean traffic moves.

7. Name and locate six of the leading canals of the world. These may be transit canals or terminal ones—ending at an inland "seaport."

8. What kinds of products may be shipped by air?

9. Compare the patterns of airways with the patterns of landways.

10. What is the importance of military aircraft to the activity of the airplane-manufacturing industry of the world?

11. What are the service "industries" or activities?

12. Explain the twentieth-century expansion of the recreational industry. What manufacturing industries have arisen to importance recently, ones whose market is mainly the serving of recreational or luxury demands?

XXIII A World of Change and Increasing

Interdependence

The economic geography of the world is subject to constant change; some changes are slow and are trends that occur over a long period of time. Others are rapid and dynamic. The economic world is not static, but is subject to many changes induced by man himself through his technology or through his laws or political manipulations. Nevertheless man works within the broad framework of the natural environment. Most of his basic raw materials and fuels are distributed in relationship to climatic, terrain, or geological conditions, and their geographical distribution is generally a known factor. But man has the choice of the use of the materials, the substitution of one for another, the transfer or assembly of materials from several source regions, and the redistribution of his manufactured products with respect to markets. Thus he works within an economic framework as well as a geographical one. The competitive situation of the moment, the supply of and demand for a given good at a particular time, the attitude of the government of a country toward tariffs, quotas, or subsidization of enterprises, the comparative costs of labor and production in competing regions, and many other factors are conducive to change.

The changes in the commercial world have been profound when measured from any given date line, and particularly striking since the beginning of the present century. The development of the automobile, the airplane, the present large-scale mining of metals for use in the machines of industry, commerce, agriculture, fishing, and mining, and the developments in the petroleum industry have been particularly significant. However, changes continue in the commercial and highly developed world. The rise of the chemical and petrochemical industries to their present importance has been relatively recent; the multitude of products of these industries—mainly materials for use by other manufacturers—has added hundreds of materials to everyday use in both the capital-goods and consumer-goods fields. More recently, the development of radar, the technical advances in the entire electronics industry, and the development of computers, the missiles field, and others, has added new undertakings to the activities of man in the highly developed countries. But the significant fact of recent times has been the continuance of the broad *geographical patterns;* nearly all technological changes have occurred in the previously highly developed regions of the world save for some in the Soviet Union—which was perhaps best described as "underdeveloped" prior to the inauguration of the Five Year Plans (rather than undeveloped). And it is from the highly developed regions, through capital investment, that some of the outlying districts, particularly mineralized regions, have been brought into the commercial world.

► BROAD GEOGRAPHICAL PATTERNS

The basic or broad regions that furnish raw materials, foods, feeds, and other commodities are reasonably well known or outlined. This does not mean that all details are known for all parts of the world.

Agricultural Patterns of the World

The agricultural regions of the middle latitudes are almost completely occupied by farmers. The last major areas to be settled or cultivated were the prairie grasslands of the subhumid-semi-arid border zone of the dry continental lands. These areas, formerly pastured under a livestock-ranching economy, came under major cultivation beginning in about the 1870's, with the advent of the steel breaking-plow which could cut the tough prairie sod, with the development of well-drilling machinery, the barbed-wire fence, and with the building of railroads to and through the grasslands. The railroads transported the wheat and other grains to market and ports and in turn brought in manufactured products and settlers. The American, Russian, Argentine, Australian, and South African prairies became important agricultural regions; the grain they furnished to the growing urban and manufactural centers played no small part in feeding the dense populations, permitting further expansion of cities without pressure on the food supply. The "final" settlement of the similar prairies of Canada and Manchuria continued into the present century and was not "completed" until the 1910's in Canada, the 1920's in Manchuria.

The fact that the farm lands of the middle latitudes are occupied does not mean that their capacity for producing foods, feeds, and raw materials for manufacturing cannot be increased. True, the best subregions or districts—those with the most suitable terrain, the best soils, or favorable access to markets—are highly productive at present. But yields per acre can be increased, soils better managed, fertilizers added, pastures managed and fertilized, and better seed and animals selected. These things are being done at present. Unfortunately in some districts the increases in productivity are offset by the losses of top-grade agricultural land to the urban and suburban sprawl of growing cities. And, also within the middle latitudes—and particularly in the New World and the Soviet Union—there remains land of lesser quality and land in poor woodlots, fallow land, and land unused within the boundaries of existing farms. The placing of these presently unused or not completely used areas under cultivation or in managed pastures can result in increases in the food supply. The United States is said to contain, on its present farm land—that included within farm boundaries—more unused land than any other country, and more than is actually under cultivation in many nations of the world. The current surpluses of certain crops in the United States, and the crop-control and land-retirement programs of the government, are factors keeping this land in its present status and mitigating against the expansion of crop acreage. It is a special situation in this country. But in the world as a whole (including the United States) there are only two acres of crop land for each inhabitant—the equivalent of two football fields to provide the fibers, oils, industrial crops, food crops, and meats for each person alive.

Agriculture in the tropical world, and its pattern, is very different from that of the middle latitudes. Intensive production on a commercial scale is characteristic of tropical plantations; but these occupy only a very small part of the potential area suitable for rubber, cacao, bananas, fibers, and vegetable oils. The accessible island and shore locations have been the producing regions to date. With improved transportation inland the producing areas can be expanded enormously. Tropical agriculture is intensive in certain regions; the inhabitants of India, Pakistan, Java, and part of Nigeria press upon the food supply. But the possibilities of increased yields with better husbandry—and aid from the outside—are very great. Elsewhere the shifting from subsistence to commercial agriculture, the elimination of shifting cultivation, and the introduction of modern methods and fertilizers would increase productivity. A handicap of the tropics is the poor lateritic soils; careful study and more knowledge is needed about them and their management. Attempts at commercial cultivated-crop production here and there on non-alluvial and non-volcanic soils, as the British scheme to grow peanuts extensively in East Africa, have failed because (in large part) of the lack of appreciation of the environmental conditions and especially because of the attempt to cultivate lateritic tropical soils as if they were the high-humus soils of the middle latitudes.

The potentialities for the rearing of cattle on the tropical grasslands are large. Cattle are reared in the Sudan, the Llanos, and northern Australia, but only in the last has management of the range been studied in some detail in a few districts. Not only must more be learned about tropical grassland range, but high-quality cattle suitable to the environmental conditions must be introduced or developed for the local settings, and dependable water supplies must be made available for the duration of the dry season.

Fishing and Ocean-Resource Patterns of the World

The four great fishing regions of the world, two each on either side of the North Atlantic and the North Pacific, are related not only to markets of the present but also to the quantities of edible fish present in each region, for in each there is mixing of warm and cool waters and abundant plankton and copapods for the fish to feed on.

The resources of the sea have barely been touched elsewhere in the world. Local markets are small in the middle latitudes of the Southern Hemisphere. The recent rise in importance of the fisheries of South Africa is an indication of the potentialities of the southern seas. Tropical fisheries face the problem of the variety of fish caught—many inedible or of poor quality—and the problem of refrigeration. This last can be solved, if the demand for a particular species justifies it, as has been done by the American, Mexican, and Japanese fishing fleets in the tuna fisheries of the tropical latitudes of the North Pacific Ocean. The resources of the oceans will be used by man far more in the future than they are at present. However, conservational measures must be practiced and enforced if sustained yields of these resources are to be maintained.

The desalting of ocean waters, when this becomes economically feasible on a large and relatively inexpensive scale, holds untold possibilities, both for the water supplies of coastal cities and for the irrigation of present semi-arid or desert land along the seacoasts of the world.

Forest Patterns of the World

The great Northern Coniferous Forest stretches across much of northern North America and Eurasia. It lies poleward of the important agricultural regions. Its southern portion offers occasional districts suitable for agriculture— river flood plains and old lake beds, especially. Its northern portion lies beyond the limit of farming, owing to a season of warmth which is too short to mature crops. In much even of the southern portion the growing season is less than one hundred days, and frost is expectable over lowlands in any warm month except July. Upland soils are poor podsols. In the North American forest the eastern two-thirds lies on the glaciated and rocky Canadian Shield, or Laurentian Upland. The overall environmental conditions exclude the possibility of agriculture. This forest is now and most of it will remain as one of the major forest regions of the world.

Mountain forests, woodlands in rough hill lands, and planted and managed forests on poor sandy soils in the middle latitudes will continue to provide timber products in the highly developed world. These forests, except for some farm woodlots, are now managed, are protected from fire and insects, and, in many cases, are in national, state, or private forest preserves.

The tropical forests are scattered widely in the rainy tropics. The Amazon Basin, the Congo Basin, the Indochina Peninsula, and some of the islands of the East Indies contain extensive stands of timber. To date there has been little pressure of alternative land uses for the areas they occupy. Such has not been the case in the forest areas of the wetter portions of the wet-and-dry tropics. Shifting cultivation, burning, indiscriminate cutting of trees, and—in India—the clearing of land centuries ago for farming has destroyed or damaged much of this forest. It is said that few truly virgin stands remain. The eventual use of these "forest" lands will be dependent upon a variety of circumstances impossible to forecast—the pressure of population, and the competition between an agricultural and a forest land use in the future in the wet-and-dry tropics.

Energy Resource Patterns of the World

The major patterns of the distribution of coal in the world are known; estimates of the reserves have been made but are subject to revision as detailed geological work proceeds in fields which are not fully developed, or which remain in the potential state. The total resources within inner China are, however, educated guesses in many cases. The coal of Antarctica may never be a usable resource, and, of course, the amount buried beneath the ice cap of the continent is an unknown quantity.

The accessible, or inhabited, portions of the world have been mapped into regions wherein—because of the geological age of the rocks—the existence of petroleum (or of coal) is impossible; into regions where the discovery or existence of oil fields is possible, but not probable; and into regions of younger rocks where oil resources are possible. It is in areas of this last category that all present petroleum fields exist, and wherein the oil companies spend their money and resources in investigation. Even within the possible regions the subsurface geological structures are not everywhere suited to the entrapment of petroleum. And the difficulty of working out the details of the subsurface structures are considerable, though aided now by core drilling, electric logging, study of the structures and fossils from drill cores, and by many other methods. Thus, the discovery of new fields, as the recent ones of the Sahara Desert, subject the potential petroleum resources to constant revision. Large areas of the world, too —particularly in the densely forested wet tropics, where the soil and subsoil is excessively thick and where in the area as a whole there are few rock outcrops—are known only in their broadest outlines so far as bedrock conditions are concerned. Thus much recent development has expanded from known fields onto the submerged continental shelves adjacent to producing oil fields. Nevertheless, all potential oil regions of the world are in the process of being geologically explored or examined.

Potential hydroelectric sources are greatest outside of the present highly developed countries. The Congo Basin leads all regions in its potentialities.

The actual provision of energy from all sources today is concentrated in the highly developed regions and countries. It is in these that nuclear energy was developed, and from them that power from nuclear sources will be provided for the rest of the world if and when the costs are permissive and some of the present governmental or military controls are relaxed or removed.

Mineral Resource Pattern of the World

The present pattern of the mining of the minerals of the world reflects the existence of the highly developed regions wherein the minerals are used. Originally these regions depended upon home supplies or on ones nearby and accessible. But from these regions, through exploration, capital investment, and the export of technically trained mining engineers and equipment, mines have been opened in distant regions of the world. If the minerals were in locations previously inaccessible, transportation has been provided—again by outside capital.

The first, or earliest, stage in mining activity in a given region (such as western South America, the American West, Australia, or South Africa) was associated with the precious metals, usually gold. Later stages involved the opening of metal mines—iron, copper, lead, zinc, and others. Originally only high-grade deposits of metals were worked. A later stage, now prevalent in many mining regions, is the working of low-grade ores by mass methods—by the open pit mine if possible.

Many of the metals, unlike the mineral fuels, are associated with either the oldest rocks of the world, which form "basement complexes" or are associated with rocks which have been subjected to mountain-building processes. As a result many mining regions are in the old basement complexes such as the Laurentian Upland of Canada, Angaraland of Siberia, or the Katanga of Africa, or are in mountainous terrain such as that of the Cordillera of western North and South America.

The potential resources of metalliferous ores are not known; only the potentially productive regions are known but they have not been examined in geological detail. For example, the Laurentian Upland, covered by glacial debris in many places, by lakes and swamps over some areas, and by rock-strewn boulders in others, is Canada's "mineral frontier." New discoveries are made constantly as geological exploration continues. The iron-ore development on the Quebec-Labrador boundary is one among many recently established mining districts.

The dry lands of the world and the mountains contain rock outcrops in abundance, in contrast to the basement complexes. The old-time mineral prospector operated in mountains and deserts. The modern geologist finds study of the rocks of these areas relatively easy, although the folded and faulted rock formations make the untangling of the structures a complex problem. Thus, to date, many of the world's sources of metals are from mines in mountainous country. Mountains will continue as storehouses of minerals, but probably will drop in the percentage of the world production in the future as ore bodies are discovered and developed in the basement complexes and elsewhere (as beneath certain kinds of plains) in the world.

Manufacturing Pattern of the World

The Industrial Revolution resulted in the establishment of manufacturing in England, from which it spread to western Europe and the northeastern United States. The race for colonies among European countries was in part owing to the desire to control source regions of raw materials for the home industries. Until toward the close of the nineteenth century the two "traditional" manufacturing regions faced each other across the North Atlantic. To these two Japan and the Soviet Union have been added. Outlying and small areas, mainly in the self-governing nations of the British Commonwealth, contribute some of the world's manufactured goods.

The underdeveloped countries, witnessing the success of the manufactural nations in the provision of a high standard of living for their inhabitants— through commercial agriculture as well as industry—are striving to industrialize. India has made a considerable start; China, with aid from the Soviet Union, is now engaged in a massive and stringently controlled effort to lift herself through two or three centuries of time within a few decades.

The undeveloped lands, using wishful thinking, would like to industrialize, and they ask for foreign aid—which can come only from the present highly developed countries, ones which, for many reasons, developed themselves without outside aid.

The present manufactural pattern is rather clear. The future one is uncertain. Will the present regions, through the advantage of an early start, the educational and technical knowledge of their citizens, and the financial and market contacts and strength they now possess, maintain themselves as relatively higher and stronger centers even if the rest of the world industrializes and provides itself with goods? Or will the increased manufacturing and educational facilities rising elsewhere in the future tend to level off the differential just as two reservoirs at different levels, when joined, reach a common level—one rising higher than it was previously, the other being lowered relatively? The questions cannot be answered. Not all parts of the world have the ingredients of industry. But an industrialized China and India—to mention only two—each with very large home resources of raw materials, energy, and labor, would have, after their home needs were supplied, a profound effect upon the world market patterns, the prices of goods, the differential costs of production, and the regional competition among manufacturing regions and nations.

Commercial and Transportation Patterns of the World

The commercial patterns, and the transportational patterns, recently discussed in this book are major activities within the present highly developed regions. Commercial functions of world-wide scope extend from these regions to all parts of the world, and particularly to the regions or districts wherein capital from the highly developed nations is invested. The raw-material source regions thus have daily contacts with London, New York, or other financial centers. The financing of the great ports from which raw materials are shipped, ports such as Singapore, is from the outside. And the transport networks of the world are densest and most used in the highly developed regions themselves, in connecting them with each other, and in providing tentacles from them to source regions of foods and raw materials and market regions for their surplus manufactured goods.

▶ THE FUTURE?

It is impossible to forecast the details of change in the economic geography of the future. The broad major patterns will continue. But the post-World War II world has been one of exceedingly rapid change, both within the existing highly developed regions and outside of them. The underdeveloped and undeveloped lands are awakening rapidly, are becoming self-governing, and are placing demands upon the developed countries. With the division between a world of the West and a Communist world the leaders of many of the new countries have been able to play one side against the other, and so obtain technical assistance and loans from one side or the other more rapidly and "generously" than would otherwise be the case. And these leaders have the advantage of operating in a world of rapid communication and one with world organizations of economic or political or governmental type which they have been able to use as sounding boards. The milieu is different than it was before World War II.

The advent of rapid transportation has not only shrunk the world in size (really in accessibility) but has made distant source regions of raw materials easily reached, and has expanded the markets to ones esentially world-wide in scope. Despite the "one-world" concept the rising tide of nationalism and the desire of many countries to commercialize their agriculture and emulate the traditional manufacturing regions in industry is resulting in the creation of further competitive situations in the production, transfer, and exchange of goods.

Index

Date Due